DISCOVERING ART HISTORY

Umberto Boccioni, *Unique Forms of Continuity in Space*, 1913. Bronze, 44" high (111.2 cm). The Museum of Modern Art, New York. Acquired through the Lillie P. Bliss Bequest.

DISCOVERING

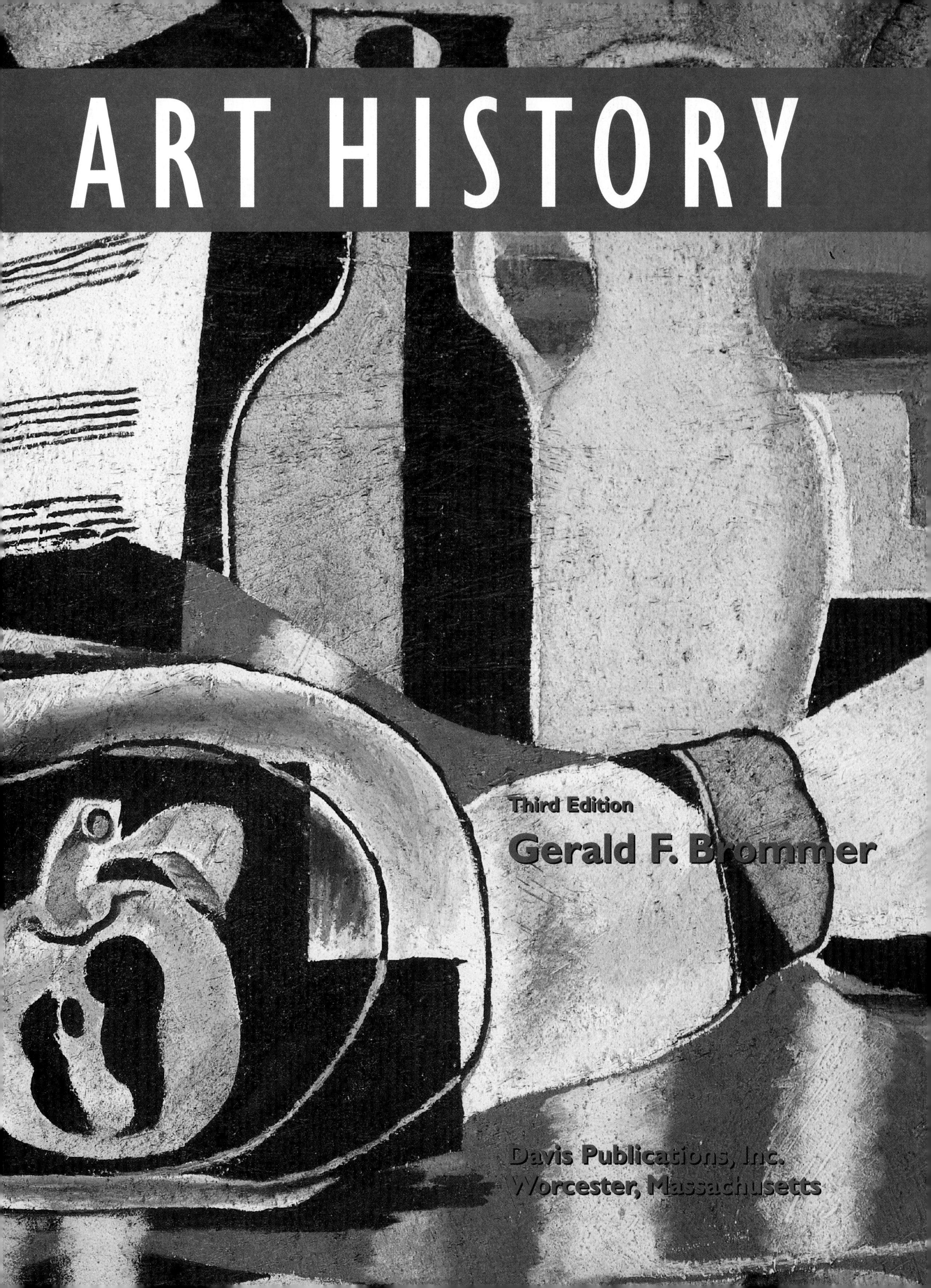

ART HISTORY

Third Edition

Gerald F. Brommer

Davis Publications, Inc.
Worcester, Massachusetts

What is Art?

"Art is like light," as a famous composer once said. "Everybody knows what it is, but few can tell you what it is."

Art *is* difficult to define. Unlike light, though, art isn't one thing or a single phenomenon. People create it, and that's enough to make it complicated and subject to many definitions.

Art can be personal, art can call for social change, and art can portray human emotions as well as evoke them. It can express harmony or disharmony, show the simple and everyday in unfamiliar ways, or be monumental, mysterious, and fantastic.

But how do we know what is good art? What makes a work good? Whatever form it takes, art is based on ideas. Art history looks at these ideas over the ages and across cultures. We learn about art objects and why they are important. We learn about artistic styles, to comprehend how style comes about through line, motion, form, texture, color and the use of space. When we read about artists, their lives, and their ideas, from century to century—how some worked in monasteries, art guilds, royal courts, and art academies, and others created art to use and wear—we can better understand the art and architecture around us.

We can discover the "good" of art when we see how new thoughts about art, new movements among artists and changes in style give us new ways of seeing the world. And that is, certainly, a kind of light.

Title page: Following spread: Georges Braque, *Still Life: The Table*, detail, 1928. Oil on canvas, 32" x 51 1/2" (81 x 130 cm). National Gallery of Art, Washington, DC. Chester Dale Collection.

Printed in U.S.A. Library of Congress Catalog Card Number: 95-068097 ISBN: 87192-299-1 10 9 8 7 6 5 4 3 2

Freeing figures in stone

Imagine Michelangelo. He is twenty-five. He chisels a huge block of marble and two lifelike figures emerge in one piece—a masterpiece. His art, in Italy, 1500, will influence European art *for the next three centuries!*

Who were the first artists?

A dog fell into a hole and some of the world's oldest known paintings were discovered. The underground paintings at Lascaux, France, have lasted more than 17,000 years. How?

The mysteries of ancient art

An art rescue project using computers, saws and giant cranes? Hundreds of people from many countries worked together to save the ancient Egyptian monuments at Abu Simbel. The art of Egypt fascinates people the world over. Why?

Page IV: Hans II Jordaens (figures by Cornelis Baellieur), *A Collection of Art and Rarities,* 1630. Oil on panel, 34" x 47" (86 x 120 cm). Kunsthistorisches Museum, Vienna.

Page V: (clockwise from top) *Hall of Bulls,* detail, about 15,000- 13,000 BC. Dordogne, France. *Ramses II,* about 1257, Abu Simbel. Michelangelo, *Pietà,* detail, 1499-1500. Marble, 68 1/2" high (1.74m). St. Peter's, Vatican, Rome.

Painting the real and the personal

History's first solo art show, in 1855, was opened out of spite. When the Paris art experts said "no" to Gustave Courbet's paintings about ordinary people and everyday life, he built a shed to exhibit his art anyway.

Early earth art

A hand-made mountain of art rises to the sky. Over a thousand years ago on the island of Java, Indonesia, Buddhists sculpted scenes of deities and demons along the path to the mountaintop. What were they trying to reach?

Showing the hard social truths

Paint from a local dimestore and other simple materials were the fabric of America's own Renaissance—the 1920s in Harlem. Artists like Jacob Lawrence captured the epic struggles of African Americans.

Page VI (clockwise from top left): Gustave Courbet, *Burial at Ornans*, detail, 1849-1850. Oil on canvas, 10' 3 1/2" x 21' 11" (3.15 x 6.68 m). Musée d'Orsay, Paris. *Borobudor*, about 850. Shailendra dynasty, Java. Jacob Lawrence, *One of the largest Race Riots Occurred in East St. Louis*, panel 52 from the *Migration of the Negro* series, 1940-1941. Tempera and gesso on composition board, 12" x 18" (30 x 46 cm). The Museum of Modern Art, New York, gift of Mrs. David M. Levy.

Page VII (clockwise from top left): Michael Graves, *Public Library of San Juan Capistrano*, 1983. San Juan Capistrano, California. Judy Chicago, *The Dinner Party*, 1979. Ceramic with handwoven cloth, each side 82' long (25 m). Through the Flower, Albuquerque, New Mexico. Dorothea Lange, *Migrant Mother, Nipomo California*, 1936. Photograph: Dorothea Lange Collection, The Oakland Museum.

What next?

"Less is more," said Mies van der Rohe. Buildings should be simple—function comes first. "Less is a bore," said Robert Venturi years later. Great architecture can be complex. Modernism followed by Post-Modernism followed by...

What is context?

A single image that changed lives. San Franciscans opened their newspapers one day in 1935 and saw Dorothea Lange's photograph of starving migrant workers. Some readers were moved and sent the workers food—an extraordinary reaction.

Women making art

Women making art

In 1979, Judy Chicago set a place at the dinner table for each of thirty-six women whose ideas and actions changed history. Did Chicago's monument to women, "The Dinner Party," change art history?

Some art might make you wonder, "Why would somebody do that?" People who study art ask the same question. That question leads to others: What was life like when and where the artist lived? What did people value? Who looked at art? What materials did artists use?

Discovering Art History addresses many questions about art. It also provides opportunities to better understand art by making it yourself. Turn the page to find out more.

Your Guide to Art History

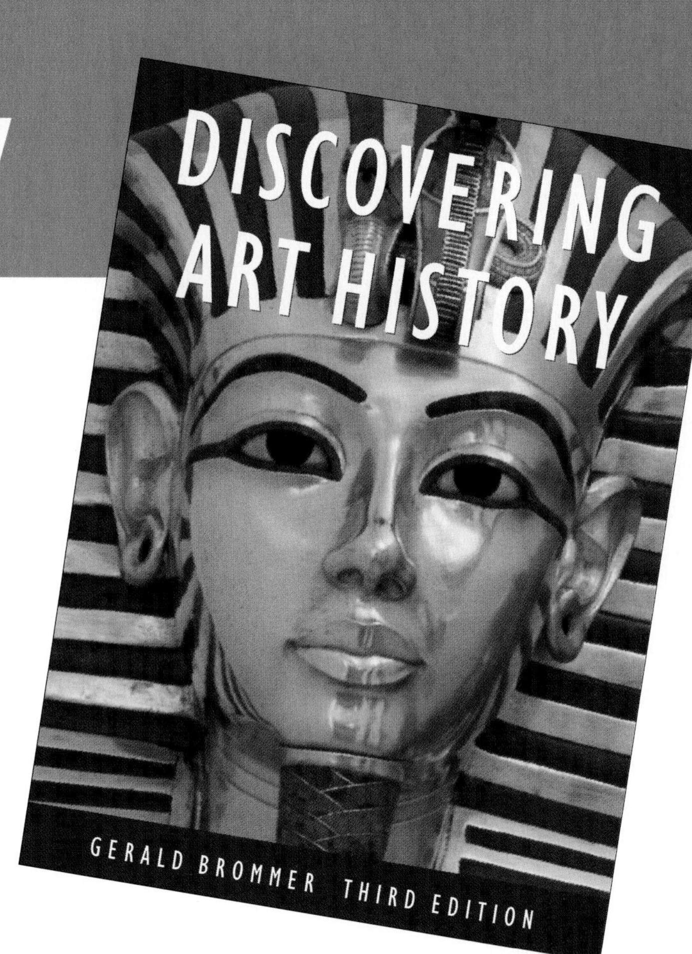

Get ready for an intriguing tour across centuries and into creative minds.

Visual art is a record of ideas and cross-cultural influences. It illuminates science, history and social customs of a particular time and place. *Discovering Art History* focuses mainly on Western art—the art of Europe and America. But, it makes important connections to non-Western art—the art of other cultures.

This book is organized to give you several options for a satisfying study. And there are many tools you can use to fully comprehend the long time spans and complex movements in art history.

Three Parts

Part One: The World and Work of the Artist introduces art-making. Understanding the choices among materials, techniques and subject matter will deepen your appreciation of the decisions artists make.

Part Two: Trends and Influences in the World of Art shows that artists around the world often pursue similar ideas. You'll learn different perspectives, too, about Native American art and about the art and cultures of India, China, Japan, Africa and others.

Part Three: Art in the Western World begins with the ancient world and concludes with a look at the fascinating kinds of art being made today.

Chapter Openers

Overview
Each of the book's seventeen chapters begins with a stand-alone overview. Text, images and captions combine to give you a sense of what will be covered in the chapter's lessons.

Read all seventeen chapter openers first and you'll get the "big picture" of art history.

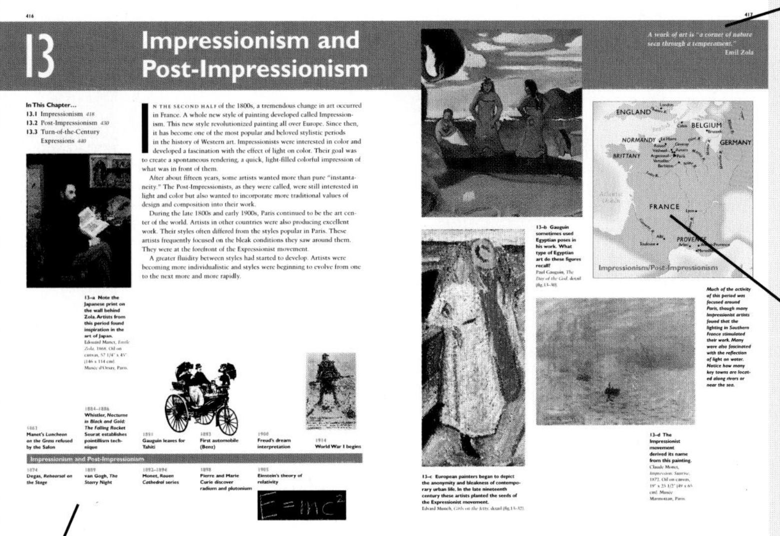
13 Impressionism and Post-Impressionism

Quotation
Sometimes a quotation sums it up well. Sometimes quotations will make you curious.

Maps
Maps help you visualize where the people lived who were making images or objects of the period.

Use the world map at the back of the book, too.

Timeline
What else is happening? The timeline points out significant European and American historical events taking place during the periods covered in the chapter. Those events can include great works of literature or music, political revolutions, inventions, or natural disasters.

Lesson Openers

Overview
The chapters are sectioned into lessons and each lesson begins with a lesson opener. Reading the lesson opener provides you with a summary of that lesson's main points and prepares you for further exploration of the topic.

15.2 The Influence of Abstraction

Special Feature
Here, Georgia O'Keeffe's life and work sets the foundation for understanding the shift to abstraction in American art. A practical example is provided in the opener to expand your understanding of the lesson's major concept.

Key Notes
The major concepts covered in the lesson appear as Key Notes in the lesson opener. Use these points as guides for your study, making sure you come away from the lesson with a clear understanding of each concept.

Vocabulary
Important terms are listed in the opener, alerting you to the fact that they will be used in the lesson. The words are highlighted as they appear in the lesson text.

Text Features

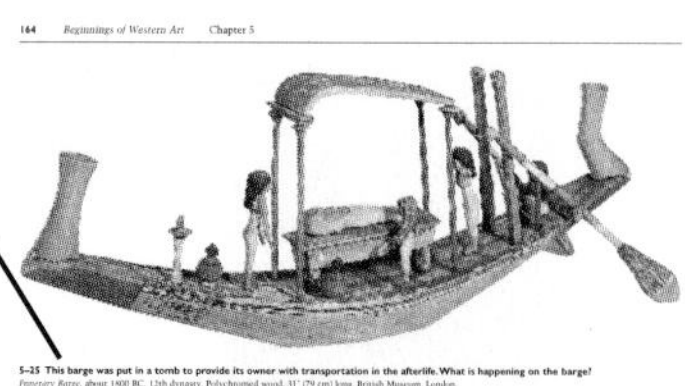

Captions
help you understand ideas in the text or help you make comparisons between art styles. When the sizes of the original art are given, take time to imagine the work in real life. Works may be as small as a postage stamp or as large as a billboard.

Window in Time
features include some of art history's exciting events and intriguing discussions.

World Cultural Timelines
show what's going on in cultures apart from the Western world.

Text
The text is the voice of the author, explaining, defining and helping you to think. It can point out things you might not otherwise notice, confirm conclusions you had reached on your own and even challenge your perspective. Use the text as a starting point, and not the end point, to your personal exploration of art history.

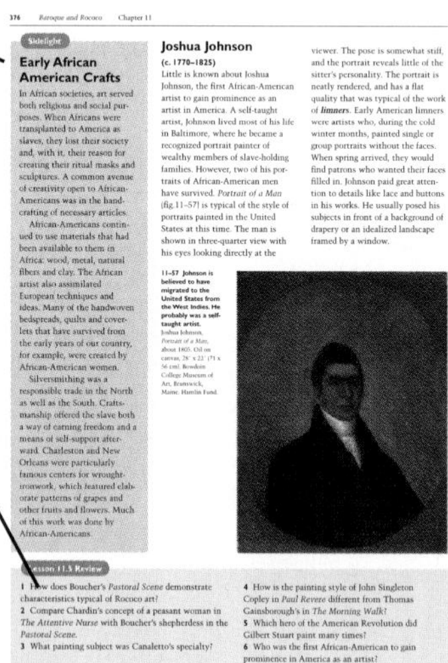

Sidelights
give a glimpse of important art-related topics. They help round out the historical view in the text.

Lesson Review
questions and Chapter Review questions help you recall and integrate what you've learned. Some questions and activities ask for interpretation. Analyze for yourself!

Primary Source
"More scope to the fancy..." Hogarth's words expand our sense of London in the early 1700s. A primary source is direct. We can make up our own minds about a period or an artist, based on the actual words said or written.

Other Tools for Learning
are just that. Use the timeline and map for keener comprehension. Or tap into electronic research.

Studio Activities

Classroom Connections
Now it's your turn to be the artist! These activities help you use what you've learned from each chapter to generate new ideas and approaches to making art.

Student Profiles
Meet a fellow student. What you read may surprise you. Find out what other students have to say about making and understanding art, as they tackle a Classroom Connections activity.

Reference

Pronunciation Guide
Klee is pronounced "clay." If you've never heard someone speak of painter Paul Klee, how would you know how to pronounce his name? The Pronunciation Guide lists all the artists in the text.

Index
The Index lists in alphabetical order the contents of *Discovering Art History* and the page number for each topic. Use it to locate artworks, artists, movements and the ideas discussed in the text.

Glossary
Words in lesson vocabulary lists are defined in the Glossary. Check this resource for proper names, place names, historical terms, art movements and words unfamiliar to you.

Part One The World and Work of the Artist

Contents

Part Two Trends and Influences in the World of Art

Looking for a Common Denominator 3

Page 60

Non-Western Art and Cultural Influences 4

Page 76

Part Three Art in the Western World

Beginnings of Western Art

Page 148

5

Greek and Roman Art

Page 172

6

Religious Conviction

Romanesque and Gothic Art

The Italian Renaissance 9

Page 260

Renaissance in the North 10

Page 302

Baroque and Rococo 11

Page 330

Three Opposing Views 12

Impressionism and Post-Impressionism 13

A Half-Century of "Isms"

American Art 1900–1950

Twentieth-Century Architecture 16

Page 522

Art from the Fifties to the Present 17

Page 548

Reference

Page 590

Part One

The World and Work of the Artist

Diego Rivera, *The Making of a Fresco Showing the Building of a City*, detail, April-June 1931. True fresco, 18 3/4' x 32 1/2' (9 5.68 x 9.91 m). San Francisco Art Institute.

1 Learning About Art

In This Chapter...

ART IS PERHAPS HUMANITY'S most essential, most universal language. While art uses visual images to communicate its messages, we use words to describe the images, reactions and feelings we have about objects of art.

All the images in this book are concerned with art. Museums around the world are filled with objects called art. Hundreds of books and magazines are filled with pictures and descriptions of fascinating objects: paintings, buildings, drawings, pottery, weavings, sculpture, prints and other things we call art. Works of art add to our enjoyment of life. And yet, some observers ask seriously, "What is so special about that chair, vase, painting or wood carving? Why is it called art?"

It is impossible to establish a definition of art that will please everyone. The term is broad; each age of humanity has different ideas about it. While we may not be able to define art to everyone's satisfaction, we can define some of the standards by which art is evaluated.

When an object is placed before a group of people, how do they come to agree it is a work of special quality? What criteria or guidelines do they use to make a judgment? And how can you learn to judge whether a work of art—your own, your peers' or a work in a museum or gallery—is good? How can you learn to think beyond "I like it" or "I don't like it" and give reasons for your preferences?

1–a Edward Hopper's painting *Early Sunday Morning* expresses some of the artist's feelings about his society. How do you respond to it? How does it make you feel? How do you think the artist created these feelings in you?
Edward Hopper, *Early Sunday Morning,* 1930. Oil on canvas, 35" x 59 3/4" (89 x 152 cm). The Whitney Museum of American Art, New York, gift of Gloria Vanderbilt Whitney.

All art consists in bringing something into existence.
Aristotle

1–b This plaque containing the figures of a warrior and his helpers is from the Benin culture of Nigeria. It was designed and cast in bronze, a complex technique the Benin learned from their neighbors, the Ife people. This relief once decorated the king's palace in Benin. The king, in the center, is flanked by two soldiers and two children making music.

Warrior and Attendants plaque, late 17th century. Benin Culture, Nigeria. Bronze, 14 1/2" x 15 1/4" (37 x 39 cm). The Nelson-Atkins Museum of Art, Kansas City, Missouri, Nelson Fund.

1.1 Evaluating Works of Art

We generally base our evaluation of works of art on such criteria as craftsmanship, design and aesthetic properties. We also consider how well the works reflect the societies in which they were created.

Craftsmanship

A craftsperson is someone who is skilled in the use of materials and tools and produces well-made objects of above-average quality (figs.1–1, 1–2).

Aesthetic Properties

Each work of art has certain *properties* that belong to it. By analyzing them, we can understand what makes the work unique.

Sensory properties are the elements of art (see pages 41–47) that we can recognize by using our sense of sight and touch. The use of *line* is a sensory property that we can see. So are the choice and blending of *colors*, the variety of *values*, and *shapes* created by color and line. Our sense of touch helps us understand the *texture* of an object, the suggestion of *space* and the *form* or *mass* of something three-dimensional.

Formal properties are the principles of art (see pages 48–54) that help us see how artists organize the elements of art to express their ideas effectively. If we are able to analyze the *unity, balance, contrast, rhythm, pattern, emphasis* and visual *movement* in works of art, we can determine how all parts of a composition work together.

Technical properties are the media, tools and equipment used to make the work of art. For example, ceramics, oil painting, bronze casting (fig.1–b) and charcoal drawing all rely on different technical skills. Studying and working with various media and methods can help you make value judgments about the quality of artists' techniques.

Expressive properties are the characteristics of an artwork that cause us to respond to it with feeling and emotion. Paintings, for example, might express moods of tension, relaxation or sadness through color, metaphor, symbolism or design (fig.1–a). Ideas, ideals, social criticism, religion, hope and compassion can be communicated through art.

Reflection of Society. Artworks also reflect the times in which they were created. Artisans created works that often provide or confirm information about cultures. The images depicted, the materials used and the style of the piece all help place the object in a particular time and place.

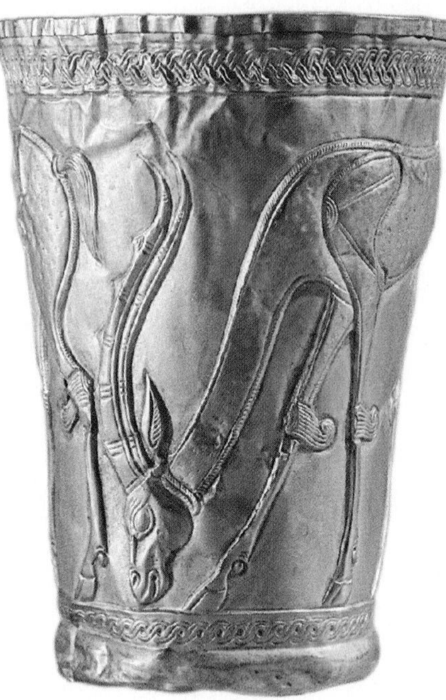

1–1 This cup was made from a thin sheet of gold and the design was probably hammered from within, against a wooden mold. The gazelle is beautifully stylized and designed to fit the space comfortably. All the details are carefully planned and executed. No cracks appear, even after this tremendous length of time. All these features tell us that the piece was made with great care and a mastery of materials and tools.

Ceremonial cup, about 1000 BC. Northwest Iran. Gold, 4 1/4" (11 cm) high. Los Angeles County Museum of Art.

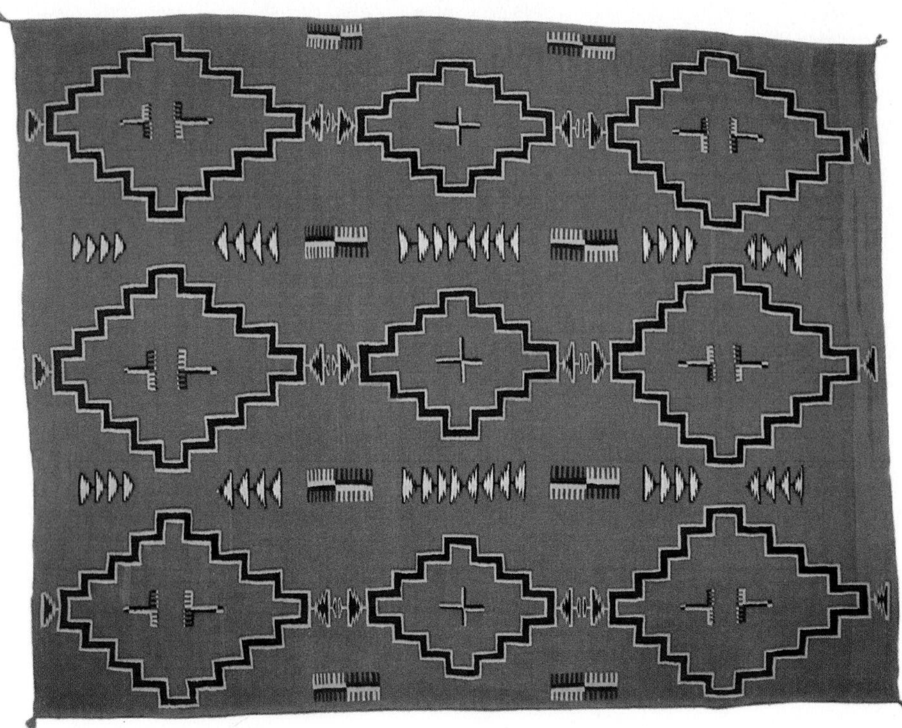

1–2 The weaver who created this blanket used line, shapes, color and texture. The blanket also shows an understanding of design principles, for it has pattern, unity, balance and contrast. The weaver used the elements of art and the principles of design to create an object that reflects the values of her cultural heritage.

Navajo rug, *Eye Dazzler*, 18th century. Wool. Hurst Gallery, Cambridge, Massachusetts.

Identifying Works of Art. Paintings and sculptures can easily be identified as works of art. But often a bowl, blanket or other functional object is also called art. Collectors or *connoisseurs* appreciate the appearance, craftsmanship or message of such objects. If a society placed a high value on a crafted object, that object may be considered an object of art today (fig.1–3). An item is not art just because it is old, but its age is one of many factors taken into consideration.

Art historians search for pieces that are good examples of the craftsmanship, aesthetic properties and societal background of a culture. They look for certain objects that seem to reflect the highest quality work. These objects stand out as *paradigms*, or classic examples (fig.1–4). You will encounter many paradigms in this book. Some already will be recognizable. Others will grow in familiarity as you encounter them here and elsewhere.

1–4 This drinking cup is considered a paradigm. This work of high quality is an outstanding example from the Archaic period in Greek art.
Exekias, *Dionysus in a Boat.* Interior of an Attic black-figured kylix, about 540 BC. Diameter, 12" (30 cm). Staatliche Antikensammlungen, Munich.

1–3 This kylix, or shallow drinking cup, shows the Greek goddess of Dawn holding the body of her son, who has just been killed by Achilles. The shape of the vessel, its high quality, and the mythological scene depicted aid the viewer in identifying the piece as a product of ancient Greece.
Douris, *Eos and Memnon.* Interior of red-figured kylix, about 490–480 BC. Diameter, 10 1/2" (27 cm). The Louvre, Paris.

Lesson 1.1 Review

1 What are some of the criteria that we should consider when evaluating a piece of art?
2 List the art elements and the principles of art. What is the relationship between these sensory and formal properties of art?
3 What are the technical properties used to create art?
4 Give some examples of art media. What medium was used to create the Nigerian *Warrior and Attendant*'s plaque (fig.1–a)?
5 What are some of the factors in a piece of art that can indicate when or where it was created?
6 Define paradigm. Give an example of a paradigm from this chapter.

1.2 Why Do People Create Art?

Why do people create art? Why do they bother to carve or paint an object? There are many reasons why people have made objects of great beauty. They may include functional considerations, religion, politics, education, aesthetics and humanity's inborn desire to create.

Utility

Utility is a term that describes an object's usefulness. Nearly all societies have needed eating utensils and storage vessels, which they have formed from clay, basketry, leather or metals.

Similarly, clothing not only protects the wearer but also indicates social rank and individual taste. Architectural forms not only provide shelter. They also enclose spaces for living, worship or public assembly, and are specifically designed and decorated to enhance those functions. Functional objects from Western culture include furniture, glassware, machinery, automobiles, office buildings, airplanes, pens and lamps. Yet, all these objects have artistic qualities in addition to their functional qualities.

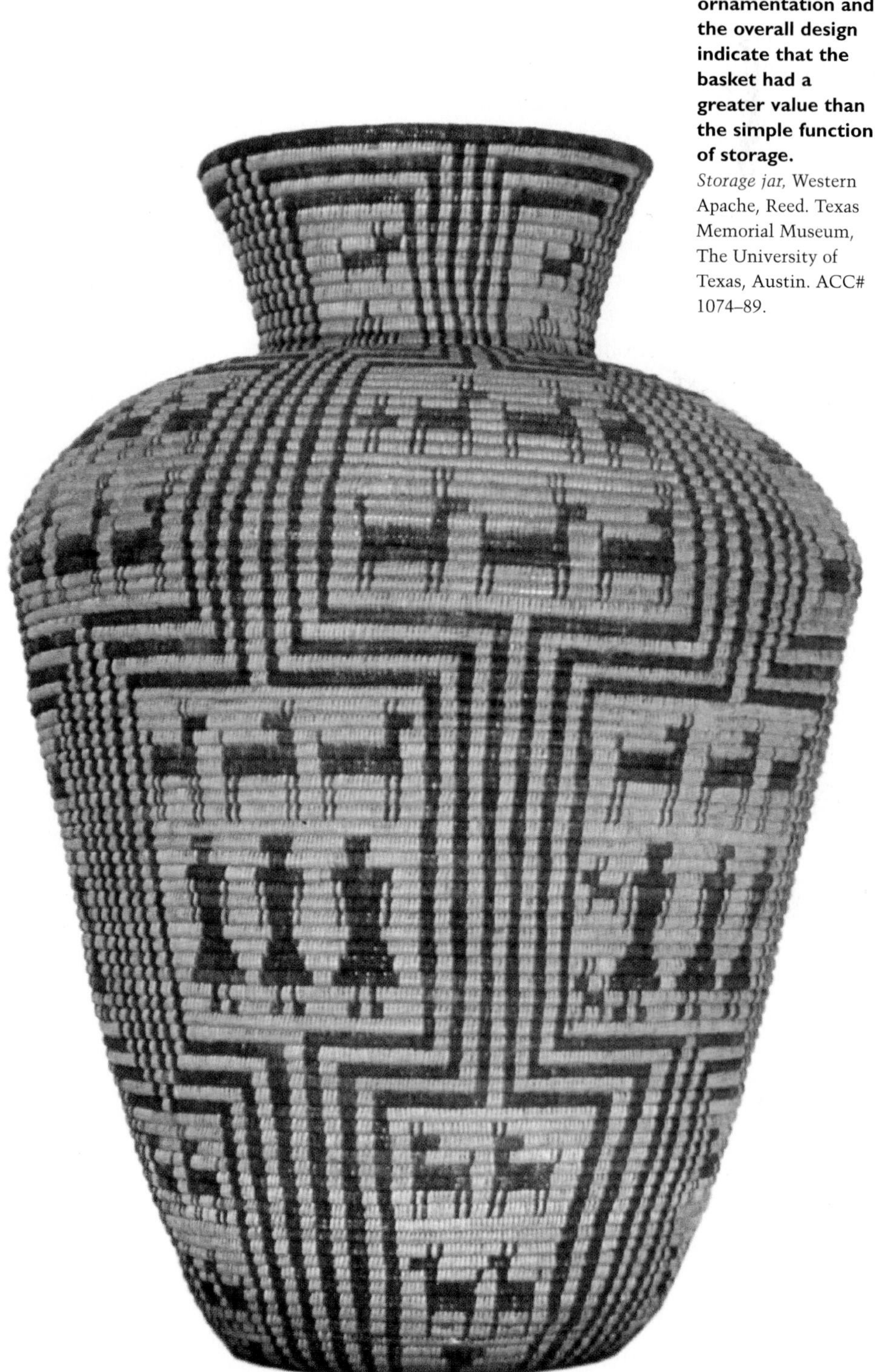

1–5 The storage jar of basketry created by a Western Apache artisan is meant to be utilitarian. Yet the intricate craftsmanship, the attention to ornamentation and the overall design indicate that the basket had a greater value than the simple function of storage.
Storage jar, Western Apache, Reed. Texas Memorial Museum, The University of Texas, Austin. ACC# 1074–89.

1–6 The Poro Society mask was worn by dancers "possessed" by the spirit of the object. The mask is meaningless until given life by the ceremony. Then, it is no longer an inanimate object, but a real force, an abode of power and a controller of life.
Poro Society mask. N'Gere Peoples, Ivory Coast, Africa. Wood, fiber and fur, about 18" (46 cm) high. Baltimore Museum of Art, gift of Mr. and Mrs. Leonard Whitehouse and Dr. and Mrs. Bernard Berk.

Religion

Religion has played an important role in the creation of objects. Many objects have been created to support religious beliefs and activities. In many cultures, the movement of stars and moon, the rising and setting of the sun, tidal activities, flooding rivers and the habits of animals have supernatural meanings. Worship is aided in many cultures through the use of magical designs or geometric shapes, and the creation of good-luck charms, or *fetishes*. Symbolic or ornamental containers on specially designed altars are used for ritual display. Priests and worshipers wear unique ornaments and coverings.

Objects may be made to represent a god and to remind the worshiper of that spirit's power, divinity, omniscience or humanity. Gods are often depicted in human or animal form. Many beautiful and impressive objects have been made as gifts to the gods by worshipers in cultures as diverse as *aborigines* and ancient Greeks. Structures for the worship of gods range from Neolithic circles of huge stones to elaborate cathedrals and temples.

1–7 Copies of holy writings may be elaborately printed in specially ornate script and bound or protected in cases or bindings of leather, precious metals and jeweled designs.
Upper cover of binding, the *Lindenau Gospels*, about 870 AD. Gold and jewels, 13 3/4" x 10 1/2" (35 x 27 cm). The Pierpont Morgan Library, New York.

1–8 This is a billboard poster used for political propaganda purposes in China.
Crush the Gang of Four! Political poster, 1977. About 59" x 79" (1.5 x 2 m). Guilin, China.

Politics

The use of art and architecture in politics goes back to ancient times. Castles and fortified cities were built to defend the people from enemies. Paintings or carvings of the ruler on walls and towers were used to perpetuate myths of the awesome power of a king. Today, political propaganda is conveyed through political cartoons, critical painting and billboard posters.

Information/History

The use of art to teach assumes great importance in societies where there is no written language or where the literacy rate is low. Paintings, sculptures, stained glass windows and symbolic abstract designs have been used to pass on a culture's history, folk tales, religious traditions, mythology and moral values. The art provides a visual record of heroes, gods, or even instructions on how to make wine or worship properly. Oral traditions are thus reinforced in a physical way.

1–9 Some of the scenes on this door relate the visit of a British colonial official to the king. Other anecdotes of Yoruba life also are depicted.
Areogun, *Door from the king's palace* at Ikerre, Yoruba, Nigeria, about 1910. Wood, approximately 6' (1.8 m) high. The British Museum, London.

1–10 Robert Swain's painting may evoke many types of thoughts to viewers, regardless of their backgrounds. And, by adding a title like *Untitled*, the possible connotations are limited only by the imagination of the viewer.
Robert Swain, *Untitled*, 1968. Acrylic on cotton duck, 105 1/2" (268 cm) per side. Collection, Stephen S. Schwartz, Columbus, Ohio. Courtesy of the artist.

Aesthetics

Today we may think of art as something meant to be pleasing to the sight or touch. *Aesthetics* is the term used to sum up the search for beauty—for a feeling of balance, proportion and pleasing arrangement; for a tasteful mixture of plain surface with textured or ornamental areas; and for a conscientious use of materials to achieve good craftsmanship and permanence. Aesthetics also includes a search for subject matter that is thought-provoking.

Lesson 1.2 Review

1 List six reasons why people create art. Give an example of art created for each reason.
2 What features of the Western Apache storage jar (fig.1–5) make it not just a useful object, but a work of art?
3 Define aesthetics and use it in a sentence.
4 Explain how an automobile can be considered a work of art.
5 Write three words that come to mind as you look at Robert Swain's painting (fig.1–10).
6 Compare your terms with those of another student. Why do you think Swain did not give this painting a title?

1.3 The Discovery and Preservation of Art

Archaeology

Archaeology is the unearthing and study of evidence from past cultures which have been hidden from human eyes for centuries (fig.1–11). Much of the ancient material seen in this book, such as statues, coins and even buildings, was dug from its earthly grave and brought to society's attention by trained archaeologists. Many of these items are now preserved in museums and universities. Archaeologists also play a key role in giving people an insight into the roots of their culture.

1–11 Students uncovering an *Etruscan object* near Siena, Italy. Bryn Mawr College Archives.

Archaeological items are usually not discovered easily. They are located after hard, plodding detective work. Research is needed to find a probable site for some undiscovered city or culture. To determine if a site is a worthwhile place for archaeological research, cores are drilled to identify the materials under the surface. Once a likely place is found, the earth is carefully dug and removed. Nothing must be disturbed or broken. All the earth must be sifted for tiny bits of pottery or jewelry. Every item uncovered is catalogued, referenced and photographed—even broken bits of jewelry or pottery fragments. Objects are dated by scientific means (carbon-14 count) or by their historical associations.

Archaeology may seem exciting and romantic, as workers excavate sites to find buried treasure. However, it requires research, analysis and a scientific approach to cultural detective work. But there is always the chance of some extraordinary and fascinating find.

In 1977, Soviet and Afghan scientists, working a dig near Afghanistan's northern border, uncovered the grave of a nobleman covered with pieces of gold. Nearby graves revealed more gold objects: bracelets, beads, pins, rings, daggers, clasps and pendants. Before winter set in, they uncovered another grave with so many golden artifacts that they covered it up and returned to it the following year, after the ground had thawed. For 2000 years, these tombs had not been discovered. They date from a culture that lived there from 100 BC to 100 AD. A stunning part of the discovery is that the objects reveal the combined influences of Greek, Bactrian, Roman, Indian and Chinese cultures. It was not known before this discovery that these cultures were ever united in one place on earth. One pendant shows Bactrian rams' heads, Chinese dragons and Mesopotamian animals on the same piece of work.

Sites around the world have revealed glimpses into past great civilizations: the Ming Tombs in China, Pompeii and Herculaneum, the Athenian Acropolis, the Roman Forum, Persepolis, Niniveh, Ur, Memphis, and Monte Alban. More will be uncovered in the future. Every time a new discovery is made, our understanding of world culture is enriched.

Museums

When people want to hear good music, they go to a concert hall, and when they want to see art, they go to a museum. This seems simple enough, but it was not always so. Throughout history, artists have created their work for patrons and collectors, not for museums. Paintings and sculpture were held in the great family collections of kings and queens, nobles and wealthy families (fig.1–12). Only after the revolutions of the eighteenth and nineteenth centuries tumbled the monarchies were the common people allowed to see these objects of art. The new governments opened the fabulous collections of art to the public. The Palace of the Louvre in Paris became the Museum of the Republic in 1793, and many other royal buildings in Europe followed suit. Sometimes new structures were designed to house collections.

Many collections in the United States belong to the cities (Museum of Fine Arts in Boston) or counties (Los Angeles County Museum of Art) or the nation (National Gallery in Washington, DC). These collections were built from gifts of art donated or loaned by individuals or groups of people. Some of the art was purchased with donated funds or by bequests. In this way, American collections have grown in the past century to equal many older collections around the world.

Often, owners of individual collections buy or build their own museums, fill them with their own collections, and open the doors to visitors. The Solomon R. Guggenheim Museum in New York and the J. Paul Getty Museum in California are two examples. Asia and Europe have similar individual collections that are open to the public.

The primary function of museums is to display works of art for the enjoyment of viewers and students of art and culture. Various collections preserve artifacts of past civilizations which contribute to the public's understanding of the history and social customs of these groups. But most museums have other functions also.

Education is of great concern. Groups of schoolchildren and adults can hear lectures and see movies and television and slide programs to aid their understanding of art. Some museums even send out materials to schools and other groups.

Museums in various parts of the country and other parts of the world often work cooperatively to arrange special exhibits for their patrons. As a result of joint efforts, treasures from Mexican and Soviet museums have traveled to museums in the United States and other countries. Some large museums and collections also sponsor exhibits from their collections that travel to smaller regional or municipal museums. In this way, the collected works of art can be enjoyed by many more people.

A program of art restoration and repair is essential to most large museums. The science of formulating pigments, matching paints and repairing canvas, bronze and marble is quite exacting. Photography is used to assure the authenticity of a work of art. Every major painting is X-rayed to record the underpainting and characteristic use of brush and pigments by the artist. This procedure aids in identification, helps prevent frauds and leads to an expanded knowledge of older painting techniques.

Museums control humidity and temperature so valuable works of art on wood or canvas do not dry out or age too rapidly. Light can also be controlled so unnecessary fading is kept to a minimum. Museums take great care to protect works of art and yet keep them on public display.

1–12 Some museum buildings are architectural works of art in themselves. The fifteenth-century Topkapi Palace in Istanbul is a magnificent structure of great historical and architectural interest. It now contains the fabulous collection of jewelry, ceramics, furniture and relics of sultans and the Ottoman Turkish Empire. Although not designed as a museum, it is a worthy setting for such a collection.
Topkapi Palace. *View of the interior,* 15th century. Istanbul.

How We Study Art

Art covers a broad spectrum of ideas and expression. It is a beginner's attempt at watercolor; the graceful design of a table; the Statue of Liberty; a tiny piece of jewelry. Clothes, cars, textbooks and television scenery are designed by artists, and their designs affect the way you live.

Art is all around you. Do you always see it? Probably not. And you probably don't understand all of what you *do* see. But the more you learn about art, the more you'll notice. And the more you notice, the more you'll understand. Understanding things helps you enjoy them and respond to them in new ways.

To grasp the various aspects of art, we can break its study into four components: *aesthetics, history, production* and *criticism.* None of these four components stands alone. All four must be used together to fully appreciate and understand a single work of art.

Aesthetics is a term that refers to our personal responses to works of art. Why do we like some visual images and dislike others? Why do we feel more comfortable with some works than with others? We each respond differently to visual images because we each have a different set of personal experiences on which our responses are based. You say, "I like that painting because..." and your reasons will be your aesthetic response to the painting.

Art History provides the setting and context for a work of art. Artworks reflect the times and cultures of the people who produced them. Art history provides a kind of timeline that shows how art has developed from early human history to the present. It also shows how artists have been influenced by previous artistic styles, by technology and social change, and how those influences show up in their artwork. Art history adds personality to works of art and helps us see artists and their times in the work they have done. We understand today's art more fully when we can trace its development through time.

1–13 Two students study Seurat's *Sunday Afternoon on the Island of La Grande Jatte* at the Art Institute of Chicago.

1–14 Caryn Kim of West Springfield High School, Fairfax County, Virginia, sculpts her self-portrait in clay.

Art Production is the creation of art. This process requires tools, media and technical ability. It involves learning to look carefully, use the materials you choose, make decisions, solve problems, learn about design, interpret what you see and feel, and criticize your own efforts. Through production and studio experiences, you'll learn to appreciate the ability, knowledge and skill of fine artists and craftspeople. By handling clay, mixing colors, working with composition, using brushes, carving wood or building a model, you'll enter the working world of artists and begin to understand some of the visual and technical problems they encounter daily.

Art Criticism is analysis. It is explaining and judging works of art. It is discovering how the artist used art elements such as line, color and texture. It is determining how the artist used balance, pattern, emphasis and other art principles to arrange the parts of the work. It is sensing how the artist used media and tools to create the work. It is also trying to understand what the artist might have meant to say in the work. In this way, we analyze the artwork's sensory, formal, technical and expressive qualities.

Lesson 1.3 Review

1 How are archaeology and art history related?
2 What was the Louvre before it became a museum? When did it become a museum?
3 How have the large public museums in the United States acquired their art?
4 Name two museums which began as individual's collections?
5 What are some of the processes that museums use to repair and restore art?
6 How can producing your own art help you to understand great works of art?

Primary Source

The Artist and the Museum

Museums are not simply places that house the art of by-gone eras. They are alive with teaching and learning and inspiration. The famous nineteenth-century artist, Degas, tells us why museums were so important to him.

"The museums are there to teach the history of art and something more as well, for, if they stimulate in the weak a desire to imitate, they furnish the strong with the means of their emancipation."

"No art was ever less spontaneous than mine. What I do is the result of reflection and study of the great masters."

Edgar Degas, *Carriages at the Races*, Museum of Fine Arts, Boston. Arthur Gordon Tompkins Fund.

Chapter Review

Review

1 What are some of the processes inherent in thoughtful art criticism?
2 Why are museums concerned about controlling the humidity, temperature and light inside their buildings?
3 In studying a work of art, why is it helpful to understand the history of that piece and others like it?
4 Briefly describe the archaeological processes of unearthing an ancient city.

Interpret

1 Select a piece of art from this chapter that appeals to you. Who made it and when was it created? Describe its technical and expressive properties. Why do you think it was created? Explain why you like it.
2 What are some of the clues in the kylix (fig.1–3) that would indicate to an art historian that it was created in Greece after 500 BC?

Other Tools for Learning

Electronic Research
Videodisc player: *National Gallery of Art*
CD-ROM drive: *Microsoft Art Gallery*

1 After viewing *The History of the National Gallery of Art (Washington, DC)* on their videodisc, describe what one of the many people involved in the founding of this museum did to help create it.
2 Browse through a museum's collection, such as the *Louvre Videodisc* or the National Gallery on the *Microsoft Art Gallery* CD-ROM. Select one piece of art to describe. Who created it? When was it made? What is its medium? Describe the effect this art has on your feelings.

Activity 1

Classroom Museum

Materials

found objects
paper strips for labels
scissors and ruler
pencil, eraser
markers

Take a look. Review all the artwork in Chapter 1 and read each caption carefully.

Think about it.

- The captions in this text generally have two parts. The first part asks a question or points out an interesting fact; the credits tell the title of the work, the artist's name and other information about the artwork. Does it make a difference in the way you look at an artwork to know what year it was made? In what country? What it was made of? How big it is?
- Archaeologists find and study evidence, or relics, of the past. Often, they display what they've found in exhibits that explain their discoveries. What clues might be discovered about you a few hundred years from now?

Do it. Make an arrangement of three objects, similar to a museum archaeology display.

- Be an archaeologist at home and find three objects that are clues to your family's past.
- Make labels for each object by cutting white paper into uniform strips and neatly writing out as much of the following information as possible: artist's name, title of the object, date it was made, country or state where it was made, physical description (medium, color, size), where you obtained the object, the owner.
- Consider ways of displaying your objects that will show off their best qualities. Arrange your display on your desk or a table, as indicated by your teacher.

Check it.

- Can your work be seen clearly from all angles? If not, is its "best side" facing the viewers?
- Do your labels contribute useful and interesting information to your viewers? Are they neat and easily read from about three feet away?

Helpful Hint: Write out your labels in pencil at first to determine what size, style and placement of letters is most effective. Do your final label in a color that complements your objects.

Activity 2

Digging for Art

Materials

magazines
poster board
markers
glue/tape
scissors

Take a look. Review the following artwork:

- Fig.1–1 *Ceremonial cup,* about 1000 BC.
- Fig.1–3 Douris, *Eos and Memnon.* Interior of red-figured kylix, about 490–480 BC.
- Fig.1–4 Exekias, *Dionysus in a Boat.* Interior of Attic black-figured kylix, about 540 BC.

Think about it. Art objects like these were created hundreds or thousands of years ago in early civilizations, then often lost to the world until their rediscovery centuries later. If you wanted to find ancient art, where would you look? How do you think old civilizations are found? What can we learn from discovered relics about the lives of our ancestors?

Do it. Make a display chart or poster illustrating steps that archaeologists use to find, identify and classify objects.

- Look through back issues of magazines like *National Geographic, Discover, Smithsonian, Archaeology,* etc., and clip pictures of archaeological activities, such as digging, sifting, reconstructing, photographing, drawing, plotting and so forth.
- Arrange your images on a large sheet of paper. On separate strips of paper, neatly write out labels that identify what's happening in the pictures. Before you glue everything down, do "Check it," below.

Check it. Have a friend look at your poster, and ask if he or she understands what's happening in the poster without your having to explain anything. If something is unclear, try another arrangement or new labels.

Helpful Hint: You might make up a story about the adventures of the archaeologist or the ancient artist to accompany your arrangement of images.

Additional Activities

- Art, design and visual images affect our lives in many ways every day. Make a list of things you use daily that artists have designed. Organize your list into general categories such as transportation, clothing, artwork, advertising, entertainment and others you discover.
- Research archaeology books or magazine articles that deal with parts of the world associated with your ethnic or religious roots. Write a brief report on your findings. Have many relics been discovered? Are excavations still going on? What are some theories about ancient lifestyles based on objects found?

Kyung-Sil Chang

Age 18
West Springfield High School
Springfield, Virginia
Favorite kinds of art: painting and sculpture
Favorite artists: Vincent van Gogh, Pablo Picasso, Leonardo da Vinci, Donatello, Wassily, Kandinsky
Activity 1, Classroom Museum

My first ancestor came from China to Korea about 750 years ago. Back then, a Chinese princess married a Korean prince and my ancestor had to take the princess to Korea safely. When he came to Korea, he liked it. He decided to stay and work for the Korean government. From that, my family's history started.

The portrait drawing is of my thirteenth ancestor. Back then, the king awarded him a self-portrait, drawn with rock powder so it would last forever. My ancestor's drawing is about 300 years old. One is when he was young and the other one is when he was old. All relics are so important to me, because it's about my family's history and it's about my ancestors.

My favorite subject is art and I've decided to go to an art college. My drawings are very important to me, because I put my spirit into them. If my house were to catch fire, first I would want to get my artworks. But before that, I would get my ancestors' relics, because I can't buy them and I can't make them either. Where else am I going to feel their spirit? My works I can do over, even though those were so precious to me.

I am taking art history now and learning about the history of art. I never thought about my family's history, and I think it's a shame of mine. If I don't even know mine, then how can I search for another's background? I never knew about my ancestors until we did this project in art history class.

My grandpa told me about our ancestor's history and our family tree. But, I couldn't understand the family tree that well, it was so complicated. I want my grandpa's brush for a relic, but I would like my dad and my brother to keep it, so my brother may tell his children about my grandpa. How great he was! I learned so much through this project and I had a chance to think about my family's background. I am proud of my family history!

Kyung-Sil Chang

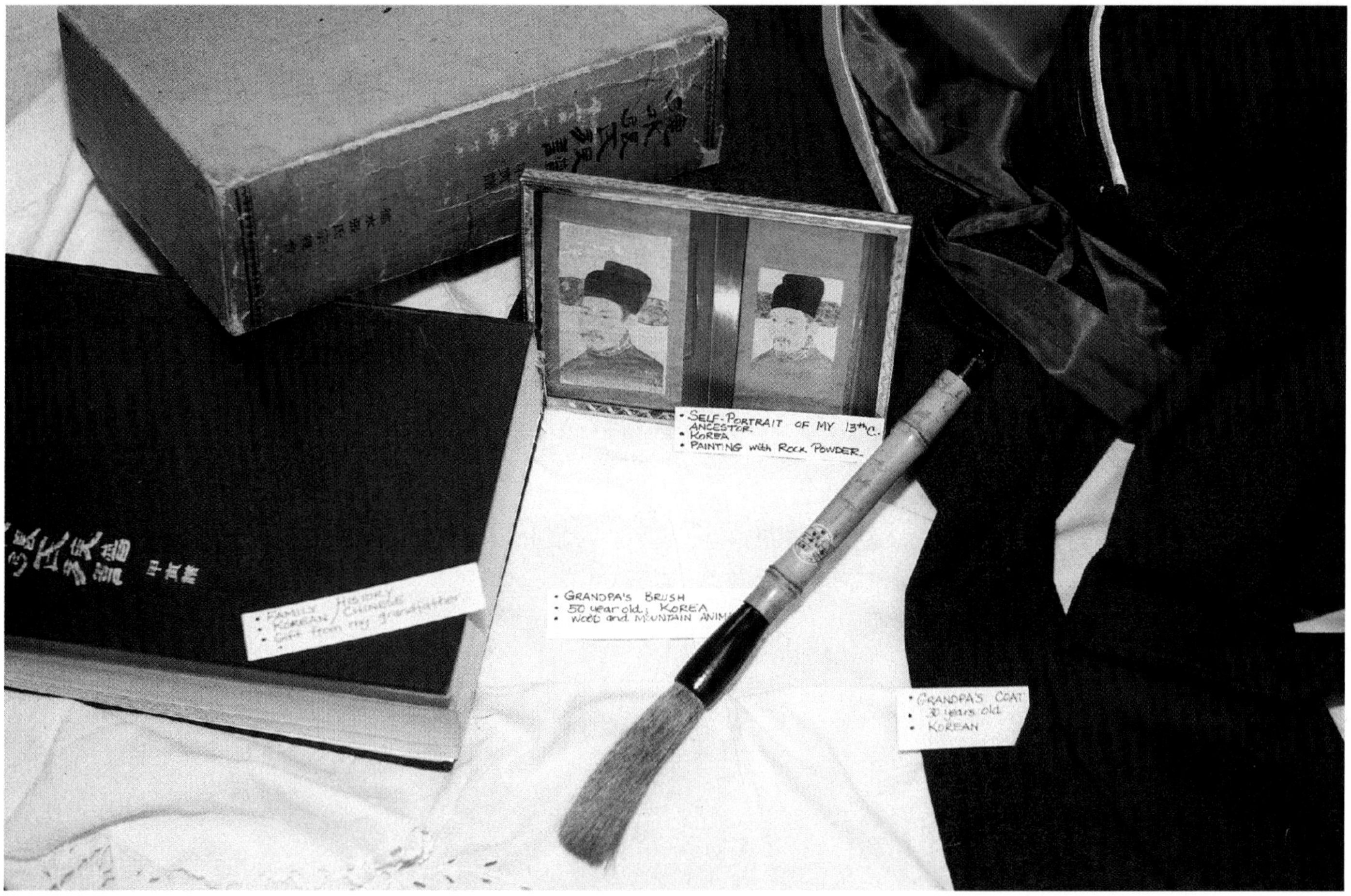

2 Visual Communication

In This Chapter...

ART IS VISUAL COMMUNICATION, with a language all its own. Artists and craftspersons communicate their ideas, concepts and responses to subject matter through their artwork.

To fully understand art and the artists' communication, it is important to learn about the entire process—subjects, techniques and styles. This chapter, therefore, explores four areas: *subject matter*—what the artist is conveying; *media*—the tools and materials the artist used; *craftsmanship*—the ability to make useful objects attractive; *design*—the grammar, or structure, of visual language.

Each of these areas could be discussed in book length. However, only the major points of each area can be covered here. This brief background should make your study of art history more interesting and meaningful, and more personally satisfying. As you learn more about the history of art, you will begin to see how the artist's use of materials and approaches to subject matter have evolved. Each era has found new ways to use the elements of art and design principles to communicate its ideas and ideals.

2–a Notice how the design and placement of the subject matter, particularly the dragon, works in such harmony with the form of this jar.
Shoulder Jar, 1522–1566. Chinese, Ming dynasty. Porcelain. Ostasiatiche Kunstabteilung Staatliche Museum, Berlin.

2–b The artist has used the medium of a fabric quilt to depict a series of Biblical images. Can you identify the subject matter of any of these scenes?
Harriet Powers, *Pictorial Quilt,* 1895–1898. American. Pieced and appliqued cotton embroidered with plain and metallic yarns, 69" x 105" (175 x 267 cm). Museum of Fine Arts, Boston, Bequest of Maxim Karolik.

All the arts are brothers; each one is a light to the others.

Voltaire

2–c The van Eyck brothers painted with extraordinary skill. The use of oil paint as a medium greatly expanded their ability to render textures with amazing accuracy. How many different materials and fabrics can you find in this painting?
Hubert and Jan van Eyck, *Ghent Altarpiece*, detail of right wing, completed 1432. Netherlandish. Oil on panel, Cathedral of St. Bavo, Ghent, Belgium.

2–e Chardin has used the student artist as his subject. What impression is he trying to convey about this laboring student?
Jean Baptiste Simeon Chardin, *Young Student Drawing*, about 1738. French. Oil on wood, 8 1/4" x 6 3/4" (21 x 17.1 cm). Kimbell Art Museum, Fort Worth, Texas.

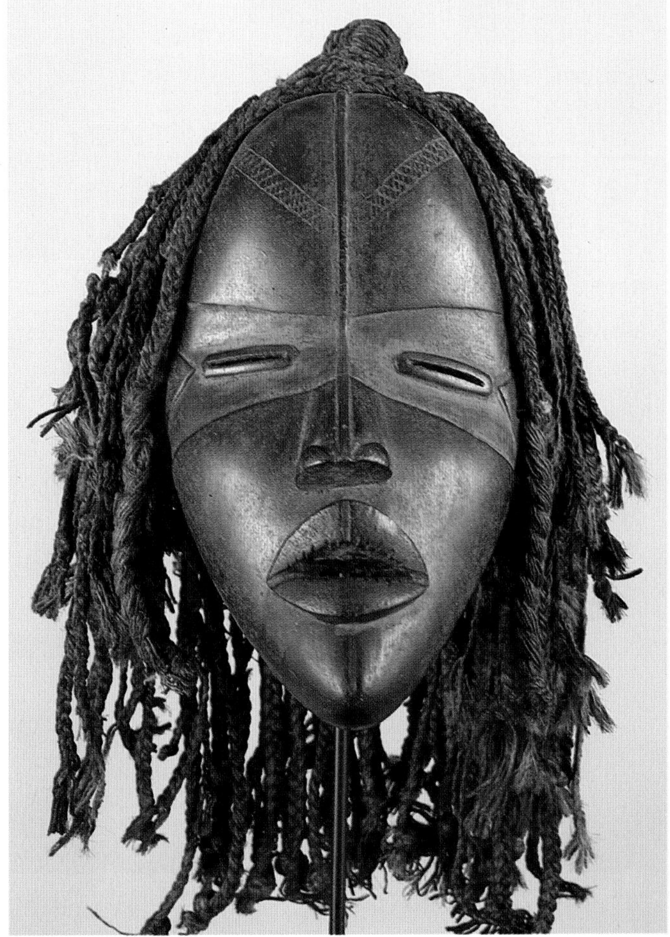

2–d How has the artist contrasted symmetry and asymmetry in this work? Do you think the contrast is effective?
Dance Mask, about 1900. African, Dan Tribe, Ivory Coast. Painted wood with vegetable fiber, 9 1/2" (24 cm) high. Collection of Charles W. and Janice R. Mack.

2.1 Subject Matter: What Is It Saying?

SUPPOSE SOMEONE HANDED YOU a pencil and told you to draw something. That *something* that you chose to draw would be the subject matter. Most artists use things as their subjects, things such as people, objects, landscape (fig.2–2) or animals. Others use ideas such as war, love, loneliness or joy. Still others are concerned with the scientific or mathematical aspects of art. Design and proportion become their subject matter.

Artists also tell something about their subject. They need a reason to paint a landscape or to sculpt a person. This reason may be as simple as liking the color of green grass or as personal as wanting to show the order and harmony of the natural world. Artists may sculpt or paint a woman because she is beautiful or because they want to show her character or her influence on her fellow humans. Throughout history, and especially in the last few decades, artists' attitudes toward subject matter have changed drastically, as you will learn in the last chapters.

Narrative Subjects

In *narrative* paintings, the artist is telling a story. The painter Pieter Brueghel of Flanders was a master storyteller. Within a large painting, he included small scenes of peasant life and little insights that can be developed into further stories. This jolly gathering is typical of his work. One can easily find the bride, but where is the groom? As Brueghel tells his own story of the wedding, he interweaves many subplots. What are they?

2–1 Pieter Brueghel, *Peasant Wedding*, 1566. Netherlandish. Oil on panel, 44 1/2" x 63 3/4" (113 x 162 cm). Kunsthistorisches Museum, Vienna.

Dürer has chosen a close-up of grass and soil as his subject matter. He presents us with a detailed view of a part of our environment that is not often subjected to careful scrutiny.

2–2 Albrecht Dürer, *The Great Piece of Turf,* 1503. German. Watercolor and tempera on paper, mounted on cardboard, 15 3/4" x 12 1/4" (40.3 x 31.1 cm). Albertina, Vienna.

Religious Subjects

Any religious figure from any religion can be the subject of a work of art. Biblical scenes dominate the Christian art of Europe. Buddhists and Hindus have a long tradition of sculpting and painting figures and scenes of their deities. The people of Africa, the Americas and the Pacific region have an extensive history of depicting their gods or sacred symbols. The Mayan maize god pictured here held great significance for the Mayan people. Maize was the main food staple of Mesoamerica. Can you distinguish any of the elements of a growing corn stalk in this figure?

2–3 *Maize God*, from Temple 22, Maya, Copan, Honduras, about 775. Limestone, 35 1/3" x 21 1/3" (90 x 54 cm). British Museum, London.

Literary Subjects

Painters may use literary sources, such as the Bible or famous myths and legends, to get ideas for their work. This painting illustrates a scene from the famous tale of Rip Van Winkle. The legend is part of Washington Irving's *Sketch Book* and illustrates that point in the story when Rip Van Winkle has awakened from his long sleep. He is bewildered by the sight of his son who stands alone by the tree. He also confronts his fellow villagers who demand to know his name. He replies: "God knows, I'm not myself—I'm somebody else—that's me yonder—no—that's somebody else got into my shoes—I was myself last night, but I fell asleep on the mountain ..."

2–4 John Quidor, *The Return of Rip Van Winkle*, 18(4?)9. American. Oil on canvas, 39 3/4" x 49 3/4" (101 x 126.5cm). National Gallery of Art, Washington, DC, Andrew W. Mellon Collection, 1942.

Landscapes

Landscapes are paintings of the natural environment. They have been a popular subject for artists through the centuries and throughout the world. The Chinese can be considered true masters of landscape painting, which has dominated their art since the fourth century AD. Here, the artist, Hsia Kuei, is able to convey a misty, evocative view of a river and mountains with only the barest use of his brush.

2–5 Hsia Kuei, *Twelve Views from a Thatched Hut*, section of handscroll, about 1180–1230. Chinese. Ink on silk, height 11" (28 cm). The Nelson-Atkins Museum of Art, Kansas City, Missouri.

Cityscapes

Views of city streets, plazas, courtyards, buildings and activities taking place in the urban environment are called *cityscapes*. Most cityscapes have been done in the twentieth century, but Corot produced this early view of Venice in 1834. Corot, a Realist painter, portrays an authentic scene from the times. He does not tell a story nor does he reveal his feelings about Venice. He simply depicts what he saw, in about the same way a photographer would take a picture of the place to send to a friend.

2–6 Jean-Baptiste-Camille Corot, *View of Venice, the Piazzetta Seen from the Quay of the Esclavons*, 1834. French. Oil on canvas, 18 1/2" x 27 1/4" (47 x 69 cm). Norton Simon Museum, Pasadena, CA.

The Figure

Artists have considered the figure a supreme subject. They appreciate the human body as both an aesthetic and sensuous form. To understand this tradition, we need to recognize that artists—and their cultures—have many reasons for portraying the nude.

Ancient Greek philosophy and religion placed the human at the center of the cosmos as the "measure of all things." In their search for ideal or divine forms it was only logical for the Greeks to place the idealized, perfect human form at the top of artistic creation. Greek athletes competed in the nude because their perfectly conditioned bodies were seen as aesthetic expressions to be admired as a good painting or sculpture would be.

At times, nudity has been seen as barbaric. One statement repeatedly made by Roman historians about the ferocity of the ancient Gauls and Britons was that they fought nude. This terrorized the Romans. During the Middle Ages, the human body was seen as corrupt and imperfect. It was not considered appropriate to portray the human body or study it.

When Renaissance artists rediscovered the Greek tradition, there was a lot of furor over the morality of portraying the nude. However, as the Western art tradition renewed its quest for naturalism, artists quickly realized that to portray people naturalistically required the study not only of the nude, but also of the cadaver. Dissection taught artists about the structure of muscles and bones.

Today, artists continue to study and portray the nude as the ultimate artistic challenge. It is a complex form that changes dramatically with the slightest shift in weight or twist in attitude. It is also capable of a tremendous range of expression and emotion.

2–7 Myron, *Discus Thrower*, Roman marble copy after Greek bronze original of about 450 BC, lifesize. Museo Nazionale Romano, Rome.

2–8 Peter Paul Rubens, *Judgment of Paris*, about 1629. Flemish. Oil on panel, 57" x 76 3/4" (145 x 195 cm). National Gallery, London.

The Portrait

Portraits come in a variety of sizes and shapes, but have one thing in common—they are representations of people. The people may be alone or in groups, young or old. They may pose formally or informally and may be set against a solid background or in the natural environment. The artist may depict the full figure, from head to toe, or only the bust, the upper body. They can be painted or sculpted. Holbein, one of the world's greatest portrait artists, painted Prince Edward VI for his father, Henry VIII. The pose is rather stiff and formal, the clothes are regal, and the inscription tells Edward to emulate his father in all things. Unfortunately, Edward died before he could become England's king.

2–9 Hans Holbein, *Edward VI as a Child*, 1538. German. Oil on panel, 22 1/2" x 17 1/4" (57 x 44 cm). National Gallery of Art, Washington, DC, Andrew Mellon Collection.

Self-Portraits

Many artists make pictures of themselves, called *self-portraits*. This nineteenth-century portraitist strongly conveys her unconventional persona in a self-portrait. The cross-legged pose, beer stein and lit cigarette fly in the face of our idea of the turn-of-the-century woman. Clearly, this is a woman who does what she wants without fear of what others will say. Indeed, Frances Benjamin Johnston was a successful and prolific photographer.

2–10 Frances Benjamin Johnston, *Self-Portrait*, 1895. American. Photograph. Library of Congress, Washington, DC.

Historical Subjects

Historical subjects have often been painted on large canvases, probably to memorialize or lend importance to an event. In 1939, Hale Woodruff painted a series of murals for a library at Talladeger College, an African-American college near Atlanta. The murals tell about the Amistad Mutiny, an important chapter of African-American history. In 1839, Africans on a Portuguese slave ship bound for Havana mutinied. Led by their Sierra Leonese chief, Cinque, they ordered the ship back to Africa. They landed instead at New London, Connecticut, where a trial was held. The Africans were acquitted and freed, and allowed to return to their homeland. In this scene, Woodruff depicts the trial.

To prepare for his work, Woodruff immersed himself in the events. He traveled to New Haven, where he discovered sketches that had been drawn of the trial. The sketches depicted the Africans and the Amistad costumes and weapons of the time. These documents helped the artist bring historical accuracy to a mural painted one hundred years after the event occurred.

2–11 Hale Woodruff, *The Amistad Slaves on Trial at New Haven*, 1840. American. Oil on canvas, 12" x 40" (31 x 102 cm). Aaron Douglas Collection. Amistad Research Center at Tulane University, New Orleans.

Genre Subjects

Genre painting refers to normal, everyday activities of ordinary people. A king and queen riding in a royal carriage is not a genre subject, but a poor family riding on the local public transportation is. Farmers working in the fields, children in school, people sitting in a café, or a woman peeling potatoes are genre subjects. In this scene, the Korean painter, Ham Yundok, depicts a man on his donkey. The bent head and splayed legs of the exhausted donkey make us wonder about the nature and length of the man's journey.

2–12 Ham Yundok, *Man Riding a Donkey*, 16th century. Korean. Album leaf, ink and color on silk, 6 1/8" x 7 5/8" (15.5 x 19.4 cm). National Museum of Korea, Seoul.

Still Life

A *still life* is a painting of inanimate objects—things that cannot move. Bottles, bowls, fruit, flowers and cloth often appear in these works. The objects are usually arranged by the artist on a table top in the studio. Still-life paintings can be elaborate (fig.13–22) or extremely simple, as in this ink drawing of persimmons.

2–14 Mu-ch'i, *Six Persimmons*, 13th century. Chinese. Ink on paper. Daitoku-ji, Kyoto, Japan.

Social Comment

Some artists want to make visual statements about their society or the world. They may criticize national leaders, churches, neighbors, wars or political oppression. Latin-American artists have a strong tradition of using their art to make pointed political statements. In this unflattering portrait of the presidential family, Botero criticized the colonial attitudes that still pervaded the upper classes.

2–13 Fernando Botero, *The Presidential Family*, 1967. Colombian. Oil on canvas, 80" x 77 1/8" (203 x 196 cm). The Museum of Modern Art, New York, gift of Warren D. Benedek, 1967.

Animals

Artists are often intrigued by animals. Nearly all cultures have portrayed birds and mammals with great skill, both in realistic and stylized versions. This alpaca from the early Inca civilization is made of soldered sheet silver. The artist is careful to show the fine long hair of this wool-producing animal.

2–15 *Alpaca,* Inca. Silver, 9 1/2" x 8 1/8" x 2" (24 x 21 x 5 cm). American Museum of Natural History, New York.

Expression

While some artists paint what they see when looking at their subject matter, others, like El Greco, include their feelings about the subject. When personal and emotional feelings are added to a work, it is an *expressionist* painting. El Greco lived in Toledo, Spain. Here he paints the city from a hill on the opposite side of the river. Using greens and blues in various values and mixtures, he gives his city a distinct personality. Sparkling under a supercharged sky, the city seems vibrant and full of excitement, yet mysterious and rather lonely.

2–16 El Greco, *View of Toledo,* 1600–1610. Spanish. Oil on canvas, 47 1/2" x 42 1/2" (121 x 108 cm). The Metropolitan Museum of Art, New York, bequest of Mrs. H. O. Havemeyer.

Abstraction

Abstraction is the simplification of subject matter into basic and often geometric shapes. Some modern artists, such as Picasso, so simplified the objects in a painting that the simplification, not the objects, became the subject matter. Picasso here uses his studio as a starting point. He depicts a table as simplified shapes. The whitish oval on the right may be a sculpture. The two triangles in the center are a container. Pictures are on the back wall. The artist and his easel are at the left. While viewers may identify these elements, the painting is first and foremost an abstract arrangement of lines, shapes and colors. The abstracted design was far more important to Picasso than the studio objects.

Notice that the artist in the picture has three eyes. What may Picasso be suggesting about the visual awareness of artists?

2–17 Pablo Picasso, *The Studio,* 1927–1928. Spanish. Oil on canvas, 59" x 91" (150 x 231 cm). The Museum of Modern Art, New York, gift of Walter P. Chrysler, Jr.

2–18 Jackson Pollock, *Full Fathom Five,* 1947. American. Oil on canvas, 51" x 30 1/4" (130 x 77 cm). The Museum of Modern Art, New York, gift of Peggy Guggenheim.

Nonobjective Painting

In the late nineteenth century, artists gradually created more abstract works. However, their art, like Picasso's *The Studio,* still presented recognizable objects. Even Cézanne, who stated that the painting was more important than the subject matter, included identifiable forms. During the early twentieth century, some artists painted fully abstract works that were composed of only color, shape and line. When artists such as Jackson Pollock began a painting, they did not think of trees and people. Instead, they thought of color and line. Today, such nonobjective painting is common.

Lesson 2.1 Review

1 Define subject matter, media, craftsmanship and design.
2 Name three different types of artistic subject matter. Give an example of each.
3 What is a portrait?
4 What type of subjects are in genre paintings?
5 What is abstract art?

2.2 Media: Tools and Materials

Drawing Media

Pencil

The pencil has always been one of the most versatile drawing tools. The pencil dates back to the Roman stylus, a pointed tool that made delicate lines. Lead had been used to make lines, but in 1795, the French inventor Conté found a way to mix graphite and clay, and the modern pencil was born. It can be used for quick sketches and for detailed drawings. Ingres' portrait drawing of Thomas Church combines many pencil techniques in one work. There are quickly sketched lines and heavy, firm lines. The shaded areas on the body were done with broad, flat strokes while the face was finished with careful shading under great control. Ingres was a master draftsperson, and the pencil was his favorite drawing medium.

2–19 Jean-Auguste-Dominique Ingres, *Thomas Church*, 1816. French. Graphite on paper, 7 1/2" x 6 1/4" (19 x 16 cm). Los Angeles County Museum of Art, Loula D. Lasker Estate Fund.

Charcoal

The soft, grainy quality of charcoal is evident in Seurat's drawing done on textured paper. Charcoal can be compressed into sticks, like chalk, so that the ends and sides can both be used. It can also be wrapped in wood and used in pencil form. Charcoal smudges easily and is used primarily as a sketching material. Seurat used the broad side of a charcoal crayon to capture quickly the pose he wanted. Look at Seurat's painting *Sunday Afternoon on the Island of La Grande Jatte* (fig.13–19) to find this sketched figure in final form.

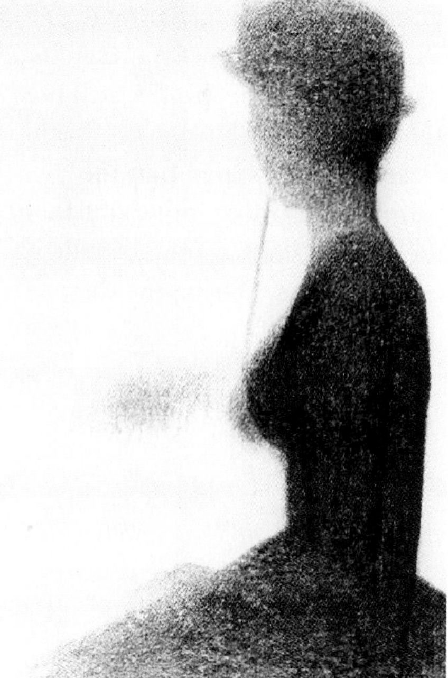

2–20 Georges Seurat, *Seated Woman*, about 1885. French. Charcoal on paper. The Museum of Modem Art, New York.

Ink

When ink is applied undiluted, it makes a solid black area. When it is mixed with water, it produces a soft gray. The more water that is added, the lighter the gray. Light grays are called *washes*—a term used to describe the dilution of inks with water. For the artists of Japan and China, ink was the preferred medium, which they applied with a brush. The technique was brought to great heights throughout the history of Asian art. The exquisite skill of the Japanese artist Sesshu is demonstrated in this landscape. The washes are subtly varied, while brushed lines define buildings, vegetation and a barely defined fisherman in his boat in the foreground.

Artists often simply use brush and ink or pen and ink to make their drawings. The hard line of comic strips and cartoons is made with these techniques. Ink is often used as a sketching medium, allowing artists to explore their subjects before painting them. Diego Rivera was an exceptional draftsperson and was very confident with his application of ink to paper. This brush drawing is simple, clean and powerful. The lines have various thicknesses, which help produce a sense of form. No shading is necessary because the lines have such visual strength.

2–21 Sesshu, *Haboku Landscape,* fifteenth century. Japanese. Ink on paper, height 28 5/16" (72 cm). Cleveland Museum of Art.

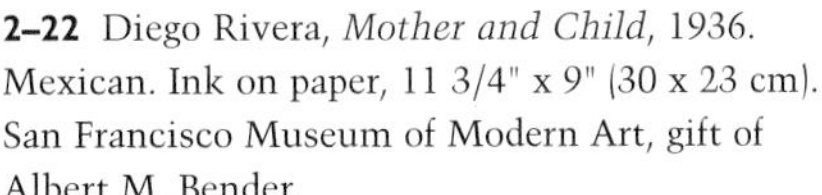

2–22 Diego Rivera, *Mother and Child,* 1936. Mexican. Ink on paper, 11 3/4" x 9" (30 x 23 cm). San Francisco Museum of Modern Art, gift of Albert M. Bender.

Pastel

Oil pastels are a dry material, almost like colored chalk. Creating with oil pastels is halfway between drawing and painting. The final result usually looks like a colored drawing and is often called a painting. Mary Cassatt was equally adept at pastels and oil painting. Her pastel *Sleeping Baby* has delicate shading, light value colors and a sketchy, dry-textured quality—all characteristic of this soft, chalky medium. The subject matter of mother and child in a casual, loving relationship is a favorite of the artist.

2–23 Mary Cassatt, *Sleeping Baby,* about 1910. American. Pastel on paper, 25 1/2" x 20 1/2" (65 x 52 cm). Dallas Museum of Fine Arts, Munger Fund.

Painting Media

Fresco

Fresco is one of the oldest painting media and one of the most difficult to master. Frescoes have been used in many parts of the world to decorate walls and ceilings. The most well-known fresco of the Western World is the Sistine Ceiling (*See* p.281).

In the fresco process, the surface to be painted is first covered with a coat of rough plaster, which is allowed to dry. Fresh, smooth plaster is applied only to the area to be painted that day. While the plaster is wet, pigment is brushed on. The pigment makes a permanent bond with the lime in the plaster. No changes can be made to this layer once it has dried. Paint added to the dried plaster is called *fresco secco* and does not have the permanence of the primary layer.

2–24 *Palace Scene,* 580 AD. Indian. Fresco. Ajanta, Grotto no. 17.

Tempera

Tempera is a type of paint that is similar to the poster paint used in elementary schools. As early as ancient Egypt, artists have used various forms of tempera paint. Some, such as the painter of this thirteenth-century cross, used egg yolk as the binding agent to stick the colored pigment to the wooden panel. Since egg tempera dries quickly, artists use small brushes to work on very small and detailed areas with tiny strokes. Building up layers of transparent color over each other creates a richly colored, luminous surface.

2–25 Master of San Francesco, *Crucifixion,* about 1280. Italian. Tempera and gold on wood, 74" high (1.88 m). Philadelphia Museum of Art, the Wilstach Collection.

Oil

Oil paint is a medium that came to dominate the history of European art. Oil painting became popular when artists needed to work on larger surfaces with larger brushes. Oil colors are pigments bound to a surface of wood or canvas with either linseed or poppy oil. The paint is usually thinned with turpentine to make it spreadable. Oil paint takes much longer to dry than tempera. It can be applied in thick, buttery layers (*impasto*) or in thinned washes, or *glazes.* The variety of techniques is tremendous. Peter Paul Rubens was a master of the medium. By using glazes of color mixed with varnish, he was able to make the tints of flesh and satin material glow in his paintings. When canvas became the main type of ground, oil paintings could become huge in size. Rubens took advantage of this advance in his many gigantic works. Deep darks and brilliant lights offer the ultimate range of value contrasts.

2–26 Peter Paul Rubens, *Garden of Love,* about 1633. Flemish. Oil on canvas, 77 1/2" x 110 1/2" (197 x 281 cm). Prado Museum, Madrid.

Watercolor

Used since ancient Egypt, watercolor only recently came into its own as a major painting medium. Many artists have used watercolor to make sketches before making oil paintings in their studios. Watercolor was not considered a major painting medium until Winslow Homer, an American artist, became famous. Homer thought of his watercolors as finished works instead of sketches, and exhibited them as such. The binding agent in watercolor is gum arabic, a water-soluble adhesive that sticks the pigments to paper. The colors are mostly transparent. Gouache and casein paints are opaque watercolor. Some artists prefer these paints for their excellent covering characteristics.

2–27 Winslow Homer, *After the Hunt*, 1892. American. Watercolor on paper, 18 3/4" x 24 3/4" (48 x 63 cm). Los Angeles County Museum of Art, Paul Rodman Mabury Collection.

Acrylic

In the last half of the twentieth century, acrylics became one of the most popular media. Instead of using natural materials for binders, acrylic paints use polymer emulsions that can adhere pigments to almost any surface—masonite, canvas, glass, paper, cardboard or wood. Thinned with water and easy to clean up, acrylics dry rapidly. They can be applied heavily like oils and transparently like watercolors. Their versatility has made them extremely popular.

2–28 Alma Thomas. *Iris, Tulips, Jonquils and Crocuses*, 1969. American. Acrylic on canvas, 60" x 50" (152.4 x 127 cm). National Museum of Women in the Arts, The Holladay Collection.

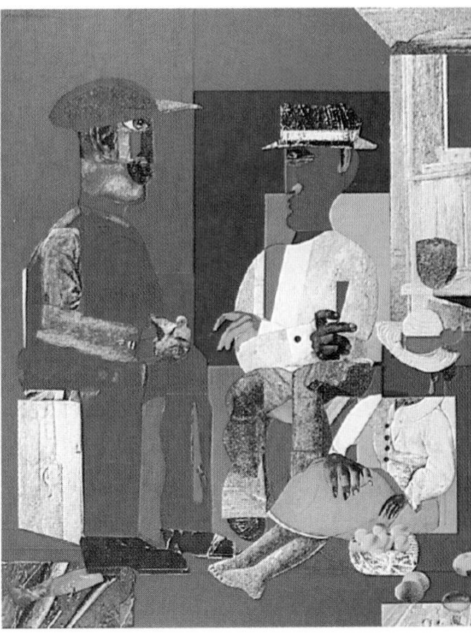

Collage

Collage is one the latest media to be developed. It was begun by Pablo Picasso and Georges Braque in France. In 1912, they started to embellish their canvases with glued materials. Collage involves pasting papers to a ground. (The word *collage* comes from the French term *papier collé*, meaning "pasted paper.") Artists have used all sorts of materials in collages, but paper continues to be the most popular. Romare Bearden cuts pictures with textures and colors from magazines to produce collages that make dynamic social statements. His reconstructed images always involve people. The chunky shapes in this rural scene are typical of Bearden's work. The shapes are cut from magazines and augmented with other painting media.

2–29 Romare Bearden, *Eastern Barn*, 1968. American. Collage of paper with glue, lacquer and oil on paper, 55 1/2" x 44" (141 x 112 cm). Whitney Museum of American Art, New York.

Printmaking Media

The various printmaking techniques began as a way to furnish art to the masses at reasonable prices. Even though many copies are made by the artist, each is signed and numbered. The edition is kept to a limited number of copies, thus ensuring that the value will remain constant.

2–31 Rembrandt van Rijn, *Christ Crucified Between the Two Thieves (The Three Crosses)*, 1653. Dutch. Fourth-state etching, approx. 15 x 18" (38.1 x 45.7 cm). Metropolitan Museum of Art, New York, gift of Felix M. Warburg and his family, 1941.

Woodcut

A woodcut is called a relief print because the image on the plate projects, or sticks up, from the surface. The artist draws on a block of wood, then cuts away the parts that will remain white. Ink is then rolled onto the remaining raised area. Then, the surface is printed to reveal a mirror image of the original cutout design. The Japanese excel at this art form. One of their most famous artists, Ando Hiroshige, designed this scene of a rain shower. This print includes a number of colors. Each color required a separate cut block. In some Japanese prints, over fifteen separate blocks were used to achieve the final result.

2–30 Ando Hiroshige, *Rain Shower on Ohashi Bridge*, 1857. Japanese. Color woodblock print, height 13 7/8" (35 cm). Cleveland Museum of Art.

Intaglio

While woodcuts are printed from the raised surface of a block, intaglio prints are made from the lines or crevices *in* a plate. To produce the design, the printmaker makes lines and scratches in the metal plate, usually zinc or copper. The indentations can be made by applying acid (etching) or by scratching (drypoint). Indentations can also be made by engraving, or removing thin V-shaped strips with a tool called a *burin.* Ink is forced into these grooves by rubbing, and the rest of the plate is wiped clean. To transfer the image, the paper is dampened and placed against the plate in a press. Under great pressure, the dampened paper picks up the ink from the grooves and the image is made. *Intaglio* refers to the ink being transferred to paper from *below the surface.* Rembrandt's intaglio print combines etching and drypoint to produce an incredible variety of lines and dark areas.

Linocut

Linocut is a relief printmaking medium that produces an image similar to a woodcut. This medium makes use of cutting tools and linoleum. Cuts are made into the smooth, even surface of the linoleum. Ink is rolled over the remaining surface with a brayer. Resulting prints can either be refined or jagged, depending on the artist's wishes and style. Elizabeth Catlett is a contemporary artist who uses the relief process to its best advantage. The marks of the cutting tools are evident.

2–32 Elizabeth Catlett, *The Survivor*, 1983. American. Linocut, 11" x 10 1/4" (28 x 26 cm). Courtesy Malcom Brown Gallery, Cleveland.

Lithograph

Lithographs may appear textured, flat, black-and-white or full-color. Toulouse-Lautrec made many large prints that advertised the cafés, bars and nightclubs of Paris. In this lithograph, a printmaker is making a lithographic print. The female client is checking it for accuracy. To make a lithograph or "stone writing," the artist draws a design on a limestone slab with a greasy crayon or ink. Then, water is spread over the stone. The water will adhere only where there is no greasy substance. A large brayer is then used to roll greasy ink onto the surface. Because grease will not mix with water, the ink sticks only where there is no water. Therefore, the ink sticks to places where the design was drawn. The image is now ready to be reproduced. As Toulouse-Lautrec's print shows, a sheet of paper is put over the slab and run through a lithographic press. Lithography is a difficult process to master. When several colors are used, each one has to have its own stone, and colors are printed one over the other.

2–33 Henri de Toulouse-Lautrec, *L'Estampe Originale*, 1893. French. Color lithograph, 17 3/4" x 23 3/4" (45 x 60.3 cm). The Metropolitan Museum of Art, Rogers Fund.

Serigraph

The newest of the printmaking media is *serigraphy*, or silkscreen printing, which developed largely in the United States. It requires a screen of silk or a similar material, stretched on a frame. A stencil is attached to the silk and ink is forced through the stencil with a rubber squeegee. The open parts of the stencil, allow the ink to pass through onto the paper or other printing surface below. Many colors can be used, but a separate stencil is needed for each one. Andy Warhol's print has been placed on canvas and is as large as one of his paintings. Each of the four colors has its own stencil, and the colors are flat and unshaded. In this print, the result seems mechanical and commercial, which is exactly the way he wanted it to appear.

2–34 Andy Warhol, *Campbell's Soup Can*, 1964. American. Silkscreen on canvas, 35 1/2" x 24" (90 x 61 cm). Leo Castelli Gallery, New York.

Sculpture Media

Sculptors work in a number of ways: by cutting away (subtractive), by putting parts together (additive), by forming with hands (modeling), and by producing from a mold (casting).

Bronze

Ancient Chinese, Egyptians, Greeks, and Ife and Benin people were expert at the complex process of casting metal. Casting is a method of reproducing a three-dimensional object by pouring a hardening liquid or molten metal into a mold bearing its impression.

In India, too, quite astonishing pieces were created. Here, the Hindu god of learning and good fortune is depicted in bronze. In temples and households, the image of Ganésa is often placed near the entrance to welcome visitors. The figure exhibits an exuberance and lightness that defies the stocky, elephantlike qualities of the god and the heaviness of the bronze.

2–36 *Dancing Ganésa,* 15th century. Indian, Karnataka. Bronze, 19 7/8" x 13" (50.3 x 32.9 cm). Los Angeles County Museum of Art, Purchase, Harry and Yvonne Lenart Funds.

Steel

Sheet steel, which can be cut and welded together, has given sculptors who enjoy the additive processes a new material to use. David Smith has produced an extensive series of sculptures by welding together flat shapes of steel into blocky forms. Because the sculptures all have cubic forms, he titled them all *Cubi,* with Roman numerals to identify each. Many of the pieces are polished to a high luster, with the machined surfaces allowed to remain scarred—a combination of industrial machinery and art. Steel can be welded into many forms and can be painted as well as polished, or allowed to rust.

2–38 David Smith, *Cubi XII,* 1963. American. Stainless steel, 109 1/2" x 32 1/4" (278 x 82 cm). Hirshhorn Museum and Sculpture Garden, Washington, DC.

Wood

Wood is a very versatile sculpture material. It can be carved and nailed, filed and drilled, sanded and glued. Artists from all over the world, from ancient times to the present, have used wood for its warm feeling, attractive color and grain. Its abundance and relative low cost have also made wood a preferred medium.

2–37 Lintel, early 18th century. Maori, New Zealand. Wood with shell, 40 1/4" (1.02 m) long. The Nelson-Atkins Museum of Art, Kansas City, Missouri.

Marble

Marble is an excellent sculptural material because it can be polished to a glasslike finish or left rough and textured. This ancient piece is from the Cyclades Islands of modern Greece. The figure and lyre have been converted into various geometric shapes (ovals, triangles and cylinders). The skillful carving of the marble, the elegance of the figure and its rather modern look make this sculpture seem very contemporary.

2–35 *Lyre Player*, from Keros, c. 2000 BC. Cycladic. Marble, 9" (22.9 cm) high. National Archaeological Museum, Athens.

Plastic

The twentieth century brought with it a bountiful array of new materials for sculptors to explore. Glass, neon lights, mirrors, plastics, acrylics and other materials have found their way into artworks. Duane Hanson combines casting techniques with plastic resins and actual clothing to produce extremely lifelike figures. The football player looks so real you might feel like talking to him. The life-size figure was cast in plastic called polyester resin, and was reinforced with fiberglass. To make molds for his sculptures, Hanson applies plaster gauze strips directly to the body of a person, whose skin and hair is heavily greased so the plaster will not stick. Then, flesh-colored resin is painted into the molds and laminated with layers of glass cloth. The hardened casts are assembled to create the finished figure. Hair and clothing are then added and painted.

2–39 Duane Hanson, *Football Player*, 1981. American. Polyvinyl, polychromed in oil with accessories, 43 1/4" x 30" x 31 1/2" (110 x 76 x 80 cm). Lowe Art Museum, University of Miami.

Crafts

Fibers

The early process of *twining* developed from a need for containers, clothing and household objects. Baskets and rugs were twined by many tribes of Native Americans. Later, weaving of fabrics on various types of *looms* was developed. This craft grew into today's huge fabric industry. Today, contemporary handweavers use fibers of many kinds to produce unique fabrics. The rug was woven by a Navajo craftsperson, using traditional tribal designs and colors. Contemporary fiber artists use all kinds of natural and synthetic fibers to knot, stitch, tie and weave their work. Such work is often sculptural. Tapestries, carpets, brocades, stitchery and fabrics of many kinds and of startling beauty have been created all over the world.

2–41 *Navajo rug,* 1850–1880. Native American. Wool, 78 3/4" x 49 1/4" (200 x 125 cm). The Indian Art Center of California, Studio City.

2–43 *Necklace of glass beads with brass beads and ornaments.* Liberia, Africa. The Peabody Museum, Harvard University.

Glass

Glass is such a common item today that it is difficult to think of it as a precious material. Yet, the Egyptians used glass and precious gems in jewelry, and it was an important part of King Tutankhamen's burial mask. The glass bottle made by an Egyptian craftsperson about 3350 years ago is a beautiful example of superb craftsmanship. It probably held valuable perfume or other precious oils for a wealthy noble.

Millions of pieces of jewelry have been made by excellent craftspersons around the world. In nomadic societies, wealthy families invested in jewelry or other portable items. Nobles and rulers who acquired great wealth often had collections of jewelry. Fine jewelry and gems in some societies became synonymous with wealth. Simple jewelry, on the other hand, can be made of any material that enhances personal appearance—string, seeds or basic metals like copper. This brass and glass bead necklace was made by the Dan people of Africa.

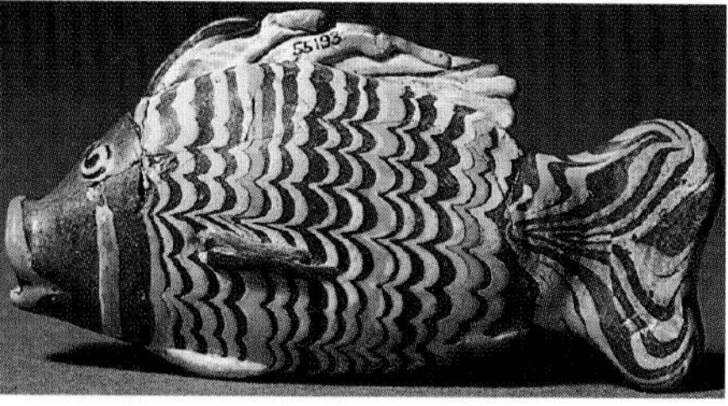

2–42 *Glass bottle shaped like a fish,* about 1370 BC. Egyptian, from el Amarna. Glass, 5 1/2" (14 cm) long. British Museum, London.

Clay

Clays of various types are dug from the earth and, when formed, dried and fired, become extremely durable. Earliest examples were *flash-fired* in open pits, but later work was heated more carefully in primitive *kilns*. Today, gas- or electric-fired kilns can be controlled carefully to create just the right temperatures, atmospheres and cooling-off times for each type of clay.

Most clay vessels are formed on a potter's wheel. Some, however, are made using the coil method. Coils of clay are added one on top of the other as the piece is slowly formed and molded by hand. Native Americans practice this technique. It is amazing to think that this was created without benefit of a wheel!

2–40 *Polacca Polychrome Style D (Sityatki Revival) jar,* 1890–1900. Hopi. Diameter 12 7/8" (32.7 cm). The Peabody Museum, Harvard University.

Furniture

Furniture, like glass, is usually taken for granted. Yet, craftspersons working with wood have produced such astounding results that they have often signed their pieces as painters and sculptors do. Like the other crafts, furniture can be as simple and stark as a Shaker chair or as elaborate as a royal throne. The commode seen here has a veneered decoration of tulipwood, burr wood and satinwood. The intricate designs are made with thin slices of wood, called veneer. When bits of veneer are cut and fitted into such designs, the craft is called *marquetry*. A fitted and shaped marble top together with gilt-bronze mounts complete this marvelous work.

2–45 Jean-Francois Oeben. *Commode,* 1761–1763. French. Veneered wood with gilt-bronze mounts, 35 3/4" (91 cm) high. The J. Paul Getty Museum, Malibu.

Mosaics

Mosaics can be made of glass, colored bits of marble, bits of ceramic tile, pieces of wood, or even seeds and paper. The walls and ceilings of early Christian churches were lined with mosaics of colored glass and even glass containing gold. Bits of glass (*tesserae*) were embedded in plaster or cement to make designs and pictures that glittered in the candlelight. Ancient Romans put thousands of incredibly small pieces of marble together to create wall decorations that were polished until smooth as glass. Often, mosaic sidewalks in front of Roman shops contained symbols or pictures of the type of business found inside.

2–44 *Apse mosaic,* c. 549. Byzantine. St. Apollinare in Classe, Ravenna.

Metalwork

Craftspersons working with metals have produced artwork for their societies ever since bronze could be worked. As with other crafts, the competence of the craftspersons provides a good indication of the sophistication of the society and its level of technology. Working in gold, silver, copper, bronze, iron, steel and aluminum, artisans have created their metal magic for centuries.

2–46 *Candlestick,* 13th century. Islamic. Engraved brass with silver and gold inlays, 9 3/8" (23.8 cm). The Nelson-Atkins Museum of Art, Kansas City, Missouri.

Lesson 2.2 Review

1 List four different drawing media and five painting media.
2 Why is charcoal used primarily as a sketching medium?
3 What is an ink wash? Name two countries whose painters created mainly in ink.
4 Describe the process of fresco painting.
5 Why did medieval artists add egg yolk to their tempera colors?
6 Explain the difference between impasto and glazes.
7 What are the binding agents for watercolors and oil and acrylic paints?
8 List five printmaking techniques.
9 How are woodcut and linocut printmaking techniques similar?
10 What is another term for serigraph? Describe the serigraph printing technique.

2.3 Design: The Structure of Art

VISUAL LANGUAGE, like verbal language, needs structure to make it understandable. The principles of design are the basic structure, or grammar, of visual language. These principles guide artists in their use of the elements of design—line, shape, form, texture, value, color and space. These elements of design are the vocabulary with which artists work. Artists usually use all the elements and principles in concert to produce an effective visual statement.

When studying and analyzing a work of art, ask yourself questions like the following to help you understand the work's content and properties.

Content can be determined by asking: Why has the artist made the work? What is he or she trying to tell me about the subject? What is the major theme? Are there minor themes also?

Sensory properties are the things we experience with our senses, such as line, shape, form, color, value, texture, space and light. These are the elements of art. Ask yourself: Which art element dominates the work? What kinds of line are used? How is form indicated? How is space felt? Is there texture? Are colors bright or dull? Which color dominates?

Formal properties tell us how the art elements are organized through the use of pattern, balance, movement, rhythm, unity, variety, emphasis, contrast and proportion. These are the principles of art. Ask yourself: What (if anything) is the center of interest? How does my eye move to it in the work? How did the artist establish the center of interest? Does the work have a sense of rhythm? Why? Is the composition vertical or horizontal? How is balance achieved? How is unity achieved? What shapes are repeated? Is a pattern evident? Are the figures in proportion?

Technical properties refer to the use of tools, media and techniques. Ask yourself: What materials and tools were used to make the work? Are the wood grains used effectively? What kinds of brushstrokes and pencil lines are used? Is it a finished work or a sketch for a later work? Are all parts treated with the same detail? Why or why not? Are there contrasts in value? What types of marks did the artist use? How is light indicated?

Expressive properties tell us what the work says, literally, metaphorically and symbolically. These properties are the mood language of the artist. Ask yourself: What mood does the work convey? Is the work timid or bold? Serious or comic? Does it establish a time of year? Does the work have social or religious significance? Is it a literal statement or a symbolic subject? How does the artist feel about the subject? How do I feel about the subject and its treatment?

Look at El Greco's painting of *St. Martin and the Beggar.* The subject matter is a narrative account of St. Martin, who is giving his own cloak to a naked, starving beggar. El Greco used all the elements of art in this composition. It is easy to find *line* in the work. The horse is a white *shape.* The beggar is shaded, so he seems to have three-dimensional *form.* The costume of St. Martin has a different *texture* than the horse. There are light, dark and medium *values* of color. The *colors* used (green and blues) are predominantly cool. Deep *space* is indicated by the small scale of the distant town. These elements are the vocabulary of the artist. But, what about the grammar?

When El Greco structured this composition, he had to decide where to place each part to make it most effective. The parts are in *balance* because there is just about the same visual activity and weight on both sides of the central axis. Because of the limited use of color and the elongated distortion that El Greco uses throughout, the painting has a sense of *unity. Emphasis* is placed on the good deed of giving to the poor and on the dominant blue-green color. There are many *contrasts:* between light and dark, textured and smooth areas, and rich and poor. The flickering light on the elongated shapes, which are repeated in the painting, forms a *pattern* of lights and darks. El Greco controls the visual *movement* so that the viewer's eyes always end at the face of St. Martin, the center of interest. The repeated vertical shapes develop a sense of *rhythm* in the painting. These principles—balance, unity, emphasis, contrast, pattern, movement and rhythm—are the grammar of the artist. They are the ways that the artist can best use the elements to create a pleasing composition.

2–47 El Greco. *St. Martin and the Beggar,* 1597–1599. Spanish. Oil on canvas, 76 1/2" x 40 1/2" (194 x 103 cm). National Gallery of Art, Washington, DC, Widener Collection.

The Elements of Design

Line

Lines are seen every day. They can be two-dimensional like those on a sheet of writing paper or three-dimensional like the branches of a tree.

The woodblock print by Hiroshige contains a marvelous variety of line. Some lines are thin or thick; continuous or interrupted; straight or curved; vertical, horizontal or diagonal; geometric or organic. Even *calligraphic* lines can be seen in the signature and description in the upper corners of the print. Some lines are massed together to create gray or textured areas. Other lines are used singly or in pairs. Some lines are black, while others are colored.

2–48 Ando Hiroshige, *Night Rain on Kirasaki Pine*, 1834. Japanese. Woodblock print, 9" x 14 1/4" (23 x 36 cm). Los Angeles County Museum of Art, gift of Mr. and Mrs. Nathan V. Hammer.

Shape

If a line on paper wanders around and finally crosses itself, the enclosed area is called a *shape*. Shapes have only two dimensions. They can be geometric, like a triangle, circle, square or rectangle. Or they can be organic—free form, irregular, pear-shaped or amoeba-like.

Montenegro used shape as the dominant element in his design. Some shapes are organic and others are geometric. The hard edges and sharp breaks between values and colors set off the various shapes. The elegant, flowing heads of the women contrast with the angularity of their white blouses and the houses behind them.

2–49 Roberto Montenegro, *Maya Women*, 1926. Mexican. Oil on canvas, 31 1/2" x 27 1/2" (80 x 70 cm). The Museum of Modern Art, New York, gift of Nelson A. Rockefeller, 1941.

Form

A *form* is three-dimensional and encloses volume. Like shapes, forms can be geometric (cubes, pyramids, boxlike, cones) or irregular (eggs, pears, horses, people, bottles). Form, the volume or mass of objects, is the most important art element for sculptors. While sculptors and potters work with form, painters work with shapes. Painters often use shading to make shapes look like forms.

This head from the Nok culture of western Africa shows an emphasis on simple yet full form. The pursed lips seem ready to whistle or blow out a flame.

The long, attenuated limbs of the figure by Giacometti are deflated by contrast. Yet, the near abstraction of the human form makes it very expressive and poignant.

2–51 Alberto Giacometti, *Man Pointing*, 1947. Swiss. Bronze, 70 1/2" high (179 cm). The Museum of Modern Art, New York, gift of Mrs. John D. Rockefeller.

2–50 *Head of Jemaa*, 510 BC. Nigeria, Nok Culture. Terracotta. National Museum, Lagos.

Texture

The surfaces of things have *texture*. Sandpaper, wool, cloth, leather and asphalt have textures. A painting may simulate textures by using color and value contrasts to make the surface *seem* textured.

Nicholas de Staël greatly simplified the landscape of Vaucluse so that only shapes and colors remain. The shapes, perhaps, remind one of cliffs and trees, sky and water, or other elements of the landscape. When the French artist put down his oil paint on canvas, he wanted to use another element of design besides color and shape—texture. One can immediately see the texture in this work. It actually exists. The paint was buttered onto the canvas with a painting knife, like a small spatula. The artist may not have used a regular brush at all on this *impasto* surface. It appears that he also added textural material like sand and sawdust to his paint. If a viewer were able to rub the surface of the painting, even with eyes closed, it would reveal the coarse textural quality.

2–52 Nicholas de Staël, *Landscape in Vaucluse, No. 2,* 1953. French. Oil on canvas, 25 1/4" x 31 3/4" (64 x 81 cm). Albright-Knox Art Gallery, Buffalo, gift of Seymour H. Knox Foundation Inc.

Simulated Texture

Although the surface of Gustav Klimt's painting looks more textured than de Staël's, it is not. The surface, which is painted to look like texture, in reality is relatively smooth. The textures are simulated. Klimt was a master at creating unusual and convincing textures. Flat surfaces often appear textured because of the value contrasts the artist used. Usually, paintings have a variety of simulated textures so the surface is not monotonous, but Klimt gives us little relief. The viewer is overpowered by the dense forest of uniform texture. Klimt and de Staël both enjoyed texture for its own sake. The two paintings are not representations of real textures in nature but are abstracted works which emphasize texture.

2–53 Gustav Klimt, *The Park,* before 1910. Austrian. Oil on canvas, 43 1/4" x 43 1/4" (110 x 110 cm). The Museum of Modern Art, New York, Gertrude A. Mellon Fund.

Space: Perspective

Space is where people live. Real space is three-dimensional. But space also refers to the illusion of depth in a painting or drawing. Actual space in a painting is two-dimensional. Leonardo da Vinci believed that true art makes the viewer feel three-dimensional space on a two-dimensional surface.

Artists use *perspective* to show depth or space in a painting. If two objects overlap on a flat surface, one is clearly behind and the other is in front. A sense of depth is created. Painters also use *aerial perspective* to show depth. In Duncanson's painting, the bright haze hides distant details. The mountains are seen as being far away. The darker values are up close, and the lighter values are far away. The colors also are more intense up close, while the edges become softer farther away.

2–54 Robert Scott Duncanson, *Loch Long*, 1867. American. Oil on canvas, 7" x 12" (18 x 30 cm). National Museum of American Art, gift of Donald J. Shein, 1983.

Canaletto used *linear perspective* to help the viewer experience the space he saw at Venice. All parallel lines run toward invisible vanishing points which are off the canvas. With mathematical precision, the artist depicts the diminishing size of arches, columns and people as they recede. In both paintings, there is a strong feeling of depth or space, yet each artist used different means.

2–55 Canaletto, *The Square of St. Mark's*, about 1730. Italian. Oil on canvas, 45 1/4" x 60 1/2" (115 x 154 cm). National Gallery of Art, Washington, DC, gift of Mrs. Barbara Hutton.

Color

Color is the one phase of art that is also a science. There are three terms that artists use in talking about color: hue, value and intensity. *Hue* is the name of the color. For example, yellow is a hue. *Value* is the dark or light quality of a color. Pink is a light value of red because white has been added to it. *Intensity* is the brightness or saturation of a color. The pure color is most intense; if one adds its *complement* and grays it, it is less intense. The color wheel is a good place to begin learning about color.

- *Primary hues* are red, yellow, blue. From these, all other colors can be made.
- *Secondary/Intermediate colors* are produced by mixing two primaries. For example, red and yellow make orange. If a primary and secondary color are mixed together, an intermediate color is created. Blue and green make blue-green.
- *Complementary colors* are colors directly opposite on the color wheel (yellow and violet). If they are mixed together, the original hue is grayer and less intense. A little green mixed with red will lessen the intensity of red and make it a grayed or muted color.
- *Warm colors* are hues containing red and orange. Warm colors seem to advance or come forward in a painting. Sunlight is often painted with warm colors.
- *Cool colors* are hues containing green or blue. Cool colors seem to recede or go back into a painting. Shadows are often painted with cool colors.

Painters also refer to the *local color* of objects. Local color is the color of objects when they are lit by uniform white light. If the source of light is colored, the local color will change. For example, under yellow light, objects will take on a yellowish hue. Think of how the colors in nature change when the sunset casts an orange hue over everything.

Objects also absorb colors from surrounding objects. These absorbed colors are called *reflected colors*. If two colored objects are next to each other, each will contain reflected colors as well as its own local color.

Color is the most important art element for the painter. How artists have seen color in nature has greatly determined their painting techniques and styles.

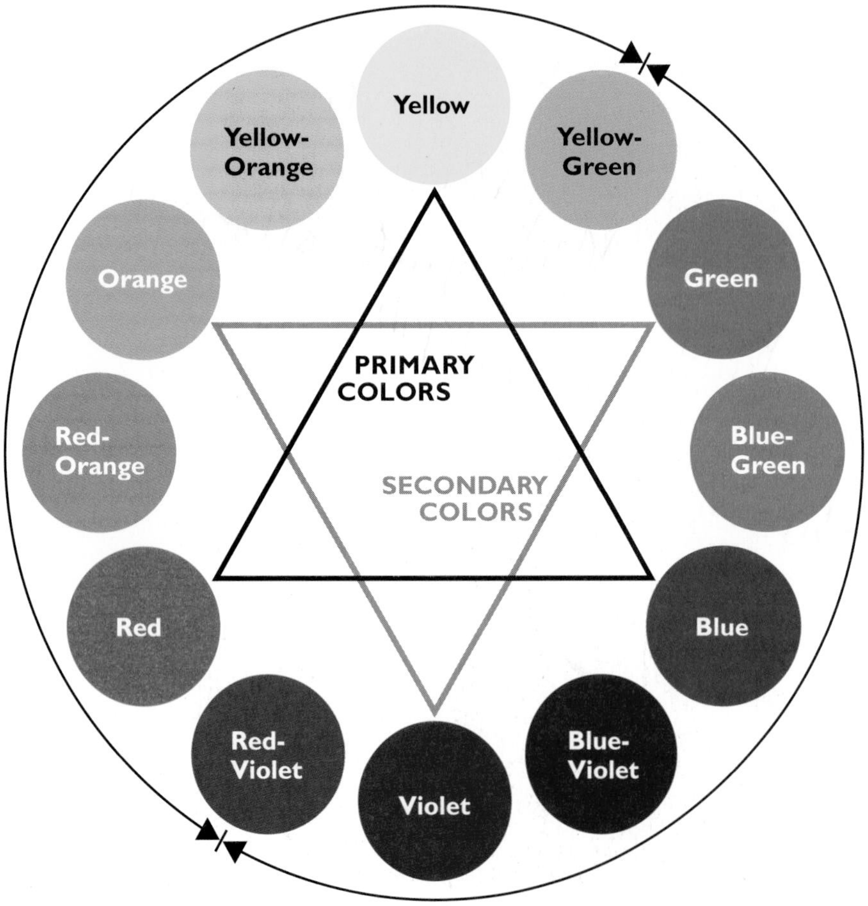

2–56 Color Wheel

Value

Value refers to the light or dark quality of a color or shape in a painting. Black is the darkest value; white is the lightest. When a basic color is mixed with white, its value is lightened; if black is added, its value is darkened. If a painting were all dark values, it would be difficult to read. Most successful paintings have a contrast of values. The stronger the contrast, the more dramatic the painting seems.

Notice the light and dark values in Zurbarán's still life. In the black-and-white print, the middle values are gray. In the color reproduction, they are variations of the dominant hues. The artist has used values to create a feeling of form, an illusion of three-dimensionality. The rounded lemons and oranges look like they have volume and take up space because of their gradual value

changes from light to dark. The rims of the plates and cup have sharp edges because the value changes are sudden. The still life is dramatic because of the strong value contrasts from deepest dark to lightest light. Paintings that have mostly light values are called *high-keyed* and those of mostly dark values, *low-keyed.*

2–57 Francisco Zurbarán, *Still Life with Lemons, Oranges and a Rose,* 1633. Spanish. Oil on canvas, 23 1/4" x 41 1/4" (59 x 105 cm). The Norton Simon Foundation, Los Angeles.

Principles of Design

The principles of design describe the general ways in which artists arrange the parts of their compositions. These organizers are balance, unity, emphasis, contrast, pattern, movement and rhythm.

The principles are never used in isolation, but always in concert. A design may use balance, but it may also contrast certain areas, emphasize one part, achieve rhythm and movement, or produce an overall pattern. One principle may dominate, but when an overall unity is achieved, all the principles have probably been employed. Look again at El Greco's painting of *St. Martin and the Beggar* (fig.2–47) to see how these principles work together.

There are many ways to use the elements to achieve each design principle. However, only a few can be explored here. Readers may want to return to this section often to reinforce their understanding of design terms and dynamics.

Balance: Symmetrical

Symmetrical (or formal) balance is a roughly even distribution of visual weight or activity on each side of a central axis—like two equally sized children on a seesaw. Much art is not perfectly balanced symmetrically because one side would be a mirror image of the other. Symmetry is an integral part of the design of this mask and many other objects created by Native Americans. Colors, shapes and lines are repeated exactly. Though the creatures depicted have a potential of being frightening, the perfect symmetry, or balance, of the work has a calm, stabilizing effect.

2–58 *Raven sun clan mask with beak: transformation mask, open,* 19th century. Harbledown Island, British Columbia. Kwakiutl. The Peabody Museum, Harvard University.

Balance: Asymmetrical

Asymmetrical balance means that larger masses on one side of the painting may be balanced by smaller, contrasting parts on the other side. An asymmetrical painting is informally balanced and is usually more exciting than a formally balanced composition. Many of Degas' ballet paintings show an asymmetrical balance. By covering first one half and then the other half of the painting the viewer can see how different they are. It is sometimes difficult to see the balance in an asymmetrical design. However, if the overall effect is comfortable, the work is probably balanced.

2–59 Edgar Degas. *The Star,* or *Dancer on Stage,* about 1876–1877. Pastel on monotype on paper, 23 5/8" x 17 5/8" (60 x 44 cm). Musée d'Orsay, Paris.

Unity

Unity combines the principles of design and the physical aspects of a painting to create a single, harmonious work. Unity in a painting is like music played by an orchestra. All notes and chords produced by the instruments combine to make a single beautiful passage of sound. Artists can use various means to achieve unity.

Turner achieved unity in his dramatic painting of the great London fire in three ways: (1) the values are mostly high-keyed; (2) feathery brushstrokes appear throughout; and (3) all forms are rendered abstractly. The painting also has color unity. Turner used a limited palette of yellows and oranges so that all the hues are related.

2–60 Joseph Mallord William Turner, *Burning of the Houses of Parliament*, 1835. English. Oil on canvas, 36 1/4" x 48 1/2" (92 x 123 cm). Philadelphia Museum of Art, The McFadden Collection.

2–61 Winslow Homer, *The Carnival*, 1877. American. Oil on canvas, 20" x 30" (51 x 76 cm). The Metropolitan Museum of Art, New York, Lazarus Fund.

Homer's subject and methods of obtaining unity are quite different from Turner's. In *The Carnival*, Homer uses a single strong light source, entering from the left. The colors on the carnival figures are more intense than the muted background hues. The figures are, therefore, dominant while the background is subordinate. The figures also contain more detail and value contrasts than the background. The central three figures are strongest and the act of sewing up the torn costume is the center of interest. All eye movement in the painting is directed to the central figures and center of interest. A strong repetition of vertical shapes establishes a rhythm that unifies the work.

But, there is also a secondary horizontal movement, established by the fence and the ground shadows, which tie the verticals together. The little girl on the left is placed to delicately balance the asymmetrically arranged elements. Finally, the visual story, or narrative, helps to unify the subject matter and, therefore, the painting.

Emphasis

Emphasis is the way of developing the main theme in a work of art. It answers the question, "What is the artist trying to say?" The answers can be obvious or obscure. Artists may emphasize one or more of the art elements—such as color, line or texture—and subordinate the rest. Artists may also emphasize a particular subject or concept—symbolism, daily life, material wealth or historical fact.

Jan Vermeer emphasizes light in his work. The natural light entering from the open window floods the wall, girl and table. Vermeer also depicts the various reflected lights and different intensities of shadow. The room, officer and girl are simply props for Vermeer's beautiful study of light.

2–62 Jan Vermeer. *Officer and Laughing Girl*, 1655–1660. Dutch. Oil on canvas, 19 1/2" x 18" (50 x 46 cm). The Frick Collection, New York.

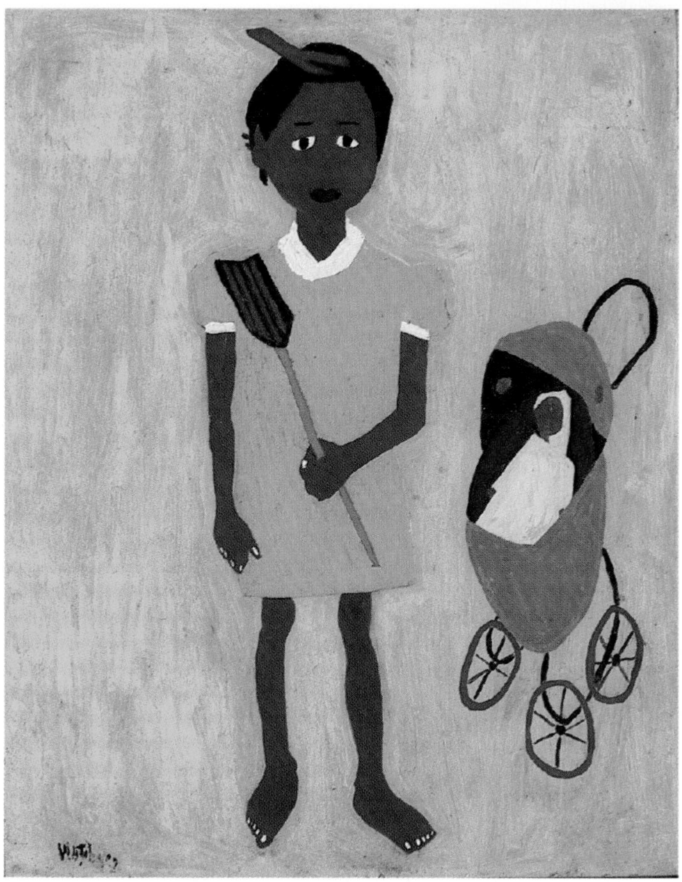

William H. Johnson placed emphasis on the little girl and her doll carriage simply by placing the figure on a plain, bright yellow background. The artist also emphasizes shape. There are very few lines, only blocks of flat, bright colors.

2–63 William H. Johnson, *Li'l Sis*, about 1944. American. Oil on canvas, 26" x 21 1/4" (66 x 54 cm). National Museum of American Art, gift of The Harmon Foundation.

Contrast

If all parts of a painting were alike, it would be monotonous and the viewer would lose interest quickly. To avoid monotony and to make the painting as visually interesting and exciting as possible, artists use contrasts of various kinds.

In Tiepolo's painting of the wise men visiting Mary and the Christ Child, he used many contrasts. It is easy to find contrast of light and dark values. These contrasts in values accompany the contrast in color between warms and cools. Soft, curving shapes of fabric contrast with the hard edges of the building. Small areas of light or dark contrast with large shapes. Textured areas contrast with smooth. Earthly elements contrast with heavenly; richness contrasts with poverty; youth contrasts with age. There are even ethnic contrasts in the people represented. Vertical movement contrasts with horizontal. The entire structure of the painting, which is superbly designed and painted, revolves around contrasts.

The abstract portrait by Jacques Villon is remarkably like Tiepolo's painting in design. To see this similarity, study both paintings with squinted eyes. Although Tiepolo's style is more representational, Villon's use of contrasting art elements is about the same. The contrast of light and dark is readily apparent. Note also the similar contrasts of size and shape in both works. Textures subtly contrast with the angular and curved shapes.

Because Villon was working solely with abstract shapes and ideas, his chief focus was on the design and arrangement of elements.

2–65 Jacques Villon, *Portrait of Mlle. Y.D.*, 1913. French. Oil on canvas, 51 1/4" x 35" (130 x 89 cm). Los Angeles County Museum of Art, gift of Anna Bing Arnold.

2–64 Giovanni Battista Tiepolo, *Adoration of the Magi*, 1753. Italian. Oil on canvas, 144" x 82 1/4" (366 x 209 cm). Alte Pinakothek, Munich.

Rhythm

Rhythm is established in a work when elements of the composition, such as curves, angles, or vertical or horizontal lines, are repeated. Repetitions can occur at either regular or irregular intervals. Rhythm and movement, like rhythm and pattern, are inseparable.

In Siqueiros' painting of the woman clasping her hands, there is strong movement up to and around her face. Her haunting eyes become the center of interest. Siqueiros repeats the gently curving shapes in regular intervals to create a strong rhythmic beat. He emphasizes the roundness of the folds so that they almost appear to be made of metal or concrete instead of cloth. Notice how the fingers and the hair repeat the rhythm established in the folds.

2–67 David Alfaro Siqueiros, *Portrait of a Woman,* 1934. Mexican. Oil on masonite, 59 1/2" x 30 3/4" (151 x 78 cm). Los Angeles County Museum of Art, gift of Morton D. May.

Pattern

Pattern can be produced by the repetition of motifs, colors, shapes or lines. Many cultures of the world rely heavily on pattern. Notice the repetition of the catlike animal motif, as well as the use of the repeated line and color in this Indonesian batik. What other elements related to pattern do you see?

2–66 *Indonesian batik,* 1980s.

Movement

Movement can be conveyed in many ways. Movement in painting directs the eyes of the viewer to the center of interest. Sculpture can come alive with the infusion of movement.

The eye, moving across the surface, creates visual movement in a painting. Movement is directed by linkage or passage across like values or colors.

In sculpture, movement is directed along edges and contours to a focal area.

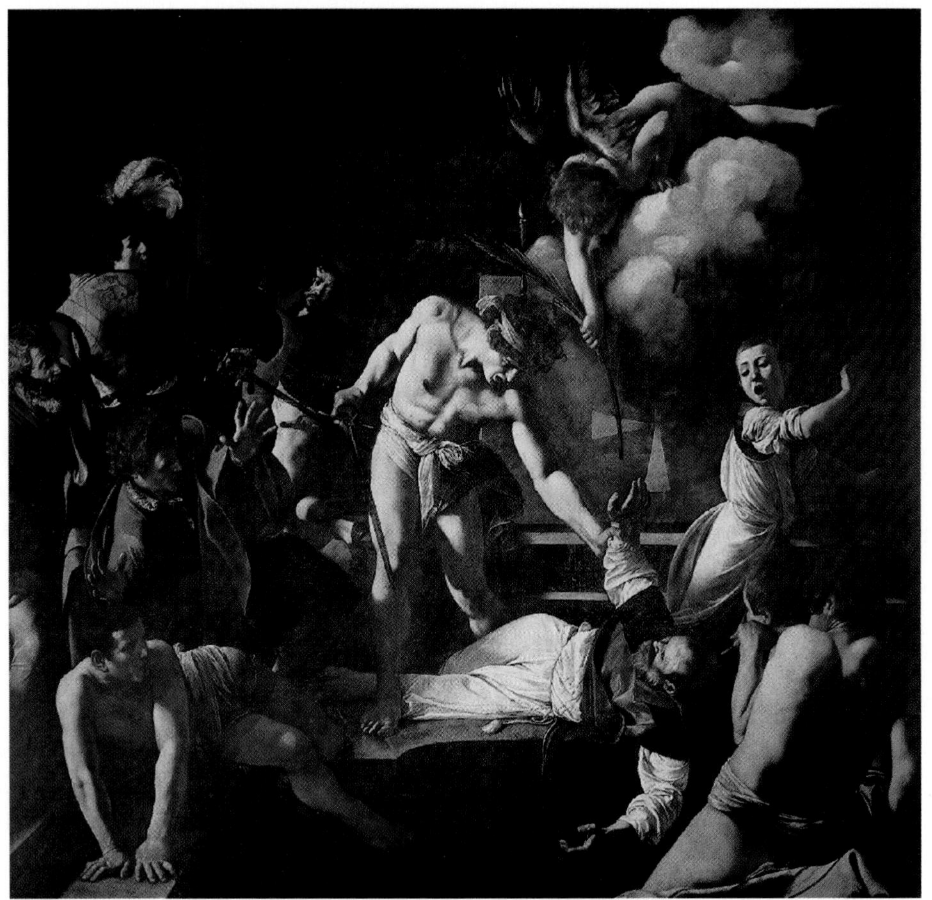

2–68 Caravaggio. *Martyrdom of St. Matthew,* 1599–1600. Approximately 10' 9" x 11' 5" (3.28 x 3.48 m). S. Luigi dei Francesi, Rome.

2–69 Niccolo dell'Arca. *The Lamentation*, detail of one of mourning figures, about 1485–1490. Italian. Terra-cotta, life-size. Santa Maria della Vita, Bologna.

Lesson 2.3 Review

1 List the art principles and elements. How are the principles of art related to the elements of design?
2 Define texture.
3 Describe three methods that artists use to show depth on a flat surface.
4 Define hue, value and intensity.
5 List the primary, secondary and intermediate colors. How are secondary and intermediate colors made?
6 What is local color?
7 What does high key and low key refer to in a painting?
8 Explain unity and emphasis in art.
9 What function does movement in a painting often play?

Primary Source

Artists Explain Why

Occasionally, artists tell us why they depict certain subjects or favor a particular medium. Their statements help us better understand their work and give us insight into the creative process.

Jacob Lawrence, a contemporary African-American artist who paints scenes about African-American life and history, explains why he has chosen this subject matter:

"My pictures express my life and experience. I paint the things I know about and the things I have experienced. The things I have experienced extend into my national, racial and class group. So I paint the American scene."

Louise Nevelson, a prominent woman sculptor of the twentieth century tells us why she worked so often with wood:

"I just automatically went to wood. I wanted a medium that was immediate. Wood was the thing that I could communicate with almost spontaneously and get what I was looking for...when I'm working with wood, it's very alive. The fact that it's wood means it has another life...."

Chapter Review

Review

1 What are some of the characteristics that have made acrylic paints popular with many contemporary painters? Which of the painting and drawing media have you used?

2 What is the difference between additive and subtractive sculpture processes? Name a medium that is often additive, one that is usually subtractive, one that is modeled, and one that is cast.

3 What medium is Duane Hanson's *Football Player*? How does Hanson create an exact likeness of his model?

4 How does Vermeer emphasize light in his *Officer and Laughing Girl*?

5 Describe the contrasts in Tiepolo's *Adoration of the Magi.*

Interpretation

1 Select one of the paintings in this chapter to analyze. Answer the questions about content and sensory, formal and technical properties on page 40.

2 Use hue, value and intensity to describe the colors in de Staël's *Landscape in Vancluse.*

3 Select a painting that uses mainly cool colors. Now choose another that features primarily warm hues.

4 Describe symmetrical and asymmetrical balance. Cite an example of art in this chapter with symmetrical balance and another with asymmetrical balance.

5 Take a stand. Is Mary Cassatt's *Sleeping Baby* a painting or a drawing? Explain your choice.

Other Tools for Learning

Electronic Research

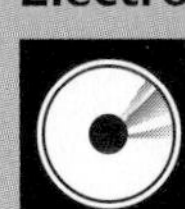

CD-ROM drive: *Microsoft Art Gallery*
Videodisc player: *National Gallery of Art, Louvre Videodisc*

1 Browse through one of the gallery collections on either videodisc or CD-ROM. After viewing a number of works by one artist, analyze the style of this artist using the art elements and principles. In your review, tell what media this artist usually used.

2 Give one fact that you found interesting about pictorial composition and another fact about perspective. (Composition and Perspective Guided Tour)

Activity 1

A New Spin on Color

Materials

11" x 14" white paper (or larger)
tempera, watercolor, prismacolor or acrylic paint
brushes
surface for mixing paint
containers of water

Take a look. Study the color wheel on page 46.

Think about it. What is the purpose of a color wheel? How is it useful in creating art? Can you think of other ways to display color relationships?

Do it. Do one or more of the following projects:

- Use tempera paints to make a color wheel that is different in design from the one on page 46. Do rough sketches of possible designs, using circles, squares or other shapes of color that you move around on a page.
- Create an original image that has twelve parts; for instance, a clown with twelve balloons. Using only primary colors, mix twelve different colors for the parts of your painting.
- Create an original image with color developed with prismacolor, using at least twelve mixed colors to complete your composition.

Check it. Are your colors clear and vibrant? Remember to rinse your brush thoroughly before switching from one color to another.

Helpful Hint: Practice mixing colors on a palette or blank sheet of paper before beginning your painting. How many shades of color can you create using just two colors at a time?

Activity 2

About Face

Materials

magazines
11" x 14" white paper
scissors
glue/tape
markers

Take a look. Review the following artwork in this chapter:

- Fig.2–9, Hans Holbein, *Edward VI as a Child*, 1538. German.
- Fig.2–10 Frances Benjamin Johnston, *Self-Portrait*, 1895. American. .
- Fig.2–19, Jean Auguste-Dominique Ingres, *Thomas Church*, 1816. French.
- Fig.2–67, David Alfaro Siqueiros, *Portrait of a Woman*, 1934. Mexican.

Think about it. Portraits have always been an important way to show how people appear to others. There are many reasons to make portraits; for instance, personal, illustration, advertising, identification, and business. What other portraits can you find in this book?

Do it.

- Clip from magazines five portraits done in each of the following ways: drawing, painting, sculpture and photography.
- You might choose portraits of people from one category for comparison, for example: sports figures, political figures, dancers or musicians. Collect both historical and contemporary examples.
- Arrange them on your paper and glue them into place. Make captions listing the probable purpose or use of each one. Tell whether you think each portrait is effective.

Check it. Do your portraits represent a range of different approaches? Are they effectively arranged on the page? Is it clear which caption goes with which image?

Helpful Hint: Consider colors, borders, type styles or other design elements you might use that would make your poster eye-catching when displayed on a wall.

Additional Activities

- Explore some of the tools and media that artists use. Find out the difference between things such as: a camel-hair and bristle brush; fine- and coarse-tooth papers; canvas and masonite; plaster and clay. In an oral presentation or video program, demonstrate such media and materials to the class.
- Nature photographers, landscape painters and landscape architects all work with nature. Write a paper describing how their work is similar and how it is different. Perhaps you can illustrate your project or present it as a videotaped documentary.
- The text identifies sixteen kinds of subject matter. Look through magazines and select advertisements, drawings or photographs that illustrate any twelve of these subjects. Label each of them and make a notebook, chart or slide/video presentation to share your findings.

Untitled, 1994. Gouache, 18" x 24" (46 x 61 cm).

A Pool of Color, 1994. Tempera paint, 8" x 8" (20 x 20 cm).

Pablo Román

Age 18
J. F. Dulles High School
Stafford, Texas
Activity 1, A New Spin on Color

This painting was my first, actually. I painted a little in junior high but never did get serious with it; I drew cartoons then.

This was a plain contour drawing of some plants I did, never supposing or planning on how I would paint it. I hadn't painted before, so I thought I would only mess it up. My teacher said it was a color assignment and that we were to experiment, using the complementary colors on the color wheel. That was a good place to start on a first painting.

Some, to look at me, might say I was slow; it's true, I did lag behind in my class. But I had a mind to work this one out with patience. I got into it. Sometimes I'd stay after school to do some extra work on it. My teacher was understanding with me, and she allowed me to go into overtime with the project. I love the patient work most of all when doing projects like these. One day I might come in and in an hour only do a few inches of detailed work. I like to take my time.

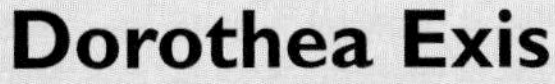

Dorothea Exis

Age 15
J. F. Dulles High School
Stafford, Texas
Activity 1, A New Spin on Color

My art project is meant to express all of the basic colors of the color wheel in a creative new way. As with all my other pieces, I put a lot of care into its creation. Because of this, I value it as a carpenter would cherish a table he crafted himself.

I enjoy the ability to create something new, to take a mere thought and be able to put it on paper. This, in my opinion, is the greatest thing about art.

Dorothea Mae Exis

Part Two

Trends & Influences in the World of Art

Chimú Tabard, detail, c. 1465. Cotton with applied feathers. The Textile Museum, Washington, DC, (91.395).

3 Common Denominators

In This Chapter...

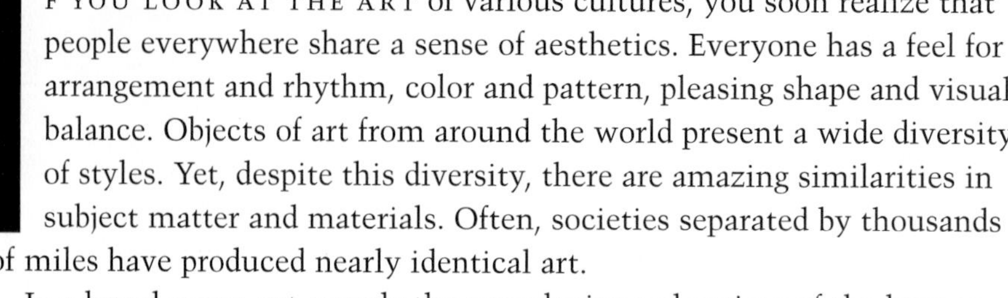

IF YOU LOOK AT THE ART of various cultures, you soon realize that people everywhere share a sense of aesthetics. Everyone has a feel for arrangement and rhythm, color and pattern, pleasing shape and visual balance. Objects of art from around the world present a wide diversity of styles. Yet, despite this diversity, there are amazing similarities in subject matter and materials. Often, societies separated by thousands of miles have produced nearly identical art.

In a broad sense, art reveals the complexity and variety of the human personality. It demonstrates the numerous relationships individuals have with each other and with society at large. Art reflects people's responses to the environment and supernatural forces. While art forms vary stylistically from culture to culture, their general messages can be understood by all.

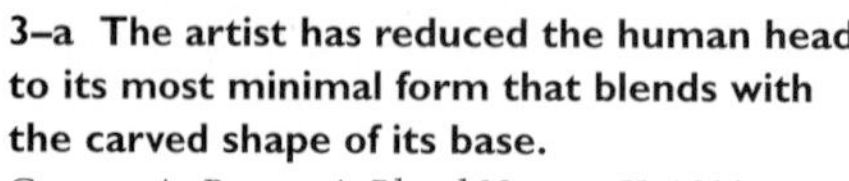

3–a The artist has reduced the human head to its most minimal form that blends with the carved shape of its base.

Constantin Brancusi, *Blond Negress II*, 1933. Bronze, 15 3/4" (40 cm) high, base: 71 1/4" (181 cm) high. The Museum of Modern Art, New York, The Philip L. Goodwin Collection.

3–b A few quick strokes of the brush outline the human figure in a skillful, animated manner.

Detail of lintel and pediment of a tomb, 50 BC–50 AD. Han Dynasty, Chinese. Earthenware, hollow tiles painted in ink and colors on a white-washed background. Museum of Fine Arts, Boston, Denman Waldo Ross Collection.

The world, harmoniously confused,
Where order in variety we see,
And where, tho' all things differ, all agree.
Alexander Pope

3–d Note that all the figures on pages 60 and 61 deal with the human form. The figures are from various parts of the world and span 2000 years. How are they similar? How are they different?
Sculpted figure, late 12th century, Toltec–Mayan culture. Chichen Itza, Mexico.

3–c Compare the many flourishing brushstrokes that this painter has used to create this portrait with the very few lines used in fig.3–b.
Francisco José de Goya, *Doña Isabel de Porcel,* 1806. Oil on canvas, 32" x 21 1/2" (81 x 55 cm). The National Gallery, London.

3–e Artists often use the human figure as the basis for creating religious or mythological figures.
Garuda, Cambodian, 10" (24.8 cm). The Detroit Institute of Arts, Gift of Albert Kahn.

3.1 Commonalities

Geometric Patterns

The use of geometric motifs is common to all societies. People the world over have had a fascination with regular, rhythmic, hard-edge patterns. For example, they have used spirals, checkerboards and wave patterns to ornament their artistic products. These designs are found in the pottery of such widely separated cultures as ancient Persia, the Indus Valley civilization, ancient Greece, Native American tribes, and the early Chinese dynasties.

Cloth woven by many cultures is often composed of colored threads woven into rhythmic patterns. From ancient civilizations of the Greeks and Romans and the Inca to the contemporary Iban tribes of Borneo, clothing has been woven with overall patterns or geometric border patterns.

3–1 Abstract geometric forms are created by Zen priests in Japanese temple grounds, where gravel is raked in patterns that aid in meditation.
Hojo Garden, Tofuku-Ji Temple, Kyoto, Japan

3–2 Animal forms are a particularly favorite motif for South American textiles.
Tabard, c. 1465. Chimú. Cotton with applied feathers, 38 1/2" x 26 3/4" (98 x 68 cm). The Textile Museum, Washington, DC.

Animal Designs

Humans have always been close to nature because they depend on plants and animals for their essential needs. Throughout history, craftspersons have used animals to represent the gods and to symbolize humans' relationship with nature. Animal designs express people's universal fascination with the animal world. Fish motifs decorate bowls of Native American, Chinese and Thai pottery. Fish are also found on the mosaic floors of early Christian basilicas and in the twentieth-century paintings of the German Expressionist Max Beckmann. In the culture of the United States, the eagle symbolizes nationalism and courage, and the bear represents strength. Wild animals, such as lions and birds, are found in the art of Persia, on ancient Greek vases, and in the weavings of North and South American tribes. Domesticated animals are used in the motifs adorning drinking vessels from Mycenae to China.

Human Figures

The human figure has been represented in art in just about every form imaginable. Peruvian potters created hollow clay water vessels in the form of bodies, while Michelangelo sculpted figures based on exacting anatomical precision.

Human activities of every kind have been depicted on the walls of ancient Egyptian, Indian and Mayan structures. People have carved monumental images of themselves, such as the huge likeness of the Roman Emperor Constantine or the United States presidents on Mount Rushmore. Conversely, minute images of people appear in the art of Tibetans and the miniature paintings of Islam.

Nude males and females have been used to portray the beauty of the human form or the creative power of God, as well as humanity's sensuous and sexual nature. Elaborately clothed figures depict wealth, social standing and cultural tastes. The facial portrait, which is the most highly individualized example of human design, has been executed in every conceivable material.

3–4 The word *pyramid* usually brings to mind the Egyptian civilization. Did you know that pyramids also were built by the Mayan culture?
Pyramid Temple, late 12th century, Toltec-Mayan culture. Chichen Itza, Mexico.

3–3 Native Americans created this vessel in the form of a human head.
Earthen Jar in Form of Human Face, painted. Fortune Mound, Poinsette County, Arkansas. 7 1/2" high (19.5 cm). Peabody Museum, Harvard University.

Architecture

Civilizations have expended tremendous energy to construct monumental architecture. The pyramids of the Egyptians, Mayans and the central Javanese were built to glorify both people and their gods. Castles of feudal Japan and Indian Hindu temples are other examples of monumental architecture.

Vertical structures have fascinated the imagination of architects throughout the world. Towers of stone have soared hundreds of feet into the sky. Ancient tribes erected enormous stones in locales as far apart as Laos and Sardinia. The ancient Egyptians carved tall needles of granite, called *obelisks*, upon which they carved historical records. The Chinese and Japanese constructed pagoda towers that function both as watch towers and Buddhist memorials. Soaring spires and towers of Gothic cathedrals testify to humankind's obsession with the vertical. Today, architects erect towers of steel and glass, perpetuating this ancient trend.

Cross-Cultural Influences

Some trends in art around the world have developed in total isolation. In many other instances, one culture has directly affected another. Cultural influence may have occurred through peaceful means, as in the Chinese and Buddhist influences upon Japanese culture. In some cases, one culture has actively sought out the aesthetic and technological expertise of another, as the Romans did when they copied Greek sculptors and techniques. The Inca had great respect for Paracas and Nazca cultures.

Ironically, military violence sometimes has been used to attain the aesthetic treasures of another society. For instance, the Japanese invaded Korea in the late sixteenth century and captured Korean potters. The Japanese transported them to the southern Japanese island of Kyushu for the crafting of tea ceremony items. The Mongols, who invaded China in the thirteenth century, did not have the artistic traditions of the Chinese. But instead of destroying Chinese art production, the Mongols encouraged Chinese potters to continue to produce the now famous blue and white ware. The Mongols then exported this ware to raise revenue throughout their far-flung empire.

Traders, missionaries, military expeditions, cultural missions and diplomatic envoys have all helped to introduce and spread the styles and motifs of one culture to another.

3–5 Osaka castle is a good example of cross-cultural influence. Chinese culture was first introduced into Japan in 552. Slowly, Chinese ideas of curved roofs and symmetrical arrangement became part of Japanese aesthetics. European traders in Japan in the 1500s taught the Japanese about fortifications built in medieval England.
Osaka Castle, late 16th century. Osaka, Japan.

3–6 The Mediterranean world changed dramatically after the rapid and militant spread of Islam in the seventh and eighth centuries. Such structures as the *Alhambra* palace in Spain reflect this radical shift in styles from a native to an imposed tradition.
The Alhambra, 13th–14th centuries. Granada, Spain.

The influence of one culture upon another is usually subtle and reveals itself slowly as styles and techniques intertwine. However, aesthetic and cultural influences may also be introduced very quickly into a society. Almost overnight, styles and tastes change.

Technology has often been imported into a culture. The use of bronze suddenly appeared in China during the *Shang* dynasty. The Chinese may have gained knowledge of the lost-wax casting process from Central Asia, from the Indus Valley, or possibly from early advanced cultures in Northern Thailand.

Ideas for forms, shapes and subjects also have been borrowed. Picasso was greatly influenced by the sculpture of African tribal peoples. Gauguin went to Tahiti hoping to see the world through the eyes of its native peoples. The French Impressionists of the mid-1800s were inspired by the woodcuts of the Japanese, who depicted the world with a different use of perspective and color.

3–7 The Chinese quickly expanded the possibilities of lost-wax casting, which they learned from outsiders. The Chinese produced such excellent works as this Mongolian figure holding two birds of jade.
Mongolian Youth, 3rd–4th centuries BC, late Zhou period, China. Bronze figure with jade birds, 11 1/2" (29 cm) high. Museum of Fine Arts, Boston, Maria Antoinette Evans Fund.

Lesson 3.1 Review

1 Name several examples of tall, vertical architectural structures built in different parts of the world.
2 How does the Osaka castle in Japan combine the architecture of different cultures?
3 What technology did the Chinese learn to use in order to produce art such as the Mongolian figure holding two birds of jade? Where might the Chinese have learned this process?
4 List three cultures whose art influenced European artists during the late nineteenth and early twentieth centuries.

3.2 Emotion vs. Intellect

In all societies and at all times in history, two extremes of visual expression have been possible: a completely emotional approach and a completely intellectual approach. An emotional or romantic approach to art features an active and colorful interpretation of the subject, violent movement, distortion, bright and vivid colors, a strong interest in nature, and a personal approach to the subject. An emotional approach has little concern for design and reason.

An intellectual or classic approach features an emphasis on design and composition; a cool, analytical approach to the subject; the use of rules; and an emphasis on neat, clean arrangements and proper proportions. An intellectual approach has little room for feelings and emotions.

Compare the sculpture by Hugo Robus (fig.3–8) with the sculpture by Henry Moore (fig.3–9). Both artists used the human form as the subject, yet each treated it with a different emphasis. Although both works have similar rounded and abstract forms, the two artists had completely different purposes in mind when working. Henry Moore's sculpture demonstrates an intellectual approach to three-dimensional form. Hugo Robus' piece suggests a romantic approach.

Henry Moore abstracted the human figure until the remaining forms are merely suggestive of the human figure. This abstracting process is an intellectual one.

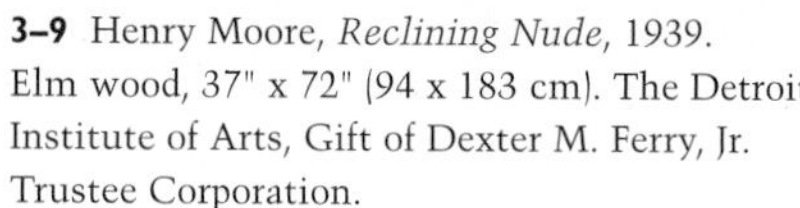

3–9 Henry Moore, *Reclining Nude,* 1939. Elm wood, 37" x 72" (94 x 183 cm). The Detroit Institute of Arts, Gift of Dexter M. Ferry, Jr. Trustee Corporation.

The finished product is cool and beautifully worked. There are no emotional overtones or hidden meanings. While the smooth curves may elicit a vague feeling of calm or sensuousness, they do not prompt a specific, overwhelming emotional response. The beauty of the form is appreciated chiefly for what it is, not for what it suggests.

The Hugo Robus sculpture is quite small, yet has a feeling of great size. It also has rounded forms and is somewhat abstracted. However, it has an emotional content that cannot be ignored. The title, *Despair,* adds an expressionist tag to the work. Viewers can feel the work's intended emotional content without knowing the title.

Artists generally choose the approach that best matches their interests. If artists work according to their natural feelings, they will express themselves in either one of the directions, although few can be found at either of the extremes. Most artists have had to try several approaches to visual expression before they feel comfortable working in their own natural way.

3–8 Hugo Robus, *Despair,* 1927. Bronze, 11 3/4" (30 cm) high. Whitney Museum of American Art, New York.

Just as individual artists have moved between emotional and intellectual approaches, so, too, has the art of various periods. In Western art, changes between the extremes at each end of the scale seem to happen in cycles. Emotional content becomes important for a while. Then, after a time, design becomes more important than emotion. When the time is right, emotion again emerges as the dominant attitude in art and expression.

Two thousand years ago, changes in style from emotional to intellectual occurred slowly, often taking hundreds of years. Then, the time span was shortened, until, today, the two extremes tend to exist simultaneously.

Sometimes, there was a period of transition as one phase of a cycle came to an end and the other quality began to emerge. At other times, a sudden, almost physical, reaction against the waning style occurred and the succeeding style became dominant instantly.

The simplified chart illustrates the cyclical development and dominance of the intellectual or emotional approaches to art. Such a generalization is not totally accurate. However, it does help to explain why Romantic painters looked back to Baroque artists for ideas and why Neoclassic artists studied Greek and Roman art for aesthetic ideas akin to their own.

A brief look at some examples of art from different places and various periods will highlight how much the styles have in common. Emotional art is always expressionist. No matter when the work was painted and no matter what the subject, emotional art is usually a strong personal statement by an artist. Intellectual art always appears cool and carefully designed. Many of these examples may contain both qualities at the same time, but one dominates the other.

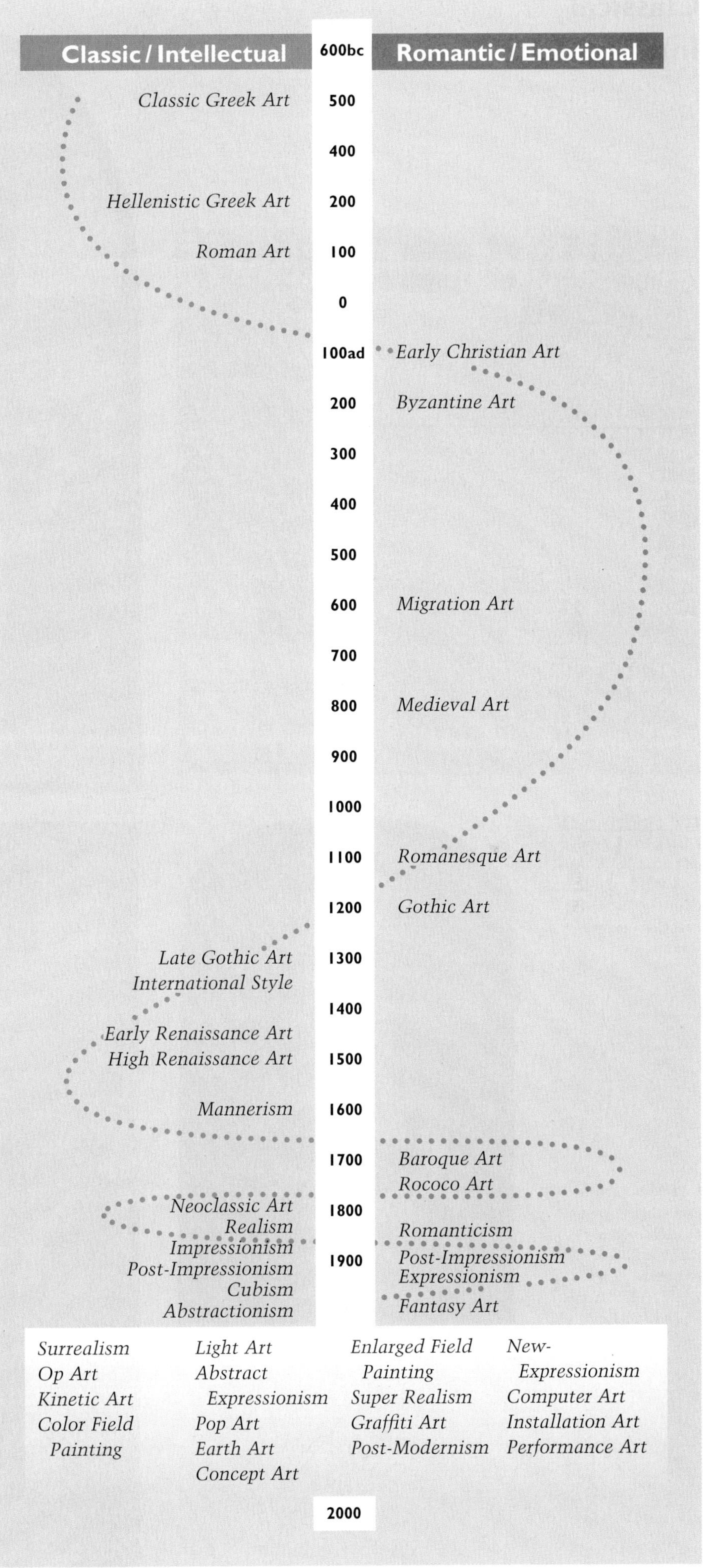

Classical Intellectual

3–10 Victor Vasarely, *Edetta*, 1984. Acrylic on canvas, 39 3/4" x 39 3/4" (101 x 101 cm). Courtesy Circle Fine Arts Corporation, Chicago.

3–11 Raphael Sanzio, *The Marriage of the Virgin*, 1504. Panel, 67" x 46" (170 x 117 cm). Pinacoteca di Brera, Milan.

3–12 Jean Auguste Dominique Ingres, *Mademoiselle Caroline Riviere.* Oil on canvas, 39 1/4" x 27 1/2" (100 x 70 cm). The Louvre, Paris.

3–13 Georges Braque, *Violin and Palette*, 1909–10. Oil on canvas, 36 1/4" x 17" (92 x 43 cm). Solomon R. Guggenheim Museum, New York.

Romantic Emotional Expressionist

3–14 Käthe Kollwitz, *Bread!* 1924. Lithograph. Courtesy Galerie St. Etienne, New York.

3–15 Willem de Kooning, *Woman I,* 1950–52. 6'4" x 4'10" (193 x 147 cm). Collection, The Museum of Modern Art, New York.

3–16 El Greco, *View of Toledo,* 1600–1610. Oil on canvas, 42 1/2" x 45" (121 x 108 cm). The Metropolitan Museum of Art, New York, bequest of Mrs. H. O. Havemeyer.

3–17 Eugene Delacroix, *Arabs Skirmishing in the Mountains,* 1863. Oil on canvas, 36 3/8" x 29 1/2" (92 x 75 cm). The National Gallery of Art, Washington, DC (Chester Dale Fund).

Lesson 3.2 Review

1 What are some features usually found in emotional art and some that are in intellectual art?

2 Why do you think the transition from one art style to another has become so rapid in recent years?

3 Study the pictures on pages 68 and 69. How are the classical/ intellectual examples alike and how are the Romantic examples alike?

3.3 Style

In the history of art, there are many styles. Some are obvious while others are subtle. Although art communicates in a universal language, the styles that characterize individuals, countries, regions and periods may vary drastically. Each develops a style best suited to its needs.

Individual Style

Artists throughout history, if they have developed in an environment free of rules and directives, have worked out their own personal styles, which are as individual as their handwriting. Many of the artists illustrated in this book can be identified by characteristic features of their work. Individual style is the result of many influences. An artist's teachers, friends, environment and exposure to art of the past can all affect the artist. These influences can cause changes in methods, subject matter and approaches to art. Often, the style of an artist changes during a lifetime of such influences and during periods of experimentation. Rembrandt van Rijn, Joseph Mallord William Turner, Jean-Baptiste-Camille Corot and Pablo Picasso are some examples of artists with changing individual styles. An awareness of style and stylistic differences will help you analyze and evaluate art.

3–18 The work of El Greco is immediately recognizable because of his distinctive style—a concentration on Biblical subject matter; an elongated distortion of the figures; writhing movement; and powerful value contrasts that create flamelike lights and darks. El Greco, *Christ and the Moneychangers from the Temple*, 1600. Spanish. Oil on canvas, 41 3/4" x 51 1/4" (106 x 130 cm). The National Gallery, London.

3–19 Jacob van Ruisdael's painting *Wheatfields* is characteristic of both the artist and the Baroque period in the Netherlands. Many Baroque artists painted such nature scenes with turbulent skies, small human figures and carefully controlled light.
Jacob van Ruisdael, *Wheatfields,* about 1660. Dutch. Oil on canvas, 39" x 51" (100 x 130 cm). The Metropolitan Museum of Art, New York, bequest of Benjamin Altman.

Period Style

Art of certain periods is often alike. Egyptian art, for example, was determined by a rigid set of conventions. Images remained strikingly similar for 2500 years. While some styles lasted for centuries, others endured for only decades or less. Within one period, a dominant style may undergo subtle changes. The Italian Renaissance, for example, can be broken up into Early, High and Mannerist periods. Despite differences, these individual styles are sufficiently alike to be grouped together for study.

3–20 In the view of Vienna, the domed structure in the foreground and the towering cathedral represent two period styles. The dome and other architectural details set that building in the Baroque period. The forms, details, spires and vertical emphasis of the cathedral place it in the Gothic period.
View of downtown Vienna, Austria. *St. Peter's Church* in the foreground, *St. Stephen's Cathedral* in the background.

National Style and Regional Style

Sometimes a country has a national style. National style is not part of any period style, but evolves gradually over a long time. Probably arising from older forms of native culture, it often has ethnic overtones and may be part of a country's political movement.

Regional styles often evolve from the influence of a single, strong local artist or a group of people working the same locale and in similar styles and techniques.

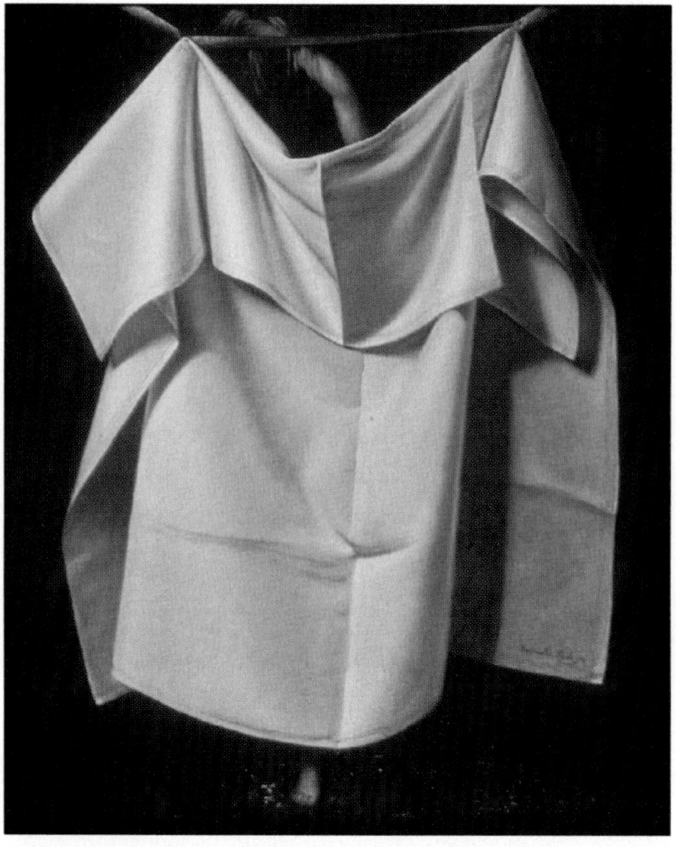

3–22 Raphaelle Peale, an early-nineteenth-century American, painted a towel with such realism that people were tempted to pluck it from the canvas in order to see the nude figure behind it.
Raphaelle Peale, *Venus Rising from the Sea—A Deception (After the Bath).* Oil on canvas, 29" x 24" (74 x 61 cm). The Nelson-Atkins Museum of Art, Kansas City, Missouri.

3–21 The style of Diego Rivera is rooted in ancient Mexican styles, but has a modern feeling. The forms are rounded, monumental and simplified. Rivera's style became a Mexican national style, the foundation for several generations of Mexican and Mexican-American artists who still work in a similar manner.
Diego Rivera, *Flower Day,* 1925. Mexican. Oil on canvas, 57 3/4" x 47 1/2" (147 x 121 cm). Los Angeles County Museum of Art.

Technique Style

A certain type of painting may emerge in several periods. It may be based on a particular technique or presentation of subject matter. One of these technique styles is *trompe l'oeil*—the French term for "fool the eye." An object painted in this style is so lifelike that viewers think it is real.

There have been many trompe l'oeil painters throughout the centuries. In the late 1970s and early 1980s, a style called Super-Realism carried on this tradition. Although such technique styles appear in many periods, they are not the dominant style of the period.

Lesson 3.3 Review

1 List four major categories of styles in art.
2 What are some of the things that can influence an artist's style?
3 Which artist's painting style became a national Mexican style?
4 Define trompe l'oeil. Describe an example of trompe l'oeil.

Primary Source

David and Kollwitz—A Contrast in Approach

Artists take a variety of approaches to art. In this chapter, two approaches, intellectual and emotional, are described and illustrated. Some artists have verbalized their thoughts on this matter. Jacques Louis David, an artist of the Classic tradition had this to say in 1796:

"I want to work in a pure Greek style. I feed my eyes on antique statues, I even have the intention of imitating some of them. The Greeks had no scruples about imitating a composition, a gesture, a type that had already been accepted and used. They put all their art on perfecting an idea that had already been conceived."

Käthe Kollwitz, a twentieth-century artist who lived during the first half of the century, witnessed a time when Europe was torn by war and strife. Her art and words reflected the emotion she felt:

"...when I became acquainted with the difficulties and tragedies underlying proletarian life, when I met the women who came to my husband for help and so, incidentally, came to me, I was gripped by the full force of the proletarian's fate. Unsolved problems such as prostitution and unemployment grieved and tormented me, and contributed to my feeling that I must keep on with my studies of the lower classes. And portraying them again and again opened a safety valve for me; it made life bearable."

Jacques-Louis David, *Oath of the Horatii*, detail (fig.12–1).

Käthe Kollwitz, *Bread!*, detail (fig.3–14).

Chapter Review

Review

1 Look through the first three chapters of this book. Select three works of art that use geometric patterns, three that portray animals, and three with human figures.

2 Describe an example of one culture influencing the art of another.

3 Why are human figures often shown nude in art? What messages can clothes convey about a figure?

Interpret

1 Compare the difference in emotional levels in Moore's *Reclining Nude* with that in Robus' *Despair*.

2 Compare El Greco's *St. Martin and the Beggar* (fig.2–47) and *Christ Driving the Money Changers from the Temple*. What clues indicate that these pictures were painted by the same artist?

Other Tools for Learning

Electronic Research

CD-ROM drive: *Microsoft Art Gallery*

1 Look at four or five works of art by one artist. What are some of the characteristics that are shared by most of these works and indicate the artist's personal style?

2 Watch the Making Paintings Guided Tour. Describe the technique of one of the artists.

Activity 1

Over the Border

Materials

stiff paper (file folders, cardboard)
11" x 14" white paper
scissors
pencils, rulers
markers
colored pencils (optional)
tempera paint
surface for mixing paint
containers of water
brushes

Take a look. Find examples in this book of paintings, blankets or pottery that use geometric patterns or borders.

Think about it. A border is a design or decorative strip around the edge or rim of something—a page, fabric, or a painting. Shapes are often repeated over and over. Notice how some patterns are intricate, some simple; some balanced, others chaotic. Where else in your environment can you find borders and geometric designs?

Do it. Create a border that will frame something (a photograph, a poem) or fill your page with a geometric design.

- Decide what shapes you will use in your border, such as crosses, circles, squares. You might want to select just two or three shapes to work with at different sizes.
- Will you be imitating the style of a particular culture? If so, identify characteristic elements or colors to use in your design.
- One approach would be to use a fairly stiff paper to draw and cut out your shapes. Then place them on your drawing paper and trace around them with a pencil, using some shapes repeatedly.
- When your pattern is complete, color it in with tempera paint, markers or pencils. You may want to select and repeat limited colors to enhance the repetition of the pattern.

Check it. Write down at least five words that you feel describe your border (ornate, colorful, energetic, etc.). Ask others to review your work and also write down five words. Compare and discuss the results. Are your perceptions similar?

Helpful Hint: You might want to imagine a pattern that would be effective made into cloth. What kinds of colors and patterns would you like to wear?

Activity 2

Side by Side

Materials

8 1/2" x 11" white paper
tempera paints
brushes
surface for mixing paint
containers of water
objects to paint, such as bottles, fruit, baskets, flowers

Take a look. Study the styles on pages 68 and 69 before you begin your project.

Think about it. Consider the categories called "classic/intellectual" versus "romantic/emotional." What qualities are distinctive in each? Do the paintings on pages 68 and 69 seem to strictly belong to each category or do you see "emotional" qualities in some of the "intellectual" paintings and vice versa? Why is it useful to classify paintings in this way?

Do it. Use tempera paint to create two small, simple still lifes of the same arrangement of three or four items.

- Arrange objects of varying size, color, shape and texture for the still life. If your teacher has arranged something for you, look at it from different perspectives to find an angle that interests you.
- Make one painting in a precise, carefully designed style, then set it aside.
- Now paint the same objects, same angle, same size, but in an expressionistic style.

Check it. Is it obvious to you and to others which painting is classical/intellectual and which is romantic/expressionistic? What other words might describe your work?

Helpful Hint: Instead of painting everything you see in the still life arrangement, you might try mentally "zooming in" on one interesting part and filling your page with it.

Additional Activities

- Find illustrations in magazines that demonstrate the influence of other cultures on American architecture. For example, trace the development of a style from Spain to Mexico to the United States.
- Study the illustrations on pages 68 and 69. Write a short paper discussing the general differences between classic and romantic styles. Then write a paragraph explaining which style you like better, and why.

Seby Ravindran

Age 16
Lake Highlands High School
Dallas, Texas
Activity 1, Over the Border

My picture is of four women gazing at a beautiful sunset. I used map pencils for the women and pastels for the background. I specially liked working with the pastels because you could combine two different colors with ease. The map pencils were harder to work with because they had to be constantly sharpened and it was harder to blend two colors.

My original idea for the background was a blue sky but instead I opted to do a sunset. Growing up in India I witnessed a lot of sunsets and I was always amazed at how sunsets conveyed a beautiful and tranquil feeling as well as a beautiful moment. I chose to use pastels for my background because I wanted a smooth transition from one color to the other in the sunset. The real challenge came when I designed a border that incorporated the images in the artwork.

The result was a picture that represents the highlight of the day for four hardworking women. At the end of a long, tiring day, they take a few seconds to admire the beauty of their surroundings. I feel this is a beautiful reminder to everyone of how short but wonderful life is and to make the most of it while you can.

Seby Ravindran

Sunset, 1994. Map pencils and pastels, 18" x 24" (45.7 cm x 61 cm).

The Sound of Music, 1994. Prismacolor, 19 1/2" x 16" (49.5 x 40.6 cm).

Beth Featherstone

Age 16
Lake Highlands High School
Dallas, Texas

This piece expresses my love for the art of music and the art of drawing. When I was developing my picture, I thought of all the different ways music can flow. It can flow smooth, choppy, loud or soft. I showed this the best way I knew how in the strokes of my pencil. I prefer smooth, mellow, soothing music that's pleasing to the ears, much like I prefer smooth, mellow soothing pictures with colors pleasing to the eye.

I mostly enjoy working with colors, shading, and free strokes. It's always a relief when you come to that final stroke that jumps out at you, and you realize that you're finished!

Beth Featherstone

4 Art of the Non-Western World

In This Chapter...

4–a Much Indian art and architecture centers around the religions of Hinduism and Buddhism. This Hindu temple complex is meant to represent the order of the universe.
Shore Temple, 7th–8th centuries. Mamallapuram (Mahabalipuram), India. Pallava style, live rock.

4–c This detail from a palace door of the Yoruba tribe shows genre scenes and anecdotes of tribal life. In this instance, the name of the sculptor has been recorded. It is often the case in African art, however, that we do not know the name of the artists of traditional works of art.
Areogun, *Door from palace at Ikerre,* detail (fig.1–9).

4–b The cultures of ancient America are famous for their work with fabrics. This mantle is made of feathers and cotton. The feathers are striking in their color and provide a strong element of contrast to the piece.
Feather Mantle, 13th–14th centuries. Feathers and cotton, 45 x 44 1/2" (114.3 x 113 cm). Chimu, Peru. The Nelson-Atkins Museum of Art, Kansas City, Missouri. Purchase: Nelson Trust [60–79].

Every country nourishes the arts.
Erasmus

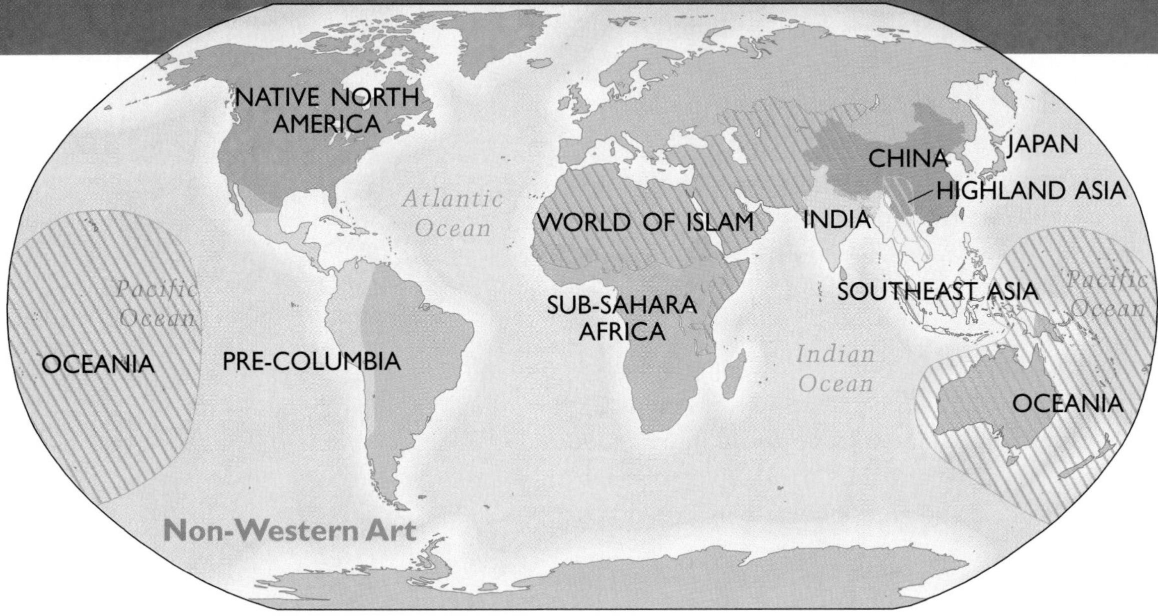

Non-Western areas of the world discussed in this chapter are highlighted on this map.

4–d How would you describe the landscape depicted here? What elements of art and principles of design has the artist used to convey this effect?
Ma Yuan, *Bare Willows and Distant Mountains,* end of 12th century. Round fan mounted as album leaf, ink and light color on silk, 9 1/2" x 9 1/2" (23.8 x 23.8 cm). Museum of Fine Arts, Boston.

4–e The Japanese have created many of the world's most beautiful and skillfully made woodcuts. The subjects of these prints often focus on scenes of everyday life.
Ando Hiroshige, *Hodogaya Station* from the Tokeido Series, 1832–1834. Collection of Bertna and Mitchel Siegel, Santa Fe, New Mexico.

4.1 A Multitude of Perspectives

ANY CULTURE THAT IS NOT RELATED TO Western civilization (the people of North America and Western Europe) is referred to as non-Western. The great civilizations of India, Asia, Islam and pre-Columbian America, and the tribal societies of Africa and North America belong to non-Western cultures.

In non-Western societies, art has many purposes, including magic, worship, status and even politics. Much of the artwork produced by these cultures features religious symbols and motifs. No understanding of art from these cultures would be complete without an understanding of their religions.

Other artwork can be understood in terms of the ways cultures have used color and perspective. But, it also helps to know something about the history and culture and people who produced it. The more you know about the experiences and attitudes that helped to shape a society, the better you can understand and appreciate its artwork.

4–2 Scholars have learned a great deal about the religious life and customs of the Mesoamerican culture by analyzing their illustrated codices.
Souche Nuttar Codex, detail (fig.4–6).

4–1 Ando Hiroshige, *Hodogaya Station,* detail (fig.4–e).

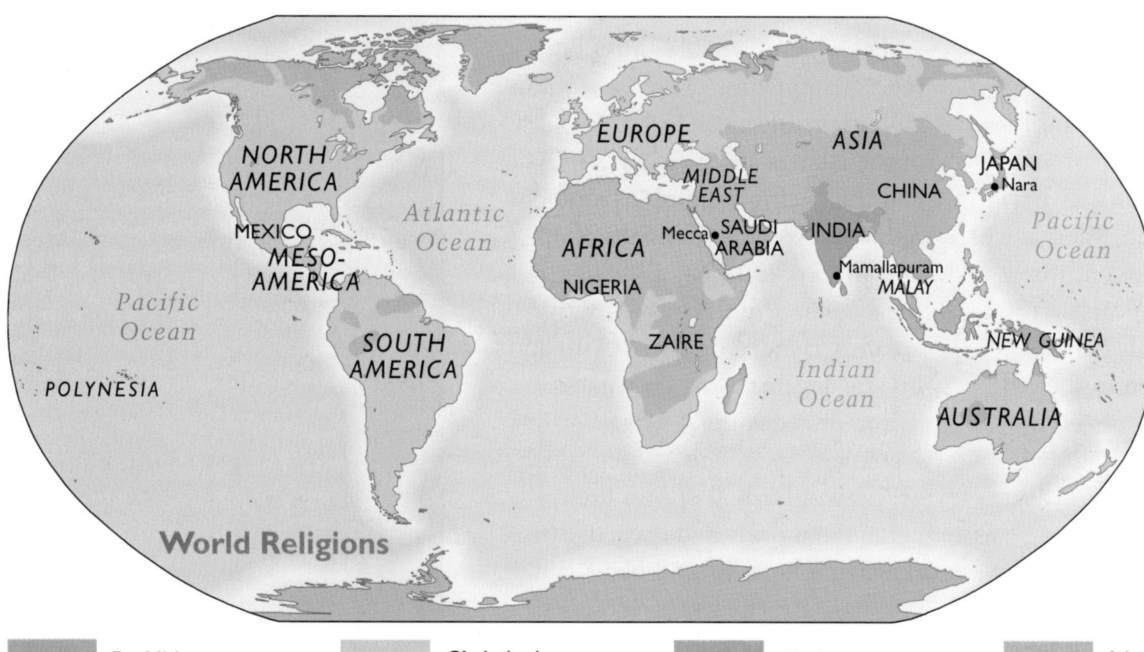

The four most widely practiced religions of the world today are shown on this map. Prior to the emergence of world-wide, organized religions, people usually followed the tribal beliefs popular in their village or local community. How did unified religions impact art around the world?

4–3 Many ancient traditions, such as the pueblo form of architecture, are still in use today.
Pueblo, Taos, New Mexico.

4–4 Bas reliefs such as this are found throughout the temple at Borobudor. They illustrate scenes from legends.
Java, *Buddhist Borobudor,* detail (fig.4–55).

Religion

Three of the world's great major religions evolved in Africa and Asia—*Hinduism*, *Buddhism* and *Islam*. Every civilization also developed religious practices. Many are based on the worship of nature, such as the planets, animals and fertility. These religious beliefs and values are reflected in the culture's art.

Western art depicts images of Christianity and ideas that reflect the Judeo-Christian tradition. Similarly, Asian art presents many images of Buddha, "the Enlightened One." African art presents images and symbols of its own religious traditions. The carved wooden figure shown here (fig.4–5) is from the Kuba tribe of Zaire. This male figure is the portrait of a king that "performs" a specific function.

While Hinduism, Buddhism and Islam are the three major religions, other religions have also had an impact on a culture's art. *Taoism* and *Confucianism* are important religions in China. The *Shinto* religion is the oldest in Japan. Peoples of the islands and highlands of Asia and the Pacific worship natural phenomena. Art and architecture of ancient civilizations of Mexico, Mesoamerica and South America are also founded on naturalism and mystic spiritualism. The manuscript, or codex (fig.4–6), is a strong statement about the Mixtec society of Mesoamerica. It shows their ceremonial dress and their use of the jaguar head as a religious symbol (fig.4–2). The game that is being played with a rubber ball is part of a ceremony, for their sports and games often revolved around religion.

4–5 Reliquary Guardian Figure, Cameroon or Gabon, c.1850. Wood, h. 23" (60 cm). Peabody Museum, Harvard University.

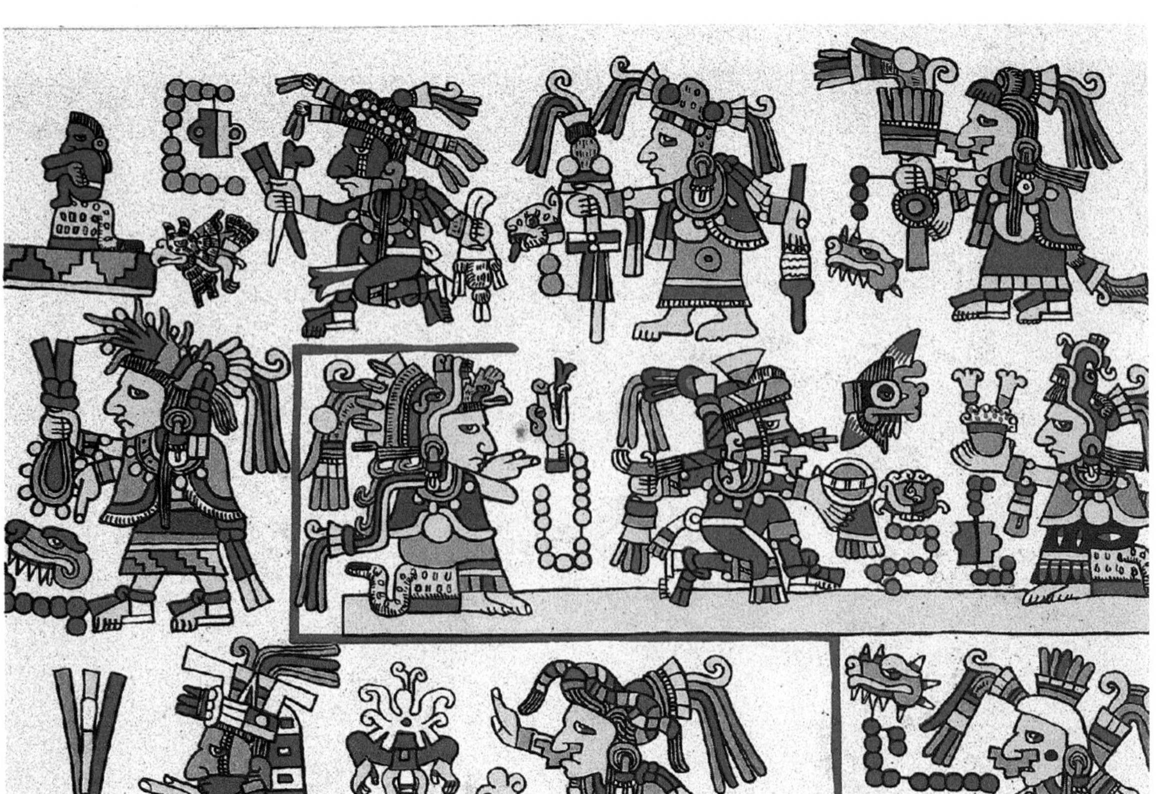

4–6 Many books of South and Central American cultures were destroyed by the Spanish conquistadors. *Souche Nuttar Codex*, one of forty-eight sheets, 14th century. Mixtec culture, Mesoamerica. Drawing and painting on deerskin, 7" x 9 3/4" (18 x 25 cm). British Museum, London.

4–8 The *Ramayana* provides us with information about the ideals, values, customs and rituals of ancient India.
Sita in the Garden of Lanka, from the *Epic of Valmaki, Ramayana.* Gold and color on paper, 22 x 31" (55.5 x 79 cm). India, Pahai, Guler School. The Cleveland Museum of Art, Gift of George P. Bickford, 66.143.

Hinduism

Hinduism, one of the world's most ancient religion, originated in ancient India about 2000 BC. Hindus believe in the gods *Brahma* the Creator, *Vishnu* the Preserver, and *Siva* the Destroyer. In artworks, Brahma appears in white robes and rides a swan. Brahma is often shown with four heads. From his four heads spring the Vedas, or sacred books, which he carries along with a scepter. Vishnu holds a discus, conch shell, mace and lotus. Siva is often entwined in snakes and wears a headdress of skulls, but, at other times, he dances in a circle of fire.

Hinduism gave order to the universe and to the structure of society. The universe was divided into three zones of earth, middle space and sky. Animals and human forms were often used to depict the powers within these three zones. In the carving *The Descent of the Ganges From Heaven* (fig.4–7), dancing and active human figures represent the source of life. The elephants in this massive work symbolize the power of nature. They have a mythological ability to call upon the clouds to produce rain. By the gigantic elephants, nature is shown as being much more powerful than humanity. The gods are portrayed as more important than humans. The different registers may correspond with social castes ruled over by a king with divine power.

One of the greatest Hindu writings of ancient India is the epic known as the *Ramayana*. The epic is about the legendary king *Rama*, who was unjustly deprived of his kingdom. The Hindus believe that Rama is a human form of their god Vishnu. Various episodes concern Rama's birth, his marriage to the beautiful *Sita*, her capture by the devil *Ravana*, and Rama's rescue of Sita and his land. The basic teaching of the *Ramayana* is that good prevails over evil. Rama and Sita are models that show Hindus how they should behave. Scenes from this tale are painted and sculpted on temples, shrines, palaces and courts throughout Asia (fig.4–8). The *Ramayana* was adopted by the Buddhists and, later, even became part of Islamic heritage. Each country has its own subtle version of this universal tale.

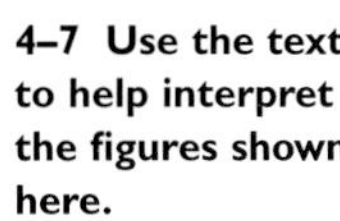

4–7 Use the text to help interpret the figures shown here.
The Descent of the River Ganges from Heaven, 10th century. Live rock carving at Mamallapuram, India.

Buddhism

Buddhism emerged in India in the sixth century BC as a Hindu reform movement. The movement was founded by Buddha, who became enlightened through years of meditation. He preached charity to all creatures, the equality of all beings, and the practice of moderation. The goal of all Buddhists is to achieve nirvana, the final state of eternal bliss. Buddha essentially reformed Hinduism without discarding the Hindu gods. However, Buddhism soon became its own strong religion and spread to other countries.

In the second century BC, a complex form of Buddhism known as *Mahayana* Buddhism developed. It preached the salvation of souls and the important role of saints, called *bodhisattvas.* These saints were believers who achieved enlightenment like Buddha, but who chose not to enter nirvana. Instead, they remained to help struggling mortals. The most popular of these bodhisattvas is *Avaloketisvara,* known in China as *Guan Yin* and, in Japan, as *Kannon.* This "goddess of mercy," with a meditative countenance and a reassuring confidence, is symbolically represented upon a lotus seat (fig.4–9). The lotus, a water lily, symbolizes purity.

Buddhism was introduced in Japan in the sixth century. There are several forms of Buddhism in Japan. The Buddhist cult of Jizo Bosatsu was introduced into Japan in the eighth century and was extremely popular from 900 to 1300. Zen Buddhism became an important cultural force in the fourteenth century.

Jizo is a compassionate deity concerned with the needs of suffering humanity and is the patron saint of children. He is usually shown as a simple monk. This carving (fig.4–10) is made of joined wood blocks. The artist used the wood grains to enhance the contours of the figure.

4–9 This goddess of mercy is said to remain on earth to help people with their earthly lives.
Nyoirin-Kannon (Bodhisattva), 645–647. Nara period. Bronze. Oka-Der-a Temple, Nara, Japan.

4–10 This monk is the patron saint of children.
Jizo Bosatsu, 12th century, late Heian period, Japan. Wood, 57 1/2" (146 cm) high. Los Angeles County Museum of Art, gift of Anna Bing Arnold.

Islam

Much of Asia is dominated by *Islam*. The religion of Islam was founded by the prophet Mohammed. In a vision, he was told that he was the messenger of Allah, the one God. Mohammed received his revelations in Mecca, a city in Saudi Arabia, during the seventh century. The spiritual writings of Mohammed are contained in the *Koran,* the sacred book of the Moslems. Mohammed preached that the way to Allah lies through learning the sacred writings and in service to him. Mohammed's followers spread his message to the Middle East, Northern Africa, China and the Malay archipelago.

Islam forbids the use of religious images of any kind. Although religious sculptures could not depict human figures, miniature paintings were allowed to include men and women as illustrations for tales about successful Islamic rulers, their loves and their adventures. This example is a single page or folio from a Shah Nama (Book of Kings), a popular illustrated history (fig.4–11).

4–11 How would you characterize the conversation in which these men are engaged? You do not know what they are saying, but do their poses give you any clues? Do other elements in the painting emphasize or repeat their poses?
Two Men Converse in a Landscape. A folio from a Shah Nama, 16th century. Sultanate period, India. Watercolor on paper, 8 1/4" x 5 1/8" (21 x 13 cm). Los Angeles County Museum of Art, gift of Doris and Ed Wiener.

Media

Non-Western cultures have produced artwork from materials similar to those used in the West. Materials such as stone, brick, wood, paint and clay are used. Oceanic peoples of New Guinea and Polynesia paint on bark, and the Chinese have used glass and silk as their grounds. American Indians have painted on hide, wood, stone and textiles. Lost-wax casting was used during the *Shang* dynasty of China and by the *Benin* culture of Nigeria. These cultures produced excellent metal sculptures with this technique. While bronze is permanent, non-Western art is also made from perishable items such as feathers, flowers, leather, grass, bark and shells.

Western painters tend to work within the limitations of a frame, but Chinese and Japanese painters worked on screens and scrolls. If they needed more space to tell their entire story, they added more sections to the screen or rolled the scroll out for several more feet.

4–12 Oceanic artists rely predominantly on natural materials for their artwork.
Painted Bark Cloth, 20th century. Melanesia, Lake Sentani (Irian Jaya). Bark cloth with pigment, 33 1/4" x 46 1/2" (84.4 x 118.1 cm). The Nelson-Atkins Museum, Kansas City, Missouri, gift of Mr. and Mrs. Morton I. Sosland.

Color

Over the centuries, Western artists have used color differently in their paintings. Roman and Renaissance artists used realistic colors. Impressionist painters dabbed in color as it was reflected from objects and approached it almost scientifically. Expressionists used color to symbolize feelings and emotions.

In Asian painting, color is arbitrary. Chinese painters painted their scrolls with monochromatic colors, often using color only for accents and emphasis (fig.4–27a,b). In woodcuts, colors were kept flat (fig.4–13). Color and value were not used together to describe form.

4–13 When they made their way west to Paris in the nineteenth century, prints like this had an enormous impact on Western art in the works of such artists as Gauguin.
Katsushika Hokusai, *The Great Wave* from *Thirty-six Views of Mt. Fuji,* Tokugawa period. Woodcut, 10" x 14 3/4" (25 x 37 cm). Spaulding Collection, Courtesy, Museum of Fine Arts, Boston.

4–14 How does your eye move through the space in this picture?
Shen Chou, *Landscape in the Style of Ni Tsan*, 1484. Ink, 54 1/2" x 24 3/4" (138 x 62.9 cm). The Nelson-Atkins Museum of Art, Kansas City, Missouri.

Perspective

Perspective was approached differently in the East and the West. Perspective is the Western term for showing realistic spatial relationships of objects in drawing or painting. Renaissance artists discovered how to show distance by using overlapping planes and lines converging at a vanishing point. (*See* fig.9–30, for example.) In some Chinese and Japanese art, receding lines remain parallel and do not converge (fig.4–14). Thus, the eye moves back into the picture, but does not eventually meet one or two specific vanishing points.

Asian artists often depict great distance by showing three planes: a foreground, a middle distance and a far distance, each parallel to the picture plane. For example, one may see land, then water, then mountains, each painted separately, not overlapping. As the viewer's eye leaps from one distance to the next, the vastness of nature is felt. Objects are often enveloped in mist or cloud to further suggest spaciousness. Details in the background become less distinct, a technique called aerial perspective. In their monochromatic ink paintings, Chinese artists often used aerial perspective to great effect.

Some non-Western artists present the front and side view of an object simultaneously. "X-ray" views of internal parts can be seen at the same time as the exterior (fig.4–15). The artist thus depicts more than the surface of things.

4–15 Why might an artist choose to depict the exterior as well as the "interior" of an animal?
X-ray Figure of Kangaroo. Aborigine, Australia. Collection of Larry Majewski.

Lesson 4.1 Review

1 When and where did Hinduism and Buddhism originate?
2 Who are Brahma, Vishnu and Siva? How are they represented in Hindu art?
3 In the carving *The Descent of the Ganges*, what do the elephants symbolize? How do we know that the artist considered nature to be more powerful than humans?
4 Who are Avaloketisvara and Jizo? How are they usually represented in Buddhist art?
5 Explain the relationship between Islam, Mohammed and the Koran.
6 Why are there no sculptures in Islamic mosques?
7 On what did traditional Chinese and Japanese artists usually paint?
8 Describe the use of color in Asian paintings.

4.2 India

INDIA WAS HOME TO ONE OF the world's oldest civilizations. Like its geography of extreme contrasts—from snow-covered mountains to steamy jungles—India has a rich mix of cultures.

Hinduism and Buddhism have dominated the art of India for over 2500 years. At times, one religion was stronger than the other, resulting in distinctly different sculpture and architecture. At other times, the two religions have co-existed, and architecture and imagery have shared similar styles. India has also received outside cultural influences at various times, but all have eventually been absorbed into the unique Indian style.

Vocabulary
stupa
harmika
live rock
gopura

4–16 This painting dates from the Mughal period, the final phase of traditional Indian art.
Rajput, Rajasthani School, *Head of Krishna.* Cartoon for mural painting, from illustration to the "Rasa Lila." Color on paper. The Metropolitan Museum of Art, New York. Rogers Fund, 1918.

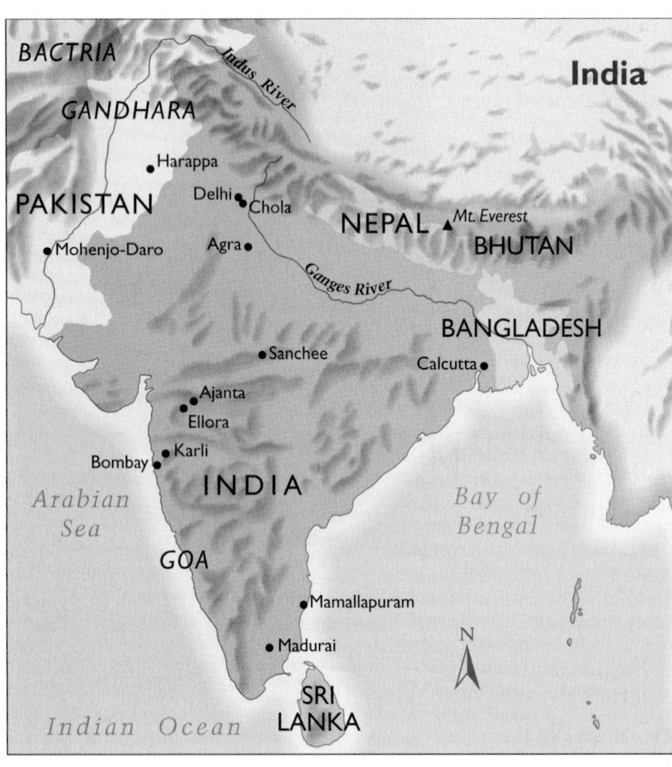

The world's highest mountains, the Himalayas, effectively separate the subcontinent of India from the rest of Asia, contributing to India's unique culture. Religious differences have resulted in the formation of new political boundaries. Islamic beliefs are more prevalent in Pakistan and Bangladesh, Buddhism in Nepal and Bhutan, Hinduism in India.

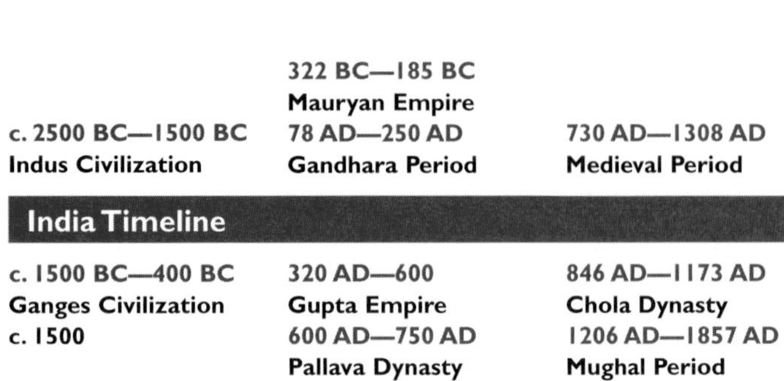

India Timeline

c. 2500 BC—1500 BC **Indus Civilization**	**322 BC—185 BC** **Mauryan Empire** **78 AD—250 AD** **Gandhara Period**	**730 AD—1308 AD** **Medieval Period**
c. 1500 BC—400 BC **Ganges Civilization** **c. 1500**	**320 AD—600** **Gupta Empire** **600 AD—750 AD** **Pallava Dynasty**	**846 AD—1173 AD** **Chola Dynasty** **1206 AD—1857 AD** **Mughal Period**

4–17 This image shows a less well-known section of the world-famous Taj Mahal. See fig.4–24 for the more familiar view.
Taj Mahal, 1632. Side building, Agra, India.

4–18 Siva often is depicted in his cosmic dance with his numerous arms rotating gracefully about his body.
Siva, Lord of the Dance, Performing the Nataraja, 10th century. Chola dynasty, India. 30" (76 cm) high. Los Angeles County Museum of Art.

Indus Valley Civilization

The earliest Indian culture is known as the *Indus Valley civilization,* a sophisticated society existing until 1500 BC. It was located along the river banks in what is modern Pakistan, stretching about two thousand kilometers, from Harappa to Mohenjo-Daro. Bronze and stone animal sculptures and small stamps, or seals, carved in stone of this culture have been discovered (fig.4–19). The seals were used to stamp signatures on official documents. The people created ceramic bowls rubbed with resin and decorated with geometric and animal motifs. They also built temples honoring popular water gods.

4–19 Scholars have been unable to decipher the script on these tiles.
Seals, from Mohenjo-Daro, Pakistan, 3000 BC. Steatite. National Museum, Delhi.

4–20 Relics of Buddha's body were placed in shrines like this, which were visited by those on pilgrimages.
Stupa I, 2nd century BC–1st century AD. Solid masonry. Sanchi, India.

The Mauryan Era

A long era, known generally as the *Ganges civilization,* followed. For one thousand years there was little evidence of Indian civilization. During this era, hymns called *Vedas* were written. These Vedas marked the beginning of Hinduism. Then, in the fourth century BC, India was united under the rule of the Maurya family. The greatest of the Maurya rulers was King Asoka. Asoka was greatly influenced by Buddhism. Through these teachings, he sought to provide his people with a better way of life, one without war. By the latter half of the second century BC, Asoka had converted many subjects to Buddhism. He had large columns built and inscribed them with Buddhist teachings. The columns were topped with magnificent seated lion sculptures, which have become the mark of Asokan art.

The Mauryans constructed the first objects of Buddhist architecture—round burial mounds known as ***stupas*** (fig.4–20), which contained relics of Buddha's body. A stupa was surrounded by a wall. Relief carvings on the walls and gateways allowed believers on pilgrimages to read Buddhist teachings. The small railed balcony atop the structure is the ***harmika***. It is topped with stylized umbrellas that symbolize the thirty-three higher heavens of Mahayana Buddhism.

The Gandhara Era

Greek armies under Alexander made conquests in Northern India and Pakistan after 326 BC. Therefore, the first significant Buddhist sculpture had a Greek influence. The first images of Buddha appeared in the Hellenistic kingdoms of Bactria and Gandhara. The sculptures were based on Greek sculptural methods and aesthetics. The sculptures had Western facial and body types. The colossal head of Buddha, made of stucco, shows a Greek-style face, except for the half-closed treatment of the eyes (fig.4–21). The hair is formed in a style similar to Greek figures of Apollo. However, distinct Buddhist motifs were developed to show Buddha's sacred nature: elongated earlobes, the *ushnisha* coil of hair protruding from the back of the head, and the third eye, or *urna,* which symbolized his omniscience.

Under the Gandhara school of art, the first Indian cave temples were cut into hillsides of ***live rock***. The form of these cave sanctuaries resembles earlier wooden constructions, except that they were hewn from solid rock.

4–21 The first images of Buddha were profoundly influenced by Greek ideas.
Colossal Head of Buddha, 2nd–3rd centuries. Gandhara school, India. Stucco, 27 1/2" (70 cm) high. Los Angeles County Museum of Art, Leo Meyer Collection.

The Gupta Era

Greek style in Indian art declined, and a new, distinctly Indian style emerged with the rise of the *Gupta* era in 320. The Gupta era is regarded as the golden age of Buddhist Indian art. Drama, literature, painting, sculpture and architecture flourished. Many beautiful and elaborate cave temples were carved and painted at Ajanta and Ellora. The style of temples mingles both Buddhist and Hindu designs. Distinctly Indian figures decorate these temples. The bodies are rounded and voluptuous and lack a characteristic Western look.

4–22 This temple was carved from some of the live rock that is found in the Mahabalipuram area.
Shore Temple. 7th–8th centuries. Mamallapuram (Mahabalipuram), India. Pallava style, live rock.

The Medieval Period

Hinduism experienced a revival toward the end of the Gupta era. From the ninth to the sixteenth centuries, a variety of kingdoms flourished simultaneously. In Southeastern India, a kingdom known as the *Pallava* produced large freestanding temples cut from live rock at Mamallapuram (fig.4–22). The monolithic structures have multistoried roofs and stone square towers developed by Hindu architects. The temple is symmetrical; the building complex is meant to represent order in the universe. Pathways are provided for worshipers and their rituals. Images of Nandi, the bull in the foreground, symbolize the god Siva.

The Pallavas also produced massive towered gateways called ***gopura,*** which were placed at entrances to temple complexes. The two gopura of the *Meenakshi Temple* (fig.4–23) are in the sacred southern city of Madurai. The temples are built in *Dravidian* style. This style is synonymous with Southern Indian architecture to this day. Each level of the rectangular

4–23 The polychromed surfaces of this temple give it a very ornate appearance.
Meenakshi Temple. 17th century. Madurai, India. Brick and stucco, painted in polychrome.

and pyramidically tapered tower is filled with sculptured and painted panels from Hindu mythology.

Bronze casting in the lost-wax method was practiced by another medieval kingdom, the *Chola.* The sculpture of Siva dancing the *nataraja,* or dance of reincarnation, is rendered in minute detail (fig.4–18). Graceful movement is depicted in metal that would be impossible to portray in stone. The flame-encrusted *halo* shows a remarkable and delicate use of line and shape.

The Mughal Period

The final phase of traditional Indian art arrived with the successive waves of Moslem invasions between the twelfth and sixteenth centuries. The greatest of the *Mughal* emperors was Akbar. Akbar reunited the divided medieval kingdoms into the mighty Mughal empire. Because the Moslem religion prohibited the use of imagery, many Hindu temples and their sculptures were destroyed during the Mughal period. The Mughals replaced them with mosques and beautiful palaces of symmetrical simplicity. Mughals brought the Persian style with them, a style mixed with Indian ideas. Mosaics of stone and ceramic decorated the floors and walls in arabesque patterns of leaves, flowers and geometric motifs. Most famous of the structures from Mughal India is the *Taj Mahal* (figs.4–17, 4–24).

Typical of Mughal art was the production of fine small objects in enamel, mother-of-pearl, glass or metalwork. Miniature paintings were made on palm leaves and paper. Here, earthly rulers (never deities) were portrayed. The faces were often in profile, and much attention was given to bodily ornament.

4–24 The Taj Mahal was built by Shah Jahan to memorialize his beloved wife. He used 20,000 workers to construct this lavish mausoleum.
Taj Mahal, 1632. Marble. Agra, India.

Lesson 4.2 Review

1 Name several types of art made by the Indus Valley civilization.
2 What are stupas and harmikas?
3 Why were the earliest Buddhist sculptures similar to classical Greek sculpture?
4 How is a temple constructed if it is carved from live rock?
5 Which era is considered the high point of Buddhist Indian art? Describe the temple art of this period.
6 Name two structures built by the Pallavas.
7 Describe the Shore Temple at Mamallapuram. What does the bull on this temple represent?
8 Who was Akbar? What was his great achievement?
9 Why did the Mughals destroy the Hindu temples and sculptures?
10 What is the most famous Mughal Indian structure?

4.3 China

CHINA IS OFTEN CLAIMED as the world's oldest continuing civilization. China developed first along the valley of the Yellow River and later in much of northern and eastern China. Many cultural and geographic differences between the Chinese north and south of the Yellow River were overcome by the common teachings of *Taoism* and *Buddhism.* Although the Chinese in different regions spoke different local dialects, the written language was the same.

Central to Chinese beliefs is their deep respect for nature. The ancient Chinese believed that nature was filled with spirits. Humanity did not become the conqueror of nature, but rather took its rightful place in it. In Chinese art, humans were seen as insignificant figures against the vastness of their natural surroundings.

The Chinese considered writing to be a form of art. The earliest writing appeared as ***pictographs*** on ***oracle bones*** (fig.4–25). A king would ask a question of the gods. The tribal *shaman* would heat a bone until it cracked, then interpret the fractures as the god's answer to the message. Questions and answers were often written down on the bones.

From these pictographs evolved the art of writing which is called ***calligraphy***. In calligraphy, there is an evolution of rhythm, similar to that in music. In China, writing and painting are closely related. Line evolved as the dominant aspect of Chinese art.

Vocabulary

pictographs
oracle bones
calligraphy
sprigging
pagoda
overglaze enamels

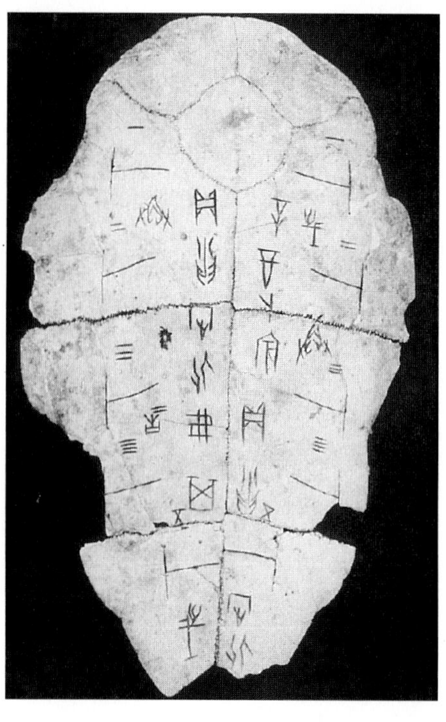

4–25 Oracle bones show early picture writing which eventually developed into modern Chinese writing.
Oracle Bones, 1200 BC. Shang dynasty, China.

4–26 During the Tang dynasty ceramic figures of people and animals were made by the thousands for the tombs of the wealthy.
Glazed horse, 618–906. Tang dynasty, China. Ceramic with three-color glaze, 29 1/8" (74 cm) high. Los Angeles County Museum of Art, gift of Mr. and Mrs. Felix Guggenheim.

c.1766 BC–1027 BC
Shang Dynasty
1028 BC–221 BC
Zhou Dynasty

206 BC–220 AD
Han Dynasty
220 AD–589 AD
Six Dynasties

960 AD–1279 AD
Song Dynasty
1279 AD–1368
Yuan Dynasty

Chinese Dynasty Timeline

221 BC–206 BC
Qin Dynasty

618 AD–907
Tang Dynasty
907 AD–960 AD
Five Dynasties

1368 AD–1644 AD
Ming Dynasty
1644 AD–1912 AD
Qing Dynasty

One-fifth of today's world population lives in China. It is thought to be the oldest civilization in the world. The Great Wall, started in the third century BC, was built by southern Chinese as protection from invading neighbors to the north.

4–28 In China jade was believed to hold spiritual qualities. From very early times, Chinese artists worked with this material.
Feline Head with Bovine Horns and Elephant Trunk, about 1200 BC. Shang dynasty. Jade, 16 1/2" (42 cm) high. The Cleveland Museum of Art, Anonymous Gift, 52.573.

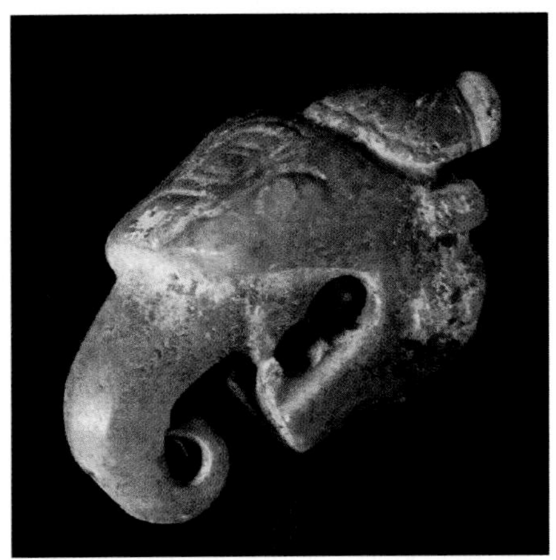

4–27a, b Working with a limited array of colors, this painter created an evocative, spacious landscape.
T'ao Ch'i, copy. *Peach Blossom Spring,* 7th century. Shang dynasty. Ink and color on paper. 9 7/8" high. Freer Gallery of Art, Washington, DC.

Shang Dynasty

The bronze age in China corresponds with the *Shang* and *Zhou* periods, from about 1600 to 221 BC. The center of the Shang culture was at the walled city of Anyang. There, fine hand-built and wheel-made gray pottery was produced. Coatings of a glasslike glaze on the pottery heralded the beginnings of modern ceramics.

Sculptures were made from ivory, stone and jade. The Chinese believed that jade has spiritual and medicinal qualities. From green, brown or white jade, craftspeople carved ritual objects and ornaments (figs.4–28, 4–29). The use of jade is found continually from ancient China to the present.

Most significantly, bronze-working became very important. Bronze ritual vessels of the highest quality were made during the Shang dynasty. They were decorated with stylized linear spiral motifs and designs that symbolized clouds, thunder and fierce animal forms (fig.4–30). These bronzes were made using the piece-mold process.

4–29 Many small ancient Chinese jade sculptures have been found. They may have been used as amulets or charms.
Jade Bird, c. 2000 BC–1500 BC. Shang dynasty. Nephrite, 1 3/4" (4.4 cm). The Nelson-Atkins Museum of Art, Kansas City, Missouri.

Ownership of bronze meant wealth and power and has been cited as one origin of the class system in Chinese history.

Zhou Dynasty

The Shang period ended around 1100 BC when the last Shang ruler was overthrown by the first Zhou king. The Zhou period marked the longest dynasty in all Chinese history, lasting until 221 BC. Pictographic symbols became more stylized and elaborate during the Zhou period. Ceramics continued to become more sophisticated. Glasslike glazes were used to create intricate geometric designs on some ware. Glass paste was melted on the surface of porous clay bodies to form geometric patterns, as in the covered jar made of stoneware shown here (fig.4–31). The brightly colored original glass has faded to soft pastel hues.

Chinese philosophy flowered during the Zhou period. Two of China's greatest thinkers lived during this time. Lao-tzu (b. 604 BC) taught that humanity needed to exist in harmony with nature. His philosophy became known as *Tao* or "The Way," the basis of Taoism. Confucius (b. 551 BC) also taught respect for nature, as well as respect for parents, ancestors, clan, state and emperor. His ideas influenced a whole culture and were followed in China to this century.

4–30 How many animals can you distinguish on this vessel? There are three: a tiger, an owl and another, unidentified bird.
Kuang, 12th century BC. Shang dynasty. Bronze, Freer Gallery of Art, Washington, DC.

4–31 How has the artist used pattern to complement the shape of the jar?
Jar with cover, 5th–3rd century BC. Late Zhou dynasty. Pottery with glass paste, 4 3/4" (12 cm) high. Museum of Fine Arts, Boston, Charles B. Hoyt Collection.

4–32 The tomb in which these figures were found is considered to be one of the greatest archaeological discoveries of modern times. An entire army of these life-sized clay figures was created to accompany the emperor into the next life.
Cavalryman and Saddle Horse, Qin dynasty (221–210 BC). Terra cotta, life-size. Xian, China. Cultural Relics Bureau PRC and The Metropolitan Museum of Art, New York.

Qin Dynasty (Ch'in)

The Chinese north of the Yang Zi (Yellow River) were united for the first time in 221 BC. The new Chinese empire was formed under the short-lived *Qin* dynasty. During this time, the system of written characters was standardized. Pottery objects were made especially for use in tombs. Burial suits of jade segments were tied together in the belief that the jade would preserve the body. In 1974, over 7000 life-size clay soldiers and horses (fig.4–32) were found in underground vaults near Xian. This clay army of imperial bodyguards was intended to serve the Qin emperor in the afterlife.

The *Great Wall* of China (fig.4–33) was also built during the Qin dynasty. The Great Wall is a massive fortification 1500 miles long, 15 to 30 feet wide and 25 feet high, designed to keep out the nomads of Mongolia and Manchuria.

4–33 The Great Wall is so enormous that it is visible to astronauts as they orbit the earth.
Great Wall of China, 3rd–2nd century BC, 1500 miles long (3971 km).

Han Dynasty

The succeeding *Han* dynasty (206 BC–220 AD) was the second longest in Chinese history. Many Chinese traditions, practices and artistic motifs became established during this period. Han rulers united several territories. The "Silk Road" connected China with Syria and Rome. Toward the end of the dynasty, Buddhism was brought by missionaries from India, where it originated, and from Indo-China.

The Han period provides the first record of Chinese architecture. Clay models of actual buildings have been discovered in royal tombs. Such models show roofs with large overhanging eaves, curved and flat clay tiles, and the inward orientation of Chinese building (fig.4–34). Houses, temples and palaces all followed a similar pattern. They had one or more courtyards, with rooms facing that space.

Han culture was as sophisticated as the contemporary Romans in the West. Ceramic sculptures and functional objects were made for rituals and daily use. Potters used a technique known as ***sprigging*** to attach preformed clay sculptural decorations into pottery. They produced vessels ornamented with frieze panels and handles with animal forms. Using lead glazes, Chinese potters produced pottery with bright and varied colors. Cosmetic boxes, cups and many other shapes were decorated in red and black lacquer. They were often inlaid with silver or mother-of-pearl. The silk industry flourished, producing woven and embroidered cloth that was colorful, elegant in appearance, and delightfully smooth and cool to the touch. Not only popular with the wealthy in China, these items were exported to royal courts throughout Asia and the Mediterranean world.

Mural painting continued in tombs, and frescoes of scenes from daily life were created. Life-size stone or clay figures lined the "spirit path" leading to these tombs, and more clay figures of sacrificial men and horses were placed inside.

4–34 Model houses like this one from tombs provide the first records of early Chinese architecture.
House model, 206 BC–221 AD. Han dynasty. Polychromed pottery, 52" (132 cm) high. The Nelson-Atkins Museum of Art, Kansas City, Missouri.

Six Dynasties Era

Although invaders overtook the Han dynasty, the ensuing period (256–589) was one of growth and change in China. Buddhism spread with zeal, and Taoism, a strong religion based on a simplistic return to nature, grew in the south. Stupa architecture merged with local Chinese watchtower forms to produce the ***pagoda***, a monument with an odd number of stories. The pagoda was thought to give protection to residents within its view. Cave temples and monasteries were hollowed out of rock and embellished with huge carved images of Buddha and bodhisattvas.

Paintings on scrolls of silk and paper first appeared, which enabled scholars to enjoy a long narrative without having to view the entire work at once. Figures were painted against plain backgrounds in a non-stylized naturalism, showing action and overlapping planes, as in *Instructress Writing Down Her Admonitions for the Benefit of Two Young Ladies* (fig.4–35). Note the undefined depth of the scene, emphasized by an absence of background and the lateral placement of the figures. This handscroll is one of the great examples of early Chinese figure painting.

Tang Dynasty

Chinese culture and art reached a golden age during the Tang (618–906) and Song (960–1279) dynasties. Buddhism flourished, and "paradise cults" of believers, anticipating a happy after-life, commissioned millions of images of Buddha. The development of woodblock printing would eventually lead to the printing of Buddhist scriptures and the world's first encyclopedia.

The Tang rulers established a great capital at Chang-An (modern Xian), an international metropolis of two million people. Many temples were built that followed codes of architectural principles. Proportional relationships for all parts of these wooden structures were required. Multistoried brick pagodas were constructed throughout the realm. Tang Buddhist missionaries introduced Chinese art, architecture and writing into Japan in 552.

Sculpture and ceramics flourished. Large tomb figures were manufactured in factories and sold to wealthy families. They often were in the form of a horse (fig.4–26), a symbol of wealth and loyalty to the emperor. "Three-color" glaze produced a profusion of colors on these figures. Sensitive figurines of court women and musicians were painted in subtle colors. These figures had a wonderfully calm quality.

Most Tang sculpture was religious. Buddhist images evolved into a fully "Chinese" style. However, in 845, Buddhism and other religions were banned because of their feared political and financial influence.

Life under the Tang was sophisticated, with a stress on Confucian values of education and respect for family and the growing bureaucracy. Learning centers, or academies, were established where scholars developed ideas about the aesthetics of painting. The expressive art of the beautiful written characters of calligraphy continued to evolve. Painting became the pastime of men who belonged to the social elite. Different "schools" of painting emerged. One school stressed monumental landscapes, while another favored natural still lifes of plants and animals. A third dealt with expressive images of Buddhist saints.

4–35 This is just one section of a long horizontal scroll. Scrolls in this format were meant to be viewed slowly, section by section.
Ku K'ai-chih, *Instructress Writing Down Her Admonitions for the Benefit of Two Young Ladies.* Six dynasties. Horizontal scroll, ink and colors on silk, 7 1/2" (19 cm) high. British Museum, London.

Song Dynasty

After the Tang empire collapsed in 906, the country was in turmoil until reunification by the Song in 960. Rulers of the Song dynasty sought to recreate the glorious politics and culture of the Tang. It was the golden age of landscape painting (fig.4–d). Painters in the north stressed bird and flower subjects while painters in the south emphasized bamboo, a plant that symbolized scholarship and wisdom.

Sculpture, while still tied to Buddhism, developed a natural appearance very different from earlier, stiff, Indian-influenced figures. The seated *Guan-Yin* (fig.4–36), the goddess of mercy, rests in a casual pose, covered with the typical elegant drapery and ornament of a bodhisattva.

Architecture of the Song period reflects the strict architectural rules developed under the Tang. Northern architecture was solid and monumental in appearance. Southern architecture evolved into a more flamboyant style with exaggerated upturned eaves.

Yuan Dynasty

The Mongols, or Yuan dynasty (1279–1368), overpowered the Song. However, the Chinese culture was so strong that, instead of imposing their own values, the Mongols supported the established culture. It was during this era that Marco Polo visited "Cathay" (his name for China) and returned to Venice to write glowing reports of Chinese urban life.

Potters, by now, had perfected the technology of porcelain that began under the Tang and, especially, the Song dynasties. Potters produced high-fired pure white ware, which was elegantly shaped and decorated. Sometimes, silver rims were added. Bold decorative floral motifs had developed under the Song, and now potters used imported Persian cobalt to create similar designs in blue. Known as *"blue-and-white,"* the objects were made for the Imperial court (fig.4–37).

4–36 Why do you suppose the pose of this figure is so casual?
Guan-Yin, about 12th century. Song dynasty. Polychromed wood, 45 1/4" (115 cm) high. Museum of Fine Arts, Boston, Henry Edward Wetzel Fund.

4–37 The Chinese for centuries have been considered masters of the art of ceramics.
Dish with flattened rim, 14th century. Yuan dynasty. Glazed porcelain, 3 1/8" x 17 7/8" (8.25 x 45 cm). Freer Gallery of Art, Washington, DC.

4–38 This hall is the best known of the buildings in the Forbidden City. It is over 200 feet long.
Hall of Supreme Harmony, Imperial Palace, Beijing. Ming dynasty, begun 15th century.

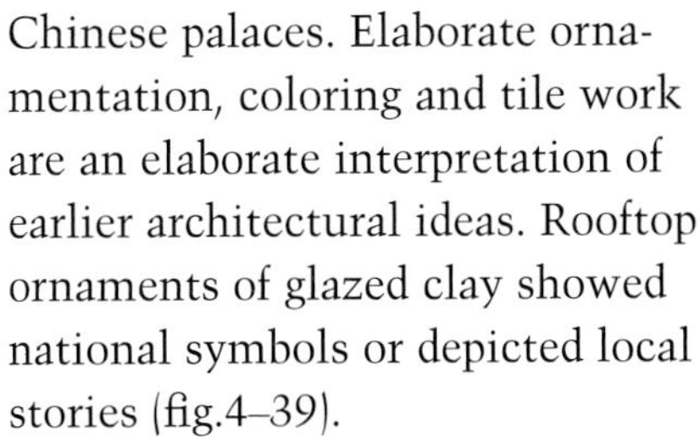

Ming Dynasty

When the Ming dynasty (1368–1644) came to power, it again tried to restore the glories of traditional China. The Imperial Palace in Beijing (called "The Forbidden City") was started in the early fifteenth century on the site of ancient palaces. Although it was often destroyed by fire and earthquakes, it was always rebuilt according to its original plans. Its many buildings are now open to visitors (fig.4–38).

Collecting older works of art became fashionable during the Ming dynasty, and many older art forms were imitated. In painting, nature scenes based on Song traditions were painted on both hanging and hand scrolls of paper and silk.

Ming ceramics saw an abundance of styles and techniques. Blue-and-white ware was produced in profusion for both local and overseas markets. Many white pieces were painted with colorful enamels and refired at lower temperatures to produce ***overglaze enamels*** of brilliant colors. Cloisonné enamel techniques were perfected, and enamels were applied to bronze surfaces to create exquisite decorative vessels.

Qing Dynasty

Tribes from Manchuria conquered the Ming in 1644. The Manchu, or Qing, dynasty (1644–1911) was regarded by the Chinese as barbarian. They absorbed and emulated Chinese culture, and their royal palace in Beijing imitated earlier Chinese palaces. Elaborate ornamentation, coloring and tile work are an elaborate interpretation of earlier architectural ideas. Rooftop ornaments of glazed clay showed national symbols or depicted local stories (fig.4–39).

Painting continued to be the main form of expression of the literary class (fig.4–27 a, b), and imperial kilns were revitalized.

During the middle of the twentieth century, art schools were shut down by the government to eliminate art as an anti-government threat. Artists were forced to work in communes as ordinary laborers to help produce food and needed supplies. In the 1970s, as China's borders were opened to the outside world, artists were again allowed to work and students could again attend art schools. In the 1990s, the government still had control over artistic production, but artists were beginning to express themselves more freely.

4–39 Scenes from mythology or operas first appeared on rooftops in the South of China during the Song dynasty.
Ceramic rooftop decoration (scene from a local opera), about 1820. Rooftop, Ap Lei Chao Temple, Hong Kong.

Lesson 4.3 Review

1 What is the world's oldest continuous civilization?
2 What is calligraphy? What do music and calligraphy have in common?
3 Why were over seven thousand life-size clay soldiers and horses buried in China during the Qin dynasty?
4 Why was the Great Wall of China built?
5 Explain some of the conventions of Chinese scroll paintings as found in *Instructress Writing Down Her Admonitions for the Benefit of Two Young Ladies.*
6 Why were so many ceramic horse sculptures created during the Tang dynasty?
7 During which dynasty did Chinese landscape painting reach its high point?
8 What is the Forbidden City?
9 How did the Chinese government affect their country's art in the middle of the twentieth century?

4.4 Japan

JAPANESE CULTURE IS THE PRODUCT of long periods of isolation followed by eras of contact with outside cultural influences. Japanese art was influenced by China and Korea from the seventh to ninth centuries; China and Europe in the sixteenth century; and the final opening of Japan to the West following 1868.

The inherent characteristics of Japanese art are simplicity of form and design (fig.4–41), attentiveness to the beauty of nature, and subtlety. The infusions of outside cultural ideas usually stimulated a development in the arts that emphasized ornamentation and elaborate refinement. In reaction, these phases were followed by periods that stressed simplicity and renewed attentiveness to natural design.

Vocabulary
haniwa
sumi-e
ukiyo-e

4–40 The Japanese always seek to blend their architecture with the natural environment surrounding it.
Nagoya Temple Complex, Japan.

4–41 This ink painting by one of Japan's greatest artists exemplifies the simplicity of form and design which are the hallmarks of Japanese art.
Katsushika Hokusai, *Flowering Squash-Vine and Bee.* Ink and tint on silk panel, 14" x 22" (35 x 55 cm). Freer Gallery of Art, Washington, DC.

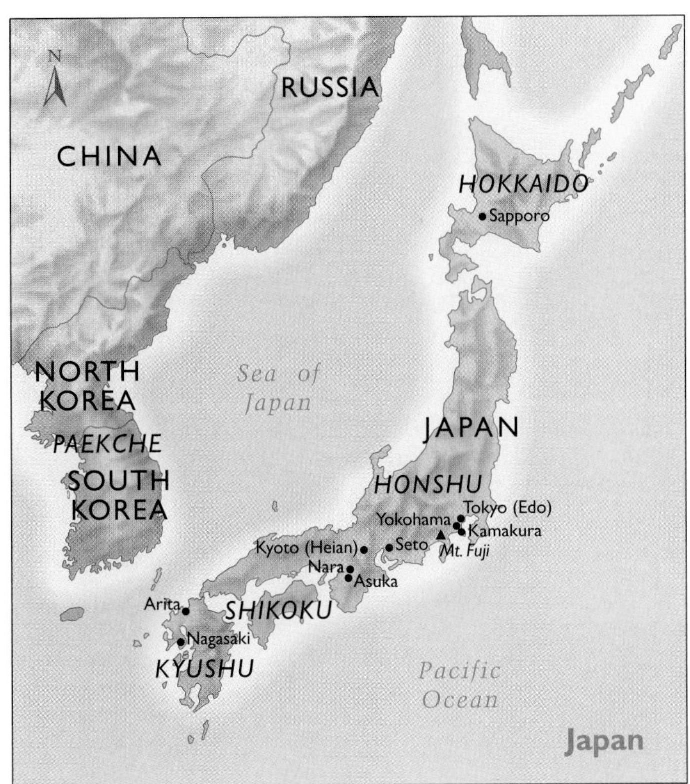

Sometimes referred to as "The Land of the Rising Sun," Japan consists of four main islands and 4000 smaller islands. Two-thirds of the land is mountainous and thickly forested. The majority of Japanese people live closely packed together in coastal regions. Japan's isolation from the Asian mainland contributed to the development of a distinct culture.

4–42 The Japanese infuse the arts and design into all phases of their lives. Household screens and slide doors often are painted with eloquent scenes from nature.
Hasegawa Tohaku, *Pine Wood,* 1539–1610 (detail from a pair of six-fold screens). Ink on paper, 61" (155 cm) high. Tokyo National Museum.

Japan Timeline

- c.9000–200 BC **Jomon Phase**
- 200 BC–300 AD **Yayoi Period**
- 552 AD–645 AD **Asuka Period**
- 645 AD–794 AD **Nara Period**
- 794 AD–1185 AD **Heian Period**
- 1185 AD–1392 AD **Kamakura Period**
- 1334 AD–1573 AD **Muromachi Period**
- 1573 AD–1615 AD **Momoyama Period**
- 1615 AD–1868 AD **Edo Period**
- 1868 AD–1912 AD **Meiji Period**
- 1912 AD–1926 AD **Taisho Period**
- 1926 AD–Present **Showa Period**

Jomon and Yayoi Cultures

Little is known of Japan's early history. Its origins may date back as far as 5000 BC during the Neolithic *Jomon* culture. This culture produced simple undecorated food vessels made of red clay. By 2000 BC, colored slip was used to create animal and human abstract patterns. By 200 BC, the *Yayoi* culture from Korea and Kyushu overtook the Jomon society. This culture created clay sculptures that were set up around gigantic burial mounds. The sculptures, called ***haniwa***, were pedestaled clay bowls, plates and unglazed ceramic cylinders with human or animal forms (fig.4–43) sculpted in their upper parts. In addition to these figures, the late Yayoi culture also produced bronze cast objects from about 300. The technique of bronze casting was likely imported from China sometime after the Han dynasty.

The area around present-day Kyoto came to be the center of political power. A statue of Buddha was sent to the Japanese court from Korea in 552. It was the beginning of Japan's acceptance of Buddhism and, with it, Chinese and Korean cultural influences. Although the Japanese borrowed many ideas from China and Korea, they did not copy them exactly.

4–44 These buildings are reproductions of Chinese Tang architecture and are the oldest wooden structures in the world.
Horyu-ji temple complex, begun 607. Asuka, Japan.

4–43 Haniwa figures were placed fencelike around burial mounds. They may have been placed there to control erosion, or perhaps to protect the dead.
Horse, Haniwa figure, 5–6th centuries AD. Terra cotta. 23" x 26" (58.4 x 66 cm). The Cleveland Museum of Art. The Norweb Collection, 57.27.

Asuka Period

Asuka became the Japanese capital from 538 to 645, giving its name to an era during which Buddhist missionaries, scriptures and beliefs were welcomed. Confucian ideals of government organization accompanied these Chinese and Korean imports. However, the older Japanese religion known as *Shinto,* "the way of the gods," continued to influence Japanese thought. Shinto, the oldest and still largest religion of Japan, began as a form of nature worship. The early Japanese believed that gods dwelled throughout the world of nature. Shinto later included the worship of ancestors.

Tang Chinese architecture was emulated in the building of the first Buddhist structures, the *Horyu-ji temple* at Asuka (fig.4–44). The main hall and an adjacent pagoda still exist as the oldest wooden structures in the world. These buildings are also regarded as a faithful reproduction of Chinese architecture of the Tang. The style reflects a calm and graceful atmosphere as well as a structural honesty in the exposure of beams and brackets.

Nara Period

When the capital was moved to nearby *Nara,* a new era began (646–784). Furniture, paintings, pottery and architecture were based on Chinese ideals. The court sponsored elaborate production and collection of art, including works from China and Persia. Buddhism became firmly entrenched, and huge temples and monasteries were constructed of wood in the Chinese style. Buddhist images were made of lacquer and bronze. The largest, a 70-foot-high, 700-ton, bronze *Dibutsu* (fig.4–45), is housed in the largest wooden temple in the world, the Todai-ji.

4–45 This figure is nearly six stories high.
Great Dibutsu (Buddha), 8th century. Bronze, 70'9" (21.6 m) high. Todai-ji temple, Nara, Japan.

Heian Period

Heian, today the modern city of Kyoto, became the capital in 784. The Heian period marked the golden age of Japanese art and lasted until 1192. Close ties with China were broken in 898, allowing Japanese artists to create their own styles of art that differed from Chinese styles.

Yamato-e painting evolved during the later Heian period. Artists created decorative horizontal scrolls with long narratives (fig.4–46). Through these scrolls, artists expressed Japanese tastes, sentiments and nationalistic feelings.

Buddhism had split into a number of factions or sects. One of these sects, the *Shingon,* stressed the veneration of images and figures of gods with multiple heads and hands. *Amida* cult Buddhists carved peaceful images, stressing spiritual sincerity. Wooden buildings of subtle proportions were constructed in natural settings, often near water. Temples and gardens were asymmetrically arranged; buildings, ponds and rock forms signified the harmony of humanity with nature.

4–46 This is a detail of a scroll that illustrates an eleventh-century Japanese novel by Lady Murasaki.
The Tale of Genji, detail. Late Heian period, 12th century. Scroll, color on paper, 8 1/2" x 15 3/4" (21.6 x 40 cm).

Kamakura Period

A military government replaced the Heian government, and the capital was moved to *Kamakura* from 1192 to 1338. Many early Nara temples were restored after the civil wars. A huge bronze Buddha (fig.4–47) was cast. Fashion and taste in the new capital were at odds with the cultural heritage of Kyoto. Kamakura art was more realistic.

During the Kamakura era, *Zen Buddhism* from China gained popularity in Japan. It was to have a far-reaching cultural impact. Zen Buddhism promoted spiritual exercises, meditation and a simple monastic lifestyle. Paintings stressed portraiture, battle scenes and incidents taken from everyday life. They also depicted torments in hell, illness and suffering. Potters who studied Song ceramic methods established kilns in Seto and other southern centers, leading to a native Japanese ceramic tradition. The objects produced there became a mainstay in the later development of the *cha-no-yu,* the Zen-inspired tea ceremony.

4–47 Compare this figure to the Khmer Buddha (fig.4–54).
Great Buddha of Kamakura, 1252. Kamakura period, Japan. Cast bronze, 42' (128 m) high.

Muromachi and Momoyama Periods

Kyoto was re-established as the capital in 1338, initiating the *Muromachi* era, which lasted until 1578. The warrior class patronized the arts and created an ostentatious court life. As a contrast to their incessant warfare, tranquil landscaped gardens provided respite with their peaceful arrangements of natural and architectural elements. Spiritual peace was also available in the *Noh* (dramas), *cha-no-yu* (tea ceremony) and *ikebana* (flower arranging). Individual works of art were displayed within special alcoves known as *tokonoma.*

Muromachi painting was dominated by the Chinese ink style, known also as ***sumi-e***. Although usually done on absorbent rice paper (washi) in quick confident strokes, the style was used on sliding door panels and screens by a family of painters named *Kano* (fig.4–48). Their style of painting was later used during the Momoyama era (1573–1615) to embellish rooms in large castles built by feudal war lords. Paintings of trees and nature scenes appear to be viewed through the pillars, adjacent to the *tatami*-matted floor.

Edo Period

Internal political turmoil caused Japanese rulers to attempt to impose order by closing Japan to the outside world. European and Christian influences were banned in 1612. The capital was moved to *Edo*, modern Tokyo (1615–1867). However, after 1868, in a period of rule called the *Meiji* Restoration, Japan again opened itself to Western influences.

In the Edo period, a unique style of genre painting evolved, known as ***ukiyo-e*** ("the art of the floating world"). This art was popular with the growing middle class. Ukiyo-e art features colorful images of daily life (fig.4–e), fashionable courtesans, and actors from the popular *kabuki* theater. These paintings were later adapted to the woodcut process. By the end of the era, multicolored prints were being produced by over two hundred artists and marketed to the middle class at very low prices. Among the best examples is Utagawa Hiroshige's *Night Rain on Kirasaki Pine,* part of a large series of prints (fig.2–48). These scenes provide vivid glimpses of Japanese life. They also came to be valued in the West for their bold design. Impressionist painters were particularly influenced by their aesthetic quality.

Modern Period

Non-Japanese painting techniques, notably oil painting, were first introduced by the Jesuits (Catholic missionary priests) and later encouraged under the Meiji era. Ming and Qing ceramics influenced Japanese pottery production. Japanese *Imari* and *Kutani* porcelain wares are brightly surfaced and boldly colored. Contemporary artists in Japan continue to reflect their traditional heritage of simplicity and elegance, but use every medium and technique available to artists around the world. Their sculpture is admired by artists in every country, and their work has been displayed in museums around the globe.

4–48 The technique of *sumi-e* involves quick, sure strokes of ink on rice paper (washi).
Kano paintings inside audience room of Nijo Castle, Kyoto, about 1603.

Lesson 4.4 Review

1 Describe haniwa sculptures.
2 What are some of the beliefs of the Shinto religion?
3 What are the oldest wooden structures in the world? How old are they?
4 Where is the great Dibutsu (Buddha)? Which is taller, your school room or this statue?
5 What modern cities did the ancient cities of Heian and Edo become?
6 What is yamato-e painting? On what type of surface were these painted?
7 How was Kamakura art different from Heian art? What were some of the subjects of Kamakura era paintings?
8 What is the Japanese term for the Zen-inspired tea ceremony? Where were the ceramics used in this ceremony first produced? Which Chinese dynasty's art influenced the production of these pieces?
9 What do Noh, ikebana and tokonoma mean?
10 What style of painting did the Kano use on the panels in the audience room of the Nijo Castle in Kyoto?

4.5 Southeast Asia

Southeast Asia is a geographic zone where different cultures have mingled, coexisted or dominated each other since the days of the Roman empire. The two dominant influences have come from India and China. Southeast Asians adapted, rather than imitated, Indian and Chinese art and government to create a way of life of their own.

Several coastal areas became *Indianized* as early as the first century. Adopting Hindu and Buddhist faiths, rulers developed a form of government known as the "cult of the god-king." The king identified himself with a god, usually the Hindu gods Siva or Vishnu. The ruler became the model for society and had the blessings of the gods in his earthly rule.

Vocabulary
wat
chedis
batik

4–49 In Thailand sculpture is the predominant art form, and Buddha is one of the most popular subjects.
Royal Palace with Gold Statue, Bangkok, Thailand.

4–50 There is a Buddha within each of the wells at the top of this monument. The figures are hidden by bell-shaped covers.
Buddha from top of Borobudor, detail (fig.4–55).

4–51 The exterior walls of many of the galleries at Angkor Wat are covered with lyrical figures. The fluid motion of this figure is characteristic of much of the relief work found at the site.
Aspara, detail of bas-relief from central structure. *Angkor Wat.* See also fig.4–52.

Thickly forested, mountainous land bathed in steamy tropical heat, Southeast Asia is home to widely diverse people speaking over 250 dialects and languages.

Thailand Timeline

- **c.550 AD–700 AD** Dvaravati Period
- **c.700 AD–1000 AD** Hindu-Javanese Style
- **1022 AD–1250 AD** Cambodian Dominance
- **1250 AD–1378 AD** Sukhotai Period
- **1378 AD–1767 AD** Ayuthia Period

Cambodia Timeline

- **c.550 BC–150 BC** Bronze Age
- **c.150 BC–600 AD** Dong Son Culture Funan
- **600 AD–802 AD** Early Khmer Style Chen–la
- **802 AD–897 AD** Koulen
- **877 AD–1002 AD** First Angkor Period
- **1002 AD–1201 AD** Second Angkor Period
- **1201 AD–1437 AD** Siamese Dominance Sack of Angkor

Cambodia

The Khmer empire had its roots in the 800s. The greatest Khmer empire was established during the twelfth and thirteenth centuries in what is now called Cambodia. Each Khmer ruler constructed his own immense national temple, or ***wat***. These temples perpetuated their divine image and later served as their mausoleums.

The finest examples of god-king temples are *Angkor Wat* (fig.4–52), built about 1150, and the Bayon at Angkor Thom. The temples reflect strong Hindu influence in the tall stone towers covered with sculptures of Hindu and local religious heroes. Many walls are decorated with images from Hindu mythology (fig.4–51). Small niches inside the temples were filled with stone or bronze images of deities. The temple of Angkor Wat was dedicated to Vishnu. The Bayon features the head of King Jayavarman VII (fig.4–53). The king is depicted as the bodhisattva *Lokeshvara* on towers throughout the temple complex.

4–53 A colossal head appears on each side of the square towers at Bayon.
Tower of Bayon, Angkor Thom, 12–13th centuries, Cambodia.

Buddhism entered Cambodia and became intermixed with older Hindu traditions. Buddhist images were cast in a unique style. Facial features were distinctly Cambodian. In the example pictured here (fig.4–54), a niche has been created for the Buddha incorporating the Hindu *kala-makara*, a serpentlike creature which devours and reproduces time. The flames, embellishments, decorations and tiny figures are part of Buddhist and Hindu iconography.

4–52 Recent research indicates that the layout of Angkor Wat may have had an astronomical significance.
Angkor Wat, 12–13th centuries, Cambodia.

Indonesia

Buddhist influences most strongly affected areas of Burma, Thailand, Sumatra and Java. Sumatra and Java are the two most important islands of the country of Indonesia. Indonesia is made up of five main islands and hundreds of smaller islands. Buddhism reached its greatest political height with the *Shailendra* kingdom in ninth-century Java. There, architects created one of the seven wonders of the ancient world in the artificial cosmic-mountain known as *Borobudor.*

Borobudor is a stupa that has ten levels (fig.4–55). Bas-relief carvings on the lower six layers symbolically represent the cosmos. The lowest of

4–55 Use the text to discover more about this cosmic mountain.
Borobudor, about 850. Shailendra dynasty. Java.

these levels represents hell and eternal torment. The images were apparently so grotesque that the Shailendras themselves covered the images with tamped earth ramparts. The next five layers represent humanity's earthly adventures. Walkways on each square level are lined with carvings of the teachings of Buddha. Sculptures show a realistic understanding of body proportion, overlapping planes to show depth, and graceful movement in the figures (fig.4–4). The sculptures provide historical records of clothing, architecture and even shipbuilding styles of the times. Four round layers finish off the top of the stupa, representing the supernatural element (fig.4–50). At the apex of Borobudor is a large solid stupa.

Buddhism declined in Java with the fall of the Shailendras in 856 but dominated the cultures of Burma, Sri Lanka, Cambodia, Thailand and Vietnam.

4–54 Hindu influences mixed with Buddhism in Cambodian portrayals of Buddha.
Buddha Enthroned, 10th century. Khmer. Bronze. Kimbell Art Museum, Fort Worth, Texas.

Burma, Thailand

Burmese art and architecture reached a high point in the twelfth century with the construction of many bell-shaped stupa-temples in the capital city of Pagan.

Distinctive Thai art and architecture originated in the late 1200s with the formation of the first Thai kingdom at *Sukothai* in the northern Chao Phraya valley. Stupas were constructed in the style of the Ceylonese, Burmese and Khmers. Ideas about architecture and sculpture came from the Khmers and from remnants of the *Dvaravati* kingdom in far southern Thailand. Immense images of Buddha were formed in clay, brick and stucco and were often covered with gold leaf.

Thai potters for the royal courts created distinctive celadon glazes. Thai equivalents of blue-and-white porcelain were made. The exquisite designs reflected the taste and traditions of the Thais. One such example is the *covered box* (fig.4–56) produced at the *Sawankhaloke* kilns near Sukothai about 1400.

4–57 Use the text to identify European architectural influences in the Thai palace.
Royal Palace, exterior view, 19th century. Bangkok, Thailand.

4–56 Exquisite designs cover this box from the Thai royal kilns.
Covered box. Sawankhaloke kilns, Thailand, 14–15th centuries. Stoneware with underglaze iron, 5 1/2" (14 cm) high. Los Angeles County Museum of Art.

Bangkok became the Thai capital in 1782. Its architecture blended Asian and European influences from Western trading nations. The *Royal Palace* (figs.4–49, 4–57) shows a European influence in the rusticated base, the segmentally arched portico, and the Classical columns and windows. The roof, however, is distinctly Thai and is topped with spirelike forms known as ***chedis***.

Vietnam, Laos, Malaysia

Chinese culture directly influenced a small area of Southeast Asia. When Vietnam became independent from China in the tenth century, the court at Hue emulated Chinese culture in its bronze castings and in the construction of Buddhist temples. This influence carried over into areas of neighboring Laos. The resulting Buddhist architecture is a mixture of Chinese, Thai and Lao traditions. *Wat Xieng Thong* (fig.4–58) is a beautiful example of these cultural blends. The concave roof is Chinese, while the overlapping roof lines are Thai. The decorative detail reflects the local Lao style.

When Islam became established in coastal Malaysia and Indonesia between the ninth and fifteenth centuries, architects produced distinctive *mosques.* Artists produced elaborate bronze weaponry (the wavy-edged *kris* dagger) and printed fabrics. The fabrics are known as ***batik*** and are made from wax-stencil dyeing processes. The elegant and sophisticated court life required well-crafted bronze utensils and bejeweled royal objects. Court musicians played the *gamelon,* an orchestra of drums, wooden wind instruments and sets of bronze gongs, all highly ornamented with geometric and curvilinear abstract patterns.

Portuguese, Dutch and British settlers arrived in Southeast Asia in the sixteenth century. Local peoples incorporated some Western ideas into their art and architecture. British and Dutch officials often provided financial support for local sultans in Malaysia and Indonesia. As a result, sultans devoted much time and newly acquired wealth to reviving traditional art forms and creating opulent courts.

4–58 Local Lao tradition combines with Chinese and Thai influences in this chapel. Can you identify them?
Wat Xieng Thong (The Chapel). Luang Prabang, Laos.

Lesson 4.5 Review

1 In what modern country was the Khmer empire located? Why did each Khmer ruler construct a wat?
2 Describe Borobudor in Java. Why did the Shailendras cover the lower levels of this stupa with dirt ramparts?
3 List seven countries in Southeast Asia and a type of art created in each area.
4 How does the Royal Palace in Bangkok combine the architecture of Thailand and the West?
5 What is an Indonesian batik? How is it made?
6 Describe the instruments found in an Indonesian gamelon.

4.6 Oceania and Highland Asia

Some of the world's most symbolic artwork has been produced in a vast area that stretches from the upper headwaters of the Mekong, Irrawaddy and Chao Phraya Rivers and south to Australia (fig.4–59) and east to Polynesia. The disparate groups of peoples throughout this area have their own traditions of sculpture (fig.4–60), fabrics (fig.4–62), architecture and pottery that are distinctive in form, style and symbolism. Many groups have had little or no contact with other cultures. They have developed artistic styles that are unique to their own cultures. Other peoples are part of larger cultural groups, most notably those within the *Oceania* area. *Oceania* is comprised of Australia, New Zealand and numerous nearby islands. Inner Pacific Islands fall into three groups: *Micronesia, Melanesia* and *Polynesia.*

Vocabulary
totem

4–59 Most of the art from the Oceania region is highly stylized and symbolic. What do you think these figures represent?
Painted Bark Cloth, detail (fig.4–12).

4–60 Tapa is a beaten bark cloth made from the paper mulberry. The inner material of this figure consists of bundles of bulrushes tied with fiber bands. Only three of these tapa figures are known to exist.
Tapa Cloth Figure. Easter Island, Polynesia. Painted mulberry bark cloth, fiber-tied bulrushes, 15 1/2" (39 cm). The Peabody Museum, Harvard University.

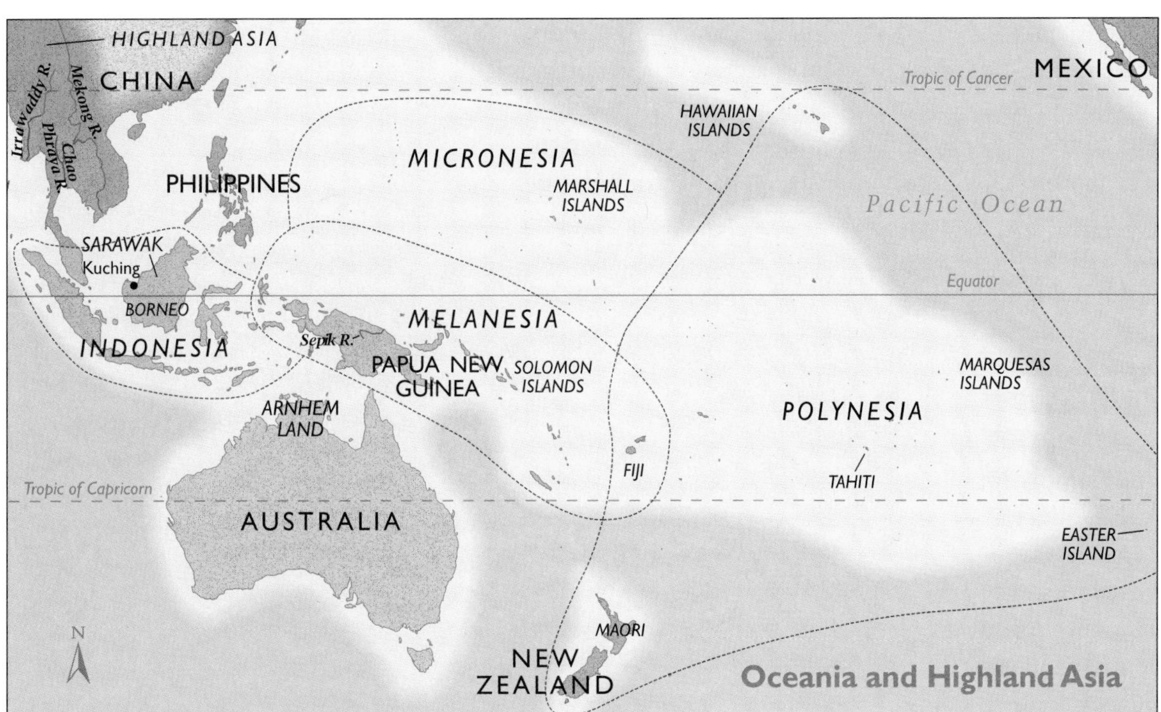

The Pacific is the largest and deepest of the world's oceans, covering a greater area of Earth's surface than all land areas combined. The numerous islands are just the uppermost tips of massive underwater mountain ranges, with trenches deep enough to cover Mount Everest.

4–61 When this mask was in use, ornaments filled the loops and small bamboo posts on each side of the head carried vari-colored feather decorations.
Malanggan Mask. New Ireland, Melanesia. Painted, carved wood, plant pith, 23" (58 cm). The Peabody Museum, Harvard University.

4–62 The higher chiefs of Hawaii wore helmets such as this one. Lesser chiefs wore unfeathered helmets. This example probably originates from either Oahu or Maui.
Hawaiian Crested Helmet, before 1841. Red, yellow, black and white feathers on wickerwork, 22" x 15" (56 x 38 cm). The Peabody Museum, Harvard University.

Highland tribes of the Southeast Asian peninsula separated themselves from the mainstream of lowland cultures at various times throughout history. The various tribes have produced similar, but distinctive, art forms. Houses built on stilts with steeply sloping thatch roofs are typical throughout the region. Peoples of the highlands share many artistic similarities with Oceanic peoples of the Pacific. They created objects not simply for their aesthetic beauty, but also for their functional purposes. Many objects are primarily used for religious purposes. Painting throughout the regions features animal and geometric symbolism and symbolic pattern. Paintings, such as those inside the communal longhouses of Borneo (fig.4–63), have highly stylized curvilinear designs.

Mystic designs in Oceanic and highland art are often empowered with spiritual energy. The woven blanket shown here (fig.4–64) is filled with mystic and *totemic* symbols. (A ***totem*** is an animal or natural object which symbolizes a clan or family.) The alligator is a common motif in Oceanic art. However, note the bird that is illustrated in the form of an army helicopter. As the indigenous people have come into contact with modern technology, their artwork has reflected the new subject matter in their world.

Masks are an important form of Oceanic art and sculpture. Masks decorate ceremonial huts and are used as objects of worship. In rituals, the person who wears the mask loses his or her own identity and becomes the spirit of the ancestor or spirit represented by the mask. Like masks, spears, boats and eating utensils are also carved. Mystic or animal motifs carved onto these objects invest them with life and power.

Wood is the commonly used sculptural material of both highland and Oceanic peoples, although almost no sculpture is known in Micronesia. Ancient examples of sculpture are rare since the materials quickly deteriorate. Most work found today is less than one hundred years old.

4–63 Boards like this, which portray mystic forces, are a part of communal longhouses.
Gableboard painting. Kenyah Tribe, Sarawak, Borneo. Vegetable dyes and earth colors on wood. Sarawak Museum, Kuching.

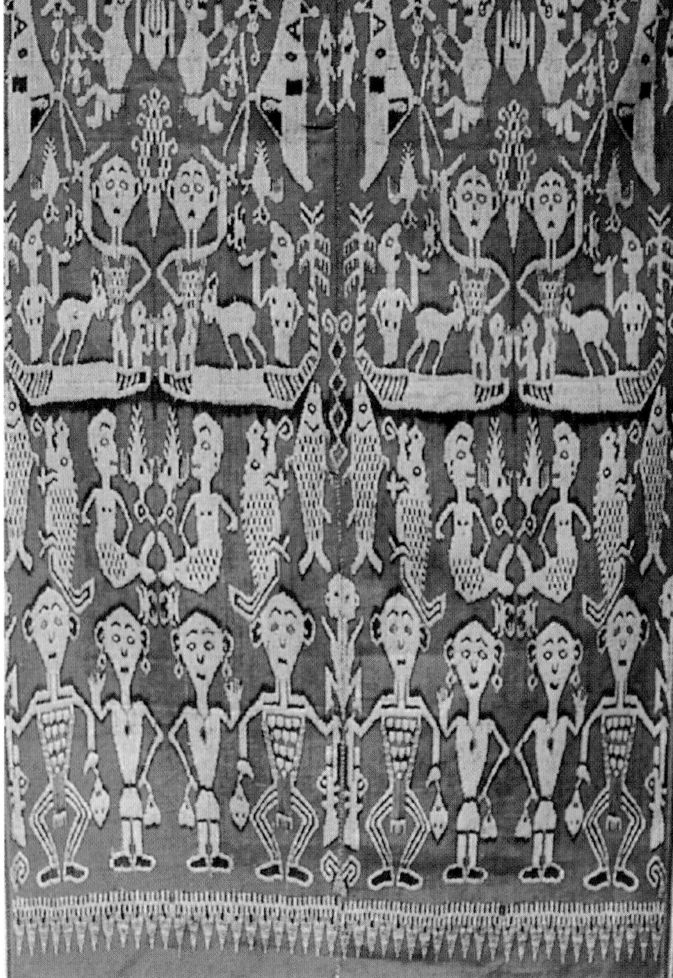

4–64 Can you find the modern helicopter which has been incorporated into this traditional totemic work?
Blanket. Iban Tribe, Sarawak, East Malaysia. Cotton and vegetable dyes, 31 3/4" x 48 1/2" (81 x 123 cm). Collection of Mr. and Mrs. David Kohl.

4–65 These figures help people remember their ancestors whom they worship.
Male ancestral figure. Sepik River, Papua, New Guinea. Wood colored with earth pigments. Collection of Mr. Vincent and Dr. Natalie Schiffano.

Painting is used to embellish carved wooden images and masks, especially in Melanesia. Papua, New Guinea, has one of the strongest artistic traditions in Melanesia. Objects for ancestor worship are ornamented in bright colors. *Ancestral figures* (fig.4–65) are carved from wood in sizes from three inches to three feet in height. The ancestral figure is embellished with white highlights and reddish brown paint. This brown paint represents blood and the continued existence of the soul of the deceased. *Totemism* is also common in Melanesia. Masks are considered as the permanent dwelling of spiritual forces. Masks, statues and other cult worship objects are used to identify kinship.

Native art in northern Papua reflects a broad blend of island, coastal and mountain cultures. Wood carvings show great variety in subject matter and free expression. Detailed and well-carved wooden images are embellished with shells, dogs' teeth, feathers, animal hair and paint or colored earth. Images are either ancestral masks, ceremonial masks or fertility images.

In Polynesia, masks and carvings and even boats represent sophisticated cult worship of gods and chiefs. Masks assume powerful worship force only when surrounded by ritual. In contrast to the carvings of Melanesia, Polynesian objects of worship stress the grain of the wood; stress is not placed on bright colors.

Unique in the art of Oceania, stone sculpture is found in Polynesia. On Easter Island are stunning stone carvings. These monumental ancestral images are made of volcanic rock. Other stone sculptures of stylized figures can be seen on the Marquesas Islands.

Woodcarving is common throughout Polynesia, from Hawaii to New Zealand. The houses of New Zealand's tribal *Maori* chiefs and priests contain intricately carved bas-relief panels (fig.4–66). Like the totem pole of Northwest American tribes, this wooden carving depicts a tribal ancestor as a warrior. His tongue is thrust out in defiance of his enemies. The small figure between his legs represents later tribal ancestors. Notice how only half of the figures are depicted. This is a distinctive feature of Oceanic art. The lattice panels of dyed vegetable fibers on each side of the carving are abstract representations of natural forms.

Tattoo work on the human body originated in the Marquesas. In an under-the-skin dyeing process taking years, men's bodies are covered in traditional geometric designs. These designs appear to be symbolic and mystic.

Australian aboriginal culture shares stylistic and media similarities with Oceanic and highland peoples. Aborigines have produced a tradition of painting on flattened bark. The bark is usually placed on the inside of their temporary shel-

4–66 Use the text to help identify the unique features of this wall panel from a chief's house.
Carved wall panel from Maori Meeting House, late 19th century. Dominion Museum, Wellington, New Zealand.

ters. Kangaroos, birds, fish, snakes, tortoises and alligators are common subjects. An "X-ray" effect is used to depict internal organs, simultaneously showing two aspects of the same subject. Designs of humans, mammals, birds, reptiles and fish are also abraded, pecked or hammered into the surface of rock outcroppings (fig.4–67). It is common to find geometric designs carved into earth or trees as part of initiation ceremonies.

The vast heritage of this entire region has only been "discovered" in the twentieth century. So far, this art heritage has been more closely studied by anthropologists than by art historians.

4–67 This X-ray painting shows both a physical and spiritual understanding of the subjects.
Aboriginal rock paintings. Gunqinggu group, Western Arnhem Land, Australia.

Lesson 4.6 Review

1 Describe the totemic symbols in the blanket in figure 4–64. What does totemic mean? How has the artist combined contemporary culture symbols with traditional design in this blanket?
2 What does the red brown paint on New Guinea wooden ancestral figures symbolize?
3 How are Melanesian wood carvings different from Polynesian wood sculptures?
4 What type of unusual art is found on Easter Island?
5 Where did the art of body tattoo originate?
6 List some of the animals painted on bark by the Australian aborigines. How did these artists show two views of an animal at the same time?

4.7 The World of Islam

THE NATION AND RELIGION of Islam has directly influenced the cultures of Europe, Africa and Asia from Spain to the Philippines. Throughout all geographic areas touched by Islam, an appreciation of crafts can be seen. Ornamentation-covered carved woodwork, crystal, bronze, textiles and weaponry. All Islamic arts remained true to the philosophical foundations of the culture. The objects are a witness to the order of creation and to the believer's submission to the will of Allah.

The Arab culture, from which Islam grew, was seminomadic and, therefore, produced no monumental architecture or paintings. Instead, these peoples valued small, portable objects with rich decoration. Arabic script became highly regarded, since it was the language through which Allah had chosen to reveal his messages to the prophet Mohammed. These inspirations were written in the Koran, and devoted scribes gave great attention in recopying that sacred text. A whole style of art developed around their calligraphy.

In metalwork, pottery, carpet making and architecture, Islamic art reveals itself as an art of ornamentation. Swirling designs known as ***arabesques*** were used to ornament objects. Imaginative, stylized designs were based on *Kufic* script, flowers and leaves, and geometric patterns. These designs fill spaces on manuscript pages, copper containers, ceramic vessels and weapons. Even the walls of holy buildings, like The Dome of the Rock in Jerusalem (fig.7–24), are covered with designs. Usually, no prominent center of interest is obvious. Instead, symmetry and tranquillity seem to be the desired goal.

Vocabulary
arabesques
mosque
qibla
minaret
madrasah
cruciform

4–68 The walls of secular and religious Islamic architecture are often covered with abstract patterns and geometric design.
Topkapi Palace, interior view, begun 1462. Istanbul.

4–69 This detail of a Persian rug shows an incredible intricacy of design that is achieved through the painstaking technique of hand-knotting.
Maqsud Kashani, *The Ardabil Carpet*, detail (fig.4–74).

Islam Timeline

622 AD
Islamic Era begins

711 AD
Muslim Conquest of Spain

800s–900s
Turks convert to Islam

1031 AD
End of Caliphate of Cordoba

c.1290 AD–1326 AD
Ottoman Empire Osman I

1453 AD
Ottoman Conquest of Constantinople

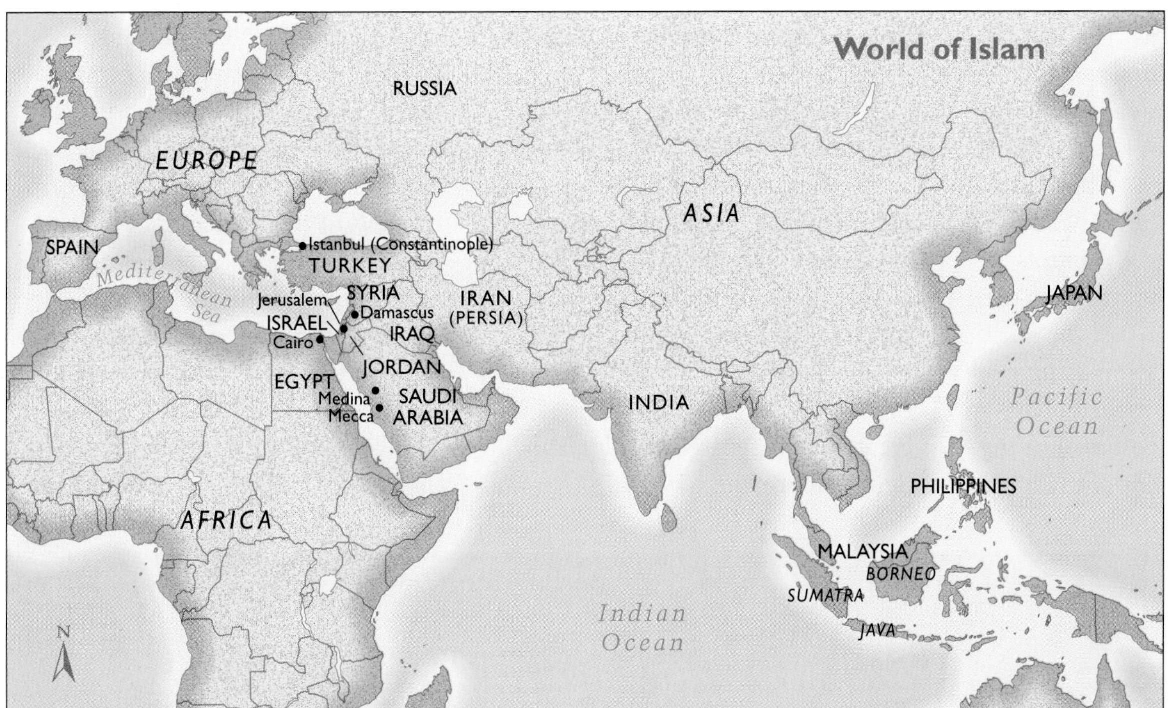

The center of Islam is Mecca, the city in Saudi Arabia where the prophet Mohammed received the revelations this religion is built upon. From the Middle East, Islam spread to encompass a wide geographic area including Northern Africa, China and the Malay archipelago.

4–70 Painting did not play a part in the Arab tradition until the technique was brought from China by the Mongols in the thirteenth century.
The Battle of Alexander with the Dragon, detail (fig.4–73).

Architecture

The major architectural form in Islam is the ***mosque***, or temple. Originally, the mosque had to have one wall facing Mecca. The wall was known as the ***qibla***, and it contained a small prayer niche. A ***minaret***, or prayer tower opposite the qibla, was used by a *muezzin* to call the faithful to prayer. Mosques in Spain centered on elaborately arched courtyards, with rows of columns facing the open space in front of the qibla. The interiors of mosques are embellished with lavish designs.

A second style of mosque emerged in Turkish and Persian areas. Called a teaching mosque, or ***madrasah*** (also spelled *medresa*), it was still open to the sky. However, the courtyard was walled in and a large semivaulted room opened into the courtyard from each of the four surrounding walls. This created an essentially ***cruciform*** (cross) floor plan.

The third style of mosque, created by the Ottoman Turks, was based on the Hagia Sophia in Constantinople (fig.7–13). The style combined the madrasah cruciform plan with the domed enclosed spaces of Byzantine architecture. The domes of the *Blue Mosque* (fig.4–71) enclose a spacious interior and, at the same time, provide a sense of rhythm. Small windows in the drum of the dome allow shafts of light to enter the ceramic-tiled

4–71 Cruciform and domed, this mosque is architecturally related to the Hagia Sophia. *Blue Mosque of Ahmet I,* 1617. Istanbul.

4–72 Use the text to help identify the unique features of this elaborate palace room.
Topkapi Palace, interior, begun 1462. Istanbul.

interior, producing a mystic atmosphere.

Court palaces featured elaborately ornamented interiors. The Alhambra in Spain (fig.7–21) and *Topkapi Palace* in Turkey testify to Islamic creativity. Rooms from the Topkapi Palace (figs.4–68, 4–72) feature Arabic calligraphy on the walls, faience wall tile, geometrically traced windows, and colorfully patterned carpets. The dais for sitting (fig.4–72) is bordered by twisted columns that support a patterned canopy.

Sculpture, particularly of humans or of God, is expressly prohibited in Islamic tradition. A few sculptured animal forms were made with an understanding that images were permitted if they were small enough so that they cast no shadows.

Painting

Painting was not originally part of the Arab tradition. Few pictorial works appeared in Islamic courts until the *Mongol* era. During the thirteenth century, Persia was invaded by the Mongols, who brought with them the sophisticated culture of the Song. Paintings, such as *The Battle of Alexander with the Dragon* (figs.4–70, 4–73), show both a Chinese subject matter and painting technique new to the Arab world. The landscape of mountains and trees is similar to Song landscapes. The sweeping curves of the mountains seem to turn back on the scene, adding drama and power to the action. The borders are Arabic, the faces are Middle Eastern, and the compacted space is Islamic. A vast quantity of painting on palm leaves, cloth and paper was created by various Islamic dynasties throughout the realm. These paintings reflected unique regional tastes and motifs.

4–73 The Mongols brought elements of Chinese culture to Persia. Use the text to guide you in finding those influences and in identifying features that are uniquely Persian.
The Battle of Alexander with the Dragon, 14th century. Mongol period in Persia. Gouache on paper, 7" x 11 1/2" (18 x 29 cm). Museum of Fine Arts, Boston, Ross Collection.

Textiles

Unique to Central Asia is the creation of beautiful and colorful rugs, carpets and textiles of wool or silk. They are often regarded as the highest achievement of Islamic craftsmanship and design. Artisans combined painstaking knotting techniques with intricate symmetric and symbolic patterns. *The Ardabil Carpet* (figs.4–69, 4–74) may have as many as three hundred knots per square inch. The complex design of sanctuary lamps, medallion and floral motifs gave the barefooted worshiper a visual as well as tactile experience.

Pottery

Potters created elegant forms and glazes, using luster, enamels and faience techniques. They decorated ceramics with Islamic motifs, adding rich color and texture to the inexpensive base materials. Turkish potters produced drinking containers, bowls and dishes such as the Isnik platter (fig.4–75). The three peonies and two tulips in the central panel are Chinese floral designs. They are surrounded by stylized cloud patterns painted in cobalt. The designer was probably influenced by imported Chinese porcelain as seen in the lobed rim. The blue, red, green, turquoise and black colors are Turkish additions to the traditional Ming blue and white.

Metalwork

Metalworking reflects the ability of Moslem artisans to render materials into intricate forms of beauty. The Persian bracelet (fig.4–76) features rows of golden birds complete with tiny beaks, wings and feather patterns. Its rhythmic alignment is in harmony with theories of symmetry and regularity typical of Islamic culture.

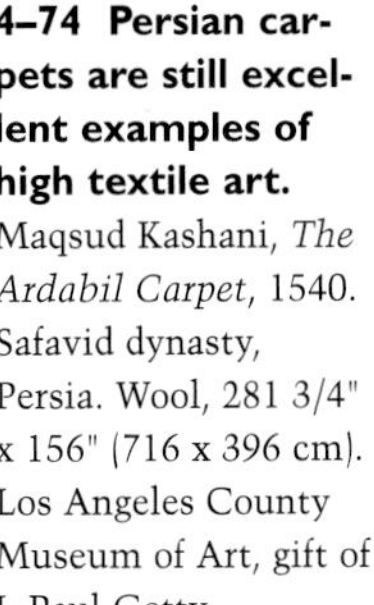

4–74 Persian carpets are still excellent examples of high textile art.
Maqsud Kashani, *The Ardabil Carpet*, 1540. Safavid dynasty, Persia. Wool, 281 3/4" x 156" (716 x 396 cm). Los Angeles County Museum of Art, gift of J. Paul Getty.

4–75 Ming influences from China combine with traditional Turkish colors.
Dish with lobed rim and flaring body, 1550–1560. Isnik (Nicaea), Turkey. Tin-glazed faience, 13 1/4" (34 cm) diameter. Los Angeles County Museum of Art, Nasli M. Heeramaneck Collection.

4–76 Rhythm and symmetry are hallmarks of Islamic aesthetics. These tiny birds are excellent examples of fine metalsmithing.
Bracelet, 10–11th centuries. Persia. Gold, 2" x 5 1/8" (5 x 13 cm). Los Angeles County Museum of Art, Nasli M. Heeramaneck Collection.

Lesson 4.7 Review

1 What is an arabesque? Give an example of arabesques in a piece of Islamic art or architecture.

2 What is a mosque, qibla, minaret and muezzin? How are these related?

3 Why were animal forms so small in Islamic architecture?

4 Describe how the art of different cultures is reflected in the Persian *Battle of Alexander with the Dragon*.

5 What form of textile art is usually regarded as the pinnacle of Islamic design and craftsmanship?

4.8 Sub-Sahara Africa

South of the Sahara there are three distinct types of societies: (1) nomadic tribes in the desert and steppe regions; (2) sedentary farming cultures in the savanna and rain-forest fringe areas; and (3) ancient, sophisticated kingdoms of Nigeria and the Guinea coast. While all three have separate art traditions, their art is similar in attention to craftsmanship, use of geometric abstraction, and a religious orientation. Religion plays a dominant part in African art forms.

Ceremony dominates much of traditional Africa's life and art. Each individual is thought to have a spirit that interrelates with the spirits of all other individuals. Spirits are everywhere, uniting the whole human race in a harmonious whole with the visible and invisible universe. A strong bond unites the individual and clan with each other and with ancestors.

Vocabulary
cult figures
fetish figures
reliquary figures

4–77 Woodcarving continues to be an important medium for contemporary African artists.
Nelson Mukhuba, *Golfer,* detail (fig.4–85).

The African continent is second only to Asia in size. The Nile, the longest river in the world, is sourced halfway across the continent in Lake Victoria.

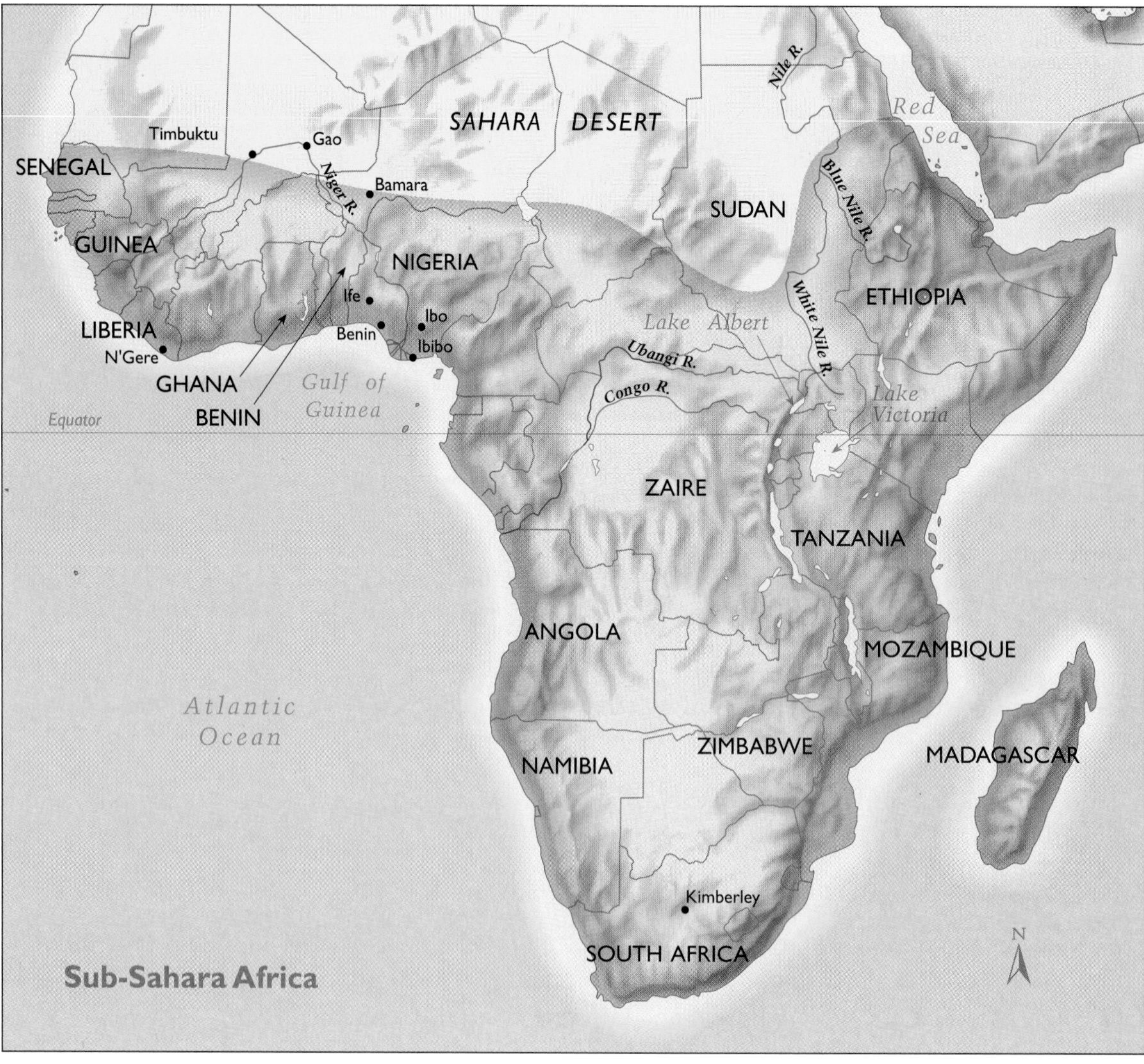

4–78 Masks are an important part of African ritual ceremonies. The multitude of materials and styles make masks one of the most exciting art forms in Africa. *Leopard Mask*, Grasslands, Bamileke, Cameroon. Raffia splints, cloth, glass beads, 31" x 48" (80 x 122 cm). Collection of Charles W. and Janice R. Mack.

Sub-Sahara Africa Timeline

500 BC–200 BC
Nok Culture

300 AD–1203 AD
Ghana Empire

1235 AD–c.1464 AD
Mali Empire
King Sundiata

1300s –1600s AD
Kongo Kingdom

1307 AD–1332 AD
Mansa Musa

1200 AD–1500 AD
Ife Kingdom (Nigeria)

1464 AD–1590 AD
Songhai Empire

1500 AD–1700 AD
Benin Kingdom

Nomadic Cultures

The wandering peoples of the semi-arid regions do not produce large sculpture, as their roaming lifestyle does not permit the accumulation of material possessions. However, they do create masks. Masks and sculpture are used in religious ceremonies. Sculpture includes ancestors or cult figures, fetishes and reliquary figures.

Sedentary Farming Cultures

A much more permanent and long-lived tradition of sculpture and masks is present among the agricultural groups of the tropical savanna regions. Masks are used in ritual ceremonies to embody spiritual forces (fig.4–78). Some are used in dance rituals, such as the wooden one from a tribe in French Guinea (fig.4–79). The stylized geometric and naturalistic shapes combine to represent a recognizable human face. By contrast, other masks only faintly resemble natural forms. The wart-hog masks of the N'Gere people of Liberia are highly stylized representations. The N'Gere use a wide range of materials to construct the masks. Wood, paint, fabric, tin, cotton cord, fiber, cloth and woolen ornaments are combined with nails. The result is an assemblage that accentuates the mysticism of the mask (fig.1–6).

4–79 A dancer puts on a mask and becomes the spirit that the mask represents.
Banda Mask, Nalu or Baga peoples, Guinea, 20th century. Wood, metal, paint. The Brooklyn Museum, New York, Caroline A. L. Pratt Fund.

Ancestor or ***cult figures*** are full-body images kept in homes and shrines. As part of a ritual, individuals present offerings to them. Sometimes these figures indicate social rank or may function as fertility images (fig.4–81). Figures may be carved on the legs of a stool and support the seat. Other cult figures may be carved holding an offering bowl or as mother and child figures (fig.4–80).

Fetish figures are designed to hold ingredients that are endowed with mystical powers. The figures are human forms that are affixed with many types of material such as rope, string, feathers or shells. ***Reliquary figures*** are carved guardians that stand above basket receptacles for ancestral remains. In these figures, the human form has a geometric stylization. Some are concave and convex surfaces, cylinders, cubes and cones symbolize (not represent) the guardian spirits.

4–80 Figures of this type are removed annually from their shrines, washed, oiled and adorned with beads and cloth.
Mother and Child, Mali, Bamana People, 19–20th centuries. Wood, 48 1/2" (123.5 cm) high. The Metropolitan Museum of Art, New York. The Michael C. Rockefeller Memorial Collection, Bequest of Nelson A. Rockefeller, 1979.

4–81 Ashanti artists of the twentieth century were intrigued with the Ashanti combination of realism and geometric abstraction.
Akua 'ba doll, 19–20th centuries. Ashanti culture, Ghana. Wood, 11 3/4" (30 cm) high. British Museum, London.

Nigeria and the Guinea Coast

In contrast to the nomadic and sedentary agricultural tribes, the aristocratic kingdoms of Nigeria created art that reflected the tastes of the wealthy kings and courtiers, not the common people. Royal craftspersons were on the king's "staff" and produced ceremonial sculpture and household ornamental panels. They also produced artifacts used in daily living, such as bowls, stools, textiles, pottery and musical instruments.

Kingdoms flourished as early as 500 BC, when the *Nok* culture created large terra-cotta figures (fig.2–50). Nearly 2000 years later, an advanced society, known as the *Ife,* flourished in western Nigeria. Their most significant accomplishment was the production of very naturalistic human sculptures, which were cast in bronze by the lost-wax method. The bronze sculpture of the head of the king, or *oni,* is an excellent example (fig.4–82). All facial features in Ife sculpture are anatomically accurate, even to the bone structure beneath the skin. Holes allowed the application of real hair to give the original an even more lifelike appearance. Many experts once thought that Ife artists learned their sculptural naturalism and technology from the Egyptians or Greeks. Now, however, most scholars agree that Ife sculpture represents the culmination of the aristocratic style, not an outside influence.

4–82 This expert metalwork in a realistic portrait tradition can be compared to the tradition of ancient Greece.
Oni (King) of Ife, 12–14th centuries. Bronze, 14 1/2" (37 cm) high (life-size). British Museum, London.

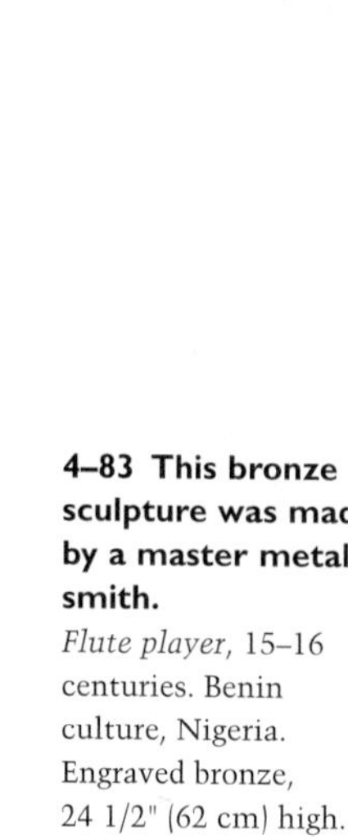

4–83 This bronze sculpture was made by a master metalsmith.
Flute player, 15–16 centuries. Benin culture, Nigeria. Engraved bronze, 24 1/2" (62 cm) high. British Museum, London.

Ife craftspeople taught artisans of the neighboring Benin kingdom the techniques of bronze casting in the fifteenth century. Figures such as the *flute player* (fig.4–83) show the Ife and Benin use of a head-to-body proportional ratio of one to four. Massive and realistic feet and legs contrast with the delicacy of the textures of cloth and helmet.

Contemporary African Art

Contemporary African art was "discovered" by Westerners near the end of the last century. Picasso, Matisse and other artists were influenced by the geometric qualities and abstract forms of African sculpture. These traditions continue to develop today. The vibrancy of the stone sculpture of the Shona people in Zimbabwe is remarkable for its extremely simple forms and quiet emotion (fig.4–84). In South Africa, artists work in a variety of styles and media (fig.4–85). Spontaneity is a hallmark of their work. The art of the African continent reflects its historic and contemporary diversity and complexity.

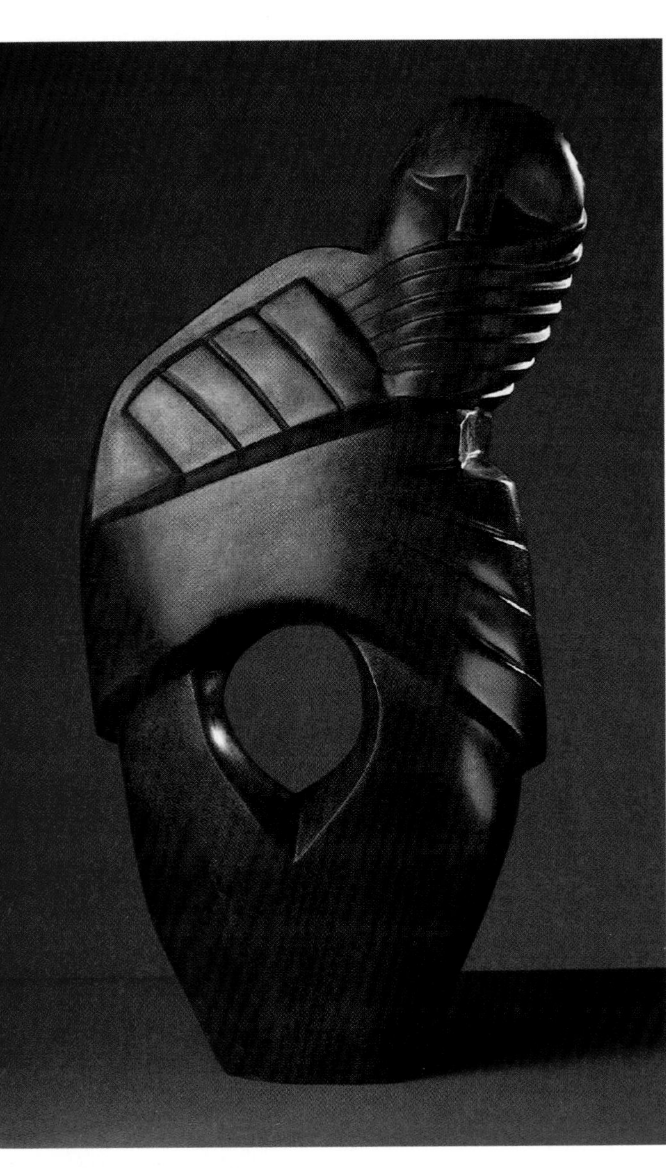

4–84 This Shona sculptor has used simplicity of form in a strikingly expressive manner. *Shona sculpture,* Richard Chirambadare, "Mweyo Mwando." Stone, h. 28" (71 cm). Gallery St. Helena, Santa Rosa, CA.

4–85 The sculptor of this piece was also a musician and a dancer. He lived in Tshakhuma Village in the Transvaal. Nelson Mukhuba, *Golfer,* Velvet corkwood, 1985. Transvaal, South Africa. Collection of Paul Stopforth and Carol Marshall.

Lesson 4.8 Review

1 What three types of societies live south of the Sahara Desert in Africa? How is their art alike?

2 What type of art do the nomadic tribes of the semi-arid regions create?

3 How are masks used in southern Africa?

4 Of what materials do the N'Gere construct their masks?

5 For which class of people was the art of the nomadic and agriculture tribes and the kingdoms of Nigeria created?

6 Who were the Nok and Ife cultures? What type of art did each group produce?

7 Measure the head of the Benin flute player. How many heads tall is he? How does this proportion compare with that of most people?

4.9 Pre-Columbian Art

CIVILIZATIONS IN THE AMERICAS flourished long before the arrival of Columbus and the conquest of the Spanish. The civilizations that flourished in Mexico, Central America and South America can be distinguished by two geographic regions: (1) *Mesoamerica*, or the areas of Mexico and the northern countries of Central America and (2) *Andean*, or the coastal and highland areas of Peru and adjacent areas in South America. Here people produced architecture, sculpture, weaving and ceramics of exceptional quality. All were technically and stylistically very different from Western traditions.

Vocabulary
corbeling
codices

4–86 The extra-ordinary quality of textiles from Paracas suggests that these were the pre-eminent art form of the society. Mantle, known as *The Paracas Textile*, detail (fig.4–93).

4–88 This garment has a checkerboard of different motifs on each of its sides. *Shirt*, or *poncho*, Inca. Interlocked tapestry, cotton and wool, 35 3/4" x 30" (91 x 76.5 cm). Dumbarton Oaks, Washington, DC.

4–87 Little is known of the origins or history of the Olmec culture. *Jadeite Mask*, Olmec. 8" x 7" (21 x 18 cm). Dumbarton Oaks, Washington, DC.

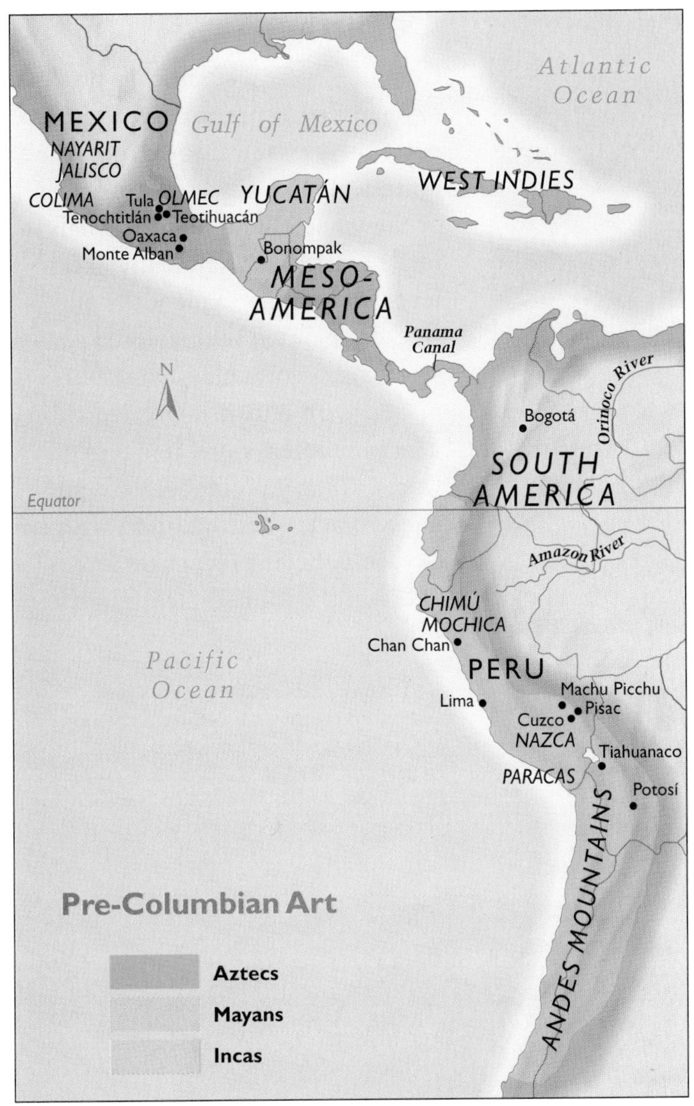

This map shows the Inca, Maya and Aztec cultures at their greatest extent. The most ancient culture, the Maya, is thought to have started as early as 1800 BC, reaching its height about 900 AD. Aztec and Inca empires flourished mostly from 1400 to 1500.

4–89 The Aztec were a highly developed civilization with great accomplishments in mathematics and astronomy, which enabled them to create this complex calendar consisting of 365 days. The year was divided into 18 months of 20 days to which were added 5 "hollow" days. The latter were considered bad luck.
The Aztec Calendar Stone, 471. Mask of Tonatiuh at center, National Museum of Anthropology, Mexico City.

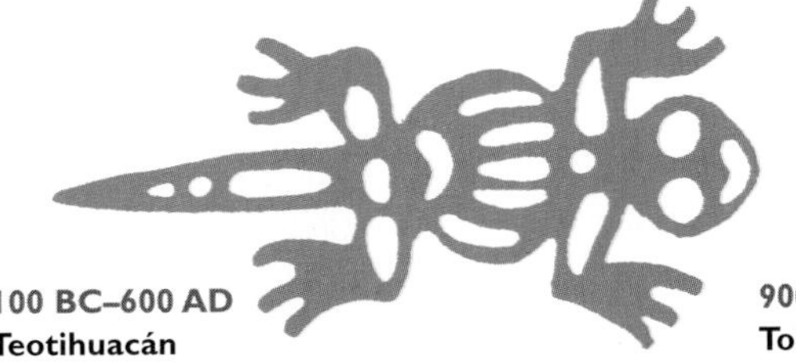

2000 BC–300 AD
Tlatlico
1500–400 BC
Olmec

100 BC–600 AD
Teotihuacán

900–1200 AD
Toltec

900–1519 AD
Mixtec

Mesoamerica Timeline

750–900 AD
Zapotec

300–900 AD
Veracruz

300–900 AD
Maya

1280–1519
Aztec

900–200 BC
Chavin

100–700 AD
Nazca

200–700 AD
Mochica

950 AD
Chimú

1476 AD–1534 AD
Inca
Machu Picchu

South America Timeline

700 BC–100 AD
Paracas

100–700 AD
Moche Culture

700 AD–1000 AD
Tiahuanaco

1000 AD–1400 AD
Chancay

4–90 The precipitous stairways of these temples seem to reach into the sky. Climbing them requires endurance. Descending them needs careful stepping and concentration.
Temple of Quetzalcoátl, 500–900. Teotihuacán, Mexico.

Architecture

In architecture, there was no knowledge of the true arch, so openings were created by ***corbeling.*** A corbeled arch cannot span a wide area. Therefore, no large openings and interior spaces are found in pre-Columbian architecture. Earthquake-proof temples and palaces were made of fitted polygonal stones that were locked and bonded into massive walls (fig.4–90). Temples were pyramidal in shape, often built of earthen mounds faced with finely fit stone or sculptured *adobe*. One or more sides of these temples were fitted with an immense stairway. Carved mythological heads depicting deities such as *Quetzalcoátl*, the feathered serpent of *Teotihuacán*, were cut and fit into the slopes.

Sculpture

Sculpture throughout the Americas was often ceremonial, with heads or full figures of gods carved in low or high relief. Very often, human or animal forms became highly stylized. Animal-human gods were carved with the type of symbolism seen on the Temple of Quetzalcoátl or in the clay funeral urn made by the *Zapotec* people of Oaxaca (fig.4–91).

Ceramics

Ceramics were a significant product of nearly all American cultures. No pottery was hand-thrown, because potters did not possess knowledge of the wheel. However, their handmade work was technically excellent, with thinly made walls and surfaces painted with colored clay slips. Terra-cotta clays were *burnished* with polished wooden cylinders to produce shiny nonglazed wares. *Chimú* potters of Peru produced black wares by firing with an oxygen-deficient reduction atmosphere in the kiln. Typically, pottery

4–91 Fierce faces with glaring eyes and bared teeth are a common theme in Central American sculpture.
Funeral urn, 600–800. Teotihuacán, Mexico. Painted clay, 23 1/2" (60 cm) high. National Museum of Anthropology, Mexico City.

Metalwork

Metalworking originated with the early cultures, which excelled at working metals such as gold and silver. Gold was associated with the sun and silver, with the moon. Tin, copper, lead and alloys were also used to make jewelry, death masks, whistles and ritual objects. Smiths hammered, shaped, soldered, inlaid, filigreed and cast these materials with lost-wax and in open molds.

Fabrics

Fabrics of cotton, wool, feathers or strips of hide and fur were produced throughout ancient America. Weaving traditions date back to at least 1500 BC in coastal Peru, where the *Paracas* culture produced the finest of all ancient American fabrics. The example shown here (figs.4–86, 4–93) was woven of cotton and wool and includes stylized figures and animal motifs worked into geometric patterns and a repeated design. This burial mantle is an excellent example of the weaver's craft.

4–92 Pots such as this have also been found in many animal forms.
Stirrup vessel, about 500–600 AD. Mochica culture.

was made for use in ritual and burial. Pots were often broken to "release" the spirit when buried with the dead. The interesting *"stirrup"-shaped vessels* (fig.4–92) have handles that bridge both sides of the pot. The handles are hollow to form a spout through which liquids were poured. Shapes included human heads, a variety of animal forms and even fish.

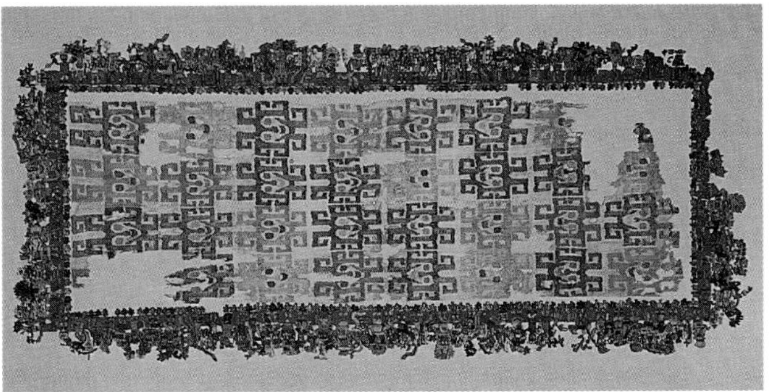

4–93 This mantle probably was included in a mummy bundle. It may have been used in important ceremonies during the life of the deceased.
Mantle, known as *The Paracas Textile,* 300–100 BC. Cotton and wool, 25" x 59" (63.5 x 150 cm). The Brooklyn Museum, New York. J. T. Underwood Memorial Fund.

4–94 Archaeologists are not sure whether the colossal heads of the Olmec are gods or rulers.
Colossal head, Olmec. 1500–300 BC. Basalt.

4–95 Ball courts have been found in the ruins of later Mesoamerican temples.
Ceremonial ball game, 100–300. Nayarit culture. Ceramic, white on red slip, 13" x 7 3/4" (33 x 20 cm). Los Angeles County Museum of Art, Proctor Stafford Collection.

Mesoamerica

The most ancient culture in Mesoamerica is the *Olmec* culture. The Olmec lived along the Gulf of Mexico from as early as 1500 BC to about 200 AD. The Olmec affected the religion, politics and art throughout the region. They carved huge monolithic basalt sculptures of faces (fig.4–94) that mixed human and catlike creatures. The jaguar became symbolic of the gods and was pictured in various forms of art.

Other ancient Mexican cultures included the *Nayarit* and *Colima* on the west coast. Their ceramic sculptures provide information about daily life. The example shown (fig.4–95) illustrates a ceremonial rubber-ball game played in a clay court. These games must have had religious significance because courts are found connected with the temples of later Mesoamerican cultures.

"Classical" Mesoamerican civilization dates from about 200 to 900. During this era, the *Teotihuacáns* built a huge stone temple-city for the use of pilgrims. *Mayan* civilization also emerged during this period, and they constructed similar pyramidal temples throughout Yucatán and much of Middle America. Frescoes were painted at Bonompak depicting life-size human figures involved in ceremonies and processions. *Zapotec* culture, noted for its ornamental clay funerary urns and incense burners, also flourished at this time.

The post-Classical era saw the rise of imperial states. First the *Toltec,* then the *Aztec* nations controlled Middle America. At Tula, the Toltec built one of the few temples to use columns, which were carved in the form of warriors and spear throwers. The Aztec reached their pinnacle of power in the later 1400s. The Aztec centered their empire at Tenochtitlán, continuing the artistic traditions of the Mixtec and Toltec. Aztec sculptors produced bas-relief calendar stones (fig.4–89) that illustrated the days of the week as well as Aztec history. Unique to this era is the development of ***codices,*** or illuminated manuscripts, painted on bark paper or deerskin parchment (figs.4–2, 4–6).

Andean

Andean civilizations trace their common origins to the *Chavin* culture of the Peruvian highlands. The stylized image of the jaguar that is featured in Andean art originated with the Chavin culture. The jaguar, which was both worshiped and feared, was one of the most powerful symbols in Andean art. Stirrup-shaped pottery vessels found in later Peruvian cultures (fig.4–92) were first made here, as were early examples of well-fitted stonework architecture.

After the Chavin era, about 500 BC, geometric decorations were used in pottery and weaving. The south coast *Paracas* culture flourished, producing thin, sculptured pottery vessels in the stirrup tradition. The pottery was covered with thick resin pigments. The Paracas culture was famous for its textiles. As mentioned, the weavings of the Paracas were the finest of all ancient American fabric art (figs.4–86, 4–93). Other coastal cultures, such as the *Mochica* and *Chimú,* constructed large pyramidal temples of adobe during this era.

From about 100 to 900, pottery production in coastal areas reached a high point in quality. Mochica potters produced naturalistic animal-shaped vessels. The vessels featured incised designs, appliquéd and pressed ornaments, and painted patterns. South coast *Nazca* potters used polychromatic decorations of bold design and color to ornament their thin, highly polished wares.

From 900 to 1200, Andean artists produced well-fitted masonry gateways covered with stylized anthropomorphic bas-reliefs. The urban Chimú kingdom reached its peak of power about 1200. Chimú goldsmiths produced fine silver and gold cups, masks, and other objects. The Chimú were also skilled architects and built urban centers organized on a grid plan. Their adobe-faced temples were ornamented with naturalistic birds, fish and geometric abstract motifs. They were also noted for their pottery, which reflected a Mochican influence.

About 1440, the *Inca* conquered the region, creating the final "imperialist" period. The Inca utilized the artistic achievements of former kingdoms for its own purposes, much as the Romans did in Europe. They were active in a number of art forms (figs.4–88, 4–96) but excelled in architecture and dry-masonry techniques. The capital at Cuzco and other cities were well-planned communities based on grid patterns. Central plazas contained public buildings and temples. Late in the Inca era, walled fortresses were built near centers like Pisac and *Machu Picchu* (fig.4–97). Despite hasty construction, huge stone blocks were expertly fitted and locked into structures that have withstood invasions and earthquakes. They stand today as a testimony to the engineering skill of the Andean civilization.

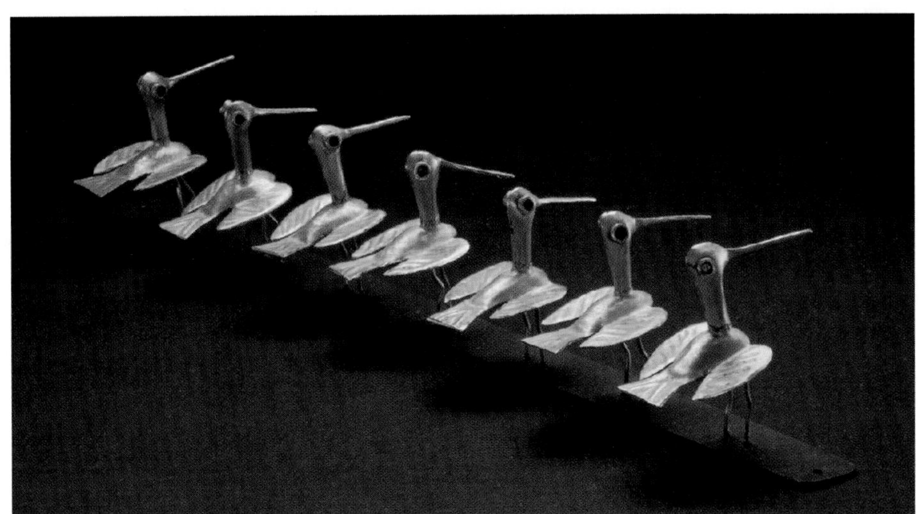

4–96 Several sets of these birds have survived, but their use is unknown.
Seven Sea Birds, Inca, 15th century. Cut and hammered gold, 2" x 10 1/4" (5 x 26 cm). American Museum of Natural History, New York.

4–97 Huge stones were cut and fitted without masonry to build this city high in the mountains.
Machu Picchu. Overall view, late 15th century. Inca culture, Peru.

Lesson 4.9 Review

1 What is corbeling? Which civilizations used this building technique and what is its limitation?
2 What shape were pre-Columbian temples? Describe the temple of Quetzalcoátl. Who was Quetzalcoátl?
3 Which pre-Columbian culture was renowned for its fine weaving?
4 List some of the metals used by pre-Columbian sculptors. What did they make with these metals?
5 What is the oldest Mesoamerican culture? What type of sculptures did they carve?
6 When was the classical Mesoamerican civilization? Which cultures were important in Mesoamerica during this classical time?
7 Which two cultures controlled the lands of Mesoamerica during the post-Classical era? What type of art did these cultures produce?
8 What animal was one of the most powerful symbols of Andean art?
9 For what type of textile art was the Paracas culture most famous?
10 What techniques did the Mochica potters use to decorate their pots?

4.10 Native America

North America supported a diverse population of Native Americans. The groups had different customs and beliefs, although all practiced a form of nature worship. Native Americans have created ceremonial and functional objects of high craftsmanship and symbolic beauty since Neolithic times. Crafts made of bark, skin (fig.4–100), wood and beads, and fine pottery and basketwork (fig.4–98) were important traditions in Native American groups. These works share several characteristics. They reflect an appreciation for the materials of nature, a close relationship with the spirit world, pictographic symbolism, and an advanced level of craftsmanship.

Vocabulary
mound builders
kivas
adobe
pueblo
tipi
petroglyphs
totem poles

4–99 The Haida people of the Northwest Coast excelled at carving wood and argillate, a black shale stone.
Haida Box. Wool. Hurst Gallery, Cambridge, MA.

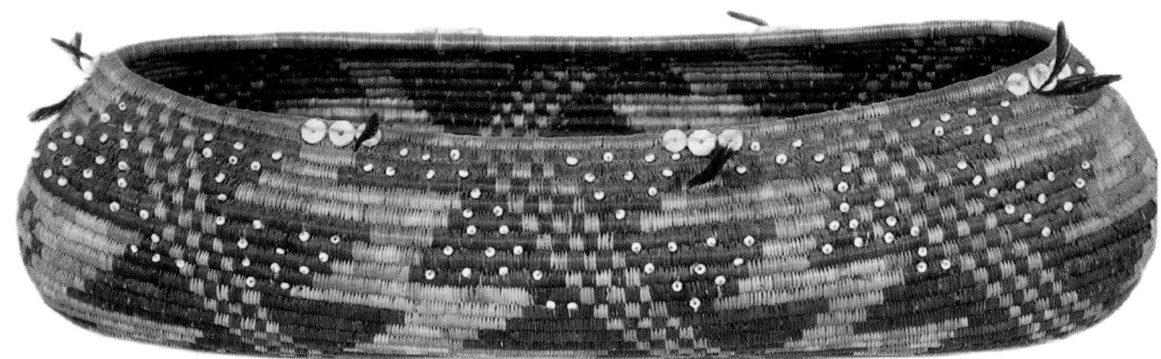

4–98 Native Americans in California have a strong tradition of basketweaving. The art flourished particularly in the late nineteenth century. The tradition continues today with women passing the techniques from one generation to the next.
Feather basket, Pomo, California. Fiber, buttons, quail topknots, 12" (30.48 cm). Hurst Gallery, Cambridge, MA.

Pre-historic Era Timeline

c.1000 BC–300 BC
Adena-Hopewell

300 AD–c.1000 AD
Ipiutak

c.1000 AD–c.1200 AD
Mesa Verde

c.1200 AD–1300 AD
Mimbres

1200 AD–1500 AD
Mississippian

1300 AD–1500 AD
Kuaua Pueblo

1700s–present
Navajo
Hopi
Chilkat, Haida, Kwkiutl, Tlingit
Iroquois
Crow
Mandan

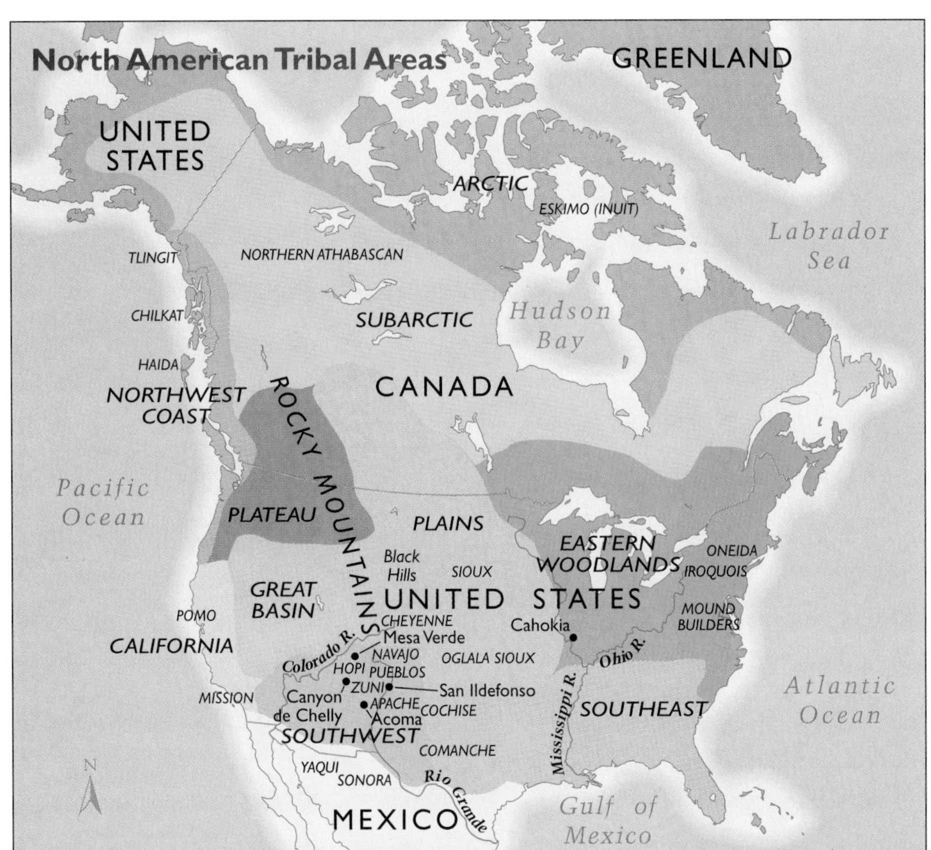

Native North American people achieved a wide cultural diversity, their tribes fanning out all over the continent. Think of the different accents, attitudes and cultures among Americans today in different parts of the country. How might geography have contributed to these differences?

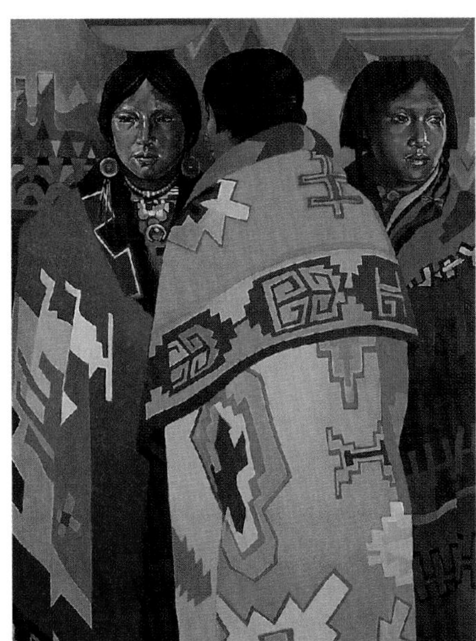

4–101 Some contemporary Native American artists choose to work with traditional materials and subjects. Others make their statements about Native American life in nontraditional ways. Compare this painting with fig.17–51.

Jon Lightfoot, *Women of Cougar Clan*, 1989. Oil on canvas, 36 x 48" (91 x 122 cm). Courtesy of the artist and the Suzanne Brown Gallery. Scottsdale, Arizona.

4–100 Men of the Plains tribes often painted hides as a means of recording important hunts and battles.

Buffalo skin robe with painted detail representing battle fought in 1797 between the Sioux and Attikara against the Mandon and Hidatsa. Peabody Museum, Harvard University.

Architecture

The ***mound builders*** of eastern America created huge earthen platforms by carrying earth in baskets and tamping it into flattened terraces. One of the largest of these is at Cahokia, Illinois, a complex of eighty-five mounds. The area is over 30 meters high, 300 meters long and over 200 meters wide.

The Anasazi people were the ancestors of the Pueblo peoples in the Southwest. They built communal apartment houses under the protecting ledges of massive cliffs. The Anasazi built *cliff dwellings at Mesa Verde* (fig.4–102) in Chaco Canyon, New Mexico, and remains are still standing. The settlement of Mesa Verde has over two hundred rooms and twenty-three meeting rooms called ***kivas***. Kivas were used as sacred worship centers. The interiors were painted with ceremonial designs.

Later, Pueblo Indians used stone and ***adobe*** (sun-dried bricks) to build square dwellings like apartment houses. They made the rooms in terraces so that the roofs of the lower rooms formed the terraces for those above. The buildings had only a few windows or T-shaped doorways high up on the walls. The openings were accessible only by retractable ladders. Thus, the ***pueblo*** could be defended, much like a fort. Round towers aided in this function. Contemporary pueblos continue the tradition in the Southwest (figs.4–3, 4–103).

Hunters of the Plains region relied on the portability of the ***tipi***, a dwelling of rawhide stretched over a conical framework of long poles. Decoration was significant, and painting on the hide included designs representing the forces of nature. Sun, rain, animals, spirits and *mandala* patterns were all rendered with earth colors and animal dyes.

4–103 Pueblo construction continues to be used today by Native Americans of the Southwest.
Pueblo, Taos, New Mexico.

4–102 This building complex is situated on a ledge above a valley floor. This location provided shelter and protection.
Cliff dwelling, Mesa Verde National Park, Colorado, about 1100.

4–104 In order to be successful, this intricate design must take into account the shape of the pot.
Acoma vase. Bird design. Polychrome pottery, 14 1/4" (36 cm) high. The Indian Art Center of California, Studio City.

Pottery

Pottery traditions of Native American peoples are exceptional for their fine craftsmanship and design. The earliest North American pottery was created by Eastern peoples about 2200 BC. The potter's wheel was not used. Instead, clay was slowly formed into symmetrical shapes using the coil method of building the form up ring by ring. Paddles were sometimes used to enlarge and shape the forms. No glaze was used, but pots were partially waterproofed by burnishing. Burnishing is a process of polishing a pot with smooth rocks or wood before the pot is completely dry. Decorations were stamped, incised or engraved into the surface. Often slip of various colors was painted onto the leather-hard clay.

Most Native American pottery was used as containers for food storage or for cooking. Its organic patterns and bird motif accent the form of the vase.

In New Mexico, in 1919, Maria Martinez with her husband, Julian, began the production of black polished pottery (fig.4–105). This pottery is made of clay that fires to a black finish. Before it is fired, it is burnished until it shines. No glazes are used in this process. Designs are then painted, or sometimes carved, on the elegant forms after polishing. The painted areas appear dull black on the polished surface and create a striking effect. Note this interaction on the upper body of this vase. Women make the basic ware; then men paint it, an unusual departure from the common Indian practice in which women make the pot from start to finish.

4–105 The matte portions of the pattern come from painting water on the burnished surface of the pot before it is fired.
Maria Martinez and Julian Martinez, *Black vase,* 1929. Polished pottery, 6" (15 cm) high. Collection of Gilbert Davis, Worcester, MA.

4–106 Petroglyphs such as these can be found on rocks throughout the American Southwest.
Petroglyphs, Arizona.

Painting

Painting can be traced to ancient rock carvings called ***petroglyphs***, found in at least forty-three states. Some petroglyphs are 5000 years old. The designs were scraped into the rock (fig.4–106), probably as part of ritual puberty, hunting, fertility or worship practices. Images of puma, serpents, bighorn owls, whales and human figures are stylized in what seem to be the beginnings of a written language. Carved patterns were often highlighted with color from clay, minerals, charred bone or plant pigments. Traditional designs are still found today in sand paintings, pottery decoration and kivas.

Weaving and Basketry

Southwestern weaving traces its unique use of the *loom* back to Cochise and Mogollon cultures, about 300 BC. Clothing and blankets are created by innovative weave patterns known as the basket, tapestry, diagonal twill or diamond twill weaves. The Navajo rug of wool (fig.4–107) has distinct designs that represent both the tribe and the individual woman who wove it.

Related to textile weaving is the more ancient craft of basketry, first practiced about 9000 years ago. One of three methods is used in their manufacture—plaiting, twining or coiling. The fibers of grass, bark, root or hemp are woven into fine, often watertight containers. Dyed or naturally colored strands are incorporated to create rhythmical geometric patterns and representations of animals like the thunderbird. Each region has produced fine work, but the outstanding baskets of the California *Hupa* and *Pomo* peoples (fig.4–108) are regarded as some of the most excellent in both craftsmanship and decoration.

4–108 Consider how the artist has combined rhythm, shape and pattern in this basket's design.
Tray, 19th century. Hupa, Northern California. Fiber, 16 1/2 x 4" (41.9 x 10.1 cm). The Nelson-Atkins Museum of Art, Kansas City, Missouri.

4–107 Compare these designs and colors to those in the *Ardabil Carpet* (fig.4–69).
Navajo rug, 1850–1880. Wool. The Indian Art Center of California, Studio City.

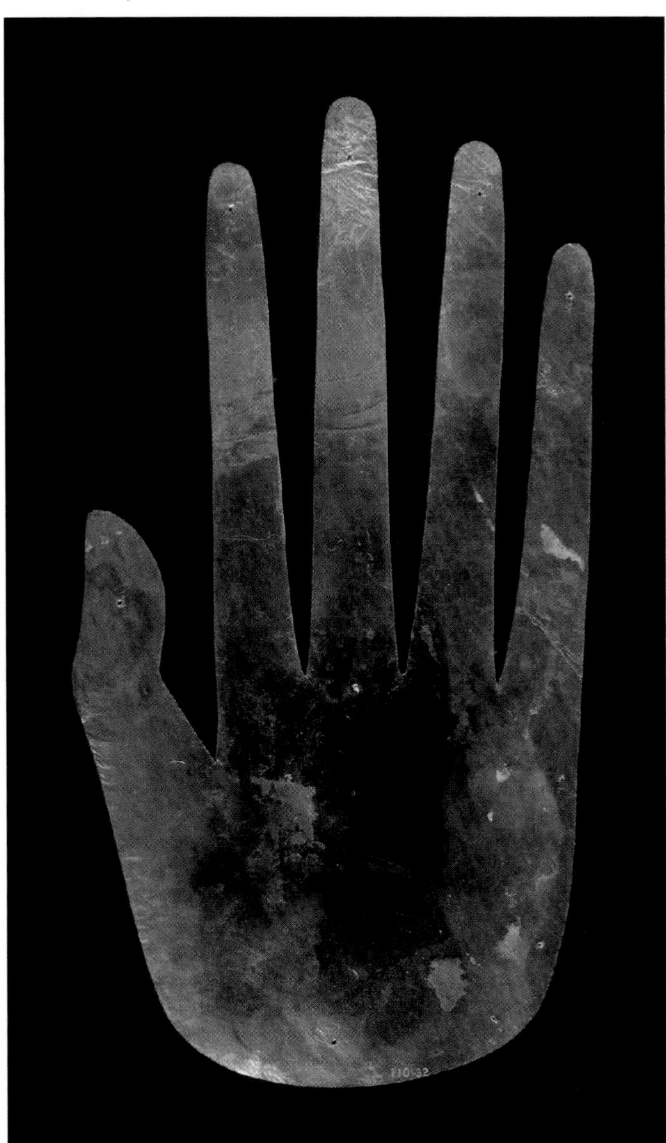

4–109 This elegant hand is very expressive in its simplicity.
Human Hand, Hopewell Mound, Ohio, 1000–1300. Cut sheet mica, 13" (33 cm) long. The Field Museum, Chicago, IL.

Metalworking

Metalworking has been practiced in copper since 3000 BC. By 1200, southeastern peoples made ceremonial plaques of eagles and costumed dancing warriors. The mound builders of Ohio hammered copper ornaments into snake heads, birds, fish and headdresses. They also fashioned mica into forms such as hands (fig.4–109). Silver was introduced by Europeans and was beaten into jewelry by the *Iroquois, Oneida* and others in the early nineteenth century. *Cheyenne* and *Sioux* created hair-plates, buckles, armbands and harness trappings during the same period. The *Navajo,* destined to become the finest of all American silversmiths, learned smithing from the Mexicans. Old silver dollars were hammered into squash-blossom necklaces and hollow beads or cast into jewelry forms (fig.4–110). *Zuni* specialized in beautiful settings for clusters of turquoise, while *Hopi* silversmiths created new techniques by adding shell and coral to their pieces.

4–110 The Navajo are the premiere American silversmiths, and they often use turquoise as an inset.
Silver bracelets, 1920–30. Navajo. The Brooklyn Museum, New York.

Woodworking

While most of the creative energy of Native Americans went into functional objects, the wood sculpture of the Northwest Coast Indians represents a contrast. The Northwest Coast is made up of the Indian tribes of the Tlingit, Haida and Kwakiutl. Carvings of the Northwest Coast represent some of the finest sculpture created by Native Americans. The ***totem poles*** and house posts of the Haida (fig.4–111) depict supernatural and legendary characters and animals associated with certain groups or clans. These poles stood in front of houses as signs of prestige and to showcase the family's totems, the animals that symbolized the family. Other Native Americans sculpted ritual masks (fig.4–112), effigy figures and utensils.

Contemporary Native American artists continue to paint, sculpt and craft in traditional fashions. Many artists also have combined tradition with modern styles (fig.4–101, 17–51).

4–111 Compare these stylized figures to those on the East Malayasian gableboard painting.
Haida totem pole. Tlingit Indians of Southeast Alaska.

4–112 Masks such as this one were carved for use in ceremonies of healing and cleansing.
Elon Webster, *False Face Mask,* 1937. Iroquois. Wood. Cranbrook Institute of Science, Bloomfield Hills, Michigan.

Lesson 4.10 Review

1 Who were the Anasazi? Describe their dwellings. Why did they build kivas?
2 Why was the tipi an ideal living structure for the hunters of the American Plains? Name several designs that were painted on these rawhide tipis.
3 When and where was the earliest North American pottery made?
4 Describe the process that Native Americans used to make their pottery partially waterproof.
5 For what type of pottery was Maria Martinez and her family famous?
6 What is a petroglyph? What images are found in petroglyphs?
7 Which craft was practiced first in the Southwest, basketry or textile weaving?
8 How did European metal-working techniques influence Native American jewelry?
9 Name three Pacific Northwest Coast Indian tribes. In what medium did they create most of their great art?
10 What subjects did the Haida carve on their totem poles?

Primary Source

Seeing What Is Not There

Chinese painting is in many ways very subtle. The viewer is frequently called upon to see what is not literally in the painting. Here the Chinese historian of art, Chang Yen-yuan, gives us a sense of the Chinese concept of color:

"Grasses and trees may display their glory without the use of reds and greens; clouds and snow may swirl and float aloft without the use of white color; mountains may show greenness without the use of the five colors. For this reason, a painter may use ink alone and, yet, all five colors may seem present in his painting."

Hsia Kuei, *Twelve Views of Landscape*, detail (fig.2–5).

Chapter Review

Review

1 Name six non-Western cultures discussed in this chapter.
2 List the three major religions that began in Africa and Asia.
3 Which religious traditions are usually reflected in Western religious art?
4 Why are there so few examples of ancient Micronesian sculptures?
5 Describe a piece of Islamic art. What was the artist trying to achieve in this art?
6 Which cultures were in power in Mesoamerica and in the Andean region when Europeans explored these lands in the sixteenth century?
7 Describe the architectural planning of Inca cities.
8 What are four characteristics common to the crafts of the various populations of Native Americans?

Interpret

1 Contrast the methods that Western and Asian artists use to indicate distance in their paintings.
2 In 200 BC, the Chinese and the Native Americans used very different methods for forming their pottery. Contrast these two methods. How did each culture decorate and glaze their pots?
3 What are the basic characteristics of Japanese art? Select one Japanese art piece in this chapter and explain how it exemplifies these characteristics.
4 Name two European artists influenced by African art. What features of African sculpture were appreciated by these European artists?
5 Rank the illustrations of Sub-Sahara African art pictured in this chapter from realistic to abstract.

Other Tools for Learning

Maps

1 What countries would a land trade route cross to connect China with Rome?
2 Find the Yellow River where Chinese culture first developed. What cities are located in this area now?
3 Find the Mekong, Irrawaddy and Chao Phraya Rivers on a map. Through which countries do these rivers flow?
4 Name three countries in Mesoamerica and three countries in the Andean region.
5 Select a culture near an ocean or in the middle of a continent. How do you think this proximity or distance from water affected this culture's art? Give an example to support your theory.

Timeline

Make a chart listing the Chinese, Indian and Japanese dynasties or cultural eras. Give an approximate date for each era and an example of art created in each time period.

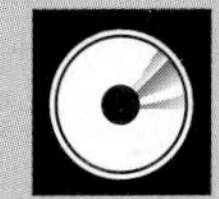

Electronic Research

CD-ROM drive: Electronic Encyclopedia (e.g., *New Grolier Multimedia* or *Microsoft Encarta*)

Research the architecture of one of the cultures in this chapter further. Look it up in one of the encyclopedias. Either get a print out or draw a structure from this culture. Why was it built?

Activity 1

Clay Vessels

Materials

newspaper or plastic cloth
containers of water
spray bottle
clay
clay tools
heavy duty plastic bags

Take a look. Look through this chapter and others for clay pots, bowls and vases found in archaeological sites.

Think about it. What similarities and differences do you see between the pottery of different cultures? How do you think each of these vessels were used by the people who made them? In what ways does the shape of a container dictate its use?

Do it. Make a clay pot, jar or bowl that you could imagine being discovered at an archaeological site.

- Roll a flat piece of clay for the base and use slip (clay thinned with water) as binding material.
- Roll the clay into long coils and place them on top of each other to shape your vessel.
- Smooth the surface with a stick or flat stone. Allow the piece to dry slowly. When "leather hard," trim it and carve designs into the surface.
- Ask your teacher for help with glazes, engobes and decorative techniques, as well as the firing process.

Check it. Is your vessel well-balanced and stable? Can others guess how you intended it to be used? Does it have the distinctive look of an ancient culture?

Helpful Hint: In a rough sketch, outline the shape of several pottery pieces found in this chapter. Try out some shapes of your own design on paper before beginning your pot.

Activity 2

Behind the Mask

Materials

Kraft paper or brown paper bags
clear glue
toothpicks for applying glue
paper, felt, buttons, yarn, etc., for decoration
scissors
mirrors
brushes

Take a look. Review the following masks in this chapter. Look for other examples.

- 4–79 *Tribal mask,* French Guinea.
- 4–112 Elon Webster, *False Face Mask,* 1937.

Think about it. Masks have been used for more than 30,000 years, on six continents. Study several kinds of masks made by native people of different cultures. Try to understand why they were made and how they were used.

Do it. Make a stylized mask that will fit your face. Work with a partner or in front of a mirror.

- Start with 1/2"-wide torn strips of Kraft paper or paper torn from heavy brown paper bags. Wrap a strip around your forehead and join (with a drop of glue) at the back, like a headband.
- Attach the next strip of paper to either side of the band, over your head, like a close-fitting hat.
- Attach two other strips to the headband on either side and join them under your chin. A narrow vertical strip covering the bridge of your nose completes the basic framework of the headband mask.
- Using your head as a mold, attach strips of torn paper to this framework. Gradually interlace more strips of paper until the mask fits your face and is strong enough to remove.
- Stuff the mask with newspaper to keep the form intact, then decide on the shape you want for eyes and other features.
- Cut with scissors to adjust the mask and/or add laminated paper strips to the basic form until it is rigid and holds its shape well. Then add paint and any other decorations.

Check it. Is your mask sturdy; does it hold together well? Ask classmates for their reaction to your mask. Do their comments match up with the effect you intended?

Helpful Hint: Wear a bandanna or stocking cap on your head to keep your hair out of the way while you work.

Additional Activities

- Use tempera paint and/or watercolor to make a design (on paper) for a blanket or rug in one of the cultural styles described in this chapter (Islamic, Navajo, etc.). Research other books or encyclopedias for examples.
- Research and write a one-page paper discussing one of the following: the effects of colonization on the arts of Asia and the Americas; the importance of masks in tribal use in Africa; the shaman's influence on the cultures of Asian or African peoples; or several ways in which Western and non-Western art seem to differ.

Marcia A. Williams

Age 16
Notre Dame Academy
Worcester, Massachusetts
Favorite kinds of art: Modern, Impressionist, Cubism
Favorite artists: Monet, Picasso, Haring, Gauguin, Escher
Activity 1, Clay Vessels

My art project is a clay pot. I made it from loops of clay that were smoothed together to form a pot. It represents a lot of creativity and hard work on my part. It took a while to think of the designs that I put on it.

While I was making this pot, I mostly thought about the composition of it. I thought about making the pot round and whether or not I would even put a neck on it. Once I decided on the neck, I had a hard time trying to keep the neck from caving in. After it was fired, I then had to think about how I wanted to do the glazing. I put all of the detail in with a watercolor-like underglaze and then covered the whole thing with clear gloss glaze. This way I was able to do very small details.

Before I did this project, I went to the Worcester Art Museum to see the display on Indian Art. I think that the pots that I saw there influenced the shape and design of my pot. It was meant to look like a water jug, although I'm not quite sure if I actually succeeded!

I think that I most enjoyed glazing the pot. I love painting, and putting the glaze on was very similar to that. It was relaxing but I still had to think about what I was doing and how I was going to accomplish it.

Other students who want to make things definitely need patience. To make something that you can truly appreciate, you have to work hard. You cannot expect to whip off a masterpiece in an hour, because it just won't happen. Also, you will appreciate something that you put a lot of time into more than something that you did in a few moments. I would say that my own personal philosophy is that if you work as hard as you can and do your best, you are bound to create something that you are proud of.

Marcia A. Williams

Pot, 1994. Clay, 4 1/2" x 4 1/2" (11.4 x 11.4 cm)

Working carefully, Marcia applies underglaze to create a colorful design on her pot.

Part Three

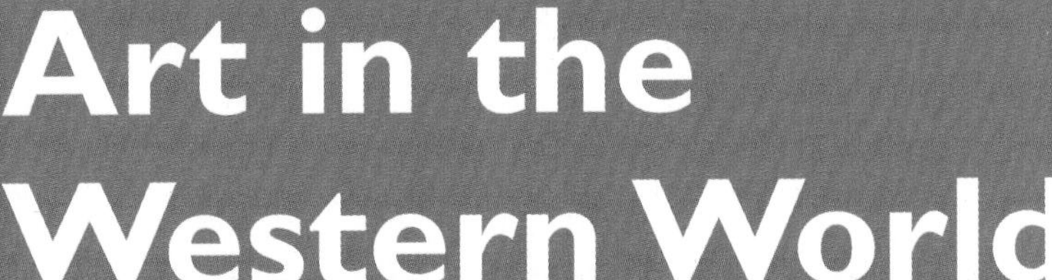

Art in the Western World

Giovanni Paolo Panini, *Interior of the Pantheon, Rome,* detail, c. 1734. Oil on canvas, 50 1/2" x 39" (128 x 99 cm). National Gallery of Art, Washington, DC, Samuel H. Kress Collection.

5 Beginnings of Western Art

In This Chapter...

EVER IMAGINE YOURSELF living thousands of years ago with people in a cave or along the Nile River in Ancient Egypt? Our best view of these people and what their lives were like comes from the art they created.

The earliest paintings we know of are in caves in Africa, Europe and Asia. The images say to us that these were highly skilled artists with keen powers of observation. They drew beautiful images of animals they hunted in order to survive.

Twenty-seven thousand years later, the first civilization we know of formed in Sumer, an area in Mesopotamia. The accomplishments of this first civilization were spectacular. The Sumerians designed and built huge temples called ziggurats which were the center of their cities. They invented writing, created sculptures of stone, and made beautiful musical instruments. They were highly accomplished artists who formalized the first style of art depicting the human form.

The second great civilization was Ancient Egypt. It thrived for several thousand years virtually unchanged in its isolated and fertile location along the Nile River. The Egyptian desire for stability and permanence led them to create huge monuments and tombs full of art meant to last forever. Although their glorious civilization did not last, we can still hear them, see them and learn from them through the art they created.

These early cultures of Mesopotamia and Egypt influenced later ones around the Mediterranean Sea, Europe and the United States. The art of these later cultures is what we call Western Art because it developed in Western Europe. It is the primary focus of the chapters that follow.

5–a Tutankhamen became Pharaoh of Egypt as a young boy, but only ruled for nine years. His tomb, discovered in 1922, was filled with precious treasures.
Tutankhamen Mummy Case, 1352 BC. Gold inlaid with enamel and semiprecious stones, h. 73" (185 cm). Egyptian Museum, Cairo.

5–b The stairways of the great Persian palace at Persepolis were carved with reliefs of royal courtiers and others who served the emperor.
Audience Hall of Darius and Xerxes, detail of relief (fig.5–17).

Truly the gods have not from the beginning revealed all things to mortals, but by long seeking mortals make progress in discovery.

Xenophanes of Colophon

Can you imagine what life in Europe might have been like before the existence of cities and countries? What kinds of climate and geographical features might be favorable for primitive civilizations?

5–c Built nearly 4000 years ago, this circle of huge stones functioned as a giant, but very accurate, calendar that was based on the movements of the sun and moon.
Stonehenge, detail (fig.5–8).

5–d Recent findings have called into question the long-accepted dating of the Sphinx. Some scholars now believe it predates by many years the Pyramid of Cheops. Additional research is necessary before final conclusions can be drawn.
The Great Sphinx, about 2500 BC, 4th dynasty, 65' (19.8 m) high, Giza.

25000–18000 BC
Last Ice Age

3500–3000 BC
Invention of the wheel, Sumeria
3300 BC
First kilns used in Mesopotamia

3300 BC
Earliest known writing, Mesopotamia
2650–2575 BC
Great Sphinx, Pyramids at Giza, Egypt

2100 BC
Ziggurat at Ur, Mesopotamia
2000 BC
Stonehenge, England

1300 BC
Moses receives the Ten Commandments, Mount Sinai, Egypt

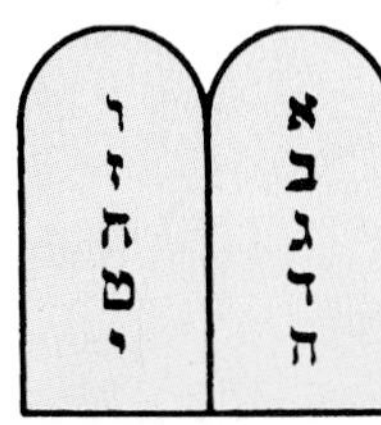

Beginnings of Western Art

15000 BC
Cave Paintings at Altamira, Spain, and Lascaux, France

1530 BC
Temple of Amun, Karnak
1352 BC
Tomb of King Tutankhamen, Egypt

705–681 BC
Height of Assyrian Empire

700 BC
Hanging Gardens of Babylon

5.1 Earliest Beginnings

CAN WE PINPOINT the beginning of art? Are its origins in the cave paintings of Africa, Spain or France? Are they still to be discovered? Or have they been lost forever? We may never know. What we do know is that the earliest known people had two recognized occupations: hunter and artist.

Hunters of the Paleolithic era (Old Stone Age, 33,000–10,000 BC) lived in the hill country of what is now Western Europe. They hunted for bison, bear, deer, reindeer, mammoth and other wild creatures. Artists drew, painted and even carved images of these animals with startling realism and vigor. We may never know why they created these pictures. Perhaps they were a means of artistic expression. The drawings may have been used in magic rituals for hunting and fertility. Perhaps they documented major hunting expeditions. Over the years there has been much argument about their actual function. But today the emphasis is on a diversity of explanations rather than on one specific answer. What is clear is that these images had a far more serious purpose than mere decoration. Whatever the reasons for their existence, the drawings, highly ***stylized*** and very simply done, are breathtakingly beautiful.

The first cave paintings were discovered in 1870 by a small girl who was exploring a cavern at Altamira in Spain. She had been taken to the cave by her father, an amateur archaeologist. Because she was so small she was able to easily look up at the ceiling. Imagine her surprise when she saw a herd of bison stampeding across it. In 1940, several small boys discovered similar paintings in a cave at Lascaux in central France, when their dog fell into a hole that led to the underground chamber.

Key Notes

- Origins of Western art are unclear.
- Earliest forms of art focussed around caves.
- Stone Age art had serious purpose and may have served several functions.

Vocabulary
stylized
cromlech
lintels

Special Feature

The Caves at Lascaux

The earliest paintings in the most famous of the caves, Lascaux, date from about 15,000 BC (figs.5–1, 5–2). The technology was crude and the working conditions were extremely difficult. Nevertheless, these first artists produced stunning work. For sheer vitality, freedom of expression and sureness of touch, these paintings have rarely been equaled. Most cave art consisted of simple outlines. The polychrome paintings of animals at Lascaux and Altamira are in fact very unusual. The colors were made from various earth hues (red, yellow, brown, violet) and lampblack (soot) from the lamps used in the cave. The pigments were ground to powder and applied directly on to the damp limestone walls and ceilings of the caves. They were probably applied with mats of moss or hair. Some colors were sprayed through tubular bones onto the walls.

In some caves, wooden scaffolding was used to enable the artists to

5–2 Most of the paintings at Lascaux are on walls far from the entrance to the caves. Some areas can only be reached by crawling on hands and knees. Because the animals could not have been in the caves, artists must have painted from memory.
Hall of Bulls, Lascaux, detail.

5–1 Many artists worked here over a long period of time. Do you think they had any plan or composition in mind for their animal images?
Hall of Bulls, Lascaux, about 15,000–13,000 BC. Dordogne, France.

reach high walls and ceilings. In the Lascaux Cave, the sockets for a platform of posts survive in one passage. The interior of the cave would have been lit by torches and by burning animal fat placed on flat or dished stones. Some beautifully carved lamps have been found at Lascaux (fig.5–3), but they are extremely rare.

Artists often took advantage of the natural formation of the cave surfaces. In an unusually large chamber at Lascaux, artists painted huge bulls, each sixteen feet long. Sometimes the natural formation of the rock-face suggested to the artist the form of animal depicted. The animals are rendered with amazing fidelity to how they actually looked. They are so lifelike that one can almost hear the thunder of the bulls' hooves as they stampede across the ceiling of the "great hall" at Lascaux.

The paintings had been sealed in the dry air of the caves for over fifteen thousand years. When the caves were opened to the public, air was let into them. The humidity, particularly from the breath of many thousands of visitors, resulted in the rapid deterioration of the paintings. The caves have been closed to the general public since 1963.

Discoveries about humankind's earliest masterpieces continue to be made. In December 1994, more cave paintings were found. These paintings are said to date from 20,000 to 17,000 BC and include the first known prehistoric portrayals of a panther and an owl. They were found near the town of Vallon-Port-d'Arc in France.

5–3 Find a picture of a modern lamp. Compare it to this one. Which do you prefer? Why?
Decorated lamp, Lascaux. Musée des Antiquités Nationale, St. Germain-en-Laye, France.

Carvings of the Paleolithic Era

Carvings, not ancient cave paintings, may be the oldest forms of art. Carvings of female figures have been discovered in many places in Europe and western Asia. The round and bulging stone carving called the *Venus of Willendorf* (fig.5–4) was found in Austria and is considered to be 25,000 years old. This small bulbous figure suggests abundant fertility and a plentiful supply of food—the two all-important needs of any society. The name of "Venus" was given by modern discoverers and does not have any connection with the later Roman goddess.

The sculptor who carved the bison (fig.5–5) out of a reindeer antler used the natural form of the found material. The turned-back head makes elegant use of the antler's existing contours. Because the piece is broken off, its original use cannot be determined.

Architecture of the Neolithic Era

Architecture became a vital concern to ancient peoples of the Neolithic era (New Stone Age, 8000–3000 BC). Humans left their caves and began to form communities. They herded cattle and raised simple crops. They lived in simple structures of grass, mud-bricks and even stone. Protection from enemies was often provided by walls around the settlement. Recent excavations have uncovered a town of mud-brick at Jericho in southern Israel, that dates from 8000 BC (fig.5–6). A rough stone wall, surrounding the village, has been dated at 7500 BC. The walls are twelve feet high and a stone tower reaches to thirty feet—the world's earliest stone fortification.

Among the ruins of Jericho, archaeologists found a group of fascinating sculpted heads (fig.5–7) dated about 7000 BC. The heads are actual human skulls with plaster applied to reconstruct the facial features. Each head is different, as though it were meant to be an actual likeness of a person. The purpose of the heads is not known. They may have had a religious function. The excavations have

5–4 Many figures like this have been found. People may have "planted" them in the ground in an effort to guarantee a good supply of food.
Venus of Willendorf, about 25,000 BC. Limestone, 4 3/8" (11 cm) high. Naturhistorisches Museum, Vienna.

5–5 Examine carefully the artist's expert use of curved lines.
Bison, about 10,000 BC. Reindeer antler, about 4" (10.15) cm long. Musée des Antiquités Nationales, St. Germain-en-Laye, France.

World Cultural Timeline

30,000 BC
Native Americans migrate from Asia to North America

25,000 BC
Cave Painting, Namibia

12,000 BC
World's first known domesticated dogs

9000 BC
World's first known pottery vessels, Japan

6500 BC
Farming and animal domestication begins, India

revealed that there was a thriving civilization in Jericho nearly 9000 years ago.

Several huge stone monuments have survived from the Neolithic era. *Stonehenge,* on the Salisbury Plain in England, was constructed about 2000 BC (fig.5–8). Stonehenge is a round grouping or ***cromlech*** of gigantic stones, some weighing fifty tons. The stones were dragged for more than twenty miles to be trimmed and stood on end. The ***lintels,*** or horizontal elements, were curved slightly to fit the circular plan (fig.5–c). Apparently a ritual site, Stonehenge was constructed to indicate the solstices and equinoxes of the calendar year, and probably the times for planting, harvest and religious ceremonies.

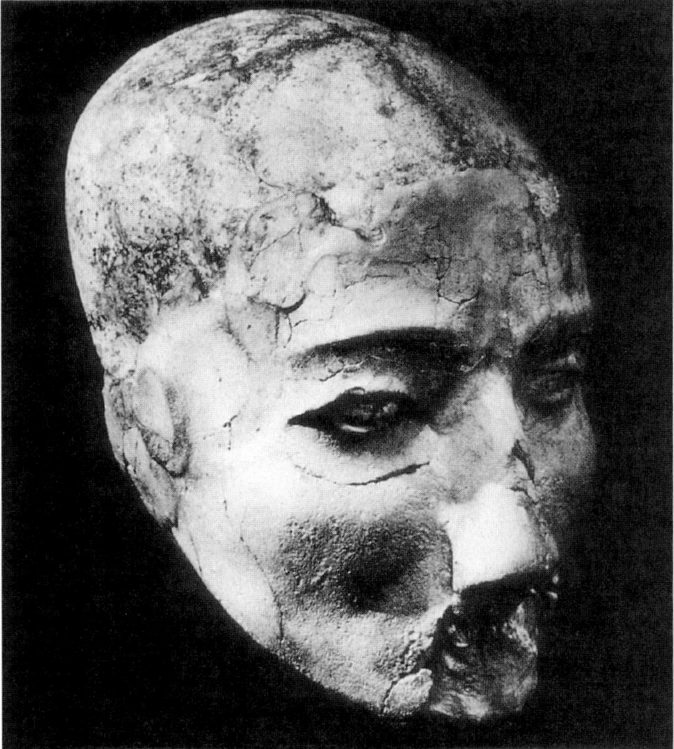

5–7 Family and community activities and stories help us remember our ancestors. This skull may have been decorated and cared for to help keep alive the memory of the person. How do modern people remember their ancestors?
Neolithic plastered skull, about 7000 BC. Life-size, from Jericho. Archaeological Museum, Amman, Jordan.

5–6 This early town with its stone walls and tower is a forerunner of medieval castles.
Fortifications and circular tower, about 7500 BC. Jericho, Israel.

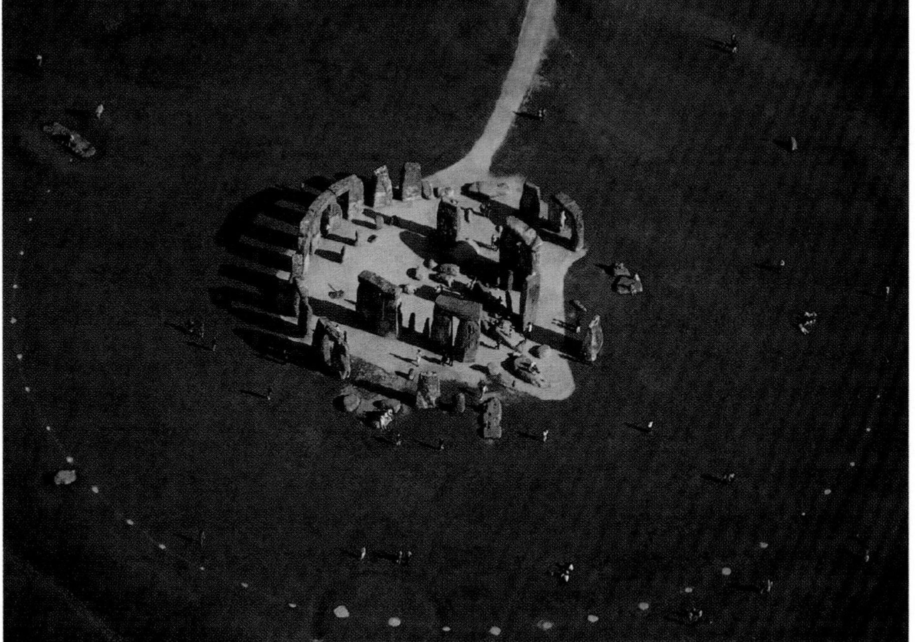

5–8 Standing to the east of the circle of stones is the "heel-stone." If someone in the center of the circle looked outward, the heel-stone marked the point at which the sun rose during the midsummer solstice.
Stonehenge, about 2000 BC. Height about 13 1/2' (4.1 m). Salisbury Plain, England.

Lesson 5.1 Review

1 Describe the tools and materials used by the artists who worked at Lascaux.
2 Why have the caves at Lascaux been closed to the public since 1963?
3 How did the earliest sculptors use the shapes found in natural materials to their advantage?
4 Where is the earliest known stone fortification located? Why did architecture gain importance during the Neolithic era?
5 Define the word "cromlech." Why was Stonehenge constructed?

5.2 The Ancient Near East: Mesopotamia

BETWEEN 3500 AND 3000 BC a great civilization arose in Mesopotamia, the flat and fertile land which lay between the Tigris and Euphrates rivers. Here a group of people called Sumerians established their first city-states. Cuneiform writing, schools, democracy, and the use of the vault and arch all originated in Sumer. For well over one thousand years the Sumerians dominated Mesopotamia. Eventually, however, the Babylonians, the Assyrians and, finally, the Persians ruled the region.

Unfortunately, little remains of the Sumerian civilization. They did not leave behind numerous tombs, like the Egyptians did, although several rich tombs have been found in the city of Ur. Also, because building stone was not available in Mesopotamia, Sumerians used mainly mud-brick. Nothing is left of their structures except the foundations.

We know that the Sumerians worshipped gods. Every city-state had its own god and human ruler who led the populace in serving the deity. Because there were no hills on which to build temples, the Sumerians constructed huge mountains of earth faced with mud-brick and sometimes fired brick. These mammoth structures were called ***ziggurats***. The ziggurat, or temple, was the center of both spiritual and city life. Everything else in the city clustered around its base. The most famous of the ziggurats, the biblical Tower of Babel, has been completely destroyed but others have survived at Warka and Ur.

Sumerians and the later inhabitants of Mesopotamia have left us numerous examples of their stone sculpture and metalwork. Early on, the Sumerians established conventions for the depiction of the human figure. With this development, art had begun to be formalized.

Key Notes

- A great civilization is born in Mesopotamia.
- Gods and rulers become central to the creation of art.
- Sumerians formalize the depiction of the human form.

Vocabulary
ziggurat
cella
stele
low relief

Special Feature

The City of Ur

Several of the ruined cities of Sumer today still are dominated by one of the most important of Sumerian art forms, the ziggurat. Ziggurat complexes were designed to make the worshiper go around as many corners as possible before reaching the ***cella***, or main room. Sacrifices were offered in the cella.

Perhaps the most interesting of all Mesopotamian ziggurats was built at Ur about 2100–2000 BC (fig.5–9). The royal architects who designed the ziggurat at Ur included stepped levels, dramatic staircases and subtly curved lines. This ziggurat also had more than the usual single staircase. There were three, and they converged at an impressive gate tower, topped perhaps by a dome. The structure's facing has withstood floods and weathering so well that it is the best preserved ziggurat in southern Mesopotamia.

The function of the ziggurat was to bridge the gap between human and divine, the earth below and the spirit world above. This explains

5–9 Keep in mind that this structure would have been part of a vast complex of other buildings that have not survived.
Ziggurat at Ur, about 2100–2000 BC. Iraq.

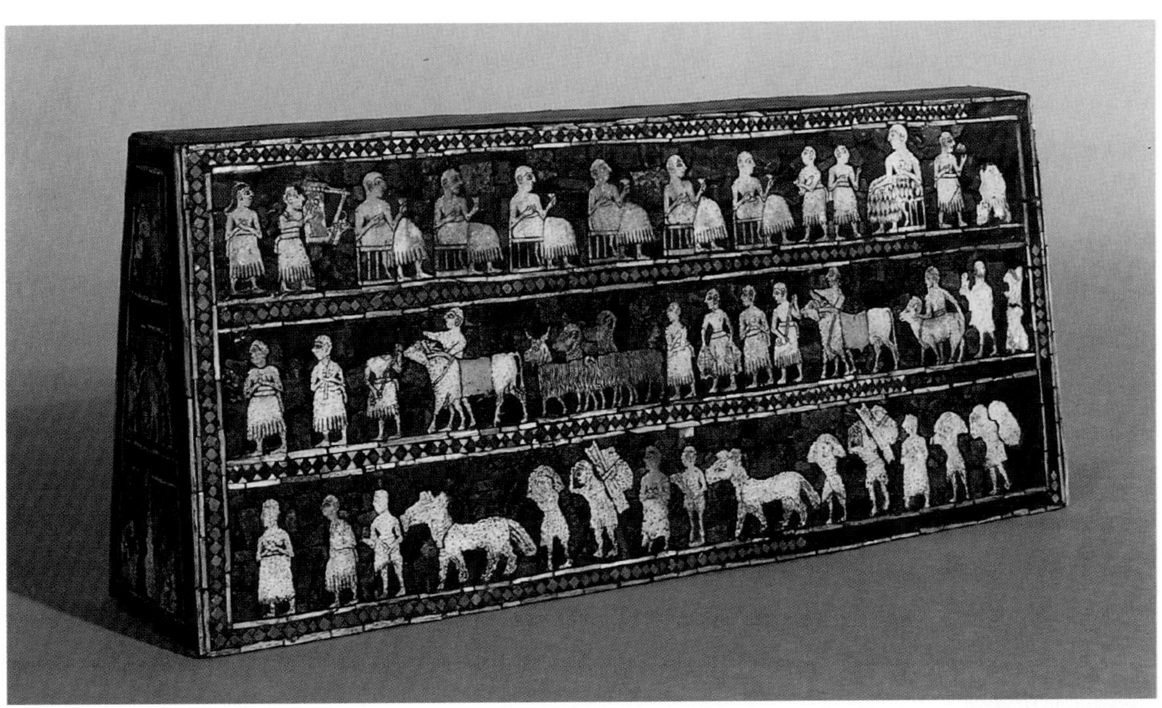

5–10 This section of the standard depicts the results of a Sumerian military battle. Prisoners and servants carry booty. How is the king celebrating his victory?
Standard of Ur: Peace, about 2685–2645 BC, Sumerian. Mosaic panel of shell and colored stones, 19" (48 cm) long, Royal Cemetery at Ur. British Museum, London.

why they went up as high as was humanly possible.

Some of the finest works of art from the Sumerian period were discovered in the royal cemetery at Ur. Archaeologists unearthed statues, panels and other artifacts. Look carefully at the *Standard of Ur: Peace* (fig.5–10). The work is a mosaic-like panel of shell and colored stones. Notice the carefully spaced figures. This is very different from the haphazard placement of figures in Paleolithic art.

5–11 This instrument was buried with its owner to provide music for him in the afterlife. It is related to the modern guitar.
Lyre, about 2600 BC, Sumerian. Wood, overlaid with silver, shell and colored stones, 38 1/2" (98 cm) high, Royal Cemetery at Ur. British Museum, London.

Sumerian kings and queens were buried in the tombs in all their finery, together with their servants (who were killed so they could accompany their royal masters into the next world) and their palace or temple furnishings. Some of these objects show marvelous workmanship. Among them is an exquisite lyre made of wood overlaid with silver, shell and colored stone (fig.5–11).

Though not found at Ur, the *Praying Nobleman* (fig.5–12) typifies the Sumerian depiction of the human form. Cut from a solid block, the figure is cylindrical and very simplified. Arms and legs have the roundness of pipes. The long skirt is straight. Notice the overly large eyes, which Sumerians believed were the windows to the soul. We are reminded of how humans have always perceived the power of the eye. Even today we are told to respect people who "look you straight in the eye" and to be wary of people with "shifty eyes."

5–12 The form of this figure is simplified and based on the cylinder.
Praying Nobleman, about 2600 BC, Sumerian. Alabaster, 14 1/4" (36 cm) high. The Nelson-Atkins Museum of Art, Kansas City, Missouri.

The Cultural Evolution of Mesopotamia

In about 2300 BC, a Semitic-speaking people, the Akkadians, moved in from the north and conquered the Sumerians. Although they tried to dominate the entire world, their rule was not long-lasting, and the Sumerians gradually regained their self-rule. The most important of the New Sumerian rulers was *Gudea of Lagash.* Many statues of Gudea still survive. The one shown here (fig.5–13) is carved in diorite, a very hard, imported black stone. The pose is relaxed and worshipful. The muscles and facial features are sculpted carefully.

After several centuries of warfare, the Babylonians emerged in 1700 BC

5–13 About twenty statues of Gudea have been found. They depict him seated or standing with hands tightly clasped. This fragment probably was part of a standing figure.
Gudea of Lagash, about 2255 BC, Neo-Sumerian. Diorite with traces of gilt, 29 1/2" (74 cm) high. British Museum, London.

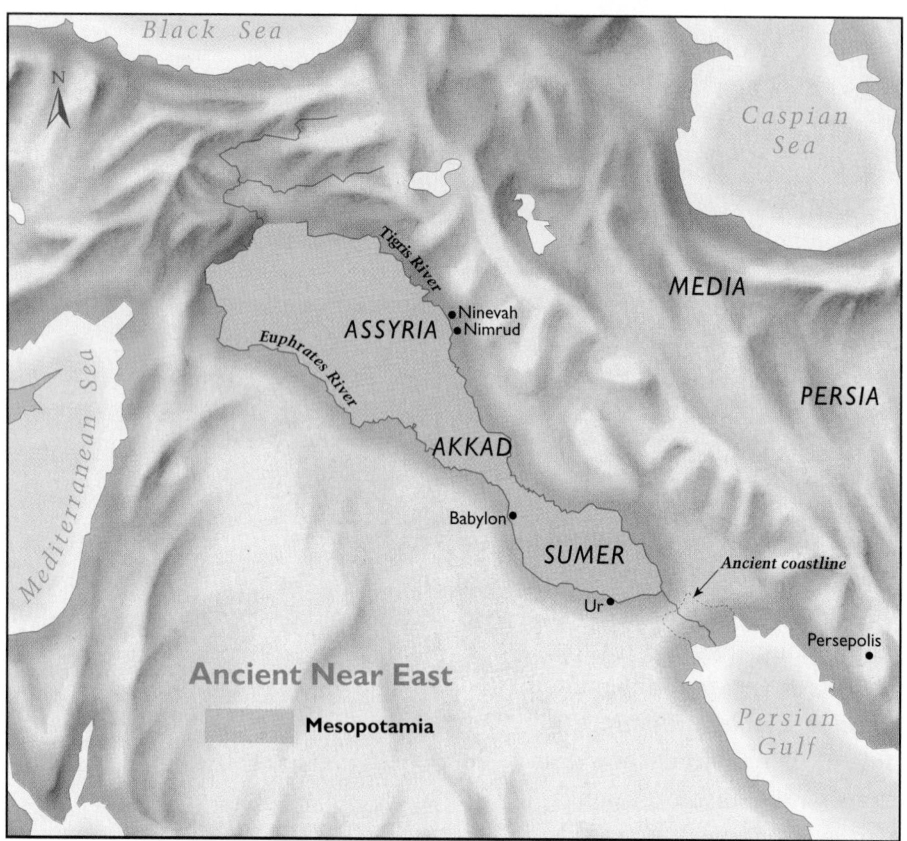

Protected by mountains and nourished by two large rivers, the area once known as Mesopotamia provided an ideal environment for a thriving culture. Why do you suppose the coastline of the Persian Gulf has changed over the years?

5–15 The Assyrians and the Sumerians had very different ideas about how to portray people. Compare this low relief sculpture to the *Praying Nobleman.*
Winged Genius, about 875 BC, Assyrian. Alabaster, 7' 9" (236 cm) high, The Palace of Ashurnasirpal II. Los Angeles County Museum of Art, gift of Anna Bing Arnold.

World Cultural Timeline

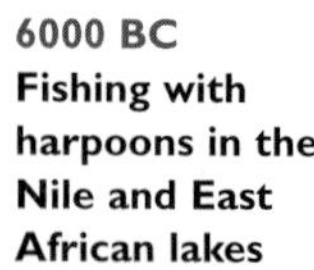

6000 BC
Fishing with harpoons in the Nile and East African lakes

5000 BC
Rice cultivation established, China

4000 BC
Village planning begins, China

3300 BC
Chili peppers domesticated, Mexico

5–14 Although these figures are in relief, the cylindrical forms seem to have great volume.
Stele of Hammurabi (upper part), about 1760 BC. Basalt, approx. 28" (71 cm) high, from Susa. Louvre, Paris.

as the masters of Mesopotamia. Their first leader was *Hammurabi*, a powerful figure, who composed a generally humane code of laws. The code of Hammurabi was inscribed on a black basalt ***stele***, or upright slab. Above the code is a relief sculpture of Hammurabi before the seated sun god (fig.5–14). It is clear that this encounter must relate to the creation of the code of laws.

The Hittites defeated the Babylonians in 1595 BC and, in turn, were overrun by a succession of warring peoples. About 900 BC, Mesopotamia was overwhelmed by the powerful Assyrians who descended on the plains from the north. They expanded their control as far away as Egypt and built marvelous palaces in the northern parts of the plain. Stone from nearby mountains was used to line these huge structures. The walls, carved in ***low relief***, showed mythical figures and the exploits of the kings (fig.5–15). The sculptors were superb craftspeople who could create a feeling of depth on a very shallow surface (fig. 5–16).

Sidelight

Hanging Gardens of Babylon

Picture it: A splendid kingdom with a huge ziggurat at its center and a royal palace overhung with luxuriant gardens. This was the fabulous city of Babylon, capital of Babylonia. It was ruled between 604–562 BC by King Nebuchadnezzar II, the greatest ruler of the late Babylonian empire.

Nebuchadnezzar II is most often remembered as the builder of The Hanging Gardens of Babylon, one of the Seven Wonders of the World. Built within the walls of the royal palace, the gardens did not actually "hang." Instead they rose into the air in a series of terraced roof gardens filled with flowers, shrubs and trees. They appeared as a miracle of greenery within a desert city. The terraces were irrigated by water pumped from the Euphrates River. It is believed that King Nebuchadnezzar II built the gardens to console his wife, Amytis, because she missed the mountains and greenery of her homeland, Media, in Persia. Babylon itself was flat and sunbaked.

Greek and Roman writers described how the terraces were lined with reeds, bitumen and lead so that there would be no seepage. The historian Diodorus Siculus wrote about the gardens in the first century BC and described them in the following manner: "This garden was 400 feet square, and the ascent up to it was as to the top of a mountain."

5–17 Stone was used for the gateways, stairs, large columns and platforms. Small columns and the roof were made of wood. The walls were constructed of brick.
Audience Hall of Darius and Xerxes, about 500 BC. Persepolis, Iran.

In 539 BC, the Persians brought an end to the Assyrian empire. Under King Darius, they built huge palaces such as the one at Persepolis (fig.5–17, 5–b). Huge, magnificent spaces had wooden ceilings supported by great columns. Atop each of the one hundred columns in a huge central room was a pair of sculpted bulls, the symbol of power (fig.5–18). Although carved from limestone, the bulls were probably covered with silver, gold leaf and lapis lazuli.

The Persians remained dominant in this area until Alexander the Great toppled them in 331 BC, thus uniting the Greek culture with the one that had slowly developed in the land between two rivers—Mesopotamia.

World Cultural Timeline

3000 BC
Silk first produced, China

2500–1500 BC
Grid pattern city built at Mohenjo-Daro, Indus Valley

2000 BC
Ice cream invented, China

3000 BC
Mummification practiced in S. America and Africa

2000 BC
First temple-pyramids built, Peru

5–16 The Assyrians depicted the hunting of big animals, especially lions, to show the power they and their kings had over nature. *Dying Lioness,* about 650 BC. Limestone, height of lion 13 3/4" (35 cm), from Nineveh (Assyria). British Museum, London.

5–18 Two of these bulls facing opposite directions formed the capital of a Persian column. *Bull capital,* about 518–460 BC, Persian. Bituminous limestone, 28" x 30" x 12" (71.1 x 76.2 x 30.5 cm) high, Persepolis. The Nelson-Atkins Museum of Art, Kansas City, Missouri (Purchase: Nelson Trust) 50–14.

Lesson 5.2 Review

1 Why does so little remain of Sumerian architecture?

2 How was the function of a ziggurat reflected in its appearance?

3 Where were some of the finest works of art from the Sumerian period found? Describe the types of objects discovered.

4 Describe the palaces built by the Assyrians.

5 Re-read the description of the Persian palace at Persepolis on page 158. Imagine, or even sketch out, how it might have looked. What impression would the central room have made on a visitor?

5.3 Egypt

EGYPT, WITH ITS extraordinarily rich history, its glorious Nile River and its gigantic monuments to eternal life, has always been a source of fascination. Imagine living in an environment both protected from your enemies and fertile enough to produce a surplus of food. This was the situation in early Egypt.

Because of the extra food not everyone had to be a hunter or farmer and the small scattered communities living along the Nile River gradually developed into complex cultures. They learned to make bricks, to use sails on the water and wheels on land. There were many different kinds of professions available in the fast-growing cities and people became soldiers, judges, priests, scribes, engineers, merchants, laborers and, naturally, artists. From the earliest times (in the Pre-Dynastic period), Egyptian craftspeople were honored and their products admired.

In their protected environment, separated from the rest of the developing world, the Egyptians evolved a unique way of life and a style of art that remained almost unaffected for several thousand years.

The Egyptians enjoyed living in their Nile-centered homeland so much that they wished to live forever. This desire for a happy eternity (afterlife) led to a prolific development of tomb art and architecture. Historians owe much of their knowledge of Egyptian society to these monuments and their contents. The god-king (Pharaoh) was buried in his tomb along with food, servants, art and equipment to accompany him in his second life. Unlike humankind of today the early Egyptians believed with great conviction that you can take it with you.

Key Notes

- Geographic isolation allows Egyptian art and culture to remain constant for several thousand years.
- Strongly held belief in afterlife helps stimulate growth of all art forms.
- Pyramid evolves as elaborate tomb for Pharaohs.

Vocabulary

mastaba
step pyramid
frontal
pylon
hypostyle hall
register
descriptive perspective

Special Feature

The Great Pyramids

The first pyramids were constructed as successors to the low rectangular tombs, called ***mastabas***, built for the Pre-Dynastic kings. King Zoser, the most important ruler of the Third Dynasty, built the first pyramid. The king asked the architect Imhotep to build his memorial tomb on a rock ledge at Sakkara, west of Memphis. Imhotep, the first artist in history whose name is known, built a solid stone structure of six huge steps rising over twenty stories in the desert air. This ***step pyramid*** at Sakkara (fig.5–20) was the first huge stone structure built on earth, and the architect Imhotep was deified for his work. The time was about 2600 BC.

During the Fourth Dynasty, pyramid building reached a climax in the three Great Pyramids at Giza (fig.5–19). Hundreds of thousands of men, many of whom died in the effort, constructed these pyramids. The stones (some weighing over forty tons!) were floated on rafts across the Nile valley during flooding season and hauled to the edge

5–20 This pyramid began as a large mastaba. It was enlarged twice before taking its final stepped form. Imhotep, *Step pyramid of King Zoser*, about 2600 BC, 3rd dynasty. Sakkara.

5–19 Note the last remains of an outer layer of polished limestone at the top of the Pyramid of Chefren.
The Great Pyramids, about 2530–2470 BC, 4th dynasty. Giza.

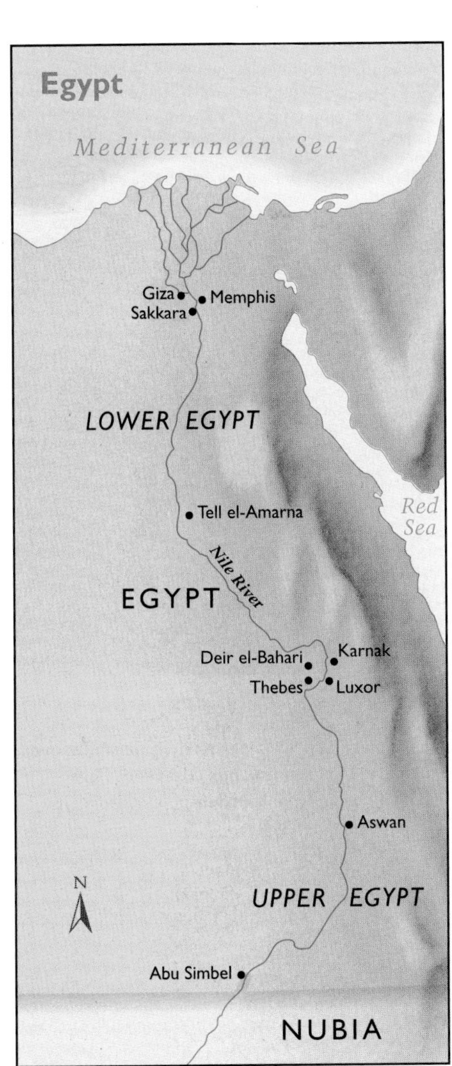

Flanked by desert to the left and mountains to the right, early Egyptian civilizations flourished on the banks of the longest river in the world.

of the desert. Only levers and rollers were employed by the workers, who constructed huge earthen ramps on which to raise the stones. This mammoth undertaking required tremendous organization and planning.

The largest of the Great Pyramids was built for Cheops about 2530 BC. It covers about 13 acres and is nearly 911 feet on each side of the base. It is over 55 stories high and was the tallest structure in the world, until modern skyscrapers pierced the skies some 4500 years later. Cheops' pyramid contains over two million blocks of limestone, most weighing over two-and-a-half tons. Originally it was faced with polished limestone to reflect the sun. The glare must have dazzled Egyptians for many miles around. The stones were cut so accurately that, even today, it is difficult to find a place where a knife blade can be forced between two surfaces. The burial chamber for the mummy of Cheops is located in the heart of the pyramid.

Besides all the possessions belonging to the dead that went into the tombs, the walls were covered with painted relief sculptures showing various activities of the persons buried there, as well as workers and relatives. The artist crammed every available space from floor to ceiling with some kind of sculpture, drawing or painting.

Two other pyramids were constructed at the same site as the Pyramid of Cheops, one for Chefren (2500 BC) and one for Mycerinus (2470 BC). Many smaller pyramids surrounded the three Great Pyramids. The Great Pyramids were all guarded by the Great Sphinx, a figure 240 feet in length, carved from the rocky ledge (fig.5–d). With the body of a lion and head of Chefren, it sat with great majesty for centuries, only to be damaged by vandalism and the sandblasting winds of the Sahara.

5–21 Mycerinus built the third and smallest of the Great Pyramids at Giza.
Mycerinus and His Queen, about 2470 BC, 4th dynasty. Slate, 56" (142 cm) high, Giza. Museum of Fine Arts, Boston

Old Kingdom

The statues unearthed in and near the great pyramids are of three types: standing, seated and sitting on the floor. The carving of the standing figures of *Mycerinus and His Queen* (fig.5–21) was cut from a single block of slate. To create the statue, the artist first drew the standing couple on all four sides of the block and then began carving toward the center. The resulting figures have a stylized and formal appearance. Arms are rigid, faces look straight ahead, and each left foot is slightly forward. There are no open spaces piercing the block; arms and legs are attached, or engaged to adjoining surfaces. Their pose is called ***frontal*** because both figures are facing and looking straight ahead. Although the faces are sculpted to describe some of the individual features of the king and queen, the bodies are stylized. They are ideal bodies and not accurate depictions of the king and queen.

The seated sculpture of *Katep and His Wife* (fig.5–22) was carved from limestone. Like other sculpture of its type, it was painted for added realism. Few Egyptian sculptures have survived with their paint intact. Here, too, the poses are frontal and the figures are stylized. Frontality and stylization are characteristics found in most Egyptian art. Katep was a nobleman, not a king, and the sculpture is an example of non-official art. The eyes are painted on, whereas the eyes of Pharaohs often contain stones or inlaid quartz.

The *Seated Scribe* (fig.5–23) sits cross-legged on the floor and is ready and eager to transcribe a message. The pose is idealized but the face is carved to appear realistic. Like artists and craftspeople, scribes who could write the language held honored positions in Egypt.

Middle Kingdom

The Old Kingdom was a period of anarchy and divided rule, in which various powerful lords controlled Egypt. In the Middle Kingdom, the princes of Thebes finally grew powerful enough to establish a comparatively peaceful rule that lasted for two dynasties (Eleventh and Twelfth).

5–22 The Egyptians painted their sculptures but little of the paint has survived. They favored realistic colors which came from colored earth.
Katep and His Wife, about 2563 BC, 4th dynasty. Painted limestone, 18 1/2" (47 cm) high, found near Memphis. British Museum, London.

Early Dynastic Period
3100–2686 BC
1st and 2nd Dynasties

First Intermediate Period
2150–2100 BC
7th–10th Dynasties

Second Intermediate Period
1700–1500 BC
14th–17th Dynasties

Dynasty Timeline

Old Kingdom
2686–2150 BC
3rd–6th Dynasties

Middle Kingdom
2100–1700 BC
11th–13th Dynasties

New Kingdom
c. 1500–1085 BC
18th–20th Dynasties

5–24 What characteristics does this temple have in common with a ziggurat and the Audience Hall at Persepolis (fig.5–17)?
Funerary Temple of Queen Hatshepsut, at Deir el-Bahari, about 1480 BC, 18th dynasty.

Architecture shifted from pyramids to the construction of funerary temples built near Thebes. These were designed to hold the mummies of the rulers and were constructed so that part was cut into the cliff and part was built outside. The temple built by Queen Hatshepsut (fig.5–24), although constructed later, was built according to these Middle Kingdom architectural styles.

Art continued to flourish in the Middle Kingdom, with craftspeople still holding an honored position in society. Many models carved throughout the country's history provide an excellent idea of Egyptian life and culture. Craftspeople carved wood into figures, boats, weapons and other items. The carvings were painted to create an illusion of reality. The wooden funerary barge (fig.5–25) is typical of boats that were buried with the dead, to be used as transportation in the afterlife. The mummy, which lies beneath the canopy, is accompanied by two women mourners, a priest and the helmsman. The painted eye at the front of the barge would help guide the craft without mishap.

The Second Intermediate Period followed the Middle Kingdom. Egypt was invaded and ruled by outsiders for 150 years. During this time, there was no harmony in the land. These outside rulers, however, did introduce Egypt to such things as the horse, chariots, wheels and weapons of war.

5–23 The Egyptians honored craftspersons and held those who could write in high esteem. At first the position of scribe was held only by the sons of Pharaohs.
Seated Scribe, about 2400 BC, 5th dynasty. Painted limestone, 21" (53 cm) high, Sakkara. The Louvre, Paris.

5–25 This barge was put in a tomb to provide its owner with transportation in the afterlife. What is happening on the barge?
Funerary Barge, about 1800 BC, 12th dynasty. Polychromed wood, 31" (79 cm) long. British Museum, London.

New Kingdom

About 1567 BC the princes of Thebes overthrew these invaders and established the New Kingdom. The New Kingdom, which began with the Eighteenth Dynasty, was a golden age in Egypt's history. More powerful than ever, Egypt became an empire and controlled lands far beyond its own borders. Not only did the kingdom flourish, but artists and architects grew in skill and creative expression. This revival in art covers a vast range of styles, from rigid and traditional approaches to brilliant inventiveness. Huge monuments were built, but tiny decorative figures also were carved.

One of the outstanding architectural works to survive is the funerary temple of Queen Hatshepsut (fig.5–24). As mentioned, the temple was built according to an architectural style first developed during the Middle Kingdom. Erected in 1480 BC the temple is partially cut into the cliffs at Deir el Bahari. Made of terraced walls, colonnades, sculptured reliefs, passageways and large open terraces, it blends harmoniously with the towering cliffs above. Egyptian rulers began constructing their tombs as soon as they were crowned, and Hatshepsut was no different. The Queen spent much of her reign constructing the temple, often strapping a false beard to her chin and wearing men's clothing when she visited the site.

All the great Egyptian structures we have examined so far have been associated with tombs and burial. But during the Eighteenth Dynasty, temples were created specifically for the worship of gods and the homes of priests. Among the greatest was the Temple of Amun at Karnak (figs.5–26, 5–27). Here a huge complex of buildings included ***pylons***, or entranceways, courtyards, a hypostyle hall and minor halls, chambers and passages.

The ***hypostyle hall*** was the most dramatic structure, consisting of 135 columns that created a forest-like feeling. There were 16 rows across the front alone. The central columns were about 69 feet high and were capped with open-flower capitals. The other capitals were in the shape of lotus buds. The columns were carved from top to bottom with relief sculptures and then painted. Stone lintels were placed atop the columns to create a sheltering roof. The higher central columns made it possible to include windows that flooded the interior with light. Because the lintel stones were of such great weight, the columns needed to be kept close together to prevent the stone slabs from breaking. Any such structure, with many columns supporting the roof (and not much open space inside), is called a hypostyle hall.

2000 BC
Iron first used for tools and weapons in the Middle East

900 BC
Chavin-style artwork produced, Peru

World Cultural Timeline

1876 BC
First recorded eclipse, China

500–200 BC
Earliest known sub-Saharan sculpture created, Nok culture, Africa

5–26 The hypostyle hall has a forest of columns. Compare it to the Audience Hall at Persepolis (fig.5–17).
Temple of Amun, Karnak, about 1530 BC.

5–27 The Egyptians used no cement. This detail shows how the huge stones were stacked one on top of the other to create a column.
Temple of Amun, Karnak, about 1530 BC, detail (fig.5–17).

Sidelight

Mummification

Because the ancient Egyptians believed that the dead lived on in the next world, they needed a way to preserve their bodies. A system of embalming was developed to help retain forever the form a body had in life. A mummy is an embalmed body that has been preserved for thousands of years. The process varied through the ages, but it always involved removing the internal organs, treating the body with resin, and wrapping it in linen bandages. In a later period the internal organs were treated and replaced inside the body.

According to ancient texts, it took seventy days to embalm and mummify a body. First, a hook was used to remove the brain through a nostril. The internal organs, except the heart and kidneys, were taken out through an incision in the side of the body. Then the body was coated in a salt-like chemical compound of sodium carbonate called natron. The natron drew out moisture and dried out the tissues in about forty days. Then the empty abdomen was packed with linen pads and sometimes with sawdust. The entire body was rubbed with spices and resin. Finally, the body was carefully wrapped in many layers of tightly wound linen bandages. It may have taken as long as fifteen days to wrap the body. Then the mummy was placed in a coffin.

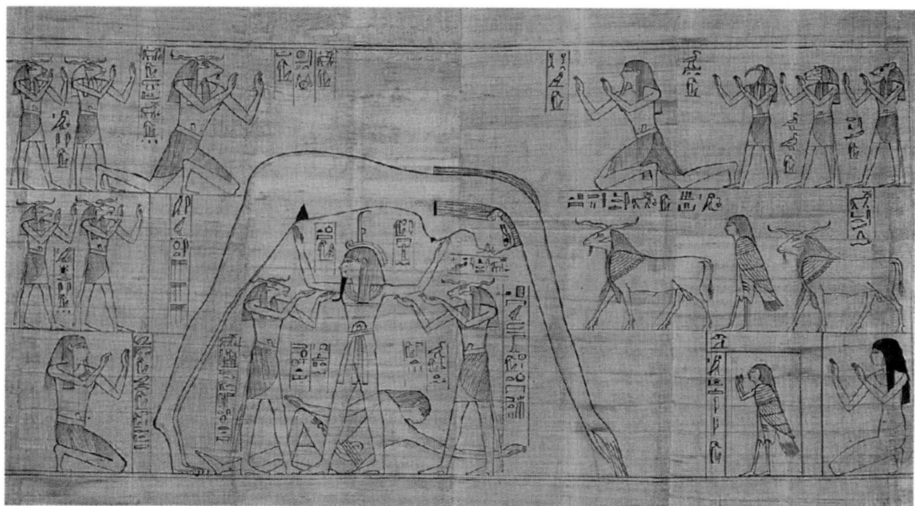

5–28 Identify the characters in this manuscript. Is there a relationship to line drawings you saw earlier, such as those at Lascaux?
Greenfield Papyrus, about 1080 BC, 21st dynasty. 19" (49 cm) high, British Museum, London.

Many huge temples and complexes were built during the New Kingdom. But other arts also flourished. The *Greenfield Papyrus* (fig.5–28) is a painted papyrus that reveals some important characteristics of Egyptian art in all ages. In the center, Shu (god of atmosphere) raises the body of Nut (goddess of sky). His arms are supported by two ram-headed gods, while Geb (god of earth) lies on the ground. In the lower right corner is the daughter of a high priest and her soul (human-headed bird). This papyrus was drawn specially for the high priest's daughter.

The drawing is sensitive and beautifully done. The figures are placed in ***registers*** (layers). Many of the gods are in the form of animals. Notice that the figures are shown so the legs, arms and faces are in profile, but the upper body is turned toward the viewer. The face is in profile, but the eye is looking directly at the viewer. ***Descriptive perspective*** also is used. This means that the more important figures are shown larger than the less important ones. The careful design and placement of figures to fill almost all available space is also characteristic of Egyptian painting and wall sculpture.

The tomb painting of a banquet scene (fig.5–29) shows guests being entertained by two female dancers, a musician, and three singers who are clapping in rhythm. The words of the song are shown directly above the singers. The guests are painted in the register directly above. (Only their feet and legs can been seen.) Is there something in this painting that is very un-Egyptian? Several figures are shown facing frontward. They are not shown in profile. The artist was attempting to paint realistically, rather than stylistically. Usually the artists worked with formulas that they knew very well, and did not depict people as they actually looked.

Stylization characterizes most of Egypt's art. However, there was a time during the reign of Akhenaton (Eighteenth Dynasty) when realism became dominant. Akhenaton stressed a realistic approach to art. The sculpture of his wife, Nefertiti, is a superb example (fig.5–30). The portrait is delicate and sensitive and shows a marvelous knowledge of the structure of the human head. In fact, Akhenaton 's artists took molds from human faces and bodies to study the structure and create carvings of anatomical perfection. The sculpture of Nefertiti, a most beautiful woman, was left abandoned in the artist's studio after the death of the king.

Akhenaton built the largest private home in the world at that time at Tel el Amarna. He changed his name and declared a single new supreme god in Aten, the sun. Most importantly, he declared himself Aten's representative on earth and a god himself. Akhenaton's successor was his nine-year-old relative, Tutankhaten. The young king was guided by advisers to move the capital back to Thebes, to reinstate the worship of Amen, and to change his name to Tutankhamen. Although

5–29 You are familiar with how the Egyptians usually depicted people. How are these figures different?
Dancing Girls at a Banquet, about 1400 BC, 18th dynasty. Wall painting, portion shown is 24" (61 cm) high, Thebes. British Museum, London.

Window in Time

The Search for the Tomb of Tutankhamen

Obsessed with finding the tomb of Tutankhamen, who had reigned more than 3,200 years before, archaeologist Howard Carter began excavating in the Valley of Kings in Egypt in the early 1900s. Thirty-three royal tombs had already been discovered in the Valley, but every one of them had been ransacked by robbers. Most experts believed that the Valley had yielded all its secrets. But Carter disagreed.

Carter believed that the tomb was located in one small area of the Valley that was filled with rubble from the excavations of other tombs. Archaeologists had not bothered to dig beneath this rubble. But even though the area was small, the task was still daunting. Just to reach the floor of the Valley, men would have to remove tens of thousands of tons of rock and sand.

After years of searching Carter had still not found anything. His patron, Lord Carnarvon, informed Carter that he would no longer renew the excavation concession from the Egyptian government. With time running out Carter decided to dig around a line of workers' huts that stood near the entrance to the tomb of Ramses VI.

By the beginning of November in 1922, the trench had been dug to bedrock. On November 4, the beginning of a staircase was discovered. At the bottom of the staircase was a door and on the door were affixed the seals of the royal necropolis—the jackal god Anubis above nine defeated foes. Carter filled in the stairway again and cabled Carnarvon in London.

Within three weeks Carnarvon arrived and the real discovery could begin. But once the door was fully uncovered the telltale marks of holes cut by thieves were revealed in the upper part of the door. The door gave onto a rubble-filled tunnel. At the end of the tunnel was another door, again marred by thieves' holes. Carter drilled a hole into the door himself and by candlelight peered in. To his great excitement, Carter was looking at the Antechamber of Tutankhamen's tomb. Robbers had indeed been there but fortunately the tomb had not been ransacked.

All the treasures, everything the eighteen-year-old king might have needed on his journey to the other world, were inside the Antechamber. The room was heaped with statues, thrones, chairs, boxes, ornaments and chests. Gold was everywhere. Clothes, bottles and paintings were also found.

***Mask of King Tutankhamen*, 1352 BC, 18th dynasty. Gold with precious stones and glass, life-size, Thebes. Egyptian Museum, Cairo.**

Some months later Carter was ready to open the Burial Chamber. As soon as he had made a large enough hole he inserted an electric torch. A wall of solid gold greeted his astonished eyes. It was one side of a shrine covering Tutankhamen's sarcophagus. The great carved stone sarcophagus in the Burial Chamber rested inside a series of four nested wooden cases covered with gold leaf. Three mummy-shaped coffins nested inside the rectangular stone coffin. The innermost coffin was solid gold. Inside was the extraordinary polished gold funerary mask covering Tutankhamen's head and shoulders.

But only Carter saw the magnificent mask. Lord Carnarvon had died in Cairo less than five months after the tomb was opened. He died of blood poisoning from a mosquito bite that had become infected. This only confirmed the rumors that an ancient curse would fall upon anyone who disturbed a Pharaoh's resting place. However, Carter, the real "disturber," died peacefully at home in England at age sixty-five.

5–30 Ideas of beauty change with time. Compare this woman to the *Venus of Willendorf* (fig.5–4).
Queen Nefertiti, about 1360 BC, 18th dynasty. Painted limestone, 20" (51 cm) high, El Amarna. Agyptische Museum, Berlin.

5–31 Ramses II erected colossal statues of himself all over his kingdom. These are carved from living rock.
Ramses II, about 1257 BC, 19th dynasty. Sculpted from cliff, each about 69 1/3' (21 m) high, Abu Simbel, Egypt.

he ruled for only nine years, he is Egypt's most famous king because of the wealth of art objects found in his tomb (fig.5–a). Over the years, Egypt's kings realized that the large burial structures only invited thievery of their buried treasures—crimes that had been going on for centuries. Now the rulers were secretly cutting their burial chambers into rock cliffs and disguising the entrances. Even these were found and rifled—all except one: that of Tutankhamen, whose tomb entrance was hidden by the debris from a later tomb.

With the end of the Eighteenth Dynasty, art again returned to traditional stylization. Ramses II (Nineteenth Dynasty) ruled for sixty-seven years and had a multitude of statues of himself placed throughout the land. His temple at Abu Simbel is the most famous (fig.5–31). Four figures of Ramses are carved directly out of the standing cliff. The temple itself recedes into the stone wall. Descriptive perspective is used to express the size, and corresponding importance, of the queen and other relatives.

The construction of the Aswan Dam in recent years caused this site to be flooded permanently. To preserve it, the entire temple and the four mammoth sculptures were cut apart, lifted to the plain above and reassembled under the direction of American engineers. Such an effort clearly shows the importance the rest of the world places on the art of ancient Egypt.

Lesson 5.3 Review

1 Explain how the Nile River influenced the development of Egyptian culture.
2 Who was Imhotep? What is his importance in the history of art?
3 Why do we know so much about Egyptian society and art?
4 Select an example of Old Kingdom sculpture illustrated in this chapter. How is it typical of the sculpture created during that period?
5 Examine the funerary barge illustrated in fig.5–25. What does it tell us about Egyptian life at that time?
6 What were the two most important types of Egyptian architecture? How were they similar? How did they differ?

Primary Source

The Code of Hammurabi King of Babylon, c.1770 BC.

The Code of Hammurabi King of Babylon was written about 1770 BC. In it we find rules about what kinds of punishment were to be given for injuries suffered by innocent victims.

#188 If an artisan takes a son for adoption and teaches him his handicraft, one may not bring claim for him.

#189 If he does not teach him his handicraft, that adopted son may return to his father's house.

#195 If a son strikes his father, they shall cut off his fingers.

#200 If a man knocks out a tooth of a man of his own rank, they shall knock out his tooth.

#202 If a man strikes the person of a man who is his superior, he shall receive sixty strokes with an ox-tail whip in public.

#209 If a man strikes a man's daughter and brings about a miscarriage, he shall pay ten shekels of silver for her miscarriage.

#213 If he strikes the female slave of a man and brings about a miscarriage, he shall pay two shekels of silver.

#218 If a physician operates on a man for a severe wound with a bronze lancet and causes the man's death; or opens an abscess (in the eye) of a man with a bronze lancet and destroys the man's eye, they shall cut off his fingers.

#228 If a builder builds a house for a man and completes it, (that man) shall give him two shekels of silver per SAR (a measurement) of the house as his wage.

#233 If a builder builds a house for a man and does not make its construction meet the requirements and a wall falls in, that builder shall strengthen that wall at his own expense.

Chapter Review

Review

1 Why is it that children were the first modern persons to encounter the cave paintings at Lascaux and Altamira?

2 What color pigments were used by the artists at Lascaux?

3 What is a lintel?

4 What human feature dominates Sumerian figure sculpture? Why?

5 How many years ago was the Pyramid of Cheops built?

Interpret

1 Compare the arrangement of figures on the Standard of Ur (fig.5–10) with the placement of figures on the walls of Lascaux (fig.5–1).

2 The art of Egypt is often described as stylized. There is a period during the 18th Dynasty, however, when the king, Akhenaton, encouraged realism in art. Compare the portrait of Akhenaton's wife, Nefertiti (fig.5–30) with the figures of Mycerinus and his queen (fig.5–21). Keep in mind the working methods of the artist of each work.

3 You have been introduced to a number of architectural monuments. Select three and describe how they relate to their environment.

Other Tools for Learning

Maps

Note the clustering of towns and cities on the maps of the ancient Near East and Egypt. Discuss the reasons for these clusters.

Timelines

The timelines within this chapter cover 25,000 years—an enormous span of time. They include events that happened all over the world. List three of the most interesting or surprising pieces of information that you can find on the timelines. Explain why you have chosen them.

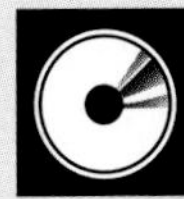

Electronic Research

CD-ROM drive: Electronic Encyclopedia (e.g., *New Grolier Multimedia* and *Microsoft Encarta*)

Explore further one of the many ancient sites introduced in this chapter. Make an effort to find more information about how it was used and who used it. Also note any differences in dates that you come across. Very often scholars disagree on the precise dating of sites as old as those discussed in this chapter.

Activity 1

Home Town Sculpture

Materials

locally available material, could be:
clay
wood
rock
scrap metal or wire
cardboard
optional: modeling clay

Take a look. Review the following artwork in this book:

- Fig. 5–4, *Venus of Willendorf*, about 25,000 BC. Limestone.
- Fig. 5–5, *Bison*, about 10,000 BC. Reindeer antler.
- Fig. 5–12, *Praying Nobleman*, about 2600 BC, Sumerian. Wood.
- Fig. 5–13, *Gudea of Lagash*, about 2255 BC, Neo-Sumerian. Diorite.
- Fig. 5–21, *Mycerinus and His Queen*, about 2470 BC, 4th dynasty. Slate.

Think about it. The size of sculpture often is determined by the materials artists have on hand. Mesopotamia lacked a ready supply of stone and artists worked on small pieces. Egypt, on the other hand, had an unlimited supply, and its artists carved gigantic figures. Is this still true in our contemporary world? What sculptural materials are readily available where you live?

Do it.

- Locate a material in your local area that is suitable for sculpture.
- Examine the material carefully. What form from nature comes to mind? Perhaps you imagine an animal like the *Bison* (fig.5–5) or a figure like the *Praying Nobleman* (fig.5–12). As you study the material, consider its surface texture and natural form.
- Do a few sketches of the image you would like to sculpt. It might be appropriate to sculpt a downsized model in clay before tackling the image at full size.
- With your teacher's guidance, create your sculpture using the necessary tools. *Stylize* the form by simplifying it and eliminating detail while retaining the beauty of the material from which it is made.

Check it.

- Does the subject you chose suit the material you used?
- Have you simplified the image but still captured the spirit of it?
- Have you taken time to finish the surface in a way that communicates good craftsmanship?

Helpful Hint: As you work, continually view the piece from all angles.

Activity 2

Weathering Time

Take a look. Look for artwork dating any time before the birth of Christ (BC) in the early chapters of this book. Note what materials they are made from and where they were found.

Think about it.

- How has climate helped to preserve ancient works of art for long periods of time?
- Would these ancient objects have endured to the present if the original cultures had been located in tropical jungles? Support your answer.
- Which climates are most favorable for the preservation of art and where in the world do they occur?
- Where have some of the more successful archaeological discoveries been made?

Do it.

Choose an area of the world which has a climate that would have preserved its ancient works.

- Research this region to find examples of pieces dating from 4000 BC to 500 BC.
- Prepare a presentation to your class, which could include photographs, samples or sketches.
- Be ready to draw comparisons between the culture you have studied and those in this chapter.

Check it.

- Did you find and use relevant examples of work that supported your ideas?
- Have you listed your sources in a bibliography?

Helpful Hint: Refer often to a good map! Become familiar with key places where art has been found around the world.

Additional Activities

- Write an essay discussing the importance of art in the development of the Egyptian civilization. Include ideas such as historical documentation, visual history, art as decoration, art as writing, celebration, family history, cultural documentation, symbolism, religion, life after death. Why were artists considered essential to Egyptian culture and life?
- Find a large open area where you can mark off the dimensions of Cheops' pyramid. Outline the shape with string, or position classmates along the edges. Make a sketch to show its size in comparison to your school campus. Ask teachers of computer technology or industrial design (or local architects) about software programs that would allow you to do this activity on the computer.

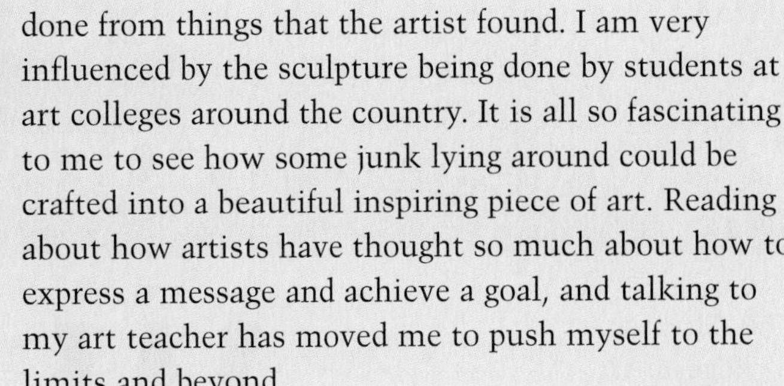

Jason Panneton

Age 17
W. T. Woodson High School
Annandale, Virginia
Favorite kinds of art: large, graffiti art; abstract
Favorite artists: Robert Rauschenberg, Hex, Al Held, any artist who sparks inspiration in me!
Activity 1, Home Town Sculpture

These pieces deal with creating a sculpture out of objects or junk or whatever else I found lying around. I was lucky enough to find a bag of blocks lying around in my garage. They were the perfect thing for me to use in doing a figurative series of sculptures.

I did a piece relating to human body parts. I wanted to do more with that idea, so I created three sculptures. The sculptures are a three-dimensional interpretation of the drawing.

I like the idea of creating sculpture from found objects. I have studied a lot of art where the art was done from things that the artist found. I am very influenced by the sculpture being done by students at art colleges around the country. It is all so fascinating to me to see how some junk lying around could be crafted into a beautiful inspiring piece of art. Reading about how artists have thought so much about how to express a message and achieve a goal, and talking to my art teacher has moved me to push myself to the limits and beyond.

I love the act of making the art. I love having my hands and mind work together. There is nothing like the little spark of happiness I feel when I draw a line that is just right or when I do a self-portrait that really expresses a feeling. So to all you young artists out there, my advice is to push yourself beyond the easy stuff, stay true to yourself as an artist, and WORK HARD!

After constructing a figure from wooden blocks found in his environment, Jason adds bands of color.

Posing Figures, 1994. Wood, cardboard and paint, 17" high (43 cm). Also *Body Parts* oil pastel with *Body Parts* sculptures.

6 Greek and Roman Art

In This Chapter...

While the Mesopotamian and Egyptian cultures prospered, two distinct cultures, the Minoans and the Mycenaeans, emerged along the Aegean Sea. The Minoans, who made their home on the island of Crete, created art that portrayed a relaxed life of luxury. On the mainland of Greece, the Mycenaeans fought to survive and left behind fortresses and monuments as proof of their struggle.

These Aegean cultures vanished, but they influenced the emergence of a great new culture in Greece which became the foundation of Western civilization. The Greeks strove for harmony and unity and placed human beings at the center of their culture. Much of their art focused on the idealized human form. It was in this form that the Greeks found the ultimate expression of beauty and harmony.

In the early 700s BC, the first Roman city-state began. It would grow to become the most powerful civilization in the Western world. The Romans created an empire which even today stands as a pinnacle of power and might.

Influenced greatly by the Greeks, the Romans made some of their greatest contributions in architecture. They were highly sophisticated, even by modern standards. They had fantastic public baths, luxurious houses, aqueducts that carried water all over the city, gigantic public arenas and marvelous bridges.

Greece and Rome provided the foundation upon which much of the art and architecture of the Western world is built. With every new generation, artists look back to see what lessons they can learn from the ancients.

6–a The Greeks often painted their sculpture, although little of the color remains today. Traces of paint can be seen on the hair of this figure.
Peplos Kore, about 530 BC. Marble, 4' (122 cm) high. Acropolis Museum, Athens.

Greek and Roman Art

1600 BC
Palace of Minos, the Labyrinth of Minotaur, Crete

1250 BC
Lion Gate, Mycenae

900 BC
Homer, *Iliad* and *Odyssey*

776 BC
First Olympic Games, Greece

700 BC
Greeks adopt alphabetic writing developed by Phoenicians

499–478 BC
Persian Wars

447–432 BC
Parthenon, Athens

386 BC
Plato founds Academy

356–323 BC
Expansion of Greek Empire under Alexander the Great

46 BC
12-month Roman calendar developed

0
Birth of Jesus Christ

72–80 AD
Colosseum, Rome

79 AD
Destruction of Pompeii

Our love of what is beautiful
does not lead to extravagance;
our love of things of the mind
does not make us soft.
Thucydides, Book II

The countries of Italy and Greece did not exist at the time of ancient Greece and Rome. They are shown on this map to provide points of reference.

6–b The Mycenaens excelled at the art of metalwork.
Vaphio Cup, one of two, see also fig.6–9.

6–c The Roman emperors frequently commissioned sculptural and architectural monuments to glorify their power and celebrate their victories.
Column of Trajan, detail (fig.6–43).

6–d Many Greek works of art were destroyed. A great deal is known about them, however, through Roman copies. This is a detail of a Roman copy (in mosaic) of a Greek painting.
Head of Alexander the Great, *The Battle of Issus*, detail (fig.6–29).

6.1 Aegean Art

While the civilizations in Egypt and Mesopotamia were flourishing, two distinct cultures developed along the Aegean Sea. One was on the island of Crete and is termed Minoan (after Minos, the Cretan king). The other was on the mainland of Greece at the city of Mycenae. For a long time both civilizations were considered mythological. They were known only through the *Iliad* by Homer. It was not until the late nineteenth century that these cities and their art were unearthed by archaeologists. These Aegean civilizations were the forerunners of Greek culture.

The Minoans were by far the richest of the Aegean civilizations. Bounded by the sea, the Cretans created a luxurious, relaxed way of life quite distinct from any other. Several "palace" centers developed on the island of Crete. The most important center was the huge complex at Knossos, called the Palace of Minos. The sprawling palace (fig.6–1) contained many rooms, running water, a sewage system, theater, storerooms (fig.6–2), terraces and elaborately decorated quarters for the rulers. Many ***frescoes*** (plaster wall paintings) decorated the interior of the palace. These frescoes provide a good idea of how these people lived.

The Mycenaeans were warriors instead of traders. They built citadels rather than pleasure palaces. Their hilltop fortresses were surrounded by walls of enormous stone blocks. The blocks were so large that later Greeks thought they were the work of the Cyclopes, a mythical race of one-eyed giants.

Key Notes

- Two distinct cultures, Minoan and Mycenaean, develop in the Aegean region.
- Minoan art is marked by a graceful ease and a delight in all forms of life.
- Mycenaean monuments reflect a protected and fortified environment.

Vocabulary
fresco

6–2 Storerooms housed jars of wine, grain, oil and honey.
View of jars in storeroom, Palace at Knossos, Crete.

Special Feature

Bull Dance Fresco

The Minoans and Mycenaeans appear to have had very different lifestyles. There is no specific historic reference that ties the two groups together. Both brought a remarkable vibrancy and extraordinary sense of beauty to their art.

These attributes are present in the *Bull Dance* (fig.6–3) fresco from the Minoan Palace of Knossos. It is the largest Minoan wall painting discovered so far. The fresco shows a ritual game in which the participants energetically vault over the bull's back. Two of the slim-waisted athletes are girls, denoted by their

lighter skin color. There are so many depictions of bulls in Minoan painting and sculpture that the bull undoubtedly was a sacred animal. It is clear that bull-vaulting had something to do with a religious custom. We see an echo of this custom in the Greek legend of the youths and maidens sacrificed to the minotaur.

There is a certain ambiguity to the fresco that prevents us from understanding exactly what is going on here. The artist has idealized the ritual by stressing its harmonious, playful aspect rather than trying to provide the viewer with a factual representation of the event.

No temple architecture has been found on Crete or in Mycenae. Objects related in some way to religion (such as the *Bull Dance* fresco) have been found. Often, however, these objects raise more questions than they answer.

6–1 The plan of this palace is so complex that it survived in Greek legend as the labyrinth of the Minotaur.
Palace at Knossos, Crete, about 1600–1400 BC.

6–3 The young vaulters in this mural may have been Minoan gymnasts.
Bull Dance, from the Palace at Knossos, about 1500 BC. Fresco, 31 1/2" (80 cm) high, including border. Archaeological Museum, Heraklion, Crete.

Minoan Art

Comfort and decoration were equally important in Minoan life. The facades of buildings appear to have been brightly colored. The plastered walls inside were painted red, yellow or blue. In the more important rooms there were figurative paintings and occasionally stucco reliefs. Unfortunately, only fragments of these works remain, but they clearly show the vigor and spontaneity of Minoan art. Minoan culture and art was greatly influenced by the sea. Minoan frescoes were characterized by lightness and freely shaped forms. The forms had a rhythmic quality inspired by the sea.

The lively spontaneity of Minoan art, so representative of their style of life, is portrayed beautifully in the Queen's Megaron in the palace of Knossos. Here, the elaborate frescoes painted on the plastered walls depict many aspects of Cretan life. There are processions and ceremonies. Images from nature appear, such as birds, animals and flowers. The sea and its creatures, such as dolphins, are also featured.

Minoan sculpture was small and, like the frescoes, probably decorated the living quarters of merchant rulers. The *Snake Goddess* (fig.6–4), carved from ivory and decorated with gold bands, may be the goddess of an unknown religion or simply a daring young woman playing with snakes.

Minoan pottery often was decorated with designs of plant and animal life. In the illustrated example, the octopus (fig.6–5) conforms so wonderfully with the contours of the vase that it seems to be floating in the open sea rather than painted on a hard, curving surface. The relief on the *Harvester Vase* (fig.6–6) brims with energy and life. Muscular men with scythes and rakes appear to be celebrating a harvest festival. Three singers, led by a fourth, have burst into song. So great is their enthusiasm that the leader's chest is swelled enough to show his ribs.

The Minoan civilization came to an abrupt halt. The people disappeared and no one really knows what happened. Perhaps future archaeologists will answer this question.

6–4 This poised young woman controls the snakes in what may have been a religious ritual.
Snake Goddess, about 1550 BC. Ivory and gold, 6" (16 cm) high, from Knossos. Museum of Fine Arts, Boston, gift of Mrs. W. Scott Fitz.

6–6 The artist of this relief has chosen to depict a joyous aspect of the human character.
Harvester Vase, about 1500 BC. Steatite, 4 1/2" (11 cm) wide, from Haiga Triada. Archaeological Museum, Herakleion.

6–5 Why do you think marine life was a favorite subject of Minoan artists?
Octopus Jar, about 1500 BC. 11" (28 cm) high, from Palaikastro. Archaeological Museum, Herakleion.

1600 BC
Colonization of the Pacific Islands

1500 BC
Spun cotton invented, India

1150 BC
Colossal basalt sculptures of human heads, Olmec Civilization, Mexico

World Cultural Timeline

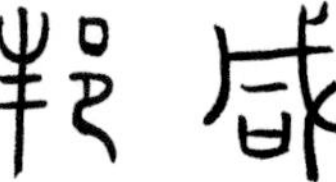

1200 BC
Pictograph writing system develops in China

6–7 These two lions flank a column which may represent the power of the Mycenaean king. Although the stone has been eroded with time, the straining muscles of the lions are still evident.
Lion Gate at Mycenae, about 1250 BC. Limestone relief sculpture, about 9 1/2' (3 m) high.

Mycenaean Art

The outer gateway of the citadel at Mycenae is called the *Lion Gate* (fig.6–7). It is topped by a huge, triangular-shaped, carved stone slab. Depicted on the stone are two majestic standing lions flanking a Minoan-type column. Notice the massive stone block that acts as a lintel over the opening. The other large blocks are cut to fit exactly together.

6–9 How does the artist make use of light and shadow to bring the relief to life?
Vaphio Cup, about 1500 BC. Gold, about 3 1/2" (9 cm) high, from Laconia. National Archaeological Museum, Athens.

In 1876, excavations at Mycenae uncovered beehive tombs of massive proportions and sunken royal graves. The graves contained a dazzling display of objects in gold, silver and other metals. The *Funeral Mask* (fig.6–8) is a thin sheet of beaten gold. It was probably intended to cover the face of a deceased ruler of about 1500 BC.

The *Vaphio Cups* (figs.6–9, 6–b) from a grave in Laconia are some of the most famous gold pieces found at Mycenae. The lively reliefs on these beautifully crafted works illustrate several ways the Mycenaeans captured wild bulls.

Recently, several ivory sculptures and some paintings have been uncovered. Still, little is known of the development of Mycenaean culture. Mycenaean history abruptly ended about 1100 BC when the Dorians invaded from the north.

By 1100 BC, the Bronze Age culture on the Greek mainland, attacked by various catastrophes, had collapsed. For the next four hundred years a dreary and subdued era swept Greece. Archaeological evidence for this period suggests material poverty and social insecurity on a grand scale. Gone was the joyful expression of the Minoans and the realistic art of the Mycenaeans.

6–8 At one time this mask was thought to be the death mask of King Agamemnon from Homer's *Iliad*.
Funeral mask, about 1500 BC. Beaten gold, about 12" (30 cm) high, from Royal Tombs, Mycenae. National Archaeological Museum, Athens.

Lesson 6.1 Review

1 Why did people suspect that the Minoan and Mycenaean civilizations had existed even before archaeologists discovered their ruins?
2 Describe the Palace of Knossos.
3 What is happening in the *Bull Dance* fresco? Of which contemporary Spanish sport does this remind you?
4 List some characteristics of Minoan frescoes.
5 Draw a sketch of the *Lion Gate at Mycenae*. Identify the lintel on your sketch.

6.2 Greek Art

HUMAN BEINGS were central to the Greek culture. They gave their gods human form. The Greek ideal was to create the perfect individual. This would be accomplished by achieving a perfect balance of intellectual and physical discipline. The Greeks considered the human body beautiful, perfectly balanced and harmonious. They made it the focal point of most of their painting and sculpture.

The key concepts of proportion, balance and unity were the driving force of many of the Greeks' achievements in architecture, mathematics, science, philosophy, poetry and architecture. Everything had its ideal form.

Greek artists worked in a cultural environment that encouraged art of all types. They were free to experiment as long as they worked toward the common goal of beauty and harmony. They even signed their works.

Vocabulary
contrapposto
frieze
pediment
architrave
cornice
metope
triglyph
entasis
caryatids
encaustic
amphora
hydria

Key Notes
- The human being was placed at the center of Greek culture.
- The Greeks encouraged all forms of art.
- Proportion, balance and unity were key Greek ideals.
- The human body was considered beautiful and perfectly proportioned.

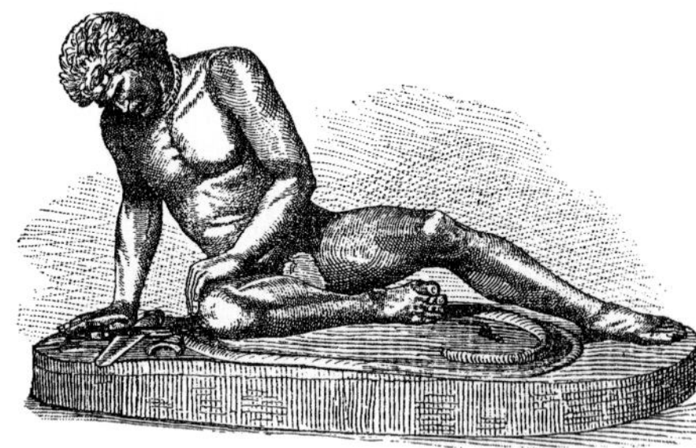

Major Periods in Greek Art

600–480 BC
The Archaic period

480–323 BC
The Classic Period

323–150 BC
Hellenistic period

Special Feature

The Kritios Boy

The development of Greek art is easily seen in its sculpture. Like Egyptian sculptures, early Greek figures were stylized. There is one sculpture that survives today, however, which shows us how artists began to move away from this rather restricted way of depicting the human form. The figure has been attributed to the Athenian sculptor Kritios and has come to be known as the *Kritios Boy* (figs.6–10, 6–11). The first important point about the *Kritios Boy* is that he really stands. His back leg is not bound to a block for balance. Openings are seen between arms and side. Previously, the figure was supported by part of the original stone block. The *Kritios Boy* stands free.

Notice how the right hip drops down and inward. The knee of the forward leg is lower than that of the other leg. The weight rests mainly on the left leg. The faint S-curve of the body causes a subtle sense of movement. The artist had grasped the concept of weight shift. Thus, the *Kritios Boy* stands in a relaxed, natural stance—as we would in the same pose.

The Italian word, ***contrapposto*** (counterpose), is used to describe this position where the engaged leg is in the forward position. Showing a truly relaxed body was a very important discovery. For only when the Greek sculptor had mastered the relaxed body could he begin to show the body in motion. Movement existed in Greek art prior to this, but it was very mechanical and inflexible. The *Kritios Boy* gives us a sense of the vitality that infuses our own bodies. The sculpture truly has come to life.

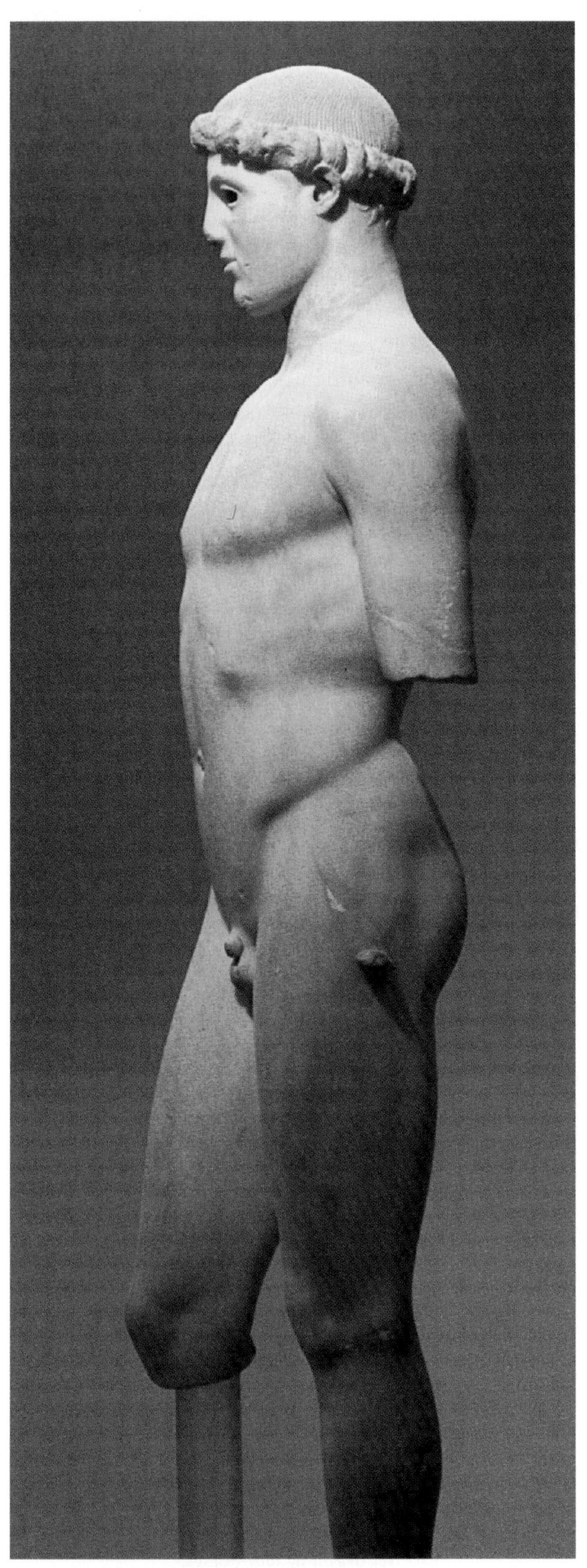

6–10 To better understand the distribution of weight represented in this figure, stand up and mimic its pose.
Kritios Boy, about 480 BC. Marble, 34" (86 cm) high. Acropolis Museum, Athens.

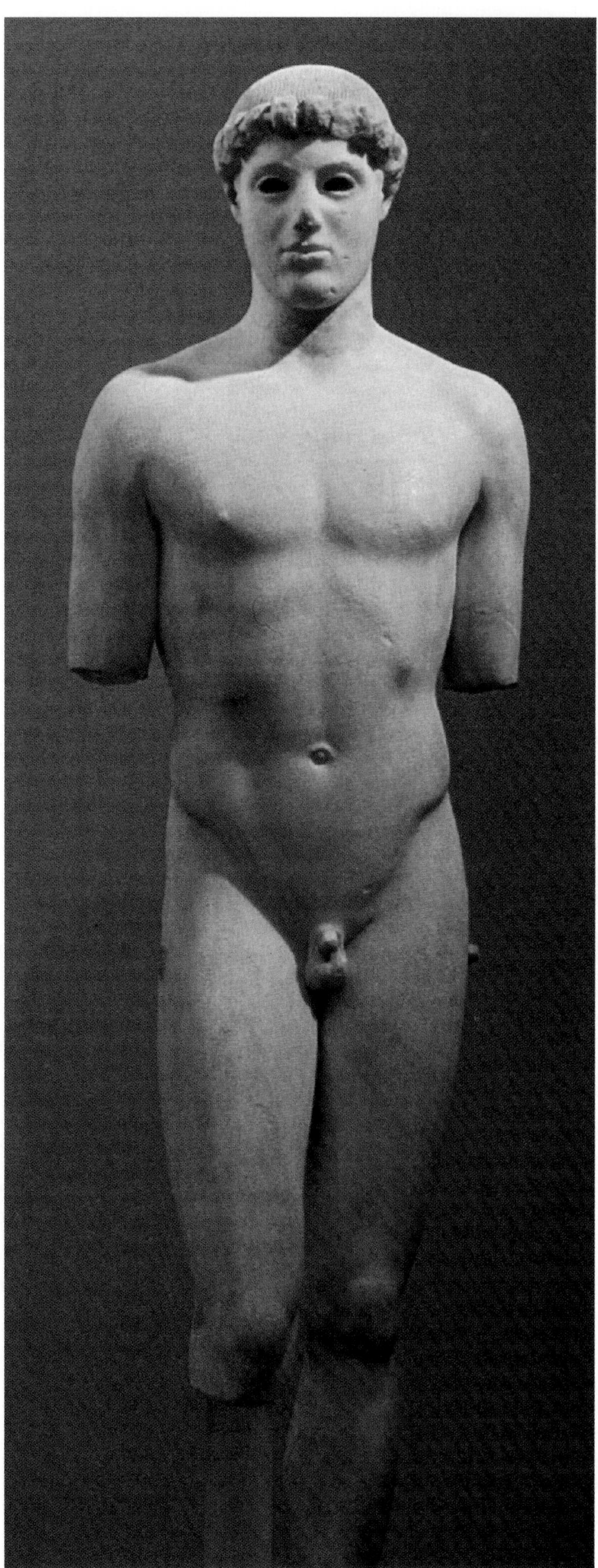

6–11 This sculpture was found amid the rubble on the Acropolis.
Kritios Boy, front view.

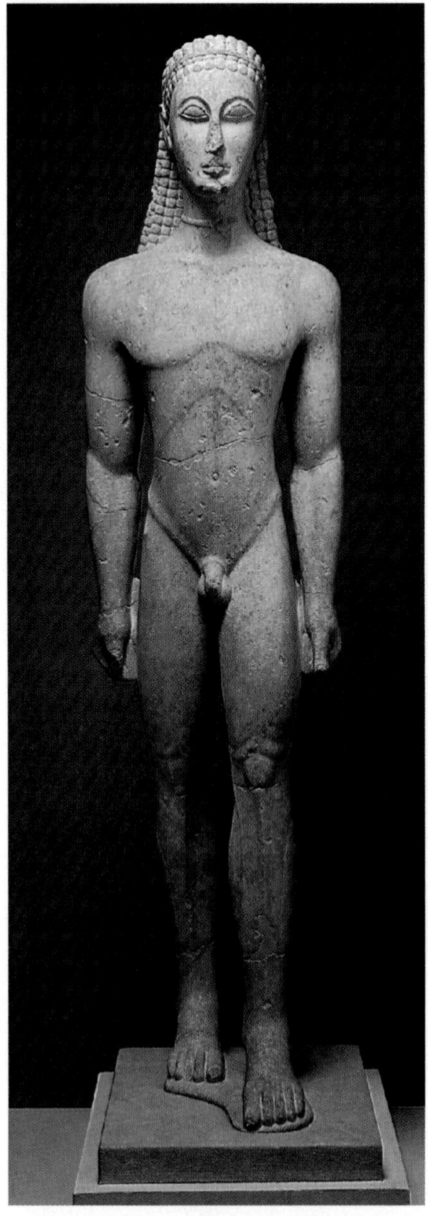

6–12 Note that this figure is free standing.
Statue of a Youth, Kouros, about 600 BC. Marble, 76" (193 cm) high. The Metropolitan Museum of Art, New York, Fletcher Fund, 1932.

Sculpture

The sculpted predecessors of the *Kritios Boy* were limited to rigid standing figures of young men and women. The sculpture of a young man was called a *Kouros* (fig.6–12). The life-size nude youth represented either Apollo or an ideal athlete. The figures were stylized and did not represent real people. The figures face toward the front. In this 600 BC example, the left foot is slightly forward. Both arms are held stiffly at their sides. Kneecaps are slightly curved. The hair is stylized into small ringlets that fall in a blocky mass to the shoulders. The mouth is set in a faint smile. In fact, the smile is so characteristic of the figures sculpted at this time, it has been termed an Archaic smile, after the name given to the period.

Over the course of the next seventy-five years, this stylization changed to a more natural and realistic representation of the human figure. Greek artists began sculpting what they saw and observed rather than creating idealized forms from memory.

The female figure, or *Kore* (fig.6–a), was a freestanding clothed figure of an idealized young girl. The clothing varied, depending upon the regions where the sculptors worked. The Kore figures were painted, as were most Greek sculptures, to appear more natural. Notice the folds of cloth, the long braided hair, the traces of color left on the work, and the hint of an Archaic smile.

The Archaic period comes to a close in about 480 BC. The *Kritios Boy* dates from this time and, as we have seen, it marks a change in how the Greeks depict the human form.

The Classic period began after 480 BC, when the Greeks defeated the Persian fleet at Salamis. In the early part of the Classic period, the Greeks enjoyed a period of peace in which the arts flourished. Individualism of ideas, thoughts and artistic representation was honored.

The *Charioteer of Delphi* (fig.6–13) is typical of the changes that took place. The figure is cast in bronze and is the earliest of the few remaining Greek bronzes. The rest were destroyed, lost or melted down for later ammunition or weapons of war. The charioteer was originally

6–13 This figure originally stood on a chariot drawn by four horses.
Charioteer of Delphi, about 470 BC. Bronze, 71" (180 cm) high. Archaeological Museum, Delphi.

750 BC
First goldworking in S. America

563 BC
Birth of Buddha, India

World Cultural Timeline

750 BC
Kingdom of Nubia founded, Africa

551 BC
Confucius born, China

6–14 Sculptors dampened the drapery of their models in order to get every fold just right to portray the form of the model.
Three Goddesses, about 435 BC. Marble, over life-size, east pediment of the Parthenon. British Museum, London.

polished. The eyes were made of glass paste, and lips and eyelashes were made of inlaid copper. In most later bronzes of Greece and Rome, these features are now missing and dark holes remain for the lost eyes. The cloth folds, muscles and facial features are natural. The Archaic smile is replaced by a look of calm and self-control, which symbolizes a classic balance of emotion, personality and physical ability. The features and pose remain a bit rigid and severe.

The Age of Pericles was the culmination of the Classic period in Greek sculpture and architecture. Athens was safe and prosperous, and the arts were admired and loved as never before and seldom since. The Athenians decorated the most prominent building in their city, the Parthenon, in their most ambitious sculptural undertaking. Both the east and west ends of the building were filled with statues that were larger than life. A continuous ***frieze*** (or sculpted band) ran for 525 feet around the top of the wall of the cella, which contained a huge statue of Athena. All the sculptures were produced in a period of twelve years by a team of sculptors under the direction of Phidias. Many of the works were later destroyed. In 1801, Lord Elgin collected most of what remained and sent them back to England for safekeeping.

Some of the sculptures were designed to fit exactly into the ***pediment***, or flat triangular area, at each end of the Parthenon. The *Three Goddesses* (from the east pediment) have remained as a group (fig.6–14). The fascinating drapery is startling in the way it seems to cling to the bodies. The clothing is no longer stylized or severe, but falls in natural folds and creases. These folds create visual movement. They lead the viewer's eye over the bodies and to the central event in the pediment composition, the birth of Athena.

The frieze around the inner wall depicts a procession, occurring once every four years, in which the youth of Athens pay tribute to Athena. The relief sculpture shows a multitude of figures and horses. One of the most impressive sections (fig.6–15) depicts horses and riders, sometimes four abreast. To sculpt this much depth in the shallow space of a few inches took great skill on the part of the Classical Greek sculptors. Anatomy, movement, rhythm and a convincing suggestion of space are all handled with superb control. The figures closest to the viewer are the most round. The second and third layers are

6–15 The parade of riders is part of a relief that continues around the entire inner wall of the Parthenon. The sculptor makes masterful use of a number of the elements of art and principles of design. Can you name at least three?
Mounted Procession (detail), 432 BC. Marble, 42" (106 cm) high, north frieze of the Parthenon. British Museum, London.

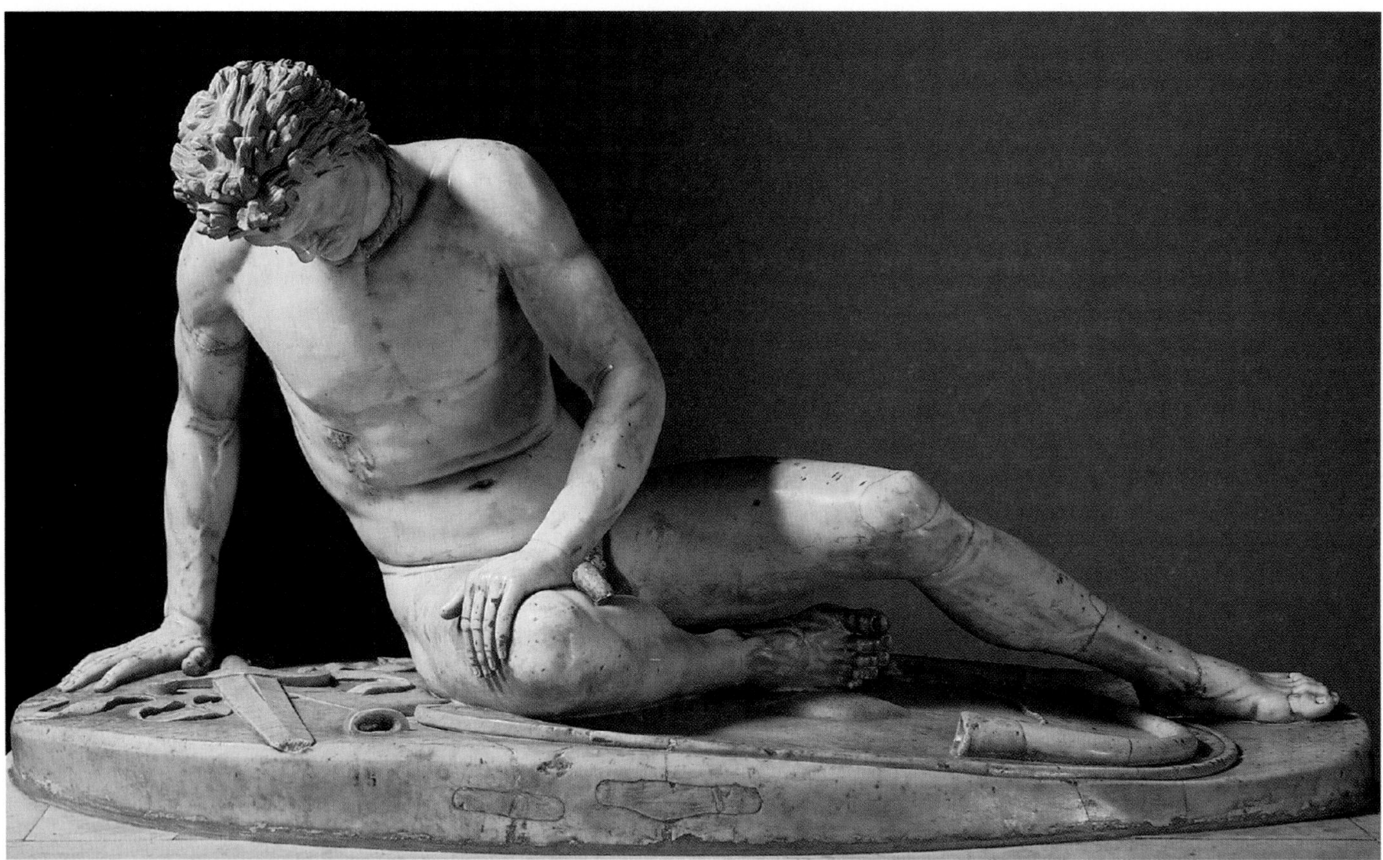

6–17 Most Greek bronzes are only known to us through Roman copies in marble such as this one.
Dying Gaul, about 230–220 BC. Roman, marble copy of bronze original, life-size, Pergamon. Capitoline Museum, Rome.

shallower, and the background is flat. Originally, the frieze, like other parts of the Parthenon, was brightly painted.

The Peloponnesian War disrupted the glory of Classical Greece. The fourth century saw a subtle change in the sculpture. A bronze figure, attributed to the Greek artist Lysippus, recently has been found in the Mediterranean Sea. Known as *The Getty Bronze* (fig.6–16), it is a victorious athlete crowning himself with a laurel wreath. Lysippus made the heads of figures slightly smaller and the bodies more slender. Notice the slight S-curve of the body caused by the centering of weight on the figure's right leg. The left leg is relaxed and does not support the weight of the body. The figure has a natural feeling. Facial features, hands and muscles are exact in their detail. The hair seems unruly and natural for an athlete. Lysippus became the official sculptor of Alexander the Great and his court.

Greek conquest of the Near East and Egypt and the spread of its civilization to the borders of India resulted in the mingling of Eastern and Western ideas. The art of this period, called Hellenistic, became more concerned with action and emotion. In art of the Classic period, these elements would have been kept under complete control.

The *Dying Gaul* (fig.6–17) is a Roman copy in marble of a Greek bronze of this time. It is life-size and shows the struggle of a wounded man about to die. The sculptor captured the ethnic features of face and hair that characterized the Gauls. The figure leans heavily on his arms because his legs no longer can help him move. There is agony in the pose and in the face of the warrior. Death seems very real and not as heroic as it might have been shown several centuries earlier.

6–16 This figure only recently came to light. There may be other Greek bronzes waiting to be discovered.
Lysippus, *Statue of a Victorious Athlete (The Getty Bronze),* about 330 BC. Bronze, life-size. The J. Paul Getty Museum, Malibu.

6–18 Powerful and just touching down to land, this Nike once overlooked the harbor at Samothrace.
Nike of Samothrace, about 190 BC. Marble, 8' (244 cm) high. The Louvre, Paris.

6–19 How has the artist used movement and line to convey the age and weariness of this woman?
Old Market Woman, 2nd century BC. Marble, 49 1/2" (126 cm) high. The Metropolitan Museum of Art, Rogers Fund, 1909.

Nike of Samothrace (fig.6–18) is perhaps one of the greatest of Hellenistic sculptures. Carved about 200 BC, it is the symbol of Winged Victory, her great wings spread wide as she lands on the prow of a ship. The force of the wind whips the drapery into wonderfully animated folds. Because of this effect, the space around the Nike, in front and behind her, become important parts of the sculpture itself—a concept that will not be used again for many centuries.

In contrast to the sweeping and energetic forward movement of the Nike is the bent and almost dragging motion of the *Old Market Woman* (fig.6–19). Here the artist's interest is in the realistic, rather painful portrayal of a tired, burdened woman. The sole focus of Greek art is no longer perfectly beautiful and ideal beings.

Architecture

Greek architecture developed from a heavy and ponderous appearance in the Archaic period to a light and airy feel in the Classic period. Most Greek architectural construction was focused around temples. Because the public generally was not allowed into the temples, architects designed impressive exteriors.

The concern of the Greeks for harmony and proportion is evident in their architecture. They saw public buildings as organic units that must be organized into orderly arrangements of parts. This attitude led to definite systems of construction that were called "the orders" (fig.6–20). The *Doric order* developed in mainland areas. The *Ionic order* evolved in the islands and the coast of Asia Minor. The *Corinthian order* was used in Hellenistic times and later in Roman civilization. The orders consisted of detailed rules for construction, based on proportions and an integration of the parts of the buildings. They were a means of breaking down complex forms into simple units that made up the whole.

In the Doric order, for example, the shaft of the column rests on the topmost step. It tapers toward the top in a slightly swelling curve. Atop the shaft is the capital, which has a round cushion-like molding capped by a square block. Resting on the capitals are the ***architrave***, frieze and ***cornice***. The architrave is the lintel that stretches horizontally above the columns. The frieze consists of oblong panels (***metopes***, often carved) and square blocks with upright channels (***triglyphs***). The crowning member of the superstructure is the cornice. The wide flat band of the cornice casts a shadow on the frieze below. The flat triangular space under the cornice is the pediment, which was often filled with sculpture.

Archaic Doric temples were powerful structures, and heavy in appearance. The *Temple of Hera* (called "The Basilica") at Paestum (fig.6–21) was built about 550 BC. The temple has very heavy columns that bulge and taper toward the top. The capitals are huge and flat.

The Doric style reached maturity during the Classic period in the

6–21 Look at the drums of the columns. What order is the temple?
"The Basilica" (*Temple of Hera*), about 550 BC. Paestum, Italy.

6–22 The Athenians' celebration of their patron goddess Athena focused on ceremonies held here.
Iktinos and Kallikrates, *The Parthenon*, 448–432 BC. The Acropolis, Athens.

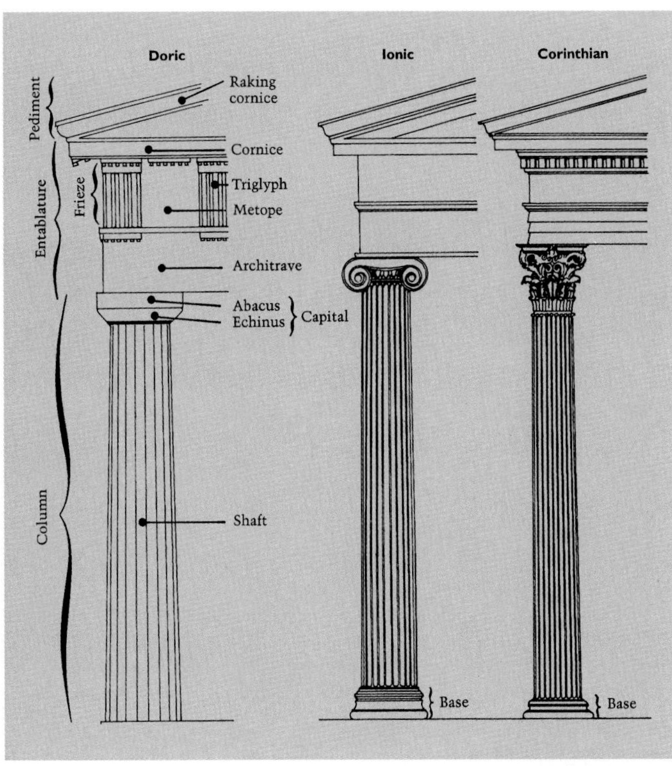

6–20 While the idea of an organized system is the same for all three orders, the particular details differ from one order to another.
Doric, Ionic and Corinthian orders. Reproduced by permission of Harcourt Brace Jovanovich, Inc., from *Art in Perspective: A Brief History* by Henri Dorra.

Parthenon (fig.6–22) in Athens. The architects Iktinus and Kallikrates built it from 448 to 432 BC, a short time for so huge a project. It is the central building of the Athenian Acropolis, which contains several other temples and Classic structures. Compare it with the *Temple of Hera* at Paestum. It is larger, but seems less massive. Proportions have been carefully readjusted. The columns are more slender, and the space between columns is wider. The slightly curved tapering (or ***entasis***) of the columns is less pronounced. Capitals are smaller and less flaring, and the cornice projects less. The columns lean slightly inward, and the corner columns are closer to their neighbors than the rest of the columns. All these visual refinements help give the structure a feeling of great harmony, balance and organic unity.

Although the ruins of the building are clean marble, originally many areas were painted, especially where sculptures were present. The cella contained a huge statue of Athena.

6–23 This small Ionic temple is very well preserved. Most temples are now only ruins.
Kallikrates, *Temple of Athena Nike,* about 425 BC. The Acropolis, Athens.

6–24 Notice how the sculptor has created figures which have a feeling of rigidity appropriate to their function as columns, yet they also have a sense of life.
The Porch of the Maidens, the Erechtheum, about 421–405 BC. The Acropolis, Athens.

6–25 The Greeks began construction of this temple, but the Romans completed it.
Cossutius, *Temple of the Olympian Zeus,* about 174 BC–2nd century AD. Athens.

The Ionic order is much lighter and more delicate than the Doric. The columns are set on a base and are more slender. The capitals are decorated with a spiral motif. The frieze is continuous, and the superstructure is lighter in appearance.

Most Ionic temples were built away from the mainland of Greece. However, the Acropolis in Athens contains several excellent ones. The *Temple of Athena Nike* (fig.6–23), built from 427 to 424 BC, is a fine example of a small Ionic building. The *Erechtheum* (421–405 BC) is a large and more complex structure. Columns are quite thin, tall and delicate in appearance, and have scroll-like capitals. *The Porch of the Maidens* (fig.6–24) uses six female figures (***caryatids***) instead of columns to support the architrave.

All of these temples, many of which are still standing in part, were constructed without mortar or cement. The stones were cut so exactly that they fit together precisely. Sometimes, metal rods were used as dowels to hold one block in place above another. The columns were built up of several drums and had flutes cut in after they were erected.

Corinthian columns were used in the *Temple of the Olympian Zeus* (fig. 6–25) in Athens. The temple was begun in 174 BC and completed in the second century under the Roman emperor Hadrian. The towering columns are crowned with decorative capitals of acanthus leaves. Only a small portion of the huge temple remains today.

The Greeks were also interested in drama and music, and constructed theaters in the larger cities. These were open-air, rounded structures that were placed into the sloping sides of hills. Theaters were constructed of carefully tiered stone seats with aisles and walkways. Theaters had a round stage area called the orchestra, where the action took place. Behind the orchestra was a low building that formed the backdrop and supported the scenery. All these features can be seen in *The Theater at Epidaurus* (fig.6–26) which still is used for dramatic productions today.

Sidelight

A Touch of Color

Because the remains of Greek statues and architecture have lost their color over the centuries, we tend to think that much of Greek art was white. This, however, is far from the truth. In early periods, bright, even garish, colors were applied to statues, judging from the scraps of original paint that have been found. Coloring grew more restrained in the Classic period but it was still used to suggest actual colors, especially in lips, hair and eyes.

A painting technique called ***encaustic*** was used on the figures. This method involved mixing the pigment with wax and applying it to the surface when hot. Colors on some of the early statues have been preserved. One reason for this is that the Athenians used fragments of broken figures as rubble fill when rebuilding the temples on the Acropolis after the Persian destruction of the fifth century BC.

Benoit, *The Parthenon*, 1879–1881. Ecole Nationale Superieure des Beaux-Arts, Paris.

Color also was used in architecture. In regions where marble was not available, limestone or sandstone temples were tinted to resemble marble. In all temples, including the marble ones, capitals and other architectural details were brightly painted. The Greeks tried always to achieve harmony in everything they did, and color was essential to the overall effect of sculpture and architecture.

6–26 Although they are outdoors, Greek theaters had excellent acoustics. Plays are still performed here.
The Theater at Epidaurus, about 350 BC, Greece.

Painting

The Greeks were proud of the large and colorful paintings decorating their walls, but not even one exists today. Only the paintings on their vases remain. Early vases of the Archaic period are of red clay and have black figures and decorations painted on them. The ***amphora*** (fig.6–27) from Attica—a large storage jar with two handles—was signed by Exekias. He considered it one of his finest works. The inscription reads, *Exekias painted and made me*, indicating that he both formed and painted the amphora. Two events are shown on the vase.

6–28 Greek vase painters portrayed stories from their mythology and history.
Meidias, *Red-Figured Hydria*, about 410 BC. 20 1/2" (52 cm) high. British Museum, The Hamilton Collection, London.

6–27 Greek vase painters often signed their work. In the case of this piece, the same artist both made the vase and painted it.
Exekias, *Black-Figured Amphora*, about 530 BC. 24" (61 cm) high. The Vatican Museum.

The one seen here shows Pollux (with the dog) and Castor (with the horse) being honored by Leda and Tyndareos. All are identified and named on the painted vase. This outstanding example of Greek vase painting represents the most refined phase of Attic black-figure ware. The figures and animals are beautifully designed, and executed with exquisite technique.

The ***hydria*** (fig.6–28)—a large jug for carrying water from the community fountain—is from 410 BC. It shows a great change in technique and style. The background is now painted black and brush lines can be drawn freely on the red figures to show exacting detail and a variety of lines. A kind of perspective is shown by having some figures higher than others. Two scenes of familiar stories are painted by the artist/potter Meidias, who signed

World Cultural Timeline

400 BC
Earliest known calendar used in Mexico

200 BC
Irrigation systems developed in N. America

400 BC
Chopsticks first used in China

105 BC
Paper invented, China

6–29 The Romans copied many Greek statues and paintings like this one. The painting has been lost, but the mosaic survives.
The Battle of Issus, about 100 BC. Marble mosaic, length 16'9" (5 m). Roman copy of Greek painting, from Pompeii. National Museum, Naples.

the vase. The upper register shows the rape, or carrying away, of the daughters of Leucippus. The lower register shows Heracles in the garden of the Hesperides. Traces of white, brown and gold have been added to suggest form and depth on this red-figured hydria.

The sophistication of later Greek painting is revealed in *The Battle of Issus* (fig.6–29), a Roman mosaic of marble chips. The mosaic is a copy of a Hellenistic wall painting of about 315 BC. Only four colors—red, yellow, white and black—are used in the mosaic. (Quite likely the original painting was painted with the same limited palette.) The subject is the victory of Alexander the Great over Darius and the Persian army. Alexander, on the left, is partly obliterated because many of the stone tesserae are lost (fig. 6-d). Note the accurate anatomy of both horses and men. The overlapping figures, the rounded forms created by shading, the foreshortening, the complicated composition, and the marvelous detail are exciting and advanced achievements in visual presentation. Later Hellenistic painting retained the natural appearance of people and animals which characterized the Classic period, but added excitement, action and emotion.

Lesson 6.2 Review

1 How did the Greek artist create a sense of movement in the *Kritios Boy*?
2 Why have so few original bronze Greek statues survived?
3 Between the Archaic and Classical Greek periods, how did Greek artists change the way they conceived a sculpture?
4 How is it that we have some idea of what Greek wall painting looked like although no example has survived?
5 How did the sculptor show depth in the Parthenon frieze?
6 Compare the *Dying Gaul* to the *Charioteer of Delphi*. What are the differences between this Classical Greek statue and this Hellenistic sculpture? Which is more emotional?
7 What art principle is most important in the *Nike of Samothrace*?
8 Draw the column capitals of the three Greek orders of architecture. Which order has the heaviest look? Which order seems tallest and most slender?
9 During which period of Greek art was the Parthenon built?
10 How were Attic black-figured ware and red-figured ware different? Which style was older?

6.3 Roman Art

THE ROMAN CITY-STATE had its first beginnings in the eighth century BC. It grew to a magnitude of unbelievable proportions. The Romans expanded their control in every direction. Eventually they dominated the Western world. To these places the Romans took their laws, religion, customs, their extraordinary ability to organize, and the Latin language. From their conquered peoples, they absorbed the cultures to make up the complex structure of Roman culture and art.

The Romans greatly admired Greek sculpture and brought back many pieces to decorate their villas. Whatever they did not import, they had copied by either Greek artists or their own Roman artists. The Romans made their greatest contribution to art in architecture—the area in which their influence is most strongly seen. They used the arch, vault and concrete to far greater advantage than previous cultures. Their architecture was a creative achievement of the highest order. In construction, planning and engineering they had no peers.

Vocabulary
arch
vault
velarium
coffered
oculus
basilica
forum

Key Notes

- Roman civilization came to dominate the Western world.
- The Romans excelled in the art of architecture.
- In painting and sculpture, the Romans often borrowed from and imitated the Greeks.

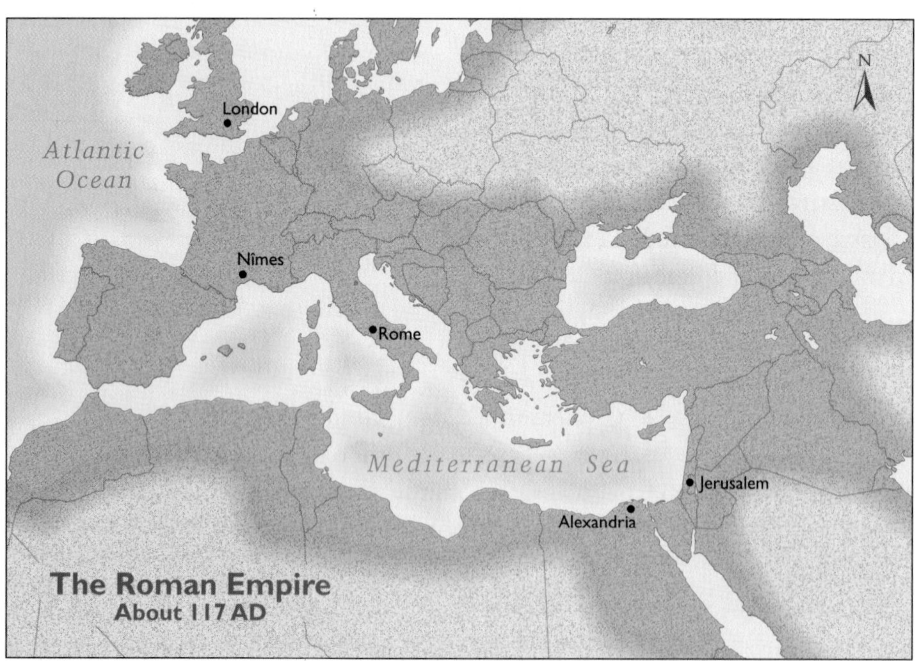

The Roman Empire eventually encompassed most of Europe. The gray boundary lines shown in this map reflect today's countries.

Special Feature

The Colosseum

Possibly the grandest of all Roman structures is *The Colosseum* (figs.6–30, 6–31). Three emperors were involved in its construction: Vespasian, Titus and Domitian. The Colosseum was originally designed for the staging of lavish spectacles, most particularly for battles between animals and gladiators. Fifty thousand Romans could be held in the marble-seated interior.

Concrete arches, walls and vaults, covered with marble or decorative plaster, made up several kilometers of passageways. The ***arch*** and ***vault*** were essential parts of monumental Roman architecture. The arch is a curved architectural element used to span an opening. The vault is an arched roof or covering made of brick, stone or concrete.

The outer wall of the Colosseum is as high as a modern sixteen-story building. This wall went completely around the structure and supported poles from which an awning could be stretched to protect spectators from sun or rain. At least 1000 men were needed to raise or lower the awning, or ***velarium***.

The exterior wall is divided into four horizontal bands, with large, arched openings piercing the lower three. The arches are framed in the standard Roman sequence for multi-storied buildings: Doric–Ionic–Corinthian, from the ground up.

6–30 Roman amphitheaters are the models for modern sports fields. Tickets were required for entrance to the Colosseum. Each of its 76 entryways had a number carved over the arch.
The Colosseum, 72–80 AD. Rome.

Statues filled the arched niches around the outside and a heavy wooden floor covered layers of cells below in which gladiators and animals were held. An amazing system of winches and lifting tackle brought the beasts from their dens into the arena. In addition, the floor area (almost 100 meters long) could be flooded and used as a shallow lake for mock naval battles.

The Colosseum is not just an architectural masterpiece. In terms of planning, engineering and organization it ranks as one of the most astonishing achievements of antiquity. Unfortunately, the Colosseum was damaged by later citizens and architects who used it as an instant quarry for marble when constructing other buildings. But other amphitheaters were constructed in every major city of the empire. Many are still in such excellent condition that they are used today as stadiums for big events.

6–31 Notice the gouged areas which are the result of centuries of pilfering by builders who took the facing stone for later constructions.
The Colosseum, detail.

Roman Predecessors: Etruscan Art

If we step back several centuries from the Romans we find that much of central Italy was dominated by the Etruscans. The origins of these people are shrouded in mystery. But we have been told by ancient Roman writers that the Etruscans were master architectural engineers and town planners. The Romans must have learned a great deal from Etruscan construction. Although little remains of Etruscan architecture, a fortified city gate (fig.6–32) in the Italian city of Perugia does survive. It shows a masterful use of the arch and masonry techniques. One reason for the lack of evidence from the Etruscan culture is that their towns are buried under present-day cities and are extremely difficult to excavate.

We also know that the Etruscan use of bronze in sculpture and other decorative items was much admired, even by the Greeks. *Statuette of a Rider* (fig.6–33) is a small, solid cast bronze sculpture. The horse is missing. Like most other Etruscan sculpture, it probably was modeled after a Greek original. The rider sits stiffly upright and wears a short toga which the Romans later adopted. A considerable understanding of anatomy was necessary for the artist to sculpt a figure with such convincingly realistic features.

Architecture

The Romans learned many lessons from the Etruscans and, as we have seen in the example of the Colosseum, the Romans advanced architecture to unrivaled heights. They constructed buildings and public works in all corners of their empire. Arenas, huge public baths and public forums were built. The Romans erected the first structures in history with vast interior spaces. These buildings are impressive because of size and practicality rather than aesthetic feeling.

One of the most astounding examples is *The Pantheon* (figs.6–34, 6–35) which was built to honor all the gods. A huge dome (an

6–32 This is one of very few surviving Etruscan architectural monuments.
Porta Augusta, 2nd century BC. Perugia.

6–33 The Etruscans were master metal workers who made statues and jewelry too.
Statuette of a Rider, about 450–425 BC. Bronze, 11" (27 cm) high, Etruscan, found at Comacchio, Italy. Detroit Institute of Arts.

6–34 The portico (porch) partly hides the Pantheon's basic geometry. What forms can you identify here?
The Pantheon, about 118–125 AD. Rome.

6–34a Plan of the Pantheon
Reproduced by permission of Harcourt Brace Jovanovich, Inc., from *Art in Perspective* by Henri Dorra.

exact hemisphere on the inside) rests on a mammoth drum, creating an interior space that is overwhelming to experience. The floor space is 144 feet in diameter, and the top of the dome is 144 feet above the floor. The concrete dome is thin at the top and thickens as it meets the walls. The dome is ***coffered***, or decorated, with a series of recessed rectangular panels. The walls of the building are over 20 feet thick and massive enough to support the tremendous weight of the dome. The only source of light is a single round, eye-like opening (***oculus***) at the top. This opening is 30 feet in diameter. Any rain that falls through it is carried away by an elaborate underground drainage system. The interior of the drum area is covered with marble columns and decorations.

Some of Italy's great artists and composers were later buried at the Pantheon. The once-gilded, huge bronze doors on gigantic hinges are the original doors. A colonnade of Corinthian columns, carved from

6–35 Light from the oculus in the coffered dome lights up the interior of this big enclosed space.
Giovanni Paolo Panini, *Interior of the Pantheon,* about 1750. Oil on canvas, 50 1/2" x 39" (128 x 99 cm) National Gallery of Art, Washington DC, Samuel H. Kress Collection.

single blocks of stone, dominates the entrance and is topped by a Greek-style pediment. The dome originally was covered with gilded bronze plates.

The Romans also built gigantic structures to house their baths. *The Baths of Caracalla* (fig.6–36) contained several pools of various temperatures, libraries, offices, meeting rooms, conversation areas and spaces for recreation. The interior of the concrete structure was roofed with vaults that spanned enormous spaces.

Large meeting halls, called ***basilicas***, were part of the civic center in each city. Many were later converted into churches. This building type will be discussed at greater length in Chapter 7.

6–36 Roman baths included pools, shops, lecture halls, libraries and running tracks.
The Baths of Caracalla, about 215 AD. Rome.

6–37 This theater was once roofed with cedar wood.
Theater of Herodes Atticus, 2nd century AD. Athens.

50 AD–500 AD
Aksum Kingdom (Ancient Ethiopia), Africa

100 AD
Mound builders, Ohio

132 AD
Seismograph invented, China

World Cultural Timeline

50 AD
Stupa at Sanchi, India

100 AD
Insecticide developed from powdered dried chrysanthemum flowers, China

271 AD
Directional compass invented, China

6–39 Romans met here and at other forums to shop and catch up on the news.
Forum Romanum. Rome.

Roman theaters differed slightly from those of the Greeks. The Romans partially cut the round Greek orchestra and constructed a raised stage area behind it. The performance was given from the stage, and important spectators were seated in the orchestra. The seating was in a semicircle rather than in the two-thirds circle of the Greeks. Theaters were often freestanding rather than placed in a concave hillside. The 5000-seat Roman *Theater of Herodes Atticus* (fig.6–37) was built on the side of the Acropolis in Athens. It is still in use today.

Several emperors built large triumphal arches to commemorate their greatest achievements. The *Arch of Constantine* (fig.6–38) celebrates Constantine's assumption of power. It is actually a large building with three arches through it. Many of the statues on it came from other monuments in Rome.

Romans loved to discuss things—politics, the weather, battles, history, art, trade business or gossip. Their ***forums*** provided a space in their cities for these discussions. The *Forum Romanum* (fig.6–39), one of many in Rome, contained temples, state buildings, open spaces, basilicas and monuments. The Via Sacra (Sacred Way) passed through it. At a later time it became a valley full of rubble from the ruins and a garbage dump for the citizens, but was later cleared and excavated.

City planning was another phase of civic engineering at which the Romans excelled. Cities were equipped with sewers, running water, city squares, shopping streets, residential areas, paved streets and warehouses.

Homes were often two stories high. They were built around atriums and contained gardens and fountains. Pompeii and Herculaneum, which were covered with volcanic ash and mud from Mt. Vesuvius in 79 AD, have been excavated to reveal urban centers of great sophistication and careful planning. Similar cities were built in nearly every corner of the Roman empire. Many European, North African and Near Eastern countries have marvelous excavations and ancient ruins where Roman civic engineering can be studied firsthand.

6–38 The Romans commemorated victories and important people in public monuments.
The Arch of Constantine, about 312–315 AD. Rome.

Sidelight

Marvels of Engineering

Roman bridges, roads and aqueducts spread from one end of the Roman Empire to the other. The roads that tied the empire together were masterpieces of engineering and are still visible in parts of Europe. Some aqueducts, partially ruined, still extend for miles outside of Rome.

The Romans were well aware that concrete is affected adversely by extremes of temperature. Repairs on aqueducts were permitted only between April 1 and November 1. *Pont du Gard,* first century BC. Near Nîmes, France.

The aqueducts, composed basically of arches and vaults, are an extraordinary example of Roman practicality on the largest scale imaginable. Rome had 11 aqueducts supplying 350 million gallons of water a day from distant mountains. Quite a feat! The oldest aqueduct dates from 312 BC, but aqueducts were constructed all over the Roman Empire, wherever water had to be brought across valleys and into cities.

The *Pont du Gard* near Nîmes, France, is a triple-storied aqueduct built of stone (without mortar) that bridges the gorge of the Gard River. The aqueduct ran for about 30 miles and supplied Nîmes daily with 22,000 tons of water.

Sculpture

Although the Romans borrowed heavily from Greek sculpture, they used original portrait sculpture to honor their emperors. These portraits helped preserve the features of the emperors and emphasized their greatness. The Roman interest in portrait sculpture, especially the bust (head and upper torso), is an important contribution to world art. Unfortunately, most of the work prior to the first century BC has been lost.

The *Head of Augustus* (fig.6–40) was part of a large full-length figure. It was probably sculpted in Alexandria, Egypt. It is cast in bronze and has eyes of glass paste. The sculpture is striking in its realistic appearance and individualized expression. It is certainly not an idealized figure. These sculptures allowed Roman subjects throughout the vast empire to know what their rulers looked like. Today a camera would assume that job.

Portrait busts of Roman people of a later date are quite realistic. *Portrait of a Lady* (fig.6–41) is carved in marble and probably was done as a commission to decorate the home of the subject. Notice the style of the coiffure and the acanthus leaf ornament at the base. Features such as these help archaeologists date such works. The bust of the *Roman Legislator* (fig.6–42) illustrates the importance placed on realism in the later Roman style. The artist makes no attempt to minimize the wrinkled and sagging skin of the aging legislator.

Relief sculptures were used to record important events in the lives of Roman emperors. The *Column of Trajan* (fig.6–43) is a splendid marble cylinder that rises to a height of over 130 feet, including the pedestal. It was originally topped by a bronze statue of Trajan; it now holds a statue of St. Peter. The base of the column is carved into a giant laurel wreath. In a spiral relief some 700 feet long, the exploits of Trajan's Dacian campaigns are carved as a narrative history in stone (fig.6–c). The column is hollow and originally contained an urn with the ashes of the emperor.

6–40 Many, many statues were made of the emperors so that their subjects in all parts of the empire would know what their ruler looked like.
Head of Augustus, 27 BC–14 AD. Bronze, 18 1/2" (47 cm) high, found at Meroe, Sudan in 1910. British Museum, London.

6–41 The realism in portraits like this one was valued in a society which revered its ancestors and tried to be accurate about its history.
Portrait of a Lady, 69 AD. Marble, 25 1/2" (64 cm) high. Nelson-Atkins Museum of Art, Kansas City.

6–42 How does this figure differ from the Greek sculpture you have studied?
The Roman Legislator, about 125 AD. Marble, 16 1/2" (42 cm) high. Nelson-Atkins Museum of Art, Kansas City.

In the piazza (square) atop the Capitoline Hill, once the center of Roman government, once stood a bronze statue of one of Rome's most notable emperors. The *Equestrian Statue of Marcus Aurelius* (fig.6–44) is the only well-preserved equestrian statue (horse and rider) from antiquity to survive and has been imitated often. Michelangelo, who designed the piazza and the surrounding buildings in the Renaissance, placed the statue here at the request of the Pope, who thought it was of Constantine, the first Christian emperor. The size of the figure is large in comparison to the horse, a characteristic of such Roman works. The bearded emperor looks out on the world, his right arm in a typical Roman oratorical gesture. The horse is superbly sculpted, showing that the artist had immense knowledge of the bone and muscle structure of horses. The balance is superb, with all the weight of the cast bronze evenly distributed over the three supporting legs.

The head of *Constantine the Great* (fig.6–45) is part of an enormous sculpture that once was

6–45 This head was part of a seated figure of the emperor that was 30 feet high. The head alone weighs over 8 tons.
Constantine the Great, about 330 AD. Marble, head about 8 1/4' (2.5 m) high. Palace of the Conservatory, Rome.

placed in his basilica. Head, arms, hands, legs and feet were of marble. The drapery was probably of bronze plates over a masonry frame. The colossal head and neck are superbly modeled, but the eyes, which seem to be fixed on some spot above our heads (perhaps on eternity), seem overly large. Such large eyes are common in the art of the early Christian period. The eyes of such late Roman sculptures were carved so that shadows, not paint, provided the definition of iris and pupil.

6–43 Trajan's ashes were buried in this column whose relief sculpture tells the story of his conquests.
Column of Trajan, 106–113 AD. Marble, over 130' (40 m) high. Rome.

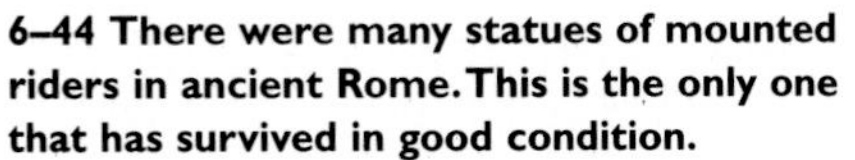

6–44 There were many statues of mounted riders in ancient Rome. This is the only one that has survived in good condition.
Equestrian Statue of Marcus Aurelius, 161–180 AD. Bronze, over life-size. Shown in the Piazza del Campidoglio, Rome.

Painting

Both the Etruscans and the Greeks made paintings which the early Romans copied. Because none of the Greek and only a few of the Etruscan paintings have survived, the extent of their influence on Roman artists cannot be determined. The Romans used paintings to decorate and color the interiors of houses. Still lifes, portraits, landscapes and mythological subjects are found on walls in Pompeii, Herculaneum and other excavated cities. Often landscapes and architectural scenes were painted to serve as "open windows" to provide a feeling of greater space in small rooms. Portraits were sometimes painted on walls to record how members of the family looked.

All Roman wall paintings were done in fresco, a method of painting wet plaster with pigment. Entire plaster-covered walls were frescoed to look like marble and wood paneling, or were gaily decorated with flowers and vines, almost like wallpaper. The *Woman Playing the Cithara* (fig.6–46) is a decorative wall fresco. The woman and child have a feeling of individuality, yet seem slightly idealized. They may be portraits. The poses are casual and intimate. The figures are shaded to create a comfortable feeling of depth. Roman painters had mastered several types of perspective to create the illusion of depth in a painting.

The girl in *Portrait of a Young Girl* (fig.6–47) is from a wall in a Pompeian house. She holds a stylus to her lips as if thinking about what to write. The painting may be a commemorative portrait of a girl who died young and whose family wished to remember her.

6–47 What do you think she is going to write?
Portrait of a Young Girl, before 79 AD. Fresco, 10" (25 cm) high, from Pompeii. National Museum, Naples.

6–46 These figures are life-sized, which could create the feeling that they were really in the room.
Woman Playing a Cithara, before 79 AD. Fresco, 6 1/2' (2 m) high, from Boscoreale. The Metropolitan Museum of Art, New York, Rogers Fund.

Window in Time

Pompeii: A City Frozen in Time

On the morning of August 24 in AD 79, a light dusting of ash from the volcano Mt. Vesuvius began falling on the prosperous city of Pompeii. But it was not until around 1:00 p.m. that, with a tremendous explosion, Vesuvius erupted, spewing out volcanic ash, great bombs of pumice and molten lava. A giant cloud of volcanic dust rose twelve miles into the sky and completely blotted out the sun. Within two to three hours Pompeii was over a foot deep in pumice and stone. All through the afternoon and evening the volcano continued to belch forth its contents. Pumice and volcanic debris accumulated at the rate of six inches every hour.

During the early hours of the outburst most of Pompeii's 20,000 inhabitants fled the city. But at least 2000 people chose to seek shelter within the town, either too terrified to leave or unwilling to abandon their homes and possessions. All who remained behind were overcome by the poisonous gases and hot ashes that clogged their lungs.

View of Mt. Vesuvius from Pompeii.

When the sky cleared three days later the once thriving port had been transformed into a huge grave, sealed beneath some 25 feet of rock and ash.

Pompeii lay locked in the earth and forgotten for many centuries. It wasn't until 1748 that serious attempts to excavate Pompeii began. In the 1860s, the archaeologist and historian Giuseppe Fiorelli, in charge of the dig from 1860–1875, began to use scientific methods to excavate Pompeii. He divided the city into regions, assigning a number to every block and every doorway. His excavation uncovered a unique view of private and public life in the Roman world. Unique because everything in Pompeii had been preserved just as it was, including its inhabitants.

Fiorelli knew that the volcanic ash had turned to mud and hardened around the fallen figures. The corpses inside the hardened mud eventually disintegrated, but left behind were molds that faithfully preserved the victims' final gestures and postures. When a workman carelessly swung his pickax and accidentally made a hole in a mold at the site, Fiorelli poured liquid plaster of Paris into the cavity. After the plaster had solidified, the cocoon of ash was removed and an uncanny lifelike figure was revealed. With the aid of the casts the last moments of the Pompeians were fixed forever: A woman falls with a baby in her arms; a man collapses as he pulls his goat along; a young man and woman are stopped in their tracks as they attempt to flee.

Just as the Pompeians had been preserved in their last living moments, so too was their city and way of life. Bakeries, inns, tanneries and wool-working shops emerged intact, providing an accurate picture of how they functioned. The food people ate was recovered. In one house, eggs and fish were found lying on a dining table. Plants, too, left cavities in the hardened lava. The archaeologist Wilhelmina Jashemski used Fiorelli's method of making casts to determine the types of plants that grew in the gardens of Pompeii.

Gloriously colored paintings and mosaics found on the walls and floors of most houses testified to the Pompeians' love of art and give tantalizing glimpses of cultural and religious life. Even information about city politics and elections could be read on the graffiti-covered walls of Pompeii.

By sealing off the area so completely, Vesuvius in effect stopped time. No one who sees these visions of the dead can fail to sense the anguish of that time.

Mosaics

Although the Greeks had used colored stones to create mosaic designs, the Romans excelled in this art. Small bits of marble were cut, polished and fitted together to make an image. Floor mosaics were made of pieces one to two centimeters across. The owner of a villa in Sicily was a Roman of extraordinary wealth. The villa boasted 7000 square feet of floor mosaics. One of the scenes (fig.6–48) depicts a group of women engaged in vigorous exercise. They almost seem to be involved in an ancient aerobic class or gym workout.

Wall mosaics were done with even more precision. Much smaller stones were used. Many stones were less than a millimeter in diameter. When done, the entire surface was polished to feel like a smooth sheet of glass. The artist of the wall mosaic *Doves* (fig.6–49) reveals an incomplete knowledge of space perception. While his shading of values is excellent, his perspective drawing is not precisely accurate. The frame and border also are done in the same mosaic techniques. Here, the stones are so tiny that 150 are used in every square centimeter.

The Battle of Issus (fig.6–29) is a mosaic from the House of the Faun in Pompeii. Huge in size for a mosaic, it is a brilliant example of this art form. Its subject matter and execution are extremely complex. The grading of colors and values to create rounded forms is difficult when the colors and values must be found in natural stones.

6–49 This whole picture is made up of tiny stones. In the space of a square centimeter, a Roman mosaicist might use 100 pieces.
Doves, 2nd century AD. Mosaic, 33 1/2" (85 cm) high, from villa of Emperor Hadrian at Tivoli. Capitoline Museum, Rome.

6–48 What details in this image remind you of life today?
Young Women Exercising, early 4th century AD. Mosaic, from the Roman villa at Piazza Armerina.

Lesson 6.3 Review

1 Who inhabited the land that became Rome before the Romans took it over?
2 Name several Roman architectural masterpieces.
3 Both *The Baths of Caracalla* and *The Pantheon* have domed roofs. Draw several arches that cross at the center to explain how a series of arches can be joined to form a dome.
4 Why was *The Pantheon* built? Describe its roof. What happens to rain water that falls into *The Pantheon*?
5 How were Roman cities similar to modern cities? How were they different?
6 How is the *Column of Trajan* like a comic strip?
7 The early Christians destroyed many of the Roman statues. Why did they preserve the statue of Marcus Aurelius?
8 Compare your height to that of the head of *Constantine the Great*. How tall are you? How tall is the head of Constantine? Guess the size of one of the feet of this statue.
9 Why are so many Roman wall paintings preserved in Pompeii and Herculaneum?

Primary Source

Vitruvius, Roman Master Builder

Vitruvius was a Roman master builder and author of volumes about standards for architecture. Because of his writings we know a great many details about Roman architecture. In this selection from Vitruvius' *Ten Books on Architecture*, he tells us how he learned from Greek literature that the Doric column was to be based on the proportion of a man's foot and height:

"Wishing to set up columns in that temple, but not having rules for their symmetry, and being in search of some way by which they could render them fit to bear a load and also of a satisfactory beauty of appearance, they measured the imprint of a man's foot and compared this with his height. On finding that, in a man, the foot was one-sixth of the height, they applied the same principle to the column, and reared the shaft, including the capital, to a height six times its thickness at its base. Thus the Doric column, as used in buildings, began to exhibit the proportions, strength, and beauty of the body of a man."

In this passage from Vitruvius' writings we learn why the caryatid figure (fig.6–24) was created:

"The Greeks...made common cause and declared war against the people of Caryae [who had sided with the Persian enemies of Greece]. They took the town, killed the men, abandoned the State to desolation, and carried off their wives into slavery, without permitting them, however, to lay aside the long robes and other marks of their rank as married women...to appear forever after as a type of slavery, burdened with the weight of their shame and so making atonement for their State. Hence, the architects of the time designed for public buildings the statues of these women, placed so as to carry a load, in order that the sin and the punishment of the people of Caryae might be known and handed down even to posterity."

Chapter Review

Review

1 What subject was central to Greek art and culture?

2 What qualities were the Greeks trying to achieve in their paintings and sculptures?

3 What was the subject of the Parthenon frieze?

4 In what area of art did the Romans make their greatest contribution?

5 How are the eyes of *Constantine the Great* (fig.6–45) different from the eyes of most of the classical Greek sculptures?

Interpret

1 Compare three Minoan works of art: the *Bull Dance* (fig.6–3), the *Octopus Jar* (fig.6–5), and the *Harvester Vase* (fig.6–6). What characteristics are common to all three?

2 How is the *Kouros* (fig.6–12) similar to *Mycerinus and His Queen* (fig.5–21). How is it different?

3 Where is most of the Parthenon sculpture now? If the Parthenon were discovered today, where do you think the art would be kept?

4 Describe a Greek theater. How did it vary from the theaters that the Romans built?

5 Analyze the difference between the types of people that the Greeks and Romans sculpted.

Other Tools for Learning

Maps

1 Notice how Greek cities are spread out over a series of islands in the Mediterranean Sea. How do you think this separation affected their government and art?

2 Find Pompeii and Rome on a map. Imagine what a southern resort town like Pompeii might have been like before Vesuvius covered it with ashes.

Timelines

During the more than 1000 years that the Greek and then the Roman civilizations developed, other world cultures were equally active and inventive. Using the timelines in this chapter, determine what events were happening simultaneously throughout the world.

Electronic Media

CD-ROM drive: Electronic Encyclopedia (e.g., *New Grolier Multimedia* or *Microsoft Encarta*)

Research one of the historic or mythological figures depicted on an object in this chapter. Which characteristics of the individual is the artist trying to emphasize? If the artist is representing a specific moment in this personality's life, is it accurately portrayed?

Activity 1

Immortalized in Clay

Materials

for preliminary drawings:
mirrors or photographs
soft lead pencils (#2 or 4B, 6B)
12" x 18" white drawing paper
for sculpture:
newspaper or plastic cloth
containers of water
spray bottle
terra cotta clay
clay tools
heavy duty plastic bags

Take a look.
- Fig.6–40, *Head of Augustus*, 27 BC–14 AD. Bronze.
- Fig.6–41, *Portrait of a Lady*, 69 AD. Marble.
- Fig.6–42, *The Roman Legislator*, about 125 AD. Marble.

Think about it. Study the ways in which these portraits reflect the individuals which they represented. Compare and contrast Greek and Roman sculpture. Study the way the Romans handled individual characteristics such as hair, clothing and facial features in their portrait sculptures.

Do it. Use terra cotta to create a miniature or lifesize self-portrait sculpture. As an option, you could portray a well-known character in literature, theater or television.
- If doing a self-portrait, use a mirror to make several drawings of yourself to record individual aspects. You may choose to portray yourself as you would have looked in Roman times.
- If choosing a living character, find photographs of him or her from different angles and do a number of sketches. To bring an imaginary character to life, make sketches from photographs and people around you to develop distinctive facial characteristics.

Check it.
Turn your sculpture as you work to look at it from all sides. You may need to make adjustments to keep the proportions realistic in three dimensions.

Helpful Hint: In your preliminary sketches, draw yourself or your subject from a variety of angles.

Activity 2

Ancient Legacy

Materials

12" x 18" white drawing paper or larger
drawing pencils (2H, 4H, 6H, HB)
rulers
kneaded erasers
drawing board (optional)

Take a look. Review the following artwork in this book:
- Fig.6–22, Iktinos and Kallikrates, *The Parthenon*, 447–432 BC.
- Fig.6–34, *The Pantheon*, about 118–125.

Think about it. The Doric style temple reached maturity during the Greek Classic period with the Parthenon, the central building of the Acropolis. The Romans built the Pantheon, a structure that honored the gods. It boasts a huge dome and a colonnade of Corinthian columns, carved from single blocks of stone.

Do it. Locate buildings in your community which use ideas and forms from ancient Greece and Rome. Look for large public buildings such as a stadium or meeting hall, or construction techniques such as domes, barrel vaults or cement construction. Do one or more of the following:
- Document the use of classical concepts in drawings, paintings or photographs.
- Do a pencil drawing of one of the buildings in your community.
- Make a drawing that incorporates the characteristics of Greek and Roman architecture to redesign a selected building. You may include pediments, friezes, columns, arches, domes and vaults.

Check it.
Trade work with a friend and talk about what you've discovered and what your drawings represent. What insights can you offer to others who selected the same building(s)?

Helpful Hint: Do the front (facade) of the building only as a flat surface (don't worry about perspective).

Additional Activities

- Read Plato's and Aristotle's thoughts about beauty in *Philosophies of Art and Beauty*. Then write your own criteria of beauty (addressing how you know that something is beautiful).
- Roman artists were masters of the mosaic medium. Experiment with this technique by using small color chips (tesserae) to make a design or picture. Make these by cutting colored construction paper or magazine colors into 1 cm squares or irregular chips. Draw the outline of your subject on a large piece of chip board or corrugated cardboard. Glue the tesserae in place.
- Design Greek-style vase paintings of American mythology, depicting folk tales such as Paul Bunyan or Big Foot, or the story of Betsy Ross or other American heroes and heroines. Paint these stylized scenes on such typical twentieth century containers as plastic bottles, gallon wine jugs, etc. Acrylic paint will stick to most surfaces.

Student Profile

Aysha Venjara

Age 17
Clarkstown High School North
New City, New York
Activity 1, Immortalized in Clay

Favorite kinds of art: pencil sketching, sculpture, watercolor
Favorite artists: van Gogh, Michelangelo, Seurat

The human face is one of the most captivating and challenging objects to render. Sculpting it makes the challenge all the more difficult; however, the experience can be one of the most rewarding you have ever had. I believe sculpting my head has been one of my greatest learning experiences.

While developing the bust, my mind was most intensely concentrated on the intricate structure of the face—its raised and lowered areas, the specific turn of the nostrils, the curve of the mouth, and every little fold of skin that formed the eye. As the bust developed, I began to concentrate not as much on every little detail, but on the overall picture, how each part of the face related to all the other parts.

Upon learning about art history in school, my view of art began to change. It is most likely a habit of mine to look at everything close up and in detail. Learning about art history taught me that great artists not only had beautiful little details, but also had beautiful pieces of art on the whole. Art history helped me in taking a step back once in a while, to take the whole piece into account. Take, for example, Michelangelo's *David*; it has the most minute details, down to every little fold in the eye, every curl in the lovely locks of hair, all the details that I admire; however, those details are just that. They supplement the entire piece, the whole. It is the whole piece, not just the details that make an impact.

Art and its influences have always been an important part of my life. My art has been an escape from everything around me, a haven. I can be in another world while I'm working on a piece and it relaxes me thus. The whole process of sculpting the bust was ever so soothing: feeling the wet clay in my hands and between my fingers, smoothing it onto the armature, using the weight of my body to sculpt it into the shape I wanted. It is a peaceful and calming process that lets you see the results of all the built-up energy inside you.

Anyone who has even the slightest bit of creativity and imagination can create beautiful and meaningful art. It simply takes some determination to see the project through. Many times, patience is the key. If an idea or method doesn't work, try again. If it doesn't work a second time, try looking at it from a different perspective. Just keep trying, never give in. And if it gets frustrating, take a step back; maybe you'll see things in terms of the whole picture, not just little details.

Aysha Venjara

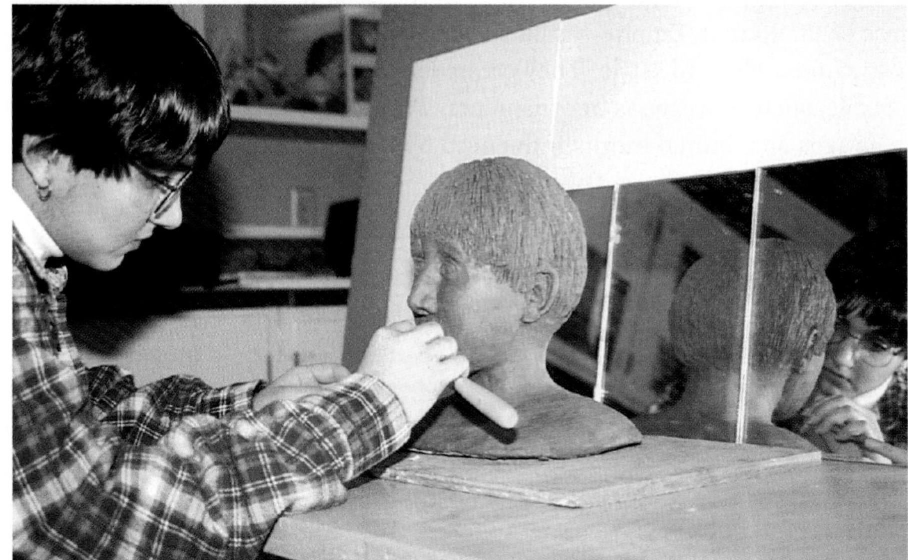

With a mirror for reference, Aysha works diligently on her own likeness in clay.

Aysha, 1994. Terra cotta, height 10" (25 cm).

7 Religious Conviction

In This Chapter...

7–a This clasp would have been used to fasten a cloak or other exterior garment. *Fibula*, 6th century, silver. Archaeological Museum, Udine, Italy.

With the emergence of Christianity on the European continent, there was a change in the kind of art produced. During the Greek and Roman period before the birth of Christ, art had been realistic. But, the early Christians were more concerned with symbolic representation.

When the Christian religion first began, it was outlawed in the Roman Empire. These early Christians worshipped and buried their dead in tunnels called catacombs where they created frescoes on the walls and ceilings.

Christianity eventually became the official religion of the Roman Empire in 313 AD. Once this happened, a church-building campaign began that would last for centuries. The earliest churches were built like the Roman civic buildings called basilicas. These churches were plain on the outside and decorated on the inside.

In 337, the Roman Empire split into two parts. The Western Empire declined, but the Eastern Empire, with its capital in Constantinople, flourished. In 527, Justinian became emperor and began the period known as the Golden Age of Byzantium. During this period, many gorgeous churches were built which had extraordinary interiors of glass mosaics. Byzantine architecture spread all over Eastern Europe all the way into what is now Russia.

Then, in the seventh century, another faith, which was to rival Christianity, started in Arabia. This was Islam (its practioners are Muslims) and it spread rapidly into the Near East and the southern Mediterranean. The Islamic religion forbade the use of the human figure in its religious artwork, so its artists turned to a more abstract form of expression.

Early medieval art began the period known as the Middle Ages. This early part of the Middle Ages lasted from the 400s to the 900s. After the collapse of the Roman Empire, various European tribes moved through Europe looking for a place to settle. They created small works of art that were portable, such as weapons or ornaments. These were decorated with geometric designs and animal motifs influenced by both Christian and Islamic art.

331
Seat of Roman Empire moves to Constantinople

570
Mohammed, founder of Islam, born

698–721
***Lindisfarne Gospel*, England**

750
Gregorian chant music, England, France and Germany

1286
Spectacles invented

1453
Constantinople conquered by Ottoman Turks

Early Christian, Byzantine, Islamic and Early Medieval

532–537
Hagia Sophia, Constantinople

643
Dome of the Rock begun, Jerusalem

700
Easter eggs come into use among Christians

800
Charlemagne crowned Holy Roman Emperor

c. 980
Vikings discover Greenland

1334–1391
The Alhambra palace, Spain

1554–1566
Cathedral of St. Basil, Moscow

Faith is the substance of things hoped for, the evidence of things not seen.

Hebrews, xi, i

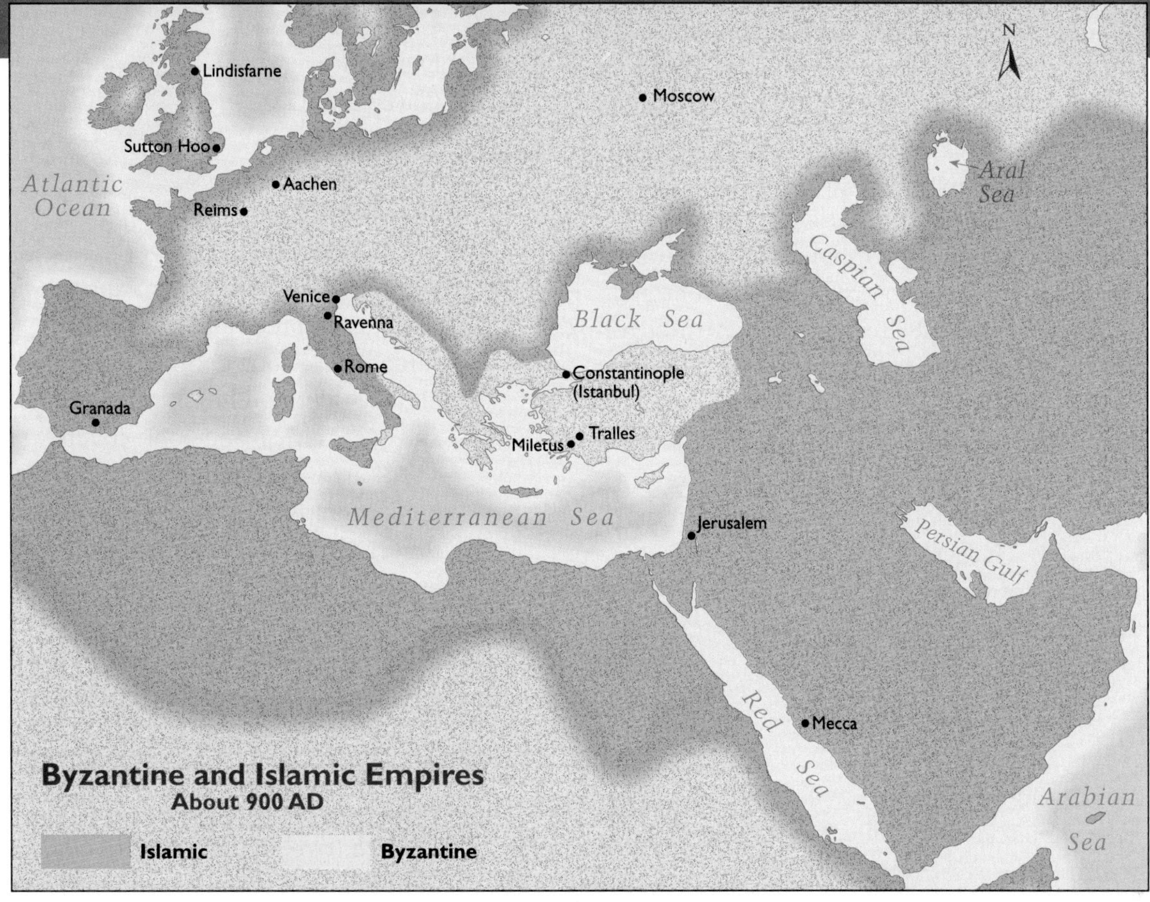

Though political borders change throughout European history, personal religious conviction crosses all boundaries. This sometimes becomes a source of conflict within countries, but many times it acts as a unifying force between different countries.

7–b Islamic monuments are decorated with abstract motifs. Human figures are prohibited in religious art and architecture.
Dome of the Rock, Jerusalem, Israel detail (fig.7–24).

7–c Can you name at least three different materials that were used to construct and decorate the interior of this church?
St. Apollinare in Classe, Ravenna, 533–549. Interior view.

7.1 Early Christian Art

Before the spread of Christianity, Romans had painted figures and scenes that were natural and realistic. The followers of Christianity, however, developed a new type of art based on their new religion. Their paintings were *symbolic.* Figures and objects suggest people and events of religious importance. Realism was not the goal of these artists. Instead, they wanted to communicate a religious thought or idea. This concept changed the course of art for several centuries.

At first, Christian artists borrowed symbols from the Romans around them. Juno's peacock became the symbol for immortality. The phoenix became the symbol for Christ's resurrection. Although first shunned as evil and deathly, the cross later became the dominant Christian symbol.

Christianity gained broad acceptance in the fourth century when the Emperor Constantine made it the state religion. This meant that the religion and its art were officially sanctioned. Large building campaigns were undertaken. The interior decoration of churches and the creation of highly crafted objects for the Christian liturgy would occupy hundreds of artists and artisans for centuries.

Vocabulary
diptych
catacombs
atrium
nave
apse
baldachin
transept
crypts
rotunda
sarcophagus

Key Notes

- Early Christian art was symbolic.
- Earliest surviving Christian art is found on frescoed walls of catacombs outside Rome.
- Acceptance of Christianity as state religion created a need for new architecture.

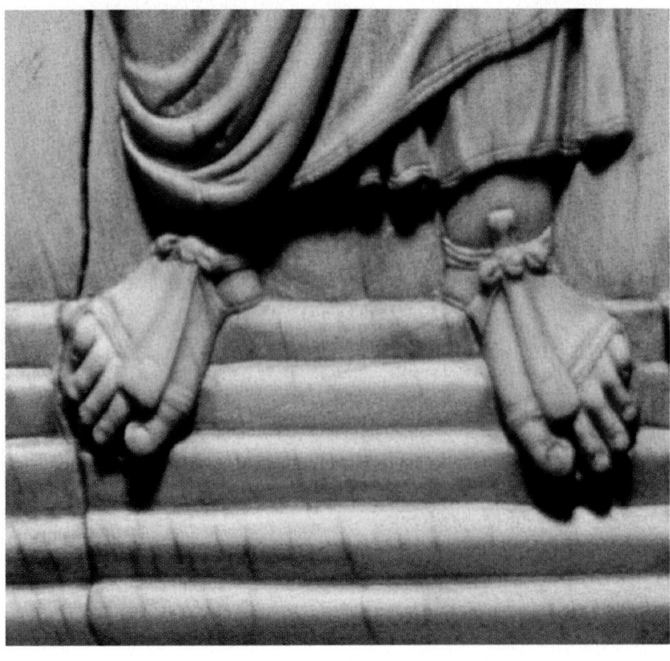

7–2 The creator of this ivory diptych was not interested in depicting real space. The niche and stairs are simply ornamental.
The Archangel Michael, detail.

Special Feature

The Archangel Michael

During the early Christian period, large sculptures were not made. However, artists did produce small pieces of exquisite craftsmanship. Artists sculpted relief carvings on sarcophagi (stone coffins), ivory panels, metalwork, church furniture and accessories, and book covers.

All art was religious and symbolic in nature, but these works also reflected the Classical ideals of beauty. Human figures were idealized, not realistic. A particularly fine example of the blend of Classical style and Christian beliefs is an ivory panel called *The Archangel Michael* (fig.7–1). The ivory panel is one half of a hinged ***diptych*** (two pieces).

In Western religions, archangels represent aspects of the divine energy. Compare this majestic archangel with a winged Victory from Greek or Roman art. The flowing folds of the robe are Classical yet naturalistic. The delicately incised wings, the features and the way the hair is styled are of the pre-Christian tradition. However, the Archangel Michael heralds a power that comes from God, not mortals. He does not inhabit an earthly space. Notice how his feet seem to hover above the stairs (fig.7–2). Clearly, Michael is not really standing on the step. The architectural setting behind him is symbolic and ornamental, not three-dimensional. The disembodied quality of the sculpture conveys the sense that Archangel Michael is a divine messenger.

7–1 What aspects of this work are naturalistic? Which are stylized?
The Archangel Michael, 5th century. Part of ivory diptych, 16 1/2" (42 cm) high. British Museum, London.

Sidelight

Thinking Like a Conservator

Faced with the task of preserving works of art, a conservator is rigorously trained in chemistry, physics and the technical aspects of treating and repairing art. The conservator also needs to know the process by which an object is made.

To make an ivory relief such as the *Archangel Michael* (fig.7–1), rectangles are sawed out of the walls of a tusk. These reliefs are seldom more than 12 inches in length. The *Archangel Michael,* nearly 50% larger, is exceptional. This relief must have been a rare and expensive item when it was created.

The conservator, very aware of the relief's uniqueness and its increasing fragility, must keep it in an optimal environment. As with most works of art, the regulation of humidity and temperature is critical. Excessive dryness causes ivory to crack. Too much moisture makes it warp. Elevated temperatures can result in color changes. Ideal conditions for the storage and display of ivory are 45% to 55% relative humidity and 65 to 72 degrees Fahrenheit. Light levels need to be kept at a minimum.

The next time you walk into a room in a museum that is a little bit chilly and rather dimly lit, keep in mind that this environment was created for a reason. The hope is that objects displayed there will be preserved for generations to come.

7–3 The catacombs functioned primarily as cemeteries. There may have been as many as four million bodies buried in the catacombs of Rome.
The Good Shepherd. Ceiling fresco, early 4th century. Catacomb of Saints Peter and Marcellinus, Rome.

Early Christian Frescoes

In Italy, Rome became the center of Christian activities, although Roman religion and traditions continued to be practiced. For a time, before the era of Constantine, the Christian religion was outlawed. Believers were persecuted and blamed for many of the troubles in the empire. In order to escape torture and death, they often inhabited the tunnel-like ***catacombs*** outside Rome. Here they met for worship, buried their dead and even lived at times in complete protection.

The earliest surviving Christian art known are frescoes that decorate the ceilings and walls of chapels within the catacombs. The ceiling fresco in the Catacomb of Saints Peter and Marcellinus shows Christ as *The Good Shepherd* (fig.7–3) in the center. (Christ had often spoken of himself as the good shepherd who gives his life for his sheep.) As in other very early Christian art, he is shown as a beardless Roman youth.

In the half-circles are several parts of the story of Jonah, an Old Testament prophet. Jonah was a significant symbol for early Christians, and his story was often used in their art. At the left, Jonah is thrown from the ship. On the right, he emerges from the whale, and, at the bottom, he is safe again on dry land. Perhaps the missing section showed him in the belly of the whale. The story was a great comfort to the Christians because it showed God's protection, care and deliverance. The standing figures with their hands raised are symbols of church members in attitudes of prayer. The circle itself represents the dome of heaven. Notice the cross formed by the bands used as connecting lines.

The Beginnings of Christian Churches

The Emperor Constantine issued the Edict of Milan in 313 AD, which made Christianity the official religion. Until his edict, worshipers had met secretly in small houses. Now, a new architecture was needed for large numbers of worshipers. The Roman basilicas (civic buildings) seemed to fit the requirements. The basilica plan seemed ideally suited for Christian worship.

The early Christian basilica (fig.7–4) was a long brick building with a timber roof. Connected to the front of the structure was an ***atrium*** (a courtyard) with a covered walkway around it. Entrances were at the rear of the atrium on the corners. Worshipers stood in the ***nave***, or central part of the basilica. On each side of the nave were side aisles. The side aisles were separated by a row of columns, usually taken from pagan temples.

7–4 Typical basilica plan.
Upper diagram reproduced by permission of Harcourt Brace Jovanovich, Inc., from *Art in Perspective* by Henri Dorra.

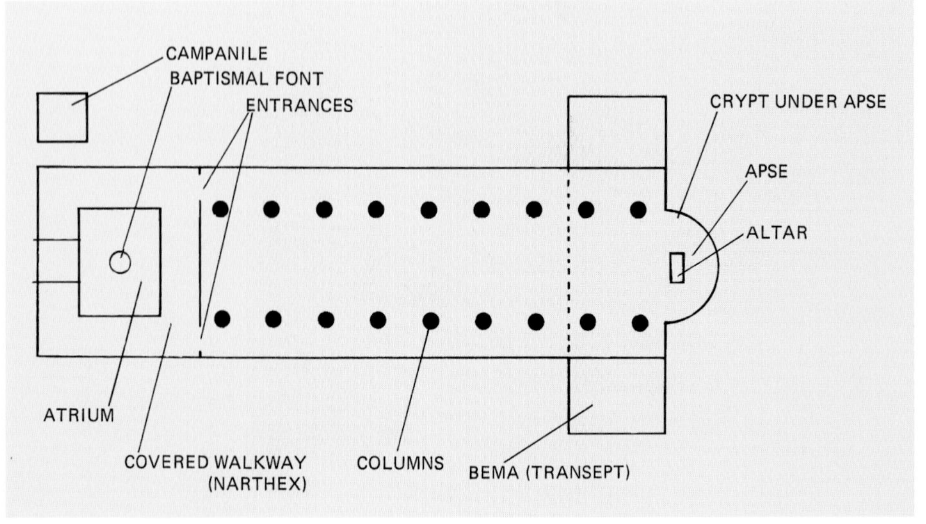

7–6 The plain exterior of this church contrasts with its rich and colorful interior (fig.7–c).
St. Apollinare in Classe. Exterior view, 533–549. Ravenna.

7–5 The long nave with its rows of columns leads the eye to the altar, the focal point of the church.
Giovanni Battista Piranesi, *St. Paul Outside the Walls.* Etching, 1749. Rome.

Windows were located above the columns to flood the interior with light. The ***apse*** was a semicircular area at the front of the nave. Above the apse was a half-dome. The altar was placed on the raised portion of the apse and always had a canopy, or ***baldachin***, over it. This was made of carved and painted wood or stone.

A triumphal arch, so-called because it symbolized the victory of Christ over eternal death, separated the nave from the apse. Later basilicas had ***transepts*** (fig.7–4) that added interior space to accommodate larger crowds and a greater number of clergy. ***Crypts*** were sometimes placed under the raised apse to provide burial space for bishops or church leaders. The general plan, enlarged and elaborated as time passed, became the basis for European cathedrals of later centuries. About forty of the original three hundred basilicas are still standing.

7–7 Early Christians identified themselves as the sheep of the Church's flock and Christ as their shepherd.
The Good Shepherd, 3rd century. Marble, half life-size. Lateran Museum, Rome.

7–8 Early Christian art uses symbols to stand for stories, people and ideas.
Chalice of Antioch, 350–500. Silver and gilt, 7 1/2" (19 cm) high, from Syria. Cloisters Collection, Metropolitan Museum of Art, New York.

The greatest basilica was Old St. Peter's in Rome. It was torn down during the Renaissance to make way for the current huge basilica of St. Peter's in the Vatican. Slightly later, *St. Paul Outside the Walls* (fig.7–5) was erected. It was destroyed by fire but was rebuilt according to old plans, paintings and drawings. Like all Christian basilicas, the interior was highly decorated. Mosaics of colored glass and gold cover the walls, creating a shimmering and sparkling surface. Even the floor is decorated with inlaid marble designs. Eighty granite columns in four rows direct the view toward the triumphal arch (also covered with mosaics) and toward the apse and altar.

In direct contrast to the glittering interiors, which symbolized the richness of spirit, the exteriors were plain brick. The exterior of *The Basilica of St. Apollinare in Classe* (fig.7–6) in Ravenna gives no hint of the mosaic-covered walls inside (fig.7–c).

Although the basilica plan was used most often in early Christian churches, it is important to note that some churches followed a central, or ***rotunda***, plan.

Sculpture and Other Metalwork

Little sculpture was produced in the early Christian church, and much of it has been destroyed. *The Good Shepherd* (fig.7–7) is a freestanding sculpture in the Roman style. It is one of the last Christian works that adheres to naturalism rather than stressing the symbolic nature of its subject. Christ is depicted as a Roman youth with his feet firmly planted on the ground. With the evolution of early Christian art, figures became more ethereal or otherworldly, as we have seen in *The Archangel Michael* (fig.7–1).

7–9 Can you identify any of the biblical scenes depicted on this sarcophagus?
Sarcophagus of Junius Bassus, about 359. Marble, 3' 10 1/2" x 8' (1.2 x 2.4 m). Museo Petriano, St. Peter's, Rome.

The Chalice of Antioch (fig.7–8) is an example of the metalwork produced during this period. Its inner, plain silver cup is set into an ornately carved silver and gilt openwork shell. The carved and footed shell has a figure of Christ depicted on each side. One is youthful and the other is more mature. Apostles, animals and birds are woven into a network of vines, branches, leaves and grapes—all symbolic of Christ and his work. The eagle on one side and the rosettes at the top are signs of immortality.

Coffin-like boxes made of stone, called *sarcophagi* (one is a ***sarcophagus***) were carved completely in relief. The sarcophagi were used as caskets for burial. The carved sarcophagus was a Roman development, but the subject matter on the Christian sarcophagi was religious (fig.7–9).

Lesson 7.1 Review

1 Name an early Christian symbol and tell what it represented.
2 Where were the earliest Christian frescoes painted?
3 What is a diptych?
4 What type of Roman buildings did the early Christians adapt to become churches?
5 How were basilicas decorated on the inside? Contrast this to their exterior appearance.
6 What was the purpose of a sarcophagus?
7 Describe how Christ was usually portrayed in the earliest Christian art.

7.2 Byzantine Art: A Shift to the East

AFTER THE DEATH of Constantine in 337, the Roman Empire was split into Eastern and Western Empires. The West went into a steady decline. Rome lost its power and was sacked by Germanic tribes. The Eastern Empire, with its capital in Constantinople, gained great political strength. In 527, Justinian ascended the throne of the Eastern Roman, or Byzantine, Empire. He recaptured most of southern Italy and established Ravenna on the east coast as the new center of power.

Justinian's reign began the so-called Golden Age of Byzantine culture and art. The number of important and beautiful church buildings constructed in Ravenna and Constantinople in the fifth and sixth centuries is amazing. Many are plain brick on the outside and look rather ordinary at first (fig.7–10). However, inside they are sumptuously encrusted with brilliant Byzantine mosaics.

Byzantine architecture spread over Eastern Europe. Gradually the exterior as well as the interior became highly imaginative, as seen in the onion-shaped domes of Russian churches.

The Byzantine tradition of art and architecture extended for centuries. For well over 1000 years artists worked to produce masterpieces of heavenly, glimmering beauty.

Key Notes

- Center of power moves to the east with Constantinople as its capital.
- First Golden Age of Byzantine begins with the reign of the Emperor Justinian.
- Mosaics made of glass become the primary means of wall decoration and completely cover the interiors of churches.

Vocabulary

tesserae
pendentives
piers
icons
iconostasis
triptych

Special Feature

The Justinian and Theodora Mosaics

Artists of the early Christian and Byzantine churches conveyed their message of salvation through mosaics. They achieved an incredible degree of expressiveness in this medium. Roman mosaics had been of polished, colored stone, but Byzantine mosaics were made of brightly colored glass (***tesserae***) pressed into wet plaster. Glass increased the color range and could be made to reflect the light. The pieces were set at a slight angle to the surface to create a shimmering effect.

One of the most striking mosaics is found in the church of San Vitale in Ravenna. The building and the mosaics inside it are extraordinary achievements of Byzantine art.

The mosaics cover almost every available surface. They sparkle with color. Green and gold are used most often, but there are also scarlets, purples and blues. Images and sym-

7–10 This building is based on the central, or rotunda, plan.
San Vitale. Interior, about 525–547. Ravenna.

7–11 Notice that the name of the bishop of Ravenna, Maximianus, is written above his head. The bishop played an important role in building the church, and he dedicated it in 547.
Emperor Justinian and Attendants, about 547. Mosaic, nearly life-size figures. San Vitale, Ravenna.

bols covering the entire sanctuary illustrate primarily Biblical subjects.

There are two mosaics flanking the altar which depict contemporary figures. *Emperor Justinian and Attendants* (fig.7–11) is on one wall, and the *Empress Theodora and Attendants* (fig.7–12) is on the other. Justinian and Theodora are participating in a church service. The bread and wine of the Eucharist are being presented. Justinian carries a vessel containing the bread, and Theodora carries the golden cup containing the wine.

7–12 Analyze how the artist has placed these figures in a particular place, yet at the same time, has negated any sense of real space.
Empress Theodora and Attendants, about 547. Mosaic, nearly life-size figures. San Vitale, Ravenna.

The emperor, with a halo around his head, is showing everyone that he is God's holy representative on earth and is therefore holy himself. Justinian is exactly at the center. The positions of the figures are very important and denote their rank. Justinian is flanked by his sources of power—court officials and the military on his right, the priesthood on his left.

The figures are generally stylized. Several of the faces are quite individualistic and are probably portraits. The bodies of these tall, slim figures disappear under flat, decorative costumes. Large eyes stare from small, almond-shaped faces. Their feet do not seem to touch the ground as they look directly ahead. They look as though they are posing rather stiffly for a photographer.

Note the monogram of Christ on the shield at left. The monogram consists of the superimposed Greek letters X and P (chi and rho) which are the first two letters of the Greek word for Christ. This symbol serves to further emphasize the divine protection the emperor believed God bestowed on his reign.

All of the figures sparkle today as they did in the sixth century. The background of gold glass tesserae (gold leaf embedded in glass) in the Justinian mosaic symbolizes the holiness and perfection of heaven and eliminates any specific spatial reference. The use of gold for this symbolic purpose was typical of Byzantine art.

Architecture

The sixth century is known as the First Golden Age of Byzantine Art. Under the reign of Justinian, the large basilica called *Hagia Sophia* (Church of the Holy Wisdom) was built in Constantinople in 532–537 (fig.7–13). Hagia Sophia is a monumental structure of completely original design. It was created by the two architects Anthemius of Tralles and Isidorus of Miletos. The unique design (fig.7–13a) combines a long open space (like a basilica) and a centralized dome (like a rotunda). The structural challenge was to place a huge round dome on square supporting walls. The diagram (fig.7–13b) shows how the problem

7–13 Compare the plan of this church to the plan of the Pantheon (fig.6–34a).
Anthemius of Tralles and Isidorus of Miletos, *Hagia Sophia,* about 532–537. Istanbul.

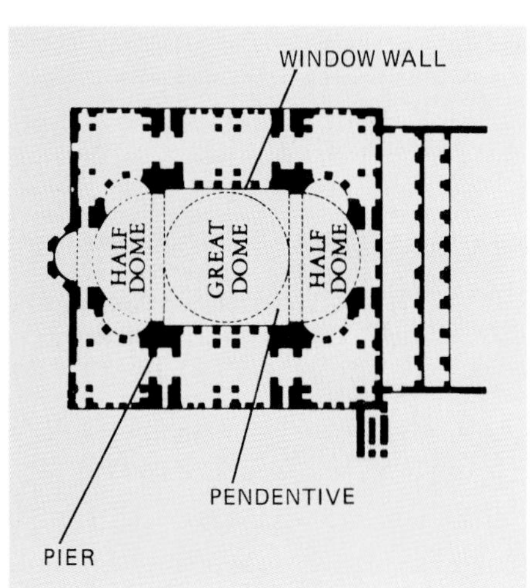

7–13a Plan of the Hagia Sophia

7–14 Notice the location of the windows and compare them to the oculus of the Pantheon (fig.6–35).
Hagia Sophia, interior.

π

190 AD
π (3.14) calculated, China

400–1240 AD
Kingdom of Ghana at its peak

450 AD
Japanese Empire founded

World Cultural Timeline

300 AD
First court ballgames played in Mesoamerica

651 AD
Koran written

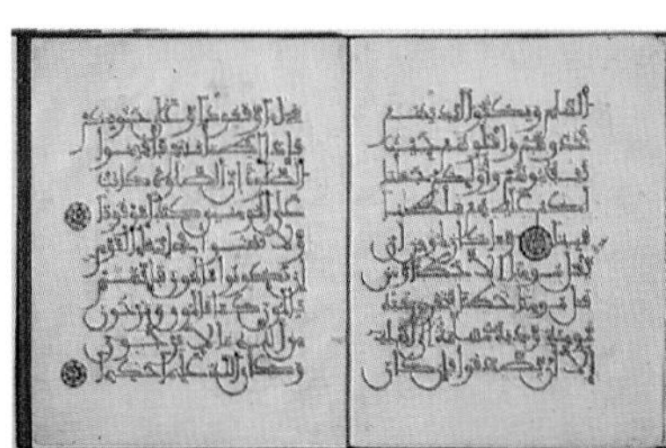

was solved. Four concave spherical triangles, called ***pendentives***, are supported by four ***piers***. These units form four arches on the walls and create a continuous circle at their top edge, on which the dome rests.

The pendentives provide a graceful transition from square base to round dome. With the four piers carrying the weight, the pendentives allow the walls to remain open under the arches. The dome seems to float above the arches. Pendentive and dome construction became a characteristic construction technique of later Byzantine churches, Renaissance domed buildings and domed structures in America and the rest of the world. This mammoth work was completed in less than six years—an incredible feat, considering the new type of construction, the gigantic size and the lack of modern machinery.

From the outside, Hagia Sophia seems to be a mountain of masonry that reaches its apex at the top of the flat dome, about 200 feet above the city. The minarets were added in 1453 when the Moslems conquered Constantinople and changed the church to a mosque. (To see how it originally looked, cover the minarets.)

The exterior of the Hagia Sophia does not prepare one for what will be seen and felt inside. The space is overpowering: 65 feet long and 130 feet wide. The inside of the dome is almost 165 feet above the floor. On either end of the dome rest two half-domes, which make the nave a long oval. The church was the largest interior space in the world at that time. Arcades and galleries open onto the main space on two levels, adding to the feeling of enormous space. Light floods the interior from many windows, although more existed in the original structure.

Originally, the interior walls (fig.7–14) were completely covered with Byzantine mosaics of brilliant colors and gold. As in Ravenna, the glass tesserae are placed irregularly and create a glittering visual sensation. Eyewitnesses tell of a feeling that the entire golden dome was hanging from heaven by a chain. As they walked past the sparkling mosaics, they felt they were walking the very streets of heaven.

When the Moslems converted the church to a mosque, they scraped the mosaics from the walls or covered them with plaster because their religion did not permit any likenesses of people. Geometric designs were painted over the plaster, completely changing the character of the interior space. Skilled workers have recently uncovered many of the mosaics.

In 1933, one of the last mosaics completed in Hagia Sophia was uncovered. It features Christ placed between John the Baptist and the Virgin Mary (fig.7–15). Christ previously often had been shown as a stern judge, but here he has a compassionate and loving look. His face is rather realistic, although his robes are stylized. Today, Hagia

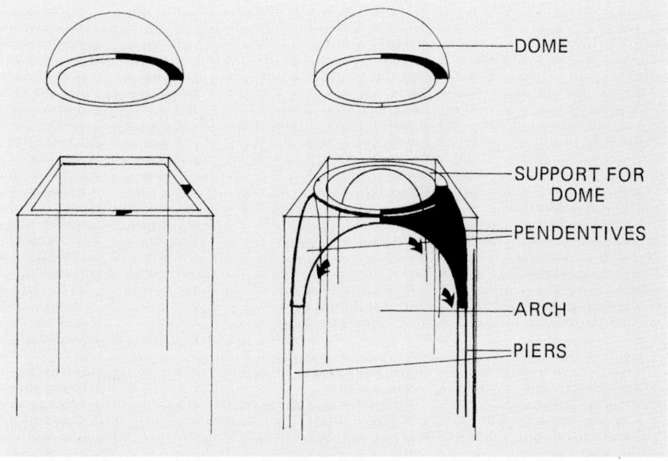

7–13b If a round dome is placed on a square base (as at left), only a small part of the dome will be supported by the existing walls. If arches are placed in the four walls (as at right) and the circle of the dome rests on the four arches, a pendentive is formed in the four corners. The massive weight of the dome is supported by this spherical triangle, which transfers the thrust to the four huge piers that support it.

7–15 The gold glass makes this mosaic shimmer. Compare it to earlier Roman mosaics.
Christ between the Virgin and Saint John the Baptist (detail), 1261. Mosaic, southern gallery, Hagia Sophia, Istanbul.

7.16 Greek cross plan.

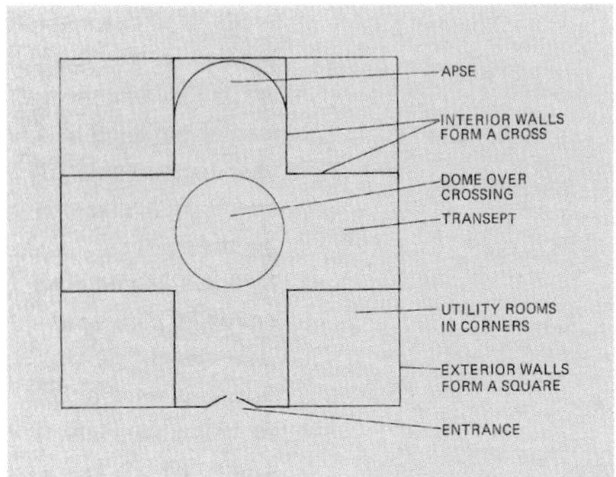

7–17 This church is dedicated to St. Mark, the patron saint of Venice.
St. Mark's, begun 1063. Venice.

7–18 Analyze the many decorative elements for their geometric shapes.
Cathedral of St. Basil, 1554–1566. Moscow.

Sophia is not used for worship, but is a huge museum of Byzantine art.

The Iconoclastic Controversy disrupted the growth of Byzantine culture after 726 and caused a split in the church. On one side were iconoclasts, who wanted to destroy religious images, or ***icons***. On the other side of the controversy were those who wanted to keep images in the church. Much of what had been created earlier was destroyed. No art was produced for over a hundred years.

The year 843 heralded the Second Golden Age of Byzantium, or the Byzantine Renaissance. No Byzantine structure rivaled Hagia Sophia in any way, although smaller churches used many of the features developed in its construction.
The plan of an Eastern European church usually was of a Greek cross (four arms of equal length) contained in a square (fig.7–16). The apse was in one of the arms. A central dome rested on a square base. Often the dome was set on a cylindrical drum that raised it high above the roof line.

The largest and most lavishly decorated church of the Second Golden Age is St. Mark's in Venice (fig.7–17). The church was begun in 1063 and built to hold the body of St. Mark, brought from Alexandria. It has the typical Greek cross plan. But in addition to the usual central dome, each arm has a dome of its own. The exterior has many mosaics and 2643 colored marble columns brought from Constantinople by Crusaders. The interior is completely covered with brilliant mosaics of both Byzantine and Venetian glass.

Four horses formerly stood above the main entrance. They also were brought from Constantinople. They are probably original Greek bronzes from about 300 BC.

Byzantine architecture, like the Eastern Orthodox faith, spread over Eastern Europe and into the center of Russia. Often churches were constructed of wood rather than brick, but the interiors still glowed with mosaics and paintings of saints and apostles. The most famous of the Russian churches is the Cathedral of St. Basil (fig.7–18) located across Red Square from the Kremlin. While Moscow contains many Byzantine-style buildings and churches, St. Basil's is unique and fantastic. Built during the rule of Ivan the Terrible, it has a large number of onion-shaped domes surrounding a central tentlike structure. The brilliantly painted domes and walls create a fairy-tale appearance that is both joyful and impressive.

Painting and Sculpture

We have seen how Byzantine artists excelled in the art of mosaics. They also had a very strong tradition of painting. Most paintings were icons (religious images) painted on wooden panels. Icons were often used as worship centers in homes. The interiors of the churches also were decorated with icons. A large screen of images (***iconostasis***) separated the sanctuary from the nave of the Byzantine church.

Byzantine painting was colorful and emotional. Artists used egg tempera as their medium. Figures were painted against a brilliant gold background. The *Enthroned Madonna and Child* (fig.7–19) is typical of the Byzantine style of work. The Madonna floats rather than sits on her throne. The Christ Child seems to be resting securely on her arm, but on closer examination the figure actually hovers in front of the elaborate design of the Virgin's garment. Indeed, the fabric of her robe takes on an abstract life of its own. The folds resemble sunbursts. The artist makes no attempt to place the figures firmly in space. The beauty of the image and emotion conveyed by the figures are the essence of this representation. The artist has adhered to the Byzantine tradition. Meaning and emotion take precedence over the depiction of reality. Icon painting continued to be important for centuries in all areas where the Eastern Orthodox church was present.

7–19 An icon's meaning is more important than an accurate depiction of reality.
Enthroned Madonna and Child, 13th century. Egg tempera on panel, 51 5/8" x 30 1/4" (131 x 77) cm. National Gallery of Art, Washington DC, gift of Mrs. Otto H. Kahn.

7–20 The hinged wings of this piece fold in on the central panel and add to its compact, portable nature.
Harbaville Triptych (Christ Enthroned with Saints), c. 950. Ivory, central panel 9 1/2" x 5 1/2" (24 x 14 cm). Louvre, Paris.

Craftspersons often decorated churches and the objects used in worship. Brilliantly colored enamels were fused to metal surfaces on crosses, boxes and chalices used in various rites. Ivory panels also were carved.

The *Harbaville Triptych* (fig.17–20), displays a series of saints with Christ enthroned at the top center between St. John and the Virgin. The ***triptych*** (three hinged pieces) is an example of the portable nature of many works of Byzantine art. Small objects like this ivory often were transported to faraway lands as gifts or as plunder. Consequently, Byzantine art and its style became known throughout Europe.

Lesson 7.2 Review

1 How are the figures stylized in *Emperor Justinian and Attendants*?
2 Analyze how the artist has made Theodora the center of attention in the mosaic *Empress Theodora and Attendants*.
3 Where is *Hagia Sophia* located? What was extraordinary about its construction?
4 What did the iconoclasts want to destroy?
5 Name the largest, most ornate church of the Second Golden Age of Byzantium.
6 From where did the horses over the entrance of St. Mark's cathedral in Venice come?
7 Describe the roof of the Cathedral of St. Basil in Moscow.
8 What is an icon?

7.3 Islamic Faith and Art

ISLAM REFERS TO BOTH the religion of the Moslems and the nations that follow the religion. In the seventh century, Islam began in Arabia and swept across the Near East and the southern Mediterranean with astonishing speed. By 732, only 100 years after the death of its founder, Mohammed, the Moslems had reached India in the east, and Spain, Portugal and southwestern France in the west. Islam created a civilization that rivaled Christianity and had a far-ranging influence in medieval Europe.

The Moslem religion prohibited the use of human figures in religious art. Therefore, artists developed elaborate geometric and abstract designs. The term ***arabesque***, which means "in the Arab style," was coined to describe their complex designs.

Islamic architecture, like Western architecture, used arches, columns and vaults. However, Islamic architects created a unique style and richly decorated their buildings with stucco reliefs.

In addition to the inventive designs and architecture, Islam developed Arabic numerals and led the way in government, philosophy, science and medicine. The splendor of the Islamic heritage, particularly its architecture, left a lasting impression on the European imagination.

Key Notes

- Islam spread rapidly in the seventh century across the Near East and the Mediterranean.
- Islamic design is complex, geometric and abstract.
- Islamic architecture is outstanding for its splendor and imaginativeness.

Vocabulary

arabesque
stucco
mosque
minarets
miniature

7–23 Stucco relief is an inexpensive means of creating elaborate architectural elements.
Court of the Lions, the Alhambra, detail of stucco work.

Special Feature

The Alhambra

Some of the most splendid Moslem architecture was built in Spain. The Alhambra Palace in Granada is an outstanding example of Islamic arch construction. *The Alhambra* (fig.7–21) is a sprawling palace with royal residential quarters, court complexes and offices, a bath and a mosque. The most famous feature of the Alhambra are the courtyards. Within the courtyards are fountains and light-reflecting water basins. The courtyards are surrounded by slender columns with decorated arches.

The most famous of the courtyards of the Alhambra is the *Court of the Lions* (fig.7–22). The courtyard is framed by rhythmically spaced single, double and triple columns. The arches above the columns are heavily decorated with ***stucco*** reliefs (fig.7–23). Stucco (wet plaster) is extremely flexible and the architecture it decorates can be made to appear very free flowing and organic. The delicate reliefs in the Court of the Lions give the building an airy, almost floating appearance. The arches themselves seem to hang from, rather than support, the ceiling. Even with the elaborate stucco work, there is a wonderful symmetry and rhythm that prevails throughout the building. Like the wonderful stories from *The Thousand and One Nights,* Islamic architecture and decoration evoke a sense of wonder and romance.

7–21 The Alhambra is a large complex that includes a variety of buildings.
The Alhambra, Granada, Spain. Overall view.

7–22 This courtyard contains some of the finest examples of stucco decoration produced in the Moslem world.
Court of the Lions, the Alhambra, 1354–1391. Granada, Spain.

Sidelight

Continuity in Islamic Art

The *Koran,* sacred book of Islam, contains both spiritual and social law. The Koran regulates not only the religion of Islam, but also acts of daily life, like brushing teeth, saying hello and eating a meal. All followers of Islam, whether they lived in Spain or Arabia, were governed by the same religious and social rules. This consistency in religious and social life was mirrored in the uniformity of Islamic art. There were certain rules that Islamic art had to follow, whatever part of Islam it may have come from. Artists in Islamic countries adhered to a single style that had been sanctioned by time and convention.

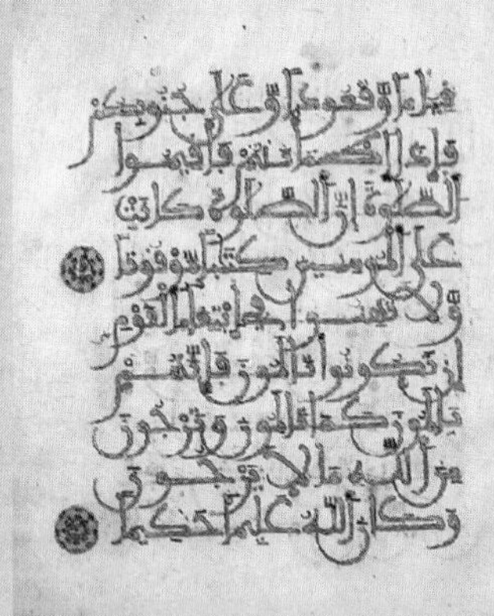

Page from the Koran.

Islamic artists are forbidden to represent humans or the Moslem god, Allah, in their art. Calligraphy, the noblest and most continuous of the arts, owes its supreme status to the fact that it transmits the Koran. Therefore, Arabic script serves as the basis for many designs.

Islamic Architecture

The Islamic architectural heritage is especially evident in the places of worship, called ***mosques***. Islamic architects constructed new buildings and also made old Christian basilicas and churches into mosques. Moslems from many countries built *The Dome of the Rock* (fig.7–24) in Jerusalem. The site of the dome marks the place where Mohammed was said to have left this earth. The dome also covers the top of the rock mountain on which Abraham attempted to sacrifice his son Isaac. This oldest Islamic monument (begun about 643) has an octagonal base. Many columns inside support the golden dome. The building is Byzantine in its rotunda form and was designed for this one particular spot. The slightly pointed dome of wood was overlaid with lead and gilded with gold, but today it reflects the brilliant sun from an anodized aluminum surface (fig. 7–b). The exterior of the mosque is covered with brightly glazed ceramic tiles. Originally, it contained mosaics of Byzantine glass.

7–24 Moslems from many countries built this monument.
Dome of the Rock, late 7th century. Jerusalem, Israel.

The earliest, huge Moslem building for congregational purposes is *The Great Mosque at Damascus* (fig.7–25), built from 705 to 711. It made use of existing Christian and Roman structures. The existing square towers were turned into the first Moslem ***minarets***. From these minarets, people were called to prayer several times a day. The huge sanctuary has many columns to support the roof. It measures about 525 feet by 328 feet. It still contains some of the original mosaic decoration. Other early Islamic mosques can be found in North Africa, Iraq, Turkey, Mesopotamia, Egypt and Spain.

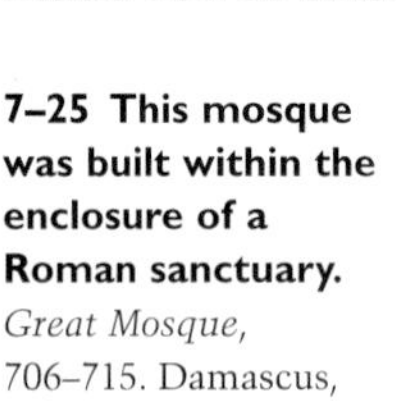

7–25 This mosque was built within the enclosure of a Roman sanctuary.
Great Mosque, 706–715. Damascus, Syria.

Islamic Book Illustration

Islamic artists greatly advanced the art of book illustration. Islamic decorative style featured elaborate geometric designs and complex patterns of intertwining lines and shapes. The use of abstract designs was highly developed because artists were forbidden to use human figures in religious art. In the page from a book shown here, a Turkish calligrapher used a lavish and inventive design to write the single word Allah (fig.7–26).

Laila and Majnun (fig.7–27) is an example of a ***miniature*** (small picture) from a manuscript. It illustrates a romantic poem. The scene is two-dimensional with little shading or perspective. The colors are bright and clear. The intertwining patterns of leaves and flowers are purely Islamic.

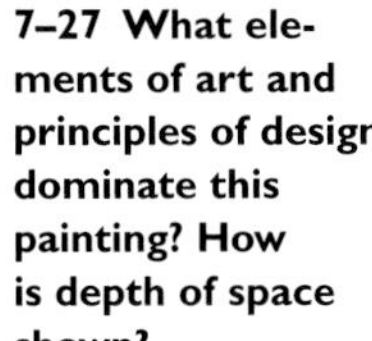

7–27 What elements of art and principles of design dominate this painting? How is depth of space shown?
Laila and Majnun at School, miniature from a manuscript of the Khamsa of Nizami, 1524–1525. Ink, colors and gold on paper. The Metropolitan Museum of Art, New York, gift of Alexander Smith Cochran, 1913.

7–26 This page has a very modern look. How would you describe it?
Calligraphic page, from the *Album of the Conqueror,* 15th century, Turkish. Topkapi Palace Museum, Istanbul.

Lesson 7.3 Review

1 Define arabesque.
2 Describe the Alhambra. What part of the Alhambra's architecture is most famous?
3 What is a mosque?
4 Why is the *Dome of the Rock* in Jerusalem important to both Christians and Moslems?
5 What were some of the characteristics of Islamic book illustration?
6 Describe the Great Mosque of Damascus.

7.4 Early Medieval Art

THE MIDDLE AGES is a period that spans over 1000 years. The first half of the medieval era was a time of much turmoil and change. The Roman empire had collapsed, having been overrun by the Visigoths, the Huns and the Vandals. Because the Roman empire no longer put up a defense against European tribes, these tribes were able to move through Europe to look for permanent homes. In this Migration period (400–600), few paintings or large buildings were produced. Tribes needed to carry their art and treasures with them. Therefore, artwork was entirely confined to portable objects such as ornaments, weapons and objects for daily use.

Most medieval tribes were Christian, but they also had a pagan tradition. Dreadful monsters and dragons were featured in their songs and epics. Animal motifs were common in their decoration and design.

Manuscript ***illumination*** became an important art form. Not only could books be easily carried, they were of great use to missionaries. Christian missionaries tried to establish the authority of the Church among the wandering tribes and bring stability. Illuminated manuscripts were drawn by monks in secluded monasteries throughout Europe.

Key Notes

- The early Middle Ages was a time of unrest as tribes moved through Europe.
- Most early medieval art was portable.
- Geometric designs and animal motifs were favored as decorative elements.
- Manuscript illumination became an important art form and reached a high point in its development.

Vocabulary
illumination
vellum

7–29 Can your eye follow the looping and curving lines of this intricate design?
Lindisfarne Gospel Book, detail of fig.7–28.

Special Feature

The *Lindisfarne Gospel Book*

Artists of the early period were influenced by Christian art of the Mediterranean. But they also were fascinated with the tribal (or barbaric) tradition of geometric motifs and interlaced designs of letters, flowers and animals. Monks in secluded monasteries spent their lifetimes illustrating pages of scripture with fantastic animals, intricate designs and infinite detail. For these artists, ornamentation represented everything that was rich and beautiful. They believed that by illustrating the holy word in this manner, they were paying tribute to the glory of God.

The *Lindisfarne Gospel Book* (fig.7–28), illustrated between 698 and 721 in Christianized Great Britain, is a volume of many ***vellum*** (parchment) pages. The page shown here is the beginning of the Gospel of St. Matthew. The X–P (chi-rho), a contraction of the Greek name for Christ, is rendered with incredible intricacy (fig.7–29) and pulsates with a life of its own. It is a fitting way for the gospel to begin. The illustration is beautifully interlaced with abstract and geometric designs of minute detail. Hidden in the curves and swirls are serpents, dragons and other fantastic animals.

7–28 This manuscript is made of a superior type of parchment (bleached animal skin) called vellum. Vellum is made of calfskin.
X-P (Chi-Rho) Page, from *Lindisfarne Gospel Book*, 698–721. Miniature on parchment, 9 1/2" x 8" (24 x 20 cm), Lindisfarne, England. British Library, London.

Migration Art

Artists of the barbaric tribes crafted ornate metalwork. Pins used to fasten garments (fig.7–a) were often inlaid with precious or semiprecious stones.

A powerful ruler probably once owned the *Purse Cover* (fig.7–30). The piece makes use of garnets, glass, enamel and gold. The lid is mounted on a slab of ivory. In 1939, it was excavated in England as part of the Sutton Hoo ship-burial. The decorations at the top are geometric and have a heavily interlaced design. The two outside groups show a man between two beasts. The inner groups show two eagles seizing two ducks.

The Classical Revival under Charlemagne

Charlemagne, the Frankish king (786–814) and emperor of the West (800–814), brought a period of stability to the north. His reign provided an opportunity for the arts to flourish. He was directly responsible for a short revival of interest in Classical studies, art and language.

Under his direction, the Palatine Chapel (fig.7–31) was built in Aachen, Germany. The Palatine Chapel, designed by the architect Odo of Metz, is the greatest surviving monument of the Carolingian era. Built from 792–805, the chapel was meant to symbolize the religious and political power of

7–31 The interior of this chapel is heavy and massive in appearance compared to early Christian and Byzantine churches. *Palatine Chapel of Charlemagne*, 792–805, interior view. Aachen, Germany.

7–30 This piece was found at the burial site of a king. *Purse Cover*, first half of 7th century. Gold, garnets, glass and enamel, 7 1/2" (19 cm) long, from Sutton Hoo, England. British Museum, London.

World Cultural Timeline

600 AD
Concept of zero invented in India

800 AD
Beginning of Inca Empire; Machu Picchu built using passive-solar energy designs

845 AD
Paper money in China leads to inflation and state bankruptcy

1000 AD
Stone quarried for first Easter Island monoliths

800–1200 AD
The Temple of Angkor Wat built, Cambodia

1312 AD
The Mali Empire reaches its height

Charlemagne. Charlemagne wanted a chapel that would rival the churches of Rome and Byzantium.

The chapel is shaped like an octagon. It was the model for several later German churches. The chapel is 105 feet high inside and is over 49 feet in diameter. The sense of space is increased by the wide walkway,

Window in Time

Monastic Life

Monasticism developed during the early Christian era, when Christians devoted themselves to solitary meditation and prayer. The earliest monks lived in small communities, each in a separate hut or cell, or in complete solitude in remote places. This hermit style of monasticism was particularly widespread in the eastern Mediterranean.

Eventually, however, some monks came together to form communities headed by an abbot. They still spent most of their time alone, but they prayed together and obeyed certain rules. This style of monastic life eventually spread into southern Europe.

In 440, St. Patrick brought the monastic tradition to Ireland, which became a refuge for Christians who fled Britain and Gaul. The site of Skellig Michael on an island off the western coast of Ireland was one of the first monastic communities. The monks lived in remote stone humps perched on steep precipices overlooking the sea. The humps were constructed from flat, unworked fieldstone and clustered around a small oratory (place for prayer) also made of stone. When not praying, the monks grew what they could in the rocky soil and supplemented their diets with any fish they could catch.

Monasteries in Ireland and Scotland became important centers of learning and the arts. In scriptoria, or writing workshops, monks produced and illuminated many Gospels and other books of sacred writings.

Following in the footsteps of St. Patrick, the Irish became fervent missionaries of their Celtic Christianity. They founded numerous important monastic communities in England, at Lindisfarne, and on the Continent, at Luxeuil in France, Saint Gall in Switzerland and Bobbio in Italy.

But it was a more regulated, less austere kind of monasticism that ultimately became most popular throughout Europe. It was established by St. Benedict of Nursia (c. 480–543) who around 529 founded a monastery at Monte Cassino in Italy. St. Benedict formulated a Benedictine Rule, which detailed how the community would be organized and how it would work. Vows were taken regarding poverty, chastity, obedience and *stabilitas loci,* which meant promising to not leave the monastery. It was important that monks stayed within the community, for sharing the manual work that made the monastery self-sufficient was of vital importance to its continued existence. St. Benedict visualized a monastery with everything the monks might need within its walls so that they would never have occasion to leave.

A plan for a medieval monastery drawn up around 820 by Abbot Heito of Reichenau is preserved in the Chapter Library at Saint Gall in Switzerland. This plan was the model used for such monasteries throughout the Middle Ages. This unique document that has survived through the centuries clearly reflects St. Benedict's wishes.

Looking at the plan we can see how every facet of life was taken care of within the monastery walls. The church is the largest structure. Close to the church were other important buildings: the dormitory, the refectory or eating hall, the kitchen and the scriptorium where manuscripts were copied. These buildings were grouped around a square courtyard or cloister. A covered walk around the four sides functioned as a sheltered walkway between essential buildings. There were various barns for livestock, workshops, a mill, a wine press and storage areas. Behind the church were an infirmary and a novitiate where young boys were trained to be monks. To the left of the church the abbot had his quarters and in front of that was a guest house for important visitors and a hostel to accommodate travelers and pilgrims.

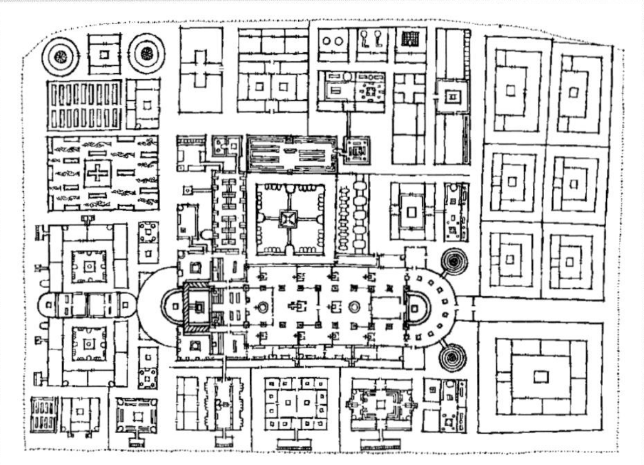

Plan of Saint Gall.

7–32 This painting reflects the strong interest in Roman civilization prevalent during Charlemagne's time.
St. Matthew the Evangelist, about 800, from the *Gospel Book*, Rhineland. Miniature on parchment, 14" x 9 1/2" (36 x 24 cm). British Museum, London.

7–33 What elements has the artist used to give this work its extraordinary energy?
St. Matthew the Evangelist, about 816–835, from the *Gospel Book of Archbishop Ebbo of Reims*. Approximately 10" x 8" (25 x 20 cm), Hautvilliers near Reims. Bibliothèque Nationale, Paris.

or ambulatory. The interior dome was originally covered with mosaics of reflecting glass tesserae. The chapel still holds the remains of Charlemagne.

Under Charlemagne's rule, monasteries were constructed to preserve the learning of the past. Monks spent their lives copying scripture and other important writings from the past. The art of manuscript illumination was very active during the Carolingian era. While some pages of these manuscripts contained no illustrations, others were filled with designs and figures. These images, or miniatures, often illustrated or embellished the written text.

St. Matthew the Evangelist was painted during Charlemagne's reign in Rhineland (now Germany). St. Matthew is writing his Gospel as he works in a Classical setting. The painting reflects the Carolingian interest in classical mathematics, architecture and perspective drawing. The canopy and building are similar to the central plan structure of both San Vitale in Ravenna and Charlemagne's Palatine Chapel.

Compare *St. Matthew the Evangelist* (fig.7–32) with another *St. Matthew* from a gospel book made for Archbishop Ebbo of Reims (fig.7–33). The first is Classical and calm; the saint is intent on setting down his own thoughts. The second is extremely expressive and is filled with energy as St. Matthew hurries to write his Gospel. He appears to be seized with divine inspiration. The contrast between these two styles shows the wide range in style that existed in the ninth century.

Lesson 7.4 Review

1 When was the Medieval period?
2 Why were nomadic tribes able to move so freely through Europe during the Middle Ages?
3 Name the main types of art produced during the Middle Ages.
4 Which medieval king revived an interest in Greek and Roman art?
5 How are the *Lindisfarne Gospel* and the Sutton Hoo purse cover similar?
6 What was the name of Charlemagne's chapel? What city is it in?
7 Compare the size of both *St. Matthew* illuminations to the size of this book. Which is larger?

Primary Source

Hagia Sophia

In the sixth century, the historian, Procopius, described Hagia Sophia (Church of the Holy Wisdom). The building was surfaced with marbles of many colors: black and white, green, silver-flecked, red and white, and yellow. Columns were gilded with gold. Brass chains from the ceiling held silver oil lamps. In the sanctuary there was a gold-plated screen with religious images. Around the altar there was a brilliant red curtain embroidered in gold.

The church was finished in less than six years by a team of ten thousand workmen gathered from all the surrounding areas. It was dedicated by the Emperor Justinian, who supplied 1006 oxen, 6000 sheep, 600 stags, 1000 swine and 10,000 birds and fowl plus 30,000 bushels of meal for the gigantic thanksgiving celebration and dedication. In his book, *On the Buildings*, Procopius describes the amazement of his contemporaries upon viewing the interior of the huge domed structure:

"So the church has become a spectacle of marvelous beauty, overwhelming to those who see it, but to those who know it by hearsay altogether incredible.…Yet it seems not to rest upon solid masonry, but to cover the space with its golden dome suspended from Heaven…though they turn their attention to every side, and look with contracted brows upon every detail, observers are still unable to understand the skillful craftsmanships, but they always depart from there overwhelmed by the sight…It was by many skillful devices that the Emperor Justinian and the master-builder Anthemius and Isidorus secured the stability of the church, hanging, as it does, in mid-air."

Chapter Review

Review

1 Describe the early Christian basilicas. Draw a basilica floor plan. Do you know a contemporary church that has a similar floor plan?

2 Describe a typical Eastern European church built during the Second Golden Age of Byzantium.

3 Name one way that Roman and Byzantine mosaics differ.

4 List several characteristics of Byzantine painting as exemplified in *Enthroned Madonna and Child.*

5 How did the iconoclasts change the development of Byzantine art?

6 What is a pendentive? Include a diagram in your explanation.

7 What material did Islamic artists use to decorate the arches in the Court of the Lion at the Alhambra?

Interpret

1 List several ways that early Christian art differed from classical Greek art.

2 How did the Edict of Milan affect architecture?

3 Compare the Roman copy of the Greek painting, *The Battle of Issus*, to *Emperor Justinian and Attendants.* Discuss medium, location and style.

4 Five illuminated manuscript pages are illustrated in this chapter. All are considered masterpieces. Which do you prefer? Why?

Other Tools for Learning

Maps

1 Look at the location of Ravenna on a map. On what sea is it located? It was surrounded by marshes and a shallow bay. Why do you think it was an important city within the Byzantine Empire?

2 Why do you think Constantinople's location has made it so important throughout history?

Timelines

1 Which is older, Dome of the Rock in Jerusalem or Hagia Sophia in Constantinople?

2 How old was Hagia Sophia when Constantinople was conquered by the Turks?

3 Name a piece of art that was made within 200 years before or after the coronation of Charlemagne.

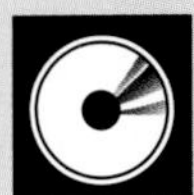

Electronic Media

CD-ROM drive: *Microsoft Art Gallery*

1 Research illuminated manuscripts. Copy an illuminated capital letter.

CD-ROM drive: Electronic Encyclopedia (e.g., *New Grolier Multimedia* or *Microsoft Encarta*)

1 Discover why Charlemagne established monasteries. How did his love of the Classics influence art and architecture?

Activity 1

Family Fresco

Materials

Styrofoam platter
tempera paint or watercolors
plaster of Paris
bucket, water
assorted brushes
terry cloth towel
vine charcoal
newspapers
paper clips

Take a look.

- Fig.7–3, *The Good Shepherd.* Ceiling fresco, early 4th century.

Think about it. Among the first Christian art known to exist are the frescoes that decorate the ceilings and walls of the catacombs. (See page 32 to refresh your memory on fresco technique). Study the fresco, *The Good Shepherd.*

- What story does this fresco tell?
- Note the simplification of the figures, animals and clothing.
- Think about yourself and your experiences with your family, school and community. What events are vivid in your mind?

Do it.

- Make a list of personal experiences that are important to you and prioritize them. Choose one of your top three as the foundation for your fresco. Do several preliminary drawings.
- Follow instructions for mixing plaster into Styrofoam platters. The side facing out will be the back of your fresco. Bend a paper clip and place it in the center of the plaster (to be used for hanging once the plaster is dry).
- After the plaster has set, remove it from the platter and turn it over. You should find a smooth surface with curved edges. Use the vine charcoal to draw your idea. You can "erase" by blotting the surface gently with a damp cloth.
- Use watercolor or tempera to paint your fresco. Place a damp terry cloth towel around the plaster for storage.

Check it. As you work, keep these questions in mind:

- Does your fresco have a center of interest? Does it have a theme? Is your composition balanced?
- Have you planned your use of color? Are your colors mixed well (not muddy)?

Helpful Hint: You may use figures or symbols in your fresco.

Activity 2

Illuminate Your Initials

Materials

White drawing paper, no larger than 4" x 6" or 6" x 9"
pencil, #3 or 4H
kneaded eraser
assorted fine-tipped markers

Take a look.

- Fig.7–28, *X-P (Chi-Rho) Page,* from *Lindisfarne Gospel Book,* 698–721.

Think about it. Whenever Islamic and European cultures clashed there were fascinating changes. The arabesques and geometric decorations of Islam contributed to manuscript illumination.

- What is the meaning of *arabesque* and *illumination*?
- Think about some characteristics of a line: its direction, curves, thickness or thinness. Does it taper at one or both ends?
- Consider the motifs and their forms. Do they repeat to create a pattern and design?

Do it.

- Visualize your initials or name. How would you illuminate them? What colors and patterns would best reflect your personality?
- Lightly sketch your initials onto a small piece of paper. Use a minimum of lines to lay out your sketch, as too many pencil marks will muddy your colors.
- Use a variety of lines to develop your design with markers. Make it look like an ancient, medieval illumination—or you may give it a more contemporary look. As you proceed, gently erase any original pencil marks when you no longer need them.

Check it. Do your letters and design elements complement each other? Do your color combinations work well together? Are there any original pencil lines showing?

Helpful Hint: Work on a small scale since this is an intricate and exacting art. After completion, laminate your illumination to intensify the color.

Additional Activities

- Perhaps there is an area in the school that would be appropriate for a mosaic. Have a school-wide design contest. Several classes could participate in the layout and development of the mural.
- Design a mural that reflects the art and cultures the class has studied. You can use icons, flags or symbols to represent each culture.
- Write an essay about famous individuals in a hypothetical situation. Use information from this and other chapters to justify your work. For example: Charlemagne and King Tutankhamen Debating ________ (you insert the topic)

Angela McPherson

Age 17
Lower Richland High School
Hopkins, South Carolina
Favorite kinds of art:
Abstract/realism
Favorite artist: Dali

Activity 2, Illuminate Your Initials

My art project symbolizes the blacks' faith in God as they struggled through slavery, hoping to one day be free. The Egyptian sign of life symbolizes freedom. The black man in chains symbolizes slavery. The Star of David symbolizes religion and belief in God. The scales symbolize the weight of the world that was against blacks.

What was your thought process when you were creating and developing your project?
What part of my history could I use to symbolize what happened, using my initials.

What have you read, seen or learned about the history of art that has influenced your approach to art?
Watching cartoons got me interested in art. At first I wanted to be a cartoonist. Now I want to go into advertising design.

What do you enjoy most about the artistic process?
Being able to create the impossible or unimaginable. A purple sky, a horse with wings, whatever you desire.

What advice do you have for other students who enjoy creating art?
To keep doing it. You'll always find a career that involves what you enjoy best.

Angela (far left) and her classmates work on their drawings in Ad Design class.

Illustrated ASM, 1994. Colored pencil and felt-tip pens, 6" x 9" (15.2 x 22.8 cm).

8 Romanesque and Gothic Art

In This Chapter...

8–a This drawing is from the sketchbook of a medieval architect who visited many of the new cathedrals built during the Gothic period. He recorded architectural innovations and stylistic variations.
Villard de Honnecourt, *Sketch of flying buttresses on apse of Cathèdral of Reims.* Bibliothèque Nationale, Paris.

THE ELEVENTH CENTURY began the period of medieval art called Romanesque. Christianity was triumphing in Europe and the Church was gaining tremendous power. The Crusades were initiated to take back the Holy Land from the Moslems. As a result, many people moved back and forth across great land areas, creating an exchange of ideas and artistic styles.

Romanesque art had influences from ancient Roman, Early Christian and Byzantine times. Its expressive and emotional style was mainly religious in theme. It was designed to evoke powerful responses in the viewer. Great building campaigns started. Churches and their decoration were the primary means of employment for artists and builders.

Large population shifts also occurred in the 1100s and 1200s. During the Gothic period, people moved from country to city. Christianity continued to grow in popularity. The Church became the social, political and religious leader of the Western world. Monasteries were replaced by church-sponsored schools and universities as centers of learning. This led to new energy and freedoms.

Architecture was the principal means of artistic expression during this time. The unity between outer and inner spaces, and between God and humankind, became a central goal. The buildings of the Gothic period soar to the heavens in celebration of this ideal.

1053–1272
Pisa Cathedral
1095
First Crusade

1130–1330
Great advances in stained glass manufacture

1142
Cathedral of Chartres, France

1298
First documented use of spinning wheel in Europe
1305
Giotto advances use of pictorial space in Western painting

1387–1400
Chaucer, *Canterbury Tales*

1428
Joan of Arc leads French armies against England

Romanesque and Gothic Art

1120–1132
***The Mission of the Apostles*, tympanum of Sainte-Madeleine**

1137
Abbot Suger helps develop Gothic architecture

1220
Climax of Gothic architecture, Amiens Cathedral, France

1347
Black Death devastates Europe

1413
Limbourg Brothers, *Book of Hours*

1465
First printed music

The church shines with its middle part brightened.
For bright is that which is brightly coupled with the bright,
And bright is the noble edifice which is pervaded by the new light.
Abbot Suger

The development of Romanesque and Gothic art included nearly all of Western Europe.

8–b During the medieval era there was extensive sculptural activity. Over the centuries, medieval sculptors became more and more interested in carving realistic figures.
Claus Sluter, *Moses*, detail from the *Well of Moses* (fig.8–37).

8–c This tapestry is unique in Romanesque art because it depicts in detail a contemporary event shortly after it occurred.
The Battle of Hastings, detail of *Bayeux Tapestry* (fig. 8–13).

8–d Paintings on wood panels grow in popularity during the thirteenth and fourteenth centuries. Artists used gold leaf and brilliant colors to depict religious scenes that begin to show human emotion.
Duccio, *Christ Raising Lazarus from the Dead*, detail (fig.8–44).

8.1 Romanesque Art

THE NAME ROMANESQUE was coined in the nineteenth century to cover all art from Roman times until the Gothic period. Today, the term applies to the eleventh and twelfth centuries in western Europe.

A variety of factors contributed to the growth and development of Romanesque art. The threat of Islam had waned, the barbarian raids from the north had subsided, the eastern tribes were held in check, and Christianity was triumphing everywhere in Europe. Monasteries began to exert influence in business and the social services. There was a growing spirit of religious fervor. More and more people were undertaking pilgrimages to holy sites. Then along came the Crusades, a bloody movement organized to liberate the Holy Land from the Moslems and recapture it for Christendom. The Crusades moved huge numbers of people back and forth across Europe. This resulted in a great mingling of cultures and ideas.

All of these factors produced a new phenomenon. We now encounter a period in art and architecture when certain traits, or characteristic features, appear throughout what we today call Europe. This happened without the backing or influence of any one particular political ruler, as was the case, for instance, during the Roman Empire. It was the movement of people and artists and the influence of the Church that provided the opportunity for artistic ideas and innovations to travel great distances.

Building campaigns were undertaken everywhere. Major efforts were directed toward constructing churches and carving sculpture to decorate them. Romanesque art reflected the activity and religious enthusiasm that characterized medieval life from about 1050 to 1200.

Vocabulary
tympanum
narthex
mandorla
crossings
lantern
ambulatory
buttresses
choir
abbey
cloister
cathedra
campanile

Key Notes

- The movement of people across Europe because of pilgrimages and the Crusades resulted in an exchange of ideas and styles.
- Church building and sculptural decoration were the principal activities of artists during the Romanesque period.
- Romanesque art is characterized by its expressive nature and by the religious fervor it represents.

Special Feature

Sainte-Madeleine Tympanum

Sculpture, like all Romanesque art, most often was associated with the church. It was intended to help the people of the faith understand the teachings of the church. Sculptures appeared on capitals of columns and around portals. They were placed in niches both inside and outside the church. The exterior of Romanesque churches provided many areas for sculptures. The doorways were important focal points. The ***tympanum***, or arched area below the arch and above the lintel of a doorway, was a large space that could be filled with a scene sculpted in relief. Anyone entering the church would notice its decoration.

One of the most beautiful of all Romanesque churches is Sainte-Madeleine in Vezelay. Its crowning glory is a set of three sculptured portals opening into the nave and side aisles from the ***narthex***, or vestibule. The central tympanum contains *The Mission of the Apostles* (fig.8–1). Here Christ is shown sending his disciples to preach to the entire world. This was a fitting subject for a church from which many Crusades departed. The huge figure of Christ is placed in an almond-shaped form, or ***mandorla***, his knees turned in a zig-zag position. From the hands (one is missing) of the majestic Christ, we see the rays of the Holy Spirit pouring down upon the apostles. The apostles, who are all equipped with copies of the Gospels, are receiving their assignments, or missions.

The lintel and the compartments around the central group are filled with grotesque people (fig.8–2). They represent the heathen, or unconverted, from many lands. There are people with dog heads, people with enormous ears, others are covered in hair, some have snoutlike noses and some are so small they have to use a ladder to mount a horse. There are also the blind, the lame, mutes and hunchbacks. All of them are awaiting conversion, which the Christians believed would bring them salvation. The arch framing the tympanum contains the signs of the zodiac and the labors for each month of the year. The whole composition is crowded and agitated, a common feature of Romanesque relief sculpture.

Relief work dominated Romanesque sculpture. At Vezelay the figures are in such high relief that many of them are carved almost in the round. The Christ also is an outstanding example of the Romanesque skill with decorative line. At Vezelay we can see how the technical expertise of centuries of working with small portable art is beautifully translated by Romanesque artists into a monumental scale.

8–1 Vezelay was the church most closely associated with the crusades. The Third Crusade left from here.
The Mission of the Apostles. Tympanum of the central portal of the narthex, 1120–1132. Sainte-Madeleine, Vezelay, France.

8–2 The title of this relief refers to the Christian belief that the apostles and all the faithful are obligated to spread the Gospel to all nations.
The Mission of the Apostles, detail (fig.8–1).

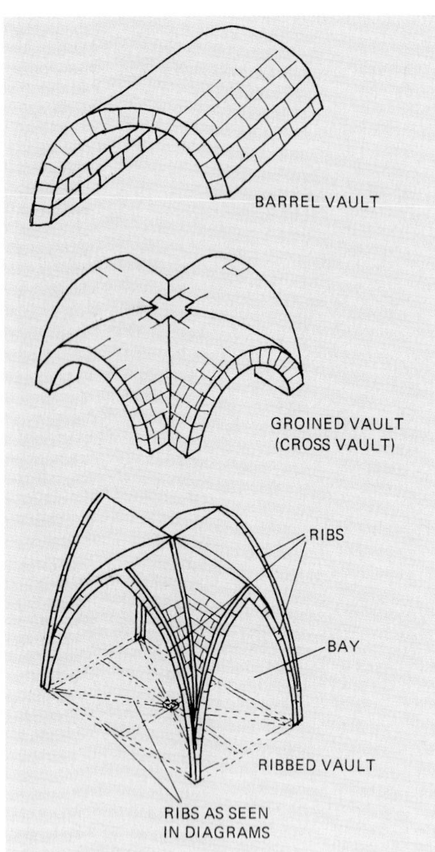

8–3 Common vaulting systems.

Romanesque Architecture

The number of Romanesque churches still standing after almost a thousand years is remarkable. They are scattered all over western Europe but most are in France, Germany and Italy. The churches were built of carefully cut local stone, which varied in color and texture from place to place. The entrances were usually at the west end. Worshipers faced toward the east (and symbolically toward Jerusalem). The ***crossings***, or the place where nave and transept intersect, are often topped with towers, or domes with ***lanterns***. These intersecting spaces produced the shape of a Latin cross with one arm longer than the other three.

Ambulatories, or walkways, were built around the apse to allow for large processions. Often small chapels were added to the outside of these ambulatories to hold relics of saints brought back in the Crusades. Interior columns separated the nave from side aisles. The columns divided the side walls into a series of rectangular units that created a strong feeling of rhythm as one looked down the nave.

The wooden roofs of previous ages were replaced by masonry barrel vaults (fig.8–3). These vaults eliminated the danger of fire and produced better acoustics. The stone vaults, similar to those used by the Romans, were extremely heavy. They spanned the naves and produced tremendous outward thrust, requiring massive exterior ***buttresses*** and thick walls for support. Groin vaults (cross vaults) were often used to stabilize the naves or to add strength over the side aisles (fig.8–3). Interior space could never attain great height because the problem of weight and thrust was simply too difficult to overcome with existing engineering skills. Windows were kept small so as not to weaken the walls. Therefore, interiors were quite dark and had a rather heavy feeling.

Rounded arches, also a Roman feature, were used over windows and over niches that contained sculpture. They also appeared in arcades, supports and side aisles.

To accommodate a larger clergy and more ritual, the apse area was greatly enlarged. The apse included a ***choir,*** a raised area for the singing clergy. Large crypts were built under the choir to hold the remains of high-ranking clergy and other important personages.

When a monastery accompanied a church, the complex of buildings was called an ***abbey***. A ***cloister***, or open courtyard, with an arcaded ambulatory usually connected the church with the living quarters of the monks. The home church of a bishop always contained a special chair or throne for him. The chair was called a ***cathedra***. It is from this term that the word cathedral is derived. Churches that do not contain such chairs cannot be correctly called cathedrals, no matter how beautiful or large the building.

Romanesque architecture was a dynamic art form. It was always changing to meet new situations and to solve new problems in construction. Often different architects worked on successive phases of a project and brought completely new ideas. A few examples will provide a

8–4 These towers are closely related to the towers of castles.
Worms Cathedral, about 1016–1181. Worms, Germany.

900–1300
5000 temples built in Burma

1000
Lady Murasaki Shikibu, *Tales of Genji*

World Cultural Timeline

1000
Zimbabwe culture; with the walled city of Great Zimbabwe at its center, dominant in Africa.

1009
First illustrated book written in Iran

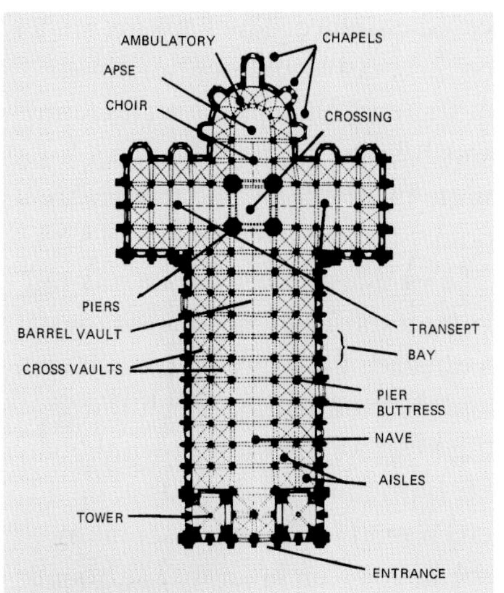

8–5a Diagram of Sainte-Sernin. Toulouse, France.

8–5 This church was designed with a long nave and transept to accommodate vast numbers of pilgrims.
Saint-Sernin, about 1080–1120. Toulouse, France.

8–6 Locate the clerestory windows. How do they make the interior different from most Romanesque churches?
Interior, *Sainte-Madeleine*, about 1104–1132. Vezelay, France.

basic understanding of this architecture—its variety and characteristic features.

Worms Cathedral (fig.8–4) typifies Romanesque architecture in Germany. Based on earlier structures built during the reigns of Charlemagne and Otto the Great, it is heavy and fortress-like, with strong geometric forms. The church has an apse on each end. The towers resemble the turrets used in castles and are repeated at the other end of the building.

The exterior view of *Saint-Sernin* in Toulouse, France (fig.8–5), shows a huge tower over the crossing and an exterior view of one arm of the large transept. This structure was a pilgrimage church. That is, it was built to hold multitudes of travelers on their way to sacred shrines. A large apse and ambulatory, many small chapels, and double side aisles helped control the crowds that moved through the church (fig.8–5a).

The interior of *Sainte-Madeleine* at Vezelay (fig.8–6) exhibits some expected Romanesque features as well as some surprises. Instead of using single barrel vaults, the architect used groin vaults. With these vaults, the architect was able to open large windows in the upper level, allowing light to flood the interior. Even with the added strength of the groin vaults, the church had to be reinforced from the outside in the following centuries. The compound piers (many columns massed together) have sculpted capitals of white limestone. Soft golden limestone and light pink granite blocks were used in the piers. The striking two-color effect created by these blocks is a direct influence of the Islamic mosques built in Spain. The brightly lit choir is a later renovation.

Notre-Dame-la-Grande in Poitiers, France, is a low and wide church (fig.8–7). The barrel-vaulted interior has small windows, and is

Sidelight

Pilgrimage Roads

During the Middle Ages, Christians in search of salvation made pilgrimages to important shrines. Although there were many shrines that people traveled to, three destinations were the most important: St. Peter's Church in Rome; the Holy Land; and the shrine of Santiago, or St. James, at Compostela in northwest Spain. The "Way of St. James" was a challenging journey to the major Romanesque churches in France and northern Spain with the shrine of St. James as a final destination.

A pilgrimage could mean a dangerous trip of hundreds, or even thousands, of miles. The trek could take many months or sometimes years. Pilgrims from many different ranks in life traveled in groups along established routes, stopping at inns along the way. They traveled on horseback or on foot, and were often prey to bandits and the forces of nature. The monks at the monastery of St. Bernard, with the help of their famous dogs, saved countless pilgrims caught in the treacherous snows of the Alpine pass.

Pilgrims traveled to churches to see the relics, or remnants of a saint's clothing, hair or bones, which they believed had the power to cure disease, forgive sins and perform miracles. Like tourist centers today, people in the various towns where shrines were located made their living from the tourist trade and sold souvenirs and fake relics to the weary pilgrims.

8–7 The helmet roofs on the towers were added after the church was finished. Do you think they are a positive addition?
Notre-Dame-la-Grande, about 1162–1271. Poitiers, France.

heavy and dark. The exterior has more sculpture than many Romanesque churches. The west facade contains fourteen large sculpted figures in niches formed by round arches and stumpy columns. Directly above the entrance is a frieze of many figures illustrating scenes from the life of Christ. Taller columns are bunched at the corners and lead upward to cone-shaped helmets. The helmets were added at a later time and do not seem to belong to the rest of the church. A heavy tower sits on the roof at the crossing. It, too, is capped with a cone-shaped top. The church is smaller than many others of the time and has only one portal, or grand entrance. The flanking arches are decorative and not functional.

Italian Romanesque architecture was brighter, more colorful and more highly decorated than contemporary buildings north of the Alps. The grandest in central Italy is the complex at Pisa, made up of the cathedral, the baptistry (not shown) and the ***campanile***, or bell tower (fig.8–8). All are built of white marble with horizontal bands of inlaid green marble. They are set off by the huge green lawn that surrounds them. The campanile—the famous Leaning Tower—started leaning during early construction. Efforts were made, unsuccessfully, to straighten it. Settling causes further tilting each year. Even extreme efforts have not stopped its continued leaning toward eventual destruction.

The cathedral is built on a Latin cross plan with an apse at each end of the transept and a pointed dome crowning the crossing. The facade consists of tiers of superimposed arcades. The interior has been strongly influenced by Early Christian basilicas, with rows of columns and a wooden roof. The baptistry is a freestanding building that was completed in the late thirteenth century.

Most Romanesque construction effort was spent on cathedrals. Much of the labor was donated by pious Christians from every level of society, who were eager to help earn

8–8 The tower keeps leaning more and more and may collapse despite efforts to reinforce it. Tourists are no longer permitted to climb to the top of this famous landmark.
Cathedral (begun 1063) *and Campanile* (begun 1174). Pisa, Italy.

8–9 Romanesque castles and churches shared many features of form and detail. What similarities do you see?
Marksburg Castle, 12th century. Braubach, Germany.

their way into heaven. However, powerful secular rulers constructed strong fortresses for themselves and their knights in France, Germany, England, Italy and Spain. The majestic *Marksburg Castle* (fig.8–9) is typical of twelfth-century fortifications in Germany. The castle stands on a cliff 495 feet above the Rhine River. Its main tower reaches another 130 feet into the air. Still intact, the castle resembles churches of the period in its towers, cones, thick walls, stone materials and small windows.

Romanesque Sculpture

As we already have seen at Vezelay, sculpture during the Romanesque period was primarily large in scale and attached to architecture. It was expressive in nature and placed an emphasis on evoking an emotional response from the viewer.

The Abbey Church of Saint-Pierre at Moissac provides an outstanding example of Romanesque sculpture. On the central support of the south portal are interlaced lions and lionesses. Such intertwined animals reflect barbaric influences as well as the style of Islamic art. Wedged against the side of these animals is the prophet Jeremiah (fig.8–10). The figure of the prophet is thin and elongated. His legs are crossed beneath garments that fall in complex patterns. His hair and beard are long and flowing. A mustache sweeps across his face. Jeremiah's head is turned to the side; the prophet seems lost in thought. The stretched limbs and piety of the figure produce a direct emotional response from us. The sculptor has taken the problem of decorating this narrow, vertical architectural element and solved it in a way that gives perfect expression to the religious fervor of the time.

Another landmark of Romanesque sculpture is on the tympanum of the church of St. Lazare at Autun (fig.8–11). It is a carving of *The Last Judgment*, the moment at the end of the world when Christians believe all of humankind will rise from the dead. Each will be judged worthy of Heaven, or condemned forever to Hell. In the relief, the dead are shown rising up from their graves. Demons grab those that have been sent to Hell by the central figure of Christ, the Divine Judge. Angels lift the blessed into Heaven. Many of the scenes are horrific and appalling. Those who passed beneath the tympanum as they entered the church could not help but be reminded of the fate that would await them should they stray from the path of strong faith and a good life.

The tympanum at Autun also has a feature that rarely is encountered in medieval art. It is one of the earliest surviving figurative sculptures that is signed by the artist who sculpted it. An inscription runs across the top of the lintel. It includes the words GISLEBERTUS HOC FECIT (Gislebertus made this).

8–10 One of the great achievements of Romanesque artists was reviving the technique of carving large-scale stone sculptures.
The Prophet Jeremiah, 1115–1135. South portal, St. Pierre. Moissac, France.

8–11 The tympanum of the central portal of most Romanesque churches had a large figure of Christ at the center of the composition.
Giselbertus, *The Last Judgment,* about 1130. West tympanum, St. Lazare. Autun, France.

8–13 This famous work of art was embroidered by women.
The Battle of Hastings, detail of *The Bayeux Tapestry,* about 1073–1083. Wool embroidery on linen, 20" (51 cm) high. Town Hall, Bayeux, France.

Romanesque Painting and Crafts

Painting took on added importance during the Romanesque period as the fresco technique gained in popularity. Frescoes were used to decorate some interior spaces, especially in Spain and Italy. Churches in the north did not have frescoes because the interiors were too dark and the weather was too damp to use the fresco technique effectively.

Although many of the frescoes have been destroyed, some remain in excellent condition. *Virgin and Child Enthroned* (fig.8–12) was painted by the Master of Pedret (an unknown artist) in a small church in the Pyrenees Mountains of Spain. The Virgin and Child are rendered symbolically. They are placed in a mandorla to signify heaven. The archangels Michael and Gabriel are standing to their sides. The painting was originally on the half-dome of the apse. Modern techniques were used to remove the entire fresco and place it on a flat surface prior to the destruction of the church.

8–12 Although this fresco is currently in a museum, it originally was painted on the wall of a now demolished church in Spain.
Master of Pedret, *Virgin and Child Enthroned,* about 1130. Fresco, 125" (318 cm) high at center. The Metropolitan Museum of Art, New York, The Cloisters Collection, 1950.

One of the most important historic events that occurred during the Romanesque period was the Battle of Hastings. It inspired the creation of a famous work in fabric. Soon after the Battle of Hastings, Bishop Odo of Bayeux, France, commissioned the marvelous illustration of William the Conqueror's invasion of England in 1066. The wool embroidered frieze, which is 230 feet long and 20 inches high, decorated the Bayeux Cathedral. It is a documentation of the battle, with soldiers, horses, weapons, shields, towns, animals, invasion fleets and even a running commentary in Latin. It is called *The Bayeux Tapestry*, but is really a richly embroidered panel and not a true tapestry.

This small section (fig.8–13, 8–c) shows the variety of weapons used as the men ferociously fight one another: battle axes, javelins, hurling spears and crossbows. The bor-

World Cultural Timeline

1050
Foot binding first used in China

1100–1400
Lost-wax metal castings, Ife, Nigeria

1227
Genghis Khan's empire is divided among his four sons

1185–1867
Shoguns rule Japan with Emperor

8–14 The Abbot had this cup made from an ancient Roman cup. French kings continued to use it for several centuries.
Chalice of Abbot Suger of Saint-Denis, about 1140. Sardonyx cup with gilded silver mounting, adorned with filigrees set with stones, pearls, glass insets and opaque white glass pearls, 7 1/2" (19 cm) high. National Gallery of Art, Washington DC, Widener Collection.

der above the scene is purely decorative while the one below shows dead soldiers, animals and discarded weapons, all part of the story.

Many works were crafted in the service of the church. The *Chalice of Abbot Suger* (fig.8–14) is created from an ancient Roman cup that was carved from a single piece of sardonyx. The twelfth-century gilt silver mounting is studded with precious stones and pearls. The chalice has a beauty and technical expertise that resembles the craftsmanship of the barbarian peoples of earlier years. It was made for Abbot Suger of Saint-Denis in Paris, one of the originators of the Gothic style. He wished to use only the best, most precious and most beautiful things in the service of God. The chalice was admired so much that it was used by French kings for three hundred years.

Lesson 8.1 Review

1 What is happening in the scene of *The Mission of the Apostles* in the tympanum at Sainte-Madeleine in Vezelay? Why is this subject appropriate for this particular church?

2 Describe a typical Romanesque church. Include these terms in your description: ambulatory, crossings, nave, transept and apse.

3 What was the purpose of an ambulatory?

4 Name two advantages of the masonry barrel vaulted roofs found in most Romanesque churches over the wooden roofs of earlier churches.

5 Draw a Romanesque arch. Which ancient culture used this same type of arch extensively in their architecture?

6 List three characteristics of Romanesque sculpture.

7 Where is a tympanum found in a Romanesque church?

8 Why did northern European churches not have frescoes painted on their walls?

9 What event is depicted in *The Bayeux Tapestry*?

10 Who was Abbot Suger? What was his philosophy concerning objects used in the church worship service?

8.2 Gothic Art

THE TWELFTH AND THIRTEENTH centuries saw a massive shift in the population of Europe. People moved from the countryside into towns, which grew in size to become cities. Cathedrals became the religious, cultural and social centers of the growing cities. Cathedral schools and universities replaced the monasteries as learning centers. The thirteenth century represents the summit of achievement for unified Christendom. It was a time of fresh ideas and technical knowledge. From this newly found freedom emerged Gothic art and, more particularly, Gothic architecture.

Gothic was first used as a term of ridicule by Renaissance critics because the style did not conform to the standards of Classical Greece and Rome. Today, however, Gothic art is synonymous with the new energy and dynamic style of the period.

Unity is the key word in Gothic architecture. Interiors and exteriors belong together and are similarly decorated. For the first time in history, they received equal emphasis. Structure, aesthetics, purpose and meaning are fused together to present an organic whole or a unified structure. This unity was sometimes an astonishing feat considering that the buildings often took several generations to complete, required the services of several architects, and were never completed according to their original design.

Key Notes

- Cities grow during the Gothic period and cathedral building flourishes.
- The church becomes the most important influence in art and in daily life.
- Unity is the key concept in Gothic architecture.

Vocabulary

flying buttresses
clerestory
rose window
tracery
fan vaulting
cartoon

8–17 Scenes from the life of Christ surround the west portal of Chartres.
West portal, *Cathedral of Chartres,* about 1145–1170. France.

Special Feature

Chartres Cathedral

One of the best remaining examples of Gothic construction is *Chartres Cathedral* (fig.8–15). Because the basic design is so unified, it seems that it must have been planned by a single master builder. However, the construction proceeded through four centuries and was never completely finished. For this reason, the cathedral incorporates a harmony that evolved over time rather than being planned in every detail from the beginning. For instance, the west towers, though similar, are not identical. They were built fifty years apart, the plainer one first and the more elaborate one later. Their spires can be seen for miles around.

You can see by the photograph how huge Chartres is and thereby how important it was to the community. Its shadow fell over everything. It represented the group effort of all who gave their labor, skill and money to build it.

Chartres incorporated many new ideas (fig.8–16). The use of ***flying buttresses*** (flying arches combined with tower buttresses) eliminated the need for heavy, solid Romanesque walls and allowed for the construction of a self-supporting skeletal structure. This, in turn, permitted huge window walls of stained glass, which today remain virtually intact. Although the windows admit far less light than one would expect, the colored light streaming down from the upper level, or ***clerestory***, produces a magical effect.

Like the revolutionary changes in Gothic architecture, there were changes in sculpture. Gothic sculpture faced the outside world, where it clustered around and over the porches and entrance portals (fig.8–17). The exterior of Chartres boasts more than two thousand carved figures. You would think that the profusion of sculpture could lead to considerable confusion. This is prevented by the close relationship of the sculptured forms to the architectural framework. The figures look as if they are enjoying their position in a perfect system.

8–15 Name three features of Chartres that make it Gothic in style.
Cathedral of Chartres, about 1194. France.

8–16 How does this interior differ from the interior of a Romanesque church?
Interior, *Cathedral of Chartres*. France.

Gothic Architecture

8–18 The multitude of windows flood the nave with colored light to create an otherworldly affect in the nave.
Nave, *Notre Dame,* about 1163–1250. Paris, France.

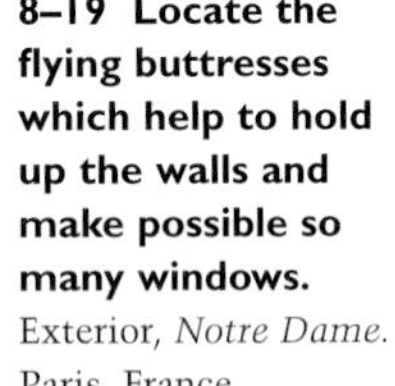

8–19 Locate the flying buttresses which help to hold up the walls and make possible so many windows.
Exterior, *Notre Dame.* Paris, France.

The Gothic style of architecture began at the royal abbey of Saint-Denis, outside Paris, in 1140, when Abbot Suger started to enlarge and redesign his small church to accommodate the many pilgrims who were visiting the chapel. (Today, little remains of its original Gothic appearance.)

Abbot Suger wished to construct a church that was as beautiful and richly decorated as possible because anything less would be unsuitable for God's house. His main concern was light because it symbolized the presence of God. He greatly enlarged the apse of his church, providing an ambulatory for the pilgrims. He designed huge windows that let in great quantities of light through stained glass. He was instrumental in developing this architecture of supports rather than walls. Columns and piers supported the vault. As we have seen at Chartres, windows replaced walls. Heavy Roman-type vaults and massive post-and-lintel construction were suddenly obsolete.

There are several features that characterize Gothic construction. There is an overall feeling of verticality as master builders tried to make the interiors as high as possible, as if reaching toward heaven. Ribbed cross vaults of several types added stability and strength and allowed for huge glass windows at the clerestory level, over the side aisles. Pointed arches provided greater height and more open area. The height-to-width ratio in round arches is about 2 to 1, but in pointed arches can be 3 to 1. The pointed arches also changed the thrust of the vault to a more vertical direction. With the addition of flying buttresses (fig.8–a), the thrust of the vault was transferred, not to the walls, but to the massive towers outside the structure, thereby eliminating the need for solid, thick walls. The arches of the flying buttresses reached over the side aisles and allowed light to enter unhindered through the clerestory windows. A Gothic church has at least three (sometimes five) portals in the facade. A huge round window (or ***rose window***) often was placed over the main portal or at the ends of the transept.

From Saint-Denis, the Gothic architectural style moved to Chartres, Paris and the rest of northern France. It spread to England, Germany and all of northern Europe. Finally it filtered into Italy, where it inspired a tremendous building boom.

On a small island in the heart of Paris is perhaps one of the best known of all Gothic cathedrals, *Notre Dame.* Construction began in 1163 and continued for about a hundred years, but was never completed. The two square towers at the front were originally to be the bases for impressive spires. The interior view (fig.8–18) from the transept shows the use of the pointed arch and ribbed vaults. The clerestory windows are huge and reach up to the roof, allowing light to flood the vault itself. Over both double side aisles is a gallery through which monks, nuns and priests walked while in prayer. The heavy, rounded columns seem Romanesque, but are well integrated into the overall construction. The thin, engaged columns extending to the vault add a feeling of lightness and help develop a visual rhythm on the side walls.

Remarkably, the openings in the galleries, the huge windows and the lower openings between the columns leave little bearing wall to hold up the great weight of the massive stone vault. By looking at the exterior view (fig.8–19), one can see how this is possible. Reaching over the side aisles and over the ambulatory of the choir and apse, flying buttresses lean against the walls at a point between the windows where the vault starts on the inside. The thrust of the vault is absorbed by the arches and buttresses. The result is functional as well as aesthetic. The exterior view also shows the huge rose window at the end of the transept and the immense choir, used for all the clergy and the pageantry of the Paris cathedral. The delicate tower over the crossing was added at a later date.

Reims Cathedral has an interior arrangement similar to Notre Dame in Paris. An immense choir takes up about half the length of the building. Because the kings of France were often crowned here, an extremely large space was needed for the pageantry.

8–20 The rose window has replaced the usual carved tympanum. Stone was carved to hold the glass in place.
West facade, *Cathedral of Reims,* about 1225–1299. France.

The west facade of the *Reims Cathedral (*fig.8–20) is fascinating. Solidity and heaviness have been replaced by openings and lightness. You can actually see through the facade (on the second level over the outside portals) to the flying buttresses of the nave. The towers are not solid at all but are carved stone openings of delicate ***tracery***. Over each portal, the usual carved tympanum is replaced by a window, also with stone tracery. Only at the third level is the facade solid and here it is full of carved niches holding full-figure, sculpted portraits of French kings. The rest of the facade is filled with sculpture: in the portals, over the portals, in other niches and on platforms. Each pinnacle is carved with knobs and protrusions to create a delicate and airy feeling. The towers were designed to hold huge spires, which were never built. The human figure at the bottom creates a sense of scale for the size of the cathedral.

Gothic architectural style reached its climax in *Amiens Cathedral* (fig.8–21). With a nave over 137 feet high, the soaring effect of its interior is dramatically overpowering. The ribbed columns, rising uninterrupted from floor to vault, seem much too slender and graceful to hold up the heavy stone vault. The clerestory windows are immense. They are separated only by the thin columns. The vault seems to float without support above the glass. These windows, the tracery openings of the middle level gallery and the large arched spaces below almost eliminate the feeling of any walls at all. This sense of openness was the ultimate goal of Abbot Suger when he started to work on his church in Saint-Denis.

The interior view is from the choir toward the entrance with the rose window (40 feet in diameter) above the main portal. By looking at the ribs in the vault, one can see where the transept crosses the nave. A view directly up at the cross vaults (fig.8–22) reveals the incredible amount of glass and the small visible columns that support the stone vault.

In Germany, the cathedral erected at Cologne (fig.8–23) is the largest in the country. Built on the site of an old Roman town on the Rhine River, the cathedral followed the plan of French cathedrals. The French plan was not a popular design in Germany. Later builders designed churches with high side aisles and wide interior spaces called *hallenkirche* or hall churches.

The ring of flying buttresses surrounding the choir appears to be a forest of stone. Notice the height of the towers and the mass of the structure when compared with the large buildings around the cathedral.

8–21 Locate the rose window, transept crossing, columns and windows.
Interior of nave, *Cathedral of Amiens*, begun about 1220. France.

8–22 The effect of lightness and effortlessness in this structure belies its heavy stone building material.
Interior, *Cathedral of Amiens*. France.

Across the channel in England, the Gothic style spread rapidly. The countryside was dotted with structures that combined French ideas and Norman influences. Compared with French cathedrals, the *Salisbury Cathedral* is low and wide (fig.8–24) because the builders did not desire a soaring effect. Sculptures fill the horizontal bands of the screen-like facade. Only a few flying buttresses can be seen. The tower over the crossing is Salisbury's crowning achievement. It reaches over 400 feet into the English sky. However, it is solid and not highly sculptured such as those in France.

A beautiful cloister (fig.8–25) is attached to the Salisbury Cathedral. The garden is visible to strollers through the carved tracery arches of the covered walkway.

1300
Anasazi abandon Canyon de Chelly National Monument, modern New Mexico

1325
Ibn Battuta journeys from North Africa to Indonesia and China

World Cultural Timeline

1325
Aztecs found Tenochtitlán

1350
Chocolate drinking popular with Aztecs

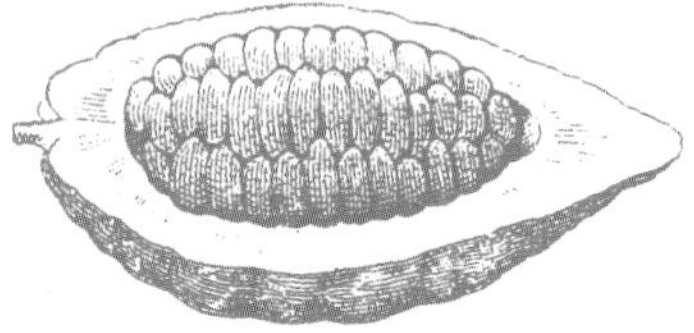

Massed columns and ribbed cross vaults are characteristic features of the early Gothic style in England. In later English Gothic architecture, the ribbing becomes extremely decorative, as in the vault of the Chapter House of the Cathedral at Wells (fig.8–26). Here small clustered columns seem to be transformed into ribs for the vault and create a feature called ***fan vaulting***. So elaborate was the rib work done at a later time that the final style of Gothic art in England is called *Flamboyant Gothic.*

8–24 This church is surrounded by an open, grassy area.
Exterior, *Salisbury Cathedral,* begun in 1220. England.

8–23 The modern city of Cologne is dominated by its cathedral.
Cathedral of Cologne, begun 1248. Germany.

8–25 A cloister is a covered walkway which allowed people to walk around the garden when the weather was bad.
Cloister, *Salisbury Cathedral.* England.

8–26 This elaborate vaulting system is called fan vaulting because it has the appearance of giant open fans.
Fan vaulting. Chapter House, *Wells Cathedral,* early 14th century. England.

8–27 Compare this Italian Gothic cathedral to the Cathedral of Reims. What similarities and differences do you see?
Cathedral of Siena, begun about 1284. Italy.

8–28 The lacy screen of the triforium on the second level adds lightness to the design.
Palazzo Ducale, 1340–1424. Venice, Italy.

In Italy, *Siena Cathedral* is a zebra-striped marble church (fig.8–27). Its elaborate facade is covered with statuary and mosaics. A dome and lantern stand over the crossing. The campanile pierces the sky. The striping continues on the interior of the church. Except for the time in history and the builders' desire to construct beautiful sanctuaries for the glory of God, most Italian Gothic churches have little in common with the French Gothic style to the north.

Although the construction of cathedrals dominated the building activity of the Gothic period, municipal buildings also were erected in major cities all over Europe. Some have the appearance of churches while others have used the features of Gothic construction in different ways. Like the cathedrals, all the buildings shown here are still in use after six hundred years or more, attesting to the skill of the architects, engineers and masons.

In Venice, the *Palazzo Ducale* (Doge's Palace) is a lacy network of marble (fig.8–28). A large arcade is on the first level and an open gallery, or triforium, is on the second level. This is similar to the interior wall plan of a French Gothic cathedral. The windows on the top story are small, but the colored pattern in marble keeps this level from seeming too heavy. The lower columns seem to be sunk in the ground, but they were not always so. The three steps on which they rest have now sunk with the subsiding Venetian ground level. The building has a very unified feeling. Light and color are reflected from its surface. These two elements would continue to fascinate Venetian artists for centuries.

In northern Europe, municipal buildings compete with cathedrals for ornateness and beauty. The town hall of Louvain, Belgium (fig.8–29), is built in the flamboyant Gothic style of the fifteenth century. It has an elaborate surface that sparkles with reflected light. There is hardly a square foot of uncarved or undecorated surface. The incredible amount of stone tracery produces a lace-like feeling in many places.

The belfry in Bruges, Belgium (fig.8–30), is an enormous brick and stone tower begun in 1376. It was completed in 1482 when the octagonal top portion was added. It dominates the small city which contains many other Gothic buildings, and its carillon of 47 bells can be heard for miles around.

8–29 In northern Europe, municipal buildings became as ornate as cathedrals.
Town Hall, 15th century. Louvain, Belgium.

8–30 The bells in this huge tower weigh a total of 27 tons.
Belfry of the City Hall, 1376–1482. Bruges, Belgium.

8–31 These figures seem very much a part of the architecture.
Four Ancestors of Christ. Jamb statues, about 1150. Stone. Cathedral of Chartres, France.

8–32 These three figures have individual expressions on their faces and gesture freely.
St. Stephen, Empress Kunigunde and Emperor Henry II. Jamb statues, about 1235–1240. Sandstone. Bamburg Cathedral, Germany.

Sculpture

The revolutionary changes in Gothic architecture were duplicated in the evolution of sculpture. The change was slow but constant. Interest in the Classic sculptural tradition was revitalized. The symbolism of Romanesque sculpture gave way to a new awareness of the natural world. Artists began to work again with increasingly natural human, animal and plant forms.

The earliest existing examples of Gothic sculpture are on the west facade of Chartres, done about 1150. The three portals are filled with sculpture on the tympanums, in the archivolts and on the door jambs. The *Four Ancestors of Christ* (fig.8–31) are from the central door jamb. The figures are extremely elongated. The drapery is still stylized and flat, often just chiseled lines. The statues appear to be part of the columns. Like Romanesque sculpture, the statues lack a sense of movement. In spite of the early date, there is some individualization of the faces. The feet seem to be floating over the sloping platforms instead of resting on them.

The figures on the door jamb of the Bamberg Cathedral (fig.8–32) illustrate the change that had occurred by the late Gothic period. Carved in sandstone about 1235, the figures are almost casual in their stance. They seem to be free of the columns and are sculpted in the round. Their faces are individual, each having a different expression. The drapery is loose and the folds are fully carved. Real bodies seem to exist beneath the garments. The figures are naturally proportioned and almost seem capable of movement. Their feet rest naturally on flat pedestals.

Not all sculpture in churches was religious in subject matter. Contemporary people and events often shared space with saints. The man with a toothache (fig.8–33) is from the capital of a column in the transept of the cathedral in Wells, England.

The highest Gothic expression in Spain occurred in magnificent altarpieces. The altarpieces were really

1350
Maori migrate from the Marquesas to New Zealand

1400
Incas develop an accounting system

1400–1591
Songhai Kingdom, Africa

World Cultural Timeline

1400
Blue and white Ming ware popular in China

8–34 The elaborate carvings tell the story of the life of Christ.
High altar, *Cathedral of Toledo*, about 1498–1504. Wood, paint and gold. Toledo, Spain.

carved screens that separated the altars from the windows behind them. The incredible detail in the *Toledo Cathedral* altarpiece (fig.8–34) was designed by Peti Juan, but carved in wood by artists from Holland, France, Germany and Spain. The figures illustrate fifteen events in the life of Christ and are painted in brilliant color. There is a multitude of other painted figures. The entire altar is woven together with incredibly detailed carvings of Gothic spires, needles, platforms and canopies that are covered with gold. It is an elaborate and decorative way of presenting the New Testament happenings to Toledo's churchgoers.

Virgin and Child (fig.8–35) is from the private chapel of a castle near Rouen, France. The sculpture is carved from limestone and was originally painted. The figures are carved completely in the round so that they can be viewed from all sides. They stand on their own as a work of art, not as part of a cathedral, chapel or column. The pose and the drapery are natural. There is a delightful interplay between the child and mother, something that is quite human.

While many artists and craftspeople of the Middle Ages worked anonymously, several became well known because of their extremely fine work. Among them are Tilman Riemenschneider of Germany (1460–1531) and Claus Sluter of Holland (active 1380–1406). Riemenschneider was the last of the great altarpiece carvers of Germany. He specialized in elaborate and detailed wood sculpture. *Group of Three Saints* (fig.8–36) is a carving of Sts. Christopher, Eustace and Erasmus. The three saints are part of a larger group of fourteen saints carved for a church altar in Würzburg, Germany. People turned to these saints for help in times of pestilence, tragedy, storm, sickness and travel. Such saints were easily identified by medieval people because the symbolism was well known. St. Christopher carries Christ on his shoulders. (Christ's head and hand, unfortunately, are missing.) St. Eustace was recognized by his knightly attire. St. Erasmus was believed to have been martyred by disembowelment, and so carries a spindle around which his entrails are wrapped.

8–33 Contemporary people and commonplace events often were portrayed on column capitals.
Toothache. Capital from south transept, Wells Cathedral, about 1250. Stone. Wells, England.

8–35 The Virgin and Child was an extremely popular subject during the Middle Ages. As in the case of this group, the artist often tried to convey the tender feeling between a mother and child.
Virgin and Child, about 1475. Limestone with traces of polychrome, 3' (90 cm) high. From castle of Gisors, near Rouen. The Nelson-Atkins Museum of Art, Kansas City.

8–36 Saints usually were depicted carrying or wearing certain objects so that they could be easily identified. These objects are known as the saints' attributes.
Hans Tilman Riemenschneider, *Group of Three Saints (St. Christopher, St. Eustace and St. Erasmus),* 15th century. Lindenwood, 21" (53 cm) high. The Metropolitan Museum of Art, New York, The Cloisters Collection, 1961.

8–37 How has the sculptor used the element of texture to enhance this figure?
Claus Sluter, *Moses with Two Prophets,* 1395–1404. Marble figures about 6 1/2' (2 m) high. From the *Well of Moses.* Carthusian Monastery of Champmol, Dijon, France.

The compact group is carved in linden wood and is unpainted. The complex interweaving of line and form in the folds of cloth and the placement of the figures are characteristic of the artist's work. It creates a rather restless feeling that is repeated in the expressive, somber faces and the long hands and fingers. Although done about 1494 while the Renaissance was exploding in Italy, it is Gothic in form and content. Northern Europe followed the Gothic style far longer than Italy.

Claus Sluter was born in Holland. His greatest work, however, was done in France, particularly at Dijon for the Duke of Burgundy. Sluter brought new zest and ultimate realism into Gothic sculpture. His work is so strong and his style so individualistic that it could be placed in the Renaissance period. *Moses with Two Prophets* (fig.8–37) is a masterful statement in marble. The facial expression is intense and powerful—more than merely natural (fig. 8–b). Moses has returned from Mt. Sinai with the tablets of the law in his right hand. The horns on his head had become a traditional symbol for the prophet as he returned from facing God. (This symbol came from an incorrect translation of the Old Testament story.) His full, parted beard and the lush, flowing robes create a dynamic rhythm and visual movement that leads up to the expressive face. The sculpture was part of a large carved monument, much of which has been lost. Because only the fountain part remains, it is known as the *Well of Moses.*

Window in Time

Black Death

Sometime during 1346, word reached Europe that a terrible plague was rife in the East. Rumors abounded and it was said that Tartary, Mesopotamia, Syria and Armenia were covered with dead bodies. By 1347 the plague, called the Black Death because blotches of blood turned black under the skin, spread to Europe.

According to an account by an Italian writer of the period, Gabriel de Mussis, the plague began in 1346 in the Tartar lands of Asia Minor. One report indicates that 80,000 people died in the Crimea alone.

One of the principal ways the plague spread was along the major trade routes from Eastern ports to the Mediterranean. Ships from plague-stricken cities in the East would dock in European ports. Sometimes these ships were quarantined and their crews forbidden to disembark. This proved to be a futile measure because, as soon as the ship's ropes were tied to a dock, infected rats carrying fleas scurried ashore. Within days the fleas would transmit the disease to the population of the city and countryside.

The Black Death, a combination of bubonic, pneumonic and septicemic plague strains, spread horror and death wherever it went. Between 1347 to 1351, it raged over the Western world, killing from 25 to 50 percent of Europe's population.

In the Italian city of Florence, more than half the population died between April and October 1348. The famous Florentine writer, Giovanni Boccaccio, places the recitation of his tales of the *Decameron* against the backdrop of the plague. He chronicles the effect of the disease on his native city and describes the physical appearance of the plague's victims for us. "...At the onset of the disease both men and women were afflicted by a sort of swelling in the groin and under the armpits which sometimes attained the size of a common apple or egg...Afterwards, the manifestation of the disease changed into black or livid spots on the arms, thighs and the whole person." These latter symptoms were an indication of certain death.

No country was spared. The plague spread from Italy to France, then to England and Germany, and then along the northward sea route to Denmark, Norway and Sweden.

Fear of the disease took many forms. Some people fled while others threw themselves into frenzies of religious excess. The Flagellants whipped themselves until they drew blood, hoping in this way to stem the pestilence. Jews were accused of spreading the Black Death by poisoning wells, and many were massacred in the Rhineland and Switzerland. Charges of sorcery and witchcraft were rife. But none of this had any effect on the disease. Rich or poor, religious or heathen, peasant or aristocrat, child or grandmother, the Black Death spared no one.

For at least a century after 1350, there were cyclical recurrences of the plague and the European population continued to decline. The population would only stabilize again in the fifteenth century.

This is a contemporary depiction of the effect of the plague that ravaged Italy in the forteenth century.
Giovanni Serambi,
The Plague, 14th century.
State Archives, Lucca.

8–39 Jean-Clement was the donor of this window. St. Denis is giving his banner to him.
St. Denis and Jean-Clement, 12th century. Stained glass. Cathedral of Chartres, France.

8–38 Chartres is the only major Gothic cathedral that retains much of its original stained glass.
Rose window and lancets, 13th century. Stained glass, 42'7" (13 m) diameter. Cathedral of Chartres, France.

Stained Glass

Abbot Suger would have been pleased to think of twelfth- and thirteenth-century cathedrals as frameworks to hold stained glass. The techniques of producing glass sheets with brilliant color began during the Romanesque period, but they reached their peak in the magnificent windows of Gothic structures. The colors glow when light passes through the glass. The glass could be cut to fit the shapes the artist required. A full-scale line drawing (called a ***cartoon***) was first put on a large board. Then sheets of glass were placed over it and cut according to the lines. These pieces were then put together like a giant jigsaw puzzle, and later soldered in place with I-shaped lead strips. Carved stone tracery or iron bars were used as supports to hold the entire window flat so that it could be set upright in place. Before assembly, paint was applied in certain places to create shading, lines and details. The individual pieces were fired in a kiln to harden the pigment.

Reds and blues dominated Gothic color schemes, although many other colors also were used. These deep hues darkened the interiors of churches, causing the windows to glow like huge jewels. Much original glass has been destroyed, but the remains indicate that the windows were brilliantly colored visual teaching aids for the church.

A huge rose window (nearly 43 feet in diameter) and lancet windows are found on the end wall of the south transept of Chartres Cathedral (fig.8–38). One of four rose windows in the church, this one features Christ at the center. The lancets symbolize the evangelists, or writers, of the New Testament. The dark spaces between the medallions that make up the rose window are carved stone that appear as silhouettes from the inside.

The single large window from Chartres (fig.8–39) is from the upper level. It shows St. Denis presenting his red banner to the knight who donated the window to the church. This interesting custom of showing the donors in the work they contributed was used in forty windows at Chartres. Donors appear with saints, Christ or the Virgin Mary. This custom also occurred in many paintings of the period and continued into the Renaissance. In this window, some of the lines and shading that were painted onto the glass can be seen. However, it is often hard to distinguish the painted lines from the lead lines.

The incredibly complex windows in *Sainte-Chapelle* in Paris (fig.8–40) are the ultimate in Gothic architectural decoration. Built by Louis IX (later known as St. Louis) in 1243, the small chapel has no side aisles and no flying buttresses—but the windows are magnificent. They are huge for the size of the small chapel. Single panels of glass extend from several feet above the ground all the way to the vault. Nowhere else is the feeling so strong that glass is holding up the vault. The columns between the windows seem incredibly thin and fragile. The pieces of glass are cut very small and illustrate Bible stories in the medallions. Those at the top are so small that viewers have difficulty reading the detailed pictures. In sunlight, all details are blurred by the brightness and the entire chapel seems to glow with brilliant color.

Late Gothic Painting

Because the huge stained glass pictures successfully illustrated the Bible in northern European cathedrals, architectural painting was kept to a minimum. Some altarpieces were painted, but most French religious painting was restricted to manuscript illumination. In *The Annunciation* page (fig.8–41) from the French *Book of Hours* (1440), the angel Gabriel is telling the Virgin Mary that she will be the mother of Christ. In the single illustration is a tiny landscape outside and a cathedral-like setting inside. God the Father (at the top) presides over all the events. The words are Mary's response to the angel. Surrounding the scene is an extremely complex and interwoven decoration of angels playing instruments. The fantastic border includes flowers, leaves, scrolls, birds and fanciful designs.

The page from a manuscript (fig.8–42) was painted in tempera and gold leaf by Goffredo da Viterbo in Italy. Many late Gothic illustrators were not monks or nuns but talented lay people working in studios such as Goffredo in Viterbo. They also illustrated nonreligious and civic books.

8–40 Describe how you think it must feel standing in the center of Sainte-Chapelle.
Interior, *Sainte-Chapelle*, 1243–1248. Paris, France.

8–41 Manuscript painting was the dominant form of painting in Gothic France.
The Annunciation page from French *Book of Hours*, 1440. Tempera and gold on parchment. Huntington Art Gallery, Pasadena.

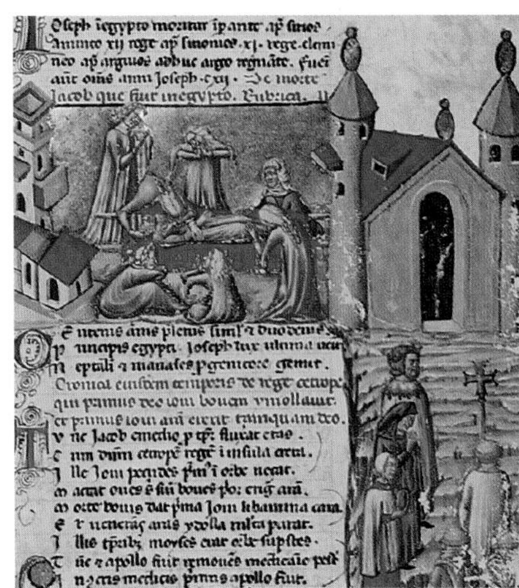

8–42 Many late Gothic illustrators were lay people in an occupation traditionally done by members of religious orders.
Goffredo da Viterbo, *detail from a manuscript*, 1331. Bibliothèque Nationale, Paris.

An exciting departure in Italian painting took place in the thirteenth century because of a change in the religious ceremony of the church. Until then the mass had been celebrated with the priest behind the altar, facing the people (as it is done again now). Then the priest's position was changed so that he faced the altar from the front. This freed the space behind and above the altar for large paintings on wood panels. Like the manuscript illuminations, these works were painted with egg tempera.

8–43 Note how Giotto has used the large figures seated at the front edge of the scene to draw the viewer right into the picture. Giotto, *Lamentation,* 1305–1306. Fresco. Arena Chapel, Padua.

8–44 What details has Duccio used to make the scene seem more human and believable? Duccio, *Christ Raising Lazarus from the Dead,* 1309–1311. Tempera on panel, 17" x 18" (43 x 46 cm). Kimbell Art Museum, Fort Worth.

Giotto

(about 1267–1337)

According to legend, when Giotto was a boy of ten, he drew pictures of his father's sheep that he was tending. He was seen by Cimabue, one of the most respected painters in Florence from 1272 to 1302. Cimabue went to Giotto's father to ask permission to make the boy one of his apprentices. Florence, soon to become a leading center of the Renaissance, was already vigorous, dynamic and experimental. Here, Giotto became recognized in his own day as one of the great men of Florence. He revolutionized painting by reviving the art of working from nature. Giotto's paintings may not seem revolutionary today, but since Roman times, few artists had been interested in painting from nature because an emphasis had been placed on the symbolic.

Giotto's masterpiece is a series of frescoes that decorate the walls of a small chapel. Working between 1305 and 1306 in the Arena Chapel in Padua, not far from Venice, Giotto illustrated the lives of Christ and the Virgin. He used the fresco technique to fill the walls of the chapel with three powerful bands of paint. The *Lamentation* (fig.8–43) is one painting in the series. The scene appears to be played out by a group of real people. The figures are in active, natural poses: leaning, holding, sitting and bending. They are monumental and solid. The large folds in their robes suggest weight and mass. Notice how the shading creates a sense of roundness and natural light coming from above. Finally, a hint of natural landscape and sky (not a gold background) enhances the reality of the event.

The center of interest in the painting is Christ, who has been taken down from the cross and is being held by several figures. His mother Mary grieves as she searches his lifeless face. Sorrow is expressed on every face.

The composition of *Lamentation* is asymmetrically balanced. A huge rock form leads the viewer's eyes diagonally across the painting directly to Christ's face. There are many other shapes and lines that also lead there. The bare tree in the upper right, separated from the figures, helps create a feeling of desolation. It also recalls a legend known by all at the time: the Tree of Knowledge in Eden withered when Adam and Eve sinned, and would come back to life when Christ fulfilled his work of redeeming humanity.

Giotto's students continued his techniques, but with less power and waning conviction. Giotto's spirit and ideas on painting would normally place him in the Renaissance, but it was almost a century before that searching and dynamic era would begin.

8–45 Paintings are often re-framed hundreds of years after they were created. This frame is from the nineteenth century.
Simone Martini, *Annunciation*, 1333. Tempera and gold on panel, 10' 1" x 8' 8 3/4" (270 x 300 cm). Uffizi Gallery, Florence.

Duccio

(active 1278–1319)

The town of Siena was a short distance from Florence. Here, the Byzantine tradition remained a strong influence into the fourteenth century, although some drastic changes were made. Duccio was asked to paint a large altarpiece for the cathedral of Siena. He worked on it for three years. When it was finished, a holiday was declared. The artist and his masterpiece were paraded through the city, from his studio to the cathedral, accompanied by the ringing of church bells and the blare of trumpets. The altarpiece, called the *Maesta* (*Madonna in Majesty*), was freestanding, about 13 feet wide, and painted on both sides. The front contained Mary and the Christ Child as large central figures, surrounded by dozens of apostles, prophets and saints. Each figure is individualized to a great degree. Such a work had never been seen before. The back side was covered with panels that illustrated the life of Christ. Painted in tempera, they were much more detailed than Giotto's large frescoes at Padua.

In the panel called *Christ Raising Lazarus from the Dead* (fig.8–44), a crowd of people surround Christ. Faces are individualized and the overlapping bodies suggest spatial depth. Although there seems to be a single light source to create the forms of faces and figures, there are no shadows cast on the ground. They are not as massive as Giotto's and yet they seem to have weight. Small brushes were used in the tempera technique, allowing Duccio to create great detail in such small works. He acquired this technique while painting miniatures in his earlier years. Many of his paintings contain part of the Sienese landscape and the city itself—a delightful mixing of time and place.

Simone Martini

(about 1284–1344)

Duccio's pupil, Simone Martini, made a further break with Byzantine tradition. While working in Naples for the French king, he picked up some ideas, techniques and styles from the French Gothic painters. *Annunciation* (fig.8–45) is a panel painting over ten feet wide. The angel Gabriel is dressed in a magnificent gold brocade robe. The Virgin's blue mantle has a deep gold border. This concern for fabric detail and beautifully drawn line is a direct influence of Simone's contact with French artists of the time. Byzantine art portrayed spiritual beauty rather than such material magnificence. The angel's message, "Hail thou that art highly favored, the Lord is with thee," appears on the burnished gold background. Mary recoils from the unexpected message in a coy and graceful way.

Gentile da Fabriano

(1370–1427)

There seems to have been a steady exchange of ideas, themes and techniques between the artists of Tuscany and those of central France. By the end of the fourteenth century, French and Italian Gothic styles had merged into an International style. Claus Sluter was the foremost sculptor in this style (see p.250).

The greatest Italian painter of the International style was Gentile da Fabriano who, like Simone Martini, exchanged ideas with French artists. Gentile's tempera painting, *The Adoration of the Magi* (fig.8–46), is a superb example of the style. The richly colored and patterned fabrics are skillfully rendered. Gentile took care with natural details. The animals, for instance, are rendered in a convincing manner. There is weight in the figures, yet great attention is paid to pattern and decoration.

The world was still one step from the Renaissance—one step from a true three-dimensional feeling in painting.

8–46 The gold-leafed frame on this painting is original. The owner paid more for it than he paid for the painting itself.
Gentile da Fabriano, *The Adoration of the Magi,* 1423. Tempera on panel, 9' 11" x 9' 3" (300 x 280 cm). Uffizi Gallery, Florence.

Lesson 8.2 Review

1 How did the term *Gothic* originate?
2 What is the most important art principle in Gothic architecture?
3 When and where did the Gothic style begin?
4 What is the largest Gothic cathedral in Germany?
5 What is the most memorable architectural feature of Salisbury Cathedral?
6 Describe Moses on Sluter's *Well of Moses.*
7 Explain the process of making a stained glass window. What two colors were used most often in Gothic stained glass windows?
8 Describe the body language of the figures, particularly the angels, in Giotto's *Lamentation.*

Primary Source

The Abbey at Cluny

Monks at the Abbey of Cluny, in France, were expected to read books daily. There was a lending library within the monastery. All of these books were handwritten and, when worn out, they were copied again by hand.

Copyists were given special privileges such as exemption from church services, special foods and opportunities to stay near fires to dry their manuscripts as well as to get warm.

The following is an excerpt from the Benedictine Rule regarding copyists in the monastery:

"Artificers, if there be any in the monastery, shall practise their special arts with all humility, if the abbot permit. But if any one of them be exalted on account of his knowledge of his art, to the extent that he seems to be conferring something on the monastery, then such a one shall be deprived of his art, and shall not again return to it, unless it hap that the abbot again order it, he being humiliated."

Peter the Venerable, a Cluniac monk, described the copying of books in the following manner:

"It is more noble to set one's hand to the pen than to the plough, to trace divine letters upon the page than furrows upon the fields. Sow on the page the seed of the word of God, and when the harvest is ripe, when your books are finished, the hungry readers shall be satisfied by an abundant harvest."

Chapter Review

Review

1 Define the term *Romanesque.*

2 Name two Romanesque churches and two Gothic churches in Europe.

3 Why did Abbot Suger incorporate so many windows in his remodeling of the Cathedral of St.-Denis?

4 How did sculpture change from the Romanesque to the Gothic period?

5 Name two known Gothic sculptors. Name one sculpture that each one carved.

Interpret

1 Imagine that *The Bayeux Tapestry* was hung near the ceiling of your classroom. Would it be long enough to fit around the perimeter of the room?

2 In a chart, compare the arches, windows, wall decoration, walls and floor plans of Byzantine, Romanesque and Gothic churches.

3 Analyze the composition of Giotto's *Lamentation.* What is the center of interest? How has Giotto directed the viewers attention to this?

Other Tools for Learning

Maps

1 Find Vezelay on the map. What country is it in today?

2 Why would the art of Venice be more closely aligned with that of northern Europe than the rest of Italy?

Timelines

1 Select a discovery or invention from the 12th through the 16th centuries that has influenced your own life. Explain why you chose it.

2 How many years elapsed between the building of the first Gothic cathedral and Chaucer's writing of *The Canterbury Tales*? What styles would the churches have been that Chaucer's pilgrims visited on their trip?

Electronic Media

CD-ROM drive: *Microsoft Art Gallery*

1 Find a copy of one of John Constable's paintings of the Salisbury Cathedral. How does it compare with the photograph of the cathedral in this chapter?

2 Describe Duccio's *Maesta* altarpiece before it was disassembled. How large was it? Find another panel, other than the one in this book, from the *Maesta* and describe its subject matter.

CD-ROM drive: Electronic Encyclopedia (e.g., *New Grolier Multimedia* or *Microsoft Encarta*, etc.)

1 Why is the Tower of Pisa leaning? What is being done to stabilize it?

Classroom Connections

Activity 1

The News in Stitches

Materials
embroidery floss
embroidery needles
scissors
drawing paper
heavyweight tracing paper
embroidery transfer paper
loosely woven cotton, wool, burlap or muslin
optional: iron, ironing board, wooden hoops

Take a look.
- Fig.8–13, *The Battle of Hastings,* detail of *The Bayeux Tapestry,* about 1073–1083. Wool embroidery on linen.

Think about it. *The Bayeux Tapestry* is a narrative of the invasion of England by William the Conqueror from Normandy, France. The lively action of the piece gives a sense of the crowded battlefield and the ferocity of the fighting.
The embroidery uses line to define the figures. Notice the way borders are created at the top and bottom of the work.

Do it.
- With your classmates, select a current event or a happening from everyday life in your school or community.
- Divide the event into parts or scenes and decide how to make one relate to the next. Individuals or groups may be responsible for different scenes.
- Use contour lines to draw the figures in your narrative, noting their relationship to other figures. Classmates can pose as models.
- Once the action is drawn, put all of the scenes together on a piece of paper representing the intended size of the tapestry. Plan out any panels, check for continuity and consider the use of borders.
- Transfer the drawings to fabric. Use a variety of yarns, threads and stitches to create an embroidered tapestry.
- Assemble the narrative. Mount and stretch the completed tapestry for display.

Check it. Throughout the project, check that your scene, choice of colors and design works with those of your classmates.

Helpful Hint: Practice several different kinds of stitches using both yarn and embroidery floss. Notice how each gives a different effect and texture on the cloth.

Activity 2

Stained Glass Windows

Materials
gray chipboard
white paper
black markers
black railroad board
colored cellophane
glue
mat knife
scissors

Take a look.
- Fig.8–18, Notre Dame, nave.
- Fig.8–38, Rose windows and lancets.
- Fig.8–39, *St. Denis and Jean-Clement.*
- Fig.8–40, Interior, *Sainte-Chapelle.*

Think about it. Study the Gothic Cathedrals of England, France and Italy.
- Notice the shape and size of the windows, as well as similarities and differences.
- How is tracery (ornamental stonework) used in all these cathedrals?

Do it.
- Select and measure a window to be redesigned as a stained glass window. Use gray chipboard to create a "stone" frame to enclose your design.
- Create the stained glass design using a broad marker or heavy line to emphasize the linear quality of the drawing.
- Transfer the drawing to black railroad board and cut out the enclosed shapes, leaving black lines. Use colored cellophane to fill in the open areas.
- Put your "stained glass" windows over your selected window.

Check it. Write about the effect the colored light has on the atmosphere of the room. What kind of mood does it create?

Helpful Hint: Think of the figures in the stained glass windows you have seen. How complex or simple are these figures?

Additional Activities

- Research the shapes and materials used by various cultures for ceremonial cups (see the *Chalice of Abbot Suger,* fig.8–14). Write about the particular ceremony in which it is used.
- Arrange a print or slide show that illustrates the changing concepts in figure painting (or sculpture) from Greek to Gothic times. Cite dates and describe stylistic changes.
- The dimensions of many Gothic cathedrals are overwhelming. The German cathedral at Cologne has a nave 151' (46 m) high and towers 498' 8" (152 m) high. Devise a visual presentation that will compare the size of several buildings in your community with this gigantic Gothic structure. Research the length and width of several cathedrals (from the encyclopedia) and plot them in your neighborhood or on school grounds.

From left to right, Eve Binder, Deborah Cambetas, Tina Greenberg and Michele Wang display their completed tapestry.

Diversity, 1995. Embroidery floss on cotton cloth, 27 1/2" x 12" (70 x 30.5 cm)

Four students from:

Clarkstown High School North
New City, New York
Activity 1, The News in Stitches

Eve Binder *Age 17*
We made a tapestry with a theme that was related to the area that we live in. After brainstorming for a while we came up with many different ideas for our theme, but we settled on diversity. We chose this particular theme because all of us working on the project came from different backgrounds. There is also a wide variety of cultures in our school.

By making squares of different cultures, sewing them all together, and giving them a common border—American symbols—we demonstrate our hope for unity in our country as well as the world.

I hope that people will look at our tapestry and understand that we are all put here as equals. We all live in the same country and no problems will be solved until we work together. *(Eve stitched the Native American panel.)*

Debora Cambetas *Age 18*
For my part of this project I chose to embroider the Statue of Liberty, which represents freedom and liberty for all peoples. I appreciate its value, being an immigrant to this country.

The part I liked most about this project was the fact that there are many different stitches I could use in order to signify shadowing and texture. I believe that if anyone is really dedicated to accomplishing a project she should follow her heart and the project will be her best ever.

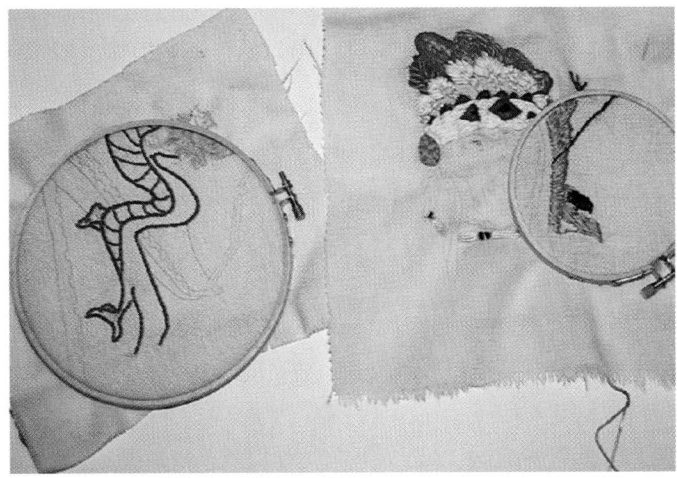

Tina Greenberg *Age 15*
In this art project, my responsibility was to embroider a drawing of a woman in India. I have learned about Indian culture and I have expanded my horizons. While I was creating my tapestry I attempted to depict Indian customs correctly. I used proper colors and patterns.

Michele Wang *Age 15*
This project meant a great deal to me. I had the privilege of doing my own culture—China. When I was doing this, I was captivated by the dragon. The dragon had an interesting form to it that really captured my thoughts.

This project helped me to explore deep into my culture. It made me realize how important it was for me to accept other people even though it was very difficult. It's very difficult for me because in the past I wasn't accepted by people in this country. People laughed and scorned me for my culture and my skin. I used to hate myself mostly being Chinese. Now, I realize that being Chinese is what makes me special.

9 The Italian Renaissance

In This Chapter...

9–a Leonardo da Vinci was the quintessential Renaissance individual. He was knowledgeable not only in the arts, but also was an expert in many of the technical and natural sciences. He left behind ten thousand pages of drawings, sketches and notes.
Leonardo da Vinci, *Five Heads*. Department of Drawings and Prints, Uffizi Gallery, Florence.

RENAISSANCE MEANS REBIRTH. In the early 1400s, a cultural rebirth created a period of intense artistic activity throughout Europe that would last for 200 years.

Leaders in this artistic flowering lived in the city of Florence which was dominated by the Medici, a powerful family who were great patrons of the arts. The Florentine artists, fueled by a renewed interest in the ancient Romans and Greeks as well as in science and math, created a city of extraordinary beauty. Though magnificent sculpture and architecture were produced, painting dominated the art of the Renaissance.

The High Renaissance was a very short period in Rome and Venice. The primary center was Rome where popes commissioned artists, like Michelangelo, who were considered geniuses. Their work was more expressive than the earlier Renaissance artists and is probably some of the most well known in the world.

The last period to be discussed in this chapter is Mannerism, a transitional period which fell between the end of the High Renaissance and the beginning of the Baroque period. Mannerism is more a grouping of various individual artists' styles than a single style.

1401
Baptistry door competition, Florence

1492
Death of Lorenzo de Medici

1498
da Vinci, *The Last Supper*

1517
Protestant Reformation begun by Martin Luther
1527
The sack of Rome by Emperor Charles V

1536–1541
Michelangelo, *Last Judgment*, Sistine Chapel

1586
El Greco, *The Burial of Count Orgaz*

The Italian Renaissance

1420–1436
Donatello, *David*
1440
Gutenberg invents printing press with movable type

1492
Columbus arrives on the island of San Salvador

1516
Titian succeeds Bellini as official painter to Venetian Republic

1527
Center of art shifts to Venice

1575
Beginning of modern botany

1600
Wigs and dress trains become fashionable

Men can do all things if they will.
Leon Battista Alberti

During the 15th and 16th centuries, a creative force rippled across the Italian peninsula and produced the Renaissance. What Italian cities do we most often associate with the Renaissance?

9–b Science and mathematics became tools for artists in the early Renaissance. There was a strong interest in the use of linear perspective.
Paolo Uccello, *Battle of San Romano*, detail (fig.9–15).

9–c This is a detail of one of the most well known works of art from the Renaissance. It is a symbol of the enduring beauty and appeal of the period.
Michelangelo, *Pietà*, detail (fig.9–25).

9.1 Early Renaissance

WHEN WE LOOK AT WORKS from the early Renaissance, they appear so calm and harmonious that we might be fooled into thinking that they were a reflection of the period. This is far from the truth. Like so many other creative periods, the early Renaissance was an era of extreme stress and conflict.

The city of Florence became the political and intellectual leader among Italian cities—a "new Athens." It was the epicenter of a tremendous creative force that swept the Italian peninsula. Nevertheless, the city was still a beleaguered place. Led by the Medici family, Florence warded off conquering armies from the north and south of Italy in the early fifteenth century. Only in their great monuments and works of art did the Florentines achieve the harmony and serenity they so desired.

Despite threats to the city's safety, the people embarked on programs to finish the cathedral, build beautiful doors for their baptistry, line the streets with magnificent homes and plan a city of extraordinary beauty. The Florentines took tremendous pride in the advances made by their native artists. They were well aware of the great beauty of their city, which remains timeless and breathtaking even today.

Key Notes

- Florence is the birthplace of the Renaissance.
- Science and mathematics become tools for artists.
- Ancient Rome and Greece are sources of inspiration for artists.

Vocabulary
cupola
tondo
foreshortening

Special Feature

Filippo Brunelleschi

(1377–1446)

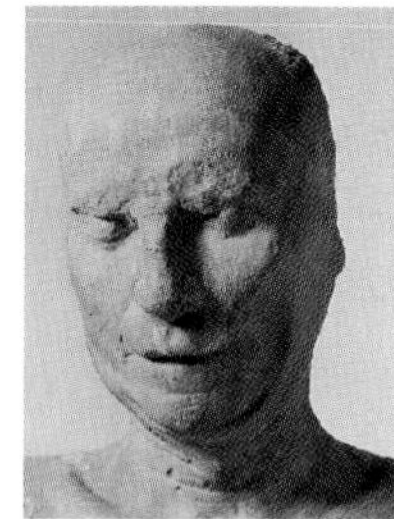

The crowning jewel of the Florentine cityscape is the ***cupola***, or dome, of its cathedral (fig.9–1). Designed by Filippo Brunelleschi (1377–1466), the dome is an architectural and engineering wonder.

Typical of the artistic genius of the Renaissance, Brunelleschi was a goldsmith, sculptor, mathematician, clock builder and architect. (His death mask is pictured above.) Trained as a sculptor, he discovered scientific perspective, a way of accurately showing three-dimensional buildings or objects on a flat sheet of paper. His greatest achievement, however, was in architecture, where he initiated a new style of building.

9–1 The transept was so huge that it could not be domed by any known system so Brunelleschi had to invent a new way to construct the dome.
Filippo Brunelleschi. Dome, *Cathedral of Florence,* 1420–1436. Florence.

9–2 Compare this interior to that of Notre Dame in Paris (fig.8–18). Look for similarities as well as differences.
Filippo Brunelleschi. Nave and choir, *San Lorenzo*, 1421–1469. Florence.

At some time between 1402 and the beginning of his architectural career, Brunelleschi had gone to Rome to study and accurately measure the remains of ancient Roman buildings. He came back to Florence with his own ideas about how ancient elements could be utilized. In 1418, he won a competition to design the mammoth dome over the cathedral.

The dome was built as two shells, one inside the other. The shells were ingeniously linked with ribs and supports so that each helped support the other. The dome is enormous. It is 140 feet in diameter and rises 300 feet above the floor.

Usually ramps were used to lift building materials to such height, but Brunelleschi designed a system of hoists that eliminated the need for ramps and scaffolding. He showed succeeding generations of architects that technical problems can be solved with scientific approaches. This was a new concept in the building trades. Previously, builders had looked at earlier structures for help in solving problems.

Brunelleschi, like the Greeks and Romans, used basic geometrical shapes and simple proportions. While Gothic interiors had become decorative and elaborate, Brunelleschi simplified. In the Church of San Lorenzo, built for the Medici family, he went back to the basilica plan for a simple framework (fig.9–2). Lines are clean and walls are uncluttered. Brunelleschi's work is in dramatic contrast to previous Gothic detail and movement. His work tends toward cool and static perfection—a drastic change. His experience in measuring the ancient Roman buildings helped him arrive at his concept of architectural design. Brunelleschi concluded that discipline of thought, clarity of design, the proportion of one part to another and a constant awareness of regular visual rhythm are essential to fine architecture.

9–3 Brunelleschi did not win the competition for the Baptistry doors with this panel. Can you "read" the story from this panel by studying it? What clues do you find?
Filippo Brunelleschi, *Sacrifice of Isaac,* 1401–1402. Gilt bronze relief, 21" x 17" (53 x 43 cm). National Museum, Florence.

Sculpture

The Classical tradition inspired not only Brunelleschi and his new architecture. Sculptors in the early part of the fifteenth century also learned many lessons from ancient Rome. When they looked at Roman sculpture they found a realism and spirit that reflected their own interest in humans and their achievements. Sculptures from antiquity were large and lifelike, celebrating the beauty, harmony and proportions of the human figure. In the early fifteenth century, sculptors once again began to place an emphasis on these values. They were commissioned to create works for public buildings, homes, palaces and churches.

Lorenzo Ghiberti

(1381–1455)

We encounter Brunelleschi at an earlier point in his career when, in 1401, a competition was held for the design and sculpting of the north doors of the baptistry of Florence. Lorenzo Ghiberti, Brunelleschi and many other artists competed intensely for this commission. The seven final contestants were assigned to sculpt the sacrifice of Isaac. Only the panels by Brunelleschi and Ghiberti have survived.

9–4 Compare this to Brunelleschi's panel which tells the same story. Which do you prefer?
Lorenzo Ghiberti, *Sacrifice of Isaac,* 1401–1402. Gilt bronze relief, 21" x 17" (53 x 43 cm). National Museum, Florence.

9–5 These panels are designed to work with light to help create the sense of three-dimensional space. Can you explain how Ghiberti did that?
Lorenzo Ghiberti, *Gates of Paradise,* 1425–1452. Gilt bronze relief, 15' (4.57 m). Baptistry, Florence.

9–6 Locate this panel on the illustration of the complete door. How does it relate to the other panels? Compare it to the relief sculptures from the Parthenon.
Lorenzo Ghiberti, *The Story of Jacob and Esau* (detail, baptistry doors), 1425–1452. Gilt bronze relief, 31 1/2" x 31 1/2" (80 x 80 cm). Florence.

Brunelleschi's panel (fig.9–3) is filled with energy and high drama. The angel rushes in and grabs Abraham's arm just as he is about to plunge the knife into his son's neck. Daring and original, it lacks the Renaissance qualities of harmony and balance—qualities Brunelleschi particularly expressed in his architecture. Ghiberti's panel (fig.9–4) is perhaps less dramatic, but more unified. Abraham's knife is poised to strike but does not touch Isaac. Figures are classical. The nude Isaac is beautifully proportioned, like the sculptures of ancient Greece.

The twenty-one-year-old Ghiberti won the competition. The two doors took more than twenty years to complete. The twenty-eight panels illustrate stories from the New Testament as well as other figures. They were received so well that Ghiberti was commissioned to do the final set of doors on the east side of the baptistry. These doors (fig.9–5) were to become his masterpiece. Later called *The Gates of Paradise* by Florentines, they were very different from the previous work. Instead of so many small panels, Ghiberti divided the space into ten large, square panels. He used pictorial space and one-point perspective (originated by Brunelleschi) to produce convincing depths on relief surfaces.

Look particularly at the panel *The Story of Jacob and Esau* (fig.9–6). Notice how the space creates an illusion of reality. The figures diminish in size as they recede in space. Parallel lines lead to a single vanishing point, and detail becomes simpler as it gets farther away. Several of the closer figures seem to project out in space in front of the panel. While his first doors contained remnants of Gothic sculpture, these doors are truly works of Renaissance art and thinking. The doors are cast in bronze, covered with gold. Said Ghiberti, "I did my best to observe the correct proportions, and endeavored to imitate nature as much as possible."

9–7 Compare this statue with the Greek sculpture, the *Kritios Boy* (fig.6–10). How are they similar? How do they differ?
Donatello, *David,* 1430–1432. Bronze, 62 1/4" (159 cm) high. National Museum, Florence.

Donatello

(1386–1466)

In a city where competition was keen among the artists, Donatello emerged as the greatest sculptor of his time and as one of the greatest ever to live. His work was a combination of Classic style and Renaissance expression. He used the contraposto of the Greeks to suggest action. His figures seem capable of movement. The facial expressions provide images of pride, dignity and self-reliance—attitudes that were a part of the Renaissance. Although most were sculpted to stand in niches, they are no longer a part of the architecture. Many of Donatello's figures, sculpted in either marble or bronze, looked out over the daily life of the Florentines.

Among his outstanding later works, his bronze *David* (fig.9–7) is unique. It was the first life-size, freestanding nude statue since ancient times. It must have seemed

9–9 Donatello never met Gattamelata. This is an idealized portrait of a military leader. What characteristics has the sculptor tried to portray in the face of the figure?
Donatello, *Gattamelata,* detail of head.

9–8 Gattamelata requested in his will that this monument be built. His family had to get a waiver from the Venetian State in order to commission the work. Previously this type of monument had been reserved for rulers.
Donatello, *Gattamelata,* Equestrian Statue of Erasmo da Narni, about 1445–1450. Bronze, approximately 11' x 13' (3.4 x 4 m). Piazza del Santo, Padua.

revolutionary. It stands in a classic contraposto, its body in a slight S-curve with its weight firmly carried by the right leg. The youth's relaxed left foot toys with the severed head of Goliath. The body of the young David is wiry and smooth. Its gently swelling muscles contrast vividly with the crisp, straight edge of the sword and the shaggy head below. Donatello's faces are usually very expressive, but David's face seems calm and serene—almost Classical—while the face of Goliath is horrifying.

Commissioned by Cosimo de Medici, *David* was designed to be viewed from all angles and to stand free of any wall or niche. David's head is crowned with contemporary fighting headgear and a laurel wreath—another combination of ancient and contemporary traditions. Throughout the Middle Ages, David's victory over Goliath was symbolic of Christ's victory over sin and death. Yet, to the Florentines, it became symbolic of the victory of the small and self-sufficient over the brute force of much larger opponents.

In 1443, Donatello was commissioned to sculpt a huge equestrian statue to place before the Basilica in Padua, where it still stands (fig.9–8). The subject was a Venetian general, nicknamed *Gattamelata* ("Honeyed Cat"), who had died before the artist arrived in Padua. Donatello undoubtedly drew his ideas from the Classic statue of Marcus Aurelius in Rome. Donatello's bronze creation is huge in size and mounted on a high pedestal. The horse is gigantic, but is controlled by the domineering will of its rider. The rider's face (fig.9–9) is a powerful and idealized portrait of the general. The visual rhythms are beautifully coordinated, from the arched tail to the arched flank to the arched neck. It was the first large equestrian statue of the Renaissance and the first larger-than-life horse and rider since ancient Rome.

Sidelight

Medici Patronage

The competition among artists of the early Renaissance was no less intense than the competition among wealthy Florentine leaders for political power. The Medici family emerged as the clear victor for political control of Florence. They were also highly important patrons of the arts. Three generations of Medici "princes"—Giovanni, Cosimo and Lorenzo—commissioned sculptures and architecture that turned Florence into a city of unsurpassed beauty. Their commissions provided artists with the income and freedom they needed to create some of the greatest works the world has known.

To be favored by the Medici assured success for any artist in Florence. In 1491, Giovanni commissioned Brunelleschi to design a parish church and sacristy space near the family home to honor the Medici patron saint, San Lorenzo. Donatello designed the sculpted ornament for the sacristy and also supplied a bronze pulpit.

In mid-century, political power passed to Giovanni's son, Cosimo de Medici. Cosimo continued the building and decoration of San Lorenzo (fig.9–2). In addition, Cosimo undertook the construction of a massive urban palace nearby.

Cosimo's grandson, Lorenzo the Magnificent, became the greatest patron, encouraging Michelangelo and Botticelli. During his rule, Florence flowered. When Lorenzo died in 1492, the greatest period in Renaissance art was also ending.

Painting

Almost a hundred years had passed since Giotto painted his magnificent and daring frescoes on the chapel walls in Padua. Gentile da Fabriano had brought a new realism in painting to Florence with his International style, which blended French and Italian Gothic style. It was only when a young man named Masaccio painted a chapel wall in Florence that Renaissance painting began. Painting would soon become the dominant art form of the Renaissance.

9–10 This painting shows three scenes from the biblical story of the Tribute Money. Can you identify them?
Masaccio, *Tribute Money*, about 1427. Fresco. Brancacci Chapel, Santa Maria del Carmine, Florence.

9–11 How has Masaccio used light to give the figures such a strong sense of realism?
Masaccio, *Tribute Money*, detail of figures.

Masaccio

(1401–1428)

Masaccio revolutionized the art of painting when he was in his mid-twenties. He studied the International style of Gentile da Fabriano and combined visual perspective and fascination with texture with the monumental forms of Giotto to initiate Renaissance painting in Florence.

Tribute Money (fig.9–10), a fresco in the church of Santa Maria del Carmine, is one of only several paintings done by the young genius before his death at the age of twenty-seven. The New Testament illustration depicts three succeeding events at the same time. In the central group of figures (fig.9–11), Christ and his disciples are confronted by a Roman tax collector and asked to pay tribute to Caesar. Christ sends Peter to the Sea of Galilee where he finds the tribute money in the mouth of a fish (at the left). Peter is seen paying the tax collector (at the right).

Masaccio used light as never before seen in a painting. There is a single source of light coming from the right side. Notice how it brightens the right part of most of the figures and casts a dark shadow on the left sides. It appears to make the rounded legs, massive folds, expressive faces and three-dimensional bodies occupy real space.

No longer is there any indication of flatness or invented light. Masaccio used atmospheric perspective to add to the sense of depth. Adding to the appearance of reality, the figures appear to be illuminated by the very real light coming from a window just to the right of where the fresco was painted.

Giotto's paintings had an illusionary depth of only a few feet, but Masaccio's depth seems endless. Look past the figures to the lake and the diminishing trees. The parallel lines of the building converge to a single vanishing point above the head of Christ. Christ's face was used as a model by painters for many years.

The halos still persist, but the bodies are no longer of the Middle Ages. They are solid and sculptural, convincing and natural under the folds of the cloaks.

Fra Angelico

(1400–1455)

Before Guido di Piero entered the Dominican order and changed his name to Fra Angelico ("Fra" means "Brother"), he was already a painter in the Late Gothic tradition. He became a prior, or high ranking administrator, of the Monastery of San Marco in Florence and filled its walls with lyrical frescoes, such as *The Annunciation* (fig.9–12). Unlike the powerful work of Masaccio or Giotto, the figures of the angel Gabriel and the Virgin Mary seem tender and frail. They are placed in an arched and vaulted porch that is painted in careful perspective.

Fra Angelico was the Florentine master of landscape painting, as seen in the *Adoration of the Magi* (fig.9–13), a ***tondo*** (a painting round in shape) painted in tempera on wood. It is the work of both Fra Angelico and Fra Filippo Lippi, a Florentine contemporary who finished it when Fra Angelico went to Rome. It reflects the past in its decorative color and line, but also foretells the future of Renaissance painting. Mary and the Christ Child are the focal point. A richly dressed group of wise men, together with hordes of other figures in fine clothing, are paying them homage. Although the perspective is not accurate in every way, it shows great depth of space. The introduction of nearly naked figures of boys watching the procession hints at the future Florentine fascination with figure painting. The animals and people in the stable foretell the painting of common, everyday subjects. The landscape elements of flowers, trees, mountains and sky indicate the Renaissance interest in nature.

9–13 During the Renaissance, artists frequently collaborated on commissions.
Fra Angelico and Fra Filippo Lippi, *Adoration of the Magi.* Tempera on wood, 54" (137 cm) diameter. National Gallery of Art, Washington DC, Samuel H. Kress Collection.

9–12 Can you identify the two types of Classical capitals the artist has placed atop the columns?
Fra Angelico, *The Annunciation,* 1440–1450. Fresco. Monastery of San Marco, Florence.

Paolo Uccello

(1397–1475)

Perspective was of such great concern to Paolo Uccello that he once made a linear diagram of a seventy-two-sided polyhedron. Here, we see a perspective drawing of a chalice that Uccello made in pen and ink (fig.9–14).

His fascination with this scientific aspect of painting is seen in *The Battle of San Romano* (fig.9–15). This complex composition is one part of a three-panel painting now in three separate museums. It was once a continuous work in the Medici Palace. *The Battle of San Romano* is a study in pattern, contrasting values and perspective (fig.9–b). The foreground becomes a stage for the main action. Riders joust with each other—left and right, into the picture plane and out. The horses are plump and artificial-looking as they prance on the stage. The landscape near San Romano in the Arno Valley is distant and contains many small figures. The fallen warrior is also in perspective. Here, Uccello has used ***foreshortening*** to create the feeling of the body pointing toward the viewer.

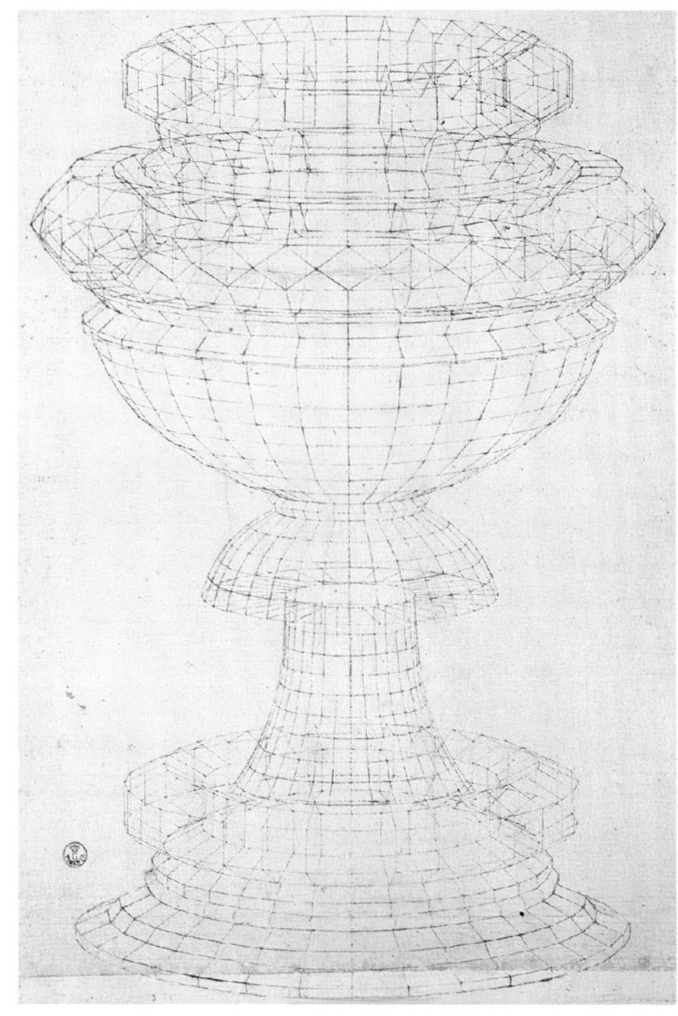

9–14 Today, wire frame models similar to this are generated by computer.
Paolo Uccello, *Perspective Study of a Chalice*, 1430–1440. Pen and ink, 13 3/8" x 9 1/2" (34 x 24 cm). Department of Drawings and Prints, Uffizi Gallery, Florence.

9–15 Does this battle scene seem real? Why or why not?
Paolo Uccello, *Battle of San Romano*, 1445. Tempera on panel, 6' x 10' 5 3/4" (1.82 x 3.2 m). National Gallery, London.

Piero della Francesca

(1420–1492)

Piero spent several years around 1439 studying in Florence. He was an apt student. From Masaccio's paintings, he learned about form. From Fra Angelico, he learned about light. From Brunelleschi, he learned scientific perspective. In fact, Piero also wrote an extensive book describing methods of working with perspective and proving its geometric exactness.

His painting has a cool and severe character, almost like the classical severity of Greek sculpture. Piero used mathematics to design his pictorial space effectively. In his emphasis on mathematical precision, he is closely related to many of today's contemporary abstract artists. His figures are scientifically accurate, but are unemotional and possess no warmth. The poses and facial expressions produce a "frozen-in-action" feeling. The light in his paintings seems to be at a low angle, like early morning, and produces solid and rounded forms.

Piero della Francesca's masterpiece is the huge wall of the Church of San Francesco in Arezzo. Several tiers of paintings relate the entire story of *The Legend of the True Cross.* In the scene reproduced here (fig.9–16), Piero depicts the actual discovery and proving of the True Cross. On the left side, the cross of Christ is found by Helena, the mother of Constantine the Great. On the right side, it is proved the True Cross by the miracles of healing it causes. Even though such a discovery would normally cause tremendous joy and excitement, Piero's figures are cool and calm. In this fresco, you can see how interested Piero was in light and how he used it to create solid geometric forms. With accurate perspective, both linear and aerial, the artist also produces a feeling of great depth in space.

9–16 Describe the narrative (story) the artist has depicted.
Piero della Francesca, *The Discovery and Proving of the True Cross,* about 1453–1454. Fresco. Church of San Francesco, Arezzo.

9–17 Use the text to identify the characters here. What elements are classical?
Sandro Botticelli, *Birth of Venus*, after 1482. Tempera on canvas, 5' 8 7/8" x 9' (1.75 x 2.8 m). Uffizi Gallery, Florence.

Sandro Botticelli

(1445–1510)

In the last third of the fifteenth century, few of the founders of the Renaissance were still living. The Florentine struggle for survival had eased, and the patricians lived lives of luxury. Artists continued to explore the Renaissance scientific appreciation of nature and the human body. They also often used the poetic and unreal subject matter of allegories and myths.

Botticelli's huge painting of the *Birth of Venus* (fig.9–17) is an example of a scene based on traditional mythology. Venus, the goddess of love, rises from the sea and emerges from a shell. On the left, West Winds, looking like puffing angels, push her toward land. The figure on the right is Spring, ready to toss a robe around Venus's unclothed body.

Often mythological and allegorical scenes were considered metaphors for Christian ideas. In this case, Venus, the water and Spring could symbolize Christ, baptism and John the Baptist. Baptism, like the birth of the celestial Venus, signifies the rebirth of humanity.

Botticelli was a master of delicate lines. His figures and fabrics are beautifully drawn. The figures seem outlined with an extremely fine line. The pale colors and the floating appearance of the figures add to the unreality of the subject. Notice the stylized waves in the sea and the spring flowers blown by the wind. It is one of the first Italian works on canvas instead of wood panel. Botticelli used gold to heighten the color of hair and robes and to add a feeling of elegant refinement.

Botticelli's *The Adoration of the Magi* (fig.9–18) reveals another characteristic of some late-fifteenth-century painting. The wise men and many others who have come to see the Holy Family are actually portraits of Italian contemporaries. Each is painted with very individualized features. Notice the figure on the far right of the painting that gazes directly at us. It is believed that this is a self-portrait of the

World Cultural Timeline

1400s
Tea ceremony, Japan

1403
22,937 volume encyclopedia written in China

1409
First book printed with metal type, Korea

1440–1550
***The Book of the Thousand and One Nights* written in Arabic**

artist. The arrangement of the figures is quite complex. The composition is calm at the center and active at the outside. Botticelli presents the serene Italian countryside in the background. Botticelli's scene is elegant and luxurious, especially when compared with Masaccio's and Giotto's treatments or to the events as they took place in the Bible.

Botticelli was not alone in his painting activity at the end of the century. Florence, Rome and other Italian cities enjoyed the works of artists such as Ghirlandaio, Perugino and Signorelli.

9–19 Artists sometimes placed themselves in their own paintings. These self-portraits often look out toward the viewer.
Sandro Botticelli, *The Adoration of the Magi,* detail of self-portrait.

9–18 Botticelli painted this popular subject seven times during the course of his career.
Sandro Botticelli, *The Adoration of the Magi,* early 1470s. Tempera on panel, 27 1/2" x 41" (70 x 104 cm). Uffizi Gallery, Florence.

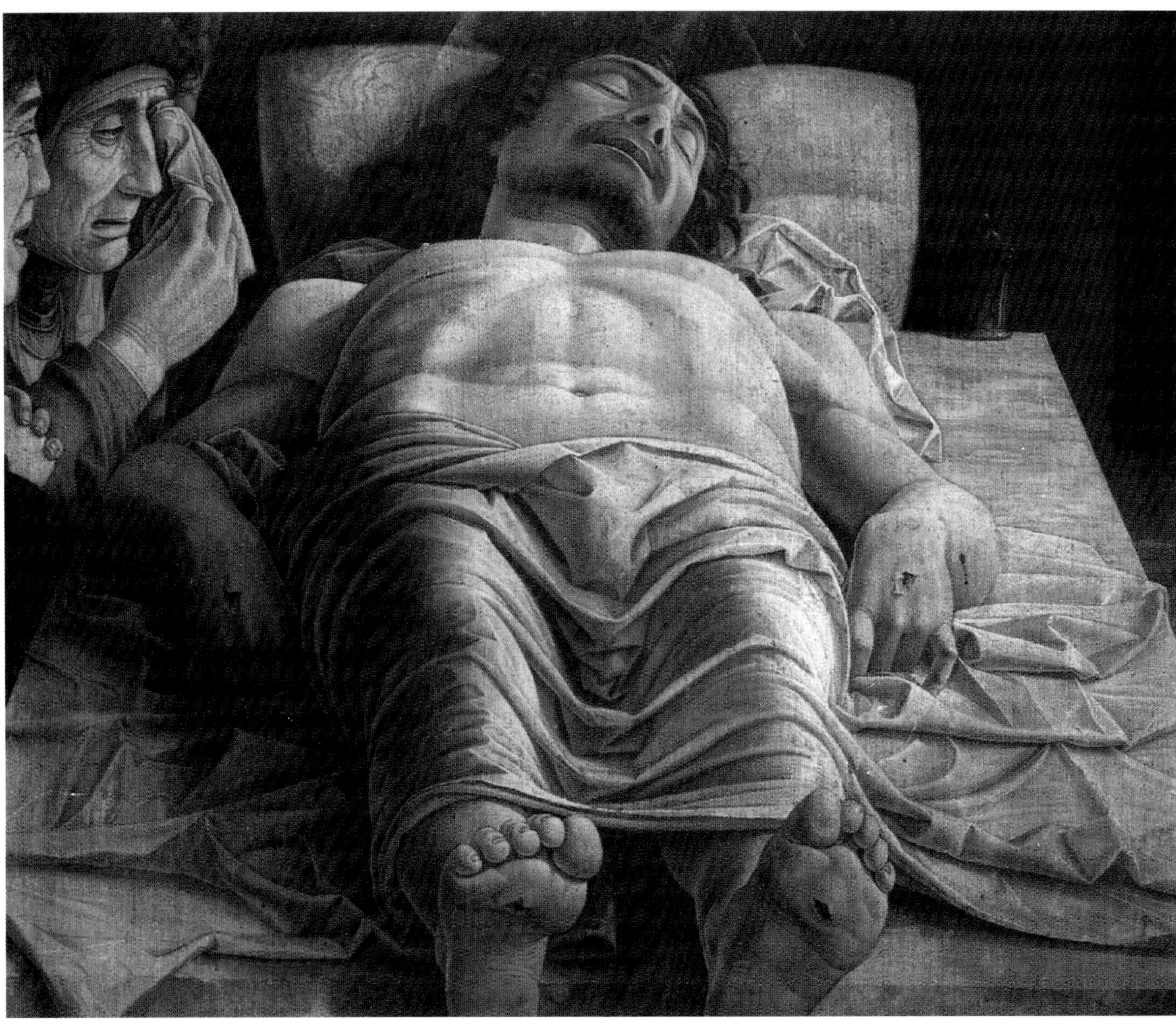

9–20 What effect does the artist's use of extreme foreshortening have on you, the viewer?
Andrea Mategna, *Dead Christ*, after 1466. Canvas, 26 3/4" x 31 7/8" (68 x 81 cm). Brera Gallery, Milan.

Venice and Northern Italy

During the early fifteenth century in northern Italy, Venice became a dominant economic and political power. Its art remained a blend of Byzantine and Gothic styles. Gentile Fabriano and Uccello visited Venice and worked there for short periods. They influenced native Venetian artists to a small extent.

It was Donatello's eleven-year stay in Padua, however, that revolutionized Venetian art. He brought the Florentine interest in perspective, form, anatomy and the classic tradition. The Venetians quickly combined these with their fascination for color and texture. Venetian artists developed a dynamic and exciting style that finally outshone Florence in its richness of expression.

Andrea Mantegna
(1431–1506)

Born in northern Italy, near Padua, Mantegna was already a polished artist by the time he was seventeen. He learned much from the Florentine artists who visited the north. He soon mastered form and anatomy. He excelled in working with perspective, especially foreshortening.

In his painting *Dead Christ* (fig.9–20), Mantegna used extreme foreshortening. The body of Christ lies on a slab of marble. The viewer can look directly into the face of Christ and at the same time see the nail holes in Christ's hands and feet.

The strong realism combined with the unusual perspective makes this image fascinating, yet unsettling, to the modern viewer. To the devout fifteenth-century Italian, however, it was an image that aided meditation. This painting, in fact, originally may have been placed outside the bedroom of a northern Italian noblewoman.

Giovanni Bellini

(1431–1516)

The master painter of Venice in the last part of the fifteenth century was Giovanni Bellini. His entire family was very artistic, and his sister married Mantegna. Bellini was greatly influenced by his brother-in-law in his early years of painting. Then with the arrival of the oil painting technique in Italy, he developed a richness of color and depth of value unequaled in Italy at the time.

In his portrait of *The Doge Leonardo Loredan* (fig.9–21), Bellini concentrated on the facial features of the Doge. The Doge was elected at age sixty-five to be the leader of the Venetian Republic. The sensitive face is beautifully captured by the artist. The light from the left softly models the forms. The extreme detail and the use of oil paints show the influence of contemporary painters in Flanders in northern Europe. Undoubtedly, works by these painters were brought to Venice at the time. Like Flemish artists, Bellini has superbly painted the luxurious brocade cloth of the Doge and contrasted the softly lit figure with the darkened and flat background. The artist signed his name as though it were on a bit of paper stuck on a piece of frame.

9–21 Locate the light source for this portrait.
Giovanni Bellini, *The Doge Leonardo Loredan*, 1502. Oil on panel, 24" x 17 1/2" (61 x 45 cm). National Gallery, London.

Lesson 9.1 Review

1 Which family ruled Florence during most of the fifteenth century?
2 Who designed the dome of the Florence cathedral?
3 Tell the story of the competition to select an artist to design the Florence baptistry doors. Describe Brunelleschi's and Ghiberti's panels for the competition.
4 What statue was the first life-size, freestanding nude made since those of classical Rome?
5 Which Roman statue was probably the inspiration for Donatello's equestrian statue of Gattamelata in Padua?
6 In what art principle was Uccello most interested in his *The Battle of San Romano*?
7 What is the subject of Piero della Francesca's frescoes in the Church of San Francisco in Arezzo, Italy?
8 Describe Botticelli's *The Adoration of the Magi.* Whose portraits were painted as the faces of the guests?
9 What means did Mantegna use to dramatize his painting of the *Dead Christ*?
10 From what city was Bellini? What characteristics in his paintings demonstrate the influence of Northern European painters?

9.2 High Renaissance

BETWEEN ABOUT 1495 AND 1527, a series of powerful and ambitious popes created a new force in Italy—a papal state, with Rome as its capital. Rome eventually took the lead from Florence and became the art capital of Europe.

The popes, living splendidly and luxuriously themselves, embellished the city with great works of art. They invited artists from all over Italy to Rome and provided them with challenging and exciting commissions. The High Renaissance lasted a very short time—a mere twenty or so years. But, during this period, artists in Rome and Venice produced great works that would influence European art for at least three centuries.

During the High Renaissance, artists began to be viewed as geniuses rather than craftspersons. It was widely believed that artists, like poets, created their work under divine inspiration. Artists of the Early Renaissance had relied on formulas, scientific perspective, ratios and proportions to structure their work. Now, the artists of the High Renaissance often disregarded those rules and let their feelings dictate their styles. Painters, sculptors and architects created works that were more expressive than those of their predecessors. Some of the most well-known artists in the history of the world worked at this time. Their achievements were so great that today we know them simply by their first names: Michelangelo, Raphael, Leonardo.

Key Notes

- Rome becomes the art center of Europe.
- The notion of artist as genius is born.
- Venetian artists make dramatic innovations in painting.

Vocabulary

chiaroscuro
sfumato
painterly

Special Feature

Leonardo da Vinci

(1452–1519)

If the ideal "Renaissance man" was to be knowledgeable in all things, then Leonardo was it! This artist-genius was ahead of his time not only in painting, sculpture and architecture, but in engineering, military science, botany, anatomy, geology, aerodynamics and optics, to mention only a few of the areas in which he made original contributions. Not only was he interested in these fields, he was considered an expert in all of them. He left *ten thousand* pages of drawing, ideas, sketches and notes, all written left-handed in reverse, or mirror, images.

Although he left only a dozen or so works, Leonardo considered painting the supreme form of art. To sculpt, he said, was simply to copy nature. To paint was to be "Lord and God" of the subject and

9–23 This painting is undergoing a long-term restoration. It is a slow, inch-by-inch process because the condition of the work is so poor. Always an experimenter, Leonardo painted on dry plaster with an oil and tempera mixture. Unfortunately, it began peeling almost immediately.
Leonardo da Vinci, *The Last Supper*, c. 1495–1498. Tempera wall mural, 15' 2" x 28' 10" (4.6 x 8.8 m). Santa Maria della Grazie, Milan.

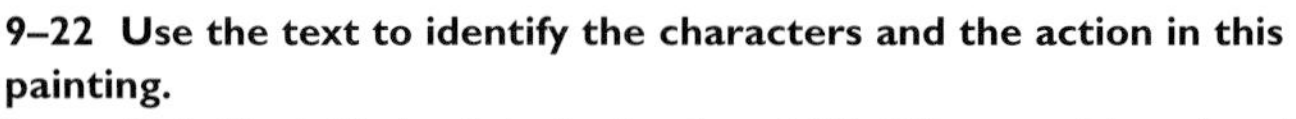

9–22 Use the text to identify the characters and the action in this painting.
Leonardo da Vinci, *Virgin of the Rocks*, about 1485. Oil on panel (transferred to canvas), 75" x 43 1/2" (190 x 110 cm). The Louvre, Paris.

9–24 How does Leonardo use chiaroscuro and sfumato in this work?
Leonardo da Vinci, *Mona Lisa*, 1503–1506. Oil on panel, 30 1/4" x 21" (77 x 53 cm). The Louvre, Paris.

art, a point on which he and Michelangelo never agreed.

Though trained in Florence, Leonardo created most of his works away from that city. *The Virgin of the Rocks* (fig.9–22) was painted in Milan. The figures in *The Virgin of the Rocks* are joined together in a triangular composition. The angel points to the infant John the Baptist, who is blessed by the Christ Child and sheltered by the Virgin's loving hand. Leonardo leads the viewer from one figure to another, but the viewer's eyes finally come to rest on the face of the Virgin. Light forms emerge from the background to create a dramatic contrast of values. This extreme contrast of dark and light values is called ***chiaroscuro***.

The Last Supper (fig.9–23) was painted on the wall of the dining hall of the monastery of Santa Maria della Grazie in Milan. Despite its ruined state, the painting is extraordinarily impressive in both form and emotion. Christ and the apostles are celebrating Passover. Suddenly a horrible announcement is made. Christ, with outstretched hands, has just said, "One of you will betray me." A shudder passes through the group as they ask themselves, "Is it I?" The intense shock and amazement is clearly visible.

The Last Supper is one of the Western world's most well-known paintings. Leonardo also painted the world's most famous portrait, the *Mona Lisa* (fig.9–24). The woman sits in a relaxed position in front of a typical Leonardo landscape. The distant hills and mountains are partially obscured by a light haze, or ***sfumato***, an effect that allowed Leonardo to create a feeling of enormous depth.

The Mona Lisa's "smile" and her identity have been the subject of endless speculation. We do know that painting must have been a particular favorite of Leonardo's. The artist carried it with him until he died.

Michelangelo Buonarroti

(1475–1564)

Recognized by his contemporaries as "the greatest man ever known to the arts," Michelangelo dominated the High Renaissance. His artistic genius influenced the Late Renaissance and beyond. Born of a poor family, he knew at an early age that he wanted to be an artist. When he was thirteen, his father finally allowed him to study with the Florentine artist, Ghirlandaio, where he learned the art of fresco painting. After a short time, Michelangelo was accepted by Lorenzo de Medici into his school for sculptors and was treated as a son in the Medici household. Here, he studied with Bertoldo, a pupil of Donatello, and developed an intense interest in Greek and Roman culture.

His earliest masterpiece, the *Pietà* (fig.9–25), was done in Rome about 1500. It is a work of profound Christian feeling. Mary holds the almost nude body of Christ on her lap. She does not grieve sorrowfully over her son, but accepts his death as the necessary fulfillment of humanity's salvation. The folds of drapery and the feeling of flesh are superbly handled. The seated mother of Christ is overly large when compared with the body of her son. Michelangelo was concerned with the overall appearance and visual effect of the pyramidal composition rather than with exact proportions.

The work was carved from a single block of marble. The sculpture is polished completely in the style of the Early Renaissance. In his later works, parts are often left in roughly chiseled condition that contrasted with polished areas. Michelangelo signed the work on the band across Mary's chest.

9–25 Michelangelo made many adjustments in the anatomy of these figures to enhance the composition of the whole.
Michelangelo, *Pietà* , 1499–1500. Marble, 68 1/2" (1.74 m) high. St. Peter's, Vatican, Rome.

Michelangelo's heroic *David* (fig.9–26) goes far beyond imitating nature. It is huge in size and superhuman in its muscular perfection. The young boy of the Bible has a manly body and an expression that is angry and defiant. The empty sling drapes over his left shoulder and a round stone is cradled in his huge right hand. He stands relaxed, but ever alert—a god-like being, half Apollo and half Hercules. It expresses Michelangelo's belief that human beauty is the outward indication of divine spirit. At only twenty-nine, Michelangelo was declared the greatest sculptor in Italy.

When finished, *David* was placed in the main square in front of the Florentine town hall, or Palazzo Vecchio. The original work is now protected indoors at the Academy in Florence. A duplicate stands in the original location in the piazza.

In 1505, Pope Julius II called Michelangelo to Rome to design his monumental tomb. The pope wanted forty over-life-size figures to be placed in St. Peter's, which was then being built. Because of innumerable interruptions, including the painting of the Sistine Chapel, the work was scaled down until only three sculptures were made, and the tomb was placed in a small church in Rome. The sculpture of *Moses* (fig.9–27) is now the dominant feature of the tomb, although it was carved to be on the second level in the original design. An incredibly powerful figure, Moses seems ready to burst into action from his seated position. The tablets of the law are only a prop as Michelangelo awes the viewer with the rippling muscles and stern glare of the prophet. Hair, beard and cloth are all deeply carved. The figure, with its dynamic power and intensity, seems ready to battle the world in defense of God's newly given law. Michelangelo had studied many ancient sculptures. From them, he gained knowledge of Classical sculpture techniques and the powerful representation of human forms.

In 1546, the seventy-one-year-old artist was in poor health. Yet, he accepted without salary the commission to finish the construction of St. Peter's. Donato Bramante, the original architect, had died while construction was underway. The huge basilica was untouched for so long that trees were growing from

9–26 The figure still holds the stone which will kill the giant, Goliath, in his hand. What moment has Michelangelo chosen to portray in the story of David and Goliath?
Michelangelo, *David*, 1501–1504. Marble, about 13' 5" (4.08 m) high. Gallery of the Academy, Florence.

9–27 This figure was meant to be placed on the second story of the tomb of Pope Julius II. The plan for the tomb was changed and cut back in size. As a result, this figure was placed on the floor where it loses the impact that Michelangelo intended.
Michelangelo, *Moses*, about 1513–1515. Marble, 7' 8 1/2" (2.35 m) high. San Pietro in Vincoli, Rome.

the huge arches. Michelangelo went to work immediately on the basilica. He slightly altered Bramante's plan. Although he retained the shape of the Greek cross, he redesigned the exterior, built the rear of the church, and designed the enormous dome (fig.9–28) which was completed after his death.

The exterior walls took on a sculptural quality that produces an upward thrust toward the dome. The hemispherical dome of Bramante's design was replaced by a high, pointed, double-shelled dome (like Brunelleschi's) placed on a tall drum. The heavily sculpted lantern completes the upward visual movement of the walls, drum and dome. The lantern is crowned by a large cross. The dome, the largest in the world, rests on four pendentives and four huge piers inside the church. Although the nave was lengthened later and a new facade was added, the imprint of Michelangelo can be easily detected in the present basilica.

Working on sculptures until six days before he died, Michelangelo said on his deathbed, "I regret that I am dying just as I am beginning to learn the alphabet of my profession."

9–28 Compare this dome to Brunelleschi's for the Cathedral of Florence.
Michelangelo. *Dome of St. Peter's,* 1546–1564. The Vatican, Rome.

1450
Great Mosque at Kilwa built, East Africa

1457
City of Edo (now Tokyo), Japan is founded

World Cultural Timeline

1453
Shin Sawba, Burma's first woman ruler, takes throne

1470
Road systems begun, Inca Empire

Window in Time

The Sistine Ceiling and Its Restoration

The painting of the Sistine Chapel ceiling was a monumental undertaking that took Michelangelo four years and five months to complete. It contains four large and five smaller Old Testament scenes. In addition, there are over 400 figures on the ceiling that fill the architectural elements and separate the main scenes.

To paint the gigantic *Last Judgment* on the end wall of the Sistine Chapel, Michelangelo had to climb between six and seven levels of scaffolding every day. Once he fell, badly injuring a leg. Between 1536 and 1541, he labored on the wall, producing an incredible work of the horror of hell and the reward of eternal life in heaven. When the *Last Judgment* was unveiled in 1541, Pope Paul III was so overcome he fell to his knees in prayer.

The Sistine Chapel ceiling and the wall with the *Last Judgment* were filled with dark tortured figures commonly believed to express the tortured genius of their creator. However, some of the darkness was due to the grime that had accumulated on the ceiling. At every papal Mass, oil lamps, incense and hundreds of candles were burned and their combined soot had collected on the ceiling. The roof also leaked and salts washed through. Attempts to undo the damage only made it worse.

The *Last Judgment*, being more accessible than the ceiling, fell more frequently into the hands of early restorers. A common fault was coating the frescoes with animal glue, or *size*. At first the glue, acting like varnish, enhanced the fresco's colors, but eventually it darkened. Then someone would add another coat of size. More torches. Candles. Salt stains. Glue, torches, candles, glue. Eventually the dark skin on the fresco was thicker than the paint beneath it.

Finally, in 1979, four hundred years after its completion, restorers began to clean the paintings of the Sistine Chapel, this time correctly. It took much experimentation and argument, but eventually a method was agreed upon. The team of experts who restored the Sistine Chapel took ten years to clean what took Michelangelo four years to paint. Using sponges soaked in a special mixture of chemicals and pure water, they carefully removed the layers of grime to reveal the original bright colors underneath. At last, the scaffolding and safety netting, which had obscured the frescoes in the Sistine Chapel for fourteen years, were removed.

Everyone, including scholars, were stunned by the results of the restoration. In place of the dark, often foreboding, colors were brilliantly rich and sparkling bright hues. Most were thrilled with the new Sistine ceiling and *Last Judgment*. Some experts, however, believed that the restoration was inaccurate and that touches of paint added by Michelangelo after the plaster had dried were removed by restorers. The controversy raged rather hotly for a while with scholars taking sides and battling with a barrage of articles and interviews.

No doubt, for as long as the frescoes exist, there will be heated arguments over how they should really look. However, the Vatican has insured that the paintings will not again suffer damage. They have installed a climate control system that filters dust and chemical pollution from the air and monitors the temperature and humidity so that no moisture can collect on the frescoes. This is a major concern in a room that receives up to 19,000 visitors a day.

Overall view of Sistine Chapel.

Raphael Sanzio

(1483–1520)

The spirit of the High Renaissance reached its peak in the work of Raphael. Raphael's paintings are masterpieces of balance and harmony. They combine the sculptural quality of Michelangelo, the grace and feeling of Leonardo and the detail and light of Perugino, who was Raphael's first teacher. While Michelangelo was a solitary genius with nothing to live for but art, Raphael (several years younger) enjoyed the social whirl of Rome and the adulation of many admirers. After working in Urbino with Perugino for several years, Raphael came to Florence in 1505, where Michelangelo and Leonardo had already established the foundations of the High Renaissance. They were too busy with large commissions to satisfy the wants of the merchants, and Raphael happily filled the gap. For eager patrons, he painted popular Madonnas and numerous flatter-

9–29 A good friend of Raphael's, Castiglione wrote a book of manners and proper behavior.
Raphael, *Baldassare Castiglione,* about 1515. Canvas, 32 1/4" x 26 1/2" (82 x 67 cm). The Louvre, Paris.

9–30 Describe how Raphael has mastered the art of perspective in this fresco.
Raphael, *School of Athens,* 1510–1511. Fresco. Stanza della Segnatura, Vatican, Rome.

ing portraits, such as the portrait of *Baldassare Castiglione* (fig.9–29).

Raphael went to Rome in 1508 at the invitation of the pope and immediately became a popular figure. Raphael was court painter in the Vatican until his early death at thirty-seven.

At the bequest of Pope Julius II, Raphael worked from 1509 to 1511 on large frescoes in the Stanza della Segnatura (Room of Signatures, where official papers were signed). The four subjects on the four walls are: *The Disputation over the Sacrament; The School of Athens; Parnassus;* and *Prudence, Force and Moderation.*

The School of Athens (fig.9–30) is probably his masterpiece. It embodies perfectly the spirit of the High Renaissance. The painting is Raphael's superb way of balancing pagan Classicism and Renaissance Christianity in one monumental work. All the masters of Classical Greek thought, science and art are in animated conversations. The two main figures, Plato and Aristotle, are deep in conversation. The figures of Socrates, Pythagoras and Euclid are actually portraits of contemporary persons. Bramante, Michelangelo and Leonardo (Plato) are included, as are many others. Raphael includes himself as a bystander.

The sculptural quality, the individual poses and the grouping of the figures in an architectural setting are influences of Michelangelo, who was painting his ceiling only a few yards away. Yet, the balance and composition are reminiscent of Leonardo's *Last Supper.* The result is a synthesis that is Raphael at his best. The architectural setting suggests the interior of the incomplete St. Peter's. The setting is dramatic and in harmony with the number and placement of the figures. The architectural perspective leads the viewer's eyes to a vanishing point between the heads of Plato and Aristotle.

The Alba Madonna (so named because it was in the collection of the Duke of Alba in Spain) was painted in 1510 and reflects the influence of Michelangelo (fig.9–31). Tondo paintings require extremely fine balance in order to keep them from seeming to roll like a wheel. Raphael used the most stable composition available, the triangle. The three solid forms of Mary, John the Baptist and the Christ Child are firmly resting on the ground. Yet, they are related to the surrounding landscape, which has a feeling of great depth. Raphael guides the viewer's eyes easily around the balanced composition, from Mary's leg, her left arm, shoulder and face, which looks at the cross and at the Baptist. The artist uses many devices (value contrast, direction of eyes and composition) so that visual movement is directed to come to rest on the cross.

Leonardo's sfumato can be detected in the portrayal of deep space, clear light and the Italian landscape. The foreshortened leg of Mary, her pose and the sculptural quality of her robes are reminiscent of Michelangelo. But the sensitive faces, graceful gestures and the balance of all elements are Raphael's.

After his early death in 1520, at the age of thirty-seven, Raphael was buried in the Pantheon in Rome. The era of the High Renaissance, which began with Leonardo's *Last Supper* twenty-five years earlier, came to an end. Although Michelangelo and Leonardo were the geniuses of the High Renaissance, it was the balance brought about by Raphael that was imitated and admired by artists in succeeding generations.

9–31 Compare this painting to Leonardo's *Virgin of the Rocks*.
Raphael, *The Alba Madonna*, c. 1510. Oil on wood panel, transferred to canvas, 37 1/5" (94 cm) diameter. The National Gallery of Art, Washington DC, Andrew W. Mellon Collection.

9–32 Can you identify Giorgione's techniques for handling light to make a unified composition?
Giorgione, *The Adoration of the Shepherds,* about 1505. Oil on panel, 35 4/5" x 43 4/5" (91 x 111 cm). National Gallery of Art, Washington DC, Samuel H. Kress Collection, 1939.

Northern Italian Art

After the death of Raphael, the sixteenth century saw a shift in the dominance in art from Florence and Rome to Venice in northern Italy. The one exception was Michelangelo, who remained the solitary genius in central Italy until his death in 1564. But Venice gradually took over the leadership in painting, building on the foundation laid down by Giovanni Bellini and benefiting from the discovery of flexible resins that made painting on canvas possible.

1500
Aztecs play early form of basketball, Mexico

1525
Raku-ware, Japan

World Cultural Timeline

1521
Aztec Empire ends

1526
Babar founds Mogul Empire

Giorgione da Castelfranco

(1478–1510)

Giorgione lived and worked only a very short lifetime and left only a relatively small number of paintings. However, he made some dramatic innovations in painting that pushed Venetian art to the forefront in Europe. Early Renaissance artists had thought of painting as colored drawings with definite contours. Forms were modeled in light and shade to suggest relief. Fifteenth-century painters realized that individual figures and objects are not seen separately, but together. The artists created interesting groupings that react with their surroundings. Yet, each part was shown as crystal clear, such as in Botticelli's *Adoration of the Magi.*

Giorgione changed this bright light that picks up all details to a soft, misty sunlight. This light helps blend all parts of a composition together to create a strong visual unity. In *The Adoration of the Shepherds* (fig.9–32), colors and values are muted for a more unifying effect. Two shepherds have come to the stable-cave to worship the Christ Child lying before Mary and Joseph. While a fairly bright light brings out the details in the principal figures, Giorgione used chiaroscuro in the cave and a soft golden light to illuminate the middle and far distance. He loved to paint landscapes. The upper left portion of the painting (fig.9–33) is not only an environment for the subject, but a jewel of a landscape painting in itself. Notice the overcast sky, which softens the light and eliminates harsh contrasts and sharp shadows. Notice, also, how the dark shadows on Mary and Joseph blend into the darks of the cave. The middle values of the shepherds blend into the middle gray values around them. By squinting, one can see how the figures seem to melt into the values around them. With these techniques, Giorgione conveyed his special feelings or moods about his subjects. While Michelangelo and Raphael excelled in creating form, Giorgione mastered mood in painting.

9–33 This detail of *The Adoration* clearly illustrates Giorgione's love for painting landscapes. Although it is only a small part of the whole, when isolated, it takes on a life of its own.
Giorgione, *The Adoration of the Shepherds,* detail.

Sidelight

Is Venice Sinking?

When the Roman empire fell in the fifth century, a group of Roman citizens fled to the safety of some muddy islands at the head of the Adriatic Sea. So began one of the greatest Italian cities: Venice. Venice is a city quite unlike any other in the world. More than 400 bridges span the network of canals that crisscross it. Boats, gondolas and barges remain, to this day, the only source of transport.

Throughout its long history, the islands comprising Venice have been threatened by high waters and flooding. The flooding occurs partly because Venice's only outlets to the sea are three large openings between the islands. The winter winds, called *sirocco,* drive huge tidal waves through these three openings into the lagoon, causing enormously high water pressure. The water that comes rushing in must drain away quickly to prevent a dramatic rise in the water level. But, this quick draining of the lagoon is no longer possible because of high industrial pollution. Another problem has been caused by the draining away of underground water reserves. As a result, the floor of the lagoon has sunk markedly and Venice risks being destroyed.

In 1966, the flooding reached critical levels when a southeasterly sirocco blowing at gale force prevented the morning tide from flowing out of the lagoon. On this occasion, the water in Venice rose to almost six and one-half feet above sea level.

Titian

(1490–1576)

The artistic giant of Venice, comparable to Michelangelo in Florence and Rome, was Tiziano Vecellio, known as Titian. Like Giovanni Bellini and Giorgione, he believed that color and mood were more important in painting than line and scientific accuracy. His painting methods were innovative. He often painted his figures in bright colors over a red-painted background, which added a warmth to the entire work. After it was dry, the surface was painted with as many as thirty or forty glazes. The glazes, transparent mixtures of color and medium, toned down the bright colors and unified the surface. Preferring not to smooth out the surface paint, he allowed brushstrokes to remain visible and let the soft edges of his figures blend into the background. In his later work, no outlines or hard edges are visible at all. Color blends into color to create form. Detail was often ignored in order to emphasize the color and movement created by rapid and powerful brushstrokes. The brushstrokes created a textured surface quality that is called ***painterly***.

Three subjects dominated Titian's imagination: events from pagan mythology, especially those involving Venus; portraits of important people and rulers from all over Europe; and religious subjects that called for great emotion, mood or physical activity.

The architectural setting of the *Madonna with Members of the Pesaro Family* (fig.9–34) is characteristic of the High Renaissance. However, unlike Leonardo's *Last Supper* or Raphael's *The School of Athens,* the composition is not symmetrical and horizontal. Instead, the composition has a drama and power that comes from the use of diagonals, angles and triangular arrangements. The Madonna, which is the focus of the composition, is placed to the right, not the center. Except for the kneeling figures, all the figures are in motion.

The figures in Titian's portraits almost always seem to have superhuman power. The *Doge Andrea Gritti* (fig.9–35) was a ruthless maritime ruler. His Venetian fleets dominated the shipping lanes of the trading world and made Venice a feared power. Yet, he also was a patron of the arts and commissioned many religious, historical and allegorical paintings from Titian.

Compare Titian's *Doge* to Bellini's (fig.9–21). Although the same robes and caps are worn by both men, Titian disregards detail and uses slashing brushstrokes to characterize the physical strength of his subject. Edges are soft, suggesting movement. A swirling motion is evident, even though the figure is sitting still. Both brushstrokes and the turn of the head contribute to this feeling. The powerful hand that holds the robes is similar to the

9–34 Jacopo Pesaro presented this painting to the Church as a thanksgiving offering for his successful expedition during a war between the Venetians and the Turks.
Titian, *Madonna with Members of the Pesaro Family,* 1526. Oil on canvas, 16' x 8' 10" (4.9 x 2.7 m). Santa Maria del Gloriosa dei Frari, Venice.

9–35 Artists often use hands to provide insight into the character of the figures they portray. Gritti's hands are quite powerful. Find two other figures in this chapter that have hands that give a clue to their personality.
Titian, *Doge Andrea Gritti,* about 1540. Oil on canvas, 52 1/2" x 40 1/2" (133 x 103 cm). National Gallery of Art, Washington DC, Samuel H. Kress Collection, 1961.

9–36 Titian painted his idea of the perfect woman. Compare her to beautiful women from other times.
Titian, *Venus with a Mirror,* 1555. Oil on canvas, 48 4/5" x 41" (124 x 105 cm). National Gallery of Art, Washington DC, Andrew W. Mellon Collection.

sculpted hand of Michelangelo's *Moses*. Bellini's fabrics and textures are very realistic. But, Titian relies on brushstrokes, deep values and vivid colors to create a robust and individualistic figure rather than simply a likeness of the Doge.

The painting of *Venus with a Mirror* (fig.9–36) was one of Titian's favorites. Painted when he was seventy-eight, the work was not easy for him to design. X-rays show that it was painted over two previous compositions; the first was horizontal with two figures and the second was of Venus with two cupids. The face and pose of the second were used in this final version. Again, the rich and glowing colors emerge from deep shadows as two cherubs are seen with the goddess of love. The figures crowd the composition as if ready to burst out of the frame. The painting expresses Titian's ideal of feminine beauty—a concept that changes throughout history.

Titian received honors from many parts of Europe in his long and productive life. Like Michelangelo and Raphael, he was quite wealthy when he died. His work was as popular in Spain and Germany as it was in Italy, making him the most sought-after artist of his time. Titian's later work, like that of Michelangelo, moved him into the trends of Mannerism and on the verge of Baroque painting.

Lesson 9.2 Review

1 When was the High Renaissance in Italy?
2 How did most people's perception of painters and sculptors change during the Renaissance?
3 Name four fields of knowledge other than art in which Leonardo da Vinci was an expert.
4 Describe Leonardo da Vinci's *Virgin of the Rocks*. What type of composition has he used? Who are the people in this painting?
5 Describe the *Mona Lisa*. What technique did Leonardo use to show distance in the background?
6 As a teenager where did Michelangelo study sculpture?
7 Why did Michelangelo carve the huge statue of *Moses*?
8 Define *chiaroscuro*.
9 Describe Titian's painting technique.
10 Compare Titian's *Doge Andrea Gritti* to Bellini's *Doge Leonardo Loredan*.

9.3 Mannerism

THE TERM *Mannerism* REFERS TO the period between the end of the High Renaissance and the beginning of the Baroque period (from 1525 to 1600). Mannerism was originally a derogatory term applied to painters who had a formal, mannered style that imitated various aspects of Raphael's and Michelangelo's works.

Included in the Mannerist style are such features as crisp and frozen shapes, elongated bodies, distorted forms and peculiar perspective views. The artists had very individual and expressionistic approaches to subject matter. Instead of a single dominant style, there was a mix of styles that were extensions of the Renaissance. Mannerism, therefore, was not a unified approach by several artists, but stressed unique approaches. Mannerism could be compared to the present-day art scene, in which there is a great variety of visual expression.

Key Notes

- Mannerism has strong ties to the High Renaissance, but rejects many of its conventions.
- Mannerism does not refer to a single style, rather to a variety of styles.

Vocabulary
genre

9–37 Note that the black-clad figures behind the burial seem to be individualized portraits of important Spanish contemporaries.
El Greco, *The Burial of Count Orgaz,* 1586. Oil on canvas, 16' x 12' (490 x 360 cm). San Tomé, Toledo, Spain.

Special Feature

El Greco

(1541–1614)

Domenikos Theotocopoulos was born in Crete but emigrated to Italy as a young man. He studied in Venice with Tintoretto and knew Titian and his work. But, when he went to Rome, he fell under the spell of Raphael, Michelangelo and the central Italian Mannerists. By 1577, he had left for Spain and settled in Toledo where he would spend the rest of his life. He was nicknamed El Greco (the Greek) there. El Greco never forgot his Byzantine heritage and continued to sign his name in Greek.

El Greco's strong personal style developed from the blending of his Byzantine background with the influence of Venetian painting and Italian Mannerist elements. His paintings are intensely emotional, which greatly appealed to the religious fervor of the Spanish. Form is often dematerialized. Color is very important and there is a strong sense of movement. His paintings featured elongated distortion and a flickering light that is much more personal than realistic. However, El Greco's style was not fully appreciated until the latter part of the nineteenth century.

Generally considered the artist's masterpiece, *The Burial of Count Orgaz* (fig.9–37) was painted in 1586 for the church of San Tomé in Toledo. The theme illustrates the legend of the Count of Orgaz. The Count, who had died some two centuries before, had been so saintly that Saints Stephen and Augustine had miraculously descended from heaven to help bury him.

The work is divided into two sections. The lower part is sixteenth century on earth, the upper is eter-

nal and in heaven. The faces of the noblemen in attendance on the lower half of the painting are portraits of El Greco's friends in Toledo. He even included himself in the group and his son in the foreground. The angel bearing Orgaz's soul to heaven (his soul looks like a small doll in the center) unites the lower part of the painting with the upper. The upward gaze of the priest at the right also makes us look up. The celestial beings in the upper half of the picture are painted differently from the lower half. The figures on earth are represented rather realistically. The heavenly figures are elongated, with fluttering draperies and on giant swirls of clouds.

El Greco painted many religious works for churches and hospitals in and around Toledo. One of the finest examples of his later mystical style is the *Resurrection* (fig.9–38). Christ soars effortlessly toward heaven, carrying the victory banner with him. He calmly observes the scene below where soldiers seem to be flung apart by the explosive power of His resurrection. The writhing movement and flickering lights and darks create a powerful and unified statement. Notice how the elongated figures and thin arms, hands and legs fill most of the available space. They draw the viewer's eyes up to the Christ figure with unrelenting magnetic force. The artist has made a personal statement powerfully expressive. Physical reality does not exist in this late work.

El Greco was concerned primarily with emotion and with the effort to express his own religious fervor. To accomplish this he, like other Mannerist painters, bent the rules of Renaissance painting to create very powerful and unique visual expressions.

9–38 Can you identify two Mannerist features in this painting?
El Greco, *Resurrection*, about 1597–1604. Oil on canvas, 9' x 4'10" (275 x 146 cm). Prado Museum, Madrid.

Rosso Fiorentino

(1494–1540)

Some of the earliest Mannerist work can be found in central Italy. About 1520, a group of Florentine painters led by Rosso shocked their fellow artists and the citizens of central Italy with works like *The Descent from the Cross* (fig.9–39). Rejecting many of the conventions of Renaissance painting, Rosso crowds figures into a tight composition with open space in the center. The impact of such spidery forms spread out against a dark sky was shocking to his contemporary Italians. The figures are agitated, yet rigid, as if quick-frozen in time and space. The acid colors and peculiar light produce a brilliant, but unreal, sensation—almost with a nightmarish quality. Rosso's mystifying work went against the Classical tradition of Renaissance painting, which emphasized balance and harmony.

9–39 How has the artist purposely avoided balance and harmony in this work?
Rosso Fiorentino, *The Descent from the Cross,* 1521. Oil on panel, 11' x 6' 5 1/2" (334 x 196 cm). Pinacoteca, Volterra.

Sofonisba Anguissola

(1535–1625)

Sofonisba was the oldest child of a wealthy family in Cremona. She was a widely recognized artist in her own long lifetime. A child prodigy, she received the attention of Michelangelo. Her paintings are charming and informal, almost like affectionate family photographs instead of formal portraits. Poses are natural. Some of her work capture small moments in everyday life, such as *Boy Pinched by a Crayfish* (fig.9–40). This lively drawing clearly conveys the small boy's painful surprise at having his finger pinched by the crayfish. The comforting older child provides a warmth and intimacy that is typical of the artist's work. The drawing, which she gave to Michelangelo, was so popular that other artists made copies of it.

9–40 This artist delighted in capturing everyday activities. Though drawn more than 350 years ago, the reaction and response of the figures seem very familiar to us.
Sofonisba Anguissola, *Boy Pinched by a Crayfish.* Museo e Gallerie di Capidimonte, Naples.

In 1559, she became court painter to Philip II of Spain. She remained in Spain for twenty years, where she was a popular portrait artist. Her self-portraits (fig.9–41), in which she often showed herself playing the spinet, were also in demand. She is credited with introducing ***genre***, or everyday activity, into formal portraiture.

9–41 Sofonisba was considered a child prodigy. Her career was quite long. She lived over 80 years.
Sofonisba Anguissola, *Self-Portrait,* Pinacoteca di Brera, Milan.

9–42 Peter leaves the boat to try to walk to Christ over the surface of the water. How does Tintoretto make you feel the emotion of the moment?
Tintoretto, *Christ at the Sea of Galilee,* about 1580. Oil on canvas, 46" x 66 1/2" (117 x 169 cm). National Gallery of Art, Washington DC, Samuel H. Kress Collection.

Tintoretto

(1518–1594)

About the middle of the sixteenth century, two Venetian painters began to crowd into Titian's dominance: Jacopo Robusti, called Tintoretto, and Paolo Caliari, called Veronese. The name Tintoretto means "Little Dyer," which was his father's occupation. Tintoretto became the most dramatic painter of the sixteenth century. He filled huge walls with canvases of soaring and hurtling figures. His subjects were mostly religious and sprang from a strong faith.

Tintoretto would arrange small models on stages and even suspend some from wires to set the composition and see the foreshortening as it should be. He made small drawings of these arrangements and enlarged them enormously on his huge canvases. Tintoretto would first paint the bright colors. Then he would add intense darks and highlights, producing the effect of a night scene illuminated with flashes of light. His brushstrokes were less controlled than Titian's, causing the nineteenth-century critic John Ruskin to accuse him of painting with a broom. Although he painted constantly, he did much of his work for charity houses at a small salary. He died almost penniless.

Christ at the Sea of Galilee (fig.9–42) presents a Biblical narrative through the eyes of Tintoretto. Christ's disciples were in a boat on the Sea of Galilee when a sudden storm arose. As the boat was being tossed about, the men saw Christ walking toward them on the water. They were astounded and afraid, but Peter asked if he could walk to Christ on the water. Christ invited him and Peter stepped from the boat. Tintoretto shows this moment of psychological tension in his painting. The artist has created a powerful composition, placing

1540
Horses introduced to the Americas from Europe

1593
The *bunraku*, a Japanese theater form using marionettes, first introduced

World Cultural Timeline

1571
Manila, The Philippines, founded

1603
Japanese Shinto priestess develops *Kabuki* theater

Christ against the left edge of the canvas. Although Christ is important in the design, the center of interest is Peter. The viewer wonders, "Will he make it? If not, why not?" The dominant hues of bluish-green are favorites of Tintoretto. The elongated figures and flickering lights are features of much of his work.

Tintoretto's masterpiece is the magnificent series of over fifty canvases in the School of San Rocco in Venice. Here, he labored for twenty-three years for a small yearly salary. He produced a monument that rivals Giotto's Arena Chapel and Michelangelo's Sistine Chapel in visual impact and sustained creative intensity. The largest canvas is the *Crucifixion* (fig.9–43) (40 feet long) which is overpowering in its visual effect. The foreground figures are over-life-size. The upward thrust of the cross seems to crush Christ against the top border. Groups of soldiers, horses, disciples and Mary are visually interlocked by their overlapping forms and the dramatic light which seems to emanate from the head of Christ. Tintoretto calls even more attention to Christ by having a great number of lines and shapes direct the visual movement toward the top center of the canvas. The use of unreal light counteracted the natural light used by Renaissance painters.

Sidelight

Thinking like a Museum Curator

A museum curator is responsible for the proper care, display, research, cataloging and publication of the objects in a collection. A "good eye" and an excellent visual memory are two of the most important qualifications that an individual must bring to the job. A good eye means that the curator is able to determine the quality, condition and authenticity of a work of art. A curator also needs to have an extensive knowledge of the history of art.

Cataloging is one of the most interesting, but often most difficult, of a curator's duties. Cataloging includes the proper documentation of an object's physical state. Cataloging also requires that the curator try to determine the artist, title and date of an object. In some cases attributing a work to an artist is quite simple because the work is signed and even dated. In many instances, however, a work of art is not signed and the curator must make a decision based on factors such as style, comparisons, surviving documents and the opinions of other scholars.

Consider the painting *Christ at the Sea of Galilee* (fig.9–42). It is usually attributed to Tintoretto, as it is here. It is not signed and no documents (such as papers commissioning Tintoretto to paint this subject) have been found. The assignment of this work to Tintoretto, therefore, has to be made purely on the basis of "eye." Is its style and technique similar to other paintings the artist executed? Is the treatment of the subject similar to any other works by Tintoretto?

The answer to the latter question is no. It is the only painting attributed to Tintoretto in which water takes up so much of the canvas. Style and technique, therefore, become the primary means of judging the work. Brushstroke, the treatment of the sky, the small figures in the boat all point to Tintoretto. But the opinions are not unanimous.

Some have suggested that the work is by El Greco. The intense blues favored by El Greco play a strong role in the painting. The elongation of the figure of Christ also recalls El Greco.

The curator at the National Gallery has weighed the opinions, carefully scrutinized the painting and made an attribution: the style and brushstroke indicate Tintoretto. What do you think?

9–43 The figures in the foreground are larger than life. The unnatural light emphasizes the importance of the event.
Tintoretto, *Crucifixion,* 1565. Oil on canvas, 17 1/2' x 40' (5.3 x 12.2 m). End wall, Sala dell'Albergo, School of San Rocco, Venice.

9–44 How does the artist make the princess the central focus of the composition?
Paolo Veronese, *The Finding of Moses,* c. 1570. Oil on canvas, 22 4/5" x 17 1/2" (58 x 44 cm). National Gallery of Art, Washington DC, Andrew W. Mellon Collection.

Veronese

(1528–1588)

Paolo Caliari was called Veronese because he came from Verona, some distance west of Venice. Tintoretto was concerned with turbulent and swirling light and action in religious scenes. Veronese emphasized the material beauty of marble, gold, textiles and other materials of superb quality and great expense. Like other Mannerist painters, he was adept at using perspective to create startling effects—such as looking straight up at figures on a ceiling or looking upward or downward diagonally. He was so skilled at foreshortening that he had no trouble portraying figures in any conceivable location and position.

His interest in the luxurious quality of fabrics can be seen in *The Finding of Moses* (fig.9–44). Although the event happened in Egypt over three thousand years earlier, Veronese placed the scene in northern Italy—the Alps and a Tyrolian town are in the background—and peopled it with a sixteenth-century princess and her court. The basis for the painting is the hiding of Moses by his mother when all first-born sons of Israel were to be put to death by the Egyptian Pharaoh. The princess, out on her daily walk, finds Moses in a basket in the reeds by the river bank. The flowing colors and spiraling, twisting figures are designed to lead the viewer's eyes to the face of the princess, even though the baby Moses is the reason for the painting. While Veronese leads the viewer's eyes along many paths, they always return to the face of the princess. Her light complexion is set off by the dark foliage behind her. The arbitrary use of light, placed just where the artist wants it, is contradictory to the use of natural light so admired by Renaissance artists.

Christ in the House of Levi (fig.9–45), like High Renaissance paintings, is symmetrically balanced. The figures, which are full of action and motion, are placed in a Classical architectural setting. Christ is seated in the center and surrounded by men of high station and their servants. The painting was originally titled *The Last Supper.* However, the Inquisition charged Veronese with impiety for including drunkards and dwarfs in such a solemn occasion. Rather than make changes in his painting, Veronese simply changed the title to one with less religious significance.

9–45 Compare this work to Leonardo's *Last Supper.*
Paolo Veronese, *Christ in the House of Levi,* c. 1573. Oil on canvas, 18' 2" x 42' (5.5 x 12.8 m). Academy, Venice.

Sidelight

Cellini's Saltcellar

Benvenuto Cellini was a sculptor and craftsman in metals who was born in Florence in the sixteenth century. He also wrote a famous autobiography that has made his life as familiar to many modern readers as his artwork. Virtuosity characterized both the art and the flamboyant life of Cellini.

Like many Florentine artists, Cellini spent much of his time away from his hometown and by 1540 went to the royal court of France at Fontainebleau. Eventually, Cellini was commissioned as goldsmith to the king. Before he left France in 1545, Cellini completed a magnificent table ornament in gold and enamel for Francis I: a *saltcellar.*

The forms of the gilded figures and the basic allegorical concept of the saltcellar derive directly from Michelangelo's work in the Medici Chapel. For the salt from the sea, Cellini provided a male Neptune (Water) figure with a trident and an accompanying ship that held the spice. Opposite him lay a reclining female Ceres (Earth), whose adjacent temple held pepper. Each of the figures is set against a field of colored enamel that includes appropriate animal companions (sea horses, dolphins and an elephant). On the ebony base, gold reliefs of the winds or seasons were depicted, as well as the times of day.

Benvenuto Cellini, *The Saltcellar of Francis I,* 1539–1543. Gold with ebony base, 10 1/4" x 13 1/8" (26 x 33.6 cm). Kunsthistorisches Museum, Vienna.

Sculpture and Architecture

Although painting was the most important medium during the late sixteenth century, several sculptors made excellent contributions to the art of the period. A slight change in style and an emphasis on luxurious elegance were characteristics of the work produced.

Benvenuto Cellini

(1500–1571)

Cellini's *Autobiography* is a book that gives us a vivid picture of life in sixteenth-century Italy. Besides being an author, Cellini was an excellent goldsmith and a sculptor in bronze. His *Perseus and Medusa*

9–46 It took Cellini nine years to devise a technique that would allow him to cast a bronze figure this size.
Benvenuto Cellini, *Perseus and Medusa,* 1545–1554. Bronze, 18' (5 1/2 m) high with base. Piazza della Signoria, Florence.

(fig.9–46) stands in the Piazza della Signoria in Florence in an honored location. The heavily muscled figure of Perseus reminds one of Michelangelo's many powerful bodies. Perseus holds the severed head of Medusa, whose blood is turning to precious coral strands as it pours from body and head. These ornamental strands and the highly decorated pedestal add the luxurious touch to a Mannerist sculpture.

Giovanni Bologna

(1529–1608)

Coming to Italy from northern Europe, Jean Boulogne (renamed Giovanni Bologna in Italy) was the most original sculptor between Michelangelo and Bernini, thus bridging the time span between the Renaissance and the Baroque. His powerfully designed *Abduction of the Sabine Woman* (fig.9–47) was carved from a single block of marble. The muscular central figure carries away the Sabine woman as her father crouches in defeat. The three figures are interwoven in a spiraling composition that seems as difficult to unravel as the groupings in many of the Mannerist paintings. All sculpture until this time was made to be viewed from front, back and profile, but Bologna's work has no front or back and viewers must constantly move around it to see the complete work. Parts of arms, legs and heads seem to flail outward at various angles, creating a feeling of violent action and tension. The monumental sculpture displays all of Bologna's considerable skills and stands close to Cellini's *Perseus* in the Palazza della Signoria in Florence.

9–47 This statue is meant to be viewed from multiple angles.
Giovanni Bologna, *Abduction of the Sabine Woman*, 1583. Marble, 13' (4 m) high. Piazza della Signoria, Florence.

9–48 Palladian architecture continues to influence the design of buildings today.
Andrea Palladio, *Villa Capra (Villa Rotunda)*, begun 1550. Vicenza, Italy.

Andrea Palladio

(1508–1580)

The only northern Italian architect that ranks with Bramante and Michelangelo was Andrea Palladio from Vicenza. Many of the buildings in his hometown (palaces, town hall and theater) were designed and built by him. Many structures in Venice, Padua and other nearby cities also were his, but none are more influential than his villas or large country homes. The *Villa Capra* (fig.9–48) (called the *Villa Rotunda* because of its dome and central plan) uses Classic forms such as a flat dome like that of the Pantheon, Ionic columns, pediments and arches. The large central cube has porches on four sides that enlarge the form to a more horizontal feeling of grace and stability. The building has the quiet elegance of Mannerism rather than the severe discipline of Renaissance architecture. In 1570, Palladio wrote and illustrated a book that contained his thoughts and ideas on architecture based on Classic ideals: a set of rules by which to build. It became the international guide for many builders up to the eighteenth century, including British and American architects, among them Thomas Jefferson (*see* p. 388). Some of the buildings seen in the next several chapters will illustrate the influence of Palladio on world architecture and the emergence of a style that bears his name—Palladian.

Lesson 9.3 Review

1 In what country did El Greco make most of his paintings?
2 Name two elements in Rosso Fiorentino's *The Descent from the Cross* that jarred most sixteenth-century viewers.
3 Which artist is credited with introducing common, everyday activities into formal portraiture?
4 Study Tintoretto's *Christ at the Sea of Galilee.* Who has Tintoretto put as the center of interest? What is happening in this picture?
5 Give an example of Veronese's art that demonstrates his love of opulent fabrics.

Primary Source

Michelangelo and the Sistine Ceiling

The Sistine ceiling took Michelangelo four years to complete. He built his own scaffolding and hired five painters from Florence to help, but their work did not meet his standards so he continued with a few assistants to mix plaster and grind colors. Day after day for four years, he stood with his face up, painting over his head. Michelangelo's friend and biographer, Condivi, says that for a time after he finished the ceiling, Michelangelo was unable to read except by holding paper over his head.

This sonnet written by Michelangelo, describes the strain and pain he suffered:

I've grown a goiter by dwelling in this den–
As cats from stagnant streams in Lombardy,
Or in what other land they hap to be–
Which drives the belly close beneath the chin;
My beard turns up to heaven; my nape falls in,
Fixed on my spine: my breast-bone visibly
Grows like a harp: a rich embroidery
Bedews my face from brush drops thick and thin.
My loins into my paunch like levers grind:
My buttock like a crupper bears my weight;
My feet unguided wander to and fro;
In front my skin grows loose and long; behind,
By bending it becomes more taut and strait;
Crosswise I strain me like a Syrian bow:
Whence false and quaint, I know,
Must be the fruit of squinting brain and eye;
For ill can aim the gun that bends awry.
Come then Giovanni, try
To succor my dead pictures and my fame,
Since foul I fare and painting is my shame.

Chapter Review

Review

1 What stance, developed by the Greeks, did Donatello use in his *David* to indicate motion?

2 List three ways Masaccio's *Tribute Money* was different from Gothic paintings.

3 Define the term *renaissance.*

4 How many times larger than you is Michelangelo's *David*?

Interpret

1 How is Brunelleschi's Church of San Lorenzo different from Gothic churches?

2 Compare Donatello's bronze *David* to Michelangelo's marble *David.*

3 Analyze the composition in Leonard da Vinci's *Last Supper.* What techniques did he use to show depth in this painting? What type of compositional balance did he use? What is the center of interest? How did he direct the viewer's gaze toward this focal point?

4 Describe Raphael's *School of Athens.* Explain why this painting is such a good example of Renaissance art. Analyze its composition. Who are the central figures in this painting?

5 Describe El Greco's *Burial of Count Orgaz.* What are some indications that this is a Mannerist painting?

Other Tools for Learning

Maps

Choose five cities from the map on p. 261. List one famous work of art or architecture that is located in each city.

Timelines

1 What were the French doing to Rome around the time that Michelangelo painted *Last Judgment*? How do you think this might have influenced the mood of this painting?

2 As Leonardo da Vinci painted *The Last Supper,* do you think he had heard about Columbus's discovery of America? Why or why not?

3 Which event was probably most significant to your ancestors? Explain why.

Electronic Research

CD-ROM drive: *Microsoft Art Gallery* (Composition and Perspective Guided Tour)

1 Select an individual object from Paolo Uccello's *The Battle of San Romano.* Describe how Uccello painted this object to give it depth or perspective.

2 Explain how Piero della Francesca directs the viewers eyes through the composition in his *Baptism of Christ.*

Activity 1

Leonardo's Sketchbook

Materials

drawing pencils or charcoal
12" x 18" white drawing paper or sketchbook
optional: colored pencil, pen and ink, conte crayon

Take a look.

- Fig.9–a, Leonardo da Vinci, *Five Heads.*
- Fig.9–22, Leonardo da Vinci, *Virgin of the Rocks.*
- Fig.9–23, Leonardo da Vinci, *The Last Supper.*
- Fig 9–24, Leonardo da Vinci, *Mona Lisa.*

Think about it. Leonardo da Vinci investigated many aspects of life in hundreds of pages in his sketchbook and journals. He would sketch his subject, then write notes in "mirror writing." This was "study" in the true sense of the word, a way of learning about life through close observation.

Do it. Find one or more subjects from life and draw them in a sketchbook or journal. Choose anything from human anatomy to objects found in nature or your everyday environment. Surround your sketches with notes and thoughts. An interesting option would be to work in a brown (burnt sienna) medium.

Check it. Do your sketches capture the essence of your subject? Try zooming in on details one at a time and drawing them separately. Ask a friend to identify the object by looking only at the details.

Helpful Hint: Find examples of Leonardo's sketches in your school or local library. Notice how he would sometimes draw an object from several angles to better understand its construction.

Activity 2

Stretching the Truth

Materials

for sculpture:
plasticine clay
newspaper or plastic
clay tools (optional)
newspaper

for painting:
white paper, 12" x 18" or larger
tempera paints
containers to mix paint
container of water
paint brushes

Take a look.

- Fig.9–37, El Greco, *The Burial of Count Orgaz*

Think about it. Research Michelangelo's late works. How did his elongated bodies and expressionistic approaches to subject matter influence visual expression?
El Greco took the distortion effect even further, exemplifying the style we call Mannerism.

Do it. Represent a stylized human figure in clay or in tempera painting based on the Mannerist style. Emphasize certain features of the individual or distort the figure through elongation.

- Select a subject to work with: family member, classmate, fairy tale figure, political figure, media celebrity or yourself. Consider the direction you have in mind and what emotion or mood you wish to express.
- If working in clay, plan your figure to be no larger than 18" or 24"—do preliminary sketches if you wish. Don't try to make things "look real."
- If painting, consider what elements you will include, such as people, a particular setting, animals, trees. Whatever you include, distort all the elements to work together in your composition. Identify what colors El Greco used to enhance his expression; plan what colors will work best to express your idea.

Check it. Does your painting reflect the Manneristic style? What primary emotion or mood is being expressed?

Helpful Hint: Be expressive! Think of people who move dramatically, such as dancers, symphony conductors or rock stars. Bring the spirit of movement and drama to your work.

Additional Activities

- Write an essay on "Why I Want to Be an Apprentice to..." (insert a Renaissance artist's name).
- Renaissance artists used the human body to show perfection by stressing muscular development, sensuality, proportion and pose. Take photographs (or do drawings) of students in gym classes or other sports activities to be labeled and used as illustrations for such concepts as loneliness, strength, thought, action, determination, dismay, exhaustion and exhilaration. Think of faces, legs, torso, hands, arms and backs as expressions of the feelings and tensions of the mind as well as the body.

Zuzana Zborilová

Age 18
J.F. Dulles High School
Stafford, Texas
Activity 1, Leonardo's Sketchbook

This is a picture which I like most from all of my work. I really like working with black pencil and doing all of the details and shadows of my shoes. Before I started with the drawing I found a contour drawing from the beginning of the year and I wanted to develop it. I drew the shoe below at first and situated it in an easier position, but I love the shoe on the left side which looks like it's kicked into the air.

What do I enjoy about the artistic process? I never know at the beginning how the picture will look like finished. I every time find new ideas during creating. I like doing art during listening to some mystical music and thinking about my dreams. I can relax and forget about the busy world around me.

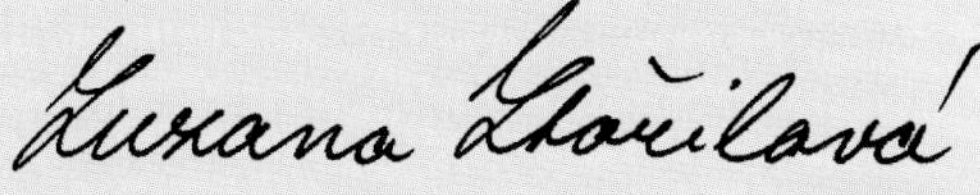

Zuzana Zborilová, *Shoes*, 1994. Pencil, 18" x 24" (46 x 61 cm).

Rich Koehler

Age: 18
J.F. Dulles High School
Stafford, Texas
Activity 2, Stretching the Truth

I enjoy doing contour lines and expanding the body parts. In this picture, I tried to expand many of the features of his body, such as his feet, and shrink his face. When I was working, I was concentrating on the lines in his clothes. I tried to put every crinkle in his clothes. When I was coloring him, I was attempting to make his clothes look real and actually folding around his body parts.

The one thing I have heard is that you cannot mess up in art. For me that statement is hard to believe, but it is true. No matter how bad I mess up it can be fixed somehow. I have also learned that not every drawing has to be life-like. Many of the famous artists did not do life-like pictures and painting.

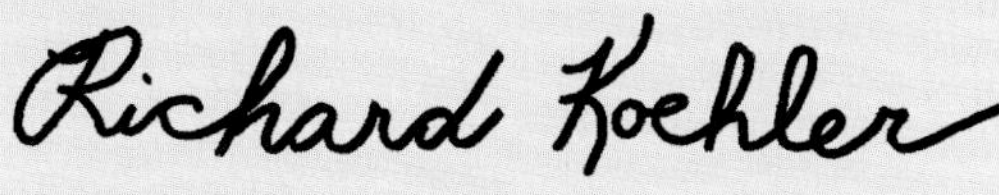

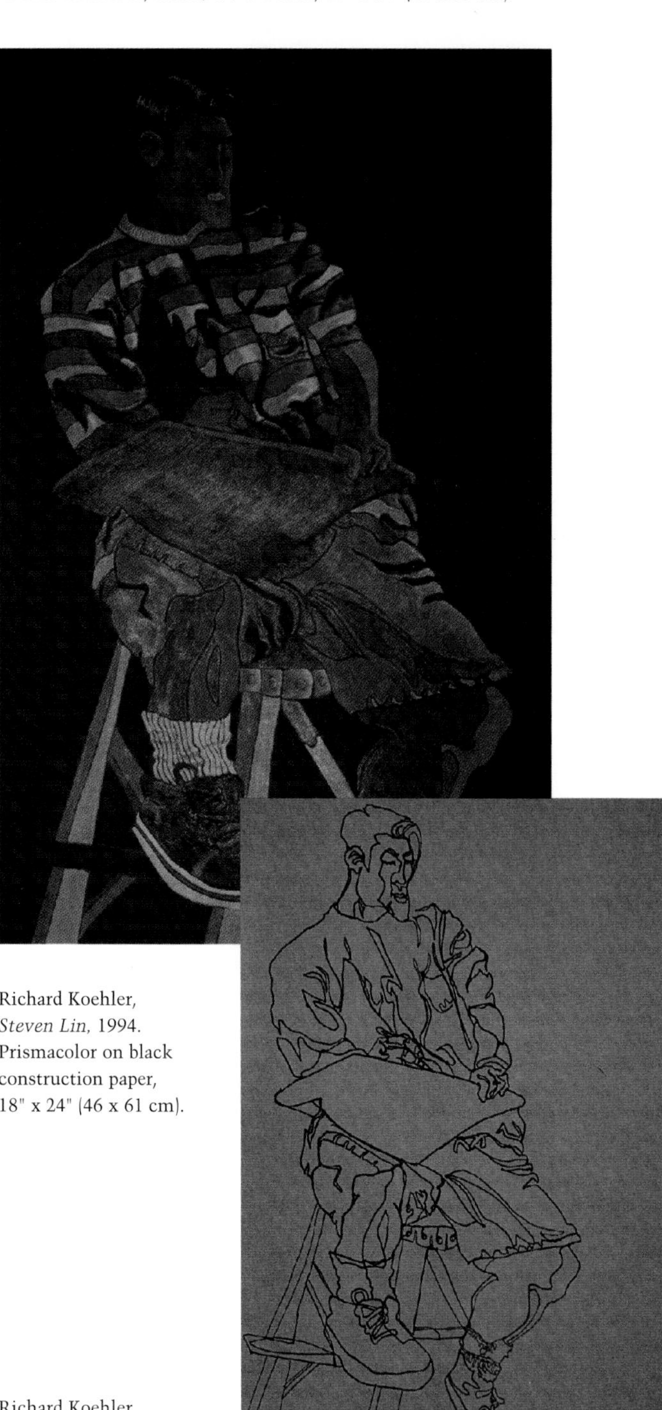

Richard Koehler, *Steven Lin*, 1994. Prismacolor on black construction paper, 18" x 24" (46 x 61 cm).

Richard Koehler, *Steven Lin*, 1994 sketch

10 Renaissance in the North

In This Chapter...

THE RENAISSANCE THAT HAD SO INSPIRED Italian painters occurred not only in Italy, but in all of Europe. In Northern Europe, however, the style of the Renaissance painters was rather different from their Italian counterparts.

Northern artists, especially those from Belgium and Holland (the Low Countries), used ordinary everyday objects to render their highly symbolic religious subject matter. There was great attention to detail. But the innovation that had the greatest impact during this period was oil paint. The new medium tremendously expanded the use of color and light and Northern Renaissance artists used it to its full advantage.

In the sixteenth century, Germany became the art center of Northern Europe. German artists were strongly individualistic, much like their contemporaries in Italy.

In England and France, painters preferred to continue with the International style that had its roots in the Gothic era. Renaissance architecture did flourish in France with the construction of many châteaux.

The great wealth of Spain drew many artists to its court. Philip II built monuments and commissioned works in a manner similar to the Medici and the popes in Italy.

10–a Northern Renaissance artists became masters of the oil painting technique. This new medium produced incredible color and permitted artists to paint with unsurpassed attention to detail.
Hans Holbein, *Sir Thomas More*, detail (fig.10–21).

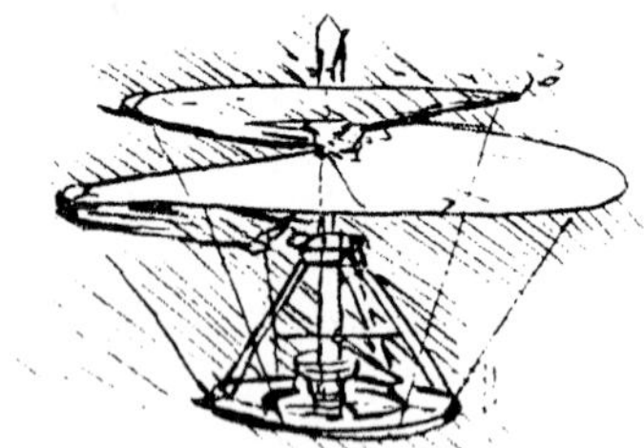

1425–1426
Master of Flémalle (Robert Campin), *Mérode Altarpiece*

1480
Leonardo invents the parachute and helicopter

1497
The Cabots reach the east coast of North America

1527
Holbein, *Sir Thomas More*

1551
Breugel becomes a master in the Antwerp painters' guild

1564
Galileo Galilei born

1594
Shakespeare, *Romeo and Juliet*

Renaissance in the North

1436
van der Weyden becomes official painter to Brussels

1480
Arrival of oil painting technique in Italy

1519
Château of Chambord begun

1543
Copernicus' planetary theory

1588
Spanish Armada defeated by the English

What beauty is I know not, though it adheres to many things...As what all the world prizes as right we hold to be right, so what all the world esteems to be beautiful that will we also hold for beautiful and strive to produce.

Albrecht Dürer

10–b Realism is an important element of Northern Renaissance art. This is a small detail from a painting that documents a wedding. The ceremony between Giovanni Arnolfini and Jeanne Cenami is witnessed by the artist and another individual. The witnesses are reflected in this mirror.
Jan van Eyck, detail of *Arnolfini Wedding,* (fig.10–6).

The Renaissance soon found its way north where it impacted the artwork and architecture of Flanders, Holland, Germany, England and France. It also moved westward to Spain (see map on page 331).

10–c The facade of this Renaissance addition to the Louvre includes a profusion of sculptured figures on the top story. The facade is considered by some to be the best example of French Renaissance architecture.
Pierre Lescot, *Square Court of the Louvre,* detail (fig.10–28).

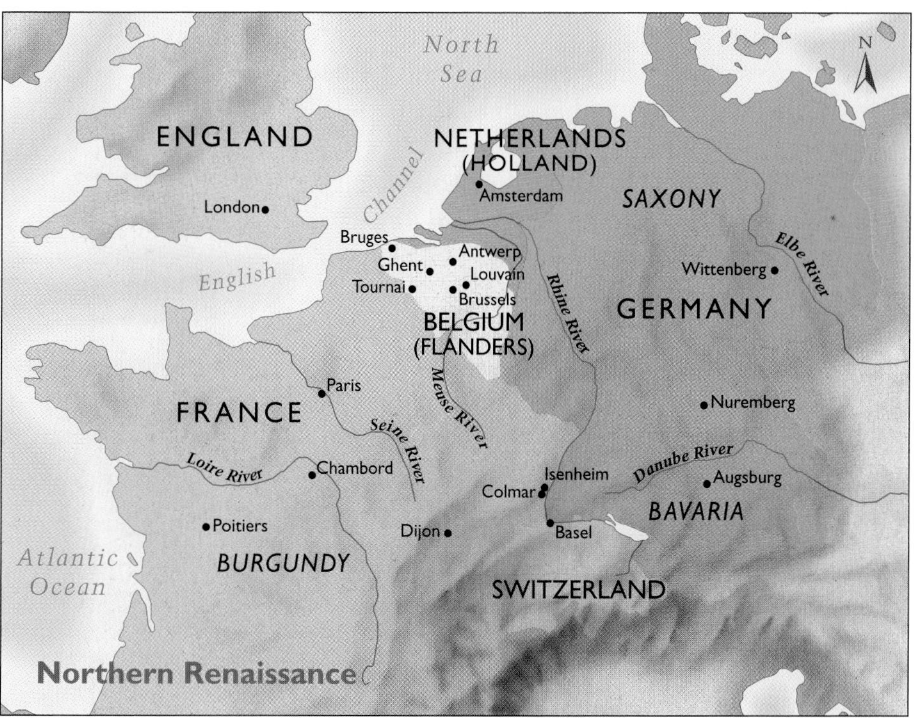

10.1 The Low Countries

THE GOTHIC STYLE OF ARCHITECTURE dominated northern Europe into the early sixteenth century. In painting, however, the Northern Renaissance painters moved in a different direction from Italian Renaissance styles. As we have seen, many Italian painters had returned to the aesthetics and ideals of Classical antiquity. Northern Renaissance artists began to direct their attention to creating works with a powerful sense of realism.

The painters of the Low Countries (Belgium and Holland) were the first to master the new medium of oil paint. With the new medium, painters were able to create richer colors than before. As a result, painting of the Low Countries in the fifteenth century is characterized by glowing colors that appear to be lit from within. This new medium revolutionized painting and allowed artists to work with an unlimited range of values and colors. Colors could be blended to produce the delicately shaded folds in cloth and the carefully observed changes in light intensity.

Painters aimed at clear, hard-edged detail in their representation of objects. Their realism was one of radiant decorative color rather than sculptural form.

All Renaissance artists tried to reconcile religious subjects with scenes and objects from everyday life. Artists in Northern Europe, particularly the Low Countries, accomplished this by using symbolism.

As had happened in Italy, the Northern painters also found a new prestige and place in society. Some women are also recorded as belonging to the art guilds of Flemish cities. To pursue a craft, individuals had to belong to the guild that controlled that craft.

Key Notes

- Northern Renaissance art is powerfully realistic.
- Oil paint, the new medium, produces marvelous color.
- Ordinary objects are used to symbolize religious subjects.

Vocabulary
realism
symbolism

Special Feature

The Master of Flémalle

Robert Campin (about 1378–1444)

Attention to detail, extreme ***realism*** and the use of commonplace settings is perfectly illustrated by the work of the Master of Flémalle. Most art historians believe that the Master of Flémalle was Robert Campin, the leading painter of the city of Tournai in Flanders (Belgium). Unfortunately, early Renaissance paintings in the Low Countries were not signed by the artist. Without signatures, names have been lost. Although there might be some doubt as to the name of the artist, there is no doubt that the *Mérode Altarpiece* (fig.10–1) is an early Renaissance masterpiece.

10–1 Notice how the top of the table is tipped up so that the viewer can clearly see everything that is on it.
The Master of Flémalle (Robert Campin), *Mérode Altarpiece*, about 1425–1426. Oil on panel, center: 25" x 25" (64 x 64 cm). The Metropolitan Museum of Art, New York, The Cloisters Collection.

10–2 Oil painting revolutionized art. It allowed artists to work with a range of values and colors and to use detail in a way not possible with tempera or fresco.
The Master of Flémalle (Robert Campin), *Mérode Altarpiece*, detail of central panel.

So named because it was in the Mérode family for many years, the *Mérode Altarpiece* is a triptych. From left to right, the three panels contain the kneeling donors of the altarpiece, an Annunciation scene with the Virgin Mary and the angel Gabriel, and Joseph in his carpenter's shop in the last panel. The *Mérode Altarpiece* belongs within the tradition of the International style yet it contains a new pictorial experience. One of the new elements is the setting of a typical contemporary Flemish dwelling. This is, in fact, the earliest Annunciation panel painting that takes place in a completely domestic interior.

The donors, a soberly dressed man and wife belonging to the middle-class, kneel in a little courtyard. The man peers through the door at the Annunciation taking place in the central panel. The donors set the tone of the painting. Discreetly set apart from the sacred scene, they take it in as a fact, as reality. They draw the viewer into looking, too. We see a very proper middle-class Mary surrounded by all the domestic details of a typical Flemish household (fig.10–2). The items are also symbols. The spotless room and the vase of lilies on the table symbolize the Virgin's purity. In the right panel, Joseph has made a mousetrap (fig.10–3). It symbolizes Christ's appearance in the world in human form as a means of fooling (baiting) and catching the Devil. So close are the sacred personages to real people that they are represented without halos.

The tonality of the painting is also different from earlier panel paintings. The color scheme is far less decorative. The artist uses subdued hues. All these effects, part of the realistic style of the Master of Flémalle, were made possible by the use of oil paint. The Master of Flémalle was among the first painters to exploit this new medium.

10–3 What is Joseph building? Why did the artist show him with that project?
The Master of Flémalle (Robert Campin), *Mérode Altarpiece*, detail of St. Joseph.

10–5 Contrast this Annunciation to the one done by Fra Angelico (fig.9–12). Which do you prefer?
Jan van Eyck, *The Annunciation,* 1434–1436. Oil on wood, transferred to canvas. 35 3/8" x 13 7/8" (90 x 35 cm). National Gallery of Art, Washington DC, Andrew W. Mellon Collection.

10–4 Compare the nude figures here to sculptures from ancient Greece.
Hubert and Jan van Eyck, *Ghent Altarpiece* (open), completed 1432. Oil on panel, 11 1/2' x 15' (3.5 x 4.6 m). Cathedral of St. Bavo, Ghent, Belgium.

Jan van Eyck

(about 1390–1441)

No painter could equal the color and light of Jan van Eyck. Like other northern European Renaissance painters, he had a fascination with detail. Yet, areas of his paintings are subordinated in order to direct attention to the most important parts. His understanding of light was far greater than that of his Italian contemporaries. Van Eyck excelled at portraying direct and diffused light, shadows falling on a variety of surfaces, and light's effect on the illusion of distance.

Philip the Good, Duke of Burgundy, considered van Eyck the world's greatest artist. Van Eyck traveled for the Duke and even went to Italy where he met Masaccio and other Florentine artists. He finally settled in Bruges in Flanders in 1430 and began to sign and date his works for the first time.

The greatest early Flemish masterpiece was *The Ghent Altarpiece* (fig.10–4). It was begun by Hubert van Eyck in 1425 and finished by his brother Jan seven years later. Art historians have spent much time trying to determine which parts were done by each, but the work largely reveals Jan's genius. The entire altarpiece is about 16 1/2 feet wide when the triptych is opened. The two wings are painted on both sides so that even when closed the altarpiece is decorative.

When the altarpiece is opened, the entire bottom section across five panels tells the story *The Adoration of the Lamb* from the Book of Revelations. Marvelous landscapes, animals, trees, people, fabrics, light and air are handled with meticulous detail, as if each part were to be studied separately. Using the new oil medium, van Eyck presents in glowing color a scene in Paradise (with Flemish buildings). The dove of the Holy Spirit sheds light on the enthroned Mystic Lamb (a symbol of Christ). The Fountain of Life pours its water into an octagonal basin and, from there, into a river in which jewels are seen. Prophets, patriarchs and kings of the Old Testament are grouped on the left, while apostles and saints are on the right.

Adam and Eve and singing angels appear in the top side panels of the altarpiece. The figures of Adam and Eve are the first almost-life-size nudes done in northern Europe. In the incredibly detailed central panel is God the Father flanked by Mary and John the Baptist.

In van Eyck's painting *The Annunciation* (fig.10–5), the angel Gabriel announces the birth of Christ to Mary. The event takes place in a fifteenth-century Gothic church. The setting could almost be the set of a play that the viewer is watching. Words coming from Gabriel's mouth ("Ave Maria...") are answered by Mary's words, which are upside down—to be read by God. Robes, building, windows, faces and the floor are painstakingly detailed. Jewels in Gabriel's crown and robe reflect the light with amazing accuracy. The panel is filled with ***symbolism***. The lilies symbolize Mary's purity and her gesture is one of submission to the will of God. Lilies on the angel's robe again symbolize Mary while pomegranates signify Christ's resurrection. From the top of the painting, the dove of the Holy Spirit descends to Mary on rays of light. Floor panels illustrate Old Testament events: David killing Goliath, Samson destroying the temple, and so on.

One of van Eyck's best-known paintings is the *Arnolfini Wedding* (fig.10–6), a work of marvelous reality and unity. Meticulous detail and incredibly realistic light share importance in the painting. Light enters at the left and softly illuminates the metal chandelier, hard walls, soft fabrics and flesh. All the detailed objects in the room have symbolic significance. The raised right hand and the little dog are symbols of fidelity. The clogs, cast aside, indicate that the couple stands on holy ground. The peaches ripening on the chest are a sign of fertility.

Jan van Eyck witnessed the ceremony, and so signed his name on the wall above the mirror with words meaning "Jan van Eyck was here in 1434." A miniature composition can be seen in the convex enlarging mirror (fig.10–b). The mirror shows not only the backs of the couple but also the front view of Jan and another person.

10–6 This painting has been described as a visual marriage license. Can you explain that description?
Jan van Eyck, *Arnolfini Wedding,* 1434. Oil on panel, 32" x 23" (82 x 59 cm). National Gallery, London.

10–8 Compare this portrait to the *Mona Lisa* (fig.9–24). Rogier van der Weyden, *Portrait of a Lady,* about 1455. Oil on panel, 14 1/2" x 10 1/2" (37 x 27 cm). National Gallery of Art, Washington DC, Andrew Mellon Collection.

Rogier van der Weyden

(1399–1464)

The third great artist of early Flemish painting was Rogier van der Weyden. Rogier van der Weyden became the official painter for the city of Brussels in 1435 and had a strong influence on countless artists that followed. He worked on larger surfaces than van Eyck and infused his detailed religious works with drama and emotion.

The large *Descent from the Cross* (probably part of a triptych) was painted for a church in Louvain in 1435 (fig.10–7). The setting (what one can see of it) is symbolic, taking place inside the sepulcher and not on a hill outside Jerusalem. Rather than use the natural light of van Eyck, Rogier lights each part carefully so that every wrinkle, tear and detail can be seen. This lighting is much like the evenly lighted treatment in the Master of Flémalle's work. The crisp folds so noticeable in the Master of Flémalle's paintings are again evident in Rogier's work. The twisted and bending bodies emphasize the strong emotional feeling expressed in each face. Notice how the limp S-curve of Christ's body is repeated in Mary's body in the foreground. Her hand almost touches the skull of Adam, which, according to legend, was discovered when the hole was dug for the cross. The entire complex composition is balanced beautifully. The figures are grouped carefully, and the almost horizontal body of Christ ties the parts together.

Jan van Eyck had been one of the first northern European artists to paint portraits. But, equally impressive are those by Rogier van der Weyden. His *Portrait of a Lady* (fig.10–8) is an excellent example. Exquisite line and delicate shading form the face. The face is set off by the beautiful white coif placed against a dark background. The folded hands are a familiar gesture in such paintings. The only bit of bright color is in the red belt, which seems much too small for the figure. The stark, simple and cool design is emphasized by the woman's aloof expression.

10–7 The twisting, turning bodies emphasize the powerful emotions of the scene.
Rogier van der Weyden, *Descent from the Cross,* about 1435. Oil on panel, 7' 2 5/8" x 8' 7 1/8" (217 x 260 cm). The Prado Museum, Madrid.

Sidelight

Tapestry

In the Middle Ages, tapestry and embroidery were widely appreciated as an art form, and women were instrumental in their making. Tapestry, which is extremely time-consuming, was a serious occupation for women. During the Middle Ages, many women used their embroidery skills to fashion some of the most significant works of their epoch. Richly colored tapestries featured scenes from history or favorite romances of the times.

Tapestries continued to be made in the Renaissance. Flemish tapestry reached a height of excellence between 1480 and 1520 that has never been equaled in Europe. Women were primarily responsible for the weaving of these masterpieces.

Tapestries had advantages over wall paintings in that they were portable and could be taken down to be rehung elsewhere. They added warmth to cold castle walls and helped reduce echoes in stone-walled halls. The materials, dyed wools and silks, and even gold and silver threads, added luxurious textures and colors to building interiors.

The process of Flemish tapestry making was long and costly. After producing a sketch, the artist would create a full-size painting on paper (cartoon). The highly skilled weavers would work from the cartoon. The entire tapestry was woven on a huge loom, thread by thread. These tapestries were found in every castle and palace in Europe.

Hans Memling

(about 1440–1494)

Born in Germany, Hans Memling (also written as Memlinc) became a citizen of Bruges and probably studied under Rogier van der Weyden for a time. Memling's work was quiet and serene, and was sometimes confused with that of Jan van Eyck.

His *Madonna and Child with Angels* (fig.10–9) is similar in theme to many works of this time. His technique is superior. The composition is symmetrically balanced. On each side of Mary and the Christ Child are two angels with musical instruments. One angel plays with the child, offering an orange. The child reaches with one hand for the orange while ruffling the pages of the book with the other, both very natural movements for a child. Notice the textural detail of the various fabrics. Some are rich brocades, others are plain and smooth. Gothic sculptures flank a rounded arch. In the distance is a medieval landscape with a castle and distant church. Every corner of the painting is carefully done. The light on each material (stone, wood, cloth, carpet, skin) is painted with knowledge and great skill.

10–9 Memling's work was sometimes confused with the work of Jan van Eyck. What similarities do you see?
Hans Memling, *Madonna and Child with Angels*, about 1480. Oil on panel, 22 5/8" x 19" (57.5 x 48 cm). National Gallery of Art, Washington DC, Andrew Mellon Collection.

World Cultural Timeline

400–1600
Kongo Kingdom

1400
Chan Chan, the largest known adobe city, built in Peru

1405
Cheng Ho begins exploration to Southeast Asia, India and Africa

1421
Chinese emperors occupy Forbidden City, Peking, China

Hieronymus Bosch

(about 1450–1516)

A Dutch painter with an incredible imagination, Hieronymus Bosch presents a world full of weird images and puzzling symbols. His work is usually packed with tiny people, mostly naked, who are engaged in dozens of activities. It is almost as if ten or more paintings were crammed into a single frame.

Probably the most complex of his busy works is the strangely wonderful *Garden of Delights* (fig.10–10), a huge triptych. The symbolism, complexity and incredible detail of the three-part story take a long time to read. The left panel is *The Garden of Eden*. Here, amid exotic animals, plants and landscape, God is introducing Adam to Eve. The

10–10 Many twentieth century artists have been influenced by Bosch's work. Hieronymus Bosch, *Garden of Delights,* about 1505–1510. Triptych, oil on panel, center panel 86 1/4" x 76 3/4" (219 x 195 cm), each wing 86 1/2" x 38" (219 x 97 cm). The Prado Museum, Madrid.

10–11 This painting could be explored inch by inch. It is crammed with fantastic figures, forms and landscapes. Hieronymus Bosch, *Garden of Delights,* detail of central panel.

right panel, *The Garden of Satan,* is a nightmare of indescribable tortures. It portrays Bosch's idea of Hell. Hundreds of figures are being tortured. The eggshell-human-tree trunk figure of Satan in the center supervises the scene. Across the River Styx, a city burns with fire and dense smoke. The huge central panel, the *Garden of Delights,* is also a huge question mark. What does it all mean? The fantastic landscape is filled with hundreds of light-pink, naked figures. They are innocently parading, riding on various beasts, sitting on giant birds, swimming, bathing, and crawling in and out of gigantic eggs and other equally amazing forms (fig.10–11).

If one reads the entire story together, Bosch is revealed as a moralist. The left panel shows God's beautiful creation. The middle panel depicts humanity's constant search to satisfy its earthly desires with overindulgence and sin. This eventually leads to Hell, shown on the right. Although it is called a *Garden of Delights,* Bosch's work is a pessimistic look at humanity. No chance of salvation is shown.

Pieter Bruegel

(about 1525–1569)

Religious wars wracked the Low Countries during the early sixteenth century. Amid this unsettling environment, Low Country painting began to discard the detail and reality of van Eyck and Rogier and to absorb the influence of Italian art.

Pieter Bruegel was the most highly acclaimed Low Country master of the sixteenth century. Born near Bosch's hometown in what is now Holland, his early work was greatly influenced by Bosch. A four-year trip to Italy changed his outlook on painting. His later work contains larger figures that often have the monumentality of Giotto or Masaccio.

Bruegel filled his painting of the *Tower of Babel* (fig.10–12) with hundreds of tiny figures that contrast with the mammoth structure set into a far-reaching landscape. According to the Old Testament, the people of Mesopotamia attempted to build a tower that reached to heaven. However, the pride of the people became so great that God could not tolerate it and confused their languages. The people could not communicate and work had to stop.

Bruegel had no knowledge of the squarish ziggurats of the Sumerians. Instead he invented a huge round structure somewhat like the Roman Colosseum. Boats and barges unload materials, which are carried up ladders and ramps to the work sites. As the mountainous structure rises into the clouds, more stone is being cut in the foreground. Bruegel emphasizes the work process, the huge scale of the tower, and the inevitable failure of the impossible task.

Very few artists have captured the silent, cold crispness of winter the way Pieter Bruegel has in *The Return of the Hunters* (fig.10–13). The painting is one of a series depicting the seasons of the year. He loved to paint peasants in their daily activities as well as at their special festivals. The world here is covered with snow. The weary hunters trudge homeward, their dogs following dejectedly behind. The hunt has been hard work, not a jolly sport, but is part of the seasonal struggle of the peasants. Below the village on the hillside, skaters frolic on the frozen ponds. Alpine peaks, which Bruegel observed on his Italian trip, are shown in the

10–12 What construction activities can you identify in this painting?
Pieter Bruegel, *The Tower of Babel,* 1563.
Oil on oakwood, 44 1/2" x 61" (113 x 155 cm).
Kunsthistoriches Museum, Vienna.

distance. The depth is felt more strongly because of the birds flying in the intervening space. The leafless trees march down the hill and help unite the foreground with the middle distance. Simple human activities and ordinary landscapes receive extreme importance and dignity in Bruegel's treatment. Humans and nature are bound together as a working unit.

10–13 Paintings of common, everyday activities were unusual in Bruegel's time. Did the hunters have a successful day?
Pieter Bruegel, *The Return of the Hunters*, 1565. Oil and tempera on panel, 46 1/2" x 63 3/4" (117 x161 cm). Kunsthistorisches Museum, Vienna.

Lesson 10.1 Review

1 What were two advantages of oil paint over tempera paint?
2 List several features of Robert Campin's *Mérode Altarpiece* that are often found in Northern European Renaissance paintings.
3 Explain the symbolism of two objects in the *Mérode Altarpiece*.
4 Which art element did Jan van Eyck understand and paint better than most of his contemporary artists?
5 Explain the symbolism of three objects in one of Jan van Eyck's paintings.
6 Describe the composition of Rogier van der Weyden's *Descent from the Cross.* How has he created unity and directed the viewer's gaze through his painting?
7 How has Bruegel created depth in *The Return of the Hunters*?

10.2 Germany

EARLY FIFTEENTH-CENTURY GERMAN ART was part of the International style. The German tradition lay in medieval expressionism and the use of line. The Italian use of nude figures and monumental forms, based on Classical Greek and Roman art, was very strange to these northern European artists. So, instead of looking to Italy for inspiration, they looked to Flanders. Van Eyck and van der Weyden were strong influences. But, the German artists did not attain the heights, in style or technique, of Flemish artists.

However, this was to change in the early sixteenth century as German art moved to the forefront of northern Europe. Now, we start to find some artists who shared the free, individualistic spirit of Italian Renaissance artists. In southern Germany, there were painters of great originality, imagination and strong individual character. Among them were artists like Albrecht Dürer from Nuremberg, Matthias Grünewald, who worked in Mainz and other centers, and Hans Holbein the Younger, who worked in Switzerland and England.

Key Notes

- In the early 1500s, Germany becomes the leader in art in northern Europe.
- German artists absorb the influence of the Italian High Renaissance and blend it with northern technique and style.

Vocabulary
polyptych

10–14 Using this painting as a guide, how would you describe Dürer's personality?
Albrecht Dürer, *Self-Portrait,* 1498. Oil on panel, 20" x 16 1/5" (51 x 41 cm). The Prado Museum, Madrid.

Special Feature

Albrecht Dürer

(1471–1528)

Albrecht Dürer was the leader of the German High Renaissance. Unlike many of his colleagues, Dürer had a strong sense of being an artist, not a craftsperson. Dürer admired the princely lifestyle enjoyed by Titian and other Italian artists. He attempted to raise the status of art in Germany and the rest of northern Europe to an equally high level. This awareness led him to date his works and sign them—a fairly unusual practice at the time. Fascinated with Classical ideas used by Italian Renaissance artists, he was the first Northern artist to travel to Italy expressly to study Italian art. He agreed strongly with Leonardo that sight is our most important faculty. He believed that through looking, truth is revealed. Dürer was also the first artist outside of Italy to become internationally acclaimed.

He was also the first Northern artist to very consciously document himself in a series of self-portraits. One of his best self-portraits was painted in 1498 (fig.10–14). Dürer is elegantly dressed. His face bears a serious, searching expression that reflects the seriousness with which he regarded his mission as an artistic reformer. The influence of Italian portraiture appears in the pose and the landscape through the window. Although the pose is Italian, the line is still German and distinctively Dürer's. Hair is not treated as a mass but as individual lines—hundreds of them. Line is also evident in the clothes, the crisp folds and edges, and the faint outlines of hands and face.

Albrecht Dürer loved animals and used them in many of his prints and paintings. In his *Young Hare* (fig.10–15), a watercolor sketch, he applied line with tender care to produce a feeling of soft fur. Dürer was a master of watercolor, a medium that, at the time, was used mostly for preliminary studies that were often discarded.

Dürer's masterpiece is the powerful oil painting of *The Four Apostles* (fig.10–16), a diptych meant as the side wings of a large triptych. The apostles John and Peter on the left with Mark and Paul on the right. The solidness and weight of these figures are more Italian influenced than any of Dürer's other works. Each part could easily stand alone. But, the two parts together produce a balanced composition of powerful expression and sculpturesque forms. The figures are crowded into the space, creating tension and a feeling of explosive energy, as if they are ready to burst from the frame and proclaim their message.

10–16 Compare the apostles above to the figures in Masaccio's *Tribute Money* (fig.9–10). Albrecht Dürer, *Four Apostles,* about 1526. Oil on panel, each part 84 3/4" x 30" (215 x 76 cm). Alte Pinakothek, Munich.

10–15 Do you think this young rabbit might have been a pet of Dürer's? Albrecht Dürer, *Young Hare,* 1502. Watercolor with opaque white, 9 7/8" x 9" (25 x 23 cm). The Albertina Museum, Vienna.

Window in Time

Dürer and Printmaking

The first artist to emerge from medieval anonymity with a distinct personality, was Albrecht Dürer (1471–1528). Dürer was the third of eighteen children and, after he had completed elementary school, he was taken on as apprentice to his goldsmith father. Dürer's thorough grounding in the goldsmith's art explains the accuracy he later displayed as an artist.

By the time he had finished his apprenticeship, Dürer had decided he was more interested in being an artist than a goldsmith. His father was not too happy about this at first, but he eventually agreed to let Dürer do another apprenticeship, this time under an artist.

Dürer proved to be extraordinarily talented in both woodcut and copper engraving. He was one of the first artists in the Western world to turn to woodcut as a major medium and, from the start, it was obvious that his technique was very original. His style was extremely precise and demanded incredible skill in cutting into the wood. In 1498, he finished a series of fifteen woodcuts illustrating events from the *Apocalypse,* the Book of Revelation (last book in the Bible) which reveals the visions of St. John. They are extremely detailed and, where other printmakers worked with single lines, Dürer massed fine lines together to produce gray-valued areas that give his prints depth and shading. The cut lines are unbelievably fine for the woodcut medium and give the appearance of being pen and ink drawings.

These cut blocks could be inked and printed in presses (Gutenberg had already invented movable type in 1446) and sold for much more modest prices than Dürer's paintings. The market for these works was huge and Dürer became a wealthy artist and honored citizen in his home town of Nuremberg. As well as writing what today we would call memoirs, he wrote a family chronicle based on the diaries of his parents. He also signed his work with an A-D monogram. Dürer was very ambitious and aimed from early on in his career for fame.

Prints like his *Four Horsemen of the Apocalypse* (one of the finest woodcuts ever made) were used as wall decorations and above altars in middle-class homes or were pasted inside trunks and travel cases as worship aids for travelers. The four horsemen seen by St. John (war, pestilence, famine and death) ride recklessly over helpless humanity. It is absolutely amazing how much detail Dürer manages to include in so small a woodcut (9 3/4" x 7 3/8"). He uses his lines to give form to the figures and horses as well as to outline, shade and indicate hair.

Another printmaking medium at which Dürer excelled was copper engraving. *Knight, Death and the Devil* is a master print made by Dürer in 1513. The subject is a knight, which symbolizes the Christian warrior, sitting astride a magnificently drawn horse. In this engraving, Dürer's comprehensive knowledge of animals and their forms is clearly demonstrated. The brave knight fears no evil and rides gallantly ahead without paying attention to Death (who holds an hourglass) or the Devil (a monster of hideous form). Dürer used incised line to outline as well as crosshatch, creating a fantastic variety of darks which appear to be solid grays rather than linear pattern. He achieved a chiaroscuro with line comparable to what the Italians did with paint.

As Dürer grew older he devoted more and more of his time to writing and teaching. He thought hard about the development and welfare of the arts and interested himself, more than any other artist of his time, in the grounding of young artists. This can be seen by the way in which he describes a little work he intended to publish as "something for budding artists to get their teeth into."

Albrecht Dürer, *Knight, Death and the Devil,* 1513. Engraving, 9 3/4" x 7 3/8" (24.8 x 18.7 cm). Graphic Arts Council Fund, 1970, Los Angeles County Museum of Art.

10–17 This painting is a documentary work. It illustrates a contemporary event, and might be compared with today's photographs of hunting parties and their catches.
Lucas Cranach, *Hunting Party in Honor of Charles V at the Castle of Torgau,* 1545. Oil on panel, 43 3/5" x 68 7/8" (111 x 175 cm). The Prado Museum, Madrid.

Lucas Cranach

(1472–1553)

Lucas Cranach (the Elder) was a Protestant painter and architect. A friend of Martin Luther, he painted several portraits of the leader of the Reformation. Cranach became official painter for the Elector of Saxony at Wittenberg, where he and his two sons, Hans and Lucas (the Younger), were responsible for dozens of paintings. Cranach painted many nudes of Adam, Eve and various gods from ancient mythology. However, he painted them as German folk posed in rugged outdoor settings rather than as Classic figures of Greek and Roman times.

His work includes a number of hunting scenes such as *Hunting Party in Honor of Charles V at the Castle of Torgau* (figs.10–17, 10–18). The painting documents a hunting event of the time. The composition is extremely complex. Assistants and dogs are driving the stags into the open and to the pond in the foreground. In the lower left, the Duke of Saxony, Emperor Charles V and a knight are waiting for the kill with their crossbows and spears. Bears are being hunted in the upper left and upper right, and above all towers the Castle of Torgau. Cranach has combined architecture, landscape, animals and people in a writhing composition. The viewer's eyes are constantly moving from one area to another, seeking a place to pause.

10–18 Notice that women took an active role in the hunt.
Lucas Cranach, *Hunting Party in Honor of Charles V at the Castle of Torgau,* detail.

10–19 Grünewald reached back to Byzantine and Gothic ideas to help him portray this scene with great spiritual power.

Matthias Grünewald, *Isenheim Altarpiece,* (closed), about 1512–1515. Oil on panel, center panel, 8' 10" x 11' 2 1/2" (2.69 x 3.4 m). Unterlinden Museum, Colmar, France.

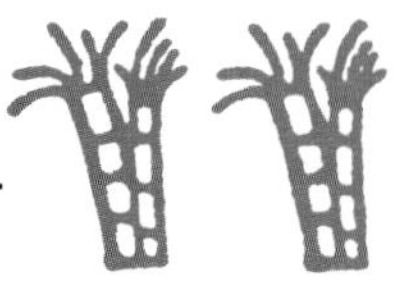

World Cultural Timeline

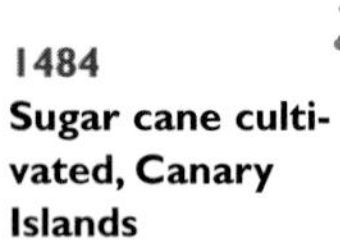

1484
Sugar cane cultivated, Canary Islands

1490
Toothbrush invented, China

1510
Major hospitals appear in Indian cities and offer free treatment

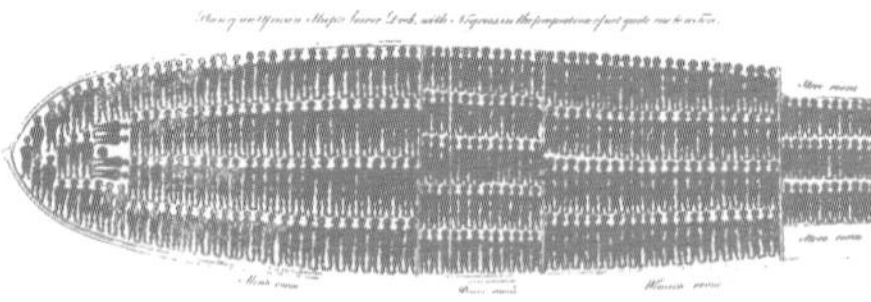

1518
Traders begin sending shiploads of African slaves to the West Indies

Matthias Grünewald

(about 1480–1528)

Although he was an excellent artist, Dürer's greatest contemporary was not a well-known figure. In fact, the real name of Matthias Grünewald (Mathis Niethardt Gothardt) was not known until this century. Grünewald was the last and most powerful of the expressive Gothic artists. He painted only a limited number of works but his single greatest masterpiece is the *Isenheim Altarpiece* (figs.10–19, 10–20). This altarpiece was done for the Hospital of St. Anthony in Isenheim, a small town now part of France. The painting is a complex ***polyptych***, made of many opening panels and wings. The polyptych was hung in two sets of paintings in front of a carved shrine to St. Anthony. When closed, the *Crucifixion* is seen, as in the illustration. As these panels are opened there are scenes of the *Annunciation*, the *Nativity*, the *Resurrection* and various saints. The saints are painted in bright orange, red, gold and blue. Finally, the carved and gilded shrine to St. Anthony appears.

The *Crucifixion* is the most dramatically powerful work ever done on the subject of Christ's suffering and death. The cross, placed slightly off-center to add to the tension, is seen as the cruelest means of death. The scarred body of the beaten Christ hangs as a broken figure, dangling from cross arms that are bent under the weight of the body and the world's sin. The pull of gravity is so strong that the fingers and hands are almost pulled apart. The bent head, bloody with the crown of thorns, seems ready to take its last breath. The drama is intensified by the black sky that adds to the feeling of death, gloom and sorrow.

On the left, St. John is consoling Mary, according to one of Christ's last wishes. Mary Magdalene shows her grief with raised clasped hands. John the Baptist is pointing to Christ as the Savior of the world. The symbolic lamb with a cross is bleeding into the chalice. The lamb was often used as a symbol of Christ and his suffering and death. The two figures standing in the side panels are St. Sebastian on the left and St. Anthony on the right. Below the central panel, under a ledge, is a horizontal composition of the *Pietà*. Christ's body has been taken down from the cross and will soon be placed in the open sarcophagus.

The entire cycle of the altarpiece is a marvel of organization. It reaches its climax in the resurrection scene in the second set of panels. Christ bursts from the tomb with the energy of an explosion. While his crucifixion is awesome, Grünewald's resurrection is the most astonishing ever painted.

10–20 Consider how the artist has used color to give this work its dynamism and supernatural qualities.
Matthias Grünewald, *Isenheim Altarpiece*, (open), about 1512–1515. Oil on panel, Unterlinden Museum, Colmar, France.

10–21 Holbein was recommended to Thomas More by the famous author Erasmus. More was the Chancellor of England under Henry VIII.
Hans Holbein, *Sir Thomas More,* 1527. Oil on panel, 29 1/2" x 23 1/5" (75 x 59 cm). The Frick Collection, New York.

10–22 The text will help you identify the objects which make a visual list of the sitters' interests. Can you see the skull?
Hans Holbein, *The French Ambassadors,* 1533. Oil on panel, 6' 8" x 6' 9 1/2" (206 x 208 cm). The National Gallery, London.

Hans Holbein

(1497–1543)

One of the finest portrait painters of all times, Hans Holbein (the Younger) was born in Germany but moved to Basel, Switzerland, when he was about thirteen and stayed there for eleven years. He enjoyed great popularity in Basel where people appreciated his paintings, prints, murals, jewelry and architectural designs. In the mid-1520s, Holbein went to England where he became court painter to Henry VIII. He painted many portraits of royalty and English contemporaries. Holbein's work provides a realistic look at sixteenth-century clothing, hair styles and general appearance.

Portraits were Holbein's strength and the source of a very handsome income. His style is characterized by extreme detail and an objective likeness of his sitters. He had a wonderful ability to describe fabrics with his brushes. Holbein painted a remarkable portrait of Sir Thomas More, the witty author and statesman (fig.10–21). No one has painted velvet or fur more convincingly (fig.10–a). More's face is beautifully rendered. Set against a green drape and dark hat, the modeling of the features is brilliant, particularly the treatment of the eyes. The face is determined and dignified. One can almost sense that this man who wrote *Utopia* could not compromise his ideals—a quality that led to his clash with Henry VIII and his beheading.

One of Holbein's greatest achievements is his double portrait, *The French Ambassadors* (fig.10–22). The French Ambassador to England, Jean de Dinteville, is on the left in a casual pose. With him is his friend, Bishop Georges de Selve. While both men are portrayed with Holbein's usual care and detail, the array of objects in the painting is fascinating. The objects are a virtual catalog of the two men's interests: eye glass, lute, celestial globe, Lutheran hymnbook, compasses, flutes, sundial, crucifix and books.

The most astounding feature is the shape that seems to grow out of the frame at the lower left in the foreground. It is impossible to tell what it is until one looks at it from below, near the left corner of the painting. Hold the book at a flat angle and view the object from the lower left to see it. Viewed from the correct angle, a skull appears. The painting was perhaps made to hang over a doorway so that when people looked up, they saw a skull.

Although England had not produced any painters of international stature, Holbein showed the world how the English looked. He established a trend in portraiture that would be long-lasting in the British empire.

Window in Time

Art and Anatomy

Artists, physicians and butchers all come under the guardianship of the same patron saint, the evangelist St. Luke. According to legend, St. Luke was both a physician and a painter.

Physicians, artists and butchers also hold in common their interest in dissecting bodies. In ancient times, people believed that the human body was sacred and to dissect it was a serious crime.

Accidents and battle wounds gave physicians information about the internal organs of human beings, but they had very little knowledge of how various organs related to each other. Pictures illustrated the internal workings of the body, but without any emphasis on showing an anatomically correct body. The more involved physicians and artists became with the workings of the human body, the more extensive became their knowledge of anatomy. For the most part, this knowledge was to come from the process of dissection. What better vehicle could there be to reveal the relationship of organs, muscles and bones than an opened corpse?

The ancient Greeks were the first people to become involved in anatomical dissections of the human body. By the third century BC, the Greeks permitted some dissections of human corpses. After the Greek civilization declined, a medical center in Alexandria, Egypt, flourished for several hundred years. It is said that, here, criminals who had been condemned to die were dissected alive. They justified this dreadful act by saying that surgeons could better understand how organs worked if they were still functioning.

In the Middle Ages, monasteries became great centers of medicine. It has been erroneously believed that in the Middle Ages and into the Renaissance the Church banned dissections. But, Leonardo da Vinci conducted dissections on as many as fifty cadavers at the ecclesiastical hospital of Santa Maria Nuova. Michelangelo was provided with corpses for anatomical study by the prior of the monastery hospital of Santo Spirito. There, he learned about the workings of the human body and its muscles, organs and skeleton. His understanding of anatomy is evident in all of his works.

If anatomical discoveries were to reach a wide audience, the anatomist had to work closely with an expert artist. The first physician to realize this was the remarkable Andreas Vesalius. In the 1500s, Vesalius revolutionized the study of anatomy. His masterwork, the *Fabrica*, became the standard anatomical textbook in use throughout Europe. The illustrations, probably done by John Stephen of Calcar, a Flemish artist, are startlingly good. The drawings of the human skeleton even include a detailed background landscape. The skeleton or "muscleman" is a standing male figure with skin, fat, connective tissue and blood vessels removed. The muscles combine beautifully with the skeleton. The posture is relaxed and "alive."

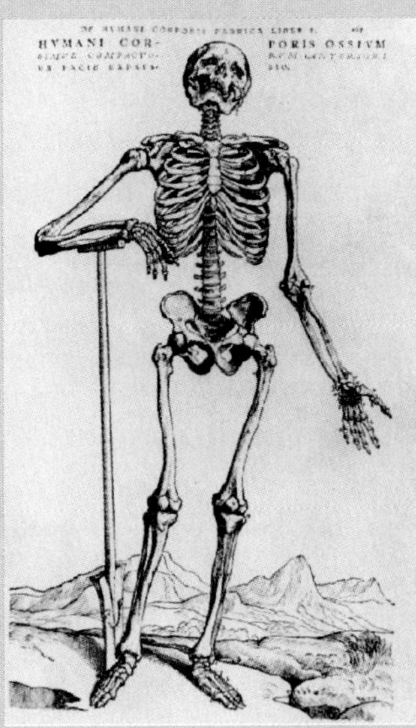

Andreas Vesalius, *Untitled*, 1555. Woodcut from *De humani corporis fabrica libri septem*, 2nd Ed. Royal College of Surgeons in Ireland, Dublin.

Lesson 10.2 Review

1 Which German Renaissance artist became a celebrity and painted many self-portraits?

2 What are two of the events happening at the *Hunting Party in Honor of Charles V* painted by Lucas Cranach?

3 Describe one of the bodies in Grünewald's *Crucifixion* from the *Isenheim Altarpiece.*

4 Which German Renaissance artist was the court painter for the English King Henry VIII?

5 What are some of the hobbies and interests of the French ambassadors displayed in Holbein's portrait of them?

6 Analyze the Italian influence found in Dürer's *Four Apostles*. Refer to paintings by Italian masters to illustrate your points.

10.3 England, France and Spain

THE RENAISSANCE IN ENGLAND brought the flowering of the English language and literature in works by Shakespeare and other writers. However, the flourishing of literature and music was not matched in the visual arts.

In France, the International style, which originated in Burgundy, continued to set the tone in painting. Two important French artists of this period were Jean Fouquet and Jean Clouet. In architecture, sixteenth-century France enjoyed a period of exceptional growth. Francis I and the French aristocracy built a group of opulent ***châteaux*** in the Loire River valley. The Square Court of the Louvre in Paris, designed as a grand palace for Francis I, was the first truly French Renaissance building.

Spain was extremely wealthy at the time. With the riches of the Old World and the unlimited resources of the New World at his command, Philip II summoned the leading artists of Europe to help build and embellish his chosen capital. His single greatest monument was the magnificent El Escorial.

Key Notes

- Music and literature were more dominant than art in England.
- In France, architecture experiences tremendous growth.
- The great wealth of Hapsburg Spain attracts artists and Philip II builds his greatest monument, El Escorial.

Vocabulary

châteaux

Special Feature

El Escorial

In the sixteenth century, Spain, under the Hapsburg Empire, was a dominant force in Europe. It ruled much of Europe and claimed vast areas of land in the Americas. With the great wealth accumulated by the Hapsburgs, the arts flourished.

The Spanish disdained the Classical ideals of purity and proportion. The need of Spanish architects to do something different with Italian form is never more magnificently visible than in *El Escorial* (fig.10–23), constructed for Philip II of Hapsburg. The main architect for this project was Juan de Herrera but the king had a lot to do with the design. Philip insisted on the right to judge the suitability of every public building undertaken during his

reign. El Escorial is a vast building complex combining a palace and court with a church. It expressed the unified Catholic spirit in Spain. The huge structure is an apt expression of Philip's passionate Catholicism, his pride in his dynasty, as well as the austerity that seems to have been very much a part of his character.

The site chosen was at the foothills of the bleak Guadarrama Mountains about thirty miles from Madrid near the village of Escorial. El Escorial is a huge square grid of corridors and courtyards with an austere basilica at its center. Beneath the high altar lie eleven Spanish kings, including Philip II. The return to Classic simplicity, the visual balance and the mathematical proportions put the stamp of Renaissance planning on the complex. It was called by Philip's contemporaries "the eighth wonder of the world."

El Escorial is gloomily grand and austerely magnificent. These characteristics perfectly represent the somber personality of Philip II. El Escorial is not a place to be trapped in alone after dark. The main entrance is built in the strict Doric order. Only the royal coat of arms and a gigantic statue of St. Lawrence holding his gridiron relieve the general starkness.

Like the whole complex of buildings, the domed church is constructed of granite. The horizontal elements used by the architect on the church facade and other buildings create the feeling of ponderous weight and mass (fig.10–24). The plainness of the facades reinforce this effect and convey a sense of starkness and severity. This contrasts sharply with the graceful elegance of Italian Renaissance architecture. (See the map on page 331 for the location of Escorial, Spain.)

10–24 Note the simplicity of the facade and the use of horizontal elements which give the building its ponderous appearance.
Juan Bautista De Toledo, *El Escorial*, detail.

10–23 The palace, court and church are combined for a completely integrated church and state that reflected the power of an absolute monarchy.
Juan Bautista De Toledo, *El Escorial*, c.1563–1584, near Madrid.

World Cultural Timeline

1520
Chocolate introduced to Spain from the Aztec Empire

1538
First plays produced in Mexico

1571
Bornu Empire in Sudan reaches its height

1585
Toyotami Hideyomi becomes Japan's military ruler

10–25 The artist spent two years in Italy and combines that influence with Flemish characteristics.
Jean Fouquet, *Etienne Chevalier and St. Stephen*, c. 1450. From a diptych now divided. Tempera on wood, 36 1/2" x 33 1/2" (93 x 85 cm). Staatliche Museen zu Berlin Preussischer Kulturbesitz Gemäldegalerie, Berlin.

French Painting

Jean Fouquet (about 1420–1481), the most important French artist of the fifteenth century, painted portraits and religious scenes and worked on manuscript illuminations. The clear details in *Etienne Chevalier and St. Stephen* (fig.10–25) reflect the Flemish influence. Fouquet was also influenced by Italian art, as can be seen in the architectural setting. Although the donor is seen with his patron, St. Stephen, the painting is more secular than religious in nature.

Jean Clouet (about 1485–1541) painted portraits, such as *Francis I* (fig.10–26). Equal emphasis is given to the face and expression and the rich brocades and silks of the king's clothing. Clouet, however, failed to reach a stature of major importance.

10–26 Note the stiff frontal pose of the king and the way his sleeves push out beyond the border of the painting.
Jean Clouet, *Francis I*, c.1525–1530. Tempera and oil on wood, approx. 38" x 29" (96 x 74 cm). The Louvre, Paris.

10–27 Compare this chateau to the castle at Marksburg (fig.8–9).
Pierre Nepveu, *Chateau of Chambord*, begun 1519.

French Architecture

The *Château of Chambord* (fig.10–27) is an excellent example of the French architecture of the sixteenth century. Started in 1519, it has a large central block that contains numerous apartments. On each corner is a rounded tower. Wings on each side contain simple hallways that terminate in huge rounded fortress-like structures with conical roofs. Viewed from afar, the entire structure has a horizontal feeling. From close up, however, the Gothic-style roof towers and the vertical elements on the exterior walls produce a vertical pull on the viewer's senses. Inside the central block is a marvelously intertwined stairway to the various apartments. It is constructed so that a person walking up the spiraling stairs can hear, but cannot see, persons coming down. The entire

structure is a remarkable combination of styles. The bottom three stories are coolly Renaissance while the roof is flamboyant Gothic. To see this dramatic contrast, cover the roof, then the lower three stories with a piece of paper.

The *Square Court of the Louvre* in Paris (fig.10–28) is the first truly French Renaissance building. It was designed by Pierre Lescot and Jean Goujon. Goujon also furnished the structure with sculptures and fine reliefs (fig.10–c). A three-story block, its large windows and steeply sloping roof are French additions to an Italian Renaissance idea. The sculptural details contrast with the Classical forms to produce a carefully balanced facade, both rich in detail, yet more restrained than Gothic flamboyance. The windows on each floor receive different treatment, yet the stories are visually tied together with vertical pilasters and Corinthian columns. Originally part of the royal palace in Paris, it is today part of the magnificent museum of the Louvre.

10–28 Use the text to help you identify the features of this palace which is now part of a famous museum.
Pierre Lescot, *Square Court of the Louvre,* 1546. Paris.

Lesson 10.3 Review

1 What was the El Escorial? Who built it? Where is it? Where did the funds come from to build it?
2 Who was the most important French artist during the 1400s?
3 Describe how two architectural styles are combined in the chateau of Chambord?
4 What was the first French Renaissance building in Paris?

Primary Source

Albrecht Dürer

Albrecht Dürer was impressed by the scientific methods and natural proportions used by Italian artists. He observed these methods on a trip to Venice. As a result, he wrote a number of books including *The Teaching of Measurements* (1525), *Fortifications of Towns, Castles, and Places* (1527) and *Four Books of Human Proportions* (1528). Dürer said that the purpose of his books was to teach Italian methods to students in his own country.

Dürer suggested that they should practice drawing many different kinds of people from life. This would eventually enable them to draw accurately proportioned figures from memory. This selection is from *Four Books on Human Proportion*, Book III, "Aesthetic Excursus:"

"...if a man accurately follows life in his imitation so that his work resembles life and is like unto nature, and especially if the thing imitated is beautiful, the work is held to be artistic, and, as it deserves, it is highly praised."

"Wherefore it follows that no powerful artist should abandon himself to one manner only; but he should be practiced in several styles and in many kinds, and should have understanding therein. Then he will be able to make whatever sort of picture is required of him."

"Therefore let no one put too much belief in himself, lest he err in his work and fail. It is very needful for one who busies himself about these things to see many good figures and especially such as have been made by the famous good masters, and that he hear them discourse therof. Howbeit you must ever observe their faults and consider how they might be bettered."

Chapter Review

Review

1 Describe three differences between Renaissance painting of Northern Europe and that of Italy.

2 Name three Northern European Renaissance artists who traveled to Italy to study Italian art. Why do you think they were interested in Italian art?

3 Discuss how the paintings of Bruegel and Bosch are alike.

Interpret

1 Explain how Bruegel's imagined *Tower of Babel* is different from the actual tower of Babel, a Sumerian ziggurat?

2 Describe a piece of clothing that seems unusual to you in one of the paintings in this chapter. Can you identify any of the fabrics from which it was made?

3 Compare El Escorial with an Italian Renaissance building you have studied.

Other Tools for Learning

Maps

1 What present-day countries make up the low countries? Why do you think they were called low? Name two towns in the low countries.

2 Notice the great rivers that the Northern European towns cluster on and around. Why do you think towns would be built near these rivers? Name a town on or near the Loire River, the Seine River and the Rhine River.

Timelines

1 The Renaissance is also known as an age of exploration. People were beginning to trade with other cultures and explore parts of the world far from their own homes. What foods or objects from non-European cultures were eagerly accepted by the sixteenth-century Europeans?

2 The Renaissance was a time of political unrest. List three wars or revolts that happened during the fifteenth and sixteenth centuries.

Electronic Research

CD-ROM drive: *Microsoft Art Gallery*

1 Explain how the distorted skull in the lower left of Holbein's *The French Ambassadors* is meant to be seen. (Composition and Perspective Guided Tour)

2 How did Jan van Eyck modify the *Arnolfini Wedding* as he painted it? (Beneath the Varnish Guided Tour)

3 Fold a piece of paper to demonstrate how triptych altarpieces such as the *Mérode* and the *Ghent Altarpiece* fold. (Look at the animation sequence in the Paintings as Objects Guided Tour to understand how this works.)

Activity 1

Symbols, Detail and Light

Materials

11" x 14" or 12" x 18" white drawing paper
assorted colored pencils

Take a look.

- Fig.10–6, Jan van Eyck, *Arnolfini Wedding,* 1434. Oil on panel.

Think about it. Northern Renaissance painters moved in a different direction from that of their Italian counterparts. Symbolism, the fascination with detail, and realistic light all share importance in *Arnolfini Wedding,* a painting by the Northern Renaissance painter Jan van Eyck. (Refer to Chapter 9 to compare and contrast the two Renaissance trends.)

- Study the detailed objects in the room and explain their significance. What might they symbolize?
- Observe how the light softly illuminates the variety of textures—skin, flesh, metal and fabrics.
- How do all of these create unity in the painting?

Do it. Using colored pencil, illustrate an important event or ceremony in your life. Incorporate symbolism, soft lighting and detail to make your composition portray the mood of the event.

Check it. Have a friend describe what he or she sees in your artwork. Is your friend's interpretation close to what you had in mind? Do the same with your friend's work. Discuss how easy or difficult it is to convey a mood or idea in images.

Helpful Hint: Make a list of symbols and their meanings.

Activity 2

Fantasy World Triptych

Materials

11" x 14" paper
assorted fine-line colored markers
optional: colored pencils, oil pastels or watercolors

Take a look.

- Fig.10–10, Hieronymus Bosch, *Garden of Delights.,* triptych, about 1505–1510.

Think about it. Hieronymus Bosch, a Dutch painter, presented a world of weird sights, fanciful images and puzzling symbols. His triptych, *Garden of Delights,* is a strange story filled with incredible detail. Bosch's painting, packed with tiny people set in a fantastic landscape, shows a pessimistic look at humanity.

Do it. Visualize your own world of fantasy and miniature images. Using fine-line colored markers, create a triptych which tells the story of your fantasy world. Make your drawing very detailed.

Check it. As you work, consider the way images, ideas and colors interact between your panels.

Helpful Hint: Relax and doodle first.

Additional Activities

- Read excerpts from Sir Thomas More's *Utopia* (1516). Create a collage showing your own personal utopia. Use photographs, illustrations and drawings. Write an essay predicting the success of your utopia.
- Using tempera, paint a picture of your favorite outdoor winter activity. Paint it in flat colors, similar to the style of Bruegel (see *The Return of the Hunters,* fig.10–13.)
- Pieter Bruegel's paintings of the four seasons are known as a cycle. He painted his Flemish community in four settings (spring, summer, autumn and winter). You (and several classmates) could depict your own community, neighborhood or school in a series of four drawings, paintings, sculptures or photographs.
- Northern European artists imitated nature by painting miniature worlds of their own. Using watercolor or colored pencils, make a tiny painting, no more than 4" wide. Work from nature (grass, flowers) or from a still life, and keep everything in proportion. Try painting with egg tempera on a wooden panel or a piece of illustration board. Use egg yolk, water and powdered pigments as your medium, and the smallest brush you can find. (Then, imagine using this exacting technique on a large altarpiece.)
- Do a miniature pen and ink line drawing of a landscape or your favorite animal. If your school has a badge-maker, turn your miniature into an art history button.

Steve Meneely

Age 17
Lower Merion High School
Ardmore, Pennsylvania
Favorite artists: Dürer, Poussin, Ingres
Activity 2,
Fantasy World Triptych

When I was a young child, I lived in a small bush village in Zaire, Africa. I can remember pausing our soccer games to chase the small whirlwinds that swept across the hard, cracked field. The tornado in the left portion of my triptych is much larger and more destructive than the ones we tried to run into.

One of the major themes in this piece is time. Time has turned what was once an unreal reality into a warm memory that slowly fades away with time. Time goes by very quickly, I am learning, and is a division, much like the cliffs and the fault line in the center piece. In all three panels, there are the two figures with torches, life and death, who are hand in hand. My fantasy is to be ruler over time, and to be with those who have vanished from my life.

To me art depends on the world surrounding us, and the inspirations and ideas of other artists. The more and more I look at art, the more I learn about what has been done, and the messages artists have conveyed in their work. This becomes a stepping block, to go on to discover new things for myself.

You should explore, expanding your horizons and your understanding. Stay away from the comforts you can create for yourself, and don't end up in a rut. Keep your eyes open at all times, be aware of the things that pass the majority by. Always improve what you do by seeing what others have done. And good luck!

Steve Meneely

Untitled, 1994. Watercolor, 30" x 42" (76 x 107 cm).

11 Baroque and Rococo

In This Chapter...

It was about 1600 when Rome emerged again as the center of the art world. The church remained all-powerful, continuing to patronize art and commission artists from all over Italy. From this hotbed of creative talent, the exuberant, emotional Baroque style was born and spread through Europe.

Throughout the 1600s, Europe was filled with an energy that inspired the production of hundreds of great paintings and sculptures and scores of architectural masterpieces. From the magnificent palace at Versailles to the world-famous canvases of Rembrandt and Rubens, Europe has seldom seen a century of such intense and widespread activity.

In the 1700s, Rococo made its first appearance in France. Its charm and lightheartedness contrasted with the power and seriousness of the Baroque. This new style was not popular in all of Europe. The English and their American colonies preferred the more serious nature of the Baroque and extended the life of that style into the later 1700s.

The late 1700s was a time of great change in Europe and America. The beginning of the industrial revolution, along with the democratic revolutions in France and America, would begin the period we consider the modern world.

11–a Part of Gianlorenzo Bernini's contribution to Baroque art in Rome was the installation of magnificent sculpted fountains. This is a detail of one of the most spectacular fountains designed during the Baroque period. It reflects the Baroque fascination with drama and emotion.
Gianlorenzo Bernini, *Fountain of the Four Rivers,* 1648–1651. Travertine and marble. Piazza Navona, Rome.

1602–1604
Caravaggio, *Deposition of Christ*
1618
30 Years War begins

1632
van Dyck becomes court painter to Charles I
1642
Rembrandt, *The Night Watch*
1656
Velazquez, *The Maids of Honor*

1666
Great Fire and Plague of London

1768–1770
Copley, *Paul Revere*
1789–1802
French Revolution
1793
The Louvre becomes a national art gallery, Paris

Baroque and Rococo

1620
The Mayflower sails to New Plymouth, Massachusetts

1675–1710
Wren, Saint Paul's Cathedral

1717–1719
Watteau, *Embarkation for Cythera*
1719
Defoe, *Robinson Crusoe*

1730
Rococo at its peak
1768
Mozart produces first opera at age 12

Nature is nearly always feeble and puny, so that if their [students'] imaginations are filled only with natural forms, they never will be able to produce anything beautiful and grand, for these qualities are not to be found in nature.

Gianlorenzo Bernini

11–c The Hall of Mirrors at Versailles is considered one of the most splendid rooms in all of Europe. Seventeen arched windows admit abundant sunlight that is reflected from seventeen mammoth mirrors.
Jules Hardouin-Mansart and Charles Lebrun, Hall of Mirrors, *Palace of Versailles,* begun 1678.

11–b In the eighteenth century wealthy travelers often purchased paintings of the cities they visited to bring home as souvenirs. This is a detail from a painting of Venice. It depicts the city in the midst of a celebration and is filled with rich and exacting details.
Antonio Canaletto, *The Basin of San Marco on Ascension Day,* detail (fig.11–48).

The widespread Baroque movement was influential in all of Europe.

11.1 The Baroque in Italy and Germany

THE TRANSFORMATION from Mannerism to Baroque took place in Rome near the end of the sixteenth century and gradually spread throughout Europe. Artists of this period were highly competent at drawing and painting the human figure from every possible angle. They reproduced the most complicated perspective and used color and value contrasts with ease. The Baroque was filled with a dynamism and opulence that contrasts with the Renaissance. Artists delighted in the theatrical and extravagant and showed incredible versatility in their work.

Around 1600, Rome became the birthplace of Baroque art, as it had been the center of the High Renaissance a century before. Artists from many regions gathered in Rome to receive challenging papal commissions. These ambitious young artists, attracted by the great activity in Rome, created the new style.

In Germany, the southern region in particular looked to Italy as its model. The leading figures of the time were architects. Though Italy was the source for many building plans, the interiors of German Baroque churches show a lavish exuberance and airiness that is a departure from Italian Baroque ideals.

Key Notes

- The Baroque is born in Italy under the patronage of the Catholic Church.
- A papal program to beautify Rome draws artists from all regions of Italy.
- The German Baroque, as seen in its churches, is exuberant and festive.

Vocabulary
tenebrism
baldachin
stucco

Special Feature

Gianlorenzo Bernini

(1598–1680)

One of the most influential and fiery artists of the Baroque period was Gianlorenzo Bernini. Too late to belong to the Renaissance period, Bernini was nevertheless a Renaissance man: sculptor, painter, architect, stage designer, dramatist and composer.

It is impossible to look at or visit St. Peter's in Rome without thinking of Bernini. Inside and out his imprint is evident. Under his supervision, thirty-nine artists carried out his sculptural plans during several years of intense activity. Bernini's largest and most impressive project was the design for a magnificent piazza in front of *St. Peter's* (fig.11–1). It begins with a trapezoidal plaza in front of the basilica's facade and opens out into a huge oval area framed by massive

11–1 This enormous piazza is frequently jammed with thousands of worshipers and tourists.
Gianlorenzo Bernini. *Piazza and colonnade of St. Peter's,* Rome, designed 1657.

11–2 The artist used a hidden window to enhance the effect of light in this sculpture.
Gianlorenzo Bernini, *Ecstasy of Saint Theresa,* 1645–1652. Marble, about 11 1/2' (3.5 m) high. Cornaro Chapel, Santa Maria della Vittoria, Rome.

11–3 Notice how Bernini chose to portray the moment just before the stone is released from the sling. The viewer is forced to imagine how the action will be completed.
Gianlorenzo Bernini, *David,* 1623. Marble, 67" (170 cm) high. Galleria Borghese, Rome.

Doric colonnades. An Egyptian obelisk stands in the center flanked by two magnificent fountains. Although grandly Classic in its style, the curves of the piazza are Baroque.

The *Ecstasy of Saint Theresa* (fig.11–2) is the work in which Bernini most completely captures the Baroque spirit. The sculpture commemorates a mystical event involving Saint Theresa, a Carmelite nun. She believed that a pain in her side was caused by an angel of God stabbing her repeatedly with a fire-tipped arrow. Her face in Bernini's sculpture shows the ecstasy of the combined pain and pleasure while her body swoons. According to her vision, the pain was dreadful, yet so sweet she wanted it to continue forever. Saint Theresa floats on a marble cloud that seems suspended in air. Rays of glimmering bronze shower down on the figures from the painted ceiling of the chapel. Bernini enhanced this sensation of light by including a hidden window to let in real light.

Bernini's *David* (fig.11–3) also expresses the Baroque spirit to perfection. It is expansive, dramatic and energetic. We see David at the beginning of the powerful pivoting motion that will propel the stone out of his sling. The space around the sculpture seems to be part of it. Viewers do not stand for long in the path of the about-to-be-hurled stone.

11–4 Caravaggio's dramatic use of light combined with naturalism influenced many other artists.
Caravaggio, *The Supper at Emmaus*, 1597. Oil on canvas, 54 1/4" x 76 1/2" (138 x 194 cm). National Gallery, London.

Caravaggio

(1571–1610)

Working about twenty-five years earlier than Bernini, Michelangelo Merisi, called Caravaggio (after his hometown) was the first giant of the Baroque. He was considered a rebel against conventional society and met an early death at thirty-seven while running from the law.

Unlike Bernini who worked as painter, sculptor and architect, Caravaggio focused solely on painting. He often tried to shock his patrons by placing his religious figures in very common, earthly settings. Figures were frequently shown barefoot, with the dirty soles of their feet presented directly to the viewer. For this reason and the fact that he used everyday citizens and common people as models, churches sometimes refused his commissioned work.

Caravaggio's work featured extreme naturalism, intense value contrasts and a hard-edged painting style. His ability to use these three elements to create intense drama strongly influenced many artists. His large paintings on canvas had a significant impact on northern European art where naturalism was already accepted.

The subjects in Caravaggio's *The Supper at Emmaus* (fig.11–4) are brilliantly lit by a single source of light. The scene is taken from the Biblical account of Easter Sunday evening. Christ had appeared and walked with two of his followers to their home at Emmaus. When Christ blessed the food on the table, the followers suddenly knew who he was—their risen Lord. Caravaggio captures them at the moment of recognition. With Christ's hand over the meal in blessing, the man on the right throws out his arms in amazement. The man on the left shoves his chair away from the table in utter astonishment. Their servant looks on in disbelief.

Set against a solid wall of dark values, the figures seem lit with a floodlight as they surround the table, acting out the drama. They are nearly life-size. Each has facial expressions and hand gestures that intensify the dramatic impact. Caravaggio is a master of foreshortening, color, light, drama and still lifes. Notice the exquisite basket of fruit, the roast chicken, the bread and the dishes on the table. All receive the same dramatic treatment as the human figures.

Caravaggio was one of the earliest artists to paint still-life subjects with such naturalism, even including rotten spots on the apples.

In his painting, *Deposition of Christ* (bringing Christ down from the cross), Caravaggio has an ideal subject for his dramatic technique (fig.11–5). The tightly composed group is made up of three women, Joseph of Arimathea and the Apostle John. They ease the lifeless body onto a huge stone slab projecting out from the canvas. Christ's limp hand and the corner of the winding cloth touch the slab, uniting it with the group of figures.

Caravaggio places the eye level right at the top of the slab so that all the action takes place above the viewer, adding to the stagelike feeling. The black background intensifies the drama. The deep shadows eat into the group of figures, making the lighter values even more powerful by contrast. The nearly nude figure of Christ contrasts with the various cloth textures. Light contrasts with dark; life with death; hunched figures with erect; and horizontal direction with vertical and diagonal.

The light plays most directly on Christ's body and highlights the faces of John and Joseph. The faces of Christ's mother and Mary Magdalene are darkened in shadow. The light again strikes the face and uplifted hands of the third Mary at the top of the composition. The exaggerated contrast of darks and lights, called ***tenebrism***, together with the naturalistic style of Caravaggio creates an overpowering work. Since the figures are slightly over life-size, viewers feel that they are watching the event take place before their eyes.

Artemisia Gentileschi

(1593–1653)

Caravaggio's followers used his dramatic staging of events set against a plain dark background as part of their own style. Among his followers was Artemisia Gentileschi. She helped spread Caravaggio's style to Florence, Genoa and Naples. By 1615, Gentileschi was a well-known artist in Florence. She moved to Rome in 1620 and painted *Judith and Maidservant with the Head of Holofernes* (fig.11–6). The story centers around the Hebrew heroine, Judith. The Babylonian army was besieging a Hebrew city when Judith surrendered herself to the enemy. Once in camp, she and her servant found and beheaded the general, Holofernes, causing the Babylonian army to retreat and lift the siege.

Instead of focusing on the violence of the killing, Gentileschi dramatizes the start of the escape from the enemy camp. The maidservant is stuffing the head of Holofernes into a sack at the bottom of the painting. Using a candle as the single light source, the artist emphasizes deep shadows and brilliant lights. The tenebrism effect highlights the forms of the figures and the satiny gold material in Judith's robe. The blacks from the background infringe on the dark shadows of the figures. The foreshortening of the figures is handled beautifully as they are shown rushing to get their work done before they are detected.

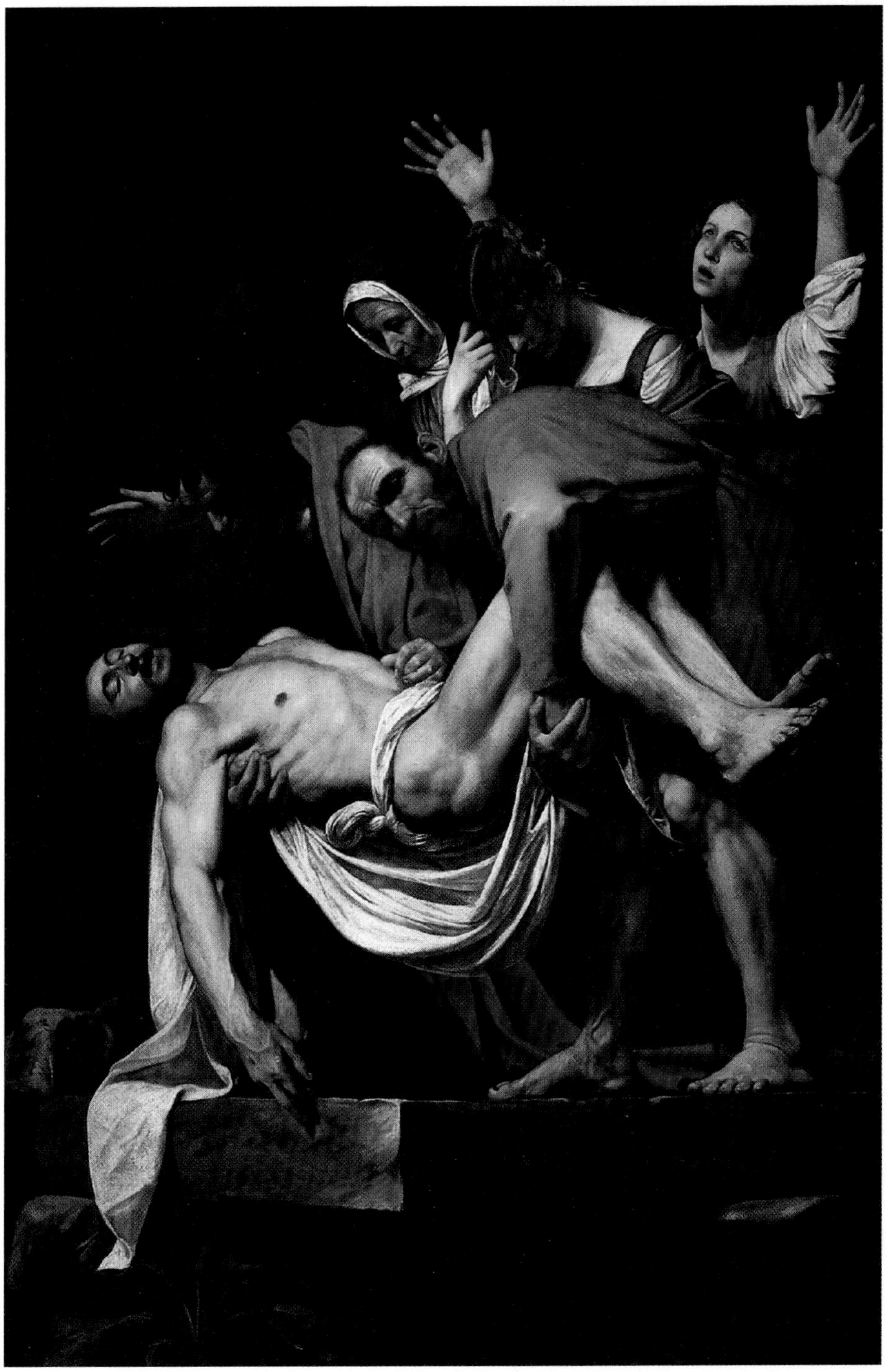

11–6 One of the first known important women painters who was important in her own right, Gentileschi was a student of her father's and of other important artists of her time.

Artemisia Gentileschi, *Judith and Maidservant with the Head of Holofernes*, about 1625. Oil on canvas, 72 3/4" x 56" (185 x 142 cm). The Detroit Institute of Arts.

11–5 Can you identify the elements of the story and the techniques used to emphasize them?

Caravaggio, *Deposition of Christ*, 1602–1604. Oil on canvas, 117 1/4" x 79 1/2" (298 x 202 cm). Vatican Museums, Rome.

11–7 The basilica of St. Peter's is an extraordinary blending of Renaissance and Baroque elements that combine to create the most impressive building in Christendom.
Carlo Maderno. *Facade of St. Peter's,* Rome, 1606–1612.

Carlo Maderno

(1556–1629)

Carlo Maderno made important contributions to the style of Baroque architecture. His work on St. Peter's in Rome brought him much fame. In 1606 Pope Paul V commissioned Maderno to add a nave to Michelangelo's building and provide a facade. Maderno moved the new facade far forward, reducing the importance of Michelangelo's dome. The dome now cannot be seen except from a distance or from the papal gardens in the rear of the basilica. The new facade (fig.11–7) has a heavy horizontal look because huge corner structures were added. Each, pierced with an arch and crowned with a clock, is a gateway to the Vatican properties behind. Maderno intended them to be the basis for massive towers. The towers were never built because the foundations were not strong enough.

The windows, five doors, columns and statues of the facade are enormous in size. But because of the careful scale and design, they work together beautifully and do not seem excessively large. Only when comparing them to a person standing by a column does one realize the massive size of the parts and the whole.

A painting by Giovanni Panini (done about 1750) shows the decoration and size of the interior of *St. Peter's* (fig.11–8). Baroque decoration can be seen in the richly gilded, coffered ceiling, the piers of colored marble and the huge sculptural monuments. Huge clear windows allow sunlight to flood the interior. Compared with the somber majesty of earlier Gothic cathedrals, the interior is startling in its brightness.

The scale is hard to believe. The parts fit together beautifully. Sizes are so carefully interrelated that, at first glance, the basilica does not seem large at all, but many steps must be taken before one reaches the high altar. The interior, from entrance to the end of the apse, is 632 feet long—longer than two football fields. Notice the size of the people in comparison with the sculpture or the thickness of the piers. To bring the scale into concrete dimensions, look at the ***baldachin*** (Bernini's creation) over the high altar, under Michelangelo's dome. It is 93 feet high or about the height of a 10-story building. Yet it is dwarfed by the hugeness of the open spaces and the massive size of the structure.

1600
Chinese tea becomes popular in Europe

1624
First theater in Tokyo, Japan, established

World Cultural Timeline

1600
Oyo Kingdom of Nigeria at height of power

1601
First strike of textile workers in China

Francesco Borromini

(1599–1667)

Borromini was a seventeenth-century Italian architect who strongly influenced succeeding generations. His buildings are marvels of Baroque feeling and are noted for their facades. The facades move in and out in great swags as though made of a plastic material. Borromini's design for Sant' Agnese in Rome (fig.11–9) combines Classic, Renaissance and Baroque styles into a unified design. This design was adopted in other parts of Europe and even Mexico. The convex sculptural quality of the dome, which rests on a high drum, is repeated in convex features of the two corner towers. The concave surface of the central part of the facade provides a gentle contrast to the dome. Notice the many places where features project out from or recede into the facade. The two corner towers are similar to those Maderno planned for St. Peter's, which were never built.

11–9 The famous *Fountain of the Four Rivers* by Bernini stands in front of Borromini's church in the Piazza Navona.
Francesco Borromini. *Facade of Sant' Agnese*, Rome, 1653–1666.

Baroque Ceilings in Rome

During the middle of the seventeenth century, several artists created illusionary paintings of tremendous complexity on the ceilings of some Baroque churches in Rome. The paintings are filled with figures that appear to be floating and soaring into infinity, like large balloons cut loose to float heavenward. A mark on the floor indicated the exact spot from which the perspective could be viewed most accurately. Several ceilings, like the barrel vault of the church of Il Gesu, contained ***stucco*** (plaster) figures in addition to the painting (fig.11–10). The reliefs gave the added illusion of figures tumbling out of the picture and into the realm of three-dimensional reality.

Painted by Giovanni Battista Gaulli (1639–1709) with sculpture by Antonio Raggi (1624–1686) and directed by Bernini, the ceiling of Il Gesu is highly gilded with a painted oval opening to the sky. Through this window one can look into heaven and see various Jesuit saints. (Il Gesu is the burial place of Ignatius Loyola, founder of the Jesuit order.) The same power that draws the faithful into heaven also casts out the unbelievers. The unbelievers tumble through the frame and seem ready to crash to the floor. The three-dimensional illusion is enhanced by the sculptures, which cast shadows on the sloping vault ceiling.

11–8 Compare this to the interior of Notre Dame in Paris. Do you see a difference in the light?
Giovanni Paolo Panini, *Interior of St. Peter's, Rome,* 1746–1754. Oil on canvas, 60 3/4" x 77 1/2" (154 x 197 cm). National Gallery of Art, Washington DC, Ailsa Mellon Bruce Fund.

11–10 Can you find the parts that are sculpture and the ones that are painted?
Giovanni Battista Gaulli and Antonio Raggi, *Triumph of the Sacred Name of Jesus.* Ceiling fresco, 1676–1679. Il Gesu, Rome.

The Baroque in Germany and Austria

While the Baroque style was developing in Italy, central Europe was engaged in the devastating Thirty Years War, which ended in 1648. Not until the eighteenth century were Austria and Germany able to begin building projects of any great size. But when they started, the activity was tremendous. Architects filled the cities and countryside of Austria and southern Germany with structures that had exteriors of stately elegance and interiors of gilded light and swirling movement.

Jacob Prandtauer

(1660–1726)

Prandtauer chose a rocky cliff above the Danube River on which to erect the *Benedictine Abbey* at Melk (fig.11–11). The imposing structure is dominated by an ornate dome and two magnificent bell towers. Each tower is topped with an onion dome so familiar in the southern German and Austrian countryside. The exterior presents a powerful appearance with curved surfaces and superb detail. The interior (fig.11–12) is filled with gilded surfaces that allow little chance for eyes to rest. Light streams into the vast space from windows in the dome. Painted areas, gilded statues and carved surfaces are all intricately woven into a huge work of art alive with swirling visual activity.

Dominikus Zimmerman

(1685–1766)

Dominikus Zimmerman created one of the finest spatial designs of the German Baroque—the Bavarian pilgrimage church called *Die Wies.* The exterior is serenely plain and was influenced by contemporary Italian building. But the interior (fig.11–13) is a sudden burst of heavenly energy. Color and light are combined with swirling decoration to create an unbelievable eruption of visual movement. Natural light from many large windows floods the interior. Marble sculptures seem to float. The pulpit appears to defy gravity. The white walls and gold decoration seem to reflect the bril-

11–11 The location of this church on a cliff above the Danube River adds to its monumentality.
Jacob Prandtauer. *Benedictine Abbey,* begun 1702. Melk, Austria.

11–12 Compare this interior with an early Renaissance church interior. Which do you prefer?
Jacob Prandtauer. Interior, *Benedictine Abbey,* begun 1702. Melk, Austria.

11–13 The plan of this church is oval in shape.
Dominikus Zimmerman. Interior, *Die Wies*, 1746–1754. Upper Bavaria.

liance of the sun. As glorious as it appears, the interior of Die Wies is typical of hundreds of similar churches in Bavaria and Austria. While Baroque in its structure, the interior decoration of Die Wies exhibits the lavishness and gaiety of an extension of the Baroque, called Rococo, that becomes popular in northern Europe during the eighteenth century.

Lesson 11.1 Review

1 At the beginning of the seventeenth century, which city became the major center of Baroque art?
2 What was Bernini's most important architectural project?
3 Describe Bernini's *Ecstasy of St. Theresa*. How does this sculpture exemplify Baroque art?
4 In your own words, what would you call a contemporary person with Caravaggio's personality?
5 If the *Deposition of Christ* by Caravaggio were on a stage, where on the stage would all the action be happening? Describe the light and motion in this painting.
6 Define *tenebrism*. Name a Baroque painting that is a good example of tenebrism.
7 Name an Italian Baroque artist who helped spread Caravaggio's style of painting to Florence, Genoa and Naples.
8 How did Giovanni Battista Gaulli and Antonio Raggi create a feeling of depth and space in the ceiling fresco, *Triumph of the Sacred Name of Jesus*?
9 Describe the interior of the Bavarian church, Die Wies.

11.2 The Baroque in France

IN THE SECOND HALF of the seventeenth century, France became the most powerful nation of Europe. Rome had been the world capital of the arts for centuries but now Paris began to take over that position. (Paris remained the center of the art world until World War II, after which the center shifted to New York.) The French regard the seventy-two-year reign of the "Sun King," Louis XIV, as their golden age. During this time, French art, fashion and etiquette were held as the standard. It was also during this period that French became the language of diplomacy. French political and cultural power reached great heights. France's influence over taste can still be felt today.

Art and architecture began to serve the king as they had once served the church. Vast projects glorifying the king's reign were embarked upon. Although the influence of Caravaggio and Bernini was felt in France, the French were not entirely comfortable with their extreme expression and enthusiasm. The French favored a more rational and balanced Classicism. The unity of style found in the art and architecture of the time is the result of the taste of Louis XIV. This taste was imposed on the whole nation through the academies that Colbert, Louis' minister, set up to regularize style in all the arts. Even though we find much that is Baroque in the "Classical" art produced in the time of the Sun King, the French preferred to call their more restrained style the Style of Louis XIV, and they continue to do so.

Key Notes

- Louis XIV sets the tone for the arts in France and, eventually, Europe.
- Paris takes over from Rome as art center of the world.
- The French favor a more balanced and Classical Baroque style.

Vocabulary

pavilions

11–15 How has the artist used light for emphasis in this scene?
Georges de La Tour, *Adoration of the Shepherds*, 1645–1650. Oil on canvas, 42" x 54" (107 x 137 cm). The Louvre, Paris.

Special Feature

Georges de La Tour

(1593–1652)

During the early part of the seventeenth century, France remained under the influence of Italy and Flanders. However, some artists of originality emerged. Among them was Georges de La Tour. The influence of Caravaggio is unmistakable in his tenebrism and realism, but La Tour developed a style that was entirely his own. La Tour was well known in his own time, but then he was completely forgotten until fairly recently. Only forty of his paintings are known to exist, yet he is now considered one of the important figures in French painting.

Often using a candle as the only source of light, La Tour built dramatic nighttime compositions. The feeling in these paintings is very intense. At first glance, the painting seems to show a genre subject, or a narrative of some happening from peasant life. However, the subject becomes charged with emotion and takes on aspects of reverence in La Tour's silent but powerful treatment. His *Magdalen with the Smoking Flame* (fig.11–14) is one of four paintings he did of this subject. Set against a flat, dark background and using a candle as the single light source, La Tour builds a striking composition in which the forms are simple and monumental. Mary Magdalen was a symbol of the Catholic doctrine of the forgiveness of sins through penance, but this picture is more than just a picture of the saint. The figure personifies a life of contemplation and mortification, devoted to the love of God. This painting was discovered and identified in 1972.

La Tour's *Adoration of the Shepherds* (fig.11–15) again shows us one of the night settings that he so favored. The painting is of a group of humbly clad men and women gathered around the Christ Child. Once again a sacred event is depicted in an ordinary, everyday way. There is little in the painting that hints at the holy nature of the scene. The figures do not have halos. There are no angels or other heavenly signs. The light that infuses the scene is natural. It comes from a candle. However, there is a reverence in the way these ordinary people contemplate the candlelit infant that tells us that the scene is holy. The great calm that pervades this picture is characteristic of La Tour's work.

11–14 Very few of La Tour's paintings are known, but he was a master of tenebrism who often used unusual light sources such as candles and moonlight.
Georges de La Tour, *Magdalen with the Smoking Flame*, about 1630–1635. Oil on canvas, 46" x 36 1/4" (117 x 92 cm). Los Angeles County Museum of Art, gift of the Ahmanson Foundation.

Nicolas Poussin

(1593/94–1665)

Even though he was the most important painter of France in the late seventeenth century, Nicolas Poussin spent most of his productive years in Rome. Poussin used the colored glazes of Titian, but employed the simplified sculptural quality of Raphael. He stressed the elimination of unnecessary detail and put emphasis on composition, balance and other qualities of Classical art which he loved. He often constructed a model stage filled with wax figures so he could obtain the best balance and movement in his painting. But, at other times, as in the *Rape of the Sabine Women* (fig.11–16), he filled his paintings with swirling activity and strong brushwork.

To Poussin, subject matter was of great importance in painting. He felt that it should be grand, heroic or divine. His *Holy Family on the Steps* (fig.11–17) illustrates his theories of painting. The theme or subject matter is divine, with Mary, Joseph, the Christ Child, Elizabeth and John the Baptist. The setting is Classical. The composition is triangular, and the design is perfectly calculated. Poussin also includes some subtle symbolism. He places Joseph and his carpentry tools, which represent the working life, in the shadow of Mary and the Christ Child, who represent the spiritual life. Asymmetrical balance is worked out carefully. Joseph's small highlighted foot balances the larger light-valued masses of Saint Elizabeth and her son John. The still-life items on the lower step are also asymmetrically balanced. Every part is considered carefully and placed to attain a perfectly balanced composition. If any part were changed in value or moved to some extent, the feeling of comfortable balance would be destroyed. With all this attention on composition, Poussin is still able to subordinate Elizabeth, John and Joseph with shadows and to center the visual emphasis on Mary and the Christ Child.

11–16 Consider how Poussin has used diagonals to give this painting its incredible motion.
Nicolas Poussin, *Rape of the Sabine Women*, about 1634. Oil on canvas, 61" x 82 1/2" (155 x 209 cm). The Metropolitan Museum of Art, New York, Harris Brisbane Dick Fund, 1946.

11–17 Compare this to Raphael's *School of Athens* (fig.9–30). Also use the text to discover Poussin's composition technique.
Nicolas Poussin, *Holy Family on the Steps*, 1648. Oil on canvas, 27 1/4" x 38 1/2" (69 x 98 cm). National Gallery of Art, Washington DC, Samuel H. Kress Collection.

World Cultural Timeline

1630
Bhutan becomes independent from Tibet

1631
Shah Jahan begins construction of Taj Mahal, Agra, India

1637
Emperor Iemitsu forbids subjects to leave Japan

1644
The Ming dynasty, the last native Chinese line of Emperors, ends

Claude Lorrain

(1600–1682)

Like Poussin, Claude Lorrain went to Rome; however, he remained there and never returned to France. He spent much time in the Italian countryside making hundreds of ink and wash sketches that he later used as subjects for studio paintings.

Claude composed his landscapes as carefully as Poussin designed his figure paintings. In *The Marriage of Isaac and Rebecca* (fig.11–18) he placed large trees in the foreground at right. These trees move in an arc to several more trees in the middle ground at the left, and then back into a spacious, sunlit countryside. The soft light creates the dreamy mood found in many of his landscapes. Claude did not enjoy painting figures and often paid fellow artists to paint them for him. Yet, the figures are important to the paintings because they provide a scale by which to see the huge size of the trees and the vastness of the landscape. The painting has also been called *The Mill* because of the buildings in the middle ground. The figures could be any group of people enjoying a party in the Italian countryside. Claude gave the work a Biblical title even though he was only interested in the landscape.

11–18 Claude Lorrain was so famous for his landscapes that compositional arrangements he used are named after him. This is a typical *Claudian* composition.
Claude Lorrain, *The Marriage of Isaac and Rebecca (The Mill)*, about 1648. Oil on canvas, 58 3/4" x 77 1/2" (149 x 197 cm). The National Gallery, London.

Sidelight

The French Royal Academy of Painting and Sculpture

Throughout antiquity and the Middle Ages, artists had been trained by apprenticeship. They learned their techniques under the personal direction and in the studio of an older and well-established master. But, as painting, sculpture and architecture gained the status of liberal arts, artists needed to supplement their "practical" training with theoretical knowledge.

In France, the history of official art is also a history of the transition from the guild-controlled arts sanctioned by the church to an academic system sponsored by the state. When Louis XIV, the "Sun King," took control of the French government in 1661, he claimed that, as the state and the king were one, all art should glorify him. Thus, the Royal Academy of Painting and Sculpture in Paris was opened to train young artists in the correct style. Instruction was based on a system of rules and formulas, with the official style being the only acceptable approach. Not surprisingly, this strict and controlling system produced no significant artists.

The French Royal Academy did set the pattern for all later academies, including their modern successors, the art schools of today. Over the centuries, there has been much change in emphasis. Today, art schools attempt to recognize all the various artistic styles and techniques connected to the making of artwork.

Window in Time

Versailles

On the site of his father's small hunting lodge, Louis XIV, the Sun King, built Versailles, Europe's greatest palace. Building began in 1661 and continued through the reigns of Louis XV and Louis XVI. Versailles, originally a symbol of the glory of the king, later became a symbol of the excesses of the monarchy and helped to bring about the French Revolution.

Although the architect, Louis Le Vau, began work on Versailles, it was Jules-Hardouin Mansart who gave Versailles its present appearance. He was responsible for designing the *Hall of Mirrors* (fig.11–c), the Chapel and the North and South Wings. The Opera House, built by Jean-Ange Gabriel under the reign of Louis XV, vies with the white and gold Chapel for theatricality.

The palace was built by an army of architects, landscape designers, sculptors, stonecutters and decorators. During the peak of construction, more than 30,000 men and 6,000 horses were needed. In today's money, Versailles would cost $10 billion.

At first, Versailles was home to the king and his court. Later, it was made the seat of government and enlarged to hold 20,000 people. Versailles was a separate world; indeed, the courtiers of Versailles always referred to it as *ce pays-ci*—"this country of ours."

From the marble courtyard can be seen the gilded balcony where the king greeted noble visitors. Inside the Grand Apartments behind the balcony are a series of six rooms where Louis XIV held court. The architecture was artfully designed to follow the movement of the sun, so that the king could move from room to room bathed in the glow of sunlight.

The Hall of Mirrors has seventeen large windows overlooking the park. The view of the park is reflected by seventeen tall mirrors on the wall opposite. The ceiling, too, sparkles with light reflected off the elaborate gold decoration. In its days of glory, the Hall was lit by 3000 candles to form a brilliant setting for ceremonies.

The palace is surrounded by formal gardens spread out over 250 acres. The Classic landscaping includes a mile-long Grand Canal. A river was even diverted to keep the 600 fountains flowing.

Two small palaces, The Grand Trianon and The Petit Trianon, housed the favorite court ladies of Louis XIV and Louis XV. On the grounds as well is Le Hameau, Marie Antoinette's model farm, where she and her companions played at being shepherds in an arcadian setting.

Louis Le Vau and Jules Hardouin-Mansart. *Palace of Versailles,* garden view, 1669–1685.

11–19 What classical elements are used here?
Claude Perrault. *East Facade of the Louvre,* 1667–1670. Paris.

11–20 Compare this dome to the one on the Cathedral of Florence. Use the text to identify all of the elements of this church.
Jules Hardouin-Mansart. Facade, *Church of the Invalides,* 1676–1706. Paris.

Architecture

The ultimate expression of the French Baroque (they called it Classic style) was the Palace of Versailles, but several major developments preceded it. The building of châteaux, begun during the Renaissance, continued and, under excellent architects, became larger and more impressively grand. In 1665, Louis XIV wanted to finish the east facade of the Louvre. The king called the Italian master Bernini to design it. But Bernini's ambitious plans were too majestic for the French. Bernini returned to Rome and the commission was turned over to Claude Perrault (1613–1688), Charles Le Brun (1619–1690) and Louis Le Vau (1612–1670), with Perrault getting most of the credit.

Often called The Colonnade, it marks a distinct victory of French Classicism over Italian Baroque (fig.11–19). The Corinthian columns, arches, pediments and low severe lines are Classic features. They are relieved somewhat by the French technique of protruding the central entrance and corner sections slightly from the facade. Such protrusions are called ***pavilions***. The ground floor is treated as a podium upon which the columns rest. Although some columns are engaged and others are freestanding, the design of the facade is simple, elegant and completely unified. It became the model for French architects for many years.

Among the most impressive Baroque buildings in Paris is the *Church of the Invalides* (fig.11–20), built by Jules Hardouin-Mansart. The vertical emphasis topped by a soaring dome is wonderfully French Baroque. The two-storied facade has graceful Corinthian columns that lead the viewer's eyes upward. The small pediment at the center is emphasized because of the treatment of the doorways below it and the drum of the dome behind it. The drum has paired columns, like St. Peter's. However, the two columns immediately behind the pediment are recessed slightly. The dome itself is highly decorated, unlike previous domes, and is topped by a square lantern, another first. Although it has no concave-convex features like those the Italians were using, the facade has a pavilion similar to some other French buildings and an unmistakable French Baroque feeling.

Lesson 11.2 Review

1 After 1650, which country became the world center for art?
2 Who was the French Sun King? What style of art did he prefer?
3 What type of setting did La Tour favor for his painted scenes?
4 Describe the subject matter, setting and composition of Poussin's *Holy Family on the Steps.*
5 What subjects did Claude Lorrain enjoy painting?
6 Describe the east facade of the Louvre.

11.3 The Baroque in Flanders and Holland

DURING THE SEVENTEENTH CENTURY, Flanders, comprising the southern part of the Low Country provinces, was Catholic and under Hapsburg and Spanish domination. Although they shared a common history and culture with the Dutch, the Flemish were separated from their northern neighbors by religion and economic and social structure. There was little large-scale construction, so Baroque architecture is not very visible in today's Belgium. But painting and, most particularly, the work of Peter Paul Rubens is another story.

Holland, the northern part of the Low Country provinces, had gained independence from Spain and had become Protestant and democratic. This produced significant changes, notably that three of the usual art patrons—the church, the court, and the nobility—were absent. Calvinist Protestantism forbade the use of art in churches. Artists were thrust into the open market, which completely revolutionized the role of art and the artist in the community. Holland, a wealthy country with new colonies and expanding commerce, developed a large middle class who wanted to buy paintings for their homes. The open-market system of artists selling their work to individual patrons led to trade in art, a method of merchandising paintings through galleries, dealers and fairs. So, artists began painting subjects that were in demand, such as landscapes, cityscapes, ideal country scenes, parties, still lifes and portraits. There are obvious parallels, here, with the modern art world.

Key Notes

- Flanders remains Catholic and is ruled by the Hapsburgs. Painting, led by Peter Paul Rubens, is dominant.
- Painting in democratic Holland becomes a commodity sought by the middle class.

Vocabulary

camera obscura

11–21 Can you detect the influence of Caravaggio in this portrait?
Judith Leyster, *Boy with Flute,* about 1635. Oil on canvas, 28 3/4" x 24 1/2" (73 x 62 cm). National Museum, Stockholm.

Special Feature

Judith Leyster

(1609–1660)

As you have seen, there has been very little reference to female artists, particularly to women who became famous. However, the Dutch artist, Judith Leyster, was probably the best-known female painter of the seventeenth century. While many women artists until this time had the advantage of having artist fathers from whom to learn, Judith Leyster's father owned a brewery and she developed her very own style. Although influenced by some artists in Utrecht who worked in the style of Caravaggio and by Frans Hals whom she knew, her style is distinctive. Leyster made her reputation as a genre painter, and she was one of the first artists to paint intimate genre scenes in Holland.

One of Leyster's freshest and most original works, *Boy with Flute* (fig.11–21), is a portrait of a young boy playing his flute. Intent on his instrument, the boy is completely self-absorbed. The composition of the painting is carefully balanced. The instruments on the wall are a counterweight to the boy sitting on the chair. An unseen window on the left provides a controlled light and is a vital part of the painting.

In Leyster's well-known *Self-Portrait* (fig.11–22), which hangs in the National Gallery in Washington, our attention is immediately caught by the ease of her pose and her obvious pleasure in her task. She is painting a violinist and the animation of both of these cheerful figures is remarkable.

Although after her death her works were often attributed to other Dutch painters, Judith Leyster's work has since gained new recognition.

11–22 The great spontaneity of this self-portrait is due in part to the pose of the artist.
Judith Leyster, *Self-Portrait, 1630.* Oil on canvas, 29" x 26" (74 x 66 cm). National Gallery of Art, Washington, DC. Gift of Mr. and Mrs. Robert Woods Bliss.

11–23 Lions were exotic and rare in Ruben's time. He used lions in private zoos for models and combined drawings from many subjects to put this painting together.
Peter Paul Rubens, *Lion Hunt*, 1616. Oil on panel, 97" x 146" (246 x 372 cm). Alte Pinakotek, Munich.

Peter Paul Rubens

(1577–1640)

While Bernini was filling Baroque Rome with sculpture, Peter Paul Rubens was flooding Flanders and the rest of Europe with magnificent Baroque paintings. Possessing enormous intelligence and an unending capacity for work, he produced over 2000 paintings. The earlier Flemish painters had specialized in detail and a cool detachment from their subjects. However, Rubens disregarded them and turned to Italy for his inspiration. He spent eight years studying the masterworks of Classic Rome, the Renaissance, Mannerism and the Baroque.

When he returned to Antwerp, he set up a painting workshop to keep up with his numerous commissions. He hired assistants (many of whom were established painters) to paint in still-life objects, flowers and landscapes. He generally painted the figures himself, but even these were often started by assistants. He would paint small studies on wooden panels. From these, his helpers painted their sections on the large canvas or wooden panels. Meanwhile, from a large balcony in the studio, Rubens directed all of their work simultaneously. He often put the finishing glazes on the works and added his characteristic brushstrokes—if the price was right. The amount he charged his patrons was in proportion to how much work he did himself.

Rubens often picked up new patrons on his travels to other countries. He also studied the work of other artists on these trips. When he first went to Italy, he met Velazquez

World Cultural Timeline

1644
Potala Palace built, Tibet

1674
Last description of live dodo, a native of Mauritius

1650
Ukiyo-e school of art begins to flourish in Japan

1660
Bambara Kingdom of the upper Niger begins to flourish

1680
Rise of the Ashanti Kingdom, West Africa

from Spain. He also made sketches and small paintings of works by Leonardo, Raphael, Titian, Tintoretto, Veronese, Mantegna and Caravaggio, among others. He even had assistants make sketches for him, so that when he returned to Antwerp he had a collection of thousands of ideas from which he would develop his personal style. His style was one of swirling physical movement, marvelous color and energetic brushwork—the epitome of Baroque painting.

From 1616 to 1618, Rubens painted a number of huge works about hunting exotic animals. Europeans were fascinated by lions, tigers, leopards, elephants and crocodiles. Many noblemen had examples in their private zoos. Whenever Rubens got the chance, he would sketch them for future use in his hunting scenes. *Lion Hunt* (fig.11–23) is typical of this phase of Rubens' painting. It boils with violent activity as turning and twisting bodies of horses, lions and humans are intertwined in a complicated knot. Rubens uses the straight lances and swords to stabilize the writhing composition and to lead the viewer's eyes back to the central area. The low eye level increases the dramatic upward thrust of the action. The confrontation would explode out of the frame if the curved necks, arms and heads did not direct the movement back to the center of the canvas. Each detail is charged with tension. The foreshortening is handled with mastery. Never before had an artist used swirling action, color and light with such complete authority and seeming ease.

In his later years, after a second stay in Madrid, Rubens' subjects became more serene and calm. Titian, whose work was much admired and abundant in the Spanish palace, became a strong influence. In his *Garden of Love* (fig.2–26), Rubens pays a superb tribute to the joy of life and love. As a widower, he had recently married the young and beautiful Helena Fourment. He and his bride are shown on the left. Four of Helena's sisters are shown also, some with their husbands. The setting is partly from Rubens' elaborate home in Antwerp and partly imaginative. Chubby cupids flit about the scene. Controlled light strikes only where the artist wants it. Yet even in a scene in which all the people are stationary and there is no evident action, Rubens still creates energetic visual movement. Light plays over and reflects from the crinkled satin gowns and translucent flesh. The painting is a portrait of happiness. The combination of reality, Classical mythology and Baroque material elegance is Rubens at his finest.

The *Castle of Steen* (fig.11–24) was a favorite painting of Rubens and one he kept until his death. After he returned from Madrid, he moved to this country estate. With tender care, he portrays the Belgian landscape with its broad receding spaces flooded with afternoon light. His earlier landscapes had been turbulent and depicted nature's violence. But, in his later years, Rubens chose to represent the quiet atmosphere surrounding his own country house. A hunter, wagon master and castle occupy the shadowy lower-left part of the scene. However, the emphasis easily shifts to the vast expanse of fields and trees that seem to reach into infinity, finally uniting with the high-keyed sky.

11–24 This is Rubens' own home. How do you think he felt about it?
Peter Paul Rubens, *Castle of Steen*, 1635. Oil on panel, 51" x 90" (131 x 230 cm). National Gallery, London.

Anthony van Dyck

(1599–1641)

Among the fine artists who painted for Rubens in his Antwerp workshop was Anthony van Dyck. Van Dyck was already an accomplished painter when only seventeen. His early work was influenced greatly by Rubens, but when he went to Italy he fell under the spell of the work of Titian, Tintoretto and Veronese.

Anthony van Dyck excelled at portraiture and worked as official court painter for Charles I of England, just as Holbein had done for Henry VIII. Van Dyck flattered his subjects, endowing them with aristocratic refinement, delicacy and elegance. It is no wonder that he became a favorite of English noblemen. In his *Portrait of Charles I in Hunting Dress* (fig.11–25), he creates the impression of regal splendor and dignity. Charles is posed dramatically with his horse and servant in an outdoor setting. With apparent ease, van Dyck accents the shimmering mane of the horse and the satin shirt of the king. They glisten with light amid the shadows of the scene. In reality the king was short and lacked a handsome appearance, but one would never suspect it after looking at van Dyck's official portrait.

Van Dyck typically placed his figures in an outdoor setting with large shaded trees, distant landscape and cloudy sky. This setting became a standard treatment for portrait paintings in England. Although a Flemish painter, van Dyck did much of his work in service of the English king and, when he died in London, he was buried there.

11–25 Van Dyck flattered his sitters. What do you think he has done here to flatter Charles I?
Anthony van Dyck, *Portrait of Charles I in Hunting Dress,* 1635. Oil on canvas, 8' 11" x 6' 11 1/2" (271 x 213 cm). The Louvre, Paris.

Jacob van Ruisdael

(1629–1682)

In Holland, Jacob van Ruisdael was a master at portraying the Dutch landscape and the drama of the sky, with its ever-changing and powerful clouds. Because Holland is so very flat, van Ruisdael places the horizon line low in the painting. The emphasis naturally is forced to the huge sky, which van Ruisdael fills with superb cumulus clouds. As in *The Mill at Wijk by Durstede* (fig.11–26), the light and dark values of the clouds lead to brightly lit highlights on the ground. These highlights contrast sharply with the dark shadowed areas. The mill is emphasized against the turbulent sky. The mill and boats pause as if held in time for the viewer to see. Even the river runs smoothly and quietly in contrast to the active sky. To drive or walk through the Dutch countryside is to experience the reality of van Ruisdael's painting.

Jan Steen

(1625–1679)

While the Dutch are noted for the immaculate order of the interiors of their homes, Jan Steen shows another side: chaos, clutter and humor. He enjoyed the unexpected and often crammed his canvases full with children, animals, drunken

11–26 The sky is the focus of the activity while the water remains calm.
Jacob van Ruisdael, *The Mill at Wijk by Durstede,* not dated. 32 1/4" x 40 1/4" (82 x 102 cm). The Rijksmuseum, Amsterdam.

folk and upset baskets. In *The Feast of St. Nicholas* (fig.11–27), Steen weaves a tender narrative of a children's festival for the viewer to enjoy. Some children are happy, having been given candy and toys. Another is crying because others are making fun of him. But, the child clutching the statue of a saint and her grandmother receive the most light and the most attention. Steen loved to portray older folks enjoying the pleasure of small children. The loose shoe and spilled fruit are almost trademarks of the clutter in his paintings. Much family interplay is taking place in the warm room. A whole story could be written about the actions and appearances of all the family members and of their relationships to each other and to the scene.

11–27 In contrast to the traditional portrayal of immaculate Dutch interiors, Steen often shows family life in action complete with clutter.
Jan Steen, *The Feast of St. Nicholas,* about 1660–1665. Oil on canvas, 32 1/4" x 27 1/2" (82 x 70 cm). Rijksmuseum, Amsterdam.

Rachel Ruysch

(1664–1750)

The daughter of an amateur painter, Ruysch became one of Holland's foremost painters of still lifes with flowers. She studied under a local artist named William van Aelst for a time before she went on to develop her own distinctive style. Her settings were not limited to a vase of flowers on a table. Instead, she often placed the flowers in a woodland setting complete with various inhabitants like mice, snails and grasshoppers. *Flower Still Life* (fig.11–28) is an excellent example of Ruysch's carefully detailed, delicate style. Each flower is rendered realistically. The flowers are asymmetrically arranged, something she learned from van Aelst. This S-curve arrangement would later be a standard for eighteenth-century flower painters.

Ruysch married Juriaen Pool, a portrait painter, and together they were appointed court painters of the Elector Palatine in Düsseldorf. She reared ten children while still devoting time to her painting. She was widely admired, and her paintings earned her from 750 to 1250 guilders each. Compare this with Rembrandt's compensation, which was seldom more than 500 guilders per painting for his later work.

11–28 The Dutch were, and still are, avid horticulturists. Can you identify some of the varieties of flowers in this vase?
Rachel Ruysch, *Flower Still Life*, c. 1782. Oil on canvas, 27" x 25" (68 x 64 cm). Academy, Vienna.

Frans Hals

(about 1580–1666)

Frans Hals was brilliantly adept at portraiture. Developing a technique using slashing brushstrokes, he captured the momentary smile and the twinkle of an eye with unerring accuracy. Although his painterly brushstrokes remain visible and his paintings appear to have been done in minutes, Hals spent much time on them to get just the right instantaneous quality. This loose feeling is completely different from the tight and exact features in the portraits of Leonardo, Holbein or Dürer.

Hals enjoyed painting the common people, especially his good friends. In *Yonker Ramp and His Sweetheart* (fig.11–29), Hals shows his friend, whom he painted often, in a happy scene at the local tavern in Haarlem. Hoisting his glass in a toast, the man is obviously enjoying his evening. His girlfriend cuddles as close as the broadbrimmed hat will allow, as if trying to get into the picture. The dashing brushstrokes add to the feeling of spontaneity and vibrant action. It is obvious that Hals enjoyed making this painting.

Although he sold many paintings and enjoyed excellent success as a portrait painter, Hals died penniless in a poorhouse. His career almost parallels the artistic development of his country. He flourished when Holland was growing and expanding her trade. However, in the second half of the seventeenth century, French painting became more in demand in Holland. Hals and many of his contemporary artist friends could find little work. After his death, agents were not able to sell his work at all, yet today there is a Frans Hals Museum in Haarlem that honors him and his vigorous painting.

Sidelight

Tulips from Amsterdam

Many people think of tulips when they think of Holland. Indeed, bulbs, not only tulip bulbs, have been a specialty of Holland since the sixteenth century. Imagine a single tulip bulb selling for $1500. This was the case during a tulip mania that rocked Europe from 1634–37. One bulb, a *Semper Augustus*, sold for $2000 plus a coach and four. Rich nobles in many lands courted bankruptcy in their eagerness to gamble on the Amsterdam tulip *bourse* (stock market) and many of them were ruined. Everyone was investing in tulips, even the poor, and sometimes life savings were lost in one season. In fact, things got so out of hand that the Netherlands government finally had to stop the madness by decree in 1637.

Rachel Ruysch, *Flower Still Life*, detail.

How did the tulip first come to Holland? Austria's ambassador to Turkey brought the first bulbs to Europe in 1554. The word *tulipa* was derived from the Turkish word for turban and is plainly descriptive. Another reason that Holland became the bulb capital of the world has to do with Holland's canal system. The canals make it possible to maintain a constant water level two and a half feet below the planted bulbs, regardless of whether droughts or floods occur.

The tulip is still in high demand and some two thousand varieties are grown in Holland today on twenty thousand acres of soil.

11–29 Describe this occasion and the relationship of these two people. Frans Hals, *Yonker Ramp and His Sweetheart,* not dated. Oil on canvas, 41 1/4" x 31" (105 x 79 cm). The Metropolitan Museum of Art, New York, bequest of Benjamin Altman, 1913.

Jan Vermeer

(1632–1675)

Even in his own day, Jan Vermeer of Delft was not well known, and after his death his name practically disappeared. In the eighteenth century, Sir Joshua Reynolds, a painter from England, saw a Vermeer painting in Holland and proclaimed it one of the greatest he had seen. Only during and after the nineteenth century was his work fully appreciated. Today he is considered one of the finest Dutch painters. All that is known of him is found in the few luminous, tranquil paintings that exist. He worked in a slow and painstaking way. Until now, only thirty-eight paintings have been attributed to him. Three of these are outdoor works; the rest are portraits or interior views. But, what views they are. Carefully designed with figures and furniture, they feature light and realistic color.

Perhaps no artist until Vermeer's time perceived natural light and color with such awareness. It is thought that he used a ***camera obscura*** to achieve this absolute realism. This device, similar to a modern camera, was a box with a small opening on one side. The image seen through the opening was transferred to the back wall of the box, in reverse of the actual scene. With a mirror and lens attachment, the user could reverse the image and focus it. With such a device, Vermeer could observe that everything in an interior scene is not on the same plane or in equal focus. He also noticed that colors from one object or area are reflected in other parts of the room. Most Northern artists had painted each object in absolute focus and disregarded reflected colors as they painted each part precisely and individually. Look back at the work of van Eyck as an example.

Woman Holding a Balance (fig.11–30) illustrates many of Vermeer's characteristics. The design of the elements is carefully planned. Vermeer often used a map or painting to back up his figures and provide a colored shape on the wall. The foreground objects—here, a large rumpled cloth—are somewhat out of focus as the viewer's steady gaze centers on the woman.

The quiet interior is lit by a window on the left. A soft light illuminates the figure and touches other objects with varying intensity. Notice the quality of the light that brushes the wall and how carefully Vermeer has observed it. The light bouncing off the clothing of the pregnant woman illuminates the objects on the table and reflects off the glass in the frame at the left. Notice how the light from the translucent window bounces off the pearls on the table and creates soft shadows elsewhere. The grays are beautifully composed through a wide range of values. No other artist had used the tones of color with such subtle distinction, or been able to indicate the light source and depth of the objects in the painting. The chiaroscuro of the Italian Renaissance is fully realized in Vermeer's work.

This simple scene also functions on a symbolic level. Notice the painting on the wall. This scene of Christ on Judgment Day, weighing the souls of humanity, makes the weighing of pearls and gold in real life take on another meaning. The pearls represent earthly possessions that account for nothing in the end.

11–30 Two levels of meaning can be read into this work. Use the text to help you identify the composition, light and symbolism of this seemingly simple genre scene.
Jan Vermeer, *Woman Holding a Balance,* about 1664. Oil on canvas, 16 3/4" x 15" (42 x 38 cm). National Gallery of Art, Washington, DC, Widener Collection.

11–31 The artist's intent in this work is not known, but there are many interpretations of it. What do you think the artist intended?
Jan Vermeer, *Allegory of the Art of Painting*, about 1665–1672.
Oil on panel, 47 1/4" x 39 1/4" (120 x 100 cm).
Kunsthistorisches Museum, Gemaeldagalerie, Vienna.

But Vermeer's woman is pregnant, about to bring new life into the world. In relation to the painting, her condition is a celebration of life. Most of Vermeer's seemingly simple paintings can be viewed on two such levels.

This double significance also is true of Vermeer's later painting (fig.11–31) *Allegory of the Art of Painting* (also called *Allegory of Fame* and, at one time, *The Artist and His Studio*). The titles, none given by the artist, depend on one's interpretation of the symbolism, also not provided by the artist. It is now thought that the model represents Clio, the Muse of history, looking at a table full of objects that symbolize other Muses. The artist in a sixteenth-century costume cannot be Vermeer... or is he? The map of Holland on the wall, surrounded by pictures of twenty cities, could symbolize that Holland is the center of world art and that the painter is the greatest creator. Whatever the meanings, this is a fine painting, again organized beautifully. Light is the most important ingredient. An unseen window on the left illuminates the model and the deep space in the work. Another source highlights the drapery in the foreground. The artist is in focus, but the foreground, the model and her space are slightly out of focus. The colors that are closest to the light source are most intense. Even with all the complex elements Vermeer uses, the painting is still clear, cool and orderly.

Window in Time

The Art of Forgery

Can an art forger ever be good enough to fool even the greatest expert? In the case of the artist Hans van Meegeren, the answer is yes.

Van Meegeren was born in Holland in 1889 and had achieved some success as a painter by 1932, when he decided on a new course for his career. Van Meegeren thought himself exceptionally talented, and he was unhappy with the response of the art world to his work. He decided to take revenge on the art critics. He would forge works by old masters and see if the art experts could detect the forgeries.

He tried his hand at various Dutch masters, but eventually he decided on Jan Vermeer. Vermeer, a seventeenth-century artist, had left behind only about three dozen paintings. A discovery of a new Vermeer would bring fabulous riches. So van Meegeren set out to produce this "new" Vermeer.

First, he had to find a way to ensure that the painting he painted would look like it was three hundred years old. He knew that the paint and canvas would be subjected to thorough testing. To get an authentic canvas, he bought a painting by a minor artist of that period, then carefully scraped and rubbed all the paint off it. Next, he experimented with various paints and techniques until he was satisfied. For subject matter, he painted a religious theme because Vermeer as a young man had been interested in such themes. Not only would he paint in the style of Vermeer, he would paint a subject that Vermeer himself might have chosen.

The actual painting took van Meegeren about six months. When the painting was completed, he invented a way to dry the paint to the requisite hardness. Normally, it takes half a century for paint to dry so that there is no trace of oil.

After completing the painting, he devised a story to explain its existence. According to his story, a family that he knew wished to sell the painting and had appointed him their agent. Just as he had planned, the painting, *Christ at Emmaus,* was acclaimed a masterpiece. The painting passed all tests of authenticity. There were many bidders for the painting, but eventually van Meegeren sold it to the Boymans Museum in Rotterdam for $285,000.

Although van Meegeren originally planned to expose his forgery and ridicule the art experts, he reconsidered his scheme after realizing how much he could earn by selling his forgeries. He continued to produce forgeries and eventually painted a series of six "Vermeers." By 1945, he was a very wealthy man.

During World War II, one of the fake Vermeers, *Christ and the Adulteress,* was acquired by Hermann Goering, Hitler's deputy. When Allied investigators found it in his collection in 1945, the Dutch members of the commission were anxious to learn how a national treasure had fallen into the enemy's hands. Their investigation led them to van Meegeren, who was charged with collaboration. Van Meegeren was subjected to some hard questioning and eventually he blurted out the truth.

But, ironically, nobody believed him. To prove he was telling the truth, van Meegeren had to paint a "Vermeer" while the experts watched. In 1947, he was tried for forgery and found guilty. He died of a heart attack before he could serve his one-year sentence.

Hans van Meegeren

11–32 Looking into a mirror, Rembrandt painted this image of himself when he was about thirty years old.
Rembrandt van Rijn, *Self-Portrait,* about 1636. Oil on canvas, 25" x 20" (64 x 51 cm). The Norton Simon Museum, Pasadena.

11–33 For this group portrait, each person paid an equal amount to the artist. Some of those who ended up in the background were not happy.
Rembrandt van Rijn, *The Shooting Company of Captain Frans Banning Cocq (The Night Watch),* 1642. Oil on canvas, 11 1/2' x 14 1/4' (3.5 x 4.37 m). Rijksmuseum, Amsterdam.

Rembrandt van Rijn

(1606–1669)

Rembrandt van Rijn was the greatest of Dutch painters and one of the great geniuses of the art world. He was the son of a miller, whose business was located on the Rijn (Rhine) River in Holland. When Rembrandt moved from Leiden to Amsterdam in 1632, he was already a competent artist. His early portraits provided him with an excellent income. When he married and bought a large house, he was seemingly well off. After several years, his wife died; he managed his income so poorly that his wealth declined and commissions dropped off. His style of painting changed and became more personal and expressionistic, which further alienated him from the public. His son and his mistress took over his business affairs as he became bankrupt. Yet, through all this adversity, his work became stronger and more powerful. He left over 600 paintings, 300 etchings and over 2000 drawings for the world to enjoy.

Rembrandt, like many other Baroque artists, painted many self-portraits. One can actually note the progress and decline of Rembrandt's fortunes by analyzing his clothes and facial expressions in dozens of such works. Using a mirror to view himself, Rembrandt would often put on one of the costumes he loved to collect, so that he could create a special mood.

The *Self-Portrait* (fig.11–32) was done in the late 1630s when the artist was just over thirty years old. His painting style was already well established, and he shows himself as successful and well dressed. The light is carefully controlled to highlight the face and collar and to shade the rest of the figure. Rembrandt used a heavy white impasto in the brightest areas. He then applied glazes over them and in the deep shadows to obtain the golden tones he desired. These light-valued passages emerge from the dark brown shadows as a brilliant use of chiaroscuro. Notice how the highlights on beads, buttons and the band of the beret help direct attention to the face. The eyes, which are always important to Rembrandt in expressing the inner feeling of the sitter, hold one's attention. Here they look confidently at the viewer and hide nothing.

A popular type of painting in Holland at this time was the group portrait, usually consisting of a number of people posed in a row or some other formal arrangement. Rembrandt accepted a commission to paint *The Shooting Company of Captain Frans Banning Cocq* (fig.11–33) and revolutionized the concept of group portrait painting. The huge painting is 11 1/2 feet high with foreground figures about life-size. He accepted equal payment from each member of the company, who expected to receive equal treatment. Rembrandt wished to make a fine painting, not produce a stereotyped group portrait. He placed Captain Cocq (in black) in a

11–35 This print combines etching and drypoint to produce an incredible variety of lines and dark areas.
Rembrandt van Rijn, *St. Jerome in an Italian Landscape*, 1653. Etching and drypoint, 10" x 8 1/4" (26 x 21 cm). Los Angeles County Museum of Art.

central position and put his lieutenant at his side. He placed the rest of the men at random to simulate natural action, as if they were preparing for a parade. Some are in shadow and some in light. Some are almost completely hidden. A little girl (who looks amazingly like the artist's wife Saskia) runs among the men and receives an ample dose of Rembrandt's mysterious light. He produced a superb painting. But, naturally, some of the men were disappointed in their portrayal, especially the man who could only see his eyes and the top of his head.

The painting at one time was brighter in color. However, oxidation of the colors and layers of soot have turned all the values darker, so it is now often called *The Night Watch*. After World War II, it was cleaned to reveal much richer color and detail, but the name remained.

The painting originally was larger. When it was moved to a new location, someone cut three feet off the left side and about a foot off the right, so it could fit between two doors. The major alteration has drastically changed the composition and balance of the work.

However, it remains a powerful, dramatic and popular painting. The pulsating light bounces off several faces and provides a number of minor centers of interest. These areas lead the viewer to the two major figures in the foreground who seem to be stepping off the stage into the viewer's presence.

The Mill (fig.11–34) is Rembrandt's greatest landscape painting. He completed it about 1650 at the height of his fame. It is a melancholy work with a mood of extreme sadness and loneliness. Details are nonexistent because a powerful chiaroscuro eliminates them. Large shapes dominate, but there are things happening in subtle ways in the shadows. Rembrandt has used the mill as the focus of a dramatic visual statement. The painting greatly influenced later English artists, who considered it a masterwork. They admired it for the artist's handling of light, its dramatic mood and its simple, powerful arrangement of elements. Design, subject, mood, spirit and technique are completely integrated in a single statement.

Even in his etchings, of which he did hundreds, Rembrandt used his favorite chiaroscuro. In *St. Jerome*

11–34 How would you describe the mood of this painting?
Rembrandt van Rijn, *The Mill*, 1650. Oil on canvas, 35" x 42" (88 x 106 cm). National Gallery of Art, Washington DC, Widener Collection.

11–36 Although they are all in similar costume, each of the sitters is shown with a unique personality.
Rembrandt van Rijn, *The Syndics of the Cloth Guild,* 1662. Oil on canvas, 75 1/4" x 109 3/4" (191 x 279 cm). Rijksmuseum, Amsterdam.

in an Italian Landscape (fig.11–35), Rembrandt combines etching and drypoint to produce a print of rich value contrasts and excellent design. He has massed lines together to produce gray-valued passages from which St. Jerome emerges as a glistening white figure. The brightness is intensified by leaving lines broken and obliterated, suggesting a glare that eliminates detail. St. Jerome's lion stands in the shadow of the huge tree while a bridge, several tiny figures, and two marvelously drawn buildings make up the setting. But Rembrandt clearly leads the viewer's eyes back to the glowing figure of St. Jerome. During his bad years, when he lost his house and art collection to his creditors, Rembrandt produced and sold many editions of such etchings at small prices for income.

In Rembrandt's late years, his work increased in power and personal expression. Sometimes, he painted friends who posed as Biblical figures. But, at the urging of close friends, he accepted one last group portrait commission. He handled this commission beautifully. *The Syndics of the Cloth Guild* (fig.11–36) is portraiture at its best—six times. The five seated figures were the officers of a trade union in Amsterdam. The bare-headed man in the background was their favorite steward whom they included at no cost to him. All faces are treated with individuality. Rembrandt interprets the inner character of each, especially in the eyes. The life-size figures are posed in a casual way. The man on the right even fondles a tiny dog. Yet, all are dignified and at ease. The controlled light makes the book and the carpet on the table seem to glow with an internal light.

Each of the five men who paid for the work received equal treatment. None is hidden as in *The Night Watch.* Here, Rembrandt conformed to tradition and the desires of the group. Yet, he produced an exceptional painting. The eye level is kept very low because the painting was meant to hang over a large fireplace, above the viewer's eyes. The viewer is immediately drawn into the work. It is as if the noise of opening the door made the syndics stop and look up. Are they pleased or dismayed? Do all handle the intrusion in the same way? In a moment, they will look down and continue their meeting, but for now Rembrandt has frozen them in time and space in his ever-glowing light.

Lesson 11.3 Review

1 What factors led to art being sold as a commodity in Holland during the seventeenth century? What subjects did the Dutch artists begin to paint as a result of having to sell their art to the middle class?
2 Who was the most famous Dutch woman artist of the seventeenth century? What type of art did she paint that established her reputation?
3 How was Rubens able to paint so many huge paintings in only one lifetime?
4 Describe Rubens' brushwork, movement and color in the *Lion Hunt.*
5 How do you think van Dyck flattered Charles I of England?
6 What subject did van Ruisdael usually paint?
7 What was a *camera obscura*? How would it have helped Vermeer make his paintings realistic?
8 Describe the light in Vermeer's *Allegory of the Art of Painting.*
9 Describe one of Rembrandt's group portraits. Who paid for this painting? Who are the people in the portrait? How are group portraits usually produced today?
10 What elements contribute to a sad, lonely mood in Rembrandt's *The Mill*?

11.4 The Baroque in Spain

SPANISH BAROQUE CANNOT BE fully understood without some knowledge of what was happening artistically in Italy and the Netherlands. Because of Spain's close contacts with Italy and the Netherlands during the sixteenth century, Spanish painters were familiar with the main trends in European art. Developments in Venice were particularly influential.

The "Golden Age" of Spanish art began shortly after 1600, when the nation's power was already beginning to decline. It was during the Baroque period that Spanish artists really seemed to come into their own. There was activity in all the visual arts of Spain during the seventeenth century, but painting dominated.

Key Notes

- The Spanish Baroque is based on developments in Italy and the Netherlands.
- The 17th century is the "Golden Age" of Spanish painting.

11–38 Notice how Velazquez avoided the use of line in his work. Color and light are used to build forms.
Diego Velazquez, *Las Meninas (The Maids of Honor)*, detail.

Special Feature

Diego Rodriguez de Silva y Velazquez

(1599–1660)

One of Spain's great artists of the Baroque period was undoubtedly Velazquez. Velazquez, who trained in Seville, came to the attention of King Philip IV as a young man, and was appointed court painter in Madrid. For more than thirty years, he painted the family and court of King Philip IV. He worked on a few religious subjects and several landscapes, but his main concentration was on portraiture. Unlike many of his Baroque contemporaries, Velazquez was interested in what was real far more than what was not.

An extraordinary example of his mastery of optical realism is his recognized masterpiece *Las Meninas (The Maids of Honor)*. Velazquez combines the formality of a royal group portrait with the informality of a more casual genre scene in his studio (fig.11–37). The painter represents himself in his studio standing in front of a very large canvas. He may be painting this very picture or perhaps the portraits of the king and queen, reflected in the mirror on the far wall. In the foreground is the five-year-old princess (fig.11–38) with her two ladies-in-waiting, her favorite dwarfs and a large dog. One of the dwarfs is poking the sleepy dog with his foot. In the middle ground are two adult chaperones. In the background, a gentleman is framed in a brightly lit open doorway.

The artist's aim is to show the movement of light and the countless ways it can be reflected. Notice

the effect of light on form and color in the painting. The indirect light in the spacious studio contrasts with the direct light that strikes the figures in the foreground and bounces and reflects from a variety of materials. Like Vermeer, Velazquez was fascinated by the quality of light and the way it interacts with the eye to create the visible world. Spots, patches of color, and light are used to define the forms. Line was seldom used by Velazquez in his work. For this reason, the closer you get to one of his canvases, the less solid are the forms.

11–37 Velazquez has been an important influence on many modern artists.
Diego Velazquez, *Las Meninas* (*The Maids of Honor*), 1656. Oil on canvas, 124 3/4" x 107 3/4" (317 x 274 cm). Prado Museum, Madrid.

Bartolomé Estaban Murillo

(1617–1682)

The last great painter of Spain's Golden Age was Bartolomé Estaban Murillo of Seville. Although he was influenced by Zurbarán and Velazquez, he developed his own warm, coloristic style. He painted relaxed and sentimentalized scenes of street urchins and flower girls in addition to religious subjects, such as the *Immaculate Conception* (fig.11–40). He painted this subject about fifteen times. The emotional quality of this painting is similar to the Flemish and Italian Baroque styles. The Virgin has a sweetness and prettiness that is especially engaging. The charm and immediacy of his style made Murillo very popular.

11–40 Murillo became famous for painting this subject. He did many versions of it during his career.
Bartolomé Murillo, *Immaculate Conception*, c.1666–1670. Oil on canvas, 6'9" x 4' 8" (2.06 x 1.42 m). Prado Museum, Madrid.

World Cultural Timeline

1687
Lima, Peru destroyed by earthquake

1691
Juana Ines de la Cruz writes *Reply to Sister Philotea* advocating expanded rights for women, Mexico

1696
Coffee growing introduced into Java from India

1700
Bantu Kingdom of Buganda develops, East Africa

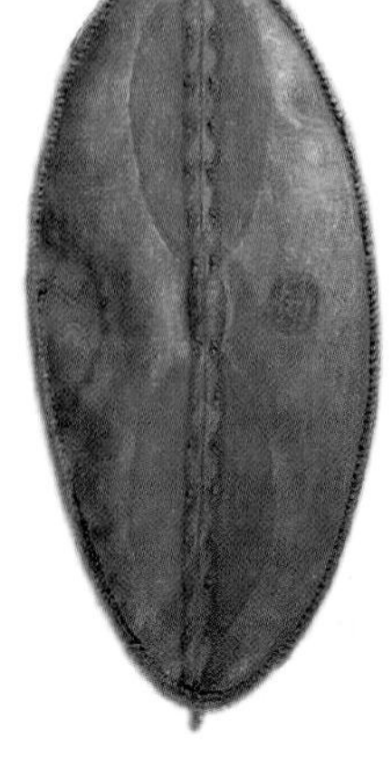

Francisco de Zurbarán

(1598–1664)

Working in Seville, Francisco de Zurbarán developed a style reminiscent of Caravaggio and La Tour. He often placed single figures against a solid, dark background, then lit them from a single source. This produced dramatic cross lighting and emphasized the simple, basic forms. *St. Francis in Meditation* (fig.11–39) is a powerful statement with Caravaggio-like tenebrism. From the black background emerges the simple sculptural form of the saint, kneeling in prayer. The strong diagonal movement is balanced by the landscape background, the skull, the book and gesturing hand, and the white paper in the foreground on which Zurbarán signed his name. All of these elements are used to stop the rushing diagonal movement and to contain it in the painting. Like Caravaggio, he also produced several still life paintings with the same dramatic light treatment. *Still Life with Lemons, Oranges and a Rose* (fig.2–57) is a beautifully designed still life by Zurbarán.

11–39 Compare this dramatically lit subject with La Tour's *Magdalen with the Smoking Flame.*
Francisco de Zurbarán, *St. Francis in Meditation*, 1639. Oil on canvas, 75 1/4" x 54 1/4" (191 x 138 cm). The National Gallery, London.

Lesson 11.4 Review

1 When did the Golden Age of Spanish art begin?
2 Describe the scene in Velazquez's *Las Meninas*. Who are the main characters and who is reflected in the mirror?
3 Name three Spanish Baroque painters and a painting by each.
4 Against what type of background did Zurbarán usually set his figures? Describe the lighting that he usually used in his portraits.
5 Which religious subject did Murillo paint many times?

11.5 The Early Eighteenth Century

THE EIGHTEENTH CENTURY was a time of great changes in every phase of European society. Industrialism was beginning, and established society was being challenged by ideas such as the rights and the dignity of the common people. Revolutions in America and France heralded the birth of modern democracy. However, during the first half of the century, the members of the European aristocracy still held much economic and social power. They continued to commission works of art that reflected their wealth and social position.

Artists and their art reflected the confusion and complexity of the times, but no artistic giants emerged to equal the Baroque standard-bearers: Caravaggio, Bernini, Rubens and Rembrandt. Instead, musical giants such as Bach, Handel, Vivaldi, Haydn and Mozart were the creative geniuses. The only new element to emerge in the visual arts was the Rococo style, which centered in France. An extension of the Baroque period, the Rococo substituted gaiety, charm and wit for Baroque grandeur. However, Classicism and Realism were not dead. It would only be a matter of time before they would appear again to dominate the art of the latter half of the century. Italy, England and America were not enticed by Rococo lavishness. These countries preferred a more dignified and serious extension of the Baroque.

Key Notes

- The eighteenth century is an age of change in Europe.
- A new style, the Rococo, emerges and is centered in France. The Baroque continues in some countries.

Vocabulary
fête galante
view painting
limners

11–42 **This detail shows the magnificent jewel-like colors Watteau created with his brush and palette.**
Antoine Watteau, *The Gamut of Love*, detail.

Special Feature

Antoine Watteau

(1684–1721)

The painter above all others whom we associate with the French Rococo was Antoine Watteau. He was actually born in Flanders shortly after it was annexed by Louis XIV. Influenced by the colorism of his countryman, Rubens, Watteau created shimmering surfaces that sparkle with life and gaiety and capture the essence of the ***fête galante*** (elegant entertainment). His work in general shows scenes of elegant society or comedic actors in parklike settings.

His technique involved underpainting the canvas with a pearly color that combined white, pale blue and rose. When this dried, he would rapidly brush in the trees and background with thin washes of color. Then, he would add the important figures in impastos of jewel-like colors, again featuring rose, pale blue, pink, yellow and white hues. Glazes would then be added over these to create a warm, atmospheric effect through which the earlier colors gleamed with sparkling richness. His technique faithfully captures the sheen of wrinkled satin and silk, favorite materials of the French aristocracy.

In *The Gamut of Love* (fig.11–41), Watteau possibly sets before us a small theatrical piece of the successive stages of love: courtship, marriage and children. He has set on

11–41 This painting is symmetrically balanced. There also are strong diagonal movements from one corner of the canvas to the other.
Antoine Watteau, *The Gamut of Love*, 1717. Oil on canvas, 20" x 23 1/4" (51 x 59 cm). The National Gallery, London.

canvas the glittering and fanciful lives of his Parisian patrons. The delicately lit scene and the shimmering surfaces are typical of Watteau's skillful handling of his subject matter and of his painting technique. Poetic and playful courtship is the main theme as a costumed gentleman of the comedic theater strums a few bars for his lady love (fig.11–42). To the right and in the distance, the viewer sees the same couple walking off together into the forest (marriage) and then again with several children (family). This is only one of several interpretations of the painting. What else do you think it could represent?

Watteau also is considered one of the world's great draughtsmen. He continually drew from life and left behind many figurative sketches.

11–43 How has the artist incorporated a sense of movement in these figures?
Antoine Watteau, *Six Figures*. Chalk, three colors, 6" x 12" (15 x 30 cm). The Louvre, Paris.

Six Figures (fig.11–43) is a study of male and female half- and quarter-length figures. Notice how the heads, topped with hats, all convey a sense of quiet, but strong, movement. Though these are only sketches, the forms of the figures are well defined.

When composing his paintings Watteau often chose figures and poses from his pages of life studies to include on the canvas. The vitality and spontaneity of the sketches are captured again in paint and embody the spirit of the French Rococo.

Francois Boucher

(1703–1770)

Most of the artists who painted the delicate and pretty decorations popular with the French nobility are forgotten, but Francois Boucher is well represented in the world's museums. Boucher's friends compared his colors to "rose petals floating in milk." His pink-fleshed nudes were in great demand. Many of his paintings dealt with mythological figures such as Venus, Diana and countless nymphs and Muses. But, he cared little about mythology and used these subjects to express his basic purpose—the painting of beautiful women. One of his largest works is *Pastoral Scene* (fig.11–44). It was probably painted for Louis XV or Madame de Pompadour, mistress to the King and patron of Boucher. It typifies the nobility's fascination with rural life in an ideal form. Instead of doing hard and dirty work, the shepherds and shepherdesses are shown in intimate conversation. The setting is romantic and idealized. The fountains and a mill house surrounded by feathery trees and backed by swirling clouds are perfectly pretty. The gorgeously costumed people are just as ideal. The pink skins and tiny delicate hands and feet are typical of the French Rococo paintings of figures. Several years after the painting was finished, it was reproduced in the form of a tapestry.

Jean-Baptiste-Simeon Chardin

(1699–1779)

While Watteau and Boucher were glorifying the earthly pleasures of the French aristocracy, Jean-Baptiste-Simeon Chardin drew on his lower middle-class background for painting subjects. Chardin used objects found in every kitchen and instilled a quiet dignity in them. His still lifes of common cooking utensils and kitchen objects were simple and strong in composition (fig.11–45). The triangular composition used so often by previous artists was used by Chardin to achieve a unified and powerful effect.

Chardin also painted servants and household workers in monumental form, giving them simple dignity and stature. How powerful Chardin's simple forms are as they are placed against a neutral and solid background. His genre subjects were the exact opposite of the typical Rococo paintings of flamboyance and delicate grace. They symbolize the power in the common people who will shortly take con-

11–44 How accurate is this view of eighteenth-century French rural life? Francois Boucher, *Pastoral Scene*, 1748. Oil on canvas, 116 1/4" x 133" (295 x 338 cm). The J. Paul Getty Museum, Malibu.

11–45 This arrangement of common objects in a pyramidal composition gives them substance and importance.
Jean-Baptiste-Simeon Chardin, *Still Life with Plums*, 1758. Oil on canvas, 16" x 19 3/4" (41 x 50 cm). The Frick Collection, New York.

trol of the government from the pleasure-seeking aristocracy.

Chardin's figures were as powerful as his still lifes. He often used nurses, servants and children as subjects. *The Attentive Nurse* (fig.11–46) is genre painting at its best. Heavy kitchen furniture, a delightful still life of ordinary items, and a charcoal heater on the floor are used for props. And what important task is the nurse performing? She is cracking a soft-boiled egg just removed from the pan. To paint such a person performing such a routine task with love and care adds importance to it. Chardin was interested in getting the common people to realize their importance and worth to society. He abandoned the painting of silky textures for the coarse homespuns of the lower classes. Instead of delicate wrinkles, his materials drape easily into heavy folds. The solidness, heaviness and simplicity of his subjects contrast directly with the frailness, delicacy and swirling of his contemporaries and their Rococo delights.

11–46 Chardin painted very different subjects than his contemporaries. Compare this genre scene to Boucher's *Pastoral Scene*.
Jean-Baptiste-Simeon Chardin, *The Attentive Nurse*, 1738. Oil on canvas, 18" x 14 1/2" (46 x 37 cm). National Gallery of Art, Washington DC, Samuel H. Kress Collection.

11–47 What features of this ceiling reflect Tiepolo's Venetian background?
Giovanni Battista Tiepolo, Interior, *Residenz Palace,* 1751–1752. Fresco. Würzburg, Germany.

Giovanni Battista Tiepolo

(1696–1770)

In Italy, only Venice continued to produce artists who could rival those of France and keep Baroque splendor alive. The finest eighteenth-century painter in Venice was Giovanni Battista Tiepolo. He did not confine his work to Venice, but fulfilled commissions in northern Italy, Germany and Spain. Tiepolo's greatest achievements were his decorative ceiling frescoes. He was probably influenced by the Baroque ceiling painters of Rome. His ceiling frescoes covered enormous surfaces, but the feeling was light and airy, not heavy and dramatic. Figures float freely and lightly in vast expanses of sky.

Leaving Venice in 1750, Tiepolo took his two sons with him to Germany to work at the Residenz Palace of the Bishop of Würzburg. The hall ceiling in *Residenz Palace,* like other frescoes by Tiepolo, is a feast for the eyes rather than a vehicle for some profound message (fig.11–47). Swirling forms, joyous color and unbelievable perspectives create a painting that seems to dissolve the architecture and continue the view up to the sky. Saints, gods and heroes of various times prance through the heavens in one of the most sumptuous ceiling decorations ever painted.

Because of Germany's damp climate and harsh winters, the fresco technique could not be used year round. Tiepolo spent those cold months working on canvases with his oils. While in Würzburg, he

1707
Mt. Fuji erupts for the last time, Japan

1727
First Brazilian coffee cultivated

1751
Ben Franklin uses the Iroquois League as model for his Albany Plan of Union

World Cultural Timeline

1720
China conquers Tibet

1735
Antonio de Ulloa discovers platinum, South America

painted the huge *Adoration of the Magi* as an altarpiece (fig.2–64). His free and slashing brushstrokes are combined with vibrant colors and a mastery of drawing to produce a startling composition. Tiepolo has made this humble event into a spectacular production. Numerous figures are crowded into the vertical format. Fabrics of various materials, from the rich silks of the kings to the coarse homespuns of the shepherds, are skillfully rendered. The clothes billow and fall effortlessly. They reflect the strong light that holds the composition together. Shadow and light are handled with surety and ease. The high-keyed emphasis naturally is placed on Mary and the Christ Child. The strong light, contrasting darker values, quivering dark lines, and flecks of light scattered throughout characterize the sparkling and joyous work of Tiepolo.

Antonio Canaletto

(1697–1768)

A new style of painting called ***view painting*** emerged in Venice early in the eighteenth century. Giovanni Antonio Canal, called Canaletto, depicted city views with incredible accuracy. Specializing in views of Venice, he sold dozens of them to the wealthy travelers. The perspective of Canaletto is very precise in many of his works. He probably made use of a camera obscura to project the correct lines and angles. In addition to his views of Venice, he painted realistic views of many of the capitals of Europe. His accuracy and detail were so carefully painted that in Warsaw, for example, the central core of the city was rebuilt after Nazi bombings according to Canaletto's painting.

Works like *The Basin of San Marco on Ascension Day* (fig.11–48) are historically important because they provide an exact picture of places as they appeared in the eighteenth century. The Grand Canal is choked with various types of gondolas and boats in celebration of the religious feast of the Ascension. The great landmarks of Venetian architecture are accurately detailed. Note the Doge's Palace in front of St. Mark's Basilica and the library on the left with the huge campanile behind it. All the buildings seen here are still in use. The huge Doge's state barge is tied up at its mooring in front of the palace. A viewer tends to be overcome by the profusion of detail (fig.11–b). Yet Canaletto was very conscious of design elements. He placed the movable parts of the composition—the figures and boats—in just the right places to provide scale, visual movement, contrast and pattern.

11–48 Many of Canaletto's landscapes were bought as souvenirs by wealthy travelers from other parts of Europe.
Antonio Canaletto, *The Basin of San Marco on Ascension Day,* about 1740. Oil on canvas. The Royal Collection, St. James' Palace, London.

Sidelight

The Great Fire

The Great Fire of London, which took place in 1666, was so catastrophic that its story has become a part of history.

On September 2,1666, a fire started in Pudding Lane, in the house of the king's baker. From here, it quickly spread through the city's closely packed, wooden buildings. Everything burned in its wake.

Some efforts were made to contain the fire, but the tightly built-up area of old timber structures burned like dry tinder. The Great Fire raged from September 2 to September 5. It decimated four-fifths of the structures that had stood within the city walls. The riverside with its warehouses of wood and its flammable stocks suffered particularly severely. The old cathedral was a complete ruin.

Contemporary Print of the Great Fire of London in 1666.

The problem of rebuilding was tackled with great will. The right man in the right place at the right time was the architect Christopher Wren. To this day Wren's spires and domes help give London its characteristic look.

Christopher Wren

(1632–1723)

In seventeenth-century England, several architects began to make important contributions to the art scene. Christopher Wren, the great English architect of the late seventeenth century and early eighteenth century, left his mark on London by virtue of the forces of nature.

The disastrous London fire leveled great portions of the city in 1666. Wren was instrumental in designing many of the major buildings that replaced those that were destroyed. His most important structure is *St. Paul's Cathedral* (fig.11–49). St. Paul's Cathedral has a basically Gothic, longitudinal floor plan (Latin cross) with a very large choir. At the center of the exterior facade, two stories of paired Corinthian columns are topped with a decorated pediment, all of which stand forward like a French-styled pavilion. The corner towers are derived from Borromini's Church of Sant' Agnese and even have similar concave features. The beautiful dome is second in size to

11–49 This cathedral was constructed after the previous one was destroyed during the Great Fire of London in 1666.
Christopher Wren. West facade, *St. Paul's Cathedral,* 1675–1710. London.

11–50 Hogarth was arrested while making sketches for this painting. Why were the French unhappy with him?
William Hogarth, *O, The Roast Beef of Old England,* 1748. Oil on canvas, 31" x 37 1/2" (79 x 95 cm). Tate Gallery, London.

St. Peter's. The dome is vertical in feeling and stands on a high, columned drum over the crossing. The dome has been copied many times in Europe and the United States, as in the Capitol in Washington.

Although Wren drew on many sources for the design of St. Paul's, his finished work is a powerful Baroque statement. The interior is not as elaborate as Italian Baroque churches, but has a restrained and simple elegance more in keeping with Anglican Protestantism. Wren's use of circles, arches and framing to emphasize certain elements creates a Classic feeling.

William Hogarth

(1697–1764)

We have seen little of English painting to this point. We have observed painters from the continent, such as Holbein and van Dyck, move to England and serve as court painters. In the eighteenth century, however, painting in England comes into its own. The real founder of the British school of painting was William Hogarth. His satiric wit emerged in most of his work. He painted many portraits and argued long and loud that English painters were equal to those on the continent. However, his fame was established by several series of narrative paintings. These works, or "morality plays," came in sets of engravings for mass distribution to the common people. They dealt with such topics as problems in marriage, the ruinous life of an English rogue, the distressing life of a harlot, political corruption, and the results of alcohol abuse. In all of these series, he criticized society and the upper class's lack of morals. His work was naturally popular with the lower classes. His caustic wit knifed deeply into the heart of London society.

Hogarth's scathing satire can be felt in the painting *O, The Roast Beef of Old England* (fig.11–50), in which he attacks England's traditional enemy, France. The scene occurs before the gate of Calais in France—a gate built by the English. A huge side of beef is being delivered to an English eating house. The size seems so tremendous to the starving Frenchmen that they stumble about in disbelief and stare as if it was a mammoth gold nugget. As a barb to Catholic clergy, the Protestant Hogarth shows the priest as the only overfed person among his starving French countrymen. Near the left border, Hogarth is sketching the scene. Actually, he was arrested while sketching here and was imprisoned briefly as a spy. When he returned to England, he made this painting to get back at the French in his own way.

Sir Joshua Reynolds

(1723–1792)

Unlike Hogarth, who stayed at home in England, Sir Joshua Reynolds traveled in Europe. While living in Rome, he absorbed the influences of Renaissance and classical painting and architecture. He returned to England and, in 1768, helped to establish and become president of the Royal Academy of Arts, based on the example of the French school. Here, he lectured on his theories of art, which he based on his own intensive studies of European art.

He received a tremendous number of portrait commissions. He soon needed assistants to stretch the huge canvases and start the background work. Often his figures were placed in Classical settings to enhance their nobility, creating an artificial feeling. In the painting *Lady Sarah Bunbury Sacrificing to the Graces* (fig.11–51), the contemporary woman seems to be living in past times. The huge size of his portraits and the grand settings he devised would often flatter the subjects, making them seem more important than they actually were.

11–51 What classical influences do you find here?
Sir Joshua Reynolds, *Lady Sarah Bunbury Sacrificing to the Graces*, 1765. Oil on canvas, 93 3/4" x 59 3/4" (238 x 152 cm). The Art Institute of Chicago, W. W. Kimball Collection. 1922.

World Cultural Timeline

1750
Indonesian dyeing technique makes multicolored batik fabrics possible

1780
***The Bengal Gazette*, first newspaper in India, begins publication**

1782
Bangkok established as seat of Thai monarchy

1795
First theater for Bengali plays opens, Calcutta, India

Thomas Gainsborough

(1727–1788)

Although he would rather have painted landscapes, Thomas Gainsborough became one of England's finest portrait artists. He often would include large areas of open landscape as backgrounds for his subjects. His patrons were getting a bonus, almost two paintings in one.

Before the invention of photography, marriage portraits were often painted. The double portrait of young Squire William Hallett and his wife Elizabeth, called *The Morning Walk* (fig.11–52), is probably Gainsborough's finest. Obviously influenced by the outdoor portraits of van Dyck, Gainsborough's figures walk with their dog through a park. Feathery trees seem to move ever so slightly in the breeze. Carefully controlling the light and dark values, the artist skillfully places the light faces against dark foliage and balances them with splashes of light in other areas. Gainsborough's loose brushstrokes masterfully catch the glint of light on rustling fabrics. Great care is taken to paint the faces accurately, but the rest of the surface shimmers with flashing brushstrokes. Gainsborough's tendency to elongate the figures slightly always made his subjects seem regal and elegant. His success can be counted in over one thousand portraits that he painted.

After his reputation as a portrait artist was established, Gainsborough reserved some time for his favorite landscape painting. Only a few of the hundreds he did were sold; the others he stored away or gave to friends. He was living in London and relied on his memory for many of the scenes such as *Wooded Landscape with Peasant Resting* (fig.11–53). In his studio, he would often arrange miniature landscapes of broccoli stalks, moss, rocks and other materials to simulate nature and would paint from them. To establish scale or set the center of interest, he often included figures like farmers and farm children. Even though they were not accepted by contemporary London society, Gainsborough's landscapes greatly influenced later generations of English painters who made landscape painting the dominant subject matter.

11–53
Gainsborough advanced the idea that nature should not just be a backdrop for human activity, but could be a subject itself.
Thomas Gainsborough, *Wooded Landscape with Peasant Resting,* 1750. Oil on canvas, 24 4/5" x 30 3/5" (63 x 78 cm). Tate Gallery, London.

11–52
Gainsborough's love of landscape painting is apparent in this double portrait.
Thomas Gainsborough, *The Morning Walk,* 1785. Oil on canvas, 91 3/4" x 70 1/2" (233 x 179 cm). National Gallery, London.

John Singleton Copley

(1738–1815)

Americans during the eighteenth century were struggling to establish their cities and farmsteads in a land that was new and challenging. They had neither the time for the frivolity of the French Rococo nor sufficient wealth to support artists of the stature of Gainsborough or Reynolds. Several fine American artists, however, did emerge and some made an impact both here and in Europe.

The early works of John Singleton Copley, such as his portrait of *Paul Revere* (fig.11–54), were competent and often forceful. While Copley lacked formal training, he had considerable natural talent. He developed his own style after carefully studying the paintings of the European artists who were working in America. Intuitively aware of color, light and form, he produced excellent portraits that penetrated the personalities of his sitters.

The portrait of Paul Revere shows the famous silversmith and patriot in a moment of concentration. He holds one of his pitchers in his left hand. With his engraving tools handy, he seems to be wondering what type of design to work into the metal. A strong light is used to model the figure, which is placed before a solid, dark background. The work is a serious study of the man. The composition is strong; the edges are hard; and the figure is solid. All these qualities were different from those found in English and French painting of the same time. Copley went to Europe in 1775 to study with Reynolds and other European artists. Although his technical skills increased, his later work lost this fresh American approach. It became softer and more English in character.

11–54 The artist did not have formal training when he painted this portrait, but he studied the works of others intently. He later went to Europe and studied with Reynolds.

John Singleton Copley, *Paul Revere*, 1768–1770. Oil on canvas, 35" x 28 1/4" (89 x 72 cm). Museum of Fine Arts, Boston, gift of Joseph W., William B., and Edward H. R. Revere.

Benjamin West

(1738–1820)

Born in the Commonwealth of Pennsylvania, Benjamin West left America in 1759, lived and painted in Rome for three years, and finally settled in London. He never returned to his native land. He became an outstanding portrait and historical painter in England. His style and work really belong in the study of English art. Adept at painting huge battle scenes, he was historical painter to King George III. He became president of the Royal Academy of Arts when Sir Joshua Reynolds died.

While in Europe, West came under the influence of Poussin. West used Poussin's grand conception of historical painting in *The Death of General Wolfe* (fig.11–55). Wolfe had died ten years earlier during the siege of Quebec in the French and Indian War. Sentiments in England about this event were strong. West decided to clothe his figures in contemporary dress and use realistic locations, but present them in an "heroic" way, like Poussin. The participants in previous historical paintings had been put in classical Roman togas and armor. West made them seem real and current. He endowed the scene with Baroque light and pathos. The work became a model for American historical paintings in the nineteenth century.

11–55 Expatriate artist, West, painted American historical events from his studio in London.
Benjamin West, *The Death of General Wolfe,* 1770. Oil on canvas, 60 3/5" x 83 4/5" (154 x 213 cm). National Gallery of Canada, Ottawa.

11–56 Stuart went to England to study with American Benjamin West.
Gilbert Stuart, *Mrs. Richard Yates,* 1793–1794. Oil on canvas, 30 1/4" x 24 3/4" (77 x 63 cm). National Gallery of Art, Washington DC, Andrew W. Mellon Collection.

Gilbert Stuart

(1755–1828)

The most inventive of early American painters was Gilbert Stuart. He arrived in London in 1775, a penniless young student. After studying with Benjamin West for a time, he exhibited a portrait of a man on ice skates that became the sensation of the Royal Academy show in 1782. With his name established, he accepted many portrait commissions at prices exceeded only by Reynolds and Gainsborough. Handling his income poorly, however, he returned to America in debt. He spent the rest of his life painting the heroes of the new Republic, including the first president, George Washington.

He did not like to flatter his subjects, but painted them as he saw them. Most Americans liked this approach. Patrons such as *Mrs. Richard Yates* (fig.11–56) wanted to see themselves as they really were. Stuart's brushstrokes were strong and sure. His use of color, especially in the skin tones, was innovative. He used almost every color to portray the living quality of flesh.

Sidelight

Early African American Crafts

In African societies, art served both religious and social purposes. When Africans were transplanted to America as slaves, they lost their society and, with it, their reason for creating their ritual masks and sculptures. A common avenue of creativity open to African-Americans was in the handcrafting of necessary articles.

African-Americans continued to use materials that had been available to them in Africa: wood, metal, natural fibers and clay. The African artist also assimilated European techniques and ideas. Many of the handwoven bedspreads, quilts and coverlets that have survived from the early years of our country, for example, were created by African-American women.

Silversmithing was a responsible trade in the North as well as the South. Craftsmanship offered the slave both a way of earning freedom and a means of self-support afterward. Charleston and New Orleans were particularly famous centers for wrought-ironwork, which featured elaborate patterns of grapes and other fruits and flowers. Much of this work was done by African-Americans.

Joshua Johnson

(c. 1770–1825)

Little is known about Joshua Johnson, the first African-American artist to gain prominence as an artist in America. A self-taught artist, Johnson lived most of his life in Baltimore, where he became a recognized portrait painter of wealthy members of slave-holding families. However, two of his portraits of African-American men have survived. *Portrait of a Man* (fig.11–57) is typical of the style of portraits painted in the United States at this time. The man is shown in three-quarter view with his eyes looking directly at the viewer. The pose is somewhat stiff, and the portrait reveals little of the sitter's personality. The portrait is neatly rendered, and has a flat quality that was typical of the work of ***limners***. Early American limners were artists who, during the cold winter months, painted single or group portraits without the faces. When spring arrived, they would find patrons who wanted their faces filled in. Johnson paid great attention to details like lace and buttons in his works. He usually posed his subjects in front of a background of drapery or an idealized landscape framed by a window.

11–57 Johnson is believed to have migrated to the United States from the West Indies. He probably was a self-taught artist.
Joshua Johnson, *Portrait of a Man,* about 1805. Oil on canvas, 28" x 22" (71 x 56 cm). Bowdoin College Museum of Art, Brunswick, Maine. Hamlin Fund.

Lesson 11.5 Review

1 How does Boucher's *Pastoral Scene* demonstrate characteristics typical of Rococo art?
2 Compare Chardin's concept of a peasant woman in *The Attentive Nurse* with Boucher's shepherdess in the *Pastoral Scene.*
3 What painting subject was Canaletto's specialty?
4 How is the painting style of John Singleton Copley in *Paul Revere* different from Thomas Gainsborough's in *The Morning Walk*?
5 Which hero of the American Revolution did Gilbert Stuart paint many times?
6 Who was the first African-American to gain prominence in America as an artist?

Primary Source

William Hogarth

Artists rarely admit that they paint to earn money, but William Hogarth, son of a poor schoolmaster, was not too proud to say that he looked for subjects that would earn money to care for his family. He decided to paint moral scenes because that subject had been overlooked by other painters and would appeal to citizens who were critical of the richer classes. Hogarth made prints of his paintings both to point out the vices and foolishness of London society and to support himself financially.

Here, he tells us why he rejected one type of subject matter in favor of another:

Why I Gave Up Conversation Pieces

I then married [1729], and commenced to be a painter of small conversation pieces, from twelve to fifteen inches high. This having novelty, succeeded for a few years. But though it gave somewhat more scope to the fancy [than engraving], was still but a less kind of drudgery; and as I could not bring myself to act like some of my brethren, and make it a sort of manufactory, to be carried on by the help of background and drapery painters; it was not sufficiently profitable to pay the expenses my family required.

I therefore turned my thoughts to a still more novel mode, viz., painting and engraving modern moral subjects, a field not broken up in any country and any age.

Chapter Review

Review

1 What part of Saint Peter's Cathedral in Rome did Michelangelo, Bernini and Maderno each design?

2 How does the style of La Tour's *Magdalen with the Smoking Flame* remind you of Caravaggio's paintings?

3 How did the Rococo style paintings and architecture differ from the Baroque?

4 In what way is Benjamin West's *The Death of General Wolfe* similar to Poussin's paintings?

5 How are the exteriors of the Benedictine Abbey at Melk and the facade of Sant' Agnese alike?

Interpretation

1 What details or family interactions in Jan Steen's *The Feast of St. Nicholas* might be present in a family home today?

2 Select one of Frans Hals' or van Ruisdael's paintings. Describe the mood of this painting. Name a song or piece of music that seems to go with this picture.

3 Write a short story about what is happening in Watteau's *The Gamut of Love.* What song are they singing or what is their conversation?

4 Compare the statues of *David* by Bernini, Michelangelo (fig.9–26) and Donatello (fig.9–7). At what point in the story did each artist show his David? Describe the motion, emotion, size and pose of each sculpture.

Other Tools for Learning

Maps

1 Why would southern Germany align itself more with Italy and Northern Germany with Scandinavia and the Netherlands?

2 Why do you think eighteenth-century American painters did not study in Europe and were often self-taught?

Timelines

1 Select an event from the non-European timelines which influenced Western art. Explain your choice.

2 Select an event in the timelines that has probably made the world a better place in which to live. Explain why you chose this event.

Electronic Research

CD-ROM drive: *Microsoft Art Gallery*
Videodisk player: *National Gallery of Art Videodisk*

1 Rubens painted other lions besides the ones in the *Lion Hunt* in this chapter. Find another lion painted by Rubens. Compare it to the ones in the 1616 *Lion Hunt.*

2 Describe Caravaggio's *Supper at Emmaus.* How has Caravaggio made this scene dramatic? Research this painting further in the *Microsoft Art Gallery's* Composition and Perspective Guided Tour. Describe the foreshortening in this painting.

Activity 1

Learning from Rembrandt

Materials
pencils
drawing paper
etching supplies

Take a look.
- Fig.11–32, Rembrandt van Rijn, *Self-Portrait*, about 1636. Dutch. Oil on panel.
- Fig.11–35, Rembrandt van Rijn, *Saint Jerome in an Italian Landscape*, 1651. Dutch. Etching and drypoint.
- Fig.11–33, Rembrandt van Rijn, *The Shooting Company of Captain Frans Banning Cocq (The Night Watch)*, 1642. Oil on canvas.
- Fig.11–36, Rembrandt van Rijn, *The Syndics of the Cloth Guild*, 1662. Oil on canvas.

Think about it. Examine the work of Rembrandt van Rijn. Known as the greatest of the Dutch painters, he was very prolific, creating thousands of pieces of art including paintings, drawings and prints. He created hundreds of self-portraits, many of them etchings and drypoints.
- What characteristics are common to both his prints and his paintings?
- Can you see a variation in his style as he develops?
- Notice his use of *chiaroscuro*, which gives his work a feeling of drama through strong lights and darks.

Do it. Create an etching or drypoint portrait or self-portrait.
- Begin by doing drawings of yourself or your selected subject in various types of lighting. Work in charcoal or a soft lead pencil to get a good range of light and dark values.
- Once you have selected the best drawing, use it as the basis for an intaglio print on a metal or plexiglass plate. You will want to do some research into the methods and materials needed by working with your art teacher or visiting a local library.

Check it. Are the shadows in your drawing consistent with the implied light source?

Helpful Hint: When making an intaglio print, the image will be backwards from the way it looks on your plate. To preview how your print will look, hold the plate up to a mirror.

Activity 2

Light and Contrast

Materials
pencils
drawing paper for sketching
construction paper: white, yellow, gray, black
glue

Take a look.
- Fig.11–6, Artemisia Gentileschi, *Judith and Maidservant with the Head of Holofernes*, about 1625. Oil on canvas.

Think about it. Artemisia Gentileschi, a follower of Caravaggio, was one of the first women painters in Western art to make an important contribution to the art of her time. Her painting, *Judith and Maidservant with the Head of Holofernes*, does not dramatize the beheading itself. Rather, she chose to emphasize the forms of Judith and her servant through the use of deep shadows and strong highlights. This technique of exaggerating the strong contrasts of light and dark is called *tenebroso*.

Do it.
- Ask a friend to pose in a casual manner. Perhaps he/she can be relaxing, reading the newspaper or reading a book. (Using a large overstuffed chair would add to the mood.)
- Using only the reading lamp or a spotlight for the source of light, sketch the model on 12" x 18" paper. Focus on the *shapes* of the lights and darks, not just the contours of the model.
- Using black, gray, white and yellow construction paper, create a cut-paper composition using your sketch as the base.

white = lightest values
yellow and/or gray paper = middle values.
black = darkest values

Check it. Evaluate your own work based on the following:
- effective use of lights and darks
- technical skill in cutting and gluing
- effort

Helpful Hint: Refer to the *tenebroso* effect in Gentileschi's painting as you develop your own composition.

Additional Activities

- Research Saskia, Rembrandt's beloved wife, and the influence she had on his life and his painting career.
- Study the three versions of *David* by Donatello (fig.9–7), Michelangelo (fig.9–26), and Bernini (fig.11–3). Compare and contrast the sculptures, considering each artist's style and the emphasis they placed on pose, movement, expression and emotion.
- Discuss in class the lives of artists: Rembrandt, Caravaggio and Artemisia Gentileschi to better explain why these Baroque painters worked in the style they did.

Erik E. Linder

Age 17
Perkiomen Valley High School
Graterford, Pennsylvania
Favorite kinds of art: anything I've never done before
Favorite artists: anyone who can draw well

Activity 2, Light and Contrast

My class assignment was to make a cut-paper likeness of a live, volunteer model, using only black, gray, yellow and white colored paper. To create the dramatic tones of light and dark, the classroom's lighting was altered using a small portable light.

While I was studying the model and setting, I became a little nervous and wondered whether I would be able to complete the project without first going insane, but after a few minutes of sketching I began to understand the concept and everything started to pull together. After I did my sketch I realized that even though I had simplified many of the shadows, some shapes were still too complicated to successfully cut out and paste down. Now that I had something to work with I toned down the shapes once more and began to cut them out.

On the subject of influences, I would have to say that I really haven't studied any modern or classical artists very heavily, and don't feel influenced by any one person or style. On the other hand, I do draw a lot of my creative energy from personal experiences, certain types of music, and what I see other students doing.

The thing that I like most about the artistic process would have to be the problem solving that is involved. With every project I've ever done I've always run into new problems that require new and creative solutions.

ERIK E. LINDER

Megan, 1994. Construction paper, 12" x 18" (30.5 x 45.7 cm).

Megan Schook, seated under a bright light for contrast, poses as model for the class activity.

12 Three Opposing Views

In This Chapter...

During the late eighteenth and early nineteenth centuries, tremendous shifts took place in the Western world. Life's tempo was speeding up and, during this relatively short period, three very different styles dominated. These were Neoclassicism, Romanticism and Realism.

Neoclassicism had its base in France, which was ruled by the dictator Napoleon Bonaparte. Napoleon's taste in art was severe. He did not like the exuberance and frivolity of the Baroque and Rococo styles and favored the more Classical approach of ancient Greece and Rome. Napoleon's word on everything was law, and art was no exception. The reaction to Baroque and Rococo was not only confined to France, however, and a general desire for something less fussy was felt all over the Continent and as far away as America.

Neoclassicism had such a firm hold on the Western world that it seemed unlikely that anything would budge it. However, some artists, irritated with the restrictions of Classicism, started working in a more emotionally evocative way. This approach, called Romanticism, had a huge impact on all the arts.

Neoclassicism looked toward the past while Romanticism dwelt in the realm of the imagination. Artists who resisted these two movements focused on direct experience, painting what they saw, whether it was pleasant or unpleasant. These artists were the Realists. The nineteenth century also saw the development of photography as an art form.

12–a The concept of a skeletal iron tower caused an uproar when it was first proposed. Nothing like it had ever been built. Despite the protests, it was constructed at the extravagant cost of one million dollars!
Alexandre-Gustave Eiffel. *Eiffel Tower,* 1889. Paris.

12–b This painter, like all the Realist artists, studied and sketched the common, everyday world.
Rosa Bonheur, *The Horse Fair,* detail (fig.12–31).

Beauty, like truth, is relative to the time when one lives and to the individual who can grasp it.
Gustave Courbet

The development of different styles often centered in France, but artists all over Europe were exploring new forms of expression.

12–c A renewed interest in classical ideas and design gave rise to a Neoclassical style in painting, sculpture and architecture. Jacques-Louis David, *Oath of the Horatii,* detail (fig.12–1).

1752
Ben Franklin invents the lightning conductor

1789
US Constitution adopted

1834
Ingres appointed director of French Academy, Rome

1848
Marx and Engels, *Communist Manifesto*

1851–1863
Walter, US Capitol

1865
Abraham Lincoln assassinated

1877
Edison invents phonograph

Three Opposing Views

1770–1784
Jefferson, Monticello

1784–1785
David, *Oath of the Horatii*

1804
Napoleon crowned emperor

1814
Goya, *Third of May, 1808*

1840–1865
Barry and Pugin, Westminster Palace

1851
Melville, *Moby Dick*

1876
Twain, *Tom Sawyer*

1876
Alexander Graham Bell invents telephone

1883
Homer paints solitude of ocean, Maine

12.1 Neoclassicism

FROM 1775 TO 1815, the Western world was in turmoil. The American Colonies gained independence from England. France was under the dictatorship of Napoleon Bonaparte. Napoleon's fierce attacks on Europe eliminated many Baroque monarchies, dissolved the Holy Roman Empire, and almost conquered Russia and England.

Comparing himself to the Roman emperors, Napoleon preferred art that drew heavily on the Classical Roman styles. Neoclassicism became not only the dominant artistic style, but also a way of life. Furniture, dress, painting, sculpture, architecture and the crafts all relied on ancient Classicism for their motifs and forms. No-nonsense Neoclassicism was partly a reaction to the lighthearted nature of Rococo. Neoclassicism became the backbone of the academies and was the official force in art well into the nineteenth century.

In 1738, Pompeii and Herculaneum were uncovered. The discovery of artifacts from these cities, together with Napoleon's fascination with Roman history and styles, led to increased interest in Classical themes, history and design. Greek, Roman and Renaissance art was studied intensely. During the Neoclassical period, this studied aspect of art was given as much weight as individual expression.

Key Notes

- Neoclassicism arises in part from a rejection of the Rococo, but particularly from a renewed interest in Classical ideas and design.
- Napoleon Bonaparte uses the Neoclassical style to reinforce his image as all-powerful ruler.
- Neoclassicism becomes firmly embedded in the academies.

Vocabulary
allegorical

Special Feature

Jacques-Louis David

(1748–1825)

Jacques-Louis David was a man perfectly in step with the spirit of the times. He began painting under Louis XVI, but, after the king was guillotined, he embraced the Neoclassical style. He became the most important artist under Napoleon. Most other Rococo artists were unable to make this change to Neoclassicism.

David began by painting in the decorative style of Boucher, who was a distant relative. After traveling to Rome in 1775, his ideas changed. In Rome, he studied and drew the Classic sculptures with infinite detail, establishing a style that was clean, crisp and hard-edged. He would not tolerate any evidence of brushstrokes in his own work or that of his students. When he returned to Paris his ***allegorical***

12–1 David was one of the few artists to successfully make the transition from the French monarchy to the republic to the empire.
Jacques-Louis David, *Oath of the Horatii*, 1784–1785. Oil on canvas, 11' x 14' (325 x 426 cm). The Louvre, Paris.

paintings began to suggest the ideals of Classic republicanism. He used Greek and Roman subject matter to show parallels with contemporary French politics. His were among the first history paintings.

The Oath of Horatii (fig.12–1) is a huge painting that uses a Roman story to arouse passion for French unity. It is a story of conflict between love and patriotism. The Horatii brothers are chosen to defend Rome in battle against neighboring Alba. But, one of the Horatii sisters is engaged to an Alban, and a brother is married to an Alban. Yet, the three brothers take an oath on the raised swords held by their father to defend Rome. They appear rigid, manly and heroic and symbolize patriotism and loyalty. The grieving sisters on the far right embody love and sorrow. As in the Classic tradition, patriotism is the clear winner over love. This painting is a perfect example of the Neoclassical style. Every figure is painted with absolute clarity. Edges are hard and crisp. The austere figures against the plain, neutral background seem almost frozen in action on a dramatically lit stage.

After Napoleon assumed power, David painted some mammoth canvases glorifying the little emperor. *Napoleon in His Study* (fig.12–2) shows the leader alone. The details are meant to reveal aspects of his personality to the French people. The burnt-down candle and the clock set at 4:13 a.m. suggest that the emperor had been working all night in the service of the country. The figure is as solid and immobile as a statue. The lighting is sharply focused. Together Napoleon and David helped define the Neoclassic style.

12–2 This pose became a model for official portraits in Western art and many men's portraits show them in this stance although without Napolean's trademark hand-in-his-vest.

Jacques-Louis David, *Napoleon in His Study*, 1812. Oil on canvas, 80 1/4" x 49 1/4" (204 x 125 cm). National Gallery of Art, Washington, D.C., Samuel H. Kress Collection.

12–3 Note the difference between the hands of the figure in this study and the finished painting. How have they changed? Can you spot any other adjustments that the artist has made?
Jean-Auguste-Dominique Ingres, *Louis Bertin*, 1832. Pencil drawing, 46" x 37 1/2" (116.7 x 95.3 cm). The Louvre, Paris.

12–4 Ingres is noted for his crisp polished portraits which have an almost photographic quality.
Jean-Auguste-Dominique Ingres, *Louis Bertin*, 1832. Oil on canvas, 46" x 37 1/2" (117 x 95 cm). The Louvre, Paris.

Jean-Auguste-Dominique Ingres

(1780–1867)

David's best pupil and primary spokesperson for Neoclassicism and its rigid rules was Jean-Auguste-Dominique Ingres. A child prodigy, Ingres entered art school at eleven and began studying with David at seventeen. Following David's instruction, he never allowed his brushwork to show. However, his style was much softer and more sensitive to texture and flesh than David's style. Ingres considered himself a historical painter, yet most of his income came from his nude paintings and cool, Classic portraits. He was a marvelous draftsman. He drew his portraits first before he painted them. An excellent example of this process can be seen in Ingres' pencil drawing and finished painting of *Louis Bertin* (figs.12–3, 12–4).

In the Classic tradition, Ingres would draw figures in the nude to make absolutely sure all the proportions were correct. Then, he would add the clothing in intricate detail. *Scipio and His Son with the Envoys of Antiochus* (fig.12–5) is a pencil drawing of small size, but immense ability. Some places are shaded to appear almost finished, while other areas are barely outlined. The poses, attitudes and drawing technique are handled masterfully.

Ingres' cool, undramatic Classicism can be seen in the huge *Apotheosis of Homer* (fig.12–6).

1800
Canton, China, is most populous city in world

World Cultural Timeline

1811
Ruler Muhammad Ali modernizes Egypt by improving irrigation and establishing industry

1815
Mt. Tambora on Sumbawa in Indonesia erupts. Volcanic dust in the atmosphere lowers temperatures worldwide

1818
Katsushika Hokusai, Japanese landscape painter, at height of his creativity

In front of an Ionic temple, the blind poet is crowned by the Muse of epic poetry. The *Iliad* is symbolized by the sword held by one of the female figures below him. The *Odyssey* is symbolized by the rudder held by the other female figure. Ingres included figures he considered Classical geniuses from various periods, such as Phidias, Pindar, Aeschylus and Apelles; Raphael, Leonardo, Fra Angelico and Poussin; Shakespeare and Molière. Ingres' use of famous figures in a Classic setting is similar to Raphael's work in *The School of Athens* (fig.9–30).

12–5 Ingres' drawings have a very sculptural effect, but retain their life and do not become stiff.
Jean-Auguste-Dominique Ingres, *Scipio and His Son with Envoys of Antiochus*, 1827. Pencil on paper, 9 1/2" x 14 1/2" (24 x 37 cm). Norton Simon Art Foundation, Pasadena, California.

12–6 An apotheosis is the glorification of an individual or an ideal.
Jean-Auguste-Dominique Ingres, *Apotheosis of Homer*, 1827. Oil on canvas, 12 1/2' x 16 4/5' (386 x 514 cm). The Louvre, Paris.

Elizabeth Vigée-Lebrun

(1755–1842)

One of the most successful of all women painters, Elizabeth Vigée-Lebrun studied first with her father. She became an excellent portrait painter before she was twenty. At twenty-four, she was called to Versailles to paint Marie Antoinette. She stayed to become Painter to the Queen, and was elected to the Academy in 1783. When the Revolution broke out, she went to Italy, Vienna, Prague, Dresden, Moscow and London before returning to Paris. Her career was a series of international triumphs; she received commissions everywhere she went. She was constantly busy during her long life. Over eight hundred paintings have been identified as her work.

Her *Mme. de Stael as Corinn Playing a Lyre* (fig.12–7) was painted in 1789. It is typical of a period when she was using landscapes as backgrounds for her sitters. Vigée-Lebrun helped establish the simple, high-waisted dresses of the Empire style shown here, which replaced the elaborate gowns of the old monarchy. David was the instigator of this Classic style, but Vigée-Lebrun's portraits of prominent people wearing such dresses helped make the new style popular throughout Europe.

12–7 The artist was unusual for being both a highly successful woman artist and for successfully surviving the political turmoil of the French Revolution. Elizabeth Vigée-Lebrun, *Mme. de Stael as Corinn Playing a Lyre*, 1789. Musée d'Art et d'Histoire, Geneva.

Vigée-Lebrun's coloring was softer than that of David and Ingres and her poses more inventive. She was not in sympathy with Napoleon and his Empire. Nor did she follow David and Ingres and their dogmatic approaches to painting. However, her beautifully drawn and painted portraits were typical of artists at the turn of the century. She was more successful than most in working through the turmoil of the times.

Sculpture

Jean Antoine Houdon

(1741–1828)

Sculpture had been so important in ancient Greece and Rome that it would seem logical for sculpture to be as important to the Neoclassic movement, but such was not the case. The best of several sculptors working during the turmoil in France was Jean Antoine Houdon. He started his work during the reign of Louis XIV. He managed to adjust to the changing political philosophies and remain unscathed.

Although Napoleon was not an admirer of Houdon, his work was greatly honored by the philosophers Voltaire and Rousseau. In fact, Houdon made excellent likenesses of each. His work is anatomically accurate. At the same time, he was able to capture the personality of the sitter. In France, he sculpted Benjamin Franklin and Thomas Jefferson. Through them, he was invited to the new country, the United States. In 1785, he carved the first president, George Washington, in marble.

Houdon's brilliant realism can be seen in his bust of Benjamin Franklin (fig.12–8). Although the drapery has Classic overtones, the sparkle of Franklin's wit is superbly expressed in both eyes and mouth. Technically perfect, Houdon's work is charged with life and is not as somber as many Roman sculptures. His sculpture seems about ready to spring to life.

12–8 Houdon did an extensive series of sculptures of America's important early statesmen.

Jean Antoine Houdon, *Bust of Benjamin Franklin*, 1780. Marble, 24" x 24" (61 x 61 cm). The Nelson-Atkins Museum of Art, Kansas City, Missouri. Purchase: Nelson Trust, 38–8.

12–9 Jefferson's home became the basic example of the American Georgian style.
Thomas Jefferson. *Monticello*, 1770–1784. Charlottesville, Virginia.

12–10 Each level of the building repeats some characteristics of the prior level, but with alterations that create a distinctive look.
Thomas U. Walter. *United States Capitol*, 1851–1863. Washington, DC.

Architecture

Baroque and Rococo architecture was exuberant. Neoclassic architects replaced the overworked surfaces of Rococo palaces and churches with Classic simplicity and balance. Twisting and curling lines were replaced by straight ones. Frills were eliminated almost completely. Not only Napoleon's France, but all the Continent and even America were ready for a change from Baroque flamboyance to Neoclassic refinement and order.

Besides being one of our early presidents and the author of the Declaration of Independence, Thomas Jefferson (1743–1826) was also an architect. He designed his own home at *Monticello* (fig.12–9) and the first buildings at the University of Virginia at Charlottesville. He was influenced by the Italian architect, Palladio, and the Roman structures he had seen in France. Monticello is a two-story structure built along Palladian lines with a flat dome over the central space. Its portico and white-painted Doric columns and trim, which stand out from the red brick surface, became characteristic of an American style called Georgian. The noble simplicity of such architecture appealed to America's growing middle classes.

Neoclassicism and its influence are evident in the *United States Capitol* (fig.12–10). The Capitol was begun as a Georgian structure and enlarged by Benjamin Latrobe (1764–1820). It was completed as a massive, super-scale structure when Thomas Walter added the cast-iron dome in 1863. Considering the many architects who worked on it, the building has a remarkable feeling of unity. The dome is raised on a high, columned drum. It has an internal diameter of slightly over 98 feet and rises 220 feet above the floor.

In Berlin, the columned *Brandenburg Gate* (fig.12–11), topped with a four-horse Roman chariot, was built by Karl Langhans (1781–1869) along the lines of some Greek gateways. The gate later stood between East and West Berlin as a symbol of a divided city, from the end of World War II until 1989, when the Berlin Wall was torn down. The Brandenburg Gate is now a symbol of unification as it straddles one of the major avenues that runs through Berlin.

Paris has many fine examples of Neoclassic architecture, but none is better than the *Church of the Madeleine* (fig.12–12), designed by Pierre Vignon (1763–1828). The colossal structure is designed as a Roman Corinthian temple. It took over thirty-five years to complete. The exterior follows Classic ideas completely, but the interior was altered to allow light and windows.

1819
Simon Bolívar defeats Spanish and enters Bogotá, Colombia

World Cultural Timeline

1820
The Hindu College founded, Calcutta, India

1828
***The Cherokee Phoenix*, a weekly newspaper, begins its seven-year run**

ᎰᏩᏒᎩ ᎡᏣᎯ, ᏕᎤᏂᏒᎩ ᎤᏙᏝᏜ Ꮎ-
ᏇᏥ ᎾᏍᎩ ᎤᏪᏒᎯᏩ ᎤᏕᏅᏲᎯ, ᎩᏎ
ᎾᏍᎩ ᏱᎪᎯᏩᏔᏍᏕ ᎤᏂᎱᎯᏍᏗᏱ ᏂᎨ-

1850
The Navajo learn silversmithing from the Mexicans

12–11 Can you name at least three Classical architectural elements that are used on this monument?
Karl Langhans. *Brandenburg Gate,* 1788–1791. Berlin.

12–12 French Neoclassical architecture took a monumental turn. Some of the buildings designed were so huge they could not be built with existing technology!
Pierre Vignon. *Church of the Madeleine,* 1806–1843. Paris.

12–13 What Classical precedents do you know for this ceremonial arch?
J. F. Chalgrin. *Arc de Triomphe de l'Etoile,* 1806–1836. Paris.

The *Arc de Triomphe de l'Etoile* (Arch of Triumph of the Star) in Paris was one of Napoleon's numerous monuments (fig.12–13). Like Imperial Rome's triumphal arches, this ponderous structure by J. F. Chalgrin (1739–1811) towers over surrounding structures. Nearly a dozen boulevards lead into the huge circular area containing the arch. The structure contains the eternal flame that honors France's unknown soldiers, as well as a list of the campaigns and victories of Napoleon.

From Leningrad to Madrid, from Copenhagen to Athens, builders used the columns, arches, domes, pediments, simplicity, order and balance of Classic architecture to create impressive Neoclassic cityscapes.

Lesson 12.1 Review

1 What was the name of the official art style when Napoleon was in power?

2 Name two reasons artists became so interested in creating art that was reminiscent of ancient Rome during the late eighteenth and nineteenth centuries.

3 Who became the leading French artist during the French Revolution?

4 How was Ingres' painting style different from his teacher David's style.

5 Name the woman artist who was Marie Antoinette's principal portrait painter.

6 Name some of the buildings designed by Thomas Jefferson.

7 What style of art influenced the design of the United States Capitol?

8 List three early leaders of the United States that Houdon sculpted.

12.2 Romanticism

THE NEOCLASSIC STYLE, begun as a protest against the Rococo style of the eighteenth-century aristocracy, was firmly entrenched in Europe. Neoclassic traditions were taught at the Paris and London academies. It did not look as if anything could budge Neoclassicism. However, some artists had had quite enough of working within the Classic restrictions of form and proportion. Their rebellious feelings erupted into a full-blown movement called Romanticism.

The name came from a widespread revival of interest in medieval stories like *King Arthur and the Knights of the Round Table* and *The Search for the Holy Grail.* These stories about great adventures and heroism were called romances and were written in French. Instead of focusing on ancient Greece and Rome as the source of all good design, the Romanticists explored the Middle Ages. They were also fascinated by Africa and the Orient. While Neoclassic painters had revered Raphael, Poussin and the ancient Romans, Romanticists admired Rubens and Rembrandt. It was individualism versus the system; emotionalism versus intellectualism; and rebellion against the academies.

Color, emotion, content and passion became key ideas in Romantic painting. They replaced the Neoclassic stress on line, intellect, form and judgment. The new emotionalism generated excitement in the arts throughout Europe. All artistic endeavor was affected by it. Romantic poets such as Wordsworth and Keats explored a new freedom in writing. In music, Romanticism was championed by Beethoven and Schubert, and Italian tragic-opera flourished.

Key Notes

- Romanticism is born as a reaction against the restrictions of Neoclassicism.
- The new style emphasizes emotion and individualism.
- Romanticism ignites excitement throughout Europe.

Vocabulary

nonrepresentational

Special Feature

Francisco Goya

(1746–1828)

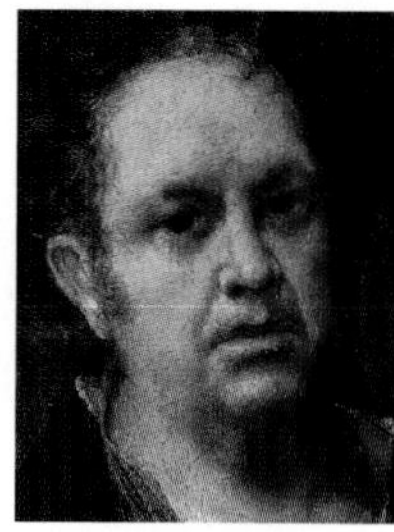

No painter worked in a style farther from Neoclassical ideals than Francisco Goya of Spain. He visited Italy, but remained unimpressed by the Classic and Renaissance masterpieces. He had no time for the restrictions that David imposed on artists. In 1786, Goya was appointed painter to King Charles IV of Spain and became responsible for the official portraits of the royal family. After a severe illness in 1792, he became totally deaf. Goya bought a home outside Madrid, known as La Quinta del Sordo ("The House of the Deaf Man"). He appears to have been an isolated, pessimistic man, but he is without doubt the genius of Romantic painting and printmaking.

12–15 A clue to the meaning of this image lies in the name Los Caprichos, Spanish for caprices, eccentricities, whims or freakishness.
Francisco Goya, *The Sleep of Reason Produces Monsters,* from *Los Caprichos* (Plate 43), c. 1794–1799. Etching and aquatint, 5" x 8" (12.7 x 20.3 cm). The Hispanic Society of America, New York.

12–14 How did Goya want you to respond to this painting?
Francisco Goya, *Third of May, 1808*, 1814. Oil on canvas, 8' 9" x 13 1/4" (2.7 x 4.1 m). Prado Museum, Madrid.

One of Goya's most powerful and emotional works is the monumental *Third of May, 1808* (fig.12–14). It shows the slaughtering of Spanish rebels by French soldiers. Done in 1814, just after the French left the country, Goya's dramatic work could be termed a "social protest" painting. Goya painted the incredible inhumanity of human beings toward each other. It is not at all allegorical, like the Neoclassic paintings. Instead, it is an emotional portrayal of the event as the artist remembered it. Goya captured its ferocity and gave it a startling sense of immediacy. The insistence on depicting real emotions, even those from our darker side, is a particularly Romantic characteristic. Compare the brushstrokes, edges of color, emotional feeling and sense of action with David's *The Oath of the Horatii.* The differences between Neoclassic and Romantic painting are readily apparent.

Goya could not always follow his internal dictates and paint what he wanted. As the royal portraitist, he had to paint the royal family. But, here, the Romantic impulse is also strongly evident. Although he paints them in very royal poses, he somehow manages to give us a good idea of what they were really like.

Goya also made several series of brilliant etchings on a variety of subjects such as war, folklore, the follies of society (fig.12–15) and bullfights. His range of expression was unmatched in his time. His powerful statements are awesome to behold.

12–16 Géricault was influenced by Michelangelo. Where do you see that influence in this painting?
Theodore Géricault, *Raft of the "Medusa"*, 1818–1819. Oil on canvas, 16' 1" x 23' 6" (4.9 x 7.2 m). The Louvre, Paris.

Theodore Géricault

(1791–1824)

The lifestyle of Theodore Géricault was pure Romanticism. He had little concern for his personal safety, loved to travel, always stood up for the less fortunate, and dedicated himself to an emotional life. He was successful in getting a painting exhibited in the Salon of the Academy when only twenty-one, a high honor. He lived and worked in Rome for several years. There he was influenced only by Michelangelo's muscular and dynamic figures and not his Classical surroundings.

When he returned to Paris, he painted his only large canvas, *Raft of the "Medusa"* (fig.12–16). It clearly shows Michelangelo's influence and Géricault's Romantic spirit. A government ship, the *Medusa,* was wrecked on the way from France to Senegal in 1816. The captain abandoned ship first, along with his crew. The 149 passengers were crowded onto a raft to be towed by the lifeboat. The raft was eventually cut adrift. After suffering extreme starvation and thirst, only fifteen survivors made it to the African coast. It was a national scandal that shook the entire country.

Géricault, always interested in humanity's struggle with nature, jumped into the subject with great enthusiasm. He interviewed the survivors, read the newspaper accounts, and made sketches and paintings of corpses and bodies at the morgue. He even had himself lashed to the mast of a small ship in a storm so he could feel the movement of the swells and the wind. Everything was done to make the painting realistic and authentic, but Géricault's Romantic treatment took him beyond realism. *Raft of the Medusa* is built around two pyramids, one of dead, dying and tragic figures and the other of hope and struggle. (Later painters would reject such an obvious attempt at organization as being too Classical and orderly.) Atop the second pyramid, several men wave clothing, trying to signal a distant ship so small and far away it can barely be seen. But, the gunboat *Argos* finally came to the rescue. Storm clouds and high seas add to the feeling of futility and constant hope in France's first great Romantic painting. Today, Géricault is known as the founder of Romanticism in France.

1851
Australian gold rush

World Cultural Timeline

1853
First railway and telegraph lines in India

1854
International trade brings Japanese prints to worldwide audience

1857
First universities founded in India

Eugene Delacroix

(1798–1863)

After Géricault's untimely death, leadership of the Romantic movement passed on to Eugene Delacroix. He and Ingres were exact contemporaries and the leaders in their separate movements. He produced thousands of paintings, sketches and watercolors.

Liberty Leading the People (fig.12–17) was inspired by the 1830 insurrection in Paris. The allegorical figure of Liberty, holding a tricolored French flag, is leading the revolutionaries over the street barricades in Paris. While he glorifies the cause of the victorious revolt, he also shows the horror and violence of fighting. In keeping with his theatrical feelings, he placed two dead figures in the foreground and blended allegory with reality. The huge painting was later purchased by the French government.

Two years after showing the painting, Delacroix made a trip to Spain and Morocco that changed his life. He experienced a way of life so different that he used the subject matter from this trip for many years. He was the first major painter in modern times to visit the Islamic world. He returned to Paris with a trunk of sketches and a head full of exotic memories. He painted a series of tiger and lion hunts from sketches made of caged animals. They swirl with incredible activity and lush color.

Compare *The Lion Hunt* (fig.12–18) with Rubens' painting of a similar subject to see why the Romantic artists admired his work. Raging animals, frightened horses and furious hunters are knotted together in an interwoven composition. The eye travels in and out as it follows the curves and counter-curves of men and beasts. Only the triangular format lends solidity to the composition and keeps the wild design under control. The slashing brushstrokes, intense colors and value contrasts are fitting for such Romantic subject matter. They point the way directly into the twentieth century.

Delacroix used photography to make studies of some subjects. He became expert at using the newly invented cameras. He was also the subject for many photographs taken by his friends, who were among the world's first photographers.

12–18 How has the artist organized his composition?
Eugene Delacroix, *The Lion Hunt*, 1861. Oil on canvas, 30" x 38 1/2" (76 x 98 cm). The Art Institute of Chicago, Potter Palmer Collection, 1922.

12–17 Delacroix has placed his self-portrait within the crowd. He is the businessman with the gun.
Eugene Delacroix, *Liberty Leading the People*, 1830. Oil on canvas, about 8' 6" x 10' 8" (259 x 324 cm). The Louvre, Paris.

John Constable

(1776–1837)

John Constable was among the first painters to paint outdoors. He made dozens of quick studies on paper. He tried to match, as closely as possible, oil colors with those of nature. He loved the English landscape and never left England to find subject matter. He once said: "... water escaping from mill dams, willows, old rotten planks, slimy posts and brickwork—I love such things." In *The Hay Wain* (fig.12–19), he shows his skill in painting huge trees, flat fields, the stream and clouds. A red hay wagon is pulled through the Stour River near a typical English farmhouse.

Constable was the first artist to paint water with such sparkling clarity and depth of shadow. He achieved this effect by adding touches of white to the canvas. While critics liked his painting generally, they often made fun of his added whites and even called them "Constable's snow." This criticism, based on a lack of knowledge of what the artist was trying to do, was the beginning of a rift between artists and the public.

The Hay Wain was one of six huge paintings that Constable did of subjects close to his home. They were the first landscapes done in a size normally used for important historical subjects. His figures are small and belong to the environment.

In his later years, Constable abandoned his careful depiction of nature. He began to paint with a great vibrancy and force. *Stoke-by-Nayland* (fig.12–20) is a large studio painting with the immediacy and verve of an outdoor sketch. The colors are applied freely. The artist even mixed and spread some of them right on the canvas with his flexible palette knife. The loose and rapid strokes and the elimination of detail create a spontaneous effect. Since the critics could not understand the white flecks of light in *The Hay Wain*, imagine how they felt about the wildness of this painting. The visual elements are similar in these two works, but *Stoke-by-Nayland* shows the drastic change in Constable's technique.

12–20 Some of this painting was done with a palette knife and not a brush.
John Constable, *Stoke-by-Nayland*, 1836. Oil on canvas, 50 1/2" x 66 1/2" (126 x 169 cm). The Art Institute of Chicago, Mr. and Mrs. W. W. Kimball Collection. 1922.

12–19 An artist's style often changes over time. Compare this painting to *Stoke-by-Nayland*.
John Constable, *The Hay Wain*, 1821. Oil on canvas, 50 3/4" x 72 3/4" (129 x 185 cm). The National Gallery, London.

12–21 The artist spent much of his early career exploring the effects of natural light.
Joseph Mallord Turner, *Sun Rising Through Vapour: Fisherman Cleaning and Selling Fish,* 1807. Oil on canvas, 52 3/4" x 70 1/5" (134 x 179 cm). The National Gallery, London.

Joseph Mallord William Turner

(1775–1851)

While Constable developed two styles, Turner developed three or more. Working in the traditional English landscape style, Turner was accepted into the Royal Academy at only twenty-four, in 1799. His contemporary, Constable, was not admitted until 1829. Turner's earliest works were all in watercolor, a medium he used all his life. He produced about 19,000 watercolor paintings. He made sketching and watercolor painting trips all over Europe. The paintings were set against backdrops of brilliantly colored, high-keyed skies of mist, sunset and sunrise. *Sun Rising Through Vapour* (fig.12–21) clearly shows Turner's interest in the effects of light.

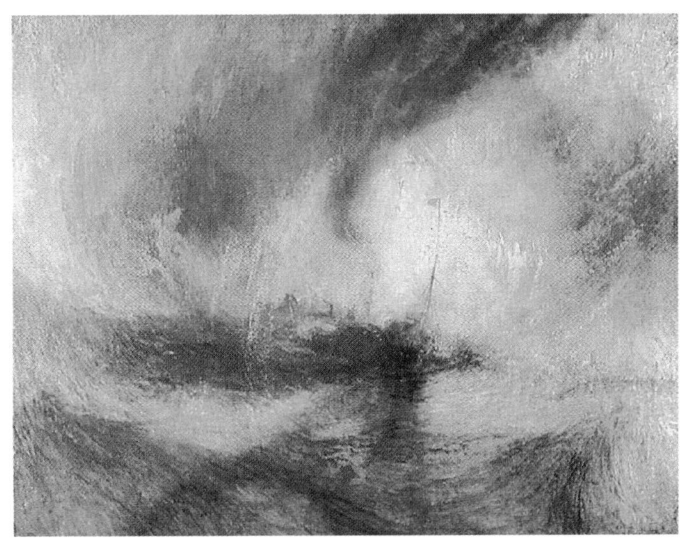

12–22 What are the subjects of this work?
Joseph Mallord William Turner, *Snow Storm: Steam-Boat off a Harbor's Mouth,* 1824. Oil on canvas, 36" x 48" (91 x 122 cm). Tate Gallery, London.

His later works are incredible compositions of swirling color and light. Turner enjoyed painting the pure movement of masses of color without representational meaning (***nonrepresentational***), although he usually had some subject in mind. Study *Snow Storm: Steam-Boat off a Harbor's Mouth* (fig.12–22) first without looking for a subject. Just enjoy the swirling fog, steam, color, water and movement. Violent action is achieved without portraying people or things. The colors and values swirl in a vortex that eventually centers on the mast of a ship. No one at that time knew anything of nonrepresentational painting, so Turner added the representation of a ship. However, the painting would be just as strong without it. Color and movement are the real subject. His work of this period anticipates the Impressionist movement. When Claude Monet spent time in London in 1870, the work of Turner had a profound impact on him and, through him, on the rest of the Impressionists.

Thomas Cole

(1801–1848)

In America, Thomas Cole was the leader of a group of painters in New York and New England called the Hudson River School. They painted a landscape that would soon vanish as the population expanded. Thomas Cole was born in England and came to America at seventeen. He returned to England to study painting and came back to America to paint. Many of his paintings depicted Classic ruins, but most, such as *View on the Catskill, Early Autumn* (fig.12–23), were painted in the studio from a series of sketches of the countryside. Like his English contemporaries, he added small figures (fig.12–24) that seem to enhance the grandeur and immensity of the landscape. To Cole, rustic beauty and ideal settings were the essence of America. His Romantic approach was adopted by his fellow artists. Other men in the group, led by an adventuresome spirit, soon left New England for the Rockies and even South America.

12–23 Cole and other Americans tried to portray both the uniqueness of the American wild landscape and the civilization of its settled land.
Thomas Cole, *View on the Catskill, Early Autumn,* 1837. Oil on canvas, 39" x 63" (99 x 160 cm). The Metropolitan Museum of Art, New York, gift in memory of Jonathan Sturges by his children, 1895.

12–24 Compare the use of figures in this painting with the figures Constable added to his landscapes. How are they similar?
Thomas Cole, *View on the Catskill, Early Autumn,* detail.

George Caleb Bingham

(1811–1879)

While Cole was content to work in his beautiful New England, George Caleb Bingham followed the American dream to the West. Even though he studied painting in Germany, he grew up by the Missouri River. Many of his paintings are based on events he saw happen there. The quiet moments and genial activity of pioneering, not the violence and hardship, are what set Bingham's brush in motion. Politicians asking for votes, Daniel Boone leading a band of pioneers, and the boat people of the rivers were his favorite subjects. In *Fur Traders Descending the Missouri* (fig.12–25), Bingham eliminates the dangers of this kind of life. He concentrates on the romance of drifting down a huge, quiet river in the early morning mist. The boat is loaded with a bale of furs for the market in St. Louis. The scene is idealized enough to make most viewers desire such work. A small black fox sits in the prow of the dugout canoe and visually balances the elegant composition. Bingham painted a Romanticist's view of the daily life of ordinary people who were part of the westward expansion. Bingham became a politician in later life and gave up most of his painting activity.

Other Americans worked with images of America in their own terms. John James Audubon (1788–1851), for instance, painted the animals and birds of America. His work was made into colored engravings that became very popular in English homes. America was beginning to develop its own painting tradition.

12–25 Compare this American genre scene to a European one such as Bruegel's *Return of the Hunters* (fig.10–13).
George Caleb Bingham, *Fur Traders Descending the Missouri,* 1845. Oil on canvas, 29 1/4" x 36 1/4" (74 x 92 cm). The Metropolitan Museum of Art, New York, Morris K. Jesup Fund, 1933.

12–26 Compare this home to Jefferson's Monticello (fig.12–9).
John Nash. *Royal Pavilion,* 1815–1818. Brighton, England.

Architecture

In architecture, England was the leader in Romanticism. English architects continued to worship the style of Palladio and to borrow ideas from his buildings. They borrowed from other times and cultures as well. No single architectural style developed. Instead, mood and individual taste were guiding principles in architecture.

One of the most fascinating structures built was the *Royal Pavilion* at Brighton (fig.12–26). It was designed by John Nash (1752–1835). Built on the south coast of England, it was to be the summer home for the prince regent, later King George IV. Using existing structures as a beginning, Nash added and enlarged them to produce an Oriental fantasy. He imitated Islamic domes and encased chimneys in minaret-like forms. Interior spaces are styled after Greek, Egyptian, Chinese and Gothic rooms. Still, the entire fun-filled structure has an overall unity even though it looks like it was transported to Brighton from India on some huge magic carpet.

After 1800, a revival of the Gothic style became very popular in England, basically because the English thought of it as *their* style. They wanted to be independent of Napoleon, Neoclassicism or anything recalling France. So when the *Houses of Parliament* were to be expanded, Gothic was the unanimous choice (fig.12–27). Sir Charles Barry (1785–1860) and A. Welby Pugin (1812–1852) were chosen as architects. The gigantic public building has the lacy feeling and perpendicular line found in Gothic cathedrals. Its Gothic feeling is so authentic that it easily blends with the nearby Westminster Abbey, a true Gothic structure.

In France, the major building activity took place in Paris. And what activity it was! Great portions of the city were rebuilt, most of it under the direction of Georges Eugene Baron Haussman (1809–1891). Along the boulevards radiating from the Arc de Triomphe, Haussman made all buildings similar in style and only six stories in height. This similarity, together with the planting of trees along the wide boulevards, gives Paris its familiar unity and striking beauty.

Several large structures stand above the six-story limit imposed by Haussman. Some were already existing, such as Notre Dame and the Church of the Madeleine, but others were new. The most striking of these new buildings was the *Opera* (fig.12–28). Designed by Charles Garnier (1825–1898), it was intended to be the central focus of the new Paris. The showy magnificence of the exterior was popular with the emerging industrial bourgeoisie. The interior is an incredible tribute to luxury and Baroque taste. The grand staircase cascades through a lobby space that is almost as large as the auditorium

12–27 What Gothic elements do you see here? Compare this building to the Town Hall of Louvain, Belgium.
Sir Charles Barry and A. Welby Pugin. *Houses of Parliament,* 1836–1860. London.

12–28 What architectural elements from earlier periods do you find here?
Charles Garnier. *Grand Staircase of the Opera,* 1861–1874. Interior view. Paris.

12–29 This is a predecessor to our shopping malls.
Giuseppe Mengoni. *Galleria Vittorio Emanuele,* 1861–1877. Milan.

itself. Colored marble columns, gigantic sculptures, elaborate light fixtures and decorative reliefs fill the space.

The Industrial Revolution made possible the use of cast iron in nineteenth-century architecture. Cast-iron frames held up the domes of the Royal Pavilion at Brighton. Since it could be formed in any required shape, it was used to make arches and spans that could leap across large spaces. However, cast iron was affected by intense heat, and many such buildings were later destroyed in fires. Among those remaining is the *Galleria Vittorio Emanuele,* a shopping arcade (fig.12–29). It was designed in Milan by Giuseppe Mengoni (1829–1877), built in England and reassembled in Milan. It is actually a glass-covered shopping street, an early relative of today's enclosed shopping malls. Four separate arcades fan out from a domed octagon. The dome tops a huge open space at the intersection.

A landmark familiar around the world is the *Eiffel Tower* (fig.12–a). Built by Alexandre-Gustave Eiffel (1832–1923) as the central feature of the Paris Exhibition of 1889, it towers 100 stories above the city. It rests on four pylons and four separate foundations. When it was completed, it was the tallest structure in the world. Still standing today, its elevators can hoist visitors to the very top to obtain a bird's-eye view of this great city.

Lesson 12.2 Review

1 How did the Romantic movement get its name?
2 Name two Romantic poets, two Romantic artists and two Romantic musicians.
3 Explain what is happening in Goya's *Third of May, 1808.* How is Napoleon connected to this story?
4 Describe some of the measures that Géricault took to ensure that his painting *Raft of the Medusa* would be authentic.
5 Which artist is now considered to be the founder of French Romanticism?
6 What new invention did Delacroix use to make studies for his paintings?
7 Describe the sky in Constable's *The Hay Wain.*
8 What was Turner most interested in painting in *Snow Storm: Steam-Boat off a Harbor's Mouth*?
9 Name the group of painters that was led by Thomas Cole.
10 During the early nineteenth century in England, why did a revival of the Gothic style become popular rather than Neoclassicism, as in Paris?
11 Which French architect is most responsible for designing the contemporary city of Paris?

12.3 Realism

IN THE FIRST HALF of the nineteenth century, while Neoclassicists tried to recall the glories of Rome and Romanticists imagined great things, another style of painting was developing. The painters in this group were called Realists. They believed that only what they could see and experience themselves was worthy subject matter. Subjects had to be treated in as natural and realistic a way as possible. Gustave Courbet said that he could not paint angels because he had never seen any. Not surprisingly, the Realists admired the work of the seventeenth-century Dutch and Flemish. Painters such as Vermeer were rediscovered and brought to light.

However, the public had some strong views themselves on the work of the Realists. And they were not favorable. They did not understand the progressive Realist philosophy that glorified the working class. According to the critics, Realist painting lacked spirit and was, therefore, not art. They showed their disapproval by not accepting the Realists' work into the Academy. But, undaunted, the Realists organized a *Salon des Refuses*, or Exhibition of Refused Art. In 1863, they showed their work in a huge tent near the Academy.

Looking at the work today, we are neither shocked nor offended by the work. The Realists painted fact, not fiction. They painted what they saw: green foliage, blue sky, brown earth, common everyday scenes of people engaged in daily labor or conversation.

Key Notes

- Realism emerges as the third style of the early nineteenth century.
- The Realists emphasize the depiction of the common, everyday world.
- Realist paintings cause anger among critics. They are rejected by the academies.

Special Feature

Rosa Bonheur

(1822–1899)

The French painter Rosa Bonheur, an important Realist painter, was both independent and unconventional. In an age when girls' education was secondary to boys', she successfully persuaded her father to let her attend boarding school with her brothers.

She worked in sculpture as well as painting, but it was her paintings of animals that brought her fame. Animals were her favorite subject (fig.12–30). She studied them carefully, even going to slaughterhouses to get pieces she could dissect. She sketched endlessly at horse fairs and cattle markets. By wearing men's clothing, she was able to move about more freely without being harassed by attendants and spectators. She kept her hair short for the same reason. Her life was dedicated to painting, and she never married.

12–30 The artist visited England and the Scottish Highlands and studied the herds of sheep that roamed the area.
Rosa Bonheur, *Sheep by the Sea*, 1869. Oil on cradled panel, 12 3/4" x 18" (32 x 46 cm). The National Museum of Women in the Arts, gift of Wallace and Wilhelmina Holladay.

Rosa Bonheur became the first woman artist to receive the coveted cross of the French Legion of Honor in 1865.

The Horse Fair (fig.12–31) is the painting that won Rosa Bonheur international acclaim. Based on many sketches done outdoors, the painting is alive with movement and tension. The horses are seen during an exercise period as trainers move them around to relieve their nervousness. The modeling of the horses that dominate the canvas is superb, and they are seen from many angles. The horses are not racing thoroughbreds, but heavy work horses. A horse fair was a common event in France at the time. Bonheur painted this scene of an annual horse fair in Paris realistically, without including a storytelling quality.

Sky and trees in this painting are treated naturally, but are kept subdued. The visual movement is strongly horizontal from left to right. The break in grouping in front of the white horses stops the movement from running out of the frame. Some of the animals are not properly broken and rear up, while others walk sedately and allow themselves to be led. The lighting is very dramatic, as is the bright white of the central horses. Bonheur was interested in light and handled it beautifully. However, she never experimented with it as the Impressionists would in the years that followed.

The Horse Fair was shown in the Salon of 1853 and then exhibited in the major cities in England. It was even taken to Buckingham Palace at Queen Victoria's personal request so she could have a private viewing. Scenes of nature were particularly popular in England at this time. There was a general desire in England and the continent for realistic work like Rosa Bonheur's.

12–31 Although we seldom see them today, work horses like the gray dappled percheron team shown here were the power for farming before tractors were invented.
Rosa Bonheur, *The Horse Fair*, 1853. Oil on canvas, 8' x 16' 3" (2.5 x 5 m). The Metropolitan Museum of Art, New York, gift of Cornelius Vanderbilt, 1887.

12–32 Leaves that seem to flutter in the light are a hallmark of Corot's landscapes.
Jean-Baptiste-Camille Corot, *Seine and Old Bridge, Limay*, 1870. Oil on canvas, 16 1/4" x 26" (41 x 66 cm). Los Angeles County Museum of Art, Paul Rodman Mabury Collection.

12–33 Why is this called a realistic portrait?
Jean-Baptiste-Camille Corot, *Agostina*, 1866. Oil on canvas, 52 1/4" x 38 1/2" (133 x 98 cm). National Gallery of Art, Washington, DC, Chester Dale Collection.

Jean-Baptiste-Camille Corot

(1796–1875)

The fascination with painting real things in real light first appeared in the early work of Jean-Baptiste-Camille Corot of France. Corot was concerned with the clearness of the light and the harmony between humans and their environment. He painted this harmony in small sketches and larger works, often done on the spot. Notice the clarity of light and form in *View of Venice, The Piazzetta Seen from the Quai of the Esclavons*. Even the title is factual (fig.2–6). Corot painted what he saw—not the pageantry of the city nor a Romantic impression of it in a misty sunrise. He simplified the detail to show what he absorbed at first glance. Corot painted patches of color in flat strokes and used only a few high-keyed, closely related colors. His limited palette helps emphasize the unity of the scene. The huge, high-keyed sky intensifies the clear light and contrasting shadow. Corot includes figures, but they are only part of the Piazzetta. They do not tell a story or emphasize an emotion. Corot treats the entire canvas in a detached way, as if he were taking a snapshot to send home.

Midstage in his career, Corot moved near the forest of Fontainebleau, near the village of Barbizon. He began painting dreamy landscapes of trees, rivers and summery scenes in grayish tones. His vivid light was changed to a purplish-gray haze. His sure, blocky strokes were changed to wispy, soft touches—a complete transformation. These poetic paintings were very popular in America where they sold as fast as Corot could paint them. Done in his studio from memory or imagination, they brought him great financial reward, even though they were not his best work. *Seine and Old Bridge at Limay* (fig.12–32) is from this period. Corot has included some structures in this work, although most include just trees, water, sky and, perhaps, a few small figures.

1869
Suez Canal begun

1898
The Capital University, later Peking University, founded, China

World Cultural Timeline

1872
Japan's first railroad opens from Tokyo to Yokohama

1895
Korean independence follows the Sino-Japanese War

Later, toward the end of his career, Corot made another about-face. He returned to solid forms, but used the figure as his theme instead of the buildings and landscapes of Italy. Few artists in history have had the ability to handle the figure and landscape with equal ease. His figures have a solid feeling and are strongly three-dimensional. His use of light was both dramatic and real, indoors as well as out. *Agostina* (fig.12–33) is a realistic portrait—no flattery, drama, romanticizing or story-telling. Rather, a standing peasant girl stares off into space. Corot seems as detached from the model as the model is from her world at the moment.

Jean François Millet

(1814–1875)

Although born of a peasant family in Normandy, Jean François Millet settled with his wife and fourteen children in the town of Barbizon and worked there for twenty years. In his early career, he painted typical Classic subjects and models. Soon, his attachment to the soil emerged in his genre paintings of the peasants in France. He painted the common activities of sowing seed, harvesting, plowing and gleaning with complete understanding. He wished to present the farm workers as dignified people, much as Chardin had done with servants in Paris. His painting of *The Gleaners* (fig.12–34) is a powerful treatment of simple workers and their daily tasks. Note how the three solid forms stand out in front of the sun-drenched background. Millet has subordinated the main harvesting activity in the bright glare. The design is simple, powerful and fitting for the subject. The light is strong and the shadows are deep. There is absolute realism in color, form and simplicity. He does not glorify or unnecessarily embellish the peasant women. He simply shows their hard, back-breaking labor as they pick over the field for any good grain the harvesting crew has left. The simple dignity of Millet's work had a direct influence on Vincent van Gogh's paintings.

12–34 Gleaning was a regular part of the harvest until recent times. How would you characterize Millet's portrayal of these women?
Jean François Millet, *The Gleaners*, 1857. Oil on canvas, 32 1/2" x 43 1/2" (83 x 111 cm). Musée d'Orsay, Paris.

Honoré Daumier

(1808–1879)

The people of Paris knew Honoré Daumier as the greatest social caricaturist in their newspapers. In his four thousand lithographic drawings for the newspaper, he took pot shots at the Royalists, the Bonapartists, politicians of all types, judges and lawyers. He was briefly imprisoned for his biting satire, but he never tempered his brilliant caricatures.

After 1848, he began to paint. His realism featured artists, performers, musicians, circus workers, dancers, audiences and the common people in daily activities. He wanted to show the people of Paris how they looked to him. His painting technique was different from his lithographic drawings. However, some of the characteristics of his caricatures carried over into his paintings.

In *Advice to a Young Artist* (fig.12–35), the young man has brought a portfolio of his work for the older artist to see and criticize. Daumier's monumental forms are powerfully simple. A strong light from the left illuminates the figures and causes them to stand forward from the neutral background. In his earlier paintings, Daumier had used oil washes applied in a thin manner. Here, the paint is heavy and the texture is sure. The simplification of features enhances the solidness of the forms, as in Chardin's work.

Daumier's painting *The Third Class Carriage* (fig.12–36) is more in the breezy style of his caricatures, but still has a marvelous solidity. As in most of his work, Daumier deals with the public where he finds them—in their urban environment. His subjects did not pose for him in his studio. Daumier used grid lines to enlarge his smaller sketches onto the canvas. Because he used thin washes of muted color, the grid lines are often visible.

12–35 What do you think the artist is telling the student? Honoré Daumier, *Advice to a Young Artist*, after 1860. Oil on canvas, 16" x 13" (41 x 33 cm). National Gallery of Art, Washington, DC, gift of Duncan Phillips, 1941.

12–36 What clues do you find to the social and economic status of these people? Honoré Daumier, *The Third Class Carriage*, 1862. Oil on canvas, 26" x 35 1/2" (65 x 90 cm). The Metropolitan Museum of Art, New York, Bequest of Mrs. H. O. Havemayer Collection.

Daumier remained poor all his life. His friends persuaded him to have an exhibition of his work only a year before he died. Thus, he received a small amount of recognition while living. Blinded by overwork, Daumier simply could not paint the last year of his life.

12–37 Notice how the artist uses patches of white to carry your eye across the composition. Gustave Courbet, *Burial at Ornans*, 1849–1850. Oil on canvas, 10' 3" x 21' 11" (315 x 668 cm). Musée d'Orsay, Paris.

Gustave Courbet

(1819–1877)

The most effective spokesperson for Realism was Gustave Courbet. He is quoted as saying, "The art of painting should consist only in the representation of objects which the artist can see and touch." This was the credo of Realism. Courbet's paintings were of events or things that he had seen and knew well. He associated himself with the working class and their search for their rights in French society. A social activist, Courbet found himself in constant trouble because of his association with admitted Socialists.

In the Salon of 1850, Courbet exhibited *Burial at Ornans* (fig.12–37). This gigantic painting is a masterpiece of Realism. There is no aristocratic funeral here or visualized soul being transported to heaven. Compare this work with El Greco's *Burial of Count Orgaz* (fig.9–37). Courbet shows the people of his home town of Ornans attending the graveside funeral of a friend. Courbet depicts the pallbearers with the coffin, the priest reading the Office of the Dead, the altar boys, the mayor standing by the dog, the grave digger kneeling next to the open grave, the mourning friends and the clergy. Ordinary people are painted doing ordinary things at a very sad time. The mood is somber. The figures and faces are solid and real. The crucifix reaches into the overcast sky, uniting it with the grouped figures below. The dog certainly adds to the common, everyday feeling of the painting. The painting was so large that Courbet could not back up from it in his studio to see the overall effect. Yet, it is amazingly unified. The simple dignity of the peasants is captured superbly.

At the 1855 Universal Exposition in Paris, works by Ingres and Delacroix were prominently displayed. The works of Courbet were rejected, including *Burial at Ornans*. Never one to stand still, Courbet, with the help of friends, built a special shed called the Pavilion of Realism. Here, he mounted an exhibition of his work alone. This became the first modern-day, one-artist exhibition.

Window in Time

Art as Documentation

Before the invention of the camera, visual records of important events were communicated worldwide by artists, whose illustrations appeared in popular magazines and periodicals. Beginning in the 1840s, these illustrated magazines provided artists with a very large audience.

Artist-reporters, or Special Artists, as they were called, worked on location, much the same way as news correspondents. The Special Artists had to have various talents. They had to be able to draw quickly on location. From everything that was happening, they had to know what was most important to capture. And, somehow, they had to be in the right place at the right time.

Winslow Homer, an american, was one of the artists who recorded the Civil War for *Harper's Weekly*, a leading periodical in the United States at the time. He did over 800 drawings of the Civil War for them, and continued illustrating for *Harper's Weekly* until 1874.

Special Artists were employed mainly to cover wars, which sold more copies of newspapers and periodicals than any other event. They spent their time traveling from one side of the world to the other, recording the tense conflicts that erupted into fighting. Special Artists often found themselves in danger when they covered wars. Their constant note-taking aroused the suspicion of citizens and officials. During the 1870–71 war between France and Germany, anyone found drawing, or with drawings on their person, was in a lot of danger. The risk was so great that artist William Simpson made his notes on cigarette papers, so that if he was caught they could either be swallowed or smoked.

Another difficulty Special Artists encountered was getting their material to their editor on time. They might have to travel up to ten miles on foot in the middle of the night or take long stagecoach journeys if they were in the American West.

For almost fifty years, the Special Artists were free from competition. Even after the invention of photography, the mechanics of taking a photograph were so cumbersome and demanded so much fragile equipment that the Special Artist was still in great demand. The South African Anglo-Boer War of 1899–1900 saw the introduction of faster film, which allowed the first action photographs. Even then, artists' drawings were still used.

By the time World War I started in 1914, photography was the preferred medium for press illustration. Nevertheless, artists—including some famous painters who fought in the war—recorded the events in drawings and prints.

As the twentieth century progressed, photography and, eventually, motion picture film and videotape became the principal means of recording newsworthy moments. Today, there are only rare occasions, such as closed courtroom proceedings, when we continue to rely solely on artists' sketches to provide us with a visual record of an event.

Winslow Homer, *Baggage Guard*, 1865. Lithographic crayon and pen and ink on paper mounted on board, 9" x 18 1/4" (23 x 46 cm). Museum of Art, Carnegie Institute, Pittsburgh, Andrew Carnegie Fund.

12–39 What compositional purpose does the ship in the distance serve?
Winslow Homer, *Breezing Up (A Fair Wind)*, 1876. Oil on canvas, 24" x 38" (61 x 97 cm). National Gallery of Art, Washington, DC, gift of the W. L. and May T. Mellon Foundation.

12–38 What effect does the sunlight have on the sense of volume in this painting?
Winslow Homer, *Croquet Scene*, 1866. Oil on canvas, 16" x 26" (41 x 66 cm). The Art Institute of Chicago, Friends of American Art Collection, 1942.

Winslow Homer

(1836–1910)

From an early age, Winslow Homer knew he had to become an artist. Mostly self-taught, he began his professional art career by making wood engravings as illustrations for *Harper's Weekly*. During the Civil War, he was a field illustrator for the magazine. When the war was over, Homer began painting. His training as a detailed wood engraver pushed him toward Realism with his oils. A trip to Europe, in 1866, gave direction to his painting. From Corot and Courbet, he learned about the use of color and light under careful value control in clear tones and the application of heavy paint to canvas.

In *Croquet Scene* (fig.12–38), Homer achieved marvelous clarity of light. He used the dazzling sunlight to generalize and flatten details. A sunny Sunday afternoon is frozen in time. The brilliant colors of the girls' dresses are locked in place against the variety of contrasting greens of grass and trees. Homer approached the painting of light and color in terms of black, white and gray values. His early paintings have the same flat shapes and intense value contrasts as early Impressionist work.

Perhaps Homer's most popular painting is *Breezing Up (A Fair Wind)* (fig.12–39). Three boys are out sailing with a New England fisherman. Each is lost in his own thoughts as the small craft skips over the Atlantic. Perhaps they dream of captaining a larger vessel like the one in the distance that so beautifully balances the painting. Those who are interested in sports relate easily to Homer and his work.

About 1873, Homer became seriously interested in watercolor (fig.2–27). He used it first to make sketches for his oils, but found that people liked them enough to purchase some of them. He spent time in England painting the sea, fishermen and their wives in oils and watercolor. He was relaxed with his watercolors. They were fresh, spontaneous and alive. Homer was the first American artist to think of his watercolors as completed statements and finished works. To him, they were not sketches or preliminary studies for oil paintings. His contribution to the use of this medium greatly influenced the development of American watercolor painting.

12–40 Eakins used photographs as references to help him get all the details in his many paintings of sports activities. Thomas Eakins, *The Biglin Brothers Racing*, 1876. Oil on canvas, 24" x 38" (61 x 91 cm). National Gallery of Art, Washington, DC, gift of Mr. and Mrs. Cornelius Vanderbilt Whitney.

Thomas Eakins

(1844–1916)

A more influential artist than Homer, Thomas Eakins is one of the finest painters America has produced. He went to Europe after studying at the Pennsylvania Academy. He returned with a dedication to paint only realistic facts and not explore imagination and sentiment. He taught drawing classes at the Pennsylvania academy and was unwavering in his stress on realism and accuracy. This determination forced his resignation when he insisted that all students, females included, draw from nude male and female models.

While Homer was concerned with nature, Eakins was interested primarily in the figure. He painted many realistic portraits of friends and approached his subjects logically and with mathematical precision. His perspectives are accurate because they were measured and plotted mathematically before the painting began. Yet in spite of such a careful system of work, his paintings have a strength and a naturalness. With his superb sense of observation, Eakins reveals a grand joy in nature and humanity.

The Biglin Brothers Racing (fig.12–40) is a fine example of Eakins' outdoor painting. He shows his two friends poised at the start of a race, waiting for the gun to sound. His realism depicts sparkling water, deep shadows, bright sunlight and muscular tension. All are perfectly integrated to make a complete and unified statement. This convincing outdoor subject was painted in Eakins' studio from sketches, photographs and his incredible memory.

Eakins' most powerful painting (and perhaps his most controversial) is *The Gross Clinic* (fig.12–41), painted for the Jefferson Medical College in Philadelphia. Dr. Samuel Gross, scalpel in hand, turns away from the beginning surgery to talk to the students. His noble portrait unites the students above with the operation below. Each face is a superb individual portrait, yet the grouping of surgeons forms a strong unit. The powerful natural light from a skylight creates intense value contrasts that focus the viewer's attention on the operation. The students are painted in dim obscurity in the background. Each part is handled with absolute realism. Yet Eakins instilled a sense of drama. The fierce concentration of the doctors creates tension. As a final realistic touch, at the left, the mother of the young man on the operating table hides her face in a gesture of intense grief.

The scene seems spontaneous, but was carefully calculated. Eakins arranged the figures and the light to create the most dramatic impact on the viewers. His fellow Philadelphians and most art critics did not like his work. They felt that the blood on Dr. Gross's hand was not necessary and made the painting too realistic and gruesome. Eakins had succeeded in his quest for realism, but his public did not appreciate his mastery. Winslow Homer and Thomas Eakins were the cornerstone of Realism in America.

12–41 How is this operating room different from a modern one?
Thomas Eakins, *The Gross Clinic*, 1875. Oil on canvas, 96" x 78" (244 x 198 cm). Jefferson Medical College of Thomas Jefferson University, Philadelphia, PA.

Lesson 12.3 Review

1 What was the philosophy of the Realist artists concerning working-class people?
2 How large is Rosa Bonheur's *The Horse Fair*? Would it fit on the wall of your art classroom?
3 What were Corot's principal subjects after he began painting near Barbizon?
4 How was Millet trying to present the peasant women in *The Gleaners*?
5 During his lifetime, for what type of art was Daumier most famous?
6 What was Courbet's response to the rejection of his *Burial at Ornans* from the 1855 Universal Exposition in Paris?
7 Why did Thomas Eakins lose his job at the Pennsylvania Academy?

12.4 Photography

Photography had its roots in the *camera obscura* of the sixteenth century. When the principles of the camera obscura were combined with lithography (invented in 1798) to make a print from an image on photo sensitive ground glass, modern photography was born. After 1839, there were many people, including artists, who considered painting to be a dead art taken over by photography. Nevertheless, few early photographers thought in terms of art. They were satisfied to simply make portraits and take pictures.

The first creative photographers came from the ranks of painters, sculptors and draftsmen in Britain and France. Once photographers realized the extent of what their cameras could portray, they were on their way to creating a visual art of their own. The camera could capture the vitality of action, the beauty of form and, most particularly, the expressiveness of a situation.

The development of photography parallels the changes in painting to some degree. Realism, Impressionism and Expressionism are common to both fields. Painters learned from photographers and photographers took hints from painters. What one developed, the other soon used.

Key Notes

- Photography becomes a new art form.
- Photography and painting experience parallel developments and styles.
- Photography permits artists to freeze motion in order to study it in detail.

Vocabulary
zoopraxiscope

12–42 To what effect has Steichen used the principle of contrast in this photograph?
Edward Steichen, *J. Pierpont Morgan.* Courtesy of Southeby's, Inc.

Special Feature

Edward Steichen

(1879–1973)

Edward Steichen, an American, was one of the early photographers who thought of photography as an art form. Trained as a lithographer, Steichen decided to leave commercial illustration to become a fine artist.

Steichen began at an early age to appreciate the subtle qualities that could make photographs into art. He did not want to merely capture physical likenesses. Steichen also argued that photographers must not try to imitate painting, but must use their cameras to find their own ways of expressing themselves.

Steichen was also a noted portrait photographer. His well-known portrait of *J. Pierpont Morgan* (fig.12–42) is one of the few surviving portraits of the financier. Some years after taking the portrait, Steichen compared encountering Morgan's gaze to watching the oncoming headlights of an express train.

The Flatiron Building (fig.12–43) is a fine example of photography as art. Design and mood are balanced as if rendered with a brush. A variety of shapes loom amidst the rain-soaked air and streets. From the tree branches, which boldly flash across the scene, to the ghostly forms of the skyscraper and other buildings, Steichen's image is evocative and memorable. All the knowledge gained by the Realist painters about light, massing of tones, shapes connecting with each other, and the flattening of forms in the absence of light are explored in this one superb photograph.

12–43 Principles of painting were also applied to photography to create works that were expressive.
Edward J. Steichen, *The Flatiron Building,* 1904. Photograph. The Metropolitan Museum of Art, New York, Alfred Stieglitz Collection, 1933.

Early Photographers

Edward Steichen followed the leadership of early photographers such as Henry Peach Robinson (1830–1901), Julia Margaret Cameron (1815–1879) (fig.12–44) and Oscar Rejlander (1818–1875) in thinking of photography as fine art.

The Realists and Romantics also were interested in photography as an aid in the study of action, form and light. In the late 1870s, Eadweard Muybridge (1830–1904) invented a device called a ***zoopraxiscope***, which produced a series of images of a moving subject (fig.12–45). Thomas Eakins also worked on it. Artists could now actually see how muscles moved when humans or animals were in motion. They learned about movement and muscles under stress. For the first time in history, action could be caught and stopped for study. For example, it was now clear that, at some times in their movement, horses had all four hooves off the ground at the same time. Eakins devised a way to mount these images, which, when rotated, made the first moving picture.

The Realists made extensive use of photography to learn how things really looked. Courbet said that he considered the camera to be his sketchbook, a prime resource for his realistic paintings.

12–44 Cameron took up photography at the age of forty-eight.
Julia Margaret Cameron, *Ellen Terry at the Age of Sixteen*, 1863. Carbon print. The Metropolitan Museum of Art, New York, Alfred Stieglitz Collection, 1949.

12–45 Muybridge's sequential photographs of human and animal movements revolutionized artists' understanding of motion.
Eadweard Muybridge, *Attitudes of Animals in Motion*, 1878. Courtesy of Sotheby's, Inc.

Lesson 12.4 Review

1 Name an American photographer who considered photography to be an art.
2 What revolutionary techniques did Eakins use in his photography?
3 How did artists of the late nineteenth century use the camera as an aid to their painting?

Primary Source

Elizabeth Vigée-Lebrun

Like many artists, past and present, Elizabeth Vigée-Lebrun found it necessary to paint portraits in order to earn a living. She traveled throughout Europe painting portraits of members of royal families, but she really wanted to paint the beautiful landscapes she saw on these travels. In this passage from her memoir, *Souvenirs*, she mentions this frustration.

"I bade adieu to the beautiful bay of Naples, the charming hills of Pausilippo and terrible Vesuvius with regret, and left for the third time to visit my dear Rome, and admire Raffaelle again in all his glory. When there, I undertook a great many portraits, which to tell the truth only partially satisfied me. I greatly regretted not having been able to employ my time, either at Naples or Rome, in painting pictures of subjects which inspired me. I had been named a member of all the Academies of Italy, which encouraged me to merit such flattering distinctions, and I was going to leave nothing in this lovely country which would add much to my reputation as an artist. These ideas were constantly on my mind—I have more than one sketch in my portfolio which could furnish the proof; but the want of money, as I had not one penny left of what I earned in France, and the natural weakness of my character, made me undertake engagements to the weary task of portrait painting. The result is that after having devoted my youth to work, with a constancy and assiduity very rare in a woman, loving my art as much as my life, I can scarcely count four works (portraits included) with which I am really pleased.

Many of the portraits which I took in Rome during my last stay there, however, procured me some gratification, amongst others, that of seeing again Mesdames de France, the aunts of Louis XVI, who at once asked me to take their portraits."

Chapter Review

Review

1 Why did Napoleon support art that was inspired by Classical Roman art?

2 Neoclassicism was a reaction to the Rococo style. Compare these two art styles in Ingres' *Apotheosis of Homer* and Watteau's *The Gamut of Love* (fig.11–42).

3 Compare Delacroix's and Rubens' *Lion Hunt* (fig.11–23). How are they alike? Try to count the lions in each.

4 Compare Courbet's *Burial at Ornans* with El Greco's *Burial of Count Orgaz* (fig.9–37). Which painting is of ordinary people?

Interpret

1 Compare Neoclassicist David's *Oath of the Horatii* to Romanticist Goya's *Third of May, 1808*. How does each artist view war?

2 Delacroix was artistically inspired by his trips to Spain and Morocco. If you could visit an exotic land to collect ideas for paintings, where would you go? Explain the reasons for your choice.

3 How would paintings like Bingham's *Fur Traders Descending the Missouri* encourage people to settle the western part of the United States?

4 Describe the scene in Homer's *Breezing Up (A Fair Wind)*. What sensations would the boys in the picture feel, smell and hear?

Other Tools for Learning

Maps

Find three cities on the map in which famous buildings of the Romantic style are located. List the names of the buildings, their architects and the cities and countries in which they are located.

Timelines

Select one event from the 1800s that eventually led to a dramatic change in the way people live. Explain why you chose this event.

Electronic Research

Videodisc player: *Louvre Videodisc* (Disk 1: Painting, Drawing)

1 Study one of the paintings in this chapter such as Géricault's *Raft of the Medusa, or David's Napoleon in his Study or Oath of the Horatii* more carefully by looking at close-up details. What do you see in these close-up views that you had not noticed before?

CD-ROM drive: *Microsoft Art Gallery*

1 Discover more about Turner's revolutionary painting techniques. (Making Paintings Guided Tour)

Activity 1

Watercolor Action

Materials

pencils
drawing paper (sketch book)
watercolor paint
watercolor paper
brushes
containers of water

Take a look.

- Fig.2–27, Winslow Homer, *After the Hunt,* 1892. Watercolor.
- Fig.12–38, Winslow Homer, *Croquet Scene,* 1866. Oil on canvas.
- Fig.12–39, Winslow Homer, *Breezing Up,* 1876. Oil on canvas.

Think about it. Compare the listed works by Winslow Homer. In each case, Homer has dealt with his subject in a realistic manner using strong value contrasts.

- In what ways are they similar? How are the paintings different?
- Notice that the watercolor painting has a sparkle to it that makes it look as though it were "lit from within." That quality is not evident in the more opaque medium of oils.

Do it.

- Choose a sport or activity that is part of your daily life.
- Take a sketch book "on site" to do drawings that capture people in motion. Consider the movement of individual figures as well as their relationship to each other.
- Record details, such as their clothing, props they may be using and the background. You may wish to take some photographs of the action to serve as a reference in the classroom.
- Develop a finished composition based on the sport or activity that you observed. Work this into a 11" x 14" watercolor painting.

Check it. Obtain feedback on your preliminary action sketches before starting to paint. See if others can tell what action you wish to portray by looking only at your figures (without clues provided by props or setting).

Helpful Hint: By using a gradual build-up of washes, you will create an image of color contrasts which will give your viewer the feeling of being there.

Activity 2

Dueling Styles

Take a look.

- Fig.12–14, Francisco Goya, *The Third of May, 1808,* 1814.
- Fig.2–19, Jean-Auguste-Dominique Ingres, *Thomas Church,* 1816.
- Fig.2–60, Joseph Mallord William Turner, *The Burning of the Houses of Parliament,* 1835.
- Fig.12–1, Jacques-Louis David, *Oath of the Horatii,* 1784–1785.
- Fig.12–7, Elizabeth Vigée-Lebrun, *Mme. de Stael as Corinn Playing a Lyre,* after 1808.
- Fig.12–17, Eugene Delacroix, *Liberty Leading the People,* 1830.
- Fig.12–22, Thomas Cole, *View on the Catskill, Early Autumn,* 1837.

Think about it. While the Neoclassic style grew out of a rebellion against the ornate styles of the eighteenth century, it soon became not only the accepted style, but dictated to artists the ways in which they should think. This, in turn, led to a new rebellion known as Romanticism.

Do it.

- Chart the differences between Neoclassicism and Romanticism.
- Consider styles, methods, emphases, techniques, influences, roots, philosophy and other features.
- Use the information to create a multimedia presentation of what you have learned. This could include a slide show, music, poetry and your own artwork.

Check it. As you work, discuss your ideas with other classmates to see what insights you can share that might broaden the scope of your presentations.

Helpful Hint: Ask your teacher or librarian for good sources of images to use in your presentation.

Additional Activities

- Many American buildings have been influenced by Neoclassic or Romantic styles. Photograph or sketch elements of architecture in your community that reflect these influences and arrange a photo essay.
- Research the Neoclassic architecture of Thomas Jefferson. Write a report tracing the roots of his style and include the works of Andrea Palladio and Robert Adam. List examples of Jefferson's work that still exist.
- Does Realism lean more toward Classicism or Romanticism, or can it go into both categories? Why do you think so? Choose a local landscape or cityscape as the subject of three drawings, each done in one of the three styles. As an artist, what style most fits your usual approach to your work? What new insights have you gained through this study?

Will Lee

Age 19
Aztec High School
Aztec, New Mexico
Activity 1, Watercolor Action

My watercolor is about kids jumping off a bridge out on Ruins Road, near where I live. To me, it symbolizes the importance of the choices we make—especially as kids.

The main things I thought about during the creation of this picture were the composition and getting the figures to stand out against the background. Also, I was really trying to capture the drama of the storm approaching.

I haven't read a whole lot about art. There are always library books and art magazines in the classroom. I spend my spare time browsing through them and looking for ideas and new things to try. I'm developing my own style and learning to express my own thought and opinions. I think the thing I like most about art is the competition. It's fun to complete a piece and see how it stacks up with the rest of the class. I also enjoy competing locally and on the state level.

My advice for other students who enjoy creating art is to express your own ideas. If the idea is fresh, the artwork will be also.

Will Lee

Dave Pazniokas

Age 17
Mansfield High School
Mansfield, Massachusetts
Favorite kinds of art: watercolor, pencil
Favorite artists: Salvador Dali, M.C. Escher
Activity 1, Watercolor Action

My painting is about finding new places with old friends.

What was your thought process when you were creating and developing your project?
To establish the background, then the foreground. I created the figures last in the area I would most like to be.

What do you enjoy most about the artistic process?
Being able to create something and have the final product look the way I intended it to look. Being able to create perspective to make it look three-dimensional.

What advice do you have for other students who enjoy creating art?
Try not to get frustrated and keep experimenting. You may find a style or media you excel in.

Follow the Leader, 1994. Watercolor, 11" x 14" (28 x 35.5 cm).

Searching for a Place, 1994. Watercolor, 11" x 14" (28 x 35.5 cm).

13 Impressionism and Post-Impressionism

In This Chapter...

13–a Note the Japanese print on the wall behind Zola. Artists from this period found inspiration in the art of Japan.
Edouard Manet, *Emile Zola,* 1868. Oil on canvas, 57 1/4" x 45" (146 x 114 cm). Musée d'Orsay, Paris.

IN THE SECOND HALF of the 1800s, a tremendous change in art occurred in France. A whole new style of painting developed called Impressionism. This new style revolutionized painting all over Europe. Since then, it has become one of the most popular and beloved stylistic periods in the history of Western art. Impressionists were interested in color and developed a fascination with the effect of light on color. Their goal was to create a spontaneous rendering, a quick, light-filled colorful impression of what was in front of them.

After about fifteen years, some artists wanted more than pure "instantaneity." The Post-Impressionists, as they were called, were still interested in light and color but also wanted to incorporate more traditional values of design and composition into their work.

During the late 1800s and early 1900s, Paris continued to be the art center of the world. Artists in other countries were also producing excellent work. Their styles often differed from the styles popular in Paris. These artists frequently focused on the bleak conditions they saw around them. They were at the forefront of the Expressionist movement.

A greater fluidity between styles had started to develop. Artists were becoming more individualistic and styles were beginning to evolve from one to the next more and more rapidly.

1863
Manet's *Luncheon on the Grass* refused by the Salon

1884–1886
Whistler, *Nocturne in Black and Gold: The Falling Rocket*
Seurat establishes pointillism technique

1891
Gauguin leaves for Tahiti

1893
First automobile (Benz)

1900
Freud's dream interpretation

1914
World War I begins

Impressionism and Post-Impressionism

1874
Degas, *Rehearsal on the Stage*

1889
van Gogh, *The Starry Night*

1892–1894
Monet, *Rouen Cathedral* series

1898
Pierre and Marie Curie discover radium and plutonium

1905
Einstein's theory of relativity

A work of art is "a corner of nature seen through a temperament."
Emil Zola

13–b Gauguin sometimes used Egyptian poses in his work. What type of Egyptian art do these figures recall?
Paul Gauguin, *The Day of the God,* detail (fig.13–30).

Much of the activity of this period was focused around Paris, though many Impressionist artists found that the lighting in Southern France stimulated their work. Many were also fascinated with the reflection of light on water. Notice how many key towns are located along rivers or near the sea.

13–c European painters began to depict the anonymity and bleakness of contemporary urban life. In the late nineteenth century these artists planted the seeds of the Expressionist movement.
Edvard Munch, *Girls on a Bridge,* detail (fig.13–32).

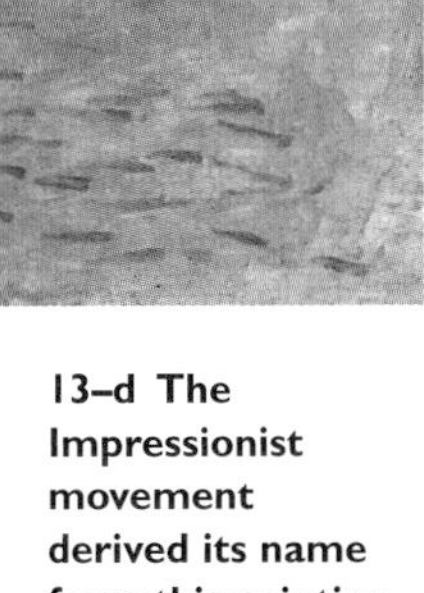

13–d The Impressionist movement derived its name from this painting.
Claude Monet, *Impression: Sunrise,* 1872. Oil on canvas, 19" x 25 1/2" (49 x 65 cm). Musée Marmottan, Paris.

13.1 Impressionism

All the Impressionist painters began as Realists. They were interested in natural colors and landscapes that they painted outdoors. Like Courbet and Corot, they painted people and things as solid, colored objects. But, they soon realized that the color of light had a tremendous effect on the color of objects. The color of the atmosphere at different times of the day changed the appearance of objects they were painting. Previous painters recorded the color of objects as they assumed them to be. The Impressionists painted color as they saw it—bright, glaring and high-keyed with colored light even penetrating the shadows. Sometimes, solid form was lost in the brilliance or mistiness of the light. The Impressionists wanted to express an immediate impression, not a detailed analysis. We all know what happens if we shut our eyes tightly and then quickly open them. That "one-second exposure" is what the Impressionists wanted to paint. Claude Monet described his goal in painting as "instantaneity."

The name Impressionism was first used in jest when Monet exhibited a work called *Impression: Sunrise* (fig.13–d) in an 1874 show. The painting's colored streaks and blobs on a pale blue ground represent what a person sees when taking a quick look at a sunrise over a harbor. Critics derisively called the works *impressions* and not paintings. The title stuck, although several Impressionists did not like it.

Impressionism was the first artistic revolution since the Renaissance and the first broad-based style to originate in France since Gothic times. It gradually built up a following throughout Europe, even in Russia. It was especially popular in the United States. Impressionism lasted about fifteen years before artists started following different directions.

Key Notes

- Impressionists revolutionize art by making light and color their subject matter.
- Artists seek to create an instant impression, not a detailed analysis.
- Impressionism originates in France and spreads throughout Europe and to America.

Vocabulary
optical mixing
broken color
series

Special Feature

Claude Monet

(1840–1926)

Claude Monet did not paint trees or fields, but simply the colors he saw—a little blue square, an oblong of pink, a streak of yellow or green dots. Monet took dabs of yellow and put them next to dabs of green and did not smear them together. Instead he let the viewer's eye blend them from a distance into a shimmering green. This technique, called ***optical mixing*** or the applying of ***broken color***, was the basis for Impressionist theories of color and light.

Monet became the leading force in the Impressionist movement, bridging the span from the Realist world to the contemporary world of abstraction. Monet loved to work outdoors and to directly confront the environment he was painting. His early work reflects his training with the landscape painter Eugene Boudin, from whom he learned the fundamentals of Realist painting. But it also shows an early fascination with light. In *Argenteuil* (fig.13–1) Monet expressed this interest with a high-keyed palette, particularly in the large portion of

13–1 What elements does this seascape share with Jacob van Ruisdael's *The Mill at Wijk by Durstede* (fig.11–26)? Also look for their differences.
Claude Monet, *Argenteuil*, 1872. Oil on canvas, 19 3/4" x 25 1/2" (50 x 65 cm). National Gallery of Art, Washington, DC, Ailsa Mellon Bruce Collection.

13–2 What time of day do you think this painting portrays?
Claude Monet, *Rouen Cathedral: The Portal (in Sun)*, 1894. Oil on canvas, 39" x 26" (99 x 66 cm). The Metropolitan Museum of Art, New York, bequest of Theodore M. Davis, 1915, Theodore M. Davis Collection.

13–3 Compare this work to fig.13–2 which depicts the same subject. There are many paintings in this series.
Claude Monet, *Rouen Cathedral, West Facade, Morning Light* 1894. Oil on canvas, 42" x 28" (107 x 72 cm). Musée d'Orsay, Paris.

sky and the reflecting water. He used flat patches of color in the foreground rather than trying to imitate the texture of the place. The heavy visual weight of the darker masses on the right is balanced by the single white sail on the left. By including such objects, Monet gave his seemingly unbalanced compositions a sense of stability.

But soon his work changed drastically. The flat brushstrokes of *Argenteuil* gave way to a shimmering effect in which the entire surface vibrated with color and light. There are no definite edges or contours to anything. The more Monet painted outdoors, the more he realized that colors were constantly changing with the moving of the sun or the interruption of clouds or haze. To analyze these changes, he decided to paint a single subject at different times of the day, at different times of the year, under different light. This is what he did with the west facade of the *Rouen Cathedral* (figs.13–2, 13–3). Here was a heavy, massive surface, built and carved of stone. Yet, under Monet's skillful handling, one no longer sees the stone and carving, but only the light and color reflected from different surfaces. Monet recorded these light and color changes on the church in more than thirty canvases.

Color and light became a new way of seeing. Monet stuck to the early credo of the Impressionist group: to depict visual sensations as experienced at a certain time and place.

Edouard Manet

(1832–1883)

Monet's predecessor as unofficial leader of the Impressionist movement was Edouard Manet. Trained as a traditional painter, Manet was particularly attracted to the paintings and the brushwork of Diego Velazquez and Francisco Goya of Spain. Like them, Manet felt that the message of the artist was the brushstrokes and patches of paint on the canvas, not the subject matter that they represented. Manet wanted the viewer to look *at* his paintings and not through them like through some magic window. He wanted to make paintings that could be enjoyed for their color and arrangement and for the fact that they were paintings and not imitations of nature.

His early work had a flatness new to the world of painting. This flatness was difficult for his contemporaries to understand. In this flat approach to design, Manet was influenced by Japanese woodcuts that were popular imports in France. His *Gare Saint-Lazare* (fig.13–4), done in mid-career, has a flatness that is fascinating. Look at the young woman's face. It is too flatly painted if the viewer looks at it with Renaissance eyes. There are no dark shadows or depth, no chiaroscuro, no roundness of form. The light source is probably directly *behind* the artist, not to the side as in most previous paintings. No black was added to make the few shadows that exist in the painting. Form is achieved by changing color slightly or lightening a value here and there.

The format of the painting is like a snapshot of a young woman and girl at the train station (*gare* is French for station). The peculiar composition, with the vertical bars dominating, is fresh and startling. The little girl looks through the bars at a train that has passed by, leaving a cloud of steam in its wake. (Manet worked on the large canvas outdoors to capture the light-through-steam effect.) The woman on the left looks at the viewer with detached interest. She will soon drop her head and go on reading as her finger in the book's pages suggests. The appealing puppy in her lap sleeps in complete contentment.

All four sides of the canvas seem to have been "cropped," much as one would "crop" a snapshot. The candid, off-hand appearance is greatly enhanced by this device. The work's occasional unfinished look also contributes to this effect. Manet's work here is different from the Realism of Corot and vastly different from the Neoclassicism of David and Ingres.

13–4 The cropped, intimate look of a snapshot is coupled with the influence of Japanese prints to create a completely new look in painting.
Edouard Manet, *Gare Saint-Lazare,* 1873. Oil on canvas, 36 1/2" x 45 1/4" (93 x 114.5 cm). National Gallery of Art, Washington, DC, gift of Horace Havemeyer in memory of his mother, Louisine W. Havemeyer, 1956.

13–5 Compare Manet's technique in this scene to Frans Hals' technique in *Yonker Ramp and His Sweetheart* (fig.11–29).
Edouard Manet, *The Waitress*, 1878. Oil on canvas, 38 1/2" x 30 1/4" (98 x 77 cm). The National Gallery, London.

Toward the end of his short life, Manet left the flat and even patches of color of his earlier work. He adopted the looser, longer strokes and vibrating color of the Impressionists. *The Waitress* (fig.13–5) was painted in Manet's studio. A real waitress at the Café de Bock in Paris posed for him. The arrangement of figures again produces a snapshot effect of an instantaneous glimpse into the café. It is almost as if the door were opened for a second and one looked quickly inside. Notice the directional brushwork in the material and on the hands and arms. Patterns of light values make the painting sparkle with light. The indefinite character of the people in the café and the band and the dancer on stage are truly impressions of the scene rather than a factual representation. Everything seems to quiver with excitement. Sparkling light transforms an everyday subject into a delightful event.

13–6 The artist is well known for his Paris street scenes. He captures a moment in time much as your eye would when quickly glancing out an upper-story window.
Camille Pissarro, *La Place du Théâtre Français*, 1898. Oil on canvas, 28 1/4" x 36 1/2" (72 x 93 cm). Los Angeles County Museum of Art, Mr. and Mrs. George Gard de Sylva Collection.

13–7 A close-up view of this painting makes the figures and objects dissolve into dabs and dashes of color
Camille Pissarro, *La Place du Théâtre Français*, detai.

Camille Pissarro

(1830–1903)

Although he was born in the West Indies, Camille Pissarro came to Paris when twenty-five, determined to be an artist. A good friend of the other Impressionists, he often bought their work to keep them from starving. He also let many of the young, struggling artists live on his property in the country and painted side by side with them. Pissarro was adept at capturing the feeling of a place through color and mood. The viewer can sense its atmosphere and even the time of year or day. His favorite subjects were scenes of the streets of Paris as viewed from second or third story windows.

13–8 This artist usually placed her subjects indoors in the direct sunlight of a window or terrace.
Berthe Morisot, *The Artist's Sister at a Window*, 1869. Oil on canvas, 21 3/4" x 18" (55 x 46 cm). National Gallery of Art, Washington, DC, Ailsa Mellon Bruce Collection.

In *Place du Théâtre Français* (fig.13–6), the viewer seems to be looking over Pissarro's shoulder, out the window and down onto the street below. The shimmering light and color of the hustle and bustle of a city street are felt immediately. People, horses and carriages appear to move as the tiny spots and dashes of color seem to melt and dissolve (fig.13–7). The viewer has to look through some leafless branches to see part of the scene. Pissarro often used this device to heighten the sense of movement and sparkle. Pissarro, like Monet, wanted to obtain an instantaneous sensation of the scene before him. He succeeded remarkably in his many refreshing and bright street scenes.

Berthe Morisot

(1841–1895)

A sister-in-law of Manet, Berthe Morisot worked and exhibited with the Impressionists, yet developed her own style. She posed for many of her friends and, in turn, painted many of them. *The Artist's Sister at a Window* (fig.13–8) expresses completely Morisot's philosophy of painting. The girl sitting by an open window, who seems to daydream while looking at her fan, creates a mood of loneliness. The application of color in flat patches reflects Manet's early influence on her work. Yet, Morisot was also influenced by her study of masterpieces of the Louvre and of Corot. Her design and composition are more solid than the off-hand, unposed look of many Impressionist works.

Sidelight

Crosscurrents with Japan

Following a long period of isolationism, in which Japan closed itself to foreign influence, Japan reopened trade relations with other nations in 1853.

By the 1860s, Japanese woodcuts became available in Paris and greatly influenced many of the French Impressionists. The beauty and economy of line in the prints caught the eye of the Impressionists and Post-Impressionists. The Japanese use of perspective and space was particularly appreciated. The woodcuts served as models for many of the formal qualities these artists were seeking to achieve in their own work.

In subject matter, Japanese *ukiyo-e* prints also were inspirational. *Ukiyo-e* was a style of genre painting that provided an informal glimpse of Japanese life. These casual scenes were just the type favored by European painters in the second half of the nineteenth century.

The Japanese themselves had been influenced in the seventeenth century by European prints which had made their way to Asia. So, when the French artists such as Manet (fig. 13–a), van Gogh, Cassatt and Gauguin started translating what they saw in Japanese prints into their own work, it was as much the result of a previous cross-fertilization as anything else. Borrowing from other traditions and producing something imaginatively new is an ongoing process in the arts.

Edgar Degas

(1834–1917)

Although Edgar Degas differed in many aspects from the Impressionists, he shared their interest in casual subjects and candid glimpses of people in action. He approached his work with intellectual curiosity. To achieve his desired instantaneity, he carefully considered design and the positioning of people and objects. Degas was a master of line and drawing and was reluctant to abandon it in favor of Impressionism's soft contours.

Degas was an excellent amateur photographer and worked with Eadweard Muybridge's and Thomas Eakins' studies of the human body and horses in motion. He applied their results to his own unique presentation of the figure in his painting.

Degas liked to paint in ***series***; that is, many paintings exploring the same theme over a period of time. One subject that he explored in great detail and in hundreds of paintings, drawings and pastels was the ballet. He captured the instantaneous glimpse of figures in action. Degas explored the indoor, controlled lighting; the lighting often comes from below as in footlights. The views are often from peculiar vantage points, such as from wings, balcony boxes or from below the stage. All these features enhance Degas' candid glimpses of dancers working at their craft.

Rehearsal on the Stage (fig.13–9) is done in pastels. He was interested in the daily routine of practice and work—the constant search for perfection. The director is instructing his ballerinas while stagehands relax and watch. The softness of the costumes is contrasted with lines and edges on figures and in the background. Degas' soft blending of

13–9 Photography and the concepts of photographic composition strongly influenced Degas' work.
Edgar Degas, *The Rehearsal on the Stage,* 1874. Pastel over brush-and-ink drawing on paper, 20 3/4" x 28 1/4" (53 x 72 cm). The Metropolitan Museum of Art, New York, bequest of Mrs. H. O. Havemeyer, 1929. The H. O. Havemeyer Collection.

13–10 How does Degas make the viewer feel like a part of this scene?
Edgar Degas, *Carriage at the Races,* 1873. Oil on canvas, 14 1/2" x 22" (36.5 x 56 cm). 1931 Purchase Fund. Museum of Fine Arts, Boston.

13–11 Trace the compositional path from the viewer to the center of interest.
Edgar Degas, *The Absinthe Drinker,* 1876. Oil on canvas, 36 1/4" x 26 3/4" (92 x 68 cm). Musée d'Orsay, Paris.

costume into background is an Impressionist technique for showing light bouncing off of form. However, as a line around a foot or down a leg suggests, Degas only uses softness to express action or to describe the material. His clustering of figures to one side or in one corner is balanced by open spaces and, perhaps, the careful placement of a separated figure or two. No matter how unbalanced or casual his groupings seem, they are always calculated to produce an asymmetric balance. This balance produces a feeling of immediacy and nonplanning. The medium of pastels is as much drawing as painting. It allowed Degas to convey the color and excitement of the ballet with more assurance than he could with oils.

Another theme that Degas covered completely in a series was racetrack activity. He treated the horses, jockeys, owners and crowds at the races with a marvelous sense of design. In *Carriage at the Races* (fig.13–10), which he painted outdoors, he used a carefully selected, high-keyed palette of pearly softness. Vibrating greens, pinks, yellows, blues and grays contrast with the crisp, darker tones of horses and the carriage. The combination definitely produces an outdoor feeling.

The carriage and the horses are placed off-center to add to the feeling of a momentary glimpse of the scene. They run out the bottom of the frame, as if cropped for some special effect. The composition is visually balanced by the partial carriage at the left edge.

While some artists saw the happy side of Parisian social life, Degas was not enchanted by what he saw. His *The Absinthe Drinker* (fig.13–11) shows a couple who have been sitting and drinking too long at their table. They no longer talk to each other but stare blankly at the activity in the café. At first, the painting has a snapshot quality and seems to lack formal composition. Yet, the more one looks, the more one realizes that everything works perfectly to attain that feeling. The zig-zag of the empty tables increases the sense of brooding and confusion. Diagonals slant in many directions. They even seem to extend forward from the picture plane, drawing the viewer into the scene. The milky green glass of absinthe becomes Degas' center of interest and the purpose for the painting.

Degas worked a great deal with pastels rather than oils. He was the first artist to exhibit them as finished works instead of preliminary sketches for paintings. As his eyesight weakened, he also spent much time working on sculptures because he enjoyed feeling the solidness of the forms and the action that they expressed. A multi-talented artist, he was a master of oils, pastels, pencil and sculpture.

Pierre Auguste Renoir

(1841–1919)

Pierre Auguste Renoir's career stretched well into the twentieth century and progressed through several developmental stages. Throughout his career, he remained interested in painting women and the nude figure.

In his first period, he was interested in the bright, cheerful effects of light and air. For the 1877 Impressionist group exhibit (their third), Renoir painted the ambitious *Dance at the Moulin de la Galette Montmartre* (fig.13–12), which is the very essence of Impressionism. Renoir, always interested in painting people, depicts a Sunday afternoon outdoor dance in a popular district of Paris, the Montmartre. Beautiful people are enjoying conversation and dancing. The viewer is caught up in the effervescence that Renoir felt and painted. Flickering light filters through the trees and speckles the people with bits of sunshine. In this delightful interplay of light and shadow, Renoir uses no black paint, but all shadows are tinged with blue. The darker the value, the deeper the blue mixed with other colors.

During the first part of his career, Renoir painted portraits, still lifes, landscapes and figures in a fantastic surge of creativity. During his second phase, after restudying the great masters, Renoir gave up the transient effects of Impressionism. He painted solid, carefully defined

13–12 No black paint is used in this work even though many areas are understood as black.
Pierre Auguste Renoir, *Dance at the Moulin de la Galette Montmartre,* 1876. Oil on canvas, 51 1/2" x 69" (131 x 175 cm). Musée d'Orsay, Paris.

13–13 The long feathery brushstrokes used here are characteristic of Renoir's late work.
Pierre Auguste Renoir, *In the Meadow,* 1892. Oil on canvas, 32" x 25 1/2" (81 x 65 cm). The Metropolitan Museum of Art, bequest of Samuel A. Lewisohn.

World Cultural Timeline

1867
Diamonds discovered, Kimberley, South Africa

1881
Japanese women perform on stage for first time since development of *Kabuki* theater in 1600

1892
Electric clocks first used to time sports events, Japan

1895
Cuba begins revolt against Spanish rule

13–14 Mothers and their children were a favorite subject for Cassatt.
Mary Cassatt, *Sleeping Baby*, about 1910. Pastel on paper, 25 1/2" x 20 1/2" (65 x 52 cm). Dallas Museum of Art, Munger Fund 1952.

forms. In his third period, he tried to unite his first two by combining the formal balance and solidity of the traditional approaches with the shimmering effects of Impressionism. *In the Meadow* (fig.13–13) was painted during this time. The figures are placed carefully in a landscape. They are shaded to produce solid, rounded forms. Cool colors are used for shadows. Yet, the two figures blend softly into their surroundings. Edges on the two girls are nonexistent. Renoir has developed a soft, longish brushstroke that is characteristic of his later work. Broken color and optical mixing are used with these strokes to create a soft, subtle and gently shimmering painting style.

In his fourth and final period, there is an exaggeration of this soft brushwork and the use of more intense colors, but the solidity remains. Whatever the period, joy never leaves Renoir's work. His fingers were crippled with arthritis at the end. Yet, Renoir still painted happy figures in sun-filled landscapes that in no way let one sense his pain.

Mary Cassatt

(1845–1926)

Mary Cassatt was born in Philadelphia. After studying art at the Pennsylvania Academy, she left for Paris in 1865 against the wishes of her parents. Here she was drawn to the work of the Impressionists, especially Degas'. In his solid design and superb draftsmanship she found the directions she wanted to take. Although influenced and helped by him, Cassatt never imitated him. She developed a style that combined the informal subject and composition of the Impressionists with her personal desire for precision and definition.

Mothers and children were Mary Cassatt's favorite subjects. She is unmatched in her ability to express, in both oils and pastels, the mutual love between the two. *Sleeping Baby* (fig.13–14), a delightful pastel, combines a seemingly casual glimpse into a nursery with a carefully designed composition. The center of interest is the tender touching of faces of the mother and her child. Arms, legs and darker values direct eye movement to this center. Like Degas, Cassatt used line along legs and arms to strengthen the design and to add solidity to the figures. Yet, the loose pastel strokes and high-keyed colors are features of the Impressionists with whom she exhibited.

Mary Cassatt was well respected among her peers in Paris, but was not recognized at home in Philadelphia, a dilemma which caused her to remain in Europe. But, she was tremendously influential in getting several American families to buy the paintings of her Impressionist friends. As a result, museums and private collections in the United States have superb collections of their work.

James Abbott McNeill Whistler

(1834–1903)

The American James Abbott McNeill Whistler moved to Paris in 1855 and four years later went to London, where he worked the rest of his life. Instead of adopting the broken color or the sunlit effects of Manet and Degas, Whistler often worked in grays and blacks. He blended his colors so carefully that he could obtain a wide range of hues and values with his limited palette. He was strongly influenced by Japanese prints and, for a while, included Oriental motifs and objects in his paintings.

By the late 1860s, Whistler returned to portraiture. He wanted to combine a realistic likeness of the sitter with an excellent sense of design. To this end, he looked to the simplification and stark arrangements of Degas and of the Japanese woodcut. An example is his best-known work, *Arrangement in Gray and Black No. 1: The Artist's Mother,* commonly known as *Whistler's Mother* (fig.13–15). The realistic portrait of the delicate woman is placed against a carefully designed background of vertical and horizontal rectangular shapes. The shapes, not the likeness, dominate the painting. Every item in the painting is an integral part of the design, including the draperies, the pictures on the wall, the floor and the placement of his mother's hands. He used the flat color areas of Manet, but not his brushwork. Instead, Whistler used thin glazes of color to build up his subtle grays. Even the title was selected to help the public see the painting as a design rather than a representational painting. Whistler often used titles that recall musical compositions, such as "arrangements," "symphonies," "harmonies" or "nocturnes."

In 1877, he exhibited *Nocturne in Black and Gold: The Falling Rocket* (fig.13–16). The painting caused a furor in London. The painting is an impressionistic view of skyrockets bursting in the English night. It swirls with muted colors and dark shadows, punctuated with vivid flecks of color. It is a symphony of color, tones, accents and dark passages. But the noted English art critic, John Ruskin, defender of traditional Realism, used his biting satire to remark that Whistler was "flinging a pot of paint in the public's face." Whistler could not let the challenge go and sued Ruskin for libel. During a lengthy trial, he struggled vainly to explain to judge and jury what he was trying to express in his painting. Whistler won the trial, but was awarded only one farthing in damages.

13–15 The composition of shapes is the subject, and the sitter is a part of the design.
James Abbott McNeill Whistler, *Arrangement in Gray and Black No. 1: The Artist's Mother,* 1871. Oil on canvas, 56 1/2" x 63 3/4" (144 x 162 cm). Musée d'Orsay, Paris.

13–16 The English art critic John Ruskin's criticism of this painting caused a lawsuit for libel.
James Abbott McNeill Whistler, *Nocturne in Black and Gold: The Falling Rocket,* 1874. Oil on panel, 23 1/2" x 18 1/2" (60 x 47 cm). The Detroit Institute of Arts.

Auguste Rodin

(1840–1917)

During the years of Impressionism, when color and light were all-important, Auguste Rodin burst on the scene with magnificent sculptural forms. He transformed the off-handedness and instantaneity of Impressionism into powerful, three-dimensional forms. Rodin's sculptures can be favorably considered with those of Donatello, Michelangelo and Bernini. Yet, they were so individual and personal that no followers imitated them.

Rodin's best works were cast in bronze, but were first formed with his hands in clay, plaster or wax. He loved the immediacy of these materials, which he could manipulate, push, stab and form. Impressionist paintings may seem unfinished, yet are complete. In the same way, Rodin often left his sculptures seemingly unfinished. He experimented with figures in action, accidental effects, and feelings of spontaneity and tension. Often the surfaces of his bronzes shimmer with light reflecting from his fingerprints and the rough surfaces.

13–17 This is Rodin's best-known work.
Auguste Rodin, *The Thinker*, 1879–1889. Bronze, 28" (71 cm high). National Gallery of Art, Washington, DC, gift of Mrs. John W. Simpson.

Like the Impressionists, Rodin's work was not popular with critics and the public because it was not smooth, finished and beautiful. He planned a gigantic work, the *Gates of Hell* (which he never finished) that would have rivaled Michelangelo's Sistine Ceiling in the amount of effort expended. Models were made, but, because of frequent interruptions, he was never able to complete the task. His famous *The Thinker* (fig.13–17) was to be a small part of the entire monumental design.

Most of Rodin's works were never completed. Others were rejected by the patrons who had commissioned them. His *Monument to Balzac* (fig.13–18) was finally put in place in 1939, long after the artist's death. The sculpture of the French author is a massive form that is both powerful and expressive. Rodin wanted to show the author at the moment he conceived a new creative idea for a novel. Balzac (whom Rodin did not know) is shown wrapped in a long cloak and lost in thought. The huge figure seems to be a mass of drapery with an unbelievably powerful head thrusting out of the folds. Again, the original concept was not appreciated by the patrons who wanted something more refined and traditional, but Rodin would not compromise his ideas. Viewed from below, the figure is overpowering. It is the summation of Rodin's sculptural expression.

13–18 Rodin's sculptures were planned and formed in clay, plaster or wax, then cast in bronze.
Auguste Rodin, *Monument to Balzac*, 1897–98. Bronze, 110 3/4" (281 cm high). The Museum of Modern Art, New York. Presented in memory of Cort Valentin by his friends.

Lesson 13.1 Review

1 From which style of art did Impressionism develop?
2 Which painting suggested the title Impressionism to the art critics?
3 Why did Monet paint so many versions of the Rouen Cathedral?
4 From what vantage point is the viewer looking at the *Place du Théâtré Français* in Pissarro's painting?
5 What medium did Degas use to draw *Rehearsal on the Stage*?
6 Which American woman Impressionist painted many pictures of mothers and children?
7 How are Rodin's sculptures similar to Impressionist paintings?

13.2 Post-Impressionism

As the nineteenth century came to an end, Impressionism had run its course as the new direction in art. The early goals of Impressionism had been abandoned and artists were exploring new aspects of the Impressionistic style. Artists who based their work on the color theory and techniques of Impressionism, but who developed their own unique styles, are loosely grouped together under the heading Post-Impressionists. They worked alongside many of the Impressionists, but they were no longer convinced by their instantaneous glimpses of nature and their seemingly unplanned canvases. They wanted to combine the color and light of Impressionism with the design and composition of traditional painting—much like Renoir's goals in his last period of work.

Two directions emerged among these artists. Cézanne and Seurat looked for permanence of form and concentrated on design. Van Gogh and Gauguin emphasized emotional and sensuous expression. The development of Impressionism had freed artists from traditional painting techniques and Renaissance concepts of space and form. Building on this new freedom, Post-Impressionism produced a variety of styles. It set the stage for the extreme range of individual expression that characterizes art in the twentieth century.

Key Notes

- Post-Impressionism combines the color and light theory of the Impressionists with the design and composition of traditional painting.
- Post-Impressionism produces a variety of unique styles.

Vocabulary

pointillism
expressionists

Special Feature

Georges Seurat

(1859–1891)

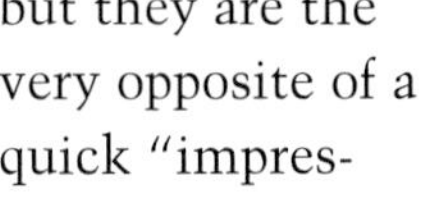

Color and light predominate in Seurat's paintings, but they are the very opposite of a quick "impression." Seurat went after a permanence of design. He used methodical and scientific techniques based on photography and the physics of light and color. Combining this knowledge with the techniques of the Impressionists, Seurat painted marvelously light-filled pictures. Before starting work on the final canvas, Seurat made many sketches in oils, charcoal and crayon to determine color, light, placement and shapes.

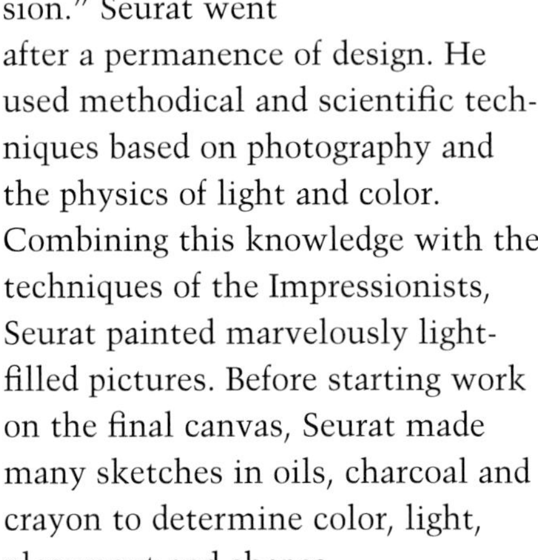

Seurat's largest and most impressive work, and a landmark in modern art, is *A Sunday on La Grande Jatte—1884* (fig.13–19). Seurat made forty preliminary studies for this painting. He placed each figure extremely carefully. The color was

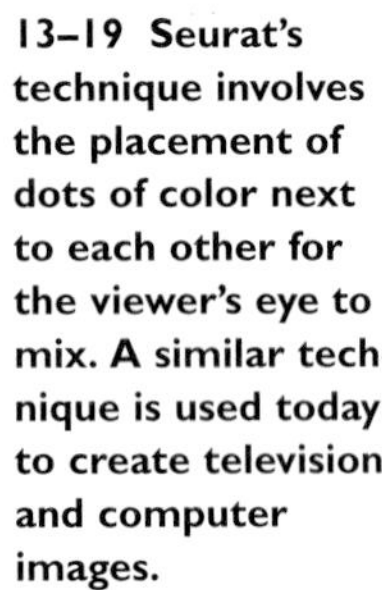

13–19 Seurat's technique involves the placement of dots of color next to each other for the viewer's eye to mix. A similar technique is used today to create television and computer images.
Georges Seurat, *A Sunday on La Grande Jatte–1884*, 1884–1886. Oil on canvas, 81 1/2" x 121" (207.5 x 308 cm). The Art Institute of Chicago, Helen Birch Bartlett Memorial Collection.

13–20 Compare this seascape to Monet's *Argenteuil*. Consider color, brushstrokes, point of view.
Georges Seurat, *Le Bec du Hoc at Grandchamp*, 1885. Oil on canvas, 21 1/2" x 25 1/2" (55 x 65 cm). Tate Gallery, London.

applied in tiny dots, each about the size of a pencil eraser. From a distance, the viewer's eyes visually mix these dots together to create the vast array of hues and values that make up the painting. For example, red dots placed next to yellow dots appear as an orange area. This technique, which is called ***pointillism***, is similar to the placing of tessarae in a mosaic. Today, we see a similar technique to pointillism in the "dots" in halftones, TV images and color printing. The result of this technique in *La Grande Jatte* is a marvelously uniform surface that sparkles with light and color.

In the painting, the people of Paris, enjoying a Sunday afternoon in the park, are carefully arranged. They face either sideways or forward and are almost Egyptian in their formality. Seurat placed figures and landscape features according to a mathematical formula similar to one the Greeks used in their designs and compositions. As you can see, this work is definitely more solid than a fleeting glimpse.

Seurat painted a series of landscapes in the late 1880s, almost all of which included views of the sea. The flickering light of pointillism is especially appropriate in depicting sparkling water. In *Le Bec du Hoc at Grandchamp* (fig.13–20), a large cliff rises to break the far horizon. The view may look quite casual but Seurat always chose his subject matter with great care. Again, hundreds of thousands of points of color are applied to build up the surface and develop the final color range. Apparently Seurat walked around an area for a long time before he started making sketches and small painting studies of the final scene. He was looking for just the right view to fit his design formula.

Like the Impressionists, Seurat focused on color and light, but, as with the other members of the Post-Impressionist group, he went beyond these very specific interests. His method was highly scientific and the results much more solid than the instantaneity of Impressionism.

Paul Cézanne

(1839–1906)

Paul Cézanne was the leading painter of the late nineteenth century in France and one of the most influential artists in Western painting. Although he worked for a short while in Paris, he spent most of his life in relative seclusion in his hometown of Aix. His early work was Romantic, and he used Delacroix as his model. He applied his colors in juicy, thick passages. In the early 1870s, he met Pissarro and adopted the Impressionists' high-keyed palette. He exhibited with them at their first exhibition in 1874 and, again, at their third showing. All of his submissions to the Salon were rejected except one, in 1882. According to the standards of his time, he was a failure.

While the Impressionists used light to capture a fleeting moment, Cézanne's light seems permanent and all-encompassing. It illuminates colors and subjects, and shadows are often nonexistent. Cézanne did not want his paintings to imitate the realistic three-dimensionality of nature. He wanted them to remain as flat canvases with paint on them. Because he was concerned with the structure of the painting, he felt free to move objects and adjust relationships of color and form to produce the best design possible, even if it meant distortion. He discarded the traditional aerial and linear perspective and painted every part of the canvas with equal intensity—foreground, middle ground, background and sky. This led to compressing of space so that the canvas remained visually flat yet the colors seemed to indicate depth.

Near the town of Aix, the large mountain *Mont Sainte-Victoire* (fig.13–21) dominates the landscape. Cézanne painted the mountain often and explored his developing techniques and painting concepts. In the version shown here, the mountain is in the background. Houses and trees fill the valley in front. Cézanne built up his painting by applying paint in flat, squarish patches or planes of color. Some of these planes may seem to be houses or trees, but were meant to be planes of color. The intensity of the colors remains strong throughout so that the sky seems as close to the viewer as the foreground. Colors and values are distributed over the picture plane to produce a visual balance. The whole painting reads as a mountain-dominated landscape. Yet it is built up of relatively equal, small, squarish, flat abstract planes of color that unify the composition.

Earlier in his life, Cézanne painted many portraits. His sitters often complained of extremely long sessions and many quit before the paintings were finished. Cézanne's approach to painting required hours

13–21 Cézanne creates a sense of perspective by overlapping planes of color.
Paul Cézanne, *Mont Sainte-Victoire,* 1904. Oil on canvas, 28" x 35 1/4" (71 x 89 cm). Philadelphia Museum of Art, George W. Elkins Collection.

13–22 Design of the painting was Cézanne's ultimate concern. Use the text to help you completely understand this design.
Paul Cézanne, *Still Life with Apples and Peaches*, 1905. Oil on canvas, 32" x 39 1/2" (81 x 100 cm). National Gallery of Art, Washington, DC, gift of Eugene and Agnes Meyer.

of looking. He was intent on making sure of the placement of color and value and its relationship to the canvas. How different his approach was from the instantaneous approach of the Impressionists! When sitters would not tolerate the long hours of posing, Cézanne began working with still lifes. His patient and tedious working process often caused fruits to spoil before the painting was finished. He finally had to resort to using wax fruit and vegetables in his set-ups. His still lifes were carefully designed and made use of brilliant color.

Still Life with Apples and Peaches (fig.13–22) is an excellent example. At first glance, the painting appears to be a simple still life with fruit and a few ceramic pieces. However, like all of Cézanne's art, it is carefully designed. The rich colors glow from the canvas. The warm hues of the fruit contrast with the cool hues of the surroundings. Rather than add black to the peach color to create a feeling of form, Cézanne used flat patches of gradually changing color to produce roundness. This careful selection of adjacent colors made his painting process lengthy. The Impressionists had used color to dissolve form. Cézanne used patches of color to build up form. Blues are distributed throughout the painting as are touches of pink, yellow and orange.

Lines are either painted on the canvas or occur as breaks in value or color. Notice the lines of the cloth and table. Their many lines seem to flow diagonally from upper right to lower left. In order to balance that strong diagonal movement, Cézanne introduced counter movement from the lower right to the upper left in several lines and in the cloths. But more important, notice the slanting of the pitcher, the distortion of the bowl, and the arrangement of the fruit. All add to the counter movement and balance the design. Every brushstroke, color change and line has a purpose in the painting. The visual movement from object to object and the rhythm established with color and value accents produce a typical painting of perfect control, careful design and brilliant use of color. To Cézanne, the design of the painting was most important, not the imitation of the original still life. If distortion produced a better design, it was the artist's privilege, or even requirement, to distort.

Henri de Toulouse-Lautrec

(1864–1901)

Born in Albi to one of the noble families of France, Henri de Toulouse-Lautrec broke both legs when fourteen. Because they did not develop properly, his growth was stunted. Since he could not participate in his family's active social life, he went off to Paris to paint. He lived in the Montmartre area, Paris's theater district and artists' quarters. He spent much of his time in the cafés, cabarets and theaters. He drew caricatures and portraits with great skill. He liked to portray dancers and circus people, such as his dancer-friend *Jane Avril* (fig.13–23). In his quick, sketchy style, he was able to capture her character in a few rapidly applied lines. Lautrec created the same feeling of spontaneity in his paintings, although they often took a long time to finish. Thin washes of color are often used in combination with a sure, dark line which was an extension of his drawing technique.

Many of his paintings are of the night life of Paris, which he saw from "elbow height," as he himself said. *At the Moulin Rouge* (fig.13–24) reveals the influence of his friend Degas. The composition recalls *The Absinthe Drinker*. A group of his friends are clustered around a table in the cabaret. Lautrec and his much taller cousin can be seen crossing the canvas in the background. The diagonal table and the woman at the right seem to move forward from the picture

13–23 Notice how the artist has sketched some parts of this figure in greater detail than others. Where has the artist placed his emphasis?
Henri de Toulouse-Lautrec, *Jane Avril*, 1892. Mounted on wood, 26 3/4" x 20 3/4" (68 x 53 cm). National Gallery of Art, Washington, DC, Chester Dale Collection.

13–25 The artist designed many posters for the cafés and cabarets of Paris' theater district.
Henri de Toulouse-Lautrec, *Moulin Rouge, La Goulue*, 1891. Poster. Indianapolis Museum of Art, Gift of the Gamboliers.

World Cultural Timeline

1904
African art begins to influence European artists

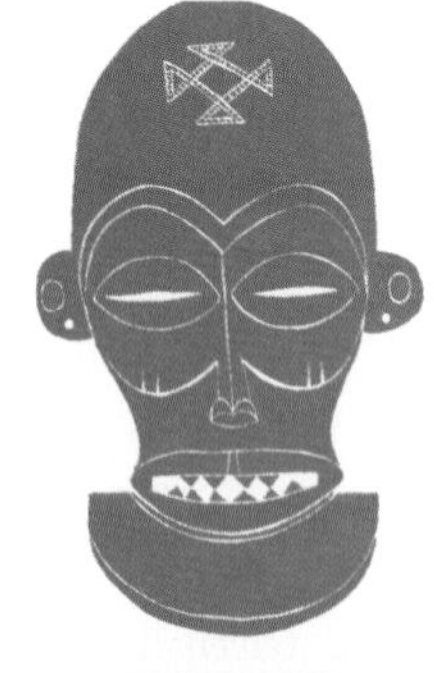

1917
Mexico adopts a new constitution

1912
First Japanese battleship built

1914
Panama Canal opens

13–24 Toulouse-Lautrec was greatly influenced by Degas. This influence is evident in the strong diagonals and asymmetrical composition of the painting.
Henri de Toulouse-Lautrec, *At the Moulin Rouge,* 1892. Oil on canvas, 48 1/2" x 55 1/2" (123 x 141 cm). The Art Institute of Chicago, Helen Birch Bartlett Memorial Collection.

plane. They bring the viewer into direct relationship with the scene. Lautrec's presentation of his lifestyle and social environment was as realistic as that of Daumier and just as biting in its social comment. He knew it well, and painted and drew it with gusto. He also lived it excessively, dying of alcoholism when only thirty-seven.

Lautrec was the first artist to produce modern posters for commercial purposes. His caricatures adorned advertisements for many of the cafes and cabarets of the Montmartre (fig.13–25). Most of his prints of dancers were used to advertise their performances and were pasted on the kiosks of Paris. These kiosks were the billboards of the time. In the poster, notice Lautrec's use of strong, black line and flat areas of lighter color. Although he enjoyed painting, he did not consider his work worthy of display. At his early death, many fine works, not seen before by his friends, were found in his studio.

Vincent van Gogh

(1853–1890)

The first great Dutch painter since the seventeenth century, Vincent van Gogh did not start out as an artist. He worked for art dealers in The Hague, London and Paris. He also had a great love for humanity and was a language teacher in England, an evangelist in Brussels, and a missionary to coal miners in Belgium. At times, he was vital and exuberant while, at other times, depressed and melancholy. During several sieges of mental depression, he even admitted himself to sanitariums for help and rest. Van Gogh began painting when he was twenty-seven. He worked feverishly for only ten years before suicide ended his tragic life. Like Cézanne, he was considered a failure. He sold only a single painting while he was alive. Yet today he is considered one of the world's more important artists. He left over eight hundred drawings and an equal number of paintings.

Van Gogh was very close to his brother, Theo, who was an art dealer in Paris. In his correspondence with Theo, van Gogh fully explained his reasons, techniques and feelings about each painting as he worked on it. These letters provide a fascinating insight into the creative processes of a deeply serious painter. Van Gogh spent most of his painting years in France, had few friends, and devoted himself fully to his painting.

His early work was traditional in technique, dark in value and somber in color. But once he saw the work of the Impressionists, his colors brightened and his brushstrokes became visible. His paintings jumped alive with brilliant color and a textured surface never seen before. Rather than use the soft strokes of Renoir or the dots of Seurat, van Gogh jabbed at his canvas with vigorous strokes, applying paint in thick impasto.

Van Gogh was not satisfied with merely painting a scene or a person. He felt he had to say something about the subject or about himself and his own emotional involvement

13–27 Trace the motion of the brushstrokes to feel van Gogh's gesture with his brush.
Vincent van Gogh, *The Starry Night*, 1889. Oil on canvas, 29 1/4" x 36 1/2" (74 x 93 cm). The Museum of Modern Art, New York, Lillie P. Bliss Bequest.

13–26 Van Gogh was one of the few artists of his generation who carried on the tradition of portraiture.
Vincent van Gogh, *Portrait of a Peasant,* 1888. Oil on canvas, 25 1/2" x 21 1/4" (65 x 54 cm). The Norton Simon Art Foundation, Pasadena, CA.

with the subject. Artists who express their feelings and emotions through their work are called ***expressionists***. Van Gogh began this movement, which was later given the logical title Expressionism.

In his portraits, van Gogh used radiant, vibrating colors to immortalize his subjects. As he said, he wanted to give them "something of the eternal which the halo used to symbolize." *Portrait of a Peasant* (fig.13–26) shows his late portrait style. Sizzling color is applied with choppy strokes to build up a textural surface. He used complementary colors (orange against blue, yellow against blue-violet, and red against green). The contrast of warm against cool creates a visual vibration that at first might seem shocking.

The Starry Night (fig.13–27) is the direct opposite of the cool and calculated paintings of Seurat, van Gogh's contemporary and friend. He tried to work in Seurat's pointillistic style for a time. However, the all-consuming passion of this painting is more in keeping with van Gogh's character. It is planned and balanced, but at the same time it has a feeling of gushing spontaneity. It is as if the brush took control of the artist. Van Gogh turns the scene of a village at night, resting peacefully under the stars, into a writhing turmoil of activity. The stars not only glow in the dark sky, but move violently, perhaps noisily, as they churn through the universe. The writhing movement from left to right is halted by the moon. The moon lends stability to the sky and sends the viewer's eyes back into the picture. The snakelike vertical cypress tree also stabilizes the scene. At the same time it adds its own writhing movement. The jabbing brushstrokes across the town, trees and hills unify the entire surface. At times, the painting seems more like a textured tapestry than a painting on canvas. The curling rhythms indicate a rapidly done painting. Van Gogh probably produced it in a creative burst of activity. This provocative work forces the viewer to ask, "What is he trying to reveal about the night?"

Sidelight

Price of Art Today

Very few artists realize large sums of money for their art during their lifetime. Take, for example, the $54,000,000 recently paid for Vincent van Gogh's *Irises*. This is an extraordinary price, yet, ironically, van Gogh was able to sell only one painting in his lifetime. His brother, Theo, who was an art dealer, recognized the quality of the work, but not even he could persuade people to buy it. Had it not been for Theo's loans, van Gogh would have been in the poorhouse.

Paul Gauguin is another artist who never knew financial success, but whose work today commands huge prices. When Gauguin went to live in Tahiti, his lack of money was so dire that he was often ill and often nearly starved. The thin gloss of color on the canvases of this period are due to the fact that he could not afford sufficient materials to lay down a thicker base. Gauguin sent paintings back to France, but no one wanted to buy them, not even cheaply. Paul Gauguin's fortunes never improved, and he died poor at the age of fifty-five.

Some artists, however, do achieve recognition and financial success in their life, particularly the popular artists of the twentieth century. Picasso's work always sold well during his lifetime, even though it did not reach the prices that it does today. Contemporary American artist Jasper Johns has seen his works sold for over a million dollars.

13–28 Gauguin searched art history for styles he felt he could meaningfully use in his work. Do you see any historical influences in this painting?
Paul Gauguin, *The Vision after the Sermon (Jacob Wrestling with the Angel)*, 1888. Oil on canvas, 28 3/4" x 36 1/4" (73 x 92 cm). The National Galleries of Scotland, Edinburgh.

13–29 Gauguin rarely used lines, preferring to build his forms through color.
Paul Gauguin, *Ia Orana Maria*, 1891. Oil on canvas, 44 1/2" x 34 1/4" (113 x 87 cm). The Metropolitan Museum of Art, New York, bequest of Samuel A. Lewisohn.

Paul Gauguin

(1848–1903)

A very successful stockbroker, Paul Gauguin became intensely interested in painting in his late twenties. At first he painted for relaxation, but soon was accepted in the Salon show in 1876. He was drawn into the Impressionists' group, exhibited with them in 1879, and studied and painted with Pissarro. In 1883, he quit his job to paint. Within a few years he could no longer support his family. They soon left for his wife's homeland of Denmark. Convinced that European urban society was incurably sick, he began a long search for a better way of life. He lived in the villages of Brittany, a remote region of France, at several different times. He lived for a time in Arles with van Gogh. He traveled to the islands of Martinique and Tahiti and finally the Marquesas Islands in the South Seas, where he died in poverty.

In his painting, he rejected the formlessness of Impressionism, the traditional Western style of naturalism, and realistic portrayal. What was left for Paul Gauguin? He wanted to return to a primitive style of art with simple forms and symbolism rendered in a decorative and stylized way. Like Egyptian, medieval and Oriental artists, he outlined his shapes. He even used Egyptian poses in several of his paintings. He flattened form into decorative shapes and combined brilliant colors to express his feelings. His color combinations were innovative. He used purples with oranges, and bright blues with yellow greens.

The search for religious experience was important to Gauguin. In *The Vision after the Sermon (Jacob Wrestling with the Angel),* he tried to show the simple, direct faith of the peasants of Brittany (fig.13–28). Shapes are flat, simplified and outlined. Modeling and perspective are minimal. Instead of natural colors, Gauguin used stained-glass colors to depict the trance-like rapture of the peasant women.

Gauguin hoped to find a simple and more meaningful lifestyle in Tahiti. Although he adopted native ways and took a native wife, he remained a sophisticated Parisian.

13–30 The artist sent his paintings to Paris to be sold so that he could support himself and continue to paint in Tahiti.
Paul Gauguin, *The Day of the Gods (Mahana No Atua),* 1894. Oil on canvas, 26 3/4" x 36 3/4" (68 x 91 cm). The Art Institute of Chicago, Helen Birch Bartlett Memorial Collection, 1926.

His painting style and colors were already established in his Brittany paintings, and Tahitian influence on his work was very small. But, the natives and their colorful surroundings fill his canvases with a fascinating beauty.

One of his earliest Tahitian paintings is *Ia Orana Maria,* translated as "We Hail Thee Mary" (fig.13–29). A native woman and her son have haloes as if they are Tahitian versions of Mary and the Christ Child. Two women stand nearby in an attitude of worship. Their poses are copied from a photograph of a Javanese temple relief. Hidden in the colorful surroundings is a protective angel. Thus, Gauguin incorporates colorful and symbolic forms with a Tahitian setting to produce a unified painting. His symbolism is completely personal, distinct from the feelings and religious convictions of the Tahitian natives. Gauguin made this work to sell in Paris to support his stay in Tahiti.

In *The Day of the God* (fig.13–30), a young native mother and her two children are near the water while a huge image of a god towers over them. Almost as in an Egyptian register, a line of other natives perform their daily tasks in the background (fig.13–b). The water takes on a decorative pattern. Gauguin outlines brilliant colors in peculiar, flat shapes which are repeated in the sky. He has again combined Tahitian subject matter with his decorative symbolism and exotic colors to produce a handsome design.

Lesson 13.2 Review

1 What did Seurat do in preparation for painting *Sunday Afternoon on the Island of La Grande Jatte*? What technique did Seurat use to paint this picture? How large is *Sunday Afternoon on the Island of La Grande Jatte*?
2 Explain what concerned Cézanne so much in his paintings that he often would distort forms? What was he trying to achieve in his art?
3 What were some of Toulouse-Lautrec's favorite subjects to paint?
4 Describe the painted surface texture of Van Gogh's paintings.
5 Why is Van Gogh considered an *expressionist*?
6 How many paintings did Van Gogh sell in his lifetime? How much have his works sold for recently?
7 Why did Gauguin travel to Tahiti and the South Sea islands?
8 Describe Gauguin's painting style in *The Day of the God.*

13.3 Turn-of-the-Century Expressions

TOWARD THE END OF the nineteenth century and the beginning of the twentieth century, France dominated the art scene. There were, of course, some marvelous painters and sculptors in other countries. Their work often reflected the sterility and pessimism that many Europeans viewed as part of contemporary urban society. A number of artists followed in the footsteps of Goya, van Gogh and Gauguin by expressing their personal dissatisfaction with their cultural environment through painting.

The first seeds of the Expressionist movement which took hold in the early twentieth century can be found in the work of these artists.

Key Notes

- France continues to dominate the art scene in the late nineteenth and early twentieth centuries.
- A number of European painters express the bleakness of contemporary urban life and help trigger the beginnings of Expressionism.

Vocabulary

primitive

13–31 Munch tried to convey the sound of a cry in color and line. Was he successful?
Edward Munch, *The Cry*, 1893. Oil and tempera on cardboard, 35 3/4" x 29" (91 x 74 cm). National Gallery, Oslo, Norway.

Special Feature

Edvard Munch

(1863–1944)

Edvard Munch learned about tragedy at an early age. When he was five, his mother died. Nine years later, his adored sister died from tuberculosis. These tragic events greatly affected his life and painting. He was obsessed with death, and it is featured continuously in his art. He borrowed some techniques from the Impressionists and Post-Impressionists, but his vision remained highly personal. He was concerned with death and dying, anxiety, loss and abandonment, and loneliness.

His first one-person show was in Berlin in 1892, and it was a total disaster. The subject matter of his paintings was too pessimistic and gloomy for most people. The exhibition caused an uproar and had to be closed after a week.

The Cry (fig.13–31) is Munch's most famous painting. It depicts a figure standing on a bridge. Her hands are on either side of her face. The scream coming out of her agonized mouth is as real as if we could hear it. She is turned away from the water and we do not know if her fright has been caused by something she saw in the water or by something she is looking at. Whatever it is, it is terrible. It is almost as if the sound waves coming out of her mouth turn into the fast flowing water. The figure is isolated at the bottom of the canvas. Behind her the river looks very ominous. This is a very disturbing painting. Even the sky is perturbed.

13–32 What mood do you feel from this work?
Edvard Munch, *Girls on a Bridge,* between 1904 and 1907. Oil on canvas, 31 1/2" x 27 1/4" (80 x 69 cm). Kimbell Art Museum, Fort Worth, Texas.

Many of Munch's works are infused with a feeling of imminent tragedy. The composition of strong diagonals and dark, foreboding shapes of *Girls on a Bridge* (fig.13–32) is characteristic of his work. The textured brushstrokes remind one of van Gogh, but the overall mood is typical of Munch's work. The faceless figures are unidentifiable and incapable of accepting one's pity or help as they stare into the dark depths of the river below (fig.13–c). Munch weaves a psychological drama, but makes no comment and offers no relief. At the time that Munch was emerging as a painter, Sigmund Freud was developing his theories of psychoanalysis. In a way, Munch was painting the states of mind Freud was studying. Clearly, *Girls on a Bridge* is more than a picture of people on a bridge, such as the Impressionists or Corot might paint. Munch was expressing his own feelings of gloom toward what he was seeing.

Pablo Picasso

(1881–1974)

Pablo Picasso came to Paris from Spain as a young man in 1900. Like Munch and van Gogh, he was affected by the tragic mood that urban society was generating. His early work has been called his Blue Period because he painted beggars, derelicts and poor families with a predominately blue palette. The color fits the mood of the paintings. *The Old Guitarist* (fig.13–33) is composed entirely in blue tones. Sadness is expressed by the color, by the attitudes of the figures, and by the mysterious sea close by. Although Picasso's name weaves itself into the fabric of many aspects of twentieth-century art, his early work in Paris coincided with the beginnings of Expressionism.

13–33 What liberties has the artist taken with the figure to achieve the effect he wanted?
Pablo Picasso, *The Old Guitarist*, 1903. Oil on wood, 48" x 32" (123 x 82 cm). The Art Institute of Chicago, Helen Birch Bartlett Memorial Collection.

Window in Time

Art Theft of the Century

Boston, March 18, 1990. The early hours of the morning. While partygoers all over Boston are still celebrating St. Patrick's Day, one of the largest art heists of the century is taking place in Boston's Isabella Stewart Gardner Museum.

Although several guards are on duty during the hours the museum is open, few guards remain on the premises at night because an elaborate security system is in place. On this night, two overnight guards, one an art student and the other a musician, were on duty. One of the guards was patrolling the galleries while the other sat behind the security console at the Palace Road service entrance. At 1:24 a.m., the bell was rung at the house's Palace Road entrance. The outside TV camera that continuously scanned Palace Road and the side entrance showed two police officers ringing the bell. The guard at the desk pushed the outdoor speaker button and asked, "What's going on?"

Edouard Manet, *Chez Tortoni*. Isabella Stewart Gardner Museum, Boston

"Boston Police," replied one of the men, adding that they had received a report of a disturbance in the outdoor compound. The museum gardens are surrounded by a high wall. The guard said he hadn't heard anything. The policeman then asked, "Any other guards on duty?"

"One," the watch desk guard replied. "He's upstairs doing rounds."

"Call him down and let us in," the policeman said. "We'll have to check out the garden compound."

This all seemed quite normal to the guard, and he did as the policeman said. The two men came in, and the three of them chatted while they waited for the other guard to join them. But, once he had, the two bogus policemen spun the guards around and flung them against the wall. Quickly, they manacled the guards' hands and covered their eyes, ears and mouths with plastic tape. Then, they hustled them down the stairs to the basement and, taking them to opposite ends of a long corridor, handcuffed them to heating pipes and left them lying on the concrete floor.

The thieves were then free to do as they wanted. Clearly, they knew how the museum security was set up. Before starting the robbery, they turned around the video cameras taping them. They also broke open the security room, destroyed the videocassettes and switched off a central computer that recorded any movements in the gallery. However, they did not manage to turn the system off completely and some of their activities in the museum were taped. The theft was discovered when the morning personnel arrived and could not get in.

The thieves stole priceless works by Rembrandt, Vermeer, Flinck, Degas and Manet. The value of the stolen art was estimated at $200 million. However, the artworks are so famous that they can never be sold, traded or displayed in a private collection without instantly being recognized.

After the robbery, art experts predicted that the paintings would either be abandoned or anonymously returned. Gardner Museum officials take comfort in the knowledge that it usually takes a number of years to recover stolen art. They also know that the more famous the work, the higher the chance of recovery.

Henri Rousseau

(1844–1910)

A customs official of France, Henri Rousseau gave up his government job at middle age and took up painting. His goal was to paint the world around him with absolute realism, in the style of Ingres. Without any formal art training, this was impossible. Instead, he presents an enchanted world of forests and tropical jungles filled with exotic flowers, fantastic animals and an occasional person or two. Fellow artists admired his directness of vision, innocence of technique and his naive spirit. His ***primitive*** style was born of technical limitations, but produced paintings of great enchantment.

Rousseau painted in a new way—innocently and truthfully. Picasso and Gauguin called him the godfather of twentieth-century painting. In *The Sleeping Gypsy* (fig.13–34), he crafted a smooth surface with no visible brushstrokes, a technique not commonly used. The meaning of the work is mysterious and is not fully explained in the painting. The final interpretation is left to the viewer. The huge moonlit sky, simplified landscape elements, multicolored coat and the sniffing lion work together to create a sense of magical calm. Recently, it has been discovered that Rousseau used children's toys, purchased on sale at a Paris store, as models for the painting. He depicted them as realistically as he could.

13–34 This painting is open to many interpretations. What story do you think the painting tells?
Henri Rousseau, *The Sleeping Gypsy*, 1897. Oil on canvas, 50 3/4" x 79" (129 x 201 cm). The Museum of Modern Art, New York, gift of Mrs. Simon Guggenheim.

The rhythmic beauty of his concepts was lost on the public. They considered him an untrained novice and laughed at his magical portrayals with outright indignation. In their derision, they overlooked the naive honesty and dreamlike expression of this delightful artist.

Lesson 13.3 Review

1 As the twentieth century began, which country was the center of Western art?
2 What themes did Edward Munch paint?
3 What is Munch's most famous painting?
4 Why is Picasso's early work called his Blue Period? Name an example of a painting from his blue period.
5 Why did Henri Rousseau paint with an innocence of technique?

Primary Source

James A. McNeill Whistler

James A. McNeill Whistler was an argumentative artist and disliked any criticism of his paintings or their titles. He rejected his friends' suggestion that he would earn more money if he simply gave his paintings names that indicated a real scene. He thought such a thing would be "a vulgar and meretricious trick." The following comments from Whistler's publication, *The Gentle Art of Making Enemies*, are his reply to these friends.

Cheyne Walk, London, May, 1878

Why should not I call my works "symphonies," "arrangements," "harmonies," and "nocturnes"? I know that many good people think my nomenclature funny and myself "eccentric." Yes, "eccentric" is the adjective they find for me.

The vast majority of English folk cannot and will not consider a picture as a picture, apart from any story which it may be supposed to tell.

As music is the poetry of sound, so is painting the poetry of sight, and the subject-matter has nothing to do with harmony of sound or of color.

Take the picture of my mother, exhibited at the Royal Academy as an *Arrangement in Grey and Black*, Now that is what it is. To me it is interesting as a picture of my mother; but what can or ought the public to care about the identity of the portrait?

Art should be independent of all clap-trap—should stand alone, and appeal to the artistic sense of eye or ear, without confounding this with emotions entirely foreign to it, as devotion, pity, love, patriotism, and the like. All these have no kind of concern with it; and that is why I insist on calling my works "arrangements" and "harmonies."

Chapter Review

Review

1 What were the Impressionists trying to achieve in their paintings?

2 What techniques did Manet use to make his paintings such as *Gare Saint-Lazare* and *The Waitress* seem like a snapshot or a view that was quickly glimpsed?

3 Explain why Renoir's *Dance at the Moulin de la Galette Montmartre* is a good example of Impressionism.

4 Describe the color and composition in Whistler's *Arrangement in Gray and Black No. 1: The Artist's Mother*. What was Whistler trying to achieve in this painting?

5 List four Post-Impressionist artists. After each one's name, write three adjectives to describe his style.

6 Describe the motion, the colors, the texture, the mood and the subject matter in van Gogh's *The Starry Night*. How large is it?

7 Describe a painting by Henri Rousseau. What did he use as his models? What is the texture of the painting surface? What is the subject?

Interpret

1 Select one of Degas' paintings; then describe how Degas directs the viewer's gaze through this composition, how he leads you into the painting and from one figure to the next. What do you think is the center of interest? What type of balance is this?

2 Explain the symbolism in Gauguin's *Ia Orana Maria*.

3 How are the composition and mood in Munch's *Girls on a Bridge* similar to Degas' *The Absinthe Drinker*?

Other Tools for Learning

Maps

1 Find Arles and Paris on the map. Why do you think van Gogh might have moved from Paris to Arles?

2 Monet's *Impression: Sunrise* was painted at Le Havre. He painted the cathedral at Rouen, and he and Renoir painted at Argenteuil. What great river runs through all these towns?

Timelines

Select one event from the non-European cultural timelines and explain how this eventually affected the countries of North America.

Electronic Research

Videodisc player: *National Gallery of Art*

1 Look at an Impressionist painting, such as one of Monet's *Rouen Cathedral* series or his *Water Lilies*, either in an art gallery or on a video disk with close-up views. What does the surface of the painting look like close-up? What does the painting look like when you back away from it?

CD-ROM drive: *Microsoft Art Gallery*

1 To understand how Seurat created with pointillism, watch the animation sequence in the Making Paintings Guided Tour. Explain the pointillism technique.

Activity 1

Still Life Pastel

Materials
vine charcoal
hard and soft pastels
pastel pencils for details
torchons
charcoal or watercolor paper
spray fixative
kneaded erasers
optional: masonite boards with bull clips, tracing paper

Take a look.
- Fig.13–22, Paul Cézanne, *Still Life With Apples and Peaches*, 1905. Oil on canvas.
- Fig.13–14, Mary Cassatt, *Sleeping Baby*, about 1910. Pastel on paper.
- Fig.13–9, Edgar Degas, *Rehearsal on the Stage*, 1874. Pastel on paper.

Think about it. Many well-known artists worked with pastels, among them Paul Cézanne, Edgar Degas, and Mary Cassatt. Study the color, line and composition in Cézanne's still life and the color blending in the pastels of Degas and Cassatt. Research other examples of pastel artwork and still lifes.

Do it.
- Choose interesting objects from your environment, ones that vary in shape, texture and color, to assemble for a still life.
- Do several practice sketches in vine charcoal before beginning your work in pastel. Draw one object at a time, concentrating on subtle details of that object; then draw thumbnail sketches of the still life to find a successful composition.
- Begin the still life with vine charcoal. Use white, black and gray hard pastels to outline the basic shapes. Draw lightly with hard pastels to build up color. Work with your teacher on the use of spray fixatives to seal the surface between layers.
- Change to soft pastels for the finishing layers.

Check it. Does your still life reflect your personal interpretation in your own style? Are the details and texture of the objects portrayed well?

Helpful Hint: Practice drawing loosely folded cloth, emphasizing the light and shadows.

Activity 2

Same Place Next Time

Materials
select from materials listed in Activity 1 as needed

Take a look.
- Fig.13–1, Claude Monet, *Argenteuil*, 1872. Oil on canvas.
- Fig.13–2, Claude Monet, *Rouen Cathedral*, 1894. Oil on canvas.
- Fig.13–3, Claude Monet, *Rouen Cathedral, West Facade, Sunlight*, 1894. Oil on canvas.

Think about it. Monet loved to work outdoors and to directly confront the environment he was painting. This was a departure from the artists of the past who might sketch outdoors but sought the comfort of their studios to do the actual painting.

Do it. Do a long-term study of the effect of light and atmosphere on a building.
- FInd a building in your neighborhood that interests you. It can be a barn, a church or even a house on your block.
- Do a number of sketches of your building until you are very familiar with its structure, its details and its surroundings.
- Work in the medium of pastel, which will be easy to transport to the site and will allow you to reproduce the Impressionist color palette.
- Create these drawings at different times of the day: early morning, midday, late afternoon and even at sunset. Choose varying weather conditions as well. A bright sunny day, an overcast day, even a foggy day will each give you the opportunity to see your building in a different way.

Check it. Each time you do a new sketch, take a fresh look from another perspective. Though Monet painted the same subject many times, he would often sit in a new location and capture it from a different angle.

Helpful Hint: Using short strokes will create the shimmering effects of color so common in Impressionist work. Also, do not use black in your drawings, but, instead, search for color in the shadows of your building.

Additional Activities

- Analyze a still life by Cézanne and one by Renoir. Compare the similarities and differences in relation to: sensory qualities of each, the formal qualities of each, the technical qualities of each, and the expressive qualities of each.
- The dot patterns of Seurat's paintings use the same principle that modern printers used in recreating the color photography in this book. If you examine any color reproduction with a magnifying glass, you should only find four colors of ink—the three primary colors and black. Using these four colors of tempera paint, experiment with dot patterns to see if you can recreate a full-color image.

Rachel Miller

Age 17
Clarkstown High School North
New City, New York
Favorite kinds of art: painting, drawing and sculpture
Favorite artists: Salvador Dali, Henry Matisse, Edvard Munch
Activity 1, Still Life Pastel

This project is especially meaningful to me since I tend to work from my imagination. The still life gave me a lot of motivation—I wanted to do it, but I didn't rush myself to get it done.

While working, I didn't have an exact plan; I let the pastels simply flow. I wanted to make the piece appear sensitive, since the still life itself had a soft, fragile, warm glow. I wasn't looking for realism, it was more for a feeling, a tenderness that these objects did not emulate on their own, but one that I knew I could bring out. Every object is an art form and creates a certain kind of uniqueness.

Besides my own creative instincts, the history of art was another factor that influenced my piece. Not until a few years ago did I realize that I wanted to pursue the arts as a career. Henry Matisse had an enormous impact on me. He created his masterpieces from his heart, not with his eyes or his hands. In my opinion, his pieces became stronger as his sight weakened. They contained more expression, beauty and emotion. Copying an object directly may be beautiful, but if it has no emotion behind it, then it is not worth the paper on which it was created.

In the artistic process, I enjoy the thought-gathering. Simply thinking about the materials, style, and technique gives me the ability to expand my mind. When I brainstorm, I don't wonder how my piece will appear ultimately, rather I visualize constantly in my mind as an ongoing process. Anyone has an artistic license to create. I feel there are no limits in art. Exposing my mind to art is most important.

To other students interested in creating, I say, "Do it. What have you got to lose?" I believe in the importance of doing what you enjoy most and never settling for anything else. Even if I do not make it as a successful artist, I know I will continue creating art for my own personal pleasure. If you have a gift and you want to share it, take full advantage of it. As you continue to develop your talent, don't let criticism discourage you. The world needs more artists and thinkers. Express yourself, create, think and let your imagination flow.

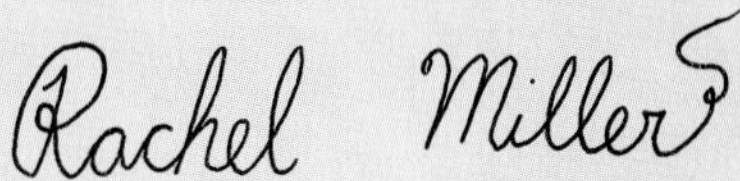

Still Life with Wine Bottle, 1994. Pastel on charcoal paper, 12" x 18" (30.5 x 45.7 cm).

14 A Half-Century of "Isms"

In This Chapter...

FROM THE SEEDS OF Impressionism and Post-Impressionism grew a variety of styles that almost defy logical organization. Several styles flourished simultaneously. New art movements began and ended with amazing speed.

During the first half of this century, the two main movements in Europe were Expressionism and Abstract art. Expressionist artists sought to express their feelings in a strong way. They often focused on the stress and alienation of modern life. Abstract artists were more interested in design than in realistic imagery.

Two other major movements were Fantasy art and Surrealism. These movements focused on the power and mystery of the fantasy world. Often, these styles left the viewer with more questions than answers, much like our dreams do.

At this same time, photographers began experimenting in new directions. They used the camera to create beautiful interpretations of everyday life and the natural world.

14–a Many early twentieth-century artists were influenced by the art of Africa. Pablo Picasso, *Les Demoiselles d'Avignon*, detail (fig.14–24).

14–b How does the photographer use space to bring this image to life? Henri Cartier-Bresson, *Woman on a Stairway Talking to a Man with Cane.* Silver print. The Detroit Institute of Arts, Michigan State Council for the Arts Exhibition Fund.

Expressionism to my way of thinking does not consist of the passion mirrored upon a human face or betrayed by a violent gesture. The whole arrangement of my picture is expressive.
— Henri Matisse

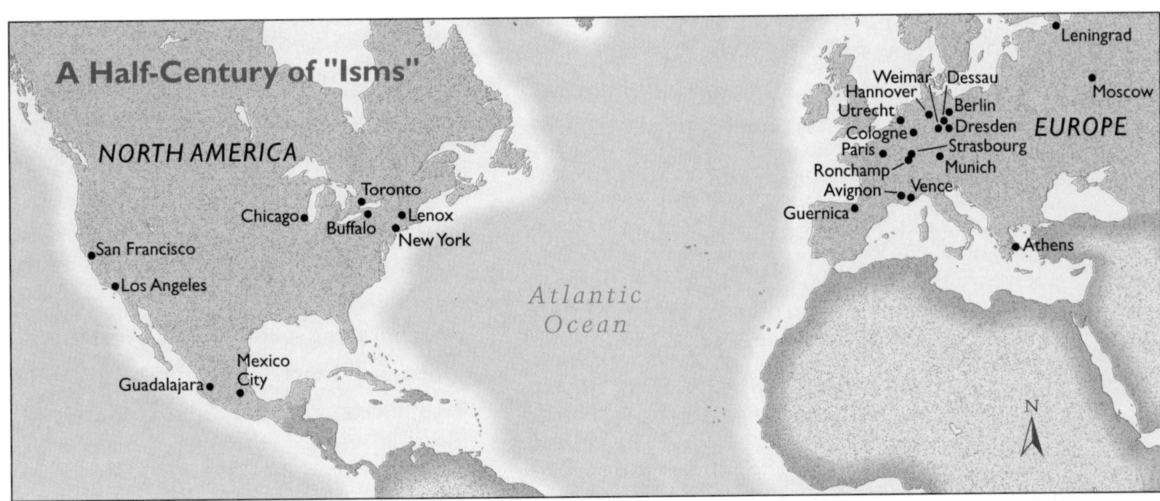

Faster, easier modes of communication and transportation provide the means for art to bridge the Atlantic. New York plays a more important role as art schools develop in the United States.

14–c Expressionism does not connote a particular style. Artists such as Beckmann sought to express emotional states in their work. What emotions does this image evoke?
Max Beckmann, *Baccarat*, detail (fig.14–17).

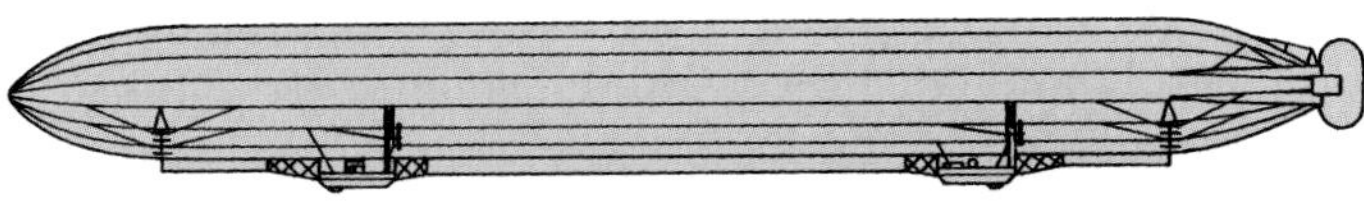

1900
First trial flight of Zeppelin

1912
Duchamp uses "ready-made" objects displayed as art

1917–1918
Stella, *Brooklyn Bridge*

1922
Klee, *The Twittering Machine*

1931
Dali, *The Persistence of Memory*

1943–1945
Cartier-Bresson photographs for the Resistance

A Half-Century of "Isms"

1907
Picasso, *Les Demoiselles d'Avignon*
1907
Triple Entente alliance between Britain, France and Russia

1913
Boccioni, *Unique Forms of Continuity in Space*

1917
Russian Revolution
1919
League of Nations

1924
Miró signs Surrealist manifesto

1939
World War II starts
1940
Discovery of penicillin

1945
United Nations founded

14.1 Expressionism

IT IS DIFFICULT TO GROUP ARTISTS according to style in the twentieth century. Each artist was trying to develop an individual style different from all other artists. But certain characteristics do group artists together for the sake of organization and study. The term *Expressionist art* refers to an attitude or philosophy of art rather than a style, because artists of many styles can be expressionistic in their work. The Expressionist artists working in the first half of the twentieth century were not interested in naturalism. They sought a means to express emotional states in their work as well as to portray the many stresses brought on by life in the modern world.

In France, there was Fauvism with its bold distortion, violent color and vigorous brushstrokes. In Germany, a number of solitary artists were setting the stage for the development of German Expressionism. Several Expressionist groups evolved in Germany. These included Die Brücke (The Bridge) and Der Blaue Reiter (The Blue Rider).

In America, artists after 1910, although familiar with Fauvism and German Expressionism, were very slow to adopt any part of the movements into their own work. Mexican artists, though, were spurred on by the fall of the dictator Porfirio Diaz. Their new freedom of expression developed into a national style "of the people" that typified the spirit of the Revolution. Combining simple, solid feeling of pre-Columbian figures and the powerful colors and forms of German Expressionism, artists decorated the walls and ceilings of Mexico City with vibrant murals.

Key Notes

- Expressionism is an attitude or philosophy of art rather than a particular style.
- Fauvism and German Expressionism dominate in Europe.
- In the Americas, Mexican artists develop their own style of Expressionism.

Vocabulary
avant-garde
nonobjective

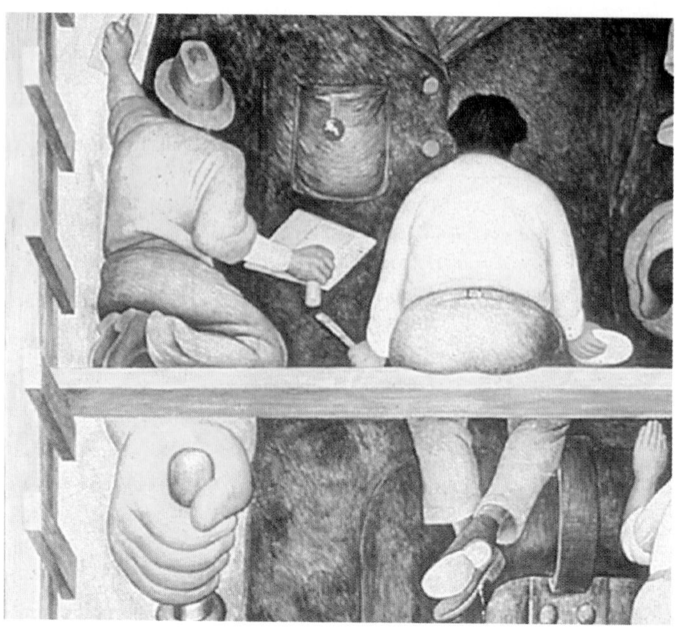

14–3 Rivera has incorporated two different activities into one painting. Can you identify them? (The title gives a hint.)
Diego Rivera, *The Making of a Fresco Showing the Building of a City*, detail.

Special Feature

Diego Rivera

(1886–1957)

Diego Rivera was influenced by many styles, but ultimately achieved his own brilliant and personal expression. Rivera studied in Paris and knew Picasso and the rest of the artists in Paris creating the newest forms of visual expression (***avant-garde***). But, he returned to Mexico in 1921 to become actively involved in its politics.

Influenced by the simple, outlined forms of Gauguin and his own cultural heritage of Mayan and Aztec sculpture, Rivera developed a powerful and unique painting style. Rivera revived the fresco technique, which had not been used extensively for centuries, and put his ideas on public walls for all to see. *Liberation of the Peon* (fig.14–1) is a strong social protest against the inhumanity of the landowners toward those who worked for them. The figures are solid, bulky and rounded, much like those of Giotto. Folds in cloth are heavy and simple. Figures are shaded in the traditional way to create a feeling of roundness and dimension.

By the late 1920s, Rivera's murals were well-known in the United States. In the early 1930s, he was one of the most sought-after artists in this country. One of his numerous commissions was for a mural for the San Francisco Art Institute. *The Making of a Fresco Showing the Building of a City* (fig.14–2) was executed from April to June 1931. The mural's theme is the design and construction of a modern industrial city in the United States. The activities of workers and planners, both

14–2 An artist of great talent, Rivera trained in Europe and brought the classical techniques of fresco back to Mexico.
Diego Rivera, *The Making of a Fresco Showing the Building of a City*, 1931. Fresco, 22'7" x 29'9" (688.3 x 906 m). San Francisco Art Institute.

above and below ground, are seen through a scaffold that supports a fresco painter (Rivera himself) and his assistants (fig.14–3). The giant helmeted worker in the background is the symbol of a technologically planned and worker-controlled industrial city. The worker is sovereign in this fresco. Rivera paints industry in an idealized setting where everyone works in harmony with each other.

Many ceilings and walls in major Mexican cities are covered with the powerful visual statements of Mexican Expressionists. These artists and their European counterparts embarked on a wide-ranging exploration of art as an expressive, emotional force.

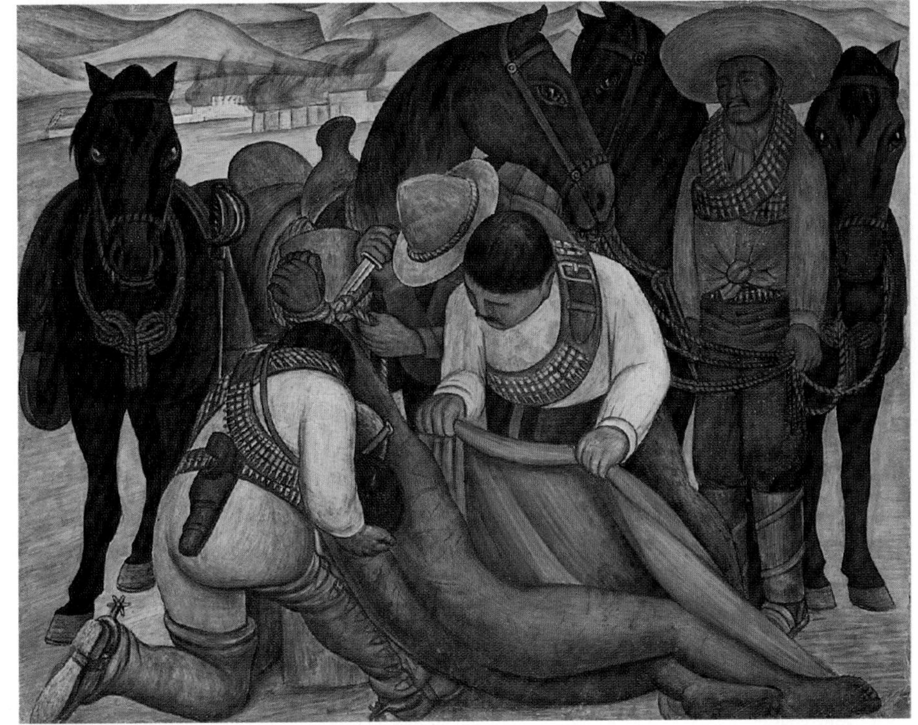

14–1 Compare this fresco to some of those from the Italian Renaissance.
Diego Rivera, *Liberation of the Peon*, 1931. Fresco, 74" x 95" (188 x 241 cm). Philadelphia Museum of Art: Given by Mr. and Mrs. Herbert Cameron Morris.

The Fauves

Between 1901 and 1906 in Paris, young artists were greatly impressed by the freedom, color and individual character of works by Cézanne, van Gogh and Gauguin. These artists filled their canvases with vigorous brushstrokes and raw, bright, hot colors that sizzled. One shocked critic described the art as the work of "wild beasts." The French word for wild beasts is Fauves, and the revolutionary artists accepted the title with pride; their work was thus called Fauvism.

Henri Matisse

(1869–1954)

While studying to become a lawyer, Henri Matisse felt the urge to paint—a feeling that completely changed his life. In the exhibition of 1905, Matisse exhibited several shocking works with the "wild beasts." He used intense colors and simplified complex subjects. This ability moved him into the forefront of Fauvism and he became spokesperson for the group. He wanted to express himself with simple color and shape rather than shading and perspective.

14–4 In this picture of his studio, and in his other work, Matisse emphasized the idea that a painting of three-dimensional space still should remain true to the fact that a canvas is really two-dimensional.

Henri Matisse, *The Red Studio*, 1911. Oil on canvas, 71" x 86" (181 x 219 cm). The Museum of Modern Art, New York, Mrs. Simon Guggenheim Fund.

Six years after the Fauves exploded on the art scene, Matisse painted *The Red Studio* (fig.14–4), which summarizes his artistic goals. The dominant color of red is used for walls, floor and many of the pieces of furniture. Matisse creates a flattened effect, enhanced by the lack of shadow and value changes. On the wall are a number of his Fauvist paintings from the previous few years. Renaissance painting concepts are almost completely eliminated and a brilliant, personal quality emerges.

In his later years, Matisse experimented with collage—pinning and pasting brightly colored flat shapes on contrasting backgrounds. When confined to his bed by illness, he used his collage technique with powerful results. In 1950, he assembled one of his most beautiful collages, *Beasts of the Sea* (fig.14–5). He cut shapes directly from colored paper without first outlining them in pencil. From the hundreds of colored scraps strewn around his bed, this charming work emerged. It is a memory of a visit he made to the South Seas twenty years earlier. By looking carefully, as if into a lagoon, one can see simplified symbolic shapes that recall sea plants, coral, sea animals, fish, water, land and sky. Matisse arranged his cutouts like a series of small enameled panels. Instead of using pastel colors for water, sky and underwater forms, Matisse used vivid hues. These heightened colors, often contrasting and dissonant for greater impact, produce a visual excitement that a realistic representation of the underwater scene could not convey.

In 1943, Matisse became quite ill and was cared for by the Dominican nuns in the southern French village of Vence. To thank them for their help, he designed, financed and built them a wonderful chapel

World Cultural Timeline

1900
The Boxers revolt against government, China

1908
Death of last Chinese Empress, Tzu-hsi

1901
Australia becomes independent country; commonwealth founded

1910
First Japanese airplane built

14–6 This chapel was a gift of thanks for care Matisse received when he was ill. The color from the windows changes as the sun moves and the weather changes.
Henri Matisse. *Chapel of the Rosary of the Dominican Nuns,* 1948–1951. Vence, France.

(fig.14–6). The chapel is white, inside and out. The only color comes from light entering through yellow, blue and green glass in the windows, casting ever-changing patterns on the floors and walls. The wall decorations are simple and linear, and are fired in black on the white tile. Matisse designed the altar, windows, wall decorations, crucifix, candelabra and even the vestments for the officiants. He provided a beautiful and uncomplicated environment for prayer and worship.

The extreme simplicity of Matisse's work is extraordinarily difficult to accomplish. The artist had a marvelous ability to look at a complex subject and then reduce it to its simplest elements using line and colored shapes. Of course, this is much more difficult to do than it looks, and few artists have ever done it as well as Matisse.

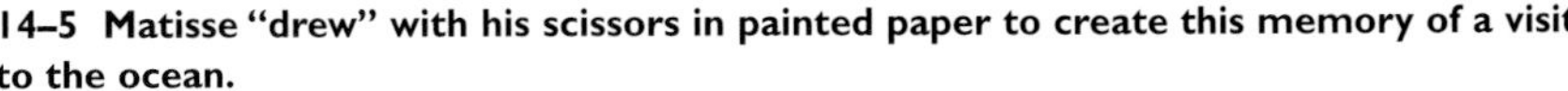

14–5 Matisse "drew" with his scissors in painted paper to create this memory of a visit to the ocean.
Henri Matisse, *Beasts of the Sea,* 1950. Paper on canvas (collage), 116 1/2" x 60 1/2" (296 x 154 cm). National Gallery of Art, Washington, DC, Ailsa Mellon Bruce Fund.

Georges Rouault

(1871–1958)

A devout Catholic, Georges Rouault used his paintings to express his deep concern over the immoral conditions of poverty and war. Rouault's expression was personal and deeply rooted in his religious background and his fascination with medieval life. His early paintings were of various religious subjects, done in traditional styles. He also spent some time working in a stained-glass studio—an experience that helped shape his mature painting style. He met Matisse and, for a while, worked with the Fauves, enjoying their unrestrained use of color. But, by 1911, his work turned darker and more subjective as he expressed his indignation at the evils around him: prostitution, injustice, poverty and corruption. He became a marvelous printmaker during this time. He used many new technical devices in several series of prints that expressed his feelings.

Rouault's numerous depictions of Christ were often limited to tragic faces as his *Head of Christ* (fig.14–7) illustrates. While Matisse insisted that his entire composition expressed his feelings, Rouault felt that his "passion" was "mirrored upon a human face." Rouault's favorite impasto technique, broad brushstrokes and massive black lines, aids his personal expression. Since Grünewald, no artist had expressed the tragedy, humility and suffering of Christ with such conviction and feeling. In such works, Rouault was leaning more toward German Expressionism than toward Fauvism.

14–8 Compare this painting to the stained glass *St. Denis and Jean-Clement* (fig.8–39) from the Cathedral of Chartres.
Georges Rouault, *The Old King*, 1937. Oil on canvas, 30" x 21" (77 x 54 cm). Museum of Art, Carnegie Institute, Pittsburgh.

Heavy black lines (like the lead in stained glass windows) are used to cage brilliant colors in *The Old King* (fig.14–8), one of Rouault's later works. This sorrowful monarch could be a figure from the Old Testament, like King David or Solomon. Glowing colors are separated by heavy lines. These lines also control eye movement and outline the half figure, separating it from the background. Rouault, using a technique vastly different from Impressionism, successfully combines his interest in medieval art and religious concepts with a personal, dynamic form of visual expression.

14–7 Do you see any similarities to medieval representations of Christ?
Georges Rouault, *Head of Christ*, not dated. Oil on panel, 23" x 19" (59 x 48 cm). Los Angeles County Museum of Art, bequest of David L. Loew in memory of his father Marcus Loew.

German Expressionism

The artists Paula Modersohn-Becker and Käthe Kollwitz set the stage for German Expressionism in their powerful and sympathetic studies of peasants and working-class people. Eventually, several groups emerged from the movement. Among these were Die Brücke and Der Blaue Reiter.

Paula Modersohn-Becker

(1876–1907)

Paula Modersohn-Becker was one of the most important German artists of her day. If Modersohn-Becker had not died at the age of 31, she would probably have become a dominant figure in the Expressionist movement. She traveled often to France to see the work of Gauguin and van Gogh, introducing Gauguin's simplified forms, exotic color and use of line to Germany. These characteristics are evident in Modersohn-Becker's *Self-Portrait with Camellia Branch* (fig.14–9) done in 1907.

Old Peasant Woman Praying (fig.14–10) is a dramatic study of a German farm woman in an ancient attitude of worship. Although Modersohn-Becker's earlier work was more realistic, this portrait shows her personal feelings about such people. The painting reflects the influence of both Gauguin and van Gogh. Such features as yellow skin, heavy-lidded eyes, a prominent nose, and a melancholy look caused the Nazis to confiscate the work. The Nazis denounced this "ugly painting" in 1937 as "degenerate art." Most German Expressionistic paintings suffered a similar fate and were later sold by the government to collectors and museums outside the country.

14–9 The artist died at the early age of thirty-one shortly after giving birth to a daughter. She painted this self-portrait the same year that she died.
Paula Modersohn-Becker, *Self-Portrait with Camellia Branch*, 1907. Oil on canvas, 24 1/2" x 12" (62 x 30 cm). Folkwang Museum, Essen.

14–10 The artist was influenced by Gauguin and van Gogh. What evidence of their influence do you see?
Paula Modersohn-Becker, *Old Peasant Woman Praying*, about 1905. Oil on canvas, 30" x 22 3/4" (76 X 58 cm). The Detroit Institute of Arts, gift of Robert H. Tannahill.

14–11 Kollwitz created many posters to express the impact of World War I and its aftermath on Germany and her children. Like many other artists she felt war could not be allowed to happen again.
Käthe Kollwitz, *Never Again War!*, 1924. Lithograph. Courtesy Galerie St. Etienne, New York.

14–12 Kollwitz did many self-portraits throughout her life. She never flinched from portraying her aging face or body.
Käthe Kollwitz, *Self-Portrait*, 1934. Charcoal and crayon on paper, 17" x 13 2/5" (43 x 34 cm). Los Angeles County Museum of Art.

Käthe Kollwitz

(1867–1945)

Käthe Kollwitz was one of the most powerfully emotional artists of this century. She worked in Berlin most of her life and was evacuated in the bombings of 1943. Her etchings, woodcuts, lithographs and drawings express her feelings about old age, hard work, war, motherhood and death. *Never Again War!* (fig.14–11) is a stirring example of this expression. She used the working-class people as her models even though she was married to a prominent Berlin doctor.

Her *Self-Portrait* (fig.14–12), one of many she did, was drawn with charcoal pencil when she was sixty-seven years old. The taut expression and lined features bear witness to a long and difficult life. The eyes and mouth are handled with special emphasis. The contrast of shadow and line is used effectively to produce a feeling of form and volume. Yet, the artist used very little detail, emphasizing instead the broad planes and the stark, powerful drama of the human face.

Die Brücke

(The Bridge)

A small brotherhood called Die Brücke (The Bridge) was formed in Dresden in 1905, the same year the colorful explosions of Fauvism were taking hold in France. The artists were ardent admirers of Munch, van Gogh and Gauguin. The group vehemently rejected academic training in art and all traditional forms of expression. They revived avid interest in the woodcut and other graphic means of expression. In their paintings and powerful and somber woodcuts, they emphasized violent color and distortion of features. They cried out against the economic and social conditions in Germany prior to World War I. They also studied African art in depth, especially the expressive masks and carvings, and tried to include some of those characteristics in their paintings. The group broke up in 1913, but in those few years exerted considerable influence on public taste.

Ernst Ludwig Kirchner

(1880–1938)

The early leader of Die Brücke was Ernst Ludwig Kirchner. He insisted that "art depends on inspiration and not on technique." In his early paintings, such as *The Street* (fig.14–13), he worked in flat color areas with bright hues and heavy black shapes. The tension and agitation of the street are expressed by sharp, angular shapes and vivid, acid colors. There is isolation and loneliness even in such crowded conditions.

14–13 What can you detect about who these people are and Kirchner's feelings about them?
Ernst Ludwig Kirchner, *The Street*, 1913. Oil on canvas, 47 3/4" x 35 3/4" (121 x 91 cm). The Museum of Modern Art, New York.

Emil Nolde

(1867–1956)

Emil Nolde was a bit older than the rest of the members of Die Brücke and remained in the group for only two years. Like Rouault, he painted many religious themes, but his slashing brushstrokes and garish colors were not pleasing to the public. His grotesque faces in *Masks* (fig.14–14) show his interest in primitive cultures and his desire to relate them to his contemporary time. He used these faces to show personal contempt for immorality, greed, avarice, lust and hypocrisy as they appeared in his society.

14–14 There were many masks from non-Western cultures in museums and private collections. Nolde used some of them as a base upon which to comment about contemporary society.
Emil Nolde, *Masks*, 1911. Oil on canvas, 28" x 30" (71 x 76 cm). The Nelson-Atkins Museum of Art, Kansas City, Missouri, gift of the Friends of Art.

Der Blaue Reiter

(The Blue Rider)

Among the many other Expressionist groups spawned in Germany prior to World War I was a small, important group of artists who called themselves Der Blaue Reiter (The Blue Rider). Centered in Munich from 1911 to 1912, it included the German Franz Marc, and the Russian Wassily Kandinsky. They were not social revolutionaries, but were strong individual artists who exerted a powerful influence as twentieth-century art unfolded.

Franz Marc

(1880–1916)

While Franz Marc painted many kinds of subjects, his animal paintings are of major importance. Marc used brilliant color in a symbolic and arbitrary way. He combined color with shape and rhythm to dramatize the integration of all creatures in nature. There probably has never been a more joyful cow than the one cavorting in his work *The Yellow Cow* (fig.14–15). Placed into the rhythmic flow of an equally colorful landscape, the happy creature fills the picture with powerful movement and an active shape. The movement of the animal seems to charge the environment with equal excitement. Marc's death during World War I cut short a very promising career.

14–15 Compare this cow to the cattle and bison painted on the cave walls at Lascaux.
Franz Marc, *The Yellow Cow*, 1911. Oil on canvas, 55 1/2" x 74 1/2" (141 x 189 cm). Solomon R. Guggenheim Museum, New York.

Wassily Kandinsky

(1866–1944)

Wassily Kandinsky was born in Moscow, but attended art school in Munich. He is credited with painting the first completely ***nonobjective*** painting about 1910. He returned to Russia, but was soon back in Germany, teaching at the Bauhaus. (The Bauhaus was a German art school where many modern concepts of design originated.)

His early paintings were similar in feeling to those of the Fauves, with recognizable houses and trees painted in vivid colors. The shapes in *Study for Composition No. 2* (fig.14–16) are already quite abstract, but many forms are still recognizable. Gradually, he simplified and abstracted these features until only shape, color and line were left. The subject matter was not recognizable. He titled these paintings with musical terminology such as "Improvisation 9" or "Composition No. 138." Kandinsky explained that improvisations were "unplanned and spontaneous expressions of inner character, non-material in nature."

Certain kinds of lines and various colors had personal meaning to Kandinsky. He wrote that to him "blue is soft and round while yellow is sharp." He developed his own personal language of color and shape to express his feelings. His later work was more geometric and more carefully organized, but just as nonobjective. His influence became very strong in the Abstract Expressionist movement following World War II. Often, the colors seem dissonant and slashing, as sounds clash in the musical compositions of his friend Igor Stravinsky.

14–16 Kandinsky was also trained as a musician. He titled his paintings with musical terminology.
Wassily Kandinsky, *Study for Composition No. 2*, 1909–1910. Oil on canvas, 51" x 38" (130 x 97 cm). The Solomon R. Guggenheim Museum, New York.

Max Beckmann

(1884–1950)

Max Beckmann started out in the traditional mainstream of art, but after World War I he began painting his nightmarish expressions of decadence and the tragedy of the human condition. Beckmann painted humanity as puppet-like figures that have been dehumanized by social conditions. Bright, raw colors are outlined with hard black lines. Like many German artists of the time, Beckmann had to flee Nazi Germany when he was officially labeled "degenerate." His last three years were spent in the United States.

His symbolism and style are personal and often unexplainable. In *Baccarat* (fig.14–17), it is difficult to explain the man with the sword in an otherwise tranquil casino setting. Yet, most of his characters seem ominous and/or evil, which is part of Beckmann's symbolic vocabulary.

Amedeo Modigliani

(1884–1920)

Amedeo Modigliani was born in Italy, but spent most of his life painting in Paris. His early work was influenced by Toulouse-Lautrec. However, he soon developed a unique style based on the elongated distortion of African sculpture, the design and brushwork of Cézanne, the sketchy line and flat shapes of Matisse, and his innate Italian interest in portraiture. He was an excellent draftsman. As *Gypsy Woman with Baby* (fig.14–18) shows, he was able to simplify human features into a dignified and simple statement. His style often recalls the Italian Mannerist distortion and elongation found in the work of El Greco. Although many outside influences can be found in Modigliani's work, his final expressions are completely unique in their design and emotional content.

14–18 Can you identify two sources of influence on Modigliani's painting?
Amedeo Modigliani, *Gypsy Woman with Baby*, 1919. Oil on canvas, 45 1/4" x 28 3/4" (115 x 73 cm). National Gallery of Art, Washington, DC, Chester Dale Collection.

14–17 Society after World War I was often characterized as decadent. Many artists commented on the degenerate self-centeredness and hinted at the dire consequences of such behavior.
Max Beckmann, *Baccarat*, 1947. Oil on canvas, 47" x 39" (119 x 100 cm). The Nelson-Atkins Museum of Art, Kansas City, Missouri, gift of the Friends of Art, 54-86.

14–19 The maguey plant is an important source of food, cloth, rope and other items for the desert people of Mexico.
José Clemente Orozco, *Mexican Landscape,* 1930. Oil on canvas, 30" x 37" (76 x 94 cm). Formerly at Los Angeles County Museum of Art, gift of Charles K. Feldman.

Expressionism in the Americas

Like Diego Rivera, other artists in Mexico combined expressionist techniques with social protest. Their works provided powerful political and social statements about the struggles of the common people, or *peons,* of Mexico.

José Clemente Orozco

(1883–1949)

Beginning with the fresco technique, José Clemente Orozco later used more modern materials to fill walls and ceilings in Guadalajara and other cities with his powerful statements. Orozco's murals are dramatic and political. They were often commissioned by revolutionary governments.

Mexican Landscape (fig.14–19) is a dramatic easel painting that features his powerful style. The forms are well rounded, like those of Rivera. However, they are painted with slashing brushstrokes and greater contrast of values, which create a more dramatic impact. Even this small canvas has the visual impact of a large mural because of the monumentality of the forms. The dominant feature is the huge maguey plant, which is a major source of food, drink, cloth, rope and other items for the desert people of Mexico. It seems as though these quiet, solitary figures are patiently waiting for more growth to sustain them a little longer. The background is treated with abstract shapes that place visual emphasis on the plant and the three human figures.

1910–17
Mexican civil war, Pancho Villa and Emiliano Zapata lead the military

1922
King Tut's tomb found

World Cultural Timeline

1918
Ottoman Empire collapses following WWI; Turkey forms

Sidelight

The Murals of East Los Angeles

Mural painting has had a long tradition in Mexico, going as far back as pre-Columbian times. Some of the greatest mural painting came out of the Mexican revolution when Diego Rivera, David Alfaro Siqueiros and José Clemente Orozco painted powerful political statements on walls in Mexican cities.

The tradition of Mexican mural painting continues on the walls of East Los Angeles. These murals have come about through the dedication of Judy Baca, a Mexican American. Hired by the city to teach art in a park in East Los Angeles, Baca made friends with the children and started studying the street life around her. As she looked at the graffiti-covered walls in the neighborhood, Baca realized that the community's history could be read on those walls. So, she formed a mural team and, for the first time in years, children from different neighborhoods and different gangs worked together. Through their murals, they expressed the issues and needs of the community as they saw them. The topics on the murals ranged from police brutality to drug abuse.

In 1976, Baca and her team started work on *The Great Wall of Los Angeles.* The longest mural in the world, this depiction of California's multicultural history from prehistoric to contemporary times runs over one-third of a mile along a flood control channel in the San Fernando Valley. The Great Wall was completed in 1983.

Judith F. Baca and others, section of *The Great Wall of Los Angeles.* SPARC.

14–20 The interior of the polyforum (not shown) contains a huge floor, ceiling and wall mural which portrays the struggle of the working class.
David Alfaro Siqueiros. Exterior, *Polyforum Cultural Siqueiros,* 1974. Acrylic enamel on asbestos-cement and steel, 50' (15 m) high. Mexico City.

David Alfaro Siqueiros

(1896–1974)

David Alfaro Siqueiros spent many years of his life in prison because of his revolutionary ideas and political connections. He worked with Rivera and Orozco on many mural projects. During the last twenty years of his life he was the only surviving member of the great triumvirate. Siqueiros designed murals of incredible dimension and powerful, emotional impact. The *Polyforum Cultural Siqueiros,* a huge structure in Mexico City, is home for many cultural arts (fig.14–20). The building is covered inside and out with mammoth murals of acrylic paint on asbestos-cement panels and sculptured steel. Its main feature is a gigantic floor, wall and ceiling mural of incredible complexity. The mural is called *The March of Humanity on Earth and Toward the Cosmos*. It is overpowering to the senses, especially when accompanied with programmed lighting and sound. The exterior is shaped like a dodecagon with over 12,000 square yards of painted surface. Each of its twelve huge facets contains a sculptured mural covering 300 square yards. Subject matter ranges from *Christ the Leader* (shown here) to *Atom as a Triumph of Peace over Destruction*. All are presented with vivid colors and surging lines. The work is a gigantic outdoor gallery for the people of Mexico.

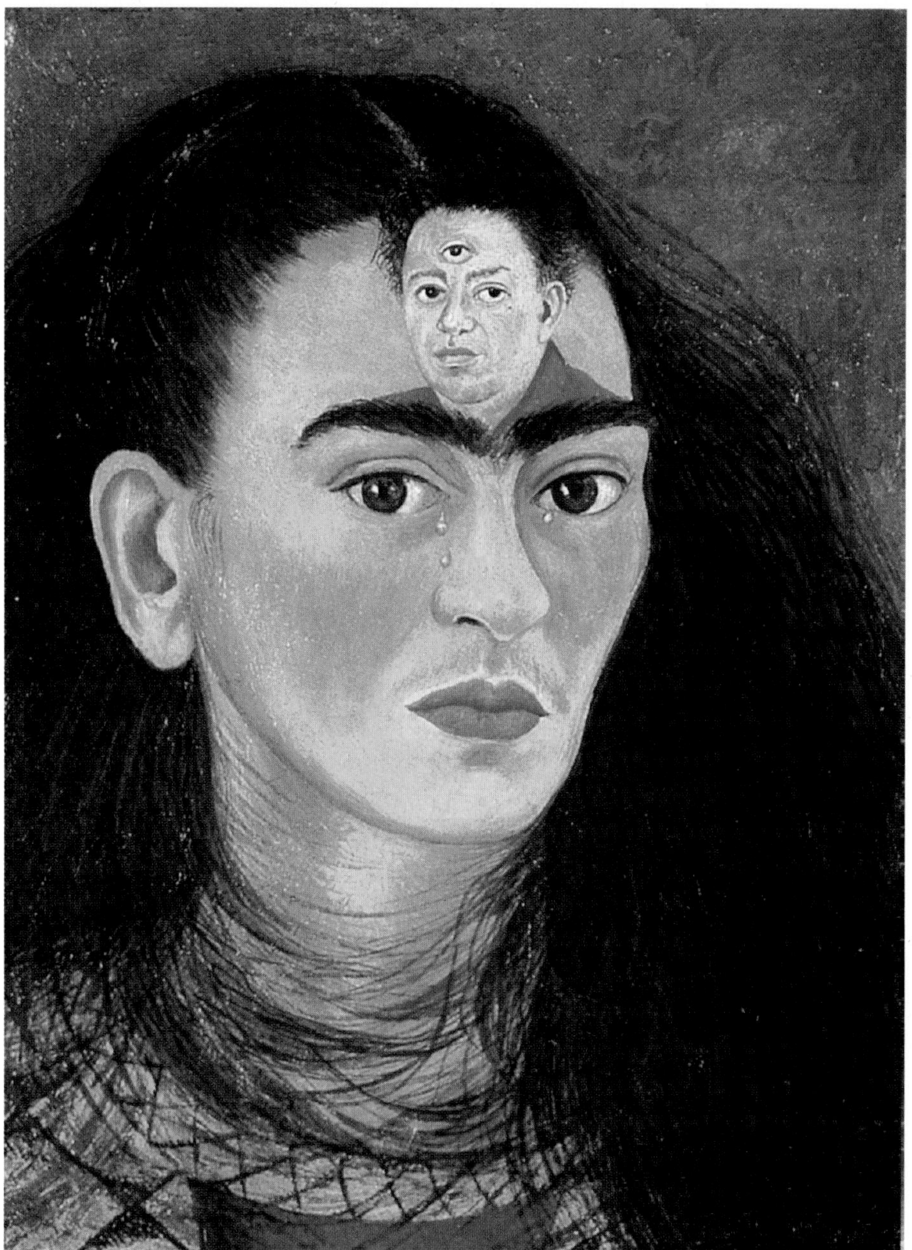

14–21 Kahlo created many paintings of her husband, Diego Rivera, and he remained a powerful influence in her life and work even after they were divorced.
Frida Kahlo, *Diego y yo*, 1940. Oil on masonite, 11 3/4" x 8 1/2" (30 x 22 cm). Courtesy, Mary Anne Martin/Fine Art, New York.

Frida Kahlo

(1907–1954)

Frida Kahlo was a self-taught artist who married Diego Rivera in 1929. Both artists were fiercely independent, and both worked feverishly at their painting. Kahlo painted works that often were psychologically mysterious, and she almost always worked with figures. Among her more than two hundred paintings are many self-portraits. In several, she showed her husband to be a powerful presence in her life. In *Diego y yo* (fig.14–21), to indicate that she was thinking about him, she painted him on her forehead. The third eye on his head is symbolic of the master artist's ability to perceive far more in life than other people. Kahlo's personal expressiveness, psychological intuition and artistic ability have placed her among Mexico's more able artists.

Lesson 14.1 Review

1 What were some of the artists and cultures that influenced Diego Rivera's art style?
2 How did Fauvism get its name?
3 What medium is Matisse's *Beasts of the Sea*?
4 What elements in Rouault's *The Old King* are similar to a stained-glass window?
5 Name two women German Expressionist artists.
6 What were some of the concerns of Die Brücke? From what artists did they draw their inspiration? What art did they reject? What were some characteristics of the art of this group?
7 Describe the mood in Kirchner's *The Street*.
8 Which artist is recognized as having painted the first nonobjective painting?
9 Name three artists or cultures that influenced Modigliani's art.
10 Explain the symbolism in Kahlo's *Diego y yo*.

14.2 Abstract Art

Expressionist artists were primarily concerned with the psychological and social drama of life. They expressed their feelings in symbolic and personal ways. Artists working with abstraction were mainly concerned with the design on the canvas and how the various parts related to each other.

Twentieth-century painters explored many avenues of expression for varying lengths of time. In 1910, almost all who were so inclined tried their hands at Cubism. Futurism, dealing with dynamic energy, was another movement explored by writers and painters during the first decades of the twentieth century. In Holland, a nonrepresentational approach to art was called "De Stijl."

Cubism, Futurism and De Stijl were three important directions that abstract art took in the first half of the twentieth century.

Key Notes

- Abstract artists are interested in the design on the canvas and how the various parts relate to each other.
- Abstract art is explored in a variety of ways, including Cubism, Futurism and De Stijl.

Vocabulary

simultaneity

Special Feature

Joseph Stella

(1880–1946)

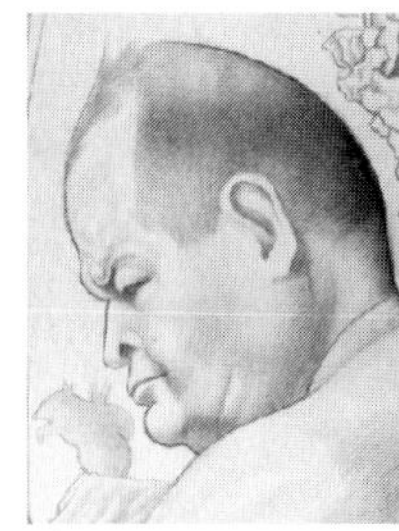

Joseph Stella came from Italy to the United States at the age of twenty-five. He returned to his homeland when Futurism was in its developmental stages. Futurism was a branch of abstract art that emphasized the lines of force or dynamism of each object.

Stella brought this particular type of abstraction to his interpretations of New York. His painting of the *Brooklyn Bridge* (fig.14–22), the construction that had become a symbol of New York, is a visual song of praise to a structure that

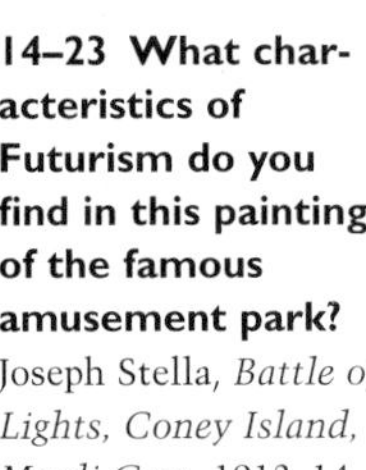

14–23 What characteristics of Futurism do you find in this painting of the famous amusement park?
Joseph Stella, *Battle of Lights, Coney Island, Mardi Gras,* 1913–14. Oil on canvas, 6'4" x 7'4" (195.2 x 215 cm). Yale University Art Gallery. Bequest of Dorothea Dreier to the Collection Société Anonyme.

14–22 The Brooklyn Bridge was a triumph of human engineering capabilities. Stella celebrates this fact in his painting. Joseph Stella, *Brooklyn Bridge*, 1918–1920. Oil on canvas, 84" x 76" (214 x 194 cm). Yale University Art Gallery, gift Collection of Société Anonyme.

was considered an industrial and engineering triumph. Towers, cables and beams of lights are all woven together with distant skyscrapers, tunnels and water. Together, they create a dynamic vision of interlocking space, light, form and color. Such glorification of industrialization is a positive expression of twentieth-century technology. It is the opposite of German Expressionism, which saw such mechanization as dehumanizing.

Like other abstract artists, Stella was concerned with the design on the canvas and how the various parts relate to one another. He often relied—as he does here—on a symmetrical balance on either side of a strong central axis to hold the composition together.

In *Battle of Lights, Coney Island, Mardi Gras, 1913–14* (fig.14–23), we are immediately struck by the energy of an amusement park filled with crowds of people. Stella's is not a literal depiction. Instead, he uses light, color and line to relate to the viewer the tumultuous nature of the scene.

As we have begun to learn, movements in art in the twentieth century follow neither a unified nor sequential path. The concept of abstraction, however, remains a vital force in art even today.

Cubism

Cubism was begun in 1907 by Pablo Picasso, who was joined shortly by his good friend Georges Braque. They used Paul Cézanne's ideas and his way of building up the surface with small squarish brushstrokes to launch a new way of seeing and painting the world. Like other abstract art, Cubism is primarily concerned with surface design, not emotion and personal feelings. What Picasso began in 1907 set the minds of artists on fire with ideas and possibilities undreamed of several years before.

Pablo Picasso

(1881–1974)

Pablo Picasso casts a long shadow across the art of the twentieth century. A creative innovator of ideas and techniques and a master of many styles, he was constantly searching and changing during his long lifetime. Born in Spain, and an excellent painter at nineteen, he moved to Paris to spend most of his years in France.

The beginning of Cubism burst onto the twentieth-century art scene with Picasso's painting *Les Demoiselles d'Avignon (The Maids of Avignon)* in 1907 (fig.14–24). Sketches reveal that Picasso at first included several other figures in the interior setting. As Picasso worked, he became aware of the relationships of shapes and colors to each other. These relationships became more important than the figures. For six months, he worked and reworked his design on the large canvas and never really finished it completely. What the viewer now sees are five fractured, nude figures and a small still life.

Picasso had been strongly impressed by his introduction to geometrical African masks. He overpainted the faces of two of the nudes with mask-like features, adding to the discordant quality of

14–24 This painting started the Cubist movement.
Pablo Picasso, *Les Demoiselles d'Avignon*, 1907. Oil on canvas, 95 1/4" x 93" (242 x 236 cm). The Museum of Modern Art, New York, acquired through the Lillie P. Bliss Bequest.

14–25 This Cubist portrait is a very different way for an artist to see his sitter. Can you find the sitter's features?
Pablo Picasso, *Daniel-Henry Kahnweiler*, 1910. Oil on canvas, 39 3/4" x 28 3/4" (101 x 73 cm). The Art Institute of Chicago, gift of Mrs. Gilbert W. Chapman.

14–26 Without the credit information, it is hard to tell from the reproduction whether this work is painted or pasted.
Pablo Picasso, *Three Musicians*, 1921. Oil on canvas, 80" x 74" (204 x 188 cm). Philadelphia Museum of Art, the A.E. Gallatin Collection.

the work. These newly introduced, sharp angles caused him to rework the entire surface, repeating the angular features of the masks in the figures and the related background. This interplay of geometric shapes led to Cubism. Cubism was given its name by critics who saw the hard edges and geometric shapes and nothing else.

Although not considered a Cubist painting, *Demoiselles* is the painting that began the Cubist movement. The unlovely ladies of Avignon had started a revolution.

Picasso began to work with Georges Braque in developing true Cubism. Big, flat shapes were replaced by small, crisp facets and nearly monochromatic hues because bright hues would detract from the design. In Picasso's painting of the art dealer *Daniel-Henry Kahnweiler* (fig.14–25), the features are broken apart and reassembled in a new and unique way. Facial features, hands and still-life objects can be discerned, but they also seem to dissolve in a shattering pattern of translucent, geometric shapes.

After World War I, the work of Picasso changed radically as one style blended into many others. His wonderful *Three Musicians* (fig.14–25) is painted to look like colorful pieces cut into flat shapes and pasted onto a surface. Recognizable images emerge again in this work: a Pierrot and a Harlequin from Italian comedic theater and a Franciscan monk. The three are making music on a violin, a clarinet and a zither. This unlikely trio is thrust forward from a neutral background as the three happily play on their instruments. The color, shapes and textures create a pleasant and happy composition, locked together as tightly as a finished jigsaw puzzle.

Following a 1917 trip to Italy, where he saw many of the works of Giotto and Piero della Francesca, Picasso developed a way of painting monumental figures in a rather Classic style. The lightning changes in his style after Cubism are too many to study here, but one work must be included. It is *Guernica* (fig.14–27), his most powerful painting and one of the most devastating social protest pictures ever composed.

Picasso painted *Guernica* as a commission for the Spanish government to exhibit at the Paris Exposition of 1937. The protest was against the massive bombing of the small Basque town of Guernica, which was a center of resistance in the ongoing civil war. By using flat, symbolic figures he was able to express extremes of suffering not possible in realistic representation. Actual destruction is shown only in a flaming building and some crumbling walls. A mother rushes screaming from a burning house, her arms flailing in the air. Agonized heads and arms reach out desperately from crumbling wreckage. At the left, a mother holds her dead child and shrieks toward the heavens. The bull, a Spanish symbol

14–27 Use the text to identify all of the elements of this painting that was created to protest the bombing of a small town.
Pablo Picasso, *Guernica*, 1937. Oil on canvas, 11 1/2' x 25 1/2' (3.5 x 7.8 m). Queen Sophia Art Centre, Madrid.

of human irrationality, surveys the scene of carnage. The screeching horse is perhaps symbolic of Spain's torment, yet it and other symbolism are never explained by the artist. The sun is mechanized with a light bulb, and textures simulate the newspaper articles that described the tragedy to a shocked world. A broken sword symbolizes the absolute defeat of the people. But, out of the handle of the sword a flower grows; hope is still alive. Pain, agony and chaos are everywhere, yet the design is solidly held together by a triangular composition. Picasso painted the enormous canvas in black, white and gray to place the visual emphasis on the message as well as to develop a somber mood. *Guernica* combines Expressionism and Cubism in a mighty voice of protest. It is Picasso's most dramatic work.

Georges Braque

(1882–1963)

Georges Braque worked closely with Picasso in developing the vocabulary of Cubism. The two artists next began adding actual bits of real objects to their canvases: newspaper clippings, pieces of rope, bits of wallpaper and even sand. These pieces added a note of realism to the designed pictorial space. The result is called collage, from the French word *collé* for glue or paste.

14–28 How would you describe the space and perspective in this painting?
Georges Braque, *Still Life: The Table*, 1928. Oil on canvas, 32" x 51" (81 x 131 cm). National Gallery of Art, Washington, DC, Chester Dale Collection.

Following World War I, Braque worked on a series of figure paintings, but finally settled on the still life as his basic subject. Braque carefully structured his space. Using the fractured planes of Cubism, he abstracted from the setups to create beautiful designs. In *Still Life: The Table* (fig.14–28), he uses several typical Braque techniques. The table top is tilted forward. It becomes a background shape for the objects, which often seem about to slide off the inclined surface. The viewer sees each object from a separate vantage point, something a camera cannot do. One can see into the top of one bottle, but not into that of its neighboring flask. The viewer looks down on the dish with the apples. The wine glass is seen straight on and in perspective at the same time. This characteristic is called ***simultaneity***. Notice how

World Cultural Timeline

1930
Mahatma Gandhi leads first significant act of passive resistance to British rule in India

1939
People's congress formed, Indonesia

1945
Arab League formed

lines from the contour of one object can be found continuing in another place, causing the shapes and lines to weave a tight pattern over the surface. Colors and textures are brighter and more developed than in earlier Cubist paintings. Braque composed a sophisticated design based on simple objects.

Marcel Duchamp

(1887–1968)

Marcel Duchamp created what was probably the most controversial Cubist painting. His *Nude Descending a Staircase, No. 2* (fig.14–29) brought him quickly to the attention of the public. Along with other European and American artists, Duchamp exhibited his painting in the famous Armory Show in New York in 1913. It was America's first chance to see Cubism, Fauvism, Impressionism and Post-Impressionism in a single exhibition. The reaction was predictable. America's artists (even those who exhibited in the show) were appalled at how far they were behind the Europeans in their expression. America's public, used to seeing realistic representation, was absolutely irate. The general public was alienated by the artists and their new forms of communication.

Duchamp's painting was the primary target of critical attack. Calling it "an explosion in a shingle factory," one critic forever made the painting famous. Duchamp had fractured the movement of a figure as it descended the stairs, and the shapes *are* very shingle-like in their character. But, Duchamp presents not one image, but an entire series of movements, stopped in successive stages of action. The result is similar to stop-action or strobe-light photography. While viewers today understand that Duchamp was painting motion, the public in 1913 could not comprehend his form of art and, out of ignorance, laughed at the result.

14–29 Compare this painting to Muybridge's photographs of motion (fig.12–45).
Marcel Duchamp, *Nude Descending a Staircase, No. 2*, 1912. Oil on canvas, 58" x 35" (148 x 89 cm). Philadelphia Museum of Art, The Louise and Walter Arensberg Collection.

Futurism

During the first decades of the twentieth century, writers and avant-garde artists began an Italian movement called Futurism. As we have seen, Joseph Stella was influenced by this group.

Futurists were interested in the mechanized advancement of society and the destruction of all symbols of the past (museums, academies and large cities) because they held up progress. Thankfully, this phase of their program was not successful. Their favorite word was "dynamism." They wanted to show the "lines of force" that characterize various objects. The sense of movement generated in Duchamp's *Nude* was basic to Futurism.

Umberto Boccioni

(1882–1916)

The young leader of Italian Futurism, Umberto Boccioni, died in an accident during World War I, and the movement died with him. In *The Noise of the Street Penetrates the House* (fig.14–30), Boccioni combines the angular facets of Cubism with a tilting of planes to create a chaotic scene, filled with agitation and motion. People are working and children are playing as other people watch from balconies in a congested urban atmosphere of noise and confusing activity.

Boccioni's finest achievement, however, was in sculpture. His *Unique Forms of Continuity in Space* (fig.14–31) is a charging male figure caught in several aspects of walking at the same time. It is Duchamp's *Nude Descending a Staircase* in three dimensions. According to Boccioni, "motion and light destroy the materiality of bodies" and his sculpture goes about proving it. The forms seem to have been shaped by rushing air, whose currents seem to extend beyond the sculpture itself and to penetrate the form in other places. Solid forms and space are merging and interlocking, causing the negative volumes to be as important as the positive. In this respect, Boccioni's figure recalls Bernini's *David*, which interacts dynamically with its surrounding space. Yet, Boccioni's work combines abstract rather than representational forms to produce a human-like result in vibrant movement.

14–30 What activities can you identify here?
Umberto Boccioni, *The Noise of the Street Penetrates the House*, 1911. Oil on canvas, 39 1/2" x 39 1/2" (100 x 100 cm). Lower Saxony National Gallery, Hannover, Germany.

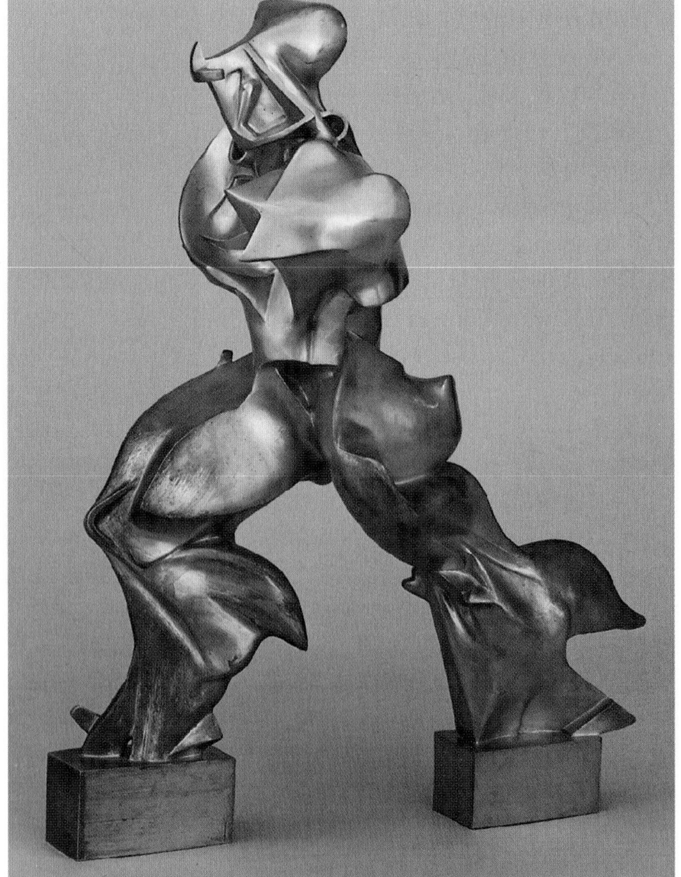

14–31 Figures in motion always intrigue sculptors. Can you think of another sculpture where motion plays an important part?
Umberto Boccioni, *Unique Forms of Continuity in Space*, 1913. Bronze, 43 3/4" (111 cm) high. Museum of Modern Art, New York, acquired through the Lillie P. Bliss Bequest.

De Stijl

(The Style)

A coldly intellectual approach to design was pioneered by another Dutch artist, Piet Mondrian. Mondrian led in the development of a nonrepresentational style, called *De Stijl*, Dutch for *The Style*. The basic precept of De Stijl was the complete reliance on design and the elimination of all feeling and emotion. It was the exact opposite of Expressionism.

14–33 The artist dispensed with images and focused on perfect relationships of color and line.
Piet Mondrian, Piet Mondrian, *Diagonal Composition*, 1921. Oil on canvas, 23 1/2" x 23 1/2" (60.1 x 60.1 cm). The Art Institute of Chicago, gift of Edgar Kaufmann, Jr.

Piet Mondrian

(1872–1944)

Coming from a tradition of Realistic painters (father and uncle), Mondrian rapidly changed styles from Realism to Impressionism, Post-Impressionism and Cubism. He was gradually flattening his natural forms and reducing them to linear patterns, as in *Tree* (fig.14–32). Natural color has been nearly eliminated as grays and blacks take over. Natural objects are reduced to lines.

Later, Mondrian restricted his design to vertical and horizontal black lines and his colors to the three primary hues (red, blue and yellow) plus black, white and gray. By doing this, all possibility of representation was eliminated. *Diagonal Composition* (fig.14–33) is one of about twenty of his paintings that are square and made to stand on one corner. It is an exercise in visual balance; the three primary colors are distributed around an imaginary center point. There is no center of interest. The viewer's eye must see the whole design at one time. Every space is a different size; each line is a different thickness; and each "white" space is a different value of very light gray. The lines establish rhythms and the various values and hues create a sense of depth.

Careful calculations and mathematical precision are essential to such a dehumanizing style of art. "But, art," Mondrian said, "systematically eliminates the world of nature and man."

14–32 Mondrian searched to find the ideal linear essence of a tree. Was he successful?
Piet Mondrian, *Tree*, 1912. Oil on canvas, 37" x 27 1/2" (94 x 70 cm). Museum of Art, Carnegie Institute, Pittsburgh, Patrons Art Fund, 61.1.

Lesson 14.2 Review

1 Describe the bridge in Joseph Stella's *Brooklyn Bridge*. What type of compositional balance is in this painting?

2 What nationality was Pablo Picasso? In what country did he spend most of his adult life?

3 Describe the musicians in Picasso's *Three Musicians*. What instrument is each one playing?

4 What is the name of the technique perfected by Braque and Picasso where bits of real objects and paper were added to paintings?

5 Describe the simultaneity in Braque's *Still Life: Table*.

6 Explain why the 1913 New York Armory Show was important.

7 What is the main subject of Duchamp's *Nude Descending a Staircase*?

14.3 Sculpture

IN THE INNOVATIVE SPIRIT of early twentieth-century art, sculptors vigorously challenged traditional interpretations of mass and space. They became interested in reducing representational images to their elemental forms.

From their wide range of sculptural expression grew the varied trends of three-dimensional expression in the later part of the century.

Key Notes

- Sculptors challenge traditional interpretations of space and mass.
- Sculpted representations are reduced to their elemental forms.

14–35 Brancusi reduced form to its essence. As he continued working, his art became more and more abstract.
Constantin Brancusi, *Sculpture for the Blind (The Beginning of the World)*, about 1916. Marble, 6 3/4" x 11 1/4" x 7" (17.14 x 28.27 x 17.78 cm). Philadelphia Museum of Art; The Louise and Walter Arensberg Collection.

Special Feature

Constantin Brancusi

(1876–1957)

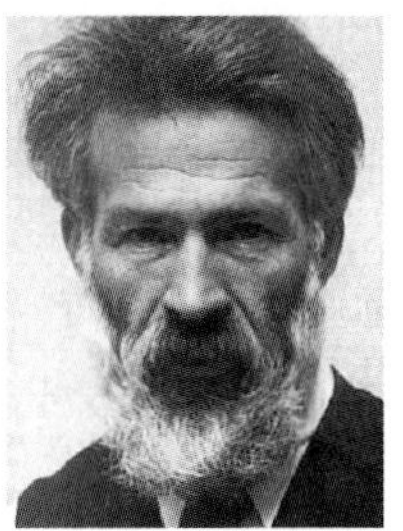

Constantin Brancusi, one of the greatest sculptors of the century, was a Rumanian who came to Paris in 1904. He became involved with the Abstractionist movement and incorporated its theories into his sculpture. Brancusi wanted to reveal the essential shape hidden in everything we see.

Brancusi's limestone carving, *The Kiss* (fig.14–34), shows his interest in simplification and elimination of detail, a characteristic of African art that he admired. He cherished the basic upright shape of the block of stone. He considered it a strong and primitive form and carved as little as possible in it. There is just enough detail for the embracing lovers to be separately visible. Anonymous and innocent, they are an enduring symbol of love.

Many of his later works stressed simplicity so much that they became abstract pieces of art. These sculptures were either based on the oval egg form (fig.14–35) or soaring, vertical bird motifs. Brancusi was particularly interested in birds and the idea of flight. He was the first sculptor of abstract forms to completely eliminate normal representational reference and to emphasize the form itself.

Brancusi's *Bird in Space* (fig.14–36) is not a sculpture of a bird, but of the essence of flight made visible and touchable. He started with a bird standing at rest with its wings folded at its sides.

Gradually, he refined the bird's shape until all its parts merged into a single vision of a bird about to soar into space. The high polish on the surface reflects surrounding space and objects and almost eliminates the form itself, uniting it with its environment.

Brancusi never really departed from working with the figure, and his themes were few, but he affected and influenced most of the major sculpture trends that followed him.

14–34 Examine the various ways the sculptor has emphasized the closeness or unity of the two figures.
Constantin Brancusi, *The Kiss*, 1912. Limestone, 22 3/4" (58 cm) high. Philadelphia Museum of Art, Louise and Walter Arensberg Collection.

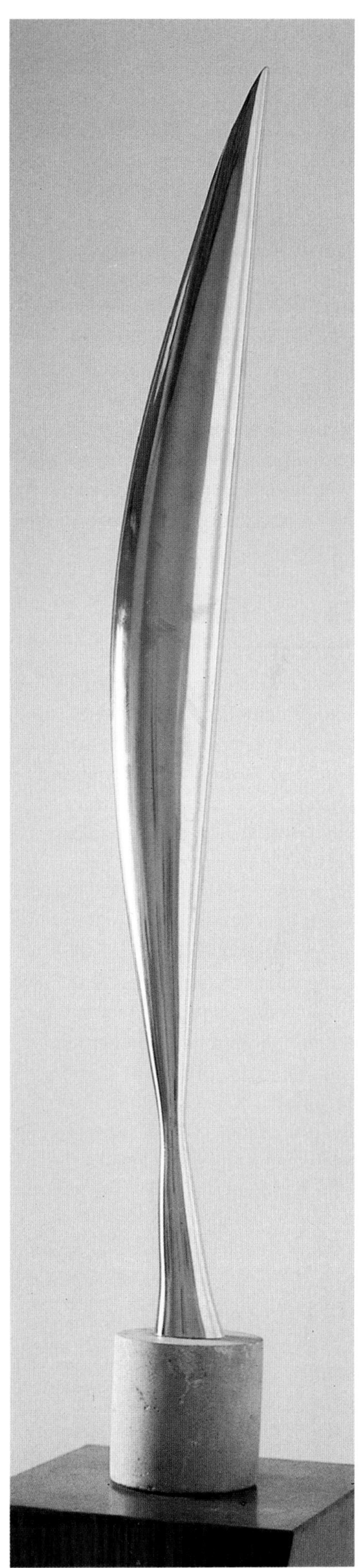

14–36 Brancusi wanted to express the essence of flight.
Constantin Brancusi, *Bird in Space*, 1928. Bronze, 54" (137 cm). The Museum of Modern Art, New York.

Aristide Maillol

(1861–1944)

Starting his art career as a painter, Aristide Maillol soon felt more at home in three-dimensional art. He admired the simple strength of early Greek sculpture, and his female figures tend toward such Classicism. Sculptures such as his bronze *Summer* (fig.14–37) have a calm and self-sufficient sense of harmony that a bustling twentieth-century world cannot destroy. While his fellow Frenchman Rodin, had emphasized movement, Maillol emphasized a static balance and feeling of serenity in his full-formed figures.

Ernst Barlach

(1870–1938)

Ernst Barlach was a German Expressionist sculptor whose simple, strong style was the result of a visit to Russia and his contact with the peasants and their folk art. He carved in wood, but also cast bronzes such as *Frenzy (Der Berserker)* (fig.14–38) that expressed basic human emotions such as anger, fear, wrath and grief. The large forms are simply sculpted. Yet, they produce powerful works when combined with such elemental human traits. Often, the figure is locked to the base and not cut free from the block, which seems to add weight and substance to the finished form.

14–38 Folk art strongly influenced this sculptor's work. His forms are simplified but powerful.
Ernst Barlach, *Frenzy (Der Berserker)*, 1910. Bronze, 21" x 27" (53 x 68 cm). The Nelson-Atkins Museum of Art, Kansas City, Missouri, gift of The Friends of Art, F65-18.

14–37 Maillol sculpted figures to represent all four seasons. Can you name an historical period that may have influenced him?
Aristide Maillol, *Summer*, 1910. Bronze, 64 1/4" (163 cm) high. National Gallery of Art, Washington, DC, Ailsa Mellon Bruce Fund.

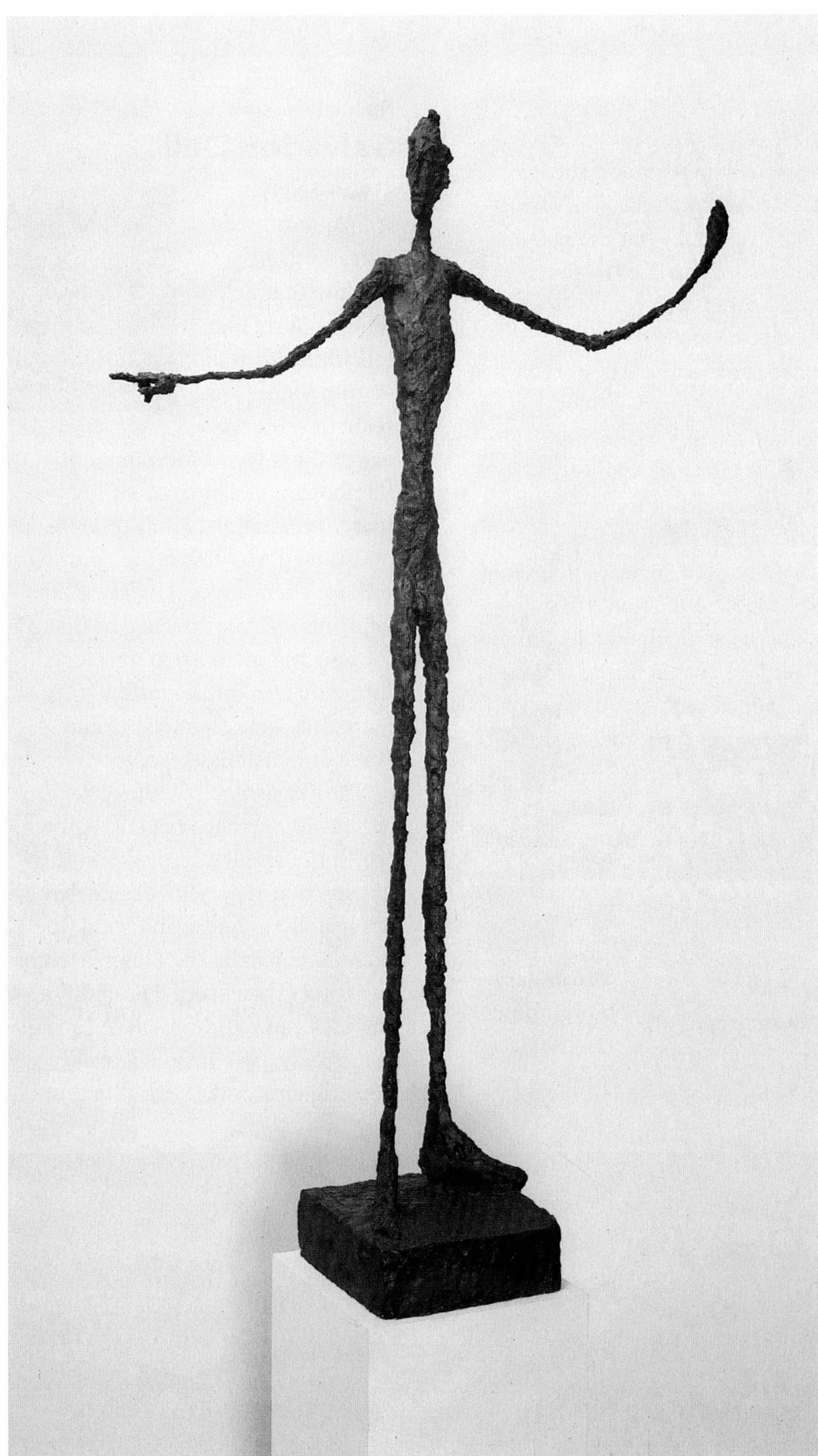

Alberto Giacometti

(1901–1966)

Alberto Giacometti was a Swiss sculptor who worked in Italy for several years before going to Paris. After 1934, he started to work on a series of figure sculptures. Their emaciated and elongated forms were first formed in plaster over a wire armature. The stick-thin figures, such as *Man Pointing* (fig.14–39), have come to be recognized as a powerful symbol of the loneliness and alienation of humanity in this century. The personal symbolism and expressive quality of his figures place Giacometti in the realm of Expressionism even though he was not formally associated with any of the groups or brotherhoods.

14–39 What emotions come to mind as you view this figure?
Alberto Giacometti, *Man Pointing*, 1947. Bronze, 70 1/2" (179 cm) high. The Museum of Modern Art, New York, gift of Mrs. John D. Rockefeller.

Lesson 14.3 Review

1 What was Brancusi trying to show in his sculpture?
2 What is the subject of Brancusi's *Bird in Space*?
3 Which historical art influenced Maillol's sculptures of female figures?
4 What did Giacometti's figure sculpture, such as *Man Pointing*, come to symbolize?
5 Name four early twentieth-century sculptors and an example of each one's work.

14.4 Fantasy Art and Surrealism

LIKE EXPRESSIONIST AND ABSTRACT ART, Fantasy art evolved from an earlier tradition. Greek mythology, the demons and monsters of the Middle Ages, the imagination of Bosch, the hideous nightmares of Goya, and even the personal symbolism of Munch were attempts to visualize the fantasy world of human imagination. In the twentieth century, many painters turned to psychological fantasy to express themselves. It was not long before groups such as the Dadaists and Surrealists were proclaiming their philosophies in paint and words.

The first Surrealist art exhibition took place in Paris in 1925. The exhibit featured artists such as Ernst, Arp, de Chirico, Klee and Picasso. Another painter who would form the heart of the Surrealist movement was Joan Miró. René Magritte and Salvador Dali would join in a few years. The work of these artists was called Surrealism because they were getting "beneath the realistic surface of life" or into a dream world of unreality. Early Surrealist work began with chance techniques such as rubbing a pencil over a paper placed on boards to see what the grain would suggest. Later, artists developed sophisticated presentations of logical or recognizable subject matter in very illogical situations or in weird associations. Much of later Surrealism developed around personal symbols that were unexplained by the artists. For example, Salvador Dali presents green giraffes that are fully ablaze and limp watches draped over a table, but he never tells the viewer what they mean.

Key Notes

- Fantasy art can be found in earlier traditions.
- Surrealists present recognizable subject matter in illogical situations.

Vocabulary
biomorphic
assemblages

Special Feature

Salvador Dali

(1904–1989)

A Spaniard, Salvador Dali became the most famous Surrealist. His life itself was so thoroughly surrealistic—his wild actions, his weird utterances, his flamboyant clothing—that his integrity as an artist has often been questioned. However, the paintings talk for themselves. His personal painting style, influenced at first by Picasso and Miró, soon developed into a magical presentation of incredible draughtmanship and three-dimensional space.

The Persistence of Memory (fig.14–40), perhaps his best-known work, is a small painting of soft objects that represent things that are usually metallic and solid. Its technique recalls the Flemish art of the fifteenth century. He said that the idea came to him while eating soft cheese. The limp watches, gigantic ants and a partial face on a

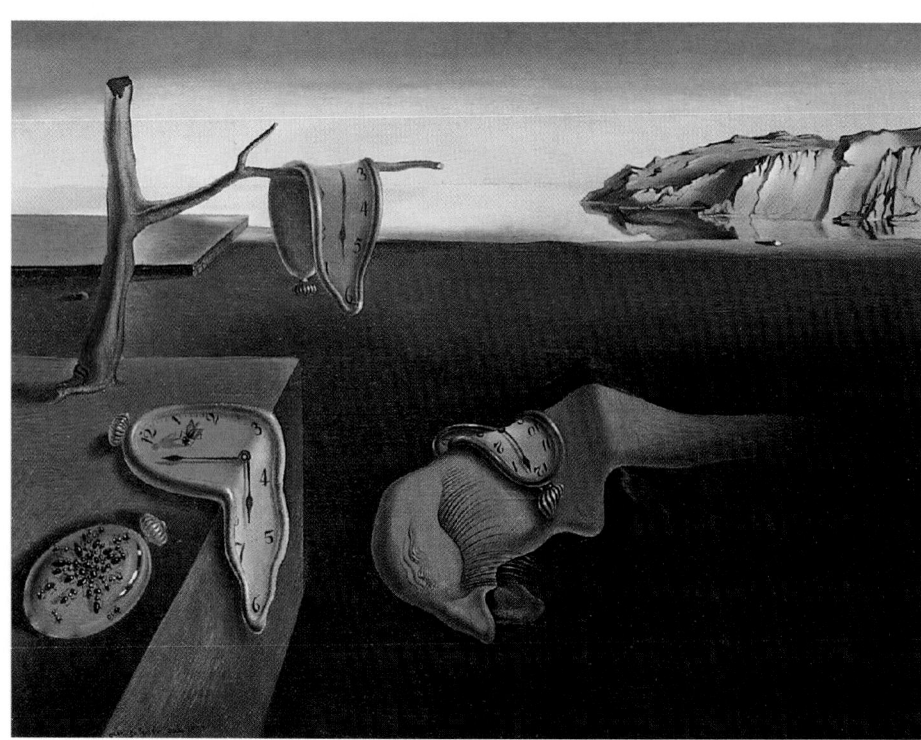

14–40 Dali's surrealism relies on the placement of objects or people in unusual surroundings, either real or imagined, to convey the personal vision of the artist.
Salvador Dali, *The Persistence of Memory*, 1931. Oil on canvas, 9 1/2" x 13" (24 x 33 cm). The Museum of Modern Art, New York.

plain of immense depth are all startling objects, even today. The images are placed in a natural setting with the rocky cliffs of Spain in the background. These cliffs and other private symbolism occur often in Dali's work. Dali uses exacting realism in every part of his paintings because he claimed to "hate simplicity in all its forms," thus rejecting abstraction and any other simplified form of art.

Later in his life, Dali began painting religious subjects with his unique style and symbolism. *Sacrament of the Last Supper* (14–41) has many features similar to the deep-spaced *Persistence of Memory*, but the subject matter is entirely different. It, at first, recalls Leonardo's *Last Supper* in Milan. Upon closer examination, Christ's body is translucent, and a partial, symbolic torso is suspended in the air above the table. The floating segment of the dodecahedron (12-sided figure) is a symbol of the universe. The detail and painting techniques are wonders of craftsmanship. The composition is designed and carried out meticulously. The image, as in all Surrealist and Fantasy art, leaves the viewer with more questions than answers.

Dali's most famous religious painting is *Christ of St. John of the Cross* (fig.14–42). The viewer sees Christ from above. This viewpoint was used by Dali to exaggerate the weight of the body hanging from the cross. What else does this unusual perspective emphasize?

14–41 Compare this to Leonardo's *Last Supper* (fig.9–23). Which do you prefer? Why? Salvador Dali, *Sacrament of the Last Supper*, 1955. Oil on canvas, 65 3/4" x 105 1/4" (167 x 267 cm). National Gallery of Art, Washington, DC, Chester Dale Collection.

14–42 Dali has used three-point perspective in this painting. The vanishing point appears at the extreme bottom of the image. Salvador Dali, *Christ of St. John of the Cross*, 1951. Oil on canvas, 6'9" x 3'10" (204.8 x 115.9 cm). The St. Mungo Museum of Religious Life and Art, Glasgow, Scotland.

Marc Chagall

(1887–1985)

Marc Chagall was born in Russia, but spent most of his life in France and the United States. He left his homeland for good after 1920 when the political climate no longer allowed personal expression and freedom of thought. Chagall's style is based somewhat on Cubism with its fractured planes, but his concepts and presentation are purely personal. His main subject is the Russia he remembered, a Russia of villages and fun-loving peasants, folklore and fairy tales. Reality is mixed with happy remembrances. The result is a delightfully personal style that has charmed viewers in countries around the globe. In *I and the Village* (fig.14–43), the cow dreams happily of a milkmaid. Lovers (one right side up, the other upside down) are on their way to the field. The village street has several upside-down houses, and a green-faced man holds a fantastic plant as he views the entire scene. Dreamlike memories, Jewish proverbs and Russian folk tales are woven to create a tapestry of Chagall's private thoughts.

The viewer need not be discouraged by failing to understand the symbolism because Chagall himself said, "I do not understand them at all. They are not literature. They are only pictorial arrangements of images which obsess me." Chagall painted fantastic murals and ceilings, designed stage settings, produced lithographs and etchings, and created imaginative stained glass windows, all in his own personal style.

14–43 Dreams, memories, folklore and fairy tales all were part of Chagall's paintings. Marc Chagall, *I and the Village*, 1911. Oil on canvas, 75 1/2" x 59 1/2" (192 x 151 cm). The Museum of Modern Art, New York, Mrs. Simon Guggenheim Fund.

14–44 What features in this painting strike you as strange, or even disturbing? Giorgio de Chirico, *The Mystery and Melancholy of a Street*, 1914. Oil on canvas, 34" x 28" (87 x 71 cm). Private Collection. Photograph courtesy Aquavella Galleries, Inc., New York. ©1996 Foundation Giorgio de Chirico/Licensed by VAGA, New York, NY.

Giorgio de Chirico

(1888–1978)

Giorgio de Chirico was an Italian artist, born in Greece, who studied in Athens and Munich before coming to Paris in 1911. He showed no interest at all in Impressionism, Cubism or Fauvism, but produced a series of disturbing cityscapes which are crisp, clean and altogether strange. Most of them, such as *The Mystery and Melancholy of a Street* (fig.14–44) have buildings of tremendous solidity that are lit from the side so that long shadows are cast. Small figures produce a feeling of loneliness and despair. They appear to be the last beings left in the otherwise deserted city. Often, an unexplained shadow creeps in from the side, a shadow without an object to cast it. Vast spaces and large flat areas of little texture create a sensation of impending doom. De Chirico changed his style in later years to more traditional approaches and failed to live up to his early promise as an experimenter and leader in personal expression.

Paul Klee

(1879–1940)

Paul Klee was a Swiss-born artist who spent most of his life in Germany. He settled in Munich in 1911 and joined Der Blaue Reiter while working in near poverty. His small watercolors, etchings and drawings were done on his kitchen table while his wife gave piano lessons. He later taught at the Bauhaus and was a close friend of Kandinsky. Always interested in children's art, he developed a style that combined his personal wit with a childlike vision of the mysteries of life. He created poetic statements of a very personal nature.

Most of his work has a happy quality, such as *Twittering Machine* (fig.14–45), a delightful exercise in imagination. If the handle is cranked, perhaps bird sounds will be produced. Or, is Klee trying to tell viewers something about their insane urge to create machines to do everything—even to make mechanical bird sounds? Or, perhaps, machines can do everything, and humanity's trust in natural things is not valid. Klee supplies no answers. He only tickles the viewers' imaginations and sets them thinking—after they first smile a bit at his art and at themselves.

14–45 What do you think happens if you turn the crank? Paul Klee, *Twittering Machine,* 1922. Watercolor, pen and ink on oil transfer drawing on paper, mounted on cardboard, 25 1/4" x 19" (64 x 41 cm). The Museum of Modern Art, New York.

Dada

During World War I, a group of artists and writers gathered in Zurich to organize a protest against the complete degradation of European society as well as the monstrous destruction of such a war. Their protest took the form of nonsense poetry. They snipped words from pages and dropped them on the table. From these random arrangements, they created poems. The name Dada originated from this nonsense attitude toward conventional language. Their anti-art doctrines spread across Europe and America. Artists used their personal styles to create spur-of-the-moment works, but the message was the same: All European culture was decadent and devoid of meaning. The Dada movement created chaos in the art world, among the public, and even in its own ranks. Members joined and left hurriedly and could not get along well with each other for any great length of time.

14–46 Arp believed that accidental and intuitive compositions were as good as those planned according to rules and conventions.
Jean (Hans) Arp, *Birds in an Aquarium*, 1920. Painted wood relief, 9 3/4" x 7 3/4" (25 x 20 cm). The Museum of Modern Art, New York.

Jean (Hans) Arp

(1887–1966)

Jean (Hans) Arp was born in Strasbourg, a city which at times was German (his name was Hans) and at times French (his name was Jean). He made collages by cutting bits of paper and floating them to the floor. Then, he made their accidental arrangement permanent by gluing them to a sheet of paper. Such unplanned work was a protest against both the design quality and the emotional expression of previous styles of art. He began cutting random bits of wood with a band saw, gluing them together, and adding paint to create relief sculptures. Some sculptures suggested visual images, such as *Birds in an Aquarium* (fig.14–46). His ***biomorphic*** (stylized and organic) shapes and scenes are often whimsical.

Max Ernst

(1891–1976)

Max Ernst was a German artist who made extensive use of collage techniques. He also worked with oils. He was associated with the Dada movement in his earlier years, but spent much of his life in the United States working with the elements of Surrealism. His painting *La Mer (The Sea)* (fig.14–47) allows one to view the sea and shore confrontation through Ernst's own eyes and inner vision. Sand, water and waves can be seen—or can they? Is that a sun and clouds above or a ball floating on water? Ernst presents a seascape of his own making, seen with unconventional eyes.

Kurt Schwitters

(1887–1948)

Kurt Schwitters was a scavenger who gathered junk items from everywhere to include in his art. The German artist glued these objects to a ground and added some paint to make images, or ***assemblages***, that were partly three-dimensional. Works such as *Construction for Noble Ladies* (fig.14–48) might contain ticket stubs, candy wrappers, announcements, bits of broken toys, wheels, boards and assorted trash. Schwitters became the ultimate Dada master. He recycled the refuse from a society he was demeaning into works of art for that same society to see. Viewers were of course disgusted at the sight of it, but the message was delivered.

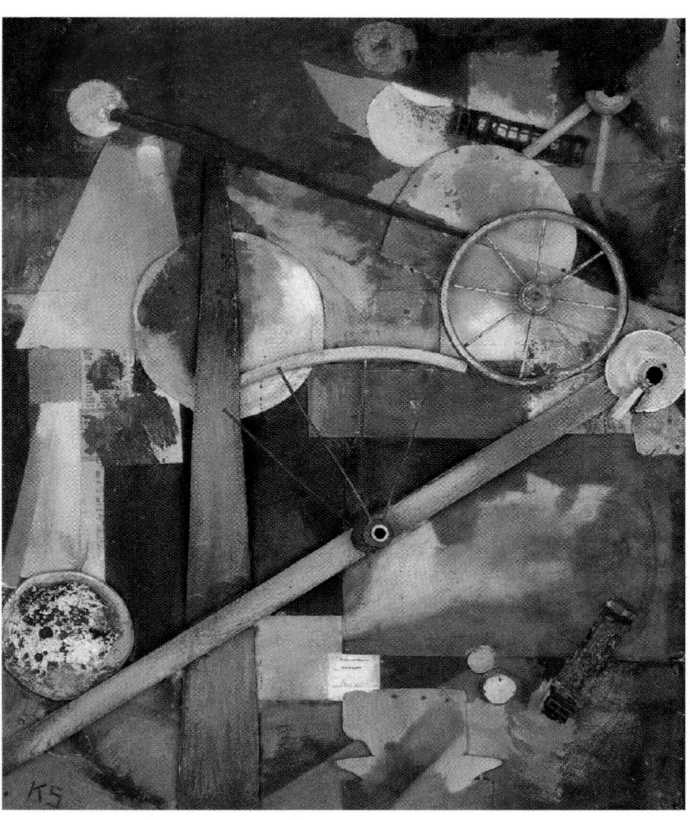

14–48 Why do you think this work is called an assemblage?
Kurt Schwitters, *Construction for Noble Ladies*, 1919. Mixed-media assemblage of wood, metal and paint, 40 1/2" x 33" (103 x 84 cm). Los Angeles County Museum of Art.

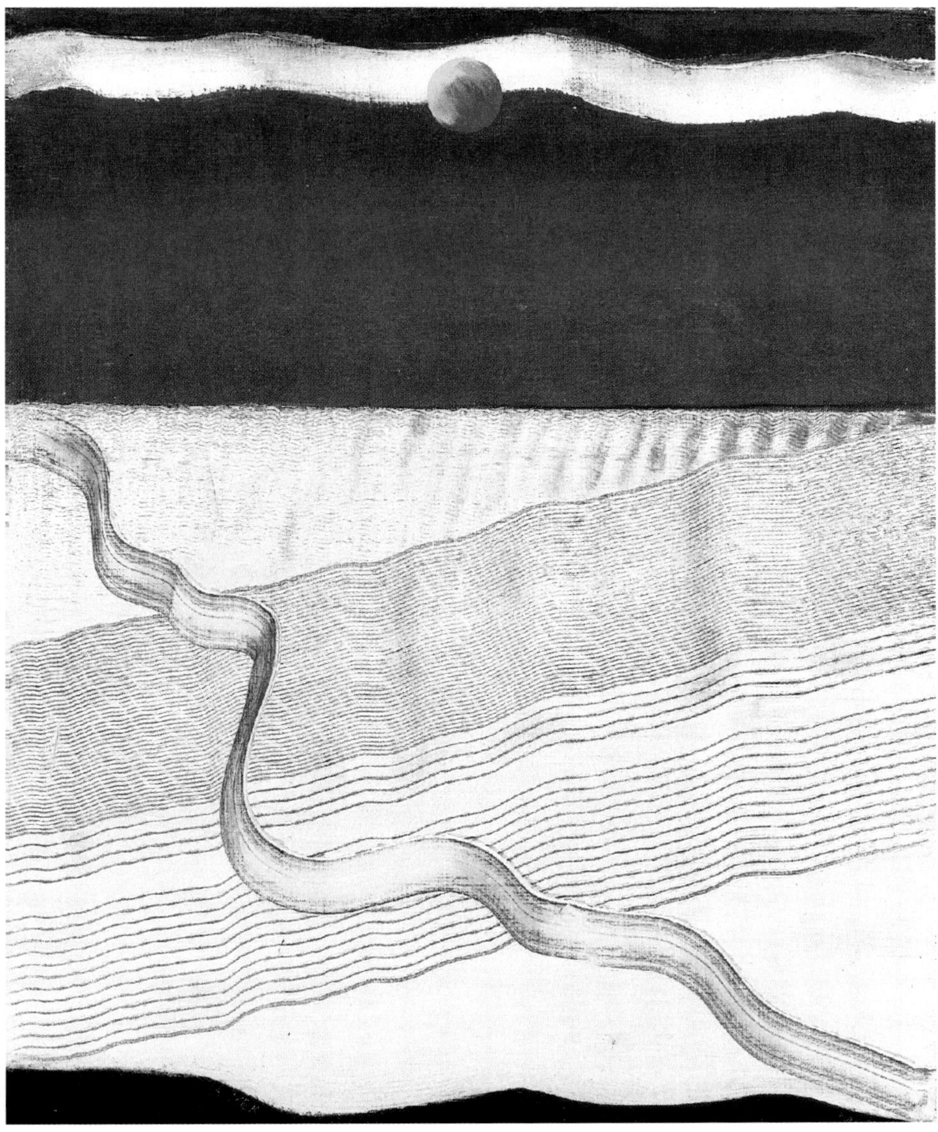

14–47 Do you see this as a seascape with the usual elements of sand, wind and water?
Max Ernst, *La Mer*, 1925. Oil on canvas, 16 1/4" x 12 1/2" (41 x 32 cm). Los Angeles County Museum of Art, Mr. and Mrs. William Preston Harrison Collection.

14–49 Miró developed a very personal symbolism for his painting, prints and tapestries.
Joan Miró, *Women at Sunrise,* 1946. Oil on canvas, 15" x 24" (38 x 61 cm). The Nelson-Atkins Museum of Art, Kansas City, Missouri, gift of the Friends of Art, 56-120.

Surrealism

As steam ran out of the Dada movement, its members began to work in varying styles and to proclaim different messages. In the rather peaceful years following the war, other movements would replace Dada, with Surrealism being the first and most direct descendant. André Breton was the instigator of Surrealism in 1924. A writer, not an artist, Breton followed the Dada philosophy of allowing things to happen naturally in his work rather than putting words together in a logical way. His emphasis on a dream world, word association games and unconscious writing was carried into the visual world of Surrealist painters and sculptors. We already have seen how Salvador Dali put his fantastic ideas and dreams on canvas. Now, we will look at three other artists who were part of the Surrealist movement.

14–50 Magritte is a popular artist. Perhaps this is because his paintings, though puzzling, often bring a smile to our faces.
René Magritte, *Time Transfixed,* 1938. Oil on canvas, 57 1/2" x 38 1/4" (146 x 97 cm). Art Institute of Chicago, Joseph Winterbotham Fund.

Joan Miró

(1893–1983)

Joan Miró charms the viewer with his Spanish wit and delightful menagerie of impossible animals and people. He uses black lines and flat shapes of red, yellow, blue, black and white that often seem cut from paper and glued to the canvas. In *Women at Sunrise* (fig.14–49), the shapes are suggestive of people, animals and a rising sun. At other times, his shapes and lines are purely abstract and suggest nothing. His biomorphic shapes seem to float on a soft background. When they overlap, they become transparent or create another shape.

In his later years, Miró also turned to abstract sculpture, using plastic and ceramic as his media. He also worked extensively with fibers, creating huge woven tapestry murals that repeat the colors, shapes and lines of his paintings. His joyful expressions of life are contagious. Viewers of his work in any media are caught up in his zest for living and his clever sense of humor.

René Magritte

(1898–1967)

René Magritte was a Belgian artist who developed his own witty style of Surrealism based on absurd combinations of realistically painted objects. These juxtapositions both amuse and puzzle the viewer. In *Time Transfixed* (fig.14–50), a partially realistic scene of a crisp, clean and detailed room is combined with a steaming train emerging from the fireplace. Each element is distinct, but, as in Dali's art, the total work raises more questions than answers. Often, Surrealist artists themselves do not know their motives for such improbable combinations.

Meret Oppenheim

(b.1913)

Meret Oppenheim exhibited the ultimate in Surrealist imaging by wrapping a cup, saucer and teaspoon with fur—recognizable objects in irrational combinations. She simply titled her controversial work *Object* (fig.14–51).

14–51 An ordinary object or grouping presented in an unusual way makes us stop and look carefully.
Meret Oppenheim, *Object*, 1936. Fur-covered cup, saucer and spoon, overall height 3" (7 cm). Museum of Modern Art, New York, Purchase.

Lesson 14.4 Review

1 Define Surrealism. List five surrealistic artists.
2 What nationality was Marc Chagall? Describe the subject of *I and the Village*.
3 In de Chirico's *The Mystery and Melancholy of a Street*, how does he create a feeling of impending doom, loneliness and despair?
4 What was Dada?
5 Describe the women in Miró's *Women at Sunrise*.
6 What unrelated objects does Magritte combine in *Time Transfixed*, and Oppenheim combine in *Object*?

14.5 Photography

WHILE PAINTERS WERE EXPERIMENTING in all directions, photographers attempted to keep pace, although they were limited by what the camera could do. While painters explored abstraction, photographers continued to work with humanity and nature. The public (which did not understand abstraction) became increasingly appreciative of photographers. Travel in foreign countries, two world wars and the publication of magazines like *Look, Life* and *National Geographic* gave photographers plenty of opportunity for reportage, an area in which they excelled. Henri Cartier-Bresson became one of the finest reportage photographers.

Creative photographers searched for ways to interpret the everyday life of humanity—human relationships, ugliness, poverty, tragedy, sympathy, love, joy and the entire range of human emotion. The work of Edward Steichen and Alfred Stieglitz dominated the American scene. Other noteworthy American photographers of the period were Ansel Adams, Dorothea Lange, Edward Weston and the great social documentarian James Van Der Zee.

Key Notes

- While painters work in many stylistic directions, photographers are bound by the limits of the camera and darkroom techniques.
- Two world wars, increased world travel, and the publication of photograph-based magazines provide many opportunities for photo reportage.
- Creative photographers interpret the human condition.

Special Feature

James Van Der Zee

(1886–1983)

Twelve-year-old James Van Der Zee was handed a simple box camera as a prize for selling twenty packets of perfume. He quickly became adept at using his camera and soon graduated to much more complex cameras.

A native of Lenox, Massachusetts, Van Der Zee lived most of his life in Harlem, New York. By 1915, he had opened a portrait studio in Harlem and started producing the enormous range of photographs depicting life in Harlem. He photographed the leading political, religious and cultural figures of the African-American community. He also recorded community events and celebrations. These included weddings, dinners and funerals. There are numerous images of the

14–53 What clues can you find in this photograph that would help you date it?
James Van Der Zee, *Couple in Raccoon Coats,* 1932. Photograph.

14–52 Why do you think this photograph is titled *Future Expectations*?
James Van Der Zee, *Future Expectations*, about 1915. Photograph.

latter which date from 1919 to 1920, the years of the great influenza epidemic. These photographs emphasize the dignity, pride and beauty of his subjects and represent our most important photographic archive of African-American life in Harlem.

A favorite technique of Van Der Zee's was to produce photographs that give us not only a physical record of the sitters, but also include a symbolic vision of their hopes and aspirations. *Future Expectations* (fig.14–52), taken about 1915, is one of those pictures. The young bridal couple is depicted with great and loving detail. The bouquet, the veil, the scalloped hem of the bride's dress, her shoes and the groom's starched white shirt are striking. Around the couple are the symbols of the home they desire. The living room with its fireplace represents the household of their dreams. Van Der Zee even places at their feet the daughter they hope to have.

Not all of Van Der Zee's photographs were so symbolic. *Couple in Raccoon Coats* (fig.14–53) is a fine example of his "straight" style. But, whether "straight" or more manipulated, his photographs record the life's work of the first great African-American photographer. They also provide an invaluable record of life in Harlem, especially during the period of the Harlem Renaissance (1919–1929), when all of the arts flourished there. Finally, the Van Der Zee archive illustrates how photography blossomed in the twentieth century and attained an important stature among the visual arts.

Window in Time

Curating Photographs

What better way to understand what a curator of photography does than to talk to one. Deborah Martin Kao is the assistant curator of photographs at the Fogg Art Museum, one of the art museums at Harvard University in Cambridge, Massachusetts. Here she explains the different types of exhibits that showcase photography.

Q: *How do you select the core of photographs that make up an exhibit?*

A: There are essentially three ways. Some exhibits are based on works of art that come out of the permanent collection. This kind of exhibit often depends on the strengths of the collection. Here at the Fogg, the strength is in twentieth-century American photography. We have a lot of documentary photography, so if we decided to do, say, a thematic exhibition based on photographers who had worked in the 1930s, that would be an example of a show coming from the strengths of an existing collection.

Another kind of show relies on borrowing works from other collections in many different locations. For instance, suppose a museum wants to mount a retrospective on a single artist, looking at all the works that artist did over a thirty- or forty-year period. The museum may have a handful of these works in its permanent collection. To complete the exhibit, the curator contacts other museums, commercial galleries or private collectors which may be willing to loan the needed works. This kind of show requires two or three years of research. Grants have to be written to obtain funding.

The third way a show can come about is when artists or experts send in suggestions. They might suggest they put on their own show, or they might want to collaborate with you. A great many suggestions come to a curator.

Deborah Martin Kao, assistant curator of photographs, Fogg Art Museum, Harvard University.

Q: *What steps do you follow for a show to be accepted?*

A: The concept is only the beginning. Once you have that, you have to sell your idea to the place where you want your show to be installed. Even if you're working in a museum, you have to present your idea. If I have an idea for a show, I write a proposal, just as I would if I were a freelancer. Then, I submit it to the director of the museum and all the other curators in the other departments.

Q: *What happens after the idea has been approved?*

A: A lot of planning! You really need to plan, even for a show that's an internal show. At an active institution like the Fogg, you need to plan a year or two in advance. First, a time slot for the show has to be found in the exhibition calendar. Six months before a show goes up, the date of the show must be set, and the title must be finalized. Four months before the show goes up, the publications department needs a list of objects. Then, using a scale model of the gallery, you cut up pieces of paper that are proportionate to the size of the objects. By laying out the works on a kind of architect's plan, you can experiment with their placement. Photographs can be placed in different-size cases instead of just being hung on the walls.

We think of photographs as being flat works on paper, but in fact you can put photographic emulsion on any material. You can even have photographic sculptures.

These are just some of the many challenges a curator of photographs must tackle. Additionally, a photography curator must always keep in mind the fragile nature of the medium, which is extremely sensitive to heat and direct light. Assistant Curator Deborah Martin Kao can attest to the variety of factors that must be juggled in caring for and exhibiting a collection of photographs.

14–54 Stieglitz regarded this as his finest photograph.
Alfred Stieglitz, *The Steerage,* 1907. Photograph. Courtesy George Eastman House.

Alfred Stieglitz

(1864–1946)

Alfred Stieglitz was a "straight" photographer, intent on recording whatever he saw around him directly, without resorting to special effects like double-exposure or double-printing. Yet, these "straight" photographs have an underlying composition of forms. Form, shape and meaning are all reflected in his best-known photograph, *The Steerage* (fig.14–54). Stieglitz captured this moment while sailing to Europe in 1907. The scene of passengers in the steerage section of the ship fascinated him. He described the scene later as "a picture based on related shapes and deepest human feelings." The drama of the people below the deck in steerage, separated from the observers on the upper deck by the white gangway, continues to affect viewers today.

Edward Weston

(1886–1958)

Edward Weston focused on the form of ordinary objects. In his tightly composed photographs, he captured the beauty in organic forms. In *Pepper* (fig.14–55), he transforms a common vegetable into a composition of flowing lines and textured surfaces.

Henri Cartier-Bresson

(b.1908)

Henri Cartier-Bresson has become one of the most influential photojournalists of his time. He has traveled around the world covering wars, occupations of countries, and the people affected by these events. His photographs are pictures that tell stories, allowing viewers to see and experience events throughout Europe and the United States.

Woman on a Stairway Talking to a Man with Cane (fig.14–b) is an excellent example of the human quality in his work. As carefully constructed as a fine painting, it has superb contrasts, aerial perspective, balance, and the touch of human interest that sparks it to life.

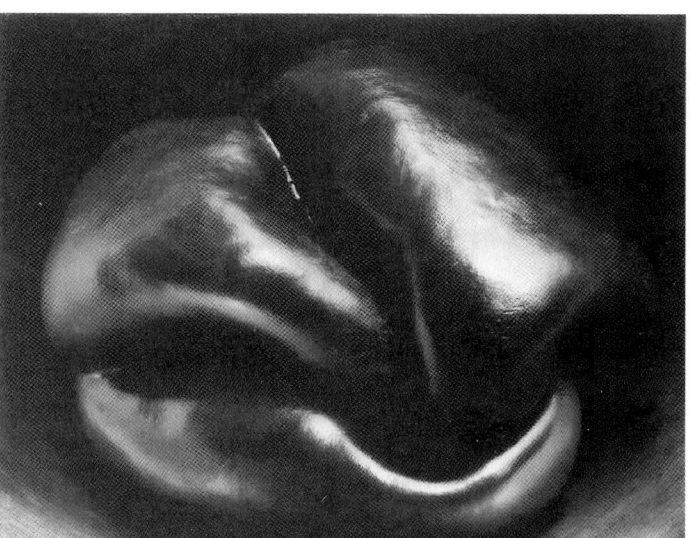

14–55 Weston did a series of ordinary vegetables photographed as monumental sculptural forms.
Edward Weston, *Pepper*. Photograph. Courtesy Sotheby's, Inc.

14–56 During his lifetime, Adams was the foremost nature photographer in the United States.
Ansel Adams, *Mt. Williamson from Manzazar*, 1944. Photograph. Courtesy of the Ansel Adams Publishing Rights Trust.

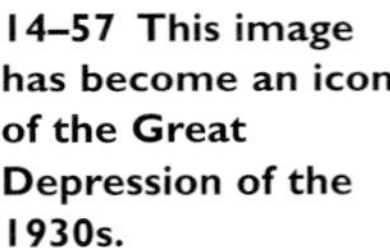

14–57 This image has become an icon of the Great Depression of the 1930s.
Dorothea Lange, *Migrant Mother, Nipomo Valley*, 1936. Gelatin silver print. Dorothea Lange Collection, Oakland Museum, Oakland, CA.

Ansel Adams

(1902–1984)

Like the nineteenth-century landscape painters in America, Ansel Adams found an emotional response in the American wilderness. San Franciscan by birth, Ansel Adams used his camera to capture the grandeur of the mountains of the West (fig.14–56), especially in Yosemite National Park. Adams was a master of photographic technology. To record the smallest detail in sharp focus, Adams used the smallest opening for his lens. His black-and-white prints have dramatic contrasts of lights and darks that he achieved by using different-colored filters.

Dorothea Lange

(1895–1965)

Dorothea Lange ranks as one of the finest documentary photographers in America. During the Great Depression in the 1930s, Lange was hired by the United States government to photograph the plight of migrant workers in California. Her photographs were intended to inform the public and the government about the sad conditions of migrant families and the programs set up to serve them. Of the photographs she took for this assignment, the best-known is *Migrant Mother, Nipomo Valley* (fig.14–57). The worried, careworn face of the mother, the baby on her lap, and the two children who cling to their mother while turning from the camera provide a powerful statement and social documentary about the workers' desperate situation.

Lesson 14.5 Review

1 What type of photographer was Henri Cartier-Bresson?

2 Describe the contrasts in Stieglitz's *The Steerage.*

3 Where did Ansel Adams take many of his most famous photographs?

4 Describe the emotions in Dorothea Lange's *Migrant Mother, Nipomo Valley.* How did this photograph affect a change in people's lives?

Primary Source

Guernica: An Eyewitness Account

The bombings and killings at the Basque town of Guernica, Spain, by Germans at the command of the Spanish government, were recorded by newspaper reporters as well as by Pablo Picasso (fig.14–27). Noel Monks, the reporter of this passage, describes the aftermath of the bombing of Guernica:

"We'd eaten our first course of beans and were waiting for our bully beef when a government official, tears streaming down his face, burst into the dismal dining room crying, 'Guernica is destroyed. The Germans bombed and bombed and bombed.'

I was the first correspondent to reach Guernica, and was immediately pressed into service by some Basque soldiers collecting charred bodies that the flames had passed over. Some of the soldiers were sobbing like children. There were flames and smoke and grit, and the smell of burning human flesh was nauseating. Houses were collapsing into the inferno.

In the Plaza, surrounded almost by a wall of fire, were about a hundred refugees. They were wailing and weeping and rocking to and fro. One middle-aged man spoke English. He told me, 'At four, before the market closed, many aeroplanes came. They dropped bombs. Some came low and shot bullets into the streets.'"

Pablo Picasso, *Guernica*, detail (fig.14–27).

Chapter Review

Review

1 Make a chart describing the painters in this chapter. Write the artists' names in a column on the left. Across the top, make column headings for nationality, style, most famous work and a one- or two-word description of his or her art.

2 What technique did Rivera use to paint many of his murals? Name an artist from the past who also used this technique to paint murals.

3 How did Matisse emphasize the flatness of the picture plane in his *Red Studio*?

4 Describe the African influence in Picasso's *Les Demoiselles d'Avignon*. What features in this painting did Picasso develop into Cubism in later paintings?

5 List six American photographers from the early twentieth century. Describe one of these artists' photographs.

Interpret

1 Describe how Orozco's art is similar to Rivera's.

2 For what event was Picasso commissioned to paint *Guernica*? What is happening in this painting? Explain three of the symbols in *Guernica*. How large is this work?

3 Explain how Miró's style of Surrealism is different from Magritte's.

4 No one really knows what Dali's *The Persistence of Memory* means. Write a short story based on this painting.

5 Draw a typical Arp shape. Explain his technique for arranging these shapes.

Other Tools for Learning

Maps

Locate on the map the cities where Diego Rivera studied and where he worked. Do the same for Wassily Kandinsky.

Timelines

Describe how one of the events in the cultural timelines relates to a piece of art in this book.

Electronic Research

Videodisc player: *National Gallery of Art*

1 Find examples of Matisse's art. Describe one of his works such as *La Negresse*.

2 Compare Brancusi's sculptures with Giacometti's.

Activity 1

The Message on the Wall

Materials
paper or cloth
acrylic paint
house paint
paintbrushes of various sizes

Take a look.
- Fig.3–21, Diego Rivera, *Flower Day*, 1925.
- Fig.14–1, Diego Rivera, *Liberation of the Peon*, 1931.
- Fig.14–19, José Clemente Orozco, *Mexican Landscape*, 1930.
- Fig.14–20, David Alfaro Siqueiros. Exterior, *Polyforum Cultural Siqueiros*, 1974.

Think about it. Social Realism is often closely allied with the labor movements and revolutions of the twentieth century. This art is often involved in controversy because of its emphasis on content and political beliefs. Diego Rivera's idealization of Lenin in the mural he was painting for Rockefeller Center in New York City so upset owner, John D. Rockefeller, that he locked Rivera out of the building and had the mural destroyed.

Do it. Create a mural which portrays some aspect of student life in this or another culture. Emphasize the way that society sees students as well as your own feelings. Are teenagers eager young contributors? Avid scholars? Dangerous revolutionaries? Economic burdens?
- Work with classmates to sketch out ideas on paper until the group agrees on the topic and general presentation. Do a "final" line drawing sketch.
- Enlarge the cartoon to full size. The mural can be painted on paper, cloth or directly on the wall. If working on a wall, grid both the wall and the cartoon. Block in the large shapes within each grid box on the wall.
- Paint the large shapes, paying careful attention to color and values.
- Add the details.
- Finish the mural with a varnish to protect it.

Check it. Throughout the project, check that your scene, your choice of colors and your design works with those of your classmates.

Helpful Hint: Murals are meant to be read by the casual observer. Use characteristic poses, clothing, settings and colors to make your message clear to your viewer.

Activity 2

Exploring Surrealism

Materials
magazines
scissors
11" x 14" white paper
pencils
colored pencils
markers

Take a look.
- Fig.14–40, Salvador Dali, *The Persistence of Memory*, 1931. Oil on canvas.
- Fig.14–50, René Magritte, *Time Transfixed*, 1939. Oil on canvas.

Think about it. Surrealism is often the result of juxtaposing realistic portrayals of unrelated objects or objects in an imaginary or out-of-context environment. Surrealist artists stretched for associations between things that ordinarily have no relationship to each other.

Do it. Try making such visual associations yourself as follows.
- From magazines and other sources, clip various types of images (objects, people, plants, landscape).
- Put these images into a box and select five random choices.
- Draw these images in an environment that makes the relationships between them puzzling to the viewer.

Check it. Are your images realistically drawn? What unlikely elements or relationships make your composition surreal?

Helpful Hint: Surrealist writers and artists played a game called "Exquisite Corpse." Try this warmup exercise of juxtaposing random objects and concepts. Fold or cover a sheet of paper so participants cannot see each other's work. The first person draws a head, the second a torso, the third legs and feet. People, animals and imaginary creatures are all fair game.

Additional Activities

- "Facet Cubism" used flat geometric planes, much like the facets of a cut gem. Make a drawing of an apple or pear, using only triangles of various sizes and shapes to indicate the changes in light and form. You could do this as a line drawing, tempera painting or collage of different values of the same color.
- Study and analyze *Guernica* by Picasso and *Third of May, 1808* by Goya (fig.12–14). Both are powerful social statements, resulting from events that occurred during the artists' lives. Compare and contrast the content, style, use of color, purpose, size, visual impact, symbolism and your personal reaction to each work.

Andrew Lee

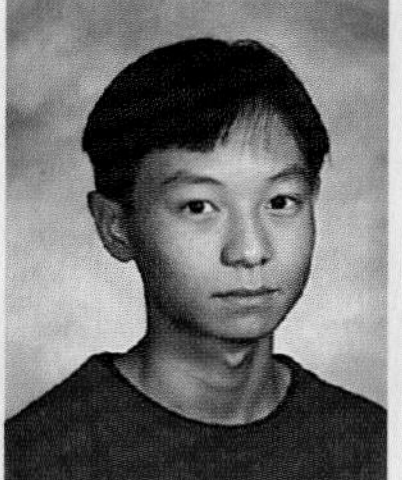

Age 15
West Potomac High School
Alexandria, Virginia
Favorite artists: Stephen Platt, Julie Bell, Tsukasa Hojo
Activity 2, Exploring Surrealism

Out of all my art projects, this one about Surrealism is one of the bigger projects that I've dealt with. It means a great deal to me because I had enough time to put an ample amount of energy into my work. It also allowed me to express my feelings that I wouldn't be able to represent or state in another assignment.

The thought process was fairly critical. After I had chosen my pictures, I had a tough time placing them on the illustration board. The positioning of the elements can become an important factor to the outcome. That was something I learned from the work of Magritte.

Some advice I would like to give to other students who enjoy creating art is not only to do your best, also to carry out the extreme of your idea or theme. Then people can feel what you were trying to say and your work can be outstanding.

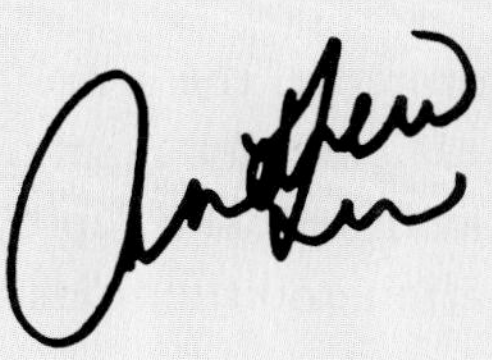

Freedom of Flight, 1994. Colored pencil, 15" x 20" (38 x 50.8 cm).

Curiosity, 1994. Colored pencil, 15" x 20" (38 x 50.8 cm).

Anita Tam

Age 16
West Potomac High School
Alexandria, Virginia
Favorite artists: Lafarge, Copley
Activity 2, Exploring Surrealism

Another student working on the same assignment came up with a playful solution: My art project is of sentimental value to me because it portrays two of my favorite things at once (cats and flowers) and it is the product of much time, effort and creativity. When I was developing my project, I wanted to combine color with a contrasting background and make my subject matter stand out. The thing I enjoy most about the artistic process is the reward of seeing my work come to life after spending a significant amount of time enhancing all the little details.

15 American Art 1900–1950

In This Chapter...

15–a The life of the city and the pulse of jazz vibrate through Davis' paintings. He used letters and words for their design quality and not their meanings.
Stuart Davis, *Something on the Eight Ball,* 1954. Oil on canvas, 56" x 44 4/5" (142 x 114 cm). Philadelphia Museum of Art. Purchased: Adele Haas Turner and Beatrice Pastorius Turner Memorial Fund. ©1996 Stuart Davis/Licensed by VAGA, New York, NY

AMERICA CHARGED INTO the first half of this century with a dynamic force, full of ideas and discoveries. It was a period of emerging brilliance for the young country. At the same time, the country experienced the Great Depression, two world wars and the harsh conditions of urbanization. The American art of this period reflects the highs and lows of these opposing forces, as well as influences from European Abstract and Expressionistic art.

American artists of the late 1800s also influenced the artists at the turn of the century. Some of the most important new artists were Realists who were part of the Ash Can School. Instead of painting romantic landscapes or portraits, these artists painted slums and other shocking scenes of everyday life.

At the same time, Abstract art from Europe captured the imagination of the American art world. It eventually received the support of the galleries and museums and went on to become the most important art movement after 1950.

The American public, on the other hand, desired a more decorative style of art. They had a difficult time supporting the artists of this period, except for the American Scene painters whose art attempted to capture the vastness, beauty and positive character of the country.

Although Abstraction would become the dominant force in the art of this period, many American artists continued to paint realistically. A group which formed after the Great Depression, called the Social Realists, depicted the dehumanizing aspects of urbanization, industrialization and the injustices of large bureaucratic institutions.

1903
Wright Brothers successfully fly a powered airplane

1912
The *Titanic* sinks

1920
Women's suffrage enacted in the United States

1928
Demuth, *I Saw the Figure Five in Gold*
1928
Mickey Mouse films

1935
Radar equipment in use
1936
Lange, *Migrant Mother*

1937
Disney's first full-length animation (*Snow White*)
1942
Hopper, *Nighthawks*

American Art 1900–1950

1908
Bellows (26) is youngest member elected to National Academy of Design

1913
The Armory Show changes American art, New York
1920
Babe Ruth sold to the Yankees for $125,000

1929
Stock Market crash
1932
Huxley, *Brave New World*

1945
The US drops atomic bombs on Hiroshima and Nagasaki

In general it can be said that a nation's art is greatest when it most reflects the character of its people.
Edward Hopper

During the twentieth century, the center of the art world gradually shifted from Paris to New York City. While different schools developed on the east coast, regionalists painted western scenes that were uniquely American.

15–b Despite the growing influence of Abstract art, many American artists continued to favor Realism.
Edward Hopper, *Nighthawks,* detail (fig.15–25).

15–c Many of Calder's works in wire are three-dimensional drawings which convey tremendous personality.
Alexander Calder, *Sow,* 1928. Wire construction, 17" (43 cm) long. The Museum of Modern Art, New York, gift of the artist.

15.1 The Early Years

America underwent tremendous change in the first half of the twentieth century. Scientific discoveries would change everyone's lifestyle, two world wars would be fought, and a depression would stagger the country. American artists were bound to reflect these changes.

Several artists were concluding their life's work as the twentieth century dawned, and they formed the springboard for the new era in painting. John Singer Sargent was a master portrait painter and watercolorist. George Inness created gentle landscapes in contrast to Albert Bierstadt, who painted dramatic pictures of the Rockies.

Several African-American artists created works that equaled or surpassed their better-known contemporaries. Among these artists were Henry Tanner (who studied under Thomas Eakins), Edward Mitchell Bannister and the sculptor Edmonia Lewis.

And, then, there were the Expressionist painters who tried to communicate their feelings about American life. Their realistic paintings of crowded city streets and ragged people created disturbing social statements. Critics derisively dubbed this style "The Ashcan School."

Key Notes

- The foundation laid by artists in the late nineteenth century provides a basis for American art of the new century.
- Young American artists keep pace with the great changes taking place in the first part of the twentieth century.
- An expressive Realism is used to describe America's growing urban centers and their inhabitants.

Special Feature

George Bellows

(1882–1925)

At the age of twenty-six, George Bellows became the youngest member ever elected to the National Academy of Design. He was a prize student of Robert Henri, the leader of the Ashcan School. Bellows was an exceptional athlete who loved to draw. His interest in sports led him to paint several boxing scenes of bouts in New York's private clubs. But, he also loved to paint the unbelievable clutter and congestion of New York's East Side slums where thousands of immigrants shouted in languages he could not understand. He painted scenes of naked boys swimming in the East River, dock workers, smoky saloons and huge horses.

15–2 The lines of the bodies create the impact that dominates this composition.
George Bellows, *Stag at Sharkey's*. Oil on canvas, 36" x 48" (91 x 122 cm). The Cleveland Museum of Art, Hinman B. Hurlbut Collection.

15–1 How has Bellows organized this chaotic scene to make it successful as a work of art?
George Bellows, *Cliff Dwellers,* 1913. Oil on canvas, 39 1/3" x 41 1/3" (100 x 105 cm). Los Angeles County Museum of Art, Los Angeles County Funds.

Cliff Dwellers (fig.15–1) is a clever title for a painting of the tenement dwellers of New York City. Bellows took the mass confusion of elements and organized a simple composition of darks and lights, eliminating much of the detail of the actual scene. The stark highlighting throws the some figures and parts of buildings into sharp relief. The activity in the painting is intense and varied yet is handled with care and compassion. Bellows felt keenly the confusion and needs of these people.

Bellows' best-known work is *Stag at Sharkey's* (fig.15–2). The painting is enormously powerful. A fight is in progress at one of the boxing clubs of which Bellows was so fond. The men are caught in action. Some areas of the canvas, like the foremost fighter's right glove, seem unfinished. This accentuates the implied motion of the moment captured by Bellows. As with the *Cliff Dwellers,* the artist makes use of sharp light and dark contrasts. The motion and force of the scene is balanced by the stable triangular formation of the three figures that Bellows has created to anchor the composition. The painting is so "real" we feel as if we are one of the dark spectators. This is a shocking and startlingly raw painting in the Realist tradition.

Because Bellows never went abroad, he was not touched by the art movements flourishing in Europe. Bellows is regarded by many as the quintessential American artist.

John Singer Sargent

(1856–1925)

Another famous American artist, John Singer Sargent, was painting during the life and times of George Bellows. However, John Singer Sargent had begun painting much earlier than Bellows and his work followed a different tradition. Sargent was born in Europe of American parents and worked both in this country and Europe. He was a master portrait painter.

Although many of his portraits were more formally arranged, his *Daughters of Edward D. Boit* (fig.15–3) is a masterful portrait painting of the four girls. Sargent painted the daughters of his artist friend with the fluid brushstrokes that characterize his portraits. Sargent was influenced by Velazquez in technique, color and the casual arrangement of his figures. Notice the large blue and white Japanese vases and the magnificent use of shadow and light that Sargent always handled with great ease. His flashy style and elegant portraits earned him many wealthy clients on two continents.

15–3 Sargent was influenced by Velazquez. Compare this portrait to Velazquez' *Las Meninas*.
John Singer Sargent, *Daughters of Edward D. Boit,* 1882. Oil on canvas, 87" x 87" (221 x 221 cm). Museum of Fine Arts, Boston, gift of the daughters of Edward D. Boit in memory of their father.

15–5 The popularity of Bierstadt's paintings helped make the Rocky Mountains a prime tourist destination.
Albert Bierstadt, *The Rocky Mountains,* Lander's Peak, 1863. Oil on canvas, 73 1/4" x 120 4/5" (186 x 307 cm). The Metropolitan Museum of Art, New York, Rogers Fund, 1907.

15–4 Notice how the artist is more concerned with the general effect of the landscape rather than the specific details.
George Inness, *The Home of the Heron*, 1893.
Oil on canvas, 30" x 45 7/16" (76 x 115 cm).
The Art Institute of Chicago, Edward B. Butler Collection, 1911.

George Inness

(1825–1894)

George Inness admired the work of the Hudson River School painters when he was only a boy. Inness also went to Europe to study and was influenced by the landscapes of Corot, Courbet, Constable and Turner. His gentle landscapes reflect his quiet personality. Inness' landscapes were faithful to nature. The general effect of a place was always more important to him than the specific details. *The Home of the Heron* (fig.15–4) is typical of the gentle moods he created. The muted colors and values of all are massed together to produce a definite feeling of place and time, without the need for specific details.

Albert Bierstadt

(1830–1902)

Albert Bierstadt was born and trained in Europe, and his paintings often reflected his interest in the Alps and other European locales. His landscapes of the American Rockies were so dramatic that they seemed to have been staged especially for his dramatic lighting. Bierstadt accompanied surveying expeditions to the Rocky Mountains and made numerous sketches and photographs. His large paintings, like *The Rocky Mountains, Lander's Peak* (fig.15–5), were composed from such sketches and painted in his New York studio. He romanticized the West to look the way easterners wanted it to look. His mountains were higher and more craggy, the gorges deeper, the reflections sharper, the waterfalls higher and the dramatic light sharper and clearer. Many critics claimed that he made the West look like the Swiss Alps with buffalo and Indians. He adds crowds of Indians and horses to the vast panorama and even shows his camera at the lower left. Such scenes soon drew people from the canyons of New York City to the new and glorious canyons of western America.

Sidelight

Thinking Like an Art Historian

Art historians tackle the problems of studying art in numerous and quite varied ways. The information, analysis or insights they offer contribute to a more complete picture of a work of art and the artist.

For instance, there are many ways in which an art historian might study a work of art such as Sargent's *Daughters of Edward D. Boit* (fig.15–3). A scholar interested in portraiture might study the history of portraiture from the Renaissance through the late twentieth century. In that case Sargent's work might be chosen to represent portraiture at the end of the nineteenth century. Another scholar might focus on just nineteenth century portraits. Yet another may only be concerned with Sargent's portraits and would study the *Daughters of Edward D. Boit* to better understand its place in Sargent's entire body of portrait work.

An art historian with different interests could research and analyze the depiction of children in art. Another might look at Sargent's work as part of a study on the history of oil painting. Or the research might be narrower in scope and study only Sargent's use of oil. A Velasquez expert might be interested in the influence of that artist on later generations, as Sargent's painting is an excellent example of this influence. The goal of all these approaches is to better understand works of art and their creators.

Edward Mitchell Bannister

(1828–1901)

The African-American painter Edward Mitchell Bannister was born in New Brunswick and later moved to Providence, Rhode Island. One of the founders of the Providence Art Club, his landscapes and seascapes were widely exhibited in his lifetime. Bannister also painted genre scenes. *Newspaper Boy* (fig.15–6) has a refreshing immediacy that causes the viewer to wonder about the life of the thoughtful young boy who sold newspapers more than 100 years ago.

15–6 Notice how the figure has been brought to the very front and to the edges of the picture plane.
Edward Mitchell Bannister, *Newspaper Boy*, 1869. Oil on canvas, 30" x 25" (76 x 63 cm). National Museum of American Art, gift of Mr. and Mrs. Norman B. Robbins.

Edmonia Lewis

(ca. 1844–1909)

Born in Ohio of a Chippewa mother and an African-American father, Edmonia Lewis was the first African American, male or female, to receive international recognition as a sculptor. In addition to portrait busts, she sculpted studies of ethnic women. Lewis once commented: "I have a strong sympathy for all women who have struggled and suffered." She was referring specifically to her marble sculpture, *Hagar* (fig.15–7). The quiet strength of the figure reinforces Lewis' statement. Hagar is an Old Testament figure who was banished with her son, Ishmael, to the desert.

15–7 Lewis was orphaned during her teens. She attended Oberlin College, perhaps on an Abolitionist scholarship.
Edmonia Lewis, *Hagar*, 1875. Marble, 52 5/8" x 15 1/4" x 17" (134 x 39 x 43 cm). National Museum of American Art, gift of Delta Sigma Theta Sorority, Inc., 1983.95.178.

1907
New Zealand becomes self-governing

1911
Sun Yat-sen overthrows ruling Manchu dynasty

1921
Chinese Communist Party forms in Mongolia

World Cultural Timeline

1911
China unifies under democratic government

1921
Japan's first census counts 77 million people

15–8 When Tanner initially decided to study art, he found it difficult to obtain art lessons because he was African-American. Finally, he did enroll in the Pennsylvania Academy of Fine Arts where he studied under Thomas Eakins.
Henry O. Tanner, *Angels Appearing Before the Shepherds,* about 1910. Oil on canvas. National Museum of American Art, gift of Mr. and Mrs. Norman B. Robbins.

Henry O. Tanner

(1859–1937)

The son of a distinguished minister, Henry Tanner often emphasized Bible stories in his paintings. At the Pennsylvania Academy of the Fine Arts in Philadelphia, he studied under Thomas Eakins, who became a strong influence on his work. Tanner went to Europe to study and work, and spent many years painting in Paris. In 1895, Tanner won an honorable mention for one of his paintings of a religious subject. His was the only American work to be so honored. Tanner continued to paint religious subjects with great frequency. Many of these works were given a very personal interpretation as in *Angels Appearing Before the Shepherds* (fig.15–8). The artist's vision of a host of angels appearing to shepherds in a landscape is extraordinary.

Genre themes were also important subjects for Tanner. *The Banjo Lesson* (fig.15–9) is a simple scene of African-American life. The figures are rendered realistically, without sentimentality, as one generation passes on knowledge to another. Tanner was the most honored of all African-American artists, here and abroad, and he was a powerful influence on others who worked with him.

15–9 What sounds might you associate with this scene?
Henry O. Tanner, *The Banjo Lesson,* 1893. Oil on canvas, 48" x 35" (123 x 89 cm). Hampton University Museum, Hampton, Virginia.

Sidelight

Realism in American Writing

Like the painters of the Ashcan School, who introduced a new realism into American painting, a new group of authors began to write books that were distinctly American in subject and realistic in tone. One of the first writers to establish this new realism was Theodore Dreiser. His first novel, *Sister Carrie,* was published in the United States in 1900 to mixed reviews and substantial opposition. Dreiser wrote straight-on about life in Chicago and New York, including its poverty, and exposed society's materialism. His characters were not heroic, nor did the novel follow conventional morality in which the bad were punished and the good rewarded.

Other writers who wrote objectively about American life included Sinclair Lewis and Upton Sinclair. Sinclair Lewis wrote of middle-class hypocrisy and conformity in his novels *Babbit* and *Main Street*. Upton Sinclair hit America in its stomach as well as its conscience by exposing the unsanitary conditions in the meat-packing industry in the nonfiction book *The Jungle.*

With characters drawn from everyday life, these writers set out to describe American life, what it was and what it was becoming; and, in so doing, raising questions about what it should be.

Robert Henri

(1865–1929)

In 1908, eight of Philadelphia's illustrators banded together to put on an exhibition of their paintings. Calling themselves *The Eight*, these Expressionist painters tried to communicate their feelings about American life in the crowded cities. Robert Henri, who pronounced his name "Hen-rye" to be as American as possible, became the leader of The Eight. They presented paintings of crowds, slums, clogged streets, ragged children, sports events, clowns and sunny afternoons. Critics jeeringly called them "The Ashcan School" because their realism became expressions of poverty and ugliness. America had always favored Realism, but such visual social statements were disturbing.

Henri's studio became a regular meeting place for The Eight as well as other young and aspiring artists whom he encouraged and helped. He urged them to paint the city and its people as they saw them and as they felt about what they saw. He encouraged his students to paint in their own way and to expand the tradition of American Realism begun by Eakins.

Henri's own style used broad brushstrokes in a direct way, much in the manner of Manet, Goya and Hals. *Snow in New York* (fig.15–10) is one of many snow-clogged cityscapes that he painted in his broad, freely brushed style. It is moody and clearly reflects Henri's knowledge and feeling about New York in winter. It is not the joyful snow scene of calendar painters, but the cold, everyday, hard-working reality of urban winters.

15–10 What devices has the artist used to create this rather gloomy feeling of winter?
Robert Henri, *Snow in New York*, 1902. Oil on canvas, 31 4/5" x 25 1/2" (81 x 65 cm). National Gallery of Art, Washington, DC, Chester Dale Collection.

15–11 Compare this painting to Renoir's *Moulin de la Galette* (fig.13–12).
John Sloan, *Renganeschi's Saturday Night*, 1912. Oil on canvas, 26 4/5" x 31 4/5" (67 x 81 cm). The Art Institute of Chicago, gift of Mrs. John E. Jenkins, 1926.

John Sloan

(1871–1951)

John Sloan was one of the most talented among The Eight. Sloan believed that a work of art need not have beautiful subject matter to be valid. To Sloan, the beauty of a painting was in the work itself, not in the subject. Sloan enjoyed painting any city scene and set up his easel in any street. People sitting on the steps, women drying their hair on a rooftop, or a woman hanging out her Monday's washing on a line could all become subject matter for Sloan's creative mind. *Renganeschi's Saturday Night* (fig.15–11) is simply a scene in an urban restaurant, rapidly brushed on canvas by an observant artist. No academic artist of the time would consider this appropriate subject matter, but Sloan filled the room with joy and delight. Sloan understood life in the city and fully enjoyed the people and their daily activities.

Lesson 15.1 Review

1 What were some scenes that George Bellows painted?
2 Describe the girls in Sargent's *Daughters of Edward D. Boit*. What are they wearing?
3 What subjects did Inness usually paint? Describe the mood in his painting *Home of the Heron*.
4 Describe the scene in Tanner's *Banjo Lesson*. What is the setting?
5 What was "The Ashcan School?" How did it get its name? Name two artists that were members of this group.
6 What was John Sloan's favorite subject to paint?

15.2 The Influence of Abstraction

If the Ashcan Eight had problems being accepted by Americans, the small group of Abstract painters had an even greater struggle. But, Abstraction persisted. In America, there was one stronghold for the young experimenters—the studio of the master photographer Alfred Stieglitz. He admired the work of Cézanne, Rodin, Brancusi and Picasso and encouraged young American Abstractionists, such as Georgia O'Keeffe and John Marin, by showing their work in his New York studio.

The 1913 New York Armory Show opened American eyes to the European art scene. American artists realized they either had to change direction or be left out. Following World War I, American artists flocked to France to study and to work. Gradually, Abstraction became an important element in American art, even though it was not yet fully accepted by the public. The American public made little attempt to understand the language and meaning of the Abstractionists. Thus, the artists worked in isolation, receiving encouragement from each other and from a small, but growing, number of patrons, museums and galleries.

Key Notes

- New York Armory Show convinces American artists that they have to change direction.
- Despite the ridicule of the public, the Abstractionists forge a new path in American art.

Vocabulary

mobiles
stabiles

Special Feature

Georgia O'Keeffe

(1887–1986)

Born and raised on a large farm in Wisconsin, Georgia O'Keeffe was an American pioneer of Abstraction. Unlike other ground-breaking artists, her training and influences were entirely American.

O'Keeffe first drew and painted representationally, but this work did not satisfy her and she began making abstract drawings of landforms from memory. She mailed some of these charcoal drawings to a friend with express instructions not to show them to anyone else. The friend took them to Alfred Stieglitz, the famous photographer, who was running an avant-garde gallery in New York. Stieglitz loved

15–12 O'Keeffe did not study in Europe, but invented her own variety of American Abstraction based on natural forms.
Georgia O'Keeffe, *From the Plains I*, 1953. Oil on canvas, 48" x 84 1/4" (122 x 214 cm). McNay Art Institute, San Antonio, Texas.

them and showed them in an exhibition with two other artists. When O'Keeffe heard about this, she rushed down to New York to confront Stieglitz and make him take down the drawings. However, Stieglitz managed to persuade her to leave them up. Eight years later, they were married.

O'Keeffe's early subjects were gigantic close-up paintings of flowers or flower parts. She said, "I'll make them big like the huge buildings going up. People will be startled; they'll have to look at them." She moved in closer and closer to blown-up images of flowers until the vibrating center of a flower was sometimes all there was on her canvas. Nature's abstract forms always pleased her and, when Stieglitz died in 1946, she settled permanently in her beloved desert landscape of New Mexico.

From the Plains I (fig.15–12) is a powerful and dramatic work that captures the austere and quiet vastness of the plains. The yellow, red and orange hues add a hot and savage feeling to a flat land. In this painting, there is no monumental mountain to break the horizon; the horizon line itself becomes monumental.

O'Keeffe always took her forms from nature, no matter how abstractly she depicted them. The 1923 charcoal drawing, *Alligator Pears in a Basket* (fig.15–13), is one of these fluid, organic images derived from nature. The deliberate ambiguity of the composition makes us want to look very carefully at the image. A close look reveals subtle shadings of grays and blacks. The grays are so luscious they seem almost to be colors. O'Keeffe often worked with an element of surprise in order to shock the viewer into seeing differently. In this drawing, the two thick charcoal lines ringing the fruit give us two different views of the pears.

Georgia O'Keeffe was one of the American artists who chose not to go to Europe to learn about abstraction. Her abstract paintings are a purely American invention.

15–13 How has the artist made full use of her medium?
Georgia O'Keeffe, *Alligator Pears in a Basket*, 1923. Charcoal drawing, 24" x 18" (61 x 46 cm). National Museum of Women in the Arts, gift of Wallace and Wilhelmina Holladay.

15–14 How do color and line create a sense of motion here?
John Marin, *Singer Building,* 1921. Watercolor on paper, 26 1/3" x 21 1/4" (67 x 54 cm). Philadelphia Museum of Art; The Alfred Stieglitz Collection.

15–15 Based on a poem by William Carlos Williams, this painting recalls a fire engine tearing through the city on a dark, wet night. How does the artist convey this image in abstract terms?
Charles Demuth, *The Figure Five in Gold,* 1928. Oil on composition board, 35 4/5" x 29 1/2" (91 x 75 cm). The Metropolitan Museum of Art, New York, Alfred Stieglitz Collection, 1949.

John Marin

(1870–1953)

John Marin studied to be an architect. However, after a trip to Europe, where he worked with Whistler, he turned to painting. Like Georgia O'Keeffe, Marin exhibited in Alfred Stieglitz's gallery. He was among the first Americans to experiment with Abstract art. His paintings have a Cubist feeling, in which soft lines break up the larger shapes. Much of his work, such as *Singer Building* (fig.15–14), explores cityscapes. He later concentrated on Maine landscapes and seascapes. He often painted in watercolor so he could work quickly in his own personal shorthand style, which expressed a sense of agitation and excitement. His paintings explode with color and line. They have a dynamic geometry that seems in constant motion. He said once that he could see and feel the "warring of great and small buildings in the city...and hear the sound of their strife." He once compared his brisk painting style to a golf game—the fewer strokes, the better. Although his paintings seem quickly done, they were carefully thought out before his brush first touched paper.

Charles Demuth

(1883–1935)

Charles Demuth was born in Pennsylvania. After studying in Philadelphia, he went to Paris. His early works were mostly Cubist watercolors of delicate, beautifully drawn houses, landscapes, grain elevators, acrobats and circus performers. Later, he painted in oils and worked on a series that he called "posters," although they were not meant to be actual posters. One was *The Figure Five in Gold* (fig.15–15), based on a poem written by his friend William Carlos Williams. Both the poem and the painting recall a shrieking fire engine tearing through the darkened city streets on a wet night. "Bill" and "Carlo" (for the name of the poet) appear in the Cubist design along with the roaring number five. The painting became Demuth's best-known work.

Charles Sheeler

(1883–1965)

After going through several phases and styles, Charles Sheeler found himself close to the thinking and design of the great and cool Renaissance designers, such as Raphael and Piero della Francesca. Instead of people, however, Sheeler used machinery, buildings and manufactured products as his subject because he enjoyed their geometric lines and solid structure. His intense interest in photography led him to believe that light is the great designer.

His carefully composed paintings combine the structure of abstraction with a realistic presentation of subject matter. *City Interior* (fig.15–16) is precisely put together and free of emotion. It combines interlocking darks and lights, verticals and horizontals, and lines and shapes. Sheeler painted the cities and the industrial scene with precision and careful attention to design and detail.

15–16 Renaissance design and concerns with realism are coupled here with industrial subjects for a very twentieth-century look.
Charles Sheeler, *City Interior*, 1936. Oil on fiberboard, 22" x 27" (56 x 69 cm). Worcester Art Museum, Massachusetts.

World Cultural Timeline

1921
First modern Chinese hospital founded, Peking

1926
Women gain right to run for political office, India

1931
First trans-African railway completed from Angola to Mozambique

1938
Oil discovered, Saudi Arabia

15–17 The title is not a clue to the meaning of this abstract work. It is up to you to make your own interpretation.
Arshile Gorky, *The Liver Is the Cock's Comb,* 1944. Oil on canvas, 71 3/5" x 97 3/5" (182 x 248 cm). Albright-Knox Art Gallery, Buffalo, gift of Seymour H. Knox.

Arshile Gorky

(1904–1948)

Gorky came to America from Armenia when he was sixteen. He became the pioneer of an American artistic revolution later called *Abstract Expressionism.* His major contribution was in developing a unique style of abstraction based on his personal feelings and inner thoughts. Some of his works are based on the abstracting of representational objects. However, the shapes are so personal that they cannot often be recognized. The viewer is forced to look at the work without recognizable symbols. The shapes, lines and colors in *The Liver Is the Cock's Comb* (fig.15–17) are organic, not geometric. They appear to be floating and turning in congested space. They seem almost human, but soon the resemblance vanishes. Only shapes, lines and colors remain. This sensation comes and goes, leaving the viewer with ambiguous feelings. Each viewer must interpret the result in his or her own way. Gorky does not provide a clue, nor does the title help. His titles are personal. Perhaps they had meaning to Gorky when he finished the work.

Stuart Davis

(1894–1964)

Stuart Davis was a student of Robert Henri and exhibited several Realistic paintings (and even sold one) in the Armory Show. But, once he was exposed to Cubism, Fauvism and the rest of European experimentation, he turned from Realism to Abstraction. The abstract style he developed formed the bridge between European Cubism and American Abstract Expressionism later in the century. From a series of experiments in color and shape, Davis finally developed a style of hard-edge abstraction that was clean, colorful and personal. It sizzled with life and a jazz beat. His works often reflected the words, numbers, shapes and colors of urban life and advertising. Works such as *Something on the Eight Ball* (fig.15–a) are bright, joyful and carefully composed.

Like Matisse and Mondrian, Davis had the rare ability to reduce the complexities of his urban environment to rhythmic and electric designs. His unique paintings have the appearance of flat cutouts of brightly colored paper, of interlocking strips overlaid with parts of words and numbers. Davis' titles, like those of Arshile Gorky, are personal and are not literal references to the paintings. Each work is to be enjoyed as seen and not for hidden meaning. Davis worked with his powerful abstractions well into the second half of the twentieth century.

Alexander Calder

(1898–1976)

American sculptors during the first half of the twentieth century worked mostly in traditional ways and media, but with ever-increasing interest in simplifying the figure. Several, including Alexander Calder, began to work with new materials and in new ways.

Calder was among the first Americans to begin working with abstract forms in space. He moved to Paris in 1926 and began creating an imaginative menagerie of animals from wire and scraps of other materials. *Sow* (fig.15–c) and other three-dimensional, linear animals and circus performers are like whimsical drawings in space.

The light and airy feeling of his space drawings was carried into more technical constructions called ***mobiles***. Calder's mobiles hung suspended from a single point. *Lobster Trap and Fish Tails* (fig.15–18) is a buoyant assemblage of shapes that is balanced so carefully that a single breath of air sets the sculpture in motion. It was constructed so that every movement produces a change in the visual configuration—with the possibilities being endless. Although this sculpture has a suggested subject matter, most of his mobiles were completely nonobjective. Calder also produced many standing sculptures that he called ***stabiles***, such as the steel *Black Widow* (fig.15–19).

15–18 Every slight motion of the air changes the configuration of this sculpture. Alexander Calder, *Lobster Trap and Fish Tails*, 1939. Painted steel wire and sheet aluminum, about 101" x 115" (257 x 292 cm). The Museum of Modern Art, New York.

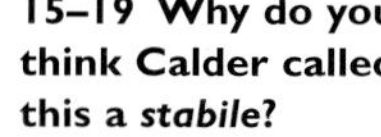

15–19 Why do you think Calder called this a *stabile*? Alexander Calder, *Black Widow*, 1959. Painted sheet steel, 7' 9" (2.34 m) high. The Museum of Modern Art, New York, Mrs. Simon Guggenheim Fund.

Lesson 15.2 Review

1 How did Alfred Stieglitz encourage American Abstractionists during the first part of the twentieth century?

2 Describe the mood of the landscape in Georgia O'Keeffe's *On the Plain I*.

3 How does Marin's *Singer Building* resemble Cubism?

4 What inspired Charles Demuth to paint *I Saw the Figure Five in Gold*?

5 What style did Arshile Gorky develop?

6 From what medium is Alexander Calder's *Sow* made?

7 What type of sculpture is Calder's *Lobster Trap and Fish Tails*?

15.3 The American Scene

THE AMERICAN ART ESTABLISHMENT made a giant swing from Realism to Abstraction following the Armory Show in 1913. However, many American artists continued to work with Realism. Because they painted the farmlands and the cities of America in a realistic way, these artists, such as Edward Hopper and Walt Kuhn, were called American Scene painters. Each had an individual style, but the message was the same: America is vast, beautiful, abundant, lonely, crowded and full of honest, hard-working people.

Another group of American Scene painters from the Midwest became known as Regionalists because they limited their subject matter to the regions in which they lived. Grant Wood painted images of rural Iowa. Thomas Hart Benton painted his native Missouri. Although they developed independent styles, the Regionalists were trying to develop an art that was truly American. These artists did not want to look to Europe for inspiration.

Key Notes

- Many American artists continue to work in Realist style.
- American Scene artists paint American farmlands and cities.
- Regionalists, a group of midwestern American Scene artists, limit their subject matter to the regions in which they live.

Special Feature

Thomas Hart Benton

(1889–1975)

Benton was the leader of the Regionalists. Born in Neosho, Missouri, Benton was the son of a United States congressman and the grandnephew of a famous senator. His childhood and adolescence were filled with talk of the forces that were shaping the Midwest. So, it is no wonder that Benton limited his subject matter to the history and activities of typical midwestern farmers. These were the subjects he knew best. Sunburned farmers, sturdy horses and furrowed fields attracted him, not the people of Paris or New York. He tried all the avant-garde

15–21 What are the arts of the West?
Thomas Hart Benton, *Arts of the West*, 1932. Tempera, 8' x 13' (2.4 x 3.9 m). New Britain Museum of American Art, Connecticut.

15–20 Why would Americans, especially Kentuckians, have found this work appealing? Thomas Hart Benton, *The Kentuckian*, 1954. Oil on canvas, 36 3/5" x 20 2/3" (93 x 52 cm). Los Angeles County Museum of Art, gift of Burt Lancaster. ©1996 T.H. Benton and R.P. Benton Testamentarry Trusts/Licensed by VAGA, New York, NY

styles, but ultimately felt comfortable only with his own brand of Realism.

The Kentuckian (fig.15–20) illustrates the type of historical subject he loved to paint. There is a slight distortion of humans, plant life and nature. However, the strongly lit forms, deep shadows and simplified design create a realistic image. The style is personal and unique. The large figure appears determined and ready to face whatever difficulties may lie ahead.

To preserve American history, Benton conceived a huge program of public mural art. The sixty-four murals would provide a complete pictorial history of the United States. Benton actually completed sixteen of these panels. In *Arts of the West* (fig.15–21), Benton wanted to present a great deal of information. The various landscapes are jammed. There is so much happening in this panel that it could easily be chaotic. Instead, it all fits together and is perfectly balanced.

Benton was a critic of modern trends in art. He forged an American art that was based on the history and folklore of the United States.

15–22 Compare Rubens' *Castle of Steen* (fig.11–24), which was his farm, to this picture of American midwestern farming.
Grant Wood, *Stone City, Iowa*, 1930. Oil on wood panel, 30 1/3" x 40" (77 x 102 cm). Joslyn Art Museum, Omaha, Nebraska. ©1996 Estate of Grant Wood/Licensed by VAGA, New York, NY

Grant Wood

(1892–1941)

Like Thomas Hart Benton, Grant Wood was a Regionalist. Wood was born on a small farm in rural Iowa and at an early age moved to Cedar Rapids. In his trips to Europe, Wood became interested in the exquisite detail of the early Flemish masters. His paintings, such as *Stone City, Iowa* (fig.15–22), reflect this fascination with detail. However, Wood used his midwestern imagination to produce trees and hills that are smoothly rounded and expertly trimmed to perfection. His work is painstakingly designed, drawn and painted to present a clean and crisp world of farmers, farms, countryside and people—an idealized American Scene. An icon of American culture, *American Gothic* (fig.15–23) is Wood's best-known work. The simple plainness of this farming couple conveys the austerity of rural American life at this time and leaves a lasting impression on the viewer.

15–23 This couple has become symbolic of America's midwestern farmers and the life they created.
Grant Wood, *American Gothic*, 1930. Oil on beaver board, 29" x 24" (76 x 63 cm). The Art Institute of Chicago, Friends of the American Art Collection, 1930. ©Estate of Grant Wood/Licensed by VAGA, New York, NY

1946
Jordan becomes independent

1947
India becomes fully independent from Britain

1948
South Africa officially adopts apartheid policy

World Cultural Timeline

1947
Dead Sea Scrolls found

1948
The Crazy Horse Memorial dedicated to all Native Americans, Black Hills, South Dakota

15–25 What does Hopper say here about life in American cities?
Edward Hopper, *Nighthawks,* 1942. Oil on canvas, 30" x 60" (76 x 152 cm). The Art Institute of Chicago, Friends of American Art Collection.

15–24 Although he was one of the organizers of the Armory Show, Kuhn stayed with his realistic painting style.
Walt Kuhn, *The Blue Clown,* 1931. Oil on canvas, 30" x 25" (76 x 64 cm). Purchase Collection of Whitney Museum of American Art, New York.

Walt Kuhn

(1880–1949)

Walt Kuhn was one of the American Scene painters. Although he was one of the organizers of the Armory Show, he could not change his painting style to adapt to the modern Abstractionism. He worked realistically, painting dramatic studies of clowns and circus performers. He had worked in circuses himself and painted his subjects with knowledge and compassion. He would catch his models, like *The Blue Clown* (fig.15–24), in off-duty moments and in moods of reflection. He was able to portray their sense of dignity and pride, of sadness and loneliness. He also captured the continuing sense of drama in which they lived and worked.

Edward Hopper

(1882–1967)

Another painter of the American Scene, Edward Hopper was one of Robert Henri's most talented pupils. He even sold a painting at the Armory Show. However, despite a trip to Europe and the increasing importance of Abstractionism in America, Hopper continued to work at his own brand of Realism. He was acutely sensitive to human emotions. He painted America from the inside out, concentrating on its feelings rather than the visibly evident. He closely observed the sadness of cheap hotel rooms, empty diners, cool nights, lonely people and cheerless houses. *Nighthawks* (fig.15–25) is a powerful and dramatic portrayal of loneliness of life in the big cities. His strong light is always garish and piercing. The subjects look exposed, as though they were put under a glaring spotlight. Hopper traveled from place to place and made mental notes of what he saw. He later put them together to visually express his feelings on American life.

Window in Time

Romanticizing the West

And ever I am leaving the city more and more, and withdrawing into the wilderness. I must walk toward Oregon, and not toward Europe. And that way the nation is moving. We go westward as into the future, with a spirit of enterprise and adventure....The West is but another name for the Wild; and in Wildness is the preservation of the World.

–Henry David Thoreau, *Walking*

The West—unspoiled, untamed, uncivilized—held Americans' imagination with a magnetic attraction. Like Thoreau, Americans saw the West and its untouched wilderness as a source of strength and truth. Nature was a reflection of both the grandeur and possibility inherent in America. The West was a state of mind as much as it was a landscape.

Images of the West have remained fixed in American lore in great part because of works by artists and writers. However, often these images are not completely accurate.

Artists such as Albert Bierstadt and Thomas Moran depicted the West in a romantic light. They wanted to show the grandeur and magnificence of what they saw, but without any harsh realities. The huge canvases were intended to be dramatic and spectacular; like the myth of the West, they were larger than life.

The Old West had largely vanished by the time Frederic Remington began to paint. Essentially, Remington created his own West, bigger and purer than what he saw. His works, which are charged with a sense of drama and excitement, are a pure celebration of the country and men who lived and worked upon it.

Both Remington and fellow artist Charles Russell transformed the cowboy from a ranch laborer who spent a lonely, monotonous life into a glamorous figure. Their cowboys are the embodiment of youthful freedom. Perhaps the cowboy, more than any other image, evokes the romantic spirit and freedom we associate with the West. He stood for the essence, not the reality, of the West.

Western American art is largely fantasy, yet in fantasy there is much truth. The works are a record of the feelings, attitudes, hopes and aspirations that objective sources cannot possibly convey. They are a vision of a better world called the West—a world of imagination and possibility.

Albert Bierstadt, *The Last of the Buffalo*, Oil on canvas, 71 1/4" x 119 1/4" (181 x 303 cm). In the collection of The Corcoran Gallery of Art, gift of Mrs. Albert Bierstadt.

Frederic Remington

(1861–1906)

Although he worked earlier in the century than the American Scene painters, Frederic Remington depicted life in the western part of the United States. He was a painter and sculptor of the great westward expansion. Although known primarily for his paintings, Remington began sculpting in bronze about 1895 and produced many fine pieces before he died in 1906. Sculptures such as *The Outlaw* (fig.15–26) show his supreme knowledge of horses, cowboys and their movement, based on countless hours of sketching and painting. Remington's work was traditional in concept because of its realism. The action and subject matter were strictly American to the point of nostalgia.

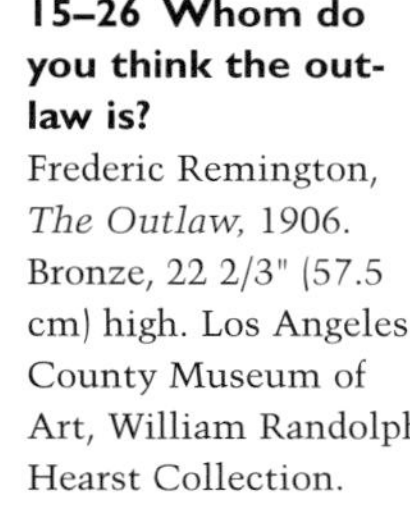

15–26 Whom do you think the outlaw is?
Frederic Remington, *The Outlaw,* 1906. Bronze, 22 2/3" (57.5 cm) high. Los Angeles County Museum of Art, William Randolph Hearst Collection.

Lesson 15.3 Review

1 Name two American Regionalists and the region or part of the country that they painted.
2 What subject did Walt Kuhn usually paint?
3 Describe how Hopper conveys a sense of loneliness in a city in his painting *Nighthawks*.
4 What is Grant Wood's most famous painting? Have you seen a parody of this?
5 What region of the United States provided Frederic Remington subjects to paint and sculpt?

15.4 Social Realism

During and immediately following the Great Depression of the early 1930s, the United States experienced a period of mass unemployment, hard times and near social panic. Outside influences, such as totalitarianism, socialism and communism cast threatening shadows over the country.

In reaction to this difficult time, many American artists rejected Abstraction, which had become increasingly fashionable. They also dismissed the Realism of Benton and Wood, who lived away from the cities' problems. Instead, these Social Realists attacked the dehumanization of industrial and urban life. They tried to use their art to influence the course of government. Their work often focused on ordinary people and the many injustices imposed on them by an uncaring society.

Led at first by Ben Shahn and Reginald Marsh, the banner of Social Realism was later picked up by artists like Jacob Lawrence and George Tooker. These artists communicated their ideas and feelings about American society in different styles, but the messages still got across. They believed that painting must describe and express the people and their lives, problems and times. This belief sums up the aesthetic philosophy of the Social Realists.

Key Notes

- The hard times brought on by the Great Depression of the 1930s are often depicted by American artists of the period.
- Many American artists reject both Abstraction and the Realism of the Regionalists.
- Social Realism shows the dehumanization of urban life.

15–28 Written statements accompany each of the sixty panels in this series. Lawrence combed history books and newspapers in order to select exactly the right statement for each scene.

Jacob Lawrence, *One of the Largest Race Riots Occurred in East St. Louis*, panel 52 from *The Migration of the Negro*, 1940–1941. Tempera and gesso on composition board, 12" x 18" (30 x 46 cm). The Museum of Modern Art, New York, gift of Mrs. David M. Levy.

Special Feature

Jacob Lawrence

(b.1917)

In the 1920s, Harlem experienced a cultural flowering known as the Harlem Renaissance. Many of the greatest African-American writers, musicians, poets and artists lived in Harlem or took their inspiration from it. When Jacob Lawrence arrived in Harlem about 1930, the greatest surge of the Harlem Renaissance had passed. But, enough stimulus remained to help turn the child of a poor family into one of the most significant American artists of his time.

Lawrence studied art at the government-sponsored Harlem Art Workshop from 1932 to 1934. By the age of twenty-one, he had already made a name for himself as an artist. His tempera paintings of the Haitian general Toussaint L'Ouverture were shown in an exhibit of African-American artists. After this exhibition, Lawrence began several series of paintings about the heritage of his people and their struggle for equality. His angular, hard-edge style was appropriate for the themes that would dominate his work. He painted the experiences of African Americans: their hardships in the ghettos, the violence that greeted their move from the South to the North, the civil rights movement.

Juke Box (fig.15–27), like most of his paintings, tells a story. A lonely woman leans against the juke box, listening sadly to its music. Is she remembering better times? Why is she alone in such a large room? Is she enjoying the

15–27 Jacob Lawrence says he chose his colors by using the ones available in the tempera sets sold at the dime store. Jacob Lawrence, *Juke Box*, 1946. Tempera on paper, 29" x 21 1/4" (74 x 54 cm). The Detroit Institute of Arts, gift of Dr. D. T. Burton, Dr. M. E. Fowler, Dr. J. B. Greene and Mr. J. J. White.

music? Why aren't others? All the answers to such questions could be narratives that Lawrence allows the viewer to imagine.

In the early 1940s, Lawrence created a sixty-panel series called *The Migration of the Negro* that dealt with the oppression of African Americans. *One of the Largest Race Riots Occurred in East St. Louis* (fig.15–28) is one of the best-known panels from that series. The race riot is not depicted realistically. Instead, Lawrence gives us a stylized and perfectly balanced dance of almost abstract shapes, which only make the work more chilling. The painting universalizes the hatred, lifting it above a more specific clash of individuals. The painting is dominated by the clenched fist holding the knife. This extremely moving and beautifully rendered painting is a searing example of Social Realism.

Sidelight

Art and Social Protest

Throughout his life, Ben Shahn was involved with political and moral issues, like those raised in the trial of Nicola Sacco and Bartolomeo Vanzetti.

Sacco and Vanzetti were Italian-American anarchists who had been charged with the robbery and murder of a paymaster and a guard in 1920. Evidence presented at the trial was far from conclusive, but still resulted in convictions. Their fate had been determined by the presiding judge, Webster Thayer. Thayer was highly biased against foreigners and anarchists and openly displayed his biases during the trial. The trial also took place during a period of national fear of anarchists and Communists.

The verdict was appealed, but in 1927 Sacco and Vanzetti were finally executed in the electric chair. The question of their guilt or innocence has never been resolved. The controversy over whether they were executed solely because of their political beliefs still remains.

Shahn did many works of the Sacco and Vanzetti trials, until as late as 1952, incurring the wrath of those who wanted the trials forgotten. His detractors said that what he was doing was not art. But, Shahn rejected art for art's sake and his willingness to comment on the life and social issues of his time never abated. As far as he was concerned, art and political action were perfectly compatible.

Ben Shahn, *The Passion of Sacco and Vanzetti*, 1931–1932. Tempera on canvas, 84 1/2" x 48" (215 x 122 cm). Collection of Whitney Museum of American Art, gift of Edith and Milton Lowenthal. ©1996 Estate of Ben Shahn/Licensed by VAGA, New York, NY

Ben Shahn

(1898–1969)

Ben Shahn grew up in a Brooklyn slum, studied art in Paris, and was the early leader of Social Realism. He hated injustice in any form. Through his art, he criticized and commented on the judicial system, racial injustice, and the plights of migratory workers and miners. His eloquent voice was heard and seen by millions. His work as a photographer, muralist and printmaker during America's rebuilding years gave him a variety of media with which to communicate.

Handball (fig.15–29) does not simply show American young people playing games. Instead, the painting indicates the tragedy of unemployment and the waste of human resources. The men have no choice but to spend their time idly. Shahn was a master at using empty space to symbolize loneliness. He could have treated this subject as an active, fun-filled sport. But the viewer feels at once that this was not his intention.

15–29 This artist worked as an apprentice for Diego Rivera and also used paintings and murals to comment on social conditions.
Ben Shahn, *Handball*, 1939. Tempera on paper over composition board, 22 1/2" x 31 1/2" (57 x 80 cm). The Museum of Modern Art, New York, Abby Aldrich Rockefeller Fund. ©Estate of Ben Shahn/Licensed by VAGA, New York, NY

15–31 For forty years, Bishop commuted every day from her suburban home to her studio in Manhattan. From the large picture window in her studio in Union Square, she observed the crowds on the streets below. Isabel Bishop, *On the Street,* about 1932. Oil on canvas, 14" x 26" (35 x 66 cm). Midtown Payson Galleries, New York City.

Reginald Marsh

(1898–1954)

Reginald Marsh painted the people of the streets during the 1930s. His subjects included crowds in the tenements, on the steps, in the streets, and at parks, beaches and theaters. His sketchy style, somewhat like Daumier's, was the result of numerous pen-and-ink sketches he made for newspaper cartoons. *The Bowery* (fig.15–30) captures the crowded living conditions and the congestion of life in parts of New York in the 1930s. Marsh's use of color, values and swirling movement creates a feeling of agitation and restlessness, even if his figures are relaxed and sleeping. The softness of his edges is drastically different from the harder edges of Shahn and Lawrence.

Isabel Bishop

(b.1902)

Although she was excited by the artists of the Armory Show, Isabel Bishop would not give up her Realistic style. She painted the workers, shoppers, derelicts and passersby outside her studio on Union Square in New York.

Bishop's paintings have a lively sense of movement that mirrors the constant flux and rhythm of people moving along crowded city streets. In paintings like *On the Street* (fig.15–31), she also captures the loneliness of the crowds. The well-dressed women look down, not around them, as they cut through the congested street. The light on the women further isolates them from the men on the fringes.

15–30 Remember that this was painted in 1930. What do you think these men are talking about? Reginald Marsh, *The Bowery,* 1930. Oil on canvas, 48" x 36" (122 x 91 cm). The Metropolitan Museum of Art, New York. Arthur H. Hearn Fund, 1932.

George Tooker

(b.1920)

Along with Jacob Lawrence, George Tooker carried the banner of Social Realism into the post-World War II period. He painted the decline in the quality of life in the growing cities by emphasizing chilling loneliness and alienation. A prison-like environment seems to engulf city-dwellers in their subways, stations, offices and governmental agencies. In his *Government Bureau* (fig.15–32), he shows the plight of a depersonalized humanity confronting a faceless bureaucracy. The same male figure is repeated three times. This repetition and the bleak architectural setting intensify the scene's impact and eerie feeling of hopelessness.

Government Bureau is the stark, almost chilling, summation of the dehumanizing of urban society that the Social Realists sought to portray.

15–32 What does this painting tell you about the relationship of the individual and the bureaucracy?
George Tooker, *Government Bureau*, 1956. Egg tempera on gesso panel, 19 1/3" x 29 1/2" (49 x 75 cm). The Metropolitan Museum of Art, New York, George A. Hearn Fund, 1956.

1948
Israel created as Jewish homeland

1949
Indonesia becomes independent from the Dutch

World Cultural Timeline

1948
Mahatma Gandhi assassinated

1949
People's Republic of China established; all China now Communist

Lesson 15.4 Review

1 Name five American Social Realist artists. What were they trying to achieve in their art?
2 What was the Harlem Renaissance? Name an artist that was involved with this movement.
3 What subjects did Jacob Lawrence paint?
4 In addition to teenagers playing, what are some of the messages in Ben Shahn's *Handball*?
5 Describe how George Tooker depersonalized people in his *Government Bureau*.

Primary Source

Jacob Lawrence: A Philosophy of Art

Jacob Lawrence consistently painted scenes from the African-American experience because he wanted his people to know their history. In this statement, which was solicited by the Whitney Museum after it acquired a painting by Lawrence, the artist describes his philosophy of art:

"Painting is a way of expressing one's thoughts and feelings. I feel that I am more articulate in painting than in any other form of expression, therefore I am always striving to perfect this particular form of art so as to reach a greater degree of articulation.

For me a painting should have three things: universality, clarity and strength. Universality so that it may be understood by all men. Clarity and strength so that it may be aesthetically good. It is necessary in creating a painting to find out as much as possible about one's subject, thereby freeing oneself of having to strive for a superficial depth.

It is more important that an artist study life than study the technique of painting exclusively. Technique will come with the desire to make oneself understood. It is more important for the artist to develop a philosophy and clarity of thought.

My pictures express my life and experience. I paint the things I know about and the things I have experienced. The things I have experienced extend into my national, racial and class group. So I paint the American scene."

Chapter Review

Review

1 List the ten pieces of art that you liked best in this chapter. Rank them from most realistic to most abstract with one being the most realistic and ten the most abstract.

2 How has Benton made *The Kentuckian* heroic?

3 List the street and city scenes and the artists who painted them in chapters 14 and 15.

4 Which do you think is the most emotional? Which is the least emotional or impersonal?

Interpret

1 How did Bierstadt romanticize the American West? What effect did this have on the westward migration?

2 Compare Sheeler's cityscape to George Bellow's *Cliff Dwellers*. What was each artist most interested in portraying?

3 Compare Gorky's *The Liver Is the Cock's Comb* to Davis' *Something on the Eight Ball*. How are they alike? How are they different? Which is hard? Which is soft? Which is larger? Describe their colors.

Other Tools for Learning

Maps

Find the regions on a map that Grant Wood, Frederic Remington and George Bellows painted.

Timelines

1 Select an event on the cultural timeline that a Social Realist would have approved. Explain why you chose this event.

2 List several events in the timelines which contributed to the sense of loneliness and alienation found in much of the art of the first half of the twentieth century.

Electronic Research

Videodisc player: *National Gallery of Art*

1 Look at Calder's sculpture in the lobby of the National Gallery in Washington, DC. Describe its size in relation to people and in relation to the space it occupies.

Activity 1

Depicting City Life

Materials
11" x 14" white paper (or larger)
tempera or acrylic paints
brushes
surface for mixing paint
containers of water

Take a look.
- Fig.15–10, Robert Henri, *Snow in New York,* 1902.
- Fig.15–1, George Bellows, *Cliff Dwellers,* 1913.
- Fig.15–16, Charles Sheeler, *City Interior,* 1936.

Think about it. Much of the artwork in this chapter represents the artists' views of city life. Some capture a realistic likeness while others aim to reflect an impression of crowds of people, linear buildings and the bustle of activity. Choose an artist you would like to emulate, and identify what makes his/her style unique; for example: use of color, brushstrokes, details, composition and emphasis.

Do it.
- Choose an active place in your community among buildings, such as a shopping mall, an outdoor restaurant or other gathering place.
- Do several drawings or take photographs as references. Carefully work out the values in your sketches.
- Use tempera or acrylic paint to create a painting in the style of your choice.

Check it. Name the elements in each of your paintings that resemble the work of the artist being emulated. What makes your work uniquely your own?

Helpful Hint: Step back from your painting occasionally to consider how it looks from a distance.

Activity 2

Balancing Act

Materials
wooden sticks
wire (assorted gauges),
fishing line or string
poster, bristol and railroad board (assorted colors)
heavy-weight white paper
scissors, mat knife
pencils, markers
straight edge
glue
templates (optional)
colored pencils, watercolors (optional)

Take a look.
- Fig.15–18, Alexander Calder, *Lobster Trap and Fish Tails,* 1939.

Think about it. Alexander Calder worked with abstract forms in space called *mobiles,* the beginning of kinetic art. Look at his artwork listed above. How would you describe the shapes he uses and their relationship to each other?

Do it.
- Choose something you enjoy as a theme for your mobile; e.g., sports, music, animals, calligraphy, geometry, food, nature.
- Bring in objects or images related to your theme. Sketch these objects and plan how they will interact in a mobile. You may want to repeat some images or shapes. Plan what colors to use.
- Use wooden sticks or stiff wire (coat-hanger weight) as a base and attach string, wire or fishing line to build the structure that will support your objects.
- Draw your objects on heavy-weight poster board or paper. Cut them out and attach them to your frame.
- Hang your mobile or have a friend hold it up for you. Adjust the position of objects and/or lengths of string until everything balances.

Check it. Is your mobile balanced both physically and visually? If not, what adjustments can you make to the weight or design to improve visual balance and keep it moving smoothly?

Helpful Hint: If you hang your objects with fishing line, which is virtually transparent, your images will stand out more clearly, as if suspended in mid-air.

Additional Activities

- With wire as his medium, Alexander Calder explored drawing in space (see *Sow,* fig.15–c). The concepts are similar to contour drawing—smooth, fluid line, carefully observed relationships and emphasis on those features unique to the subject. Likewise, his approach mimics gesture drawing—capturing the character of a motion or gesture. Use heavy gauge, soft aluminum wire to create a sculpture of a figure or animal that is a drawing in space. Preliminary sketches will help you decide how to go about this work.
- If there are murals in your library, post office or school done during the thirties and forties, find out who painted them and in what medium. Write a description of them, explaining subject matter, symbolism and style. You can film, videotape or photograph details and parts to prepare a visual presentation.

Emily Susanna Morikawa

Strath Haven High School
Wallingford, Pennsylvania
Favorite kinds of art: Impressionism, Genre painting
Favorite artists: Monet, Edward Hopper, Manet, O'Keeffe
Activity 1, Depicting City Life

My project is an image of a restaurant window in a nearby town, Media. It represents a project of hard work. I had been unfamiliar with acrylics and had little experience with window reflections, so the project proved to be a challenge for me.

In our class we use photography as a quick sketch method. Photography is an effective way to get an accurate portrayal of the subject without interference from passing people or vehicles. For example, with some subjects that are in motion you don't get the opportunity to do even quick sketches because of their movement.

The thought process behind this work was that I wanted it to look as the photo did. It was very difficult working with the reflections and with the usage of color. I was hoping to develop a finished piece that looked realistic.

I have visited many museums in my life. My mother was an art major in school, so as a child I accompanied her on museum trips. I have seen many different techniques and subject matter—it teaches me how to handle different projects. I've seen how art has evolved and changed through time. It taught me that no matter how different one artist's style is from another, it is still unique and a piece of original work.

My advice to students who also enjoy creating art is to remain patient when you're having problems. Sometimes assignments are harder than others and mean more thinking and planning behind it. Many times during this piece, I almost gave up because it never looked right. My teacher helped me throughout it all the time, pushing me to work harder, and always demanding more from me that I thought I possessed. Usually I quit when it's not easy the first time, but I'm very proud of myself for following through this time, even when it got rough.

Emily S. Morikawa

Emily photographed the reflection in a storefront window to use as the foundation for her painting.
Reflections, 1994. Acrylic, 19 1/2" x 15" (49.5 x 38.5 cm).

16 Twentieth-Century Architecture

In This Chapter...

NEW IDEAS, NEW TECHNOLOGY, scientific breakthroughs and an extraordinary outpouring of energy marked the 1900s. And, nowhere was the new dynamism better showcased than in architecture. Heavy structures of wood and stone were replaced by the modern invention of steel skyscrapers.

The new form of architecture, called Modernism, completely changed the way cities looked. The tallest structures traditionally had been church spires; the higher they soared the closer worshipers were to God. These structures were overshadowed now by taller secular buildings that were higher than anyone had ever imagined. They pierced the sky and, with it, our notions of space.

Modern architects abandoned brick and wood for steel, reinforced concrete and huge expanses of glass. Theirs was an unadorned style of architecture that sought weightlessness in all of its structures.

By the 1960s and 1970s, architects had grown tired of the pure line and impersonality of Modernism. They wanted something more vibrant and less box-like, without as many rules. Post-Modernism, the style of today, combines many styles often in clever and humorous ways. For example, Walt Disney imagery may be mixed with Doric columns. Post-Modernists take the whole environment into account when designing new structures, making this style of architecture much more personal.

16–a Using walls of windows, Wright allowed exterior space to flow into the interior space of this home. He designed many of the house's small details, such as the colored leaded glass.
Frank Lloyd Wright. *Robie House,* detail (fig.16–4).

1909
Wright initiates revolutionary style of modern architecture

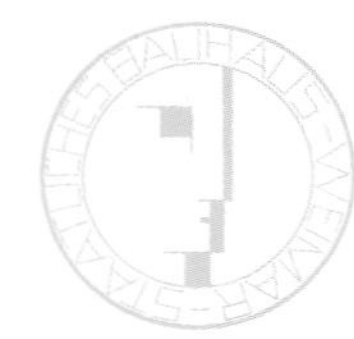

1928
Gropius, Bauhaus
1940
Hemingway, *For Whom the Bell Tolls*

1955
Le Corbusier, Notre-Dame-du-Haut

1961
Yuri Gagarin first man to orbit Earth

1980
Lech Walesa heads Solidarity Movement in Poland
1982
First artificial heart transplant

1986
Hole in ozone layer detected over Antarctica

Twentieth-Century Architecture

1909
Ford begins assembly-line auto manufacture
1918
Daylight saving time introduced in the US

1947
Flying saucers reported in the US
1947
Jackie Robinson (Brooklyn Dodgers) breaks racial barrier in sports

1959
Wright, Guggenheim Museum

1967
Buckminster Fuller, geodesic dome
1978
First personal computer

1985
Burgee and Johnson, AT&T Corporate Headquarters

1990
Break-up of the Soviet Union
1994
Construction of the Chunnel

"Less is more." Or is "Less a bore."

16–b This library is located across the street from the famous Mission of San Juan Capistrano. By incorporating elements of the Spanish mission style, it adheres to the Post-Modern intention of taking the surrounding environment into account when designing a new structure.
Michael Graves, *Public Library of San Juan Capistrano,* 1983. San Juan Capistrano, California.

16–d This architect has sought to convey the purpose of this building in a witty and appealing manner.
Frank O. Gehry & Associates. *California Aerospace Museum,* detail (fig.16–32).

16–c This museum and culture center sports its insides on its outsides. Does that appeal to you?
Renzo Piano and Richard Rogers. *Georges Pompidou National Center of Art and Culture,* 1977. Paris. (See fig.16–18.)

16.1 Modernism in Architecture

THE BIRTH OF MODERN ARCHITECTURE has much to do with breaking from the past. At the start of the twentieth century, there was a surge in construction, particularly in America. European cities had developed over centuries, while American cities underwent enormous growth and development in less than a century. Wood and stone had been the major building materials, and cast iron had been used to some degree, but these materials had severe limitations. New industries demanded a new type of architecture. Using the technology of steel and metal-frame construction, American architects developed the skyscraper, which dramatically changed the skylines and urban landscapes of Europe and America.

The steel frame, composed of vertical and horizontal beams riveted together, created a structure that was incredibly solid, rigid and strong. The structure was held together by the tensile strength of the steel instead of the enormous weight of stone. In such steel-frame structures, the walls do not have to bear the weight of the floors above. Instead, the steel became the primary support. Traditional arches and post-and-lintel elements were no longer needed. Buildings took on a gridlike appearance that echoed the supporting rectangular steel structure. The invention of high-speed elevators made it possible for skyscrapers to reach into the sky.

Architectural Modernism was based on the use of new technology and new man-made materials. Modern architects would embrace new technology and make efficient use of steel, concrete and glass construction. Lines were to be clean, without ornamentation and decoration. Function became a primary concern.

Key Notes

- Modern architecture makes a complete break with the past.
- Modernism relies on the new technology of steel and metal-frame construction.
- The lines of buildings are clean, and function becomes a primary concern.

Vocabulary
cantilevered
geodesic

6–1 Although Mies van der Rohe worked with a number of building types, his most influential contribution was to the modern evolution of the skyscraper.
Ludwig Mies van der Rohe. *Lakeshore Drive Apartments,* 1951. Chicago.

Special Feature

Ludwig Mies van der Rohe

(1866–1969)

Like many German architects and artists, Ludwig Mies van der Rohe left Germany in the thirties because of Hitler's closed attitude toward modern art. He settled in Chicago as a practicing architect. Mies was a modest man who once said of his ambitions as an architect that he did not want to be interesting, he wanted to be good. Mies had a great impact on the Modern movement in the United States. The visual artist Mies was most closely linked to was Mondrian.

Mies designed many building complexes in and around Chicago, but among his best known are the *Lakeshore Drive Apartments* (fig.16–1), constructed in 1951. The two buildings comprise two severely elegant slabs set at right angles to each other to allow the most light to strike each apartment. Mies' simplified forms usually have slight detailing on windows and employ dark colors for the metal parts. The windows here, for example, may all seem alike. However, every fourth metal division is a bit wider, adding a sense of subtle rhythm to the surface.

Mies was very attracted to skyscrapers, and his skyscraper designs of the postwar period were the most influential of the Modernist period. Together with Philip Johnson, who was mainly responsible for the interiors, Mies designed the *Seagram Building* (fig.16–2) in New York City (1954–58). The exterior of the thirty-eight-story building is made of bronze-finished steel and amber glass.

16–2 Mies designed every detail of this elegant bronze-colored building right down to the venetian blinds. Ludwig Mies van der Rohe. *Seagram Building,* 1954–1958. New York.

The rectangular building is set on a block-long plaza. Steel stilts support the building and give the bottom level an airiness that alleviates the solid form above. A pink granite pavement and lateral pools with fountains lead to a canopy and three sets of revolving doors. A visitor entering the bronze and glass-walled lobby is struck by its great simplicity and beauty. The Seagram Building is the perfect embodiment of modernism and of Mies' dictum, "Less is more."

Louis Sullivan

(1856–1924)

To find the beginnings of Modernism, we must go back to Louis Sullivan, who was one of the earliest architects to use steel construction. Sullivan believed that "form follows function." His most revolutionary work was the *Carson Pirie Scott Department Store* (fig.16–3), built in Chicago in 1901. The grid pattern of steel structure is very evident, with large windows used on all ten upper floors. The traditional heavy cornice and heavy window detail were eliminated. All ornamentation was eliminated except over the front doors at the rounded corner. Its stark simplicity heralded the beginning of modern architecture in America. America's developments would influence the entire world.

16–3 Unlike other buildings constructed at the same time, this store has decorative detail only over the front doors.
Louis Sullivan. *Carson Pirie Scott Department Store,* 1899–1901; enlarged 1899–1904. Chicago.

16–5 This famous house is popularly known as "Falling Water" because it is built over a waterfall. The sound of the falls can be heard throughout the house.
Frank Lloyd Wright. *Kaufmann House,* 1936. Bear Run, Pennsylvania.

Frank Lloyd Wright

(1867–1959)

Originally a student of Louis Sullivan, Frank Lloyd Wright was an individual genius. He developed his own style and disregarded conventional construction. His primary concern was to develop a compatible relationship between the structure and its location so that the building would seem to grow out of its environment. One of his earliest revolutionary designs was for the *Robie House* in Chicago, built in 1909 (fig.16–4). Wright disregarded the traditional plan of enclosed rooms with doors. Instead, he allowed one room to flow into another space, separated only by partial walls. He let exterior space flow into interior space (fig.16–a). Roofs here are ***cantilevered*** and seem to float without supports as they reach out from the cubic forms of the house. There is an overall horizontal feeling to the homes he built. They rest comfortably on their sites. Wright had been favorably impressed by the design of the Japanese Pavilion at the Chicago World's Fair in 1893. The simplicity of forms, the horizontal lines, and the honest use of materials in the Robie House reflect the Japanese influence.

In 1936, Wright designed and built one of the most original living spaces—the *Kaufmann House* at Bear Run, near Pittsburgh, Pennsylvania (fig.16–5). Cantilevered terraces stretch out over a stream and waterfall. These terraces echo the form and color of the natural rock terraces below. Stone, wood, color, shape, form and line are used by Wright in a perfect marriage of structure and site.

16–4 Wright was very impressed by Japanese designs he saw at the Chicago World's Fair. What evidence of that influence do you see?
Frank Lloyd Wright. *Robie House,* 1909. Chicago.

Sidelight

***Pennsylvania Railroad Station,* 1906, New York (33rd Street and Eighth Avenue).**

Great Buildings Lost

One of the greatest architectural blunders was committed in 1963, when the beautiful *Pennsylvania Railroad Station* in New York City was torn down.

The station, designed by McKim, Mead & White and completed in 1910, had been built in the grand American Neoclassical style. Scores of immense granite columns lined the perimeter of the site. From the center rose a massive near-replica of the ancient Roman Baths of Caracalla. In here were the ticket counters and the main waiting room of the station. At the west end of the waiting room was a multi-vaulted steel-and-glass concourse with stairs leading from the concourse down to the train tracks.

Once the building had been demolished, the remaining railroad station was confined to a basement concourse. All the beauty of the old building was gone. Train passengers hurried to get out of the station as quickly as possible. What had been lost was much more than just a building, for public spaces affect us in very important ways. Anyone passing through the old Penn Station could not fail to respond to its graceful and dignified monumentality or to feel a sense of pride in its existence.

The loss of this great building, however, did have a positive effect. Its demolition helped spur the beginning of the architectural preservation movement. Today a building of such architectural importance probably would not be demolished.

Gerrit Rietveld

(1888–1964)

Many Europeans were influenced by Frank Lloyd Wright and the exciting new ideas he brought to building. A Dutchman, Gerrit Rietveld combined the influence of Wright and a working relationship with the painter Mondrian to create a distinctive modern look in his architecture. The *Schröder House* in Utrecht (fig.16–6), built in the first quarter of the twentieth century, still has great appeal today. Its crisp lines and multiple surfaces look like a Mondrian work in three dimensions.

16–6 Can you see why this building might be considered a three-dimensional Mondrian painting? Gerrit Rietveld. *Schröder House,* 1924. Utrecht, The Netherlands.

Walter Gropius

(1883–1969)

and the International Style

After World War I, a style of architecture emerged in Germany, Holland and France called the *International Style.* It was the forerunner of contemporary architecture and the mass production building techniques of today. As a style, it nearly eliminated all ornamentation and avoided the use of natural materials, like wood or stone. Architects sought to produce a structure that appeared light in weight but did not have traditional architectural mass. To achieve the light appearance, flat surfaces and thin walls, they turned to glass. The result was a boxlike structure of steel, reinforced concrete and glass. The new buildings enclosed space instead of creating masses.

Walter Gropius was an early practitioner of the International Style and a powerful influence on twentieth-century art and architecture. In 1919, Gropius headed the Bauhaus. Great teachers from many countries came to the Bauhaus, where they stressed theories of the International Style. The Bauhaus taught more than just architecture. It also stressed the industrial and mechanical art processes as they related to painting, sculpture, crafts, printmaking and other art forms. Students of the Bauhaus influenced art and architecture in many countries for many years.

In 1925, Gropius moved the school from Weimar to Dessau and designed the new buildings himself. The main building (fig.16–7) is a huge glass box with flat planes of concrete and glass. Such gigantic walls of glass were used in construction until the 1970s when the energy crisis caused second thoughts. Less window space would make buildings more energy-efficient. Thus, much architecture of the 1980s used smaller windows and larger areas of masonry or concrete.

16–7 Glass walls were a hallmark of the International Style. Walter Gropius. *Bauhaus,* 1928. Dessau, Germany.

World Cultural Timeline

1920 Turkey established

1921 Iraq established

1930 Uruguay wins first World Cup Soccer title

1932 Saudi Arabia established

Le Corbusier

(Charles-Edouard Jenneret) (1887–1965)

Le Corbusier was a Swiss-born architect who grew up on the International Style. One of his earliest buildings, a residence called the *Savoye House* (fig.16–8), clearly shows the simplicity and sense of weightlessness that was possible with concrete and glass.

But Corbusier was one of the first to deviate from modern architectural principles. The concept of *Notre-Dame-du-Haut* (1955) was completely new (fig.16–9). Built on a hilltop near Ronchamp, France, the pilgrimage chapel abandons every aspect of the International Style. Using his favorite construction material, reinforced concrete, he formed an organic sculpture, not a shoe-box building. The floor plan is even irregular. The walls slope, slant and bend while the roof flares, curves and twists as if alive. Wedge-shaped windows are irregular and of different sizes. Light floods hidden chapels from recessed skylights. Around every interior turn there seems to be a surprise. Built for worship by a small number of townspeople, the interior holds about fifty people. However, the outdoor seating area can accommodate over ten thousand religious travelers.

16–9 Reinforced concrete makes the organic forms of this chapel possible.
Le Corbusier. *Notre-Dame-du-Haut,* 1950–54. Ronchamp, France.

16–8 Views of the sky and surrounding countryside are visible from everywhere in this house. The main (upper) level of the house includes a central open courtyard.
Le Corbusier. *Savoye House,* 1929–1930. Poissy-sur-Seine, France.

Wallace K. Harrison

(1895–1981)

Under the influence of the International Style, American cities (mainly New York, Philadelphia and Chicago at first) became the settings for towering skyscrapers. Wallace K. Harrison's skyscraper was the first that had a simple shaft without changes or set-backs from top to bottom. The *Secretariat Building* of the United Nations in New York (1947–1950) was designed by a firm of architects under Harrison's direction. The building (fig.16–10) has a grid of glass and steel on the wide sides and unbroken marble panels on the ends. All service units, such as elevator machinery, water towers and air-conditioning equipment, are on the roof. These units are hidden from view by the structure's extended walls.

Frank Lloyd Wright

(1867–1959)

Frank Lloyd Wright continued to exert a strong influence on architecture into the second half of the twentieth century. We have seen his work from the earliest part of the century, when he was helping give birth to Modernism. Like other great artists, Wright's work evolved throughout his life. Even at the height of Modernism in the 1950s, he continued to do ground-breaking work. The plan of the *Solomon R. Guggenheim Museum* in New York (fig.16–11) is based on a circle. Inside, the gallery unfolds like a spiral. The museum was completed only after much battling with officials. It was acclaimed only after tremendous initial criticism upon its opening.

Skidmore, Owings and Merrill

(b.1939)

Gordon Bunshaft was the chief designer for the architectural firm Skidmore, Owings and Merrill. Bunshaft was responsible for the next architectural development: the all-glass exterior of the *Lever House* (1951–52) in New York (fig.16–12). Like Gothic architecture, the design seems to defy gravity. The reflective glass tower and the two-story horizontal unit are supported by pylons above the street level. Foot traffic circulates from the pylons into a partially shaded open court. The structure itself occupies only about half of the total site, leaving room for the pleasant court. The court and space for foot traffic eliminate the feeling of congestion and crowdedness found in many urban streets. Sheathed in green-tinted glass, the Lever House reflects clouds, sky, sun and the surrounding environment. It was so successful in appearance and function that it became the model for hundreds of glass and metal skyscrapers (including Mies van der Rohe's Seagram Building) built around the world during the following quarter of a century.

16–10 The service equipment for this building is placed on the roof where it was out of the way. In the late 1940s and early 1950s, this was a new idea in architecture.
Wallace K. Harrison. *United Nations Secretariat Building,* 1947–1950. New York.

16–11 The interior of this museum is a continuous spiral with no clear delineation of levels.
Frank Lloyd Wright. *Solomon R. Guggenheim Museum,* 1956–1959. New York.

16–12 Bunshaft developed a way to create a building with an all-glass exterior. Lever House influenced architecture for years—until the cost of energy became too high.
Gordon Bunshaft and Skidmore, Owings and Merrill. *Lever House,* 1951–1952. New York.

16–13 What connections do you see between the form of this terminal and its function?
Eero Saarinen. *Trans World Airlines Terminal, John F. Kennedy International Airport,* 1962. New York.

16–14 In designing this terminal, Saarinen also solved practical problems such as transporting passengers directly to the plane through mobile lounges.
Eero Saarinen. *Dulles International Airport Terminal Building,* 1962. Washington, DC.

Eero Saarinen

(1910–1961)

Eero Saarinen was involved in the construction of many beautiful structures. But his design of several air terminals alone would be enough to make him important. Before Saarinen, airport facilities failed to equal in quality and design the advances made in the aircraft themselves. Saarinen's sculptured, organic structures were the exception. They almost seem capable of flight themselves. The *Trans World Airlines Terminal* (fig.16–13) in New York (1962) has curves that flow like air currents and suggest cloud shapes in their sculptural contours.

His magnificent terminal for *Dulles International Airport* (fig.16–14) outside Washington, DC, (1962) makes use of mobile lounges to get passengers to planes. In the structure, there is nothing left of traditional building design. Sixteen pairs of slanting concrete pillars support the enormous, hammock-shaped roof, which tilts to one side. No interior supports mar the vast enclosed space. With great window walls, the roof seems suspended from the sky. The entire building has a floating appearance. Both the Dulles and TWA air terminals are dynamic structures, perfectly expressive of their intended use.

16–15 The reflecting pools mirror the rhythm of the vaulted roof and help to create an oasis for art.
Louis I. Kahn. *Kimbell Art Museum,* 1966–1972. Fort Worth, Texas.

16–16 The geodesic dome, made of inexpensive materials which can be taken apart and reconstructed, is the signature structure of Buckminster Fuller.
R. Buckminster Fuller. *United States Pavilion, Expo 67,* 1967. Montreal, Canada.

Louis I. Kahn

(1901–1974)

Louis I. Kahn was an admirer of Le Corbusier and studied his work intensively. However, Kahn devised his own original solutions to architectural problems and had a strong influence on his contemporaries. One of his finest designs (and also his last) was the *Kimbell Art Museum* (fig.16–15) in Fort Worth, Texas (1972). The main entrance, shown here, is a tree-filled patio flanked by two open arched vaults and reflecting pools. Vaults are used to roof the entire structure. They provide a powerful sense of unity throughout. Natural light is admitted through long slits located in the vaults. The light is diffused inside by a series of baffles (adjustable panels that deflect light). The baffles provide superior lighting for the paintings. Designed to hold works of art, the structure is a work of art itself.

R. Buckminster Fuller

(1895–1983)

R. Buckminster Fuller sought to make use of inexpensive, easily manufactured materials in his constructions. Fuller is best known for his ***geodesic*** dome, like the innovative *United States Pavilion* at Expo 67 in Montreal (fig.16–16). Geodesic refers to a form of solid geometry that is the basis for structures built of interlocking polygons. Much of the dome in Montreal was destroyed by a fire. Originally it was a bubble 170 feet high and 258 feet in diameter. Thick struts, joined with knot joints, carried the weight and held up an inner net on which 2000 acrylic caps were mounted. The interior climate was controlled by motors at the joints which reacted automatically to sunlight. The motors shifted blinds and controlled the ventilating system.

Moshe Safdie

(b.1938)

Working mostly in his native Israel, Moshe Safdie has created some of the most unique and practical urban dwelling units yet conceived. Safdie created the dramatic structure called *Habitat* (fig.16–17) for Expo 67 in Montreal. Habitat was a new concept in housing. Mass-produced, precast, one-piece concrete units (each a complete apartment) were transported to the sight. They were then stacked like gigantic building blocks by huge cranes. The units came in different sizes and different interior arrangements. Therefore, the uniformity of usual apartments was avoided. Each floor has a play area for children. It is remarkable how much this contemporary structure resembles the earliest towns of Mesopotamia or the early pueblos of the Southwestern United States.

16–17 Each apartment is a ready-made module that can be stacked in a number of ways. Safdie has been very inventive in his efforts to design workable urban housing.
Moshe Safdie. *Habitat,* 1967. Montreal, Canada.

Renzo Piano

(b.1937)

and Richard Rogers

(b.1933)

The talk of the town—and the world—when it was built in the 1970s, the *Georges Pompidou National Center of Art and Culture* (fig.16–c) in Paris is the creation of Renzo Piano and Richard Rogers. It turns the functional style on its head by turning it inside out. A five-story escalator dominates the exterior along with the innards of the mechanical systems of the building (fig. 16–18). Glass walls enclose the open expanse of gallery and office space. The building still adheres to Modernist ideas, but with a visually sensational twist.

16–18 The exterior placement and lively coloring of the mechanical systems of this building suprise the viewer. They also make the viewer realize the amount of equipment, normally hidden, that is required to make a large building function.
Renzo Piano and Richard Rogers. *Georges Pompidou National Center of Art and Culture,* exterior section, (See fig.16–c).

Philip Johnson
(b.1906)
and John Burgee
(b.1933)

As the principles of an architectural firm, Philip Johnson and John Burgee were responsible for some of the most advanced thinking in major projects in the country. Instead of simply designing glass boxes, they used different solutions for different clients. *Pennzoil Place* (fig.16–19) in Houston (1976) is a dramatic example of this new direction. The two towers are separated by a ten-foot space and their tops are tapered at forty-five degrees. The glass wedge at the bottom provides a gigantic lobby that is well-lighted, but climatically controlled. The ten-foot slit of air space between the towers changes as one moves around the building to view it. The dark color, together with the unique shapes, produce a daring new outline on the Houston skyline. Pennzoil Place is like a gigantic minimal sculpture.

Another Johnson and Burgee masterpiece is the towering *I.D.S. Center* (fig.16–20) in Minneapolis (1972). Again, the usual box form was avoided. The glass shaft rises like a molded sculpture above the city. The vertical setbacks alter the regularity of the surface and add dramatic shadows and sharp contrasts. The glass-and-steel-covered courtyard allows light to enter the pedestrian levels and brings the outdoors inside all during the year, even in coldest winter.

16–19 What effect do you think reflective glass buildings of this size might have on the surrounding buildings and streets at the height of summer in Houston?
Philip Johnson/John Burgee. *Pennzoil Place,* 1976. Houston, Texas.

16–20 Compare this building to Lever House.
Philip Johnson/John Burgee. *I.D.S. Center,* 1972. Minneapolis, Minnesota.

16–22 This pyramid, like the one in Washington, DC, at the National Gallery of Art, lets light in and helps define the extensive underground space that has been added to the museum.
I. M. Pei. *Addition to the Louvre,* 1988. Paris.

I. M. Pei

(b.1917)

I. M. Pei has designed many hotels and government structures in America. One of his most dramatic buildings is the *East Building of the National Gallery* (fig.16–21) in Washington, DC (1978). Built to house part of the nation's great collection of art as well as a huge research library, the building occupies a wedge-shaped site on the Mall in Washington. The white marble structure shows a completely different face in each direction. One wall has no windows. Other walls have all windows. The huge pie-shaped section on the right rises like a white sliver when viewed from certain angles.

The solid, faceted planes do not prepare one for the marvelous open spaces inside. A mammoth skylight allows natural light to flood the interior. From various angles, one can look out at the wide vistas of the Mall and government buildings. The interior space is enhanced by sculptures and paintings prepared specifically by the artists for the spaces where they are located.

The sculptural forms in the foreground of the photograph are part of a fountain of twenty-four jets and a skylight system for the underground concourse. The concourse connects the East Building with the older structure of the National Gallery. The architecture is a perfect relationship between the form of the structure and its intended function.

Pei was also commissioned to design an addition to the Louvre Museum (fig.16–22) in France. Based on the pyramid shape, the building, like Frank Lloyd Wright's Guggenheim Museum, was greeted with dismay and criticism when it was first built. Gradually the French have grown to appreciate the structure. Today, the Parisians are proud of this modern landmark in their city.

Pei has remained a Modernist throughout his career. His most current work continues to reflect the basic tenets of the movement and is clear proof of the enduring importance of this style even as other architectural trends evolve.

16–21 Would you be surprised to learn that the inside of this building is flooded with natural light?
I. M. Pei. *East Building, National Gallery of Art*, 1978. Exterior view. Washington DC.

Lesson 16.1 Review

1 What technology did twentieth-century architects use to design and build skyscrapers?
2 Which Chicago building marked the beginning of modern architecture in the United States? When was this built?
3 Define *cantilevered*. Give an example of a cantilevered feature in architecture.
4 Name two buildings whose design was influenced by Mondrian?
5 What material did Le Corbusier use to construct Notre-Dame-du-Haut? How does this building vary from International Style structures?
6 Who designed the Guggenheim Museum in New York City? How is it different from the buildings surrounding it?
7 Describe the exterior of the Lever House in New York. Who designed this building?
8 How does the design of both Transworld Airlines Terminal in New York City and Dulles International Airport suggest their use or connection with flight? Who designed these buildings?
9 How is the Pompidou Center in Paris turned inside out?

16.2 Post-Modernism

In the 1960s and 1970s, a reaction to Modernism's pure line and uncluttered space set in. A new architectural surge called Post-Modernism emerged. Post-Modern architects shunned the glass-box ideal and began treating materials and ideals with daring and personal conviction. Post-Modern architects wanted a more vibrant and eclectic form, turning to symbolism and historical periods like Classicism. However, the new architectural style still retained its modern elements, particularly its wit, abstraction and irony.

The Modernists concentrated on function and technology. Their designs were mostly hard-edged and impersonal, and depended on right-angle geometry. Post-Modernism, on the other hand, has no fixed rules and goes for a mixture of history, popular expression, decoration and metaphor. The Post-Modernists consider the site of a building. They strive to design buildings that work in harmony with the site and its direct and indirect environment. They consider how the building will relate to the history that shaped the locale. They listen carefully to the client's specific needs.

Modernist dogma has flown out of the window to be replaced by the eclectic designs of architects like Venturi, Jahn, Johnson, Burgee and Graves.

Key Notes

- In the 1960s and 1970s, there is a reaction to the impersonality and purity of Modernism.
- Post-Modernism embraces history, symbolism, vivid ornamentation and eclecticism.

Special Feature

Michael Graves

(b.1934)

One of the leaders of Post-Modernism in the United States is Michael Graves. No other Post-Modernist architect has understood as much about Classical forms as Graves, or used them to create such strange and powerful new forms. Graves has often said that he designs as if he were a child, and the *Public Services Building* in Portland, Oregon, bears this out (fig.16–23). The Public Services Building (1980–83) is considered by many architects to be the first important monument to Post-Modernism.

On first look, the building resembles a child's colorful construction. It comprises simple blocks and very simplified classic forms. Graves also pays no heed to the usual scale rela-

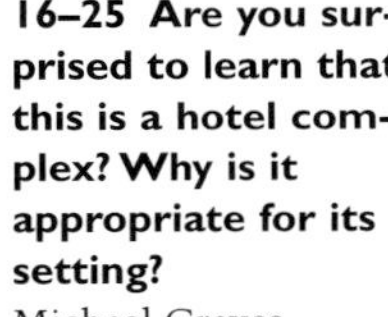

16–25 Are you surprised to learn that this is a hotel complex? Why is it appropriate for its setting?
Michael Graves. *Walt Disney World Swan Hotel,* 1989. Orlando, Florida.

16–23 Post-Modern architects often use a variety of historical styles, materials and colors on a single building. Michael Graves. *Public Services Building,* 1980–1983. Portland, Oregon.

16–24 This buiding is located in Southern California. What impact has the climate had on its design? Michael Graves, *Public Library of San Juan Capistrano,* Courtyard, detail of fig.16–b.

tionships, yet produces a marvelously sophisticated design. Graves won the commission over pure Modernists. When the purists managed to get his sculpture of civic virtue removed from over the entrance, it was restored due to popular demand.

The construction begins as a three-storied stepped base and is surmounted by twelve stories filled with a grid of small windows. In the center of the main facade are huge mirror-glass windows. The massive windows are surrounded by a gigantic maroon-colored twentieth-century version of classical elements. The design is topped by an enormous keystone. The Portland building is a civic building that embodies the dignity of the past in a completely original and present way.

The *Public Library of San Juan Capistrano,* California, is another example of Michael Graves's particular style of architecture (fig.16–b). Guidelines set by the town ordinance required new architecture to follow the indigenous Spanish mission style. As you can see, the guidelines have been perfectly carried out, but with a Post-Modern touch.

The organization of the building around a courtyard (fig.16–24) fits the Spanish style and allows light from the courtyard to filter into the rooms. At the heart of the complex, the courtyard is also a very restful place to read. The courtyard includes a stream of water that issues from the upper levels of the building. The idea here is that water, like reading, provides nourishment.

For visitors to Disney World, a familiar sight is the *Walt Disney World Swan Hotel* (fig.16–25) and its companion, *the Dolphin Hotel.* With these buildings, Graves continues to adhere to classic forms, but he embellishes them—inside and out—with an abundance of color and exuberant decoration. The humor and liveliness of these hotels delight the viewer and certainly are in keeping with the atmosphere of the nearby theme park.

16–26 Venturi believes it is important to study the everyday architecture of the United States.
Venturi, Scott Brown and Associates, Inc., *Best Products Company Catalog Showroom,* 1978. McNay Art Museum.

Robert Venturi
(b.1925)
Denise Scott Brown
(b.1931)

Proclaiming that "Less is a bore," Robert Venturi is the architect who actually led the way to the Post-Modern movement. In his book *Complexity and Contradiction in Architecture* (1966), Venturi points out that much of the great architecture of the past was not simple and classic, but elaborate and complex. Many architects agreed with Venturi, and the premiere position of Modernism began to erode.

Throughout his career, Venturi has been an avant-garde designer and thinker. In partnership with his wife, Denise Scott Brown, he fostered the notion that the commonplace, or vernacular, architecture of the United States may be as important to study as the great cathedrals of medieval Europe and monuments of ancient Greece and Rome.

16–27 Many were surprised to learn that the commission for this addition to the National Gallery of London was won by Venturi. Previously, Venturi had few major commissions, although his theory and writings were very influential.
Venturi, Scott Brown, Rauch and Associates, Inc., *Sainsbury Wing, National Gallery,* 1991, London.

Although criticized for their views, Venturi and Scott Brown have succeeded in bringing these ideas to their commissions. A store they designed for the *Best Products Company* (fig.16–26) has a plain, long, rectangular facade that faces a conventional asphalt parking lot. However, the facade is punctuated by giant, colorful flowers.

Despite their influential writings, it was not until 1986 that Venturi and Scott Brown, with their partner, John Rauch, won a major commission. It was the contract for the *Sainsbury Wing,* an addition to London's National Gallery (fig.16–27). The building is positioned on one of the world's best-known urban spaces, Trafalgar Square. The extension to England's greatest museum brought tremendous public scrutiny. It is noteworthy for its restrained, yet distinctive, appearance. The serene galleries, which house the museum's Early Renaissance collection, are filled with abundant—but indirect—natural light. The architectural elements, modern echoes of Brunelleschi, are strong and simple. They provide a most appropriate setting for the collection.

World Cultural Timeline

1958
First Chinese TV station begins broadcasting

1964
160 mph train begins running in Japan

1969
Navajo Community College, the first tribally established college, opens in Arizona

1970
First Chinese space satellite

Window in Time

Architectural Preservation

In the rush to embrace the new, buildings of historical importance and beauty have been torn down indiscriminately. Cities the world over saw and lost architecture of all styles. As look-alike skyscrapers replaced existing buildings, cities quickly lost their individual character. Today, however, the emphasis is on architectural preservation and restoration.

Architectural preservation takes several forms. In cities that once had a strong manufacturing base, old factories have been converted into shopping areas and restaurants. Projects like the Nicollet Mall in Minneapolis preserve existing architecture and often incorporate some new structures in the process.

A remarkable example of preservation is the recently restored *El Capitan Theater* in Los Angeles. El Capitan is one of the few remaining ornate movie theaters that were built in the 1930s. The theater, part of a six-floor office building, stands just across Hollywood Boulevard from the more famous Mann's Chinese Theater. El Capitan was originally designed for live performances in 1926 by G. Albert Lansburgh. In typical twenties style, it was a combination of Spanish Baroque, Moorish and East Indian elements.

***El Capitan Theater*, Los Angeles, view of marquis.**

In 1941, El Capitan was renamed the Paramount and converted into a motion-picture house. During this conversion, much of the original architecture was concealed with dropped ceilings and corrugated plaster. In the process, balcony boxes and a pair of Baroque columns were removed.

However, in 1984, Pacific Theaters, Paramount's operator, and Buena Vista Pictures, the distribution arm of Disney, recognized the theater's potential. Despite its location in a rundown neighborhood, an $8.65 million restoration was carried out by architects Fields & Devereaux. The architects consulted with organizations as diverse as the National Parks Service, the Community Redevelopment Agency and local homeowner associations.

Careful restoration and preservation has returned the El Capitan to its original form. Three curtains conceal the El Capitan's 42- by 20-foot screen and they open and close for each film. A new THX-certified sound system blares "Hooray for Hollywood" between performances. Once in this theater, all the old magic of going to the movies returns.

The Helmsley Palace Hotel complex (1980) in New York City had to work with another kind of problem. The Villard House, an 1882 townhouse and designated historical landmark, stood on the site needed for the new complex. Because the Villard House could not be moved or destroyed, the architects incorporated the house into their master plan. Entrance to the luxury 1050-room hotel-apartment tower is now through the elegant historic house. The bronze and glass tower forms a dramatic backdrop for the Villard House. Although nearly 100 years separates the two constructions, each is enhanced by the other.

***El Capitan Theater*, Los Angeles, view of lobby.**

Philip Johnson

(b.1906)

John Burgee

(b.1933)

Both Johnson and his partner, John Burgee, have maintained their influence through many decades of twentieth-century architecture right into the Post-Modern era. In New York City, their *AT&T Corporate Headquarters* (now Sony) is a thirty-seven-story pink granite building, topped with a distinctive broken pediment (fig.16–28). The latter has been referred to by critics as "Chippendale" because they believed it was reminiscent of the famous early American furniture style. The entrance to the building is through a six-story arch and colonnaded base. The ceiling of the monumental lobby is one hundred feet high.

16–29 Why was the reference to Gothic architecture such an appropriate choice for this building?
John Burgee Architects with Philip Johnson. *PPG Place,* 1984. Pittsburgh.

PPG Place (fig.16–29) in Pittsburgh is a Gothic-styled tower in glass. The design is an appropriate reflection of the company's principal product—glass—and its longevity in the industry. The task of adapting monolithic stone construction to glass was carried off with style and success. All of Johnson and Burgee's buildings reflect something about their clients. At the same time, the buildings are an individualized approach to architectural excellence.

16–28 The distinctive profile of the top of this building makes it recognizable from many miles away.
John Burgee Architects with Philip Johnson. *AT&T Corporate Headquarters,* 1985. New York.

Helmut Jahn

(b.1940)

Helmut Jahn is responsible for constructing the most dynamic terminal to be found at Chicago's O'Hare International Airport. Large glassed spaces bring light and provide a sense of constant movement to the *United Airlines Terminal* (fig.16–30). The long route from gateway to baggage claim is made less boring by walkways with cheerful blinking neon lights and pleasant chiming sounds. The lights and sounds are activated by the movement of passersby.

Jahn also has designed several skyscrapers in major American cities. In New York, *750 Lexington Avenue* (fig.16–31) is distinctive for its combination of forms stacked one upon the other. There is no doubt that eclecticism is one of the few constants in Post-Modern architecture.

16–31 Do you find the variation in form in this building appealing? Or do you prefer the regularity of the Seagram Building and the Lever House?
Helmut Jahn, *750 Lexington Avenue,* 1989. New York.

16–30 Neon light sculpture and sound, which are activated by passersby, make the journey from airplane to baggage claim rather enjoyable.
Helmut Jahn. *United Airlines Terminal,* 1987. O'Hare International Airport, Chicago.

Frank O. Gehry

(b.1929)

Frank O. Gehry and Associates of Venice, California, design buildings to capture the essence of their purpose, yet they also convey a certain wittiness. Gehry's *California Aerospace Museum* (fig.16–32) certainly reflects the building's function. Angles and planes barely seem to contain the dynamic action that the word *aerospace* implies (fig. 16–d). Its interior spaces are contained and intimate, but the overall structure is bursting with energy.

A more recent commission of Gehry's, the *Frederick R. Weisman Museum* (fig.16–33), places all of its expressive emphasis on its stainless steel facade. The remainder of the building is strictly rectangular in shape and offers an ideal space in which to exhibit works of art.

16–32 How does the form of this building express its purpose?
Frank O. Gehry & Associates. *California Aerospace Museum*, 1984. Los Angeles.

16–33 Gehry has designed the main body of this building to be an ordinary rectangle. Why do you think this form would be preferred by the museum's curators?
Frank O. Gehry & Associates. *Frederick R. Weisman Museum*, 1993. University of Minnesota, Minneapolis.

World Cultural Timeline

1975
First Indian space satellite

1976
Aboriginal Land Rights Act gives greater rights to native Australians

1979
Japanese Maglev test train sets speed record at 321.2 mph

1979
Egyptian-Israeli peace accord signed

1984
Bishop Desmond Tutu of South Africa receives Nobel Peace Prize

1997
Hong Kong reverts from a British to a Chinese territory

Arata Isozaki

(b.1931)

Headquartered in Tokyo, the firm of Arata Isozaki and Associates has designed buildings in Asia, Europe and North America. The *Museum of Contemporary Art* in Los Angeles (fig.16–34) was Isozaki's first major job outside of Japan. Situated on a narrow site in downtown Los Angeles, the commission was difficult. The requirements of the client and neighboring commercial buildings almost proved the project's undoing. However, Isozaki solved his site problem by clustering the galleries around a sunken courtyard. Solid geometric forms are relieved by French curves. These contrasting elements entice the eye to roam continuously across the structure and absorb its detail.

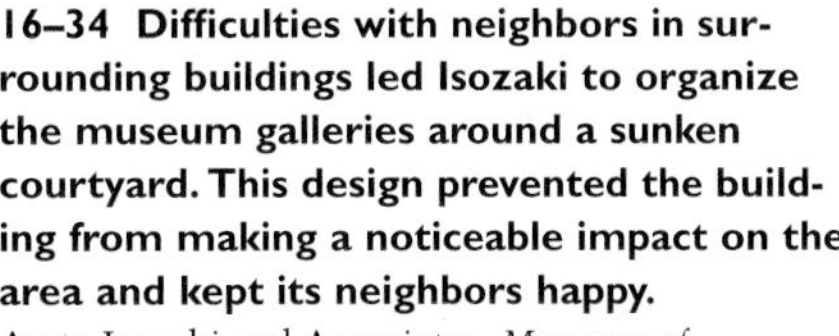

16–34 Difficulties with neighbors in surrounding buildings led Isozaki to organize the museum galleries around a sunken courtyard. This design prevented the building from making a noticeable impact on the area and kept its neighbors happy.
Arata Isozaki and Associates. *Museum of Contemporary Art,* 1986. Los Angeles.

Sidelight

C.A.D.

Computer-Aided Design

Everything that people make, whether it be a building, an automobile or a picture, has to be designed. Today, many designs are completed with the help of computer programs called CAD, or computer-aided design. Computers speed up the design process by enabling designers to try out many more ideas than before, all on the screen. CAD can also quickly find answers to problems that once took a long time to solve.

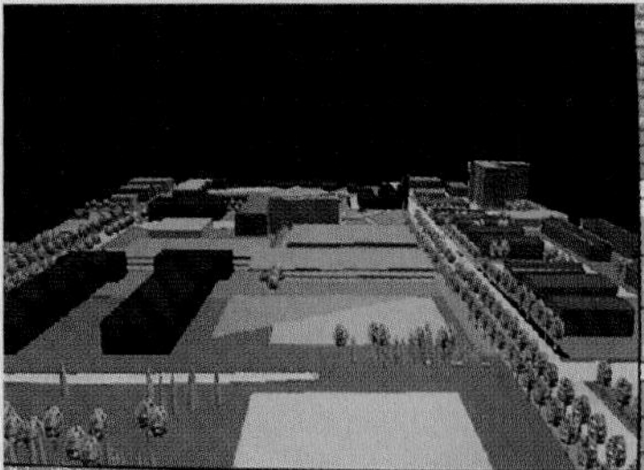

Screen from a CAD perspective

CAD programs on desktop computers have replaced the drawing board completely in many industries. One software program can produce full-color or black-and-white graphics in seconds. Another allows three-dimensional models to be constructed on the computer screen and rotated in any direction so that all sides can be seen. A program can also plot the way in which heat or electricity will flow through a structure. The computer can calculate the amount of material needed for construction and how much it will cost to make.

An architect can draw a single plan and elevation of a building and the computer will carry out calculations to produce different elevations from the same set of measurements. For something like a house or bridge, it can calculate stresses and work out whether the design is strong enough. A designer can also zoom in on a section of a design, such as the floor plan of a house, to work more closely on part of it. CAD has cut down immeasurably on the time that used to be needed to produce any design, as well as on the error factor.

Cesar Pelli

(b.1926)

Cesar Pelli was born in Argentina and immigrated to the United States in 1952. He has had a long and active career. Somewhat critical of the overuse of eclecticism in Post-Modern construction, Pelli believes in the importance of placing a building sensitively into its environment.

One of his more prominent commissions is the *World Financial Center* (fig.16–35) in Battery Park City. Located at the tip of Manhattan Island, the towers instantly became an integral part of the city's skyline. Relying on the simple elements of glass and granite, Pelli has created a classically harmonious series of towers. The stepped set-backs and variously shaped copper tops that crown each building give the work its Post-Modern flavor.

Throughout his career, Pelli has focused on city buildings. Pelli's long-standing interest in the urban environment made him a logical candidate for the design of a quintessential urban construction: one of the tallest buildings in the world.

Cesar Pelli has executed designs for an eighty-eight-story building in Malaysia (fig.16–36). But, at the same time, there are plans being made in China to begin construction of a 125-story building. It seems that the quest to build extraordinarily tall buildings is never-ending.

The technology that propels us from the twentieth century into the twenty-first century makes possible all types and forms of buildings. Perhaps this helps account for the diversity of our architecture. For how long will this variety continue? When will events, ideas or inventions help change the course of architecture once again?

16–36 A rendering of a building design is generally made to give the client a better sense of how a completed building will look.
Cesar Pelli. *Model for Kuala Lumpur City Center,* to be completed in 1996.

16–35 What makes this a Post-Modern rather than a Modern building?
Cesar Pelli. *World Financial Center,* 1988. New York.

Lesson 16.2 Review

1 How is Post-Modern architecture different from the International Style?

2 What building is recognized by most architects as the first Post-Modern building?

3 Describe one building built by Michael Graves. How is it different from anything built by Mies van der Rohe?

4 Who designed the Sainsbury Wing of London's National Gallery?

5 How did Helmut Jahn build a sense of dynamism into the terminal he designed in Chicago's O'Hare Airport?

Primary Source

Frank Lloyd Wright and the Critics

Now regarded as a great landmark of twentieth-century architecture, Frank Lloyd Wright's Solomon R. Guggenheim Museum in New York City was initially met with tremendous criticism.

Here we have an excerpt from an article written in 1960 by critic James Marston Fitch, just after the museum opened:

"Seen from the outside, the great exploding spiral is a powerful landmark; within, it appears as a magnificent vessel for containing the crowds, displaying them to far greater advantage than does the dress circle at La Scala or the grand staircase at the Paris Opera. But, it does not display painting or sculpture to equal advantage. On the contrary, with perverse if not malicious skill, Wright's museum dwarfs the art it might have been expected to magnify. He has set the individual pieces afloat in a vortex, a whirlpool, an interior volume of absolutely overpowering movement. He has taken unfair advantage of the artists: of poor dead Kandinsky, with his intersecting circles and delicate pastels; of elegant, modest Brancusi; of gay Miró. He has reduced them all to the level of lonely little shepherd boys, piping away in competition with Lohengrin. Michelangelo himself would be unsafe in Wright's museum."

Frank Lloyd Wright, Solomon R. Guggenheim Museum, detail.

Chapter Review

Review

1 Explain what Mies van der Rohe meant by "Less is more." Can you think of an example of an object that is not a building to illustrate this principle?

2 What was Frank Lloyd Wright trying to achieve in his architecture?

3 Why do you think Wright's Kaufmann House at Bear Run, Pennsylvania, is often called Falling Water?

4 How are the load-bearing characteristics of steel-frame construction different from traditional stone-building methods?

5 How does Wright's Robie House echo the prairie landscape surrounding Chicago?

6 Post-Modern architects make a point of building structures that are in harmony with their surroundings. Which Post-Modern building discussed in this chapter do you think best accomplishes this goal?

Interpret

1 How are Mies van der Rohe's Lakeshore Drive Apartments in Chicago like Mondrian's "Lozenge in Red, Yellow, and Blue"?

2 Which architect said "Less is a bore" and which said "Less is more"? Name a building to illustrate each slogan. Explain which building you like better.

3 Which architect was one of the first to stress form follows function? What does this slogan mean? Select an ordinary household object and explain how its form is related to its function.

Other Tools for Learning

Timelines

1 Select an event from the timelines near the date when you were born. Why do you think this event was included on this timeline?

2 Which event on these timelines do you think will have the most impact on people in the twenty-first century?

3 Find several events in this chapter's timelines that made the world a smaller place. How do you think this bringing people closer together affected the architecture of this time period?

Electronic Research

Look at I. M. Pei's East Building of the National Gallery on that gallery's videodisc. Describe the feeling of the interior space in the lobby.

Activity 1

Harmony Inside and Out

Materials
newsprint for preliminary sketches
#3 or 4H pencils
erasers
12" x 18" drawing paper suitable for watercolor and washes
water containers
assortment of round brushes (#2, #7, #10)
pen and ink (optional)

Take a look.
• Fig.16–5, Frank Lloyd Wright. *Kaufmann House,* 1936.

Think about it. Frank Lloyd Wright believed in developing a compatible relationship between a structure and its location, so the building seemed to grow out of its environment. Just as the exterior of buildings are often in harmony with nature, so too the interior and its furnishings can complement and be in harmony with the building's exterior.
• Consult copies of architectural magazines that provide interior views of buildings.
• How would you describe the furniture?
• Is the interior and its components a perfect marriage with the exterior? Why or why not?

Do it. After studying Frank Lloyd Wright's Falling Water, design furniture for a particular room in the house. Use watercolors to add color. If you are planning an intricate pattern you may want to use colored pencils.

Check it. Compare your final drawings with the actual furniture Frank Lloyd Wright made for Falling Water. Your design solutions will be different, but do they foster the architect's philosophy?

Helpful Hint: Research different furniture styles throughout history. Where is this furniture housed?

Activity 2

Model Community

Materials
scissors
ruler
pencil
lightweight cardboard
glue
tape

Take a look. Review the buildings shown in this chapter—notice the environment surrounding each one. What is the function of each building? How do the activities in each building contribute to and rely upon the city that surrounds it?

Think about it. Work with other students to design a model community, building or architectural complex. Take time to consider the following questions (write down your answers):
• Where would it be located (city, state)?
• What is its function or purpose?
• What year does your structure represent (present, past or future)?
• What are the components of your structure? Is there more than one building, parks, patios, archways or sidewalks?
• How large will your structure be (both real-life size and model scale)?
• What will you name it?

Do it.
• Decide on a scale for your project. Architects commonly use 1/8" = 1 foot, but you need to consider what is most practical for your project. The scale for a town square composed of one- or two-story buildings would not be appropriate for a skyscraper.
• Measure out a ground plan on a cardboard base. Consider vehicular and pedestrian traffic, use of land and landscaping.
• Decide who is responsible for the construction of each component. Plan how to work together to keep your structures harmonious with one another.
• Cut the basic structures from cardboard, measuring to scale each time. Start with basic, solid shapes, then cut away parts you don't want and/or add strips of cardboard to build up shapes in layers.

Check it. What kind of information do you need to produce accurate models? What information needs to be shared among people working together on the same project?

Helpful Hint: If possible, visit a university architectural department or an architect's studio to see how architectural models look before you begin your own design; or refer to a book on architectural design or model building.

Additional Activities

• Examine forms that are found in nature. Simplify and abstract these forms. Create several stencils based on your abstract forms. Using acrylic paint, stencil a wall, fabric, paper, or even a piece of furniture.
• Take your sketchbook or camera on an architectural tour of your community. Sketch or photograph architectural details (window treatments, doorways, cornices, pediments, columns, rooflines, domes). Prepare a display of your findings and label each item with a few sentences telling: 1) name and/or location of the example; 2) the architectural influence that is evident (Greek, Classicism, French Renaissance, for example).

Student Profile

David Michael Goodman

Clarkstown High School North
New City, New York
Activity 2, Model Community

I felt overwhelmed as I gazed at the slope of the land situated beside Bebe Lake. I strolled along the bank of the lake, trying to find the best spot to build my house. I concluded that I had two options. The first was to build on the flat, level side. I pictured an ordinary-type house overlooking the panoramic views of the lake. My second option was to attempt to construct the house on the side of a steep incline of about 24 feet. I chose to design the house on the incline because it was a more challenging task and would call for a totally innovative design.

I positioned the entrance to the home in the rear of the house because I wanted the house to be focused on the lake. In the design of the interior, I chose to use walls of transparent glass to provide views of the lake from any room of the house. In the front, I chose to use glass blocks and translucent glass. The field of architecture has always fascinated me. Ever since I was a young boy, I enjoyed building and drafting. Back then, I used blocks, Lego and Lincoln Logs. As I matured, my constructions developed into more complex and realistic structures. I plan to attend Cornell University next fall to study architecture. There I will form a foundation for a career as an architect. I can't wait to get started!

David M. Goodman

Lakeside Studio House, 1994. Corrugated cardboard, wire, chipboard, 25" x 45" (63.5 x 114 cm).

Jacob Meanley

Bakersfield High School
Bakersfield, California
Activity 1, Harmony Inside and Out

I was to draw furniture that fit the character of Frank Lloyd Wright's house over the waterfall. It was interesting to go through the process of modeling furniture after nature. I tried to keep in mind the way water flows downwards in a waterfall. I tried to incorporate the roundness and downward lines of a waterfall into the furniture.

Most people complain that they're terrible in art and can only draw stick figures. But I believe that everyone is good in at least one aspect of art. Whether it be coloring or just critiquing, it's still all part of art and its process.

Jacob Meanley

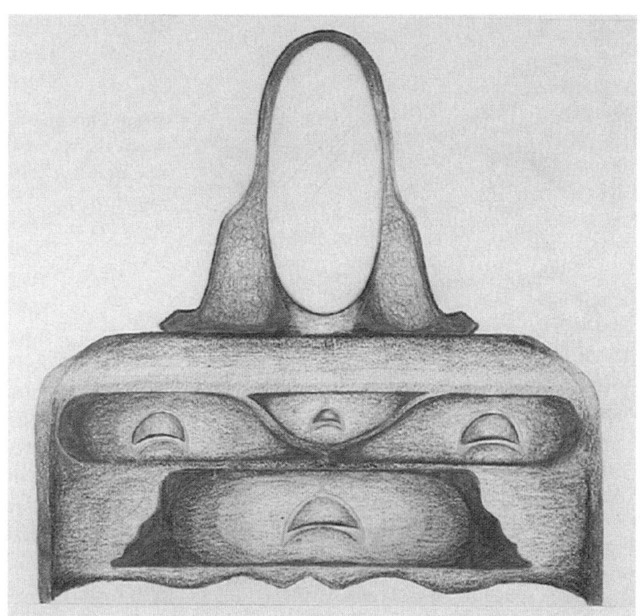

Waterfall Furniture, 1994. Colored pencil, 12" x 18" (30.5 x 45.7 cm).

17 Art from the Fifties to the Present

In This Chapter...

At the end of World War II, a dramatic shift in the art world occurred. Abstract Expressionism took New York and the Western world by storm. It was a breath of fresh air with an impact so tremendous that all eyes turned to New York, the new leader of the art world.

In the rapid pace of the post-war world, some artists tired of the emotionalism of Abstract Expressionism. These artists startled the art world with Pop Art and Op Art. Pop Art took its images from the popular culture. Op Art used scientific approaches to create motion on the canvas.

Styles began to change with greater and greater speed. In the late 1960s and into the 1970s, Color Field artists created serene paintings that relied solely on large areas of flat color. Realism reemerged in the 1970s. Like Pop artists, New Realists portrayed contemporary American life. The second half of the 1900s was also a very dynamic time for sculptors. They became much bolder and more inventive in their use of materials and space.

Diversity is the key to late-1900s art. An extraordinary array of materials, forms, interactions, juxtapositions, statements and environments has captured the imagination of many contemporary artists. As we move into the twenty-first century, we should continue to ask questions about what art is and about how we can better understand it.

17–a This Pop artist took his inspiration from the Sunday comics and oversimulated the ben-day printing dots used to print the comics.
Roy Lichtenstein, *Masterpiece*, detail (fig.17–14).

Art from the Fifties to the Present

1950
Pollock, *Lavender Mist*

1951
Double-helix DNA proposed

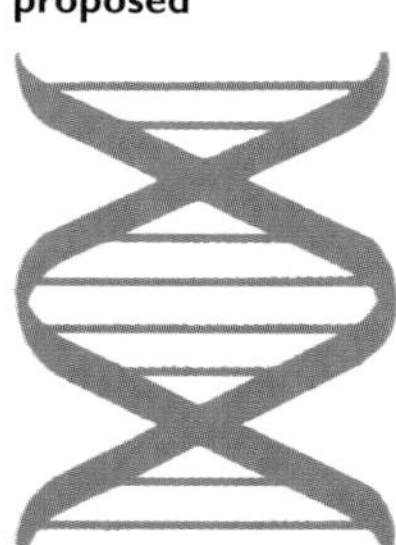

1962
Warhol, *100 Cans*

1965
Vasarely originates Op Art

1968
Martin Luther King assassinated

1969
First manned landing on the moon

1972–1976
Christo, *Running Fence*

1973
Vietnam War ends

1980
CNN offers round-the-clock news coverage

1980
Grooms, *Ruckus Rodeo*

1982
Alice Walker, *The Color Purple*

1984
Geraldine Ferraro is first woman vice-presidential candidate in the US

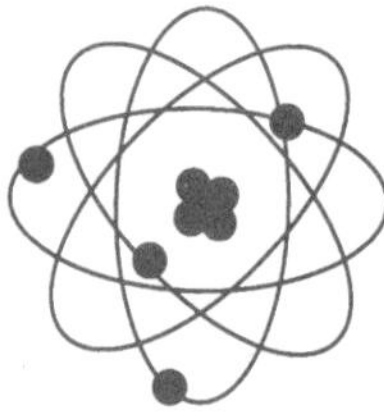

1986
Nuclear accident at Chernobyl

1989
Demolition of the Berlin Wall

1990
Violeta Barrios de Chamorro elected president of Nicaragua

Each age finds its own technique.
— Jackson Pollock

17–b Contemporary art is often very difficult to capture with still photography. How would the experience of viewing this work of art in person differ from seeing this color image of the piece?
Jennifer Bartlett, *Spiral: An Ordinary Evening in New Haven*, 1989. Oil on canvas, tables, painted wood and steel, 108" x 192" (274 x 487 cm). Paula Cooper, Inc., New York.

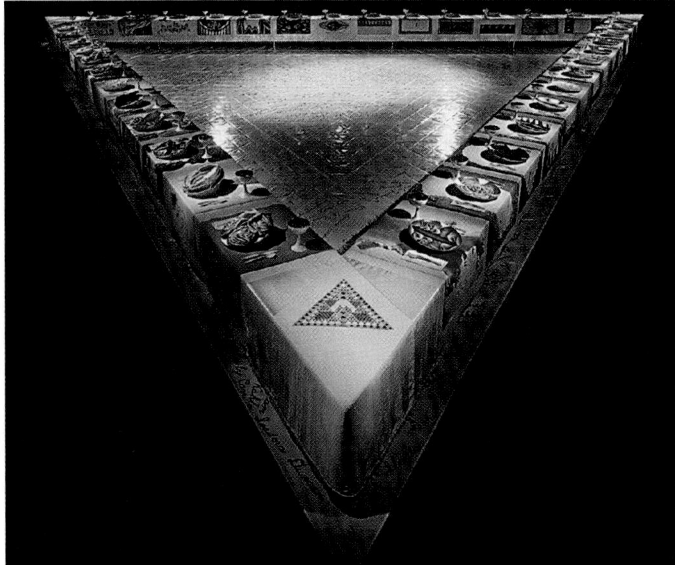

17–c Research for this project uncovered so many women of distinction that Chicago tripled the number of guests. Originally, Chicago conceived the work as a dinner attended by thirteen famous women.
Judy Chicago, *The Dinner Party*, 1979. Ceramic with handwoven cloth, each side 82' long (25 m). Through the Flower, Albuquerque, New Mexico.

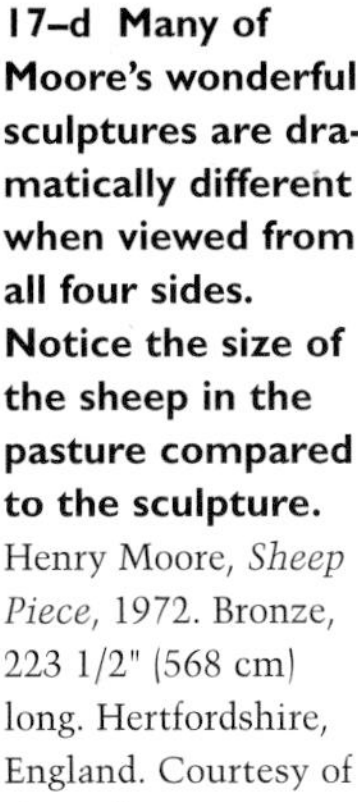

17–d Many of Moore's wonderful sculptures are dramatically different when viewed from all four sides. Notice the size of the sheep in the pasture compared to the sculpture.
Henry Moore, *Sheep Piece*, 1972. Bronze, 223 1/2" (568 cm) long. Hertfordshire, England. Courtesy of the artist.

17.1 Abstract Expressionism

WITH POWERFUL AND DYNAMIC FURY, a movement called *Abstract Expressionism* exploded in New York following World War II. Abstract Expressionism got its title because it was abstract (emphasizing shape, color and/or line with no recognizable subject matter) and expressive (stressing emotions and individual feelings more than design and form). Partly as a reaction to the times they lived in, artists turned against reason. The New York artists wanted to hold on to their humanity in the face of the insanity they perceived around them. To do this, they looked inward instead of out. Their work had a spontaneous and very fresh feel to it. It was meant to be grasped intuitively by the viewer rather than reasoned out.

The style found its roots in Kandinsky and the more recent works of Gorky. Artists from Europe, fleeing Hitler's Germany and other totalitarian regimes, settled in New York and began teaching. They and their students were the instigators of Abstract Expressionism, or *Action Painting* as it was often called. However, artists went off in individual directions and developed personal styles and techniques. Based on the freedom of individual expression, the movement soon spread from New York to the rest of the Western world. The movement lasted about fifteen years, but during that time it revolutionized the art world. America had become the art leader of the world and remains so today.

Key Notes

- Abstract Expressionism explodes in New York following World War II.
- Based on individual expression, Abstract Expressionism stresses emotions and feelings more than design and form.
- Abstract Expressionism revolutionizes painting, and America takes over as leader of the art world.

Vocabulary
drip painting

17–2 Why is the term "Action Painting" appropriate for this work?
Willem de Kooning, *Woman I*, 1950–1952. Approx. 6' 4" x 4' 10" (193 x 147 cm). Collection, The Museum of Modern Art, New York, Purchase.

Special Feature

Willem de Kooning

(b. 1904)

Willem de Kooning came to the United States from Amsterdam in 1926. Hoping to become a magazine illustrator, he found himself churning out commercial art for whoever would hire him. In the depression, he actually worked for a while as a housepainter. This experience led him to use large house-painting brushes and enamel paint in the creation of his large sprawling canvases.

After painting realistically for many years, he leapt into Abstract Expressionism with great enthusiasm and became one of its leading exponents. His slashing brush covered large canvases with color and tremendous action that became his nonobjective subject matter. His huge paintings were often frantic and violent. These features are evident in the slashing quality of the brushwork. Nothing flows easily with de Kooning. It is all crabbed and leaping, drawing in and opening out, and deliberately crude. But, at the same time, he makes abstraction appear very natural, as though there is nothing complicated about it. It's as real in his hands as going to a baseball game or taking a train ride. Because the emphasis is on the act of painting as part of the subject matter, such work was called Action Painting.

The apparent spontaneity of de Kooning's work was often the result of many days of work. In *Easter Monday* (fig.17–1), de Kooning used newspaper transfers and oils as the media of the nonobjective work.

17–1 De Kooning received a traditional education in art, and classic principles of composition provide the structure for his free brushwork and spontaneous colors. Willem de Kooning, *Easter Monday*, 1956. Oil and newspaper transfer, 96" x 74" (244 x 188 cm). The Metropolitan Museum of Art, New York, Rogers Fund.

The painting is perhaps coincidentally strewn with E's. De Kooning often used letters of the alphabet as part of his huge swinging-motion paintings.

De Kooning was one of the prophets of the new style, but at the same time he was still very interested in the figure. His famous series of *Woman* paintings was inspired in part by advertising billboards.

Woman I (fig.17–2) is an excitement-packed painting slashed out at top speed. Amid the interplay of colors and brushstrokes, the overall shape of the body is recognizable. There is an emphasis on the face with its wide, rather leering grin. Like other Action Paintings, the image constantly comes into and out of focus. This is a violent and tremendously expressive painting.

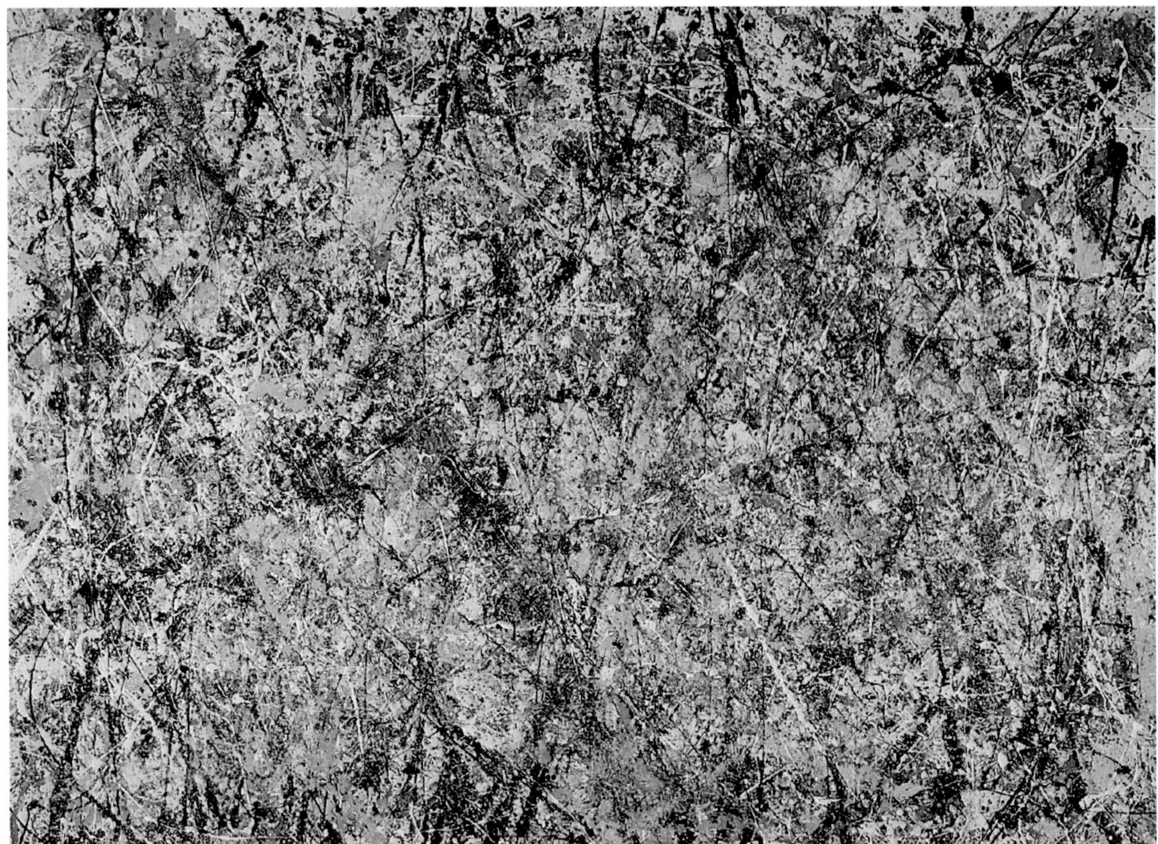

17–3 Pollock was influenced by Rubens and Orozco. What evidence of that influence do you find?
Jackson Pollock, *No. 1, 1950 (Lavender Mist).* Oil enamel and aluminum on canvas, 87" x 118" (221 x 299 cm). National Gallery of Art, Washington, Ailsa Mellon Bruce Fund.

Jackson Pollock

(1912–1956)

In 1946, after going through realistic and abstract periods, Jackson Pollock began his series of ***drip paintings***. His new working technique completely freed him from the use of traditional brushes and opened the door to Abstract Expressionism. Laying his canvas on the floor of the studio so he could walk on it, he literally put himself into his work. With a can of paint in his hand, he moved about the canvas, freely dripping, spilling and throwing the color with apparent abandon. Pollock's paintings were not haphazard. He was the force behind the paint's movement. While he could not control the paint, he completely engaged himself in releasing both his own creativity and the possibilities within the paint. The final work can thus be viewed as an interchange between the "will" of the paint and the inner forces of the artist.

Pollock's *No. 1, 1950 (Lavender Mist)* is a complex interweaving of color and line that produces an overall web of fascinating texture (fig.17–3). Pollock intended this work to be flat in appearance, as if all the color were right on the picture plane. However, overlapping lines of various values and colors add a sense of shallow depth. Some lines seem to be floating above others. The thicker, darker lines create a feeling of rhythm. Perhaps without being aware of it, Pollock was determining the flow of paint. The unanticipated depth and rhythm suggest the ways in which Pollock's subconscious interacted with the flow of paint.

World Cultural Timeline

1912
African National Congress established to promote welfare of Blacks, South Africa

1916
Hipólito Irigoyen elected president of Argentina and starts compulsory pensions, the regulation of working hours and improved factory conditions

1917
Ras Tafari (Haile Selassie) becomes ruler of Ethiopia, greatly modernizing the country

1934
Henry Puyi becomes last emperor of China

Robert Motherwell

(1915–1991)

Robert Motherwell did not use the slurred brushstrokes of de Kooning. Instead, he kept a firm clarity to the outline of his freely formed shapes. Usually his paintings have flatly painted, delicate hues. The white backgrounds and powerful, bold black shapes intensify these delicate hues. *Elegy to the Spanish Republic* (fig.17–4) is part of a series of paintings Motherwell began in 1949. The paintings reflect the horror and destruction of the Spanish Civil War. The brooding black shapes suggest a mood of anguish and a sense of doom. Usually, his gigantic canvases were laid flat on the floor. Like Pollock, Motherwell walked on them during the designing and painting process.

17–4 The spontaneity of the brushwork gives no hint that the artist actually made many small studies prior to painting the large canvases in this series.
Robert Motherwell, *Elegy to the Spanish Republic*, 1953–1954. 80" x 100" (203 x 254 cm). Albright-Knox Art Gallery, Buffalo, New York. Gift of Seymour H. Knox, 1957. ©1996 Deadalus Foundation/Licensed by VAGA, New York, NY

17–5 Can you detect images here that have been abstracted in both color and form?
Hans Hofmann, *Flowering Swamp*, 1957. Oil on wood, 48" x 36" (122 x 91 cm). Hirshhorn Museum and Sculpture Garden, Smithsonian Institution, Washington DC.

Hans Hofmann

(1880–1966)

Hans Hofmann came to New York from Germany and Paris to become one of America's most influential art teachers. He is best known for his canvases of heavily applied, brilliant color that seem to have some magical intensity. In *Flowering Swamp*, Hofmann painted several colored rectangles that seem to float over the background of softly brushed, but heavily built-up colors. *Flowering Swamp* (fig.17–5) is suggestive of water and flowers. However, the two rectangles immediately dismiss any idea of reality. They belong to Hofmann's brand of abstraction. Most of his work does not have representational aspects. While de Kooning's canvases are often violent, Hofmann's often have a sense of serenity and visual balance.

Franz Kline

(1910–1962)

In his early work, Franz Kline painted the buildings and people of New York in a representational style. Then, in 1949, he began to refine his style to a vigorous, slashing form of abstraction. At first, his forms were derived from urban structures. But soon he expressed himself freely without relying on representative subject matter.

In works like *Meryon* (fig.17–6), he found he needed larger-sized canvases and less color to project his images of the energy of the city and contemporary life. He began using gigantic slashes of black and white. He liked to tack unstretched canvas to a wall or to the floor and use large house-painting brushes to apply house-paint in powerful and energetic vertical and horizontal strokes.

Lee Krasner

(1908–1984)

Lee Krasner was a powerful influence in the development of Abstract Expressionism, although she maintained her independence on the fringes of the movement. She progressed through realism and small abstractions. Eventually, she turned to much larger-sized canvases to fully contain her expressions. With each occasional change in style, she seemed to produce stronger statements. In 1954, she was working on her brilliant collages, such as *Shattered Light.*

In creating these collages, she was actually tearing up old paintings to create dynamic new images. The resulting surfaces are rich in texture, color, movement and overall unity. They are noisy and joyous, and unique personal expressions. She was married to Jackson Pollock until his tragic death in an auto accident in 1956.

Mark Rothko

(1903–1970)

Born in Russia, Mark Rothko was an early Abstractionist. He first worked somewhat in the style of Arshile Gorky. He soon developed a style based on soft edges and blending colors. His expression was not the harsh and slashing furor of Kline or de Kooning, but a subtle and serene expression of a hushed and brooding mood. As his work became more simplified, the sizes of his canvases became larger. The color became less contrasting and less intense. He limited his large rectan-

17–6 By limiting his palette to black and white in the series to which this work belongs, this artist wanted to convey the energy of contemporary city life.
Franz Kline, *Meryon*, 1960. Oil on canvas, 93" x 77" (236 x 195 cm). The Tate Gallery, London.

17–7 The artist's collages consist of torn-up canvases. Old images are used to create new images.
Lee Krasner. *Shattered Light*, 1954. Collage, 34" x 48" (86 x 122 cm). Courtesy of the artist.

gular shapes to only two or three, as in *Blue, Orange, Red* (fig.17–8). The hazy edges give the feeling of shapes floating and vibrating in and out of the background color. When standing in front of a huge Rothko canvas, one almost has the feeling of floating along with the shapes. This sensation would be explored by the Color Field painters of the 1960s. His final works were done mostly in grays and blacks. Color, so important earlier, was completely abandoned.

17–8 Compare this painting to Gorky's *The Liver Is the Cock's Comb.*
Mark Rothko, *Blue, Orange, Red,* 1961. Oil on canvas, 90" x 81" (229 x 206 cm). Hirshhorn Museum and Sculpture Garden, Smithsonian Institution, Washington DC, gift of Joseph H. Hirshhorn Foundation, 1966.

Richard Diebenkorn

(b. 1922–1994)

Richard Diebenkorn was part of the second generation of Abstract Expressionists. Many of these painters turned from complete reliance on abstraction to representational subjects and figurative painting, but with expressive overtones. Diebenkorn combined reality with the expressive power and technique of the Abstract Expressionists. He developed a personal expression that relied on design, but was still emotional in feeling. *Cityscape I* (fig.17–9) shows the influence of Abstract Expressionism in the brushstrokes and reliance on flat shapes. However, the design is structured and not accidental or undisciplined. The muted colors are arranged in flat planes with soft edges. Often figures were included in his work. They also were treated as soft-edged planes rather than rounded forms.

17–9 Identify the artist's (and viewer's) vantage point here.
Richard Diebenkorn, *Cityscape I,* 1963. Oil on canvas, 60 1/4" x 50 3/4" (153 x 129 cm). San Francisco Museum of Modern Art.

Lesson 17.1 Review

1 Explain what the term abstract expressionism means.
2 Why did so many European artists move to New York City during the late 1930s and early 1940s? What style did these artists begin in the United States?
3 List six abstract expressionists. After each artist's name, write three words or short phrases to describe his or her art.
4 Why was de Kooning known as an Action Painter?
5 Describe Jackson Pollock's drip painting method.

17.2 Pop Art and Op Art

ABSTRACT EXPRESSIONISM held firm sway for fifteen years. But, in the early sixties, a group of artists burst on the scene. Their subjects were Coke bottles, beer and soup cans, comic strip characters and hamburgers. Because these things were so common, or popular, their movement was labeled *Pop Art*. Pop Art was not really a style because the artists were working in so many different ways. Rather, it was an attitude toward art and toward genre subjects that were reminders of supermarkets, movies, television and the comics. Pop Art answered the undisciplined emotions of Abstract Expressionism with hard edges, almost no brushstrokes in many styles, and extremely careful preparation and drawing. Pop Art expressed an impersonal attitude toward the work and subject and had a lot to do with the artists' frustration with the art establishment. It incorporated a delightful sense of wit, satire and humor.

Many artists have been fascinated by visual illusions, and some have played tricks on the viewer's eyes. But, twentieth-century *Op Art* (*Optical Art*) makes use of scientific principles to create the sensation of movement on the picture plane. There are no focal points or traditional centers of interest in an Op Art work. The overall organization creates the proper effect. Sometimes, color makes the eye detect movement, and at other times, lines or shapes do. Op Art is carefully calculated and meticulously presented.

Key Notes

- Pop Art and Op Art are both reactions to the subjective emotionalism of Abstract Expressionism.
- Pop Art uses everyday objects and references as its subject matter.
- Op Art uses scientific principles to create illusions of movement.

Vocabulary
soft sculpture
combine painting

Special Feature

Claes Oldenburg

(b.1929)

The son of a Swedish diplomat, Oldenburg grew up in Chicago. In the 1950s, he moved to Manhattan and began using found materials to make sculptures and drawings of the objects he saw around him (fig.17–10). To help the viewer see the manufactured environment with new eyes, Oldenburg worked with various sculpture media. He enlarged ordinary household objects, such as a three-way electrical plug, to enormous size. He also developed the technique of ***soft sculpture***, which added a surrealistic effect to his work.

Shoestring Potatoes Spilling from a Bag (fig.17–11) is made from painted canvas stuffed with soft kapok. The entire "sculpture" is soft to the touch. It sags humorously as it hangs limply from the ceiling. It would be startling in its soft form if it were actual size, but

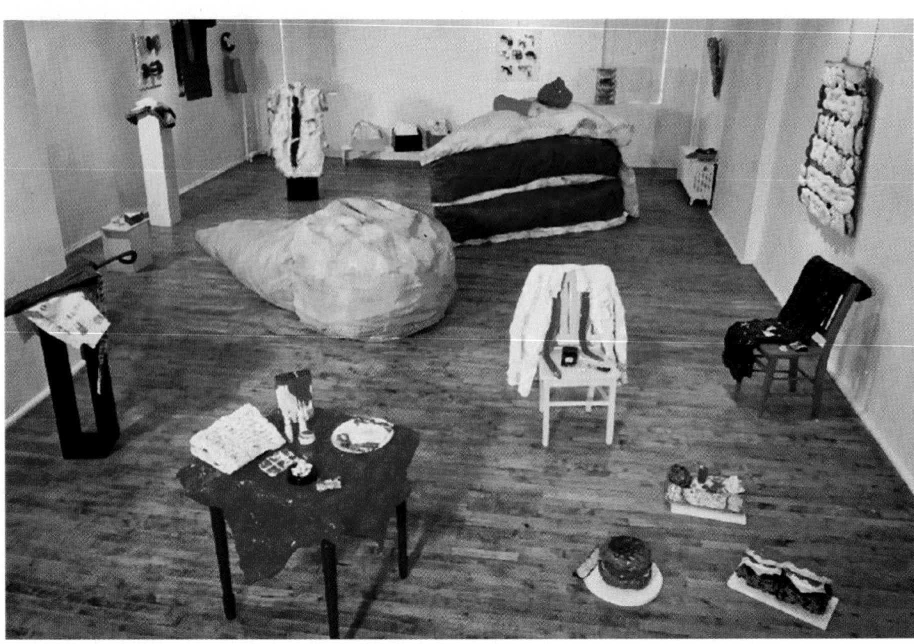

17–10 How many everyday objects can you identify in this installation of Oldenburg's work?
Claes Oldenburg, *Installation of One-Man Show,* exhibit at Green Gallery, New York, September 24–October 20, 1962.

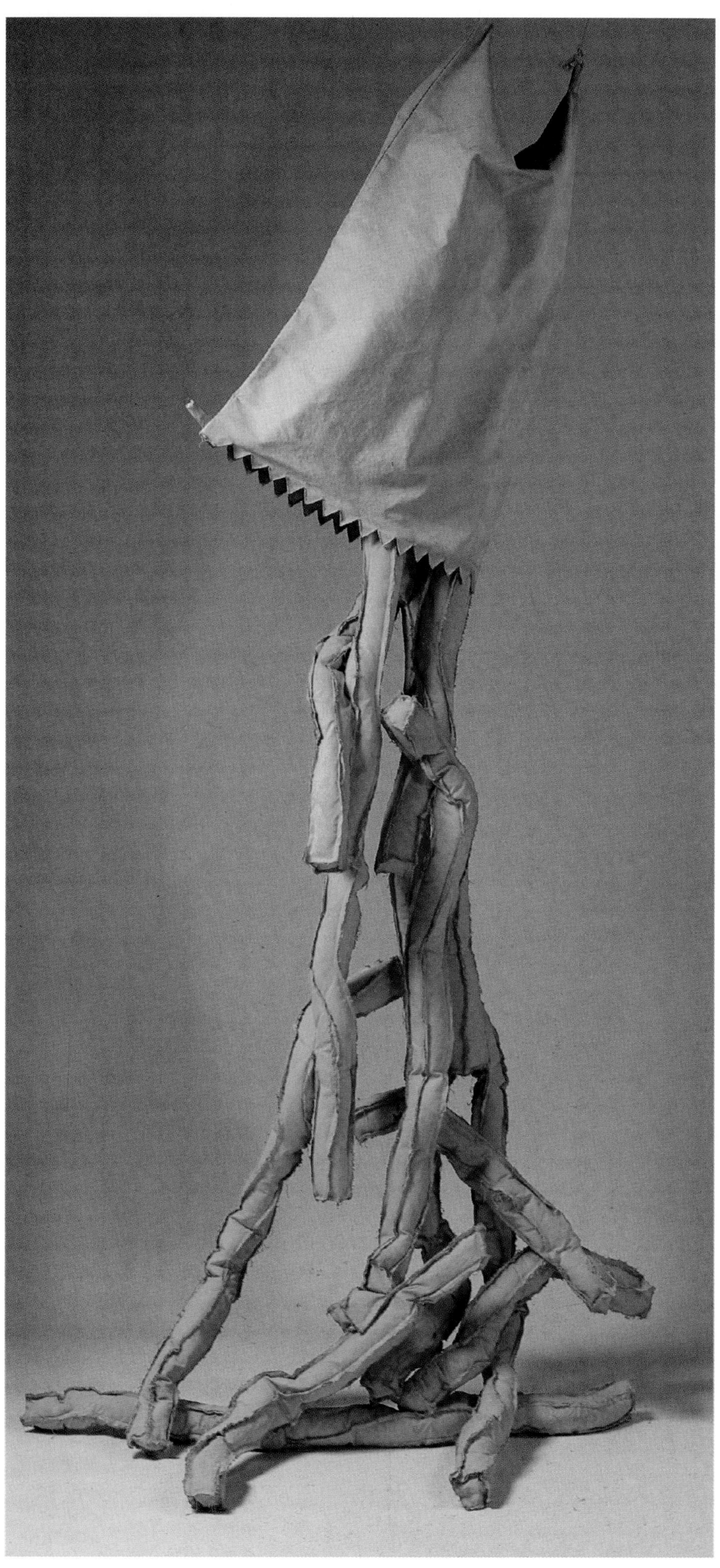

Oldenburg has enlarged it to nearly 10 feet high.

Oldenburg enjoys designing ordinary forms, like combs, trowels and typewriter erasers, and producing them as monumental-sized sculptures located in outdoor and indoor settings. There is also a great sense of humor in these sculptures. Yet, the viewer is forced to ask some questions. Do people make too much of commercialism and industrialism? Are these manufactured objects the real heroes of the twentieth century?

In 1965, Oldenburg started his "monument" proposals. A single object was to be enlarged to a gigantic scale and installed at a specific site. These objects include a huge baseball mitt, the head of a geometric mouse and a clothespin.

Oldenburg illustrates how Pop Art injected surprise, curiosity and humor into the art of the second half of the twentieth century.

17–11 Among the many everyday objects that Oldenburg has enlarged into giant sculptures are a clothespin, a baseball bat and a tube of lipstick.

Claes Oldenburg, *Shoestring Potatoes Spilling from a Bag.* Painted canvas, kapok, glue and acrylic, 107 3/4" x 46" x 42 1/8" (274 x 117 x 107 cm). Walker Art Center, Minneapolis, gift of the T. B. Walker Foundation, 1966.

Robert Rauschenberg

(b.1925)

Robert Rauschenberg acted as the bridge between Abstract Expressionism and Pop Art when he fastened such mundane objects as license plates, street signs and men's clothes to his abstract canvases. He called them ***combine paintings***. Like Picasso and Braque, he mixes reality with abstraction. Rauschenberg, however, uses the entire object, not simply scraps. He combines everything imaginable (silkscreen images, prints, objects, painting, stuffed birds and automobile tires) to create the visual sensation he desires. That sensation is often difficult for the public to comprehend. We are not used to looking at such a chaotic mixture of materials. Titles like *First Landing Jump* (fig.17–12) probably do not help either. But the artist makes the viewer look at ordinary things in a different context. The viewer is used to seeing tires on automobiles, not in "paintings." Pop artists want the viewer to see the commercial environment in a new way. By juxtaposing usually unrelated materials, Rauschenberg has succeeded.

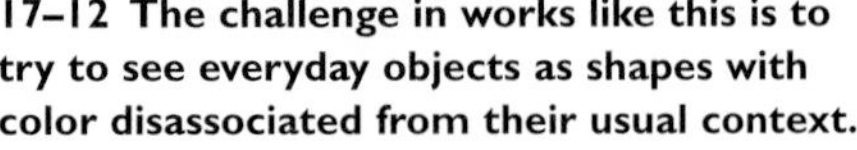

17–12 The challenge in works like this is to try to see everyday objects as shapes with color disassociated from their usual context.
Robert Rauschenberg, *First Landing Jump*, 1961. Combine painting: tire, khaki shirt, license plate, leather straps, mirror, iron street light reflector, live blue light bulb, electric cable, steel spring, tin cans, various pieces of cloth, and oil paint on composition board, 89 1/4" x 81" (227 x 206 cm). The Museum of Modern Art, New York, gift of Philip Johnson. ©1996 Robert Rauschenberg/Licensed by VAGA, New York, NY

1949
Mao Zedong becomes leader of Communist China

World Cultural Timeline

1953
Tenzing Norgay reaches summit of Mount Everest

1966
Indira Gandhi becomes India's first woman prime minister

17–14 Many of Lichtenstein's works poke fun at accepted ideas or trendy fashions of art. What is his message in this one?
Roy Lichtenstein, *Masterpiece*, 1962. Oil on canvas, 54 1/4" x 54 1/4" (138 x 138 cm). Collection of Leo Castelli Gallery, New York.

Jasper Johns

(b.1930)

Jasper Johns uses many Abstract Expressionist painting techniques, but his subject matter is as common as the American flag, targets, numbers, beer cans, flashlights and maps of the United States. Johns presents things that are often looked at, but seldom seen in detail. In *Numbers in Color* (fig.17–13), he shows numbers. He forces the viewers to look at common things that they often overlook. The complementary colors of blue and orange cry out for recognition as they seem to vibrate forward from and backward into the canvas. The overall effect is one of texture and pattern, but within that context, the individual numbers are the subject matter.

Roy Lichtenstein

(b.1923)

Roy Lichtenstein became one of the stars of Pop Art. Like other Pop artists, he wanted to play on the slick, multiple images of commercial art, its mechanical techniques and its glossy colors. Lichtenstein makes giant cartoon-like paintings. He even simulates the ben-day printing dots used to color the Sunday comics (fig.17–a). Paintings like *Masterpiece* (fig.17–14) look like they are cut from the comic page, but try to imagine this one 54 inches high. Often, he pokes gentle fun at the melodrama of the comics and the national fascination with them. Some of his works have verbal messages. His slick, machine-like style has remained the same for years. It is fun and art at the same time. His art brought Abstract Expressionism to an abrupt halt.

17–13 Johns' use of color and subject keeps your eye constantly moving over the surface with no one place to focus or rest.
Jasper Johns, *Numbers in Color*, 1959. Encaustic paint on newspaper and canvas, 66 1/4" x 49 1/4" (168 x 125 cm). Albright-Knox Art Gallery, Buffalo, New York, gift of Seymour H. Knox. ©1996 Jasper Johns/Licensed by VAGA, New York, NY

Andy Warhol

(1928–1987)

Andy Warhol and Pop Art go hand in hand; it is hard to imagine one without the other. He zeroes in on American mass production and its boring repetitions. The consumer goes into the supermarket and sees hundreds of cans of Campbell's soup. The product is instantly recognized and found in nearly every market and home in the country. Warhol painted *100 Cans* (fig.17–15) in a boring, unexciting way—just the way they are lined up on the market shelves. He even used the mechanical silkscreen process to apply paint to canvas, and had other people do the work. This is how impersonal he became with the medium. Warhol's depictions of Campbell's cans also include a series of paintings of huge, individual soup cans. They hung in the same gallery in a row to simulate the supermarket experience. Warhol is also known for his images of Marilyn Monroe and other personalities. He created the images by using the same printmaking process he used for the cans.

17–15 One soup can may be boring, but 100 of them present patterns to find. Do you find yourself reading the labels to try to find one that is different?

Andy Warhol, *100 Cans*, 1962. Oil on canvas, 71 3/4" x 52" (182 x 132 cm). Albright-Knox Art Gallery, Buffalo, New York, gift of Seymour H. Knox.

George Segal

(b.1924)

George Segal was concerned with everyday sculptural subjects the same as Claes Oldenburg. However, he uses a different medium and subjects. He uses plaster to form people in everyday activities. Segal dips surgical gauze in plaster and wraps it around the person posing for him. Each section of the fast-drying plaster is cut off as soon as it dries. The parts are assembled to make a hollow cast of the person. The ghostly white figures in *Walk, Don't Walk* (fig.17–16) are startlingly real, especially when placed in a setting with real props, such as the street sign. There is nothing amazing or dramatic about the figures or their poses. They are simply realistic slices of American life—people going about their everyday jobs and routines.

17–16 Segal placed his subjects in real-world settings. He often looked for props in junkyards.

George Segal, *Walk, Don't Walk*, 1976. Plaster, cement, painted wood and electric light, 105" x 71 3/4" x 71 3/4" (267 x 182 x 182 cm). Whitney Museum of American Art, New York. ©1996 George Segal/Licensed by VAGA, New York, NY

DONT
WALK
WALK

Bridget Riley

(b.1931)

Instead of using the common, everyday images found in Pop Art, Bridget Riley worked on pure Op Art paintings in England for many years. She created surfaces that seem to undulate before the viewer's eyes. If the viewer gazes steadily in one place, shifts eye movement, or moves the work a bit, the image itself will move. Works such as *Fall* (fig.17–17) are capable of producing a dizzy sensation in some viewers. Riley's surfaces seem to wriggle and the viewer cannot make the sensation stop, especially when confronting the work in its actual size.

Victor Vasarely

(b.1908)

Victor Vasarely is the Hungarian-born leader of the Op Art movement in America. He works with geometric shapes and brilliant colors. His works, which he does not wish to call paintings, play tricks with the viewer's eyes. His surfaces seem to bulge in or out in either subtle or unbelievably abrupt bubbles. To achieve such effects, he changes the size of shapes or the width of lines and strips, as in *Vega-Kontosh-Va* (fig.17–18). Vasarely uses thin layers of oil paint and crisp, hard edges to produce his effects. He creates fantastic illusions of optical space and depth. His experiments formed the basis for an illusionistic movement in art at the beginning of the 1980s. A museum in Aix-en-Provence, France, was built to hold his huge paintings, most of which are over twenty feet high. The effect of rooms filled with such gigantic images is overpowering for many viewers.

Richard Anuskiewicz

(1930)

Richard Anuskiewicz was another American leader in the Op Art movement. His paintings (fig.17–19) are carefully constructed with line and color to produce sensations of the same shape both advancing and receding. The placement of lines, shapes and colors is incredibly exact. His work is brilliant, balanced and optically stimulating.

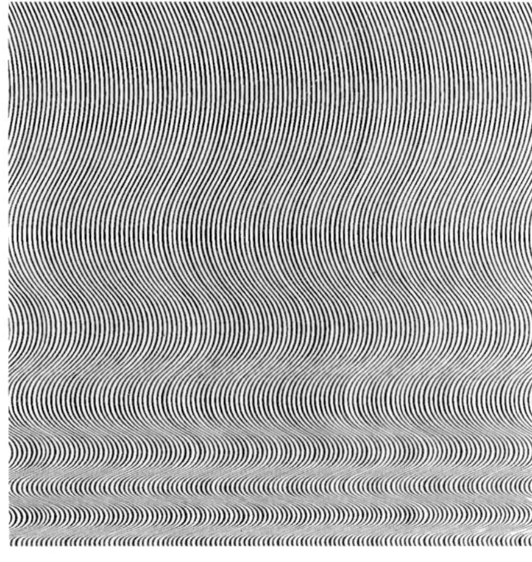

17–17 Op images like this one can seem to move and can also produce sensations of colors even though they are painted in black and white only. Bridget Riley, *Fall*, 1963. Acrylic emulsion on hardboard, 55 1/2" x 55 1/2" (141 x 141 cm). The Tate Gallery, London.

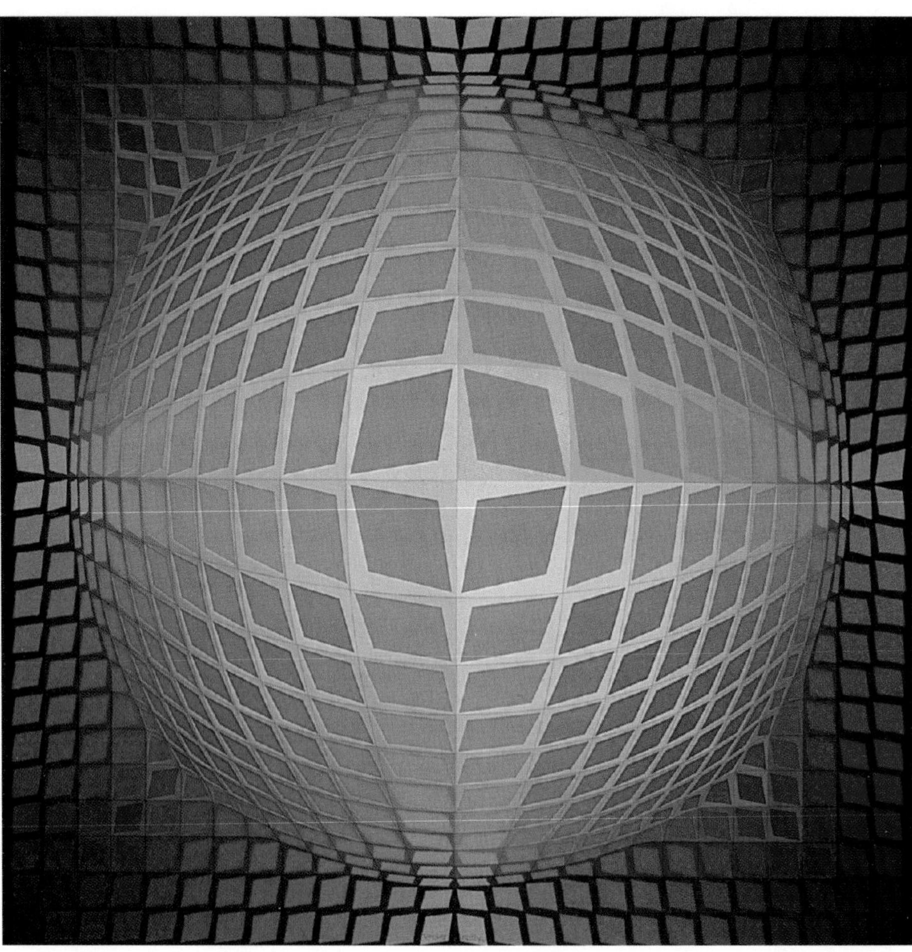

17–18 What design principles are at work here to make your eye interpret this as a three-dimensional form? Victor Vasarely, *Vega-Kontosh-Va*, 1971. Tempera on panel, 25 1/2" x 25 1/2" (65 x 65 cm). Los Angeles County Museum of Art, gift of Mr. and Mrs. Donald Winston.

17–20 Although this piece is flat, the viewer's eye insists on reading it as a three-dimensional form.
Ron Davis, *Plane Sawtooth*, 1970. Polyester resin and fiberglass, 59 3/4" x 140 1/4" (152 x 356 cm). Albright-Knox Art Gallery, Buffalo, New York, gift of Seymour H. Knox.

17–19 Why do these colors seem to shift and glow?
Richard Anuskiewicz, *Iridescence*, 1965. Acrylic on canvas, 59 3/4" x 59 3/4" (152 x 152 cm). Albright-Knox Art Gallery, Buffalo, New York, gift of Seymour H. Knox. ©1996 Richard Anuszkiewicz/Licensed by VAGA, New York, NY

Ron Davis

(b.1937)

To create his optical works, Ron Davis began using contemporary materials like acrylics or polyester resins with fiberglass. He fused colors to the rear surface of fiberglass to create astonishing works of optical illusion. *Plane Sawtooth* (fig.17–20) is absolutely flat, not three-dimensional. It is cut from a sheet of fiberglass. Its unframed, irregular shape, when placed on the wall, adds dramatically to the illusion of three-dimensionality. Even when the viewer gets close to the wall, it is difficult to visually flatten out the illusion because it is so convincing. Some parts seem shadowed while others are transparent. The viewer's eyes, accustomed to looking at three-dimensional objects, cannot separate the illusion from reality.

Lesson 17.2 Review

1 How did the Pop Art movement get its name? List some of the leaders in this movement.

2 What is Op Art? How did Op Art artists create a sense of movement within their paintings?

3 Select an Op Art painting to stare at for a full minute. Describe your feelings at the end of the minute.

4 How many times larger than life is Oldenburg's *Falling Shoestring Potatoes*?

5 In Jasper John's paintings, what is he encouraging the viewer to notice? In *Numbers in Color*, what means does he use to focus our attention on his subject?

6 What do most of Roy Lichtenstein's paintings resemble? How are they different from his source of inspiration?

7 What was the underlying message in Warhol's *100 Cans*? What means did he use to apply the paint to his canvases?

8 Describe the method that Segal used to produce the figures in *Walk, Don't Walk*. What are the people doing in this sculpture?

17.3 Color Field Painting

During the sixties and seventies, a style called *Color Field Painting* developed into a very important area of art. This style owed much to Mark Rothko's large, flat color statements. It relied solely on flat fields of color. Color Field Painting had none of the emotionalism and slashing brushwork of Abstract Expressionism. The work produced was very cool, very serene and very beautiful. Color Field Painting was often minutely planned. However, artists also worked with improvisation and accidental happenings. Color Field Painting has also been labeled *Post-Painterly Abstraction*, *Classical Abstraction* and *Hard-Edge Painting*.

After World War II, many painters started working on a larger scale until their canvases were almost mural size. When huge paintings hang on the walls of museums or other public spaces, they become an important aspect of the interior environment. They draw the viewer into active visual participation with the work. Artists then began opening up space in the work itself by leaving large portions painted white or as natural canvas. This space became active open space to which the viewer could abandon himself or herself. Some artists designed three or four canvases to work together on three or four walls, acting as a total environment. This style is sometimes called *Enlarged Field Painting*.

Key Notes

- Color Field Painting relies solely on flat fields of color.
- Enlarged field painting opens up space in works by leaving portions painted white or as natural canvas.

Vocabulary

stain painting
shaped canvas

Special Feature

Helen Frankenthaler

b. 1928

Helen Frankenthaler is one of the major contributors to Color Field Painting, particularly to Enlarged Field Painting. Many of her huge abstract paintings were painted on unprimed canvas that was stapled to the floor to make it taut. She works in a spontaneous way, pouring and spreading, pushing and flowing the stains and paints onto the canvas. What starts at the top may end up being a side or the bottom of the work. Part of the unstretched canvas may be cut off to change the shape or the dimensions. Working in such a spontaneous way is difficult for many artists, but Frankenthaler achieves wonderful results with it.

Mountains and Sea (fig.17–21) is the most famous of Frankenthaler's works. It is an important work because, with this painting, the

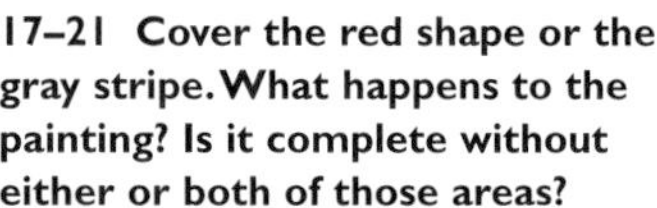

17–21 Cover the red shape or the gray stripe. What happens to the painting? Is it complete without either or both of those areas?
Helen Frankenthaler, *Mountains and Sea*, 1952. Oil on canvas, 7'2" x 9'9" (218.4 x 297 cm). Collection of the artist, on loan to the National Gallery of Art, Washington DC.

artist begins to use the technique of ***stain painting***. It forced other artists to think about and use color in a very new way. Frankenthaler made this painting after returning from a trip to Nova Scotia. On her trip, Frankenthaler was struck by the juxtaposition of mountains right beside the ocean. The painting is abstract. Nevertheless, the image does convey a sense of mass adjacent to the horizontal blue line of the ocean. The painting was not received with much enthusiasm. Priced at around a hundred dollars, it failed to sell.

The Bay (fig.17–22) is composed of an irregular blue shape looming over a field of green and gray. The blues were painted first in various horizontal gestures. The layering of different blues gives the blue shape its billowy effect. According to Frankenthaler, she had painted the blues and then left them to dry. When she came back, she added the green and thought it was done. Later that day, she put in the gray and the red dot and decided it was done. This question of whether a work is done plays an important part in her work.

Mountains and Sea and *The Bay* are both very powerful representations of Color Field Painting, particularly Enlarged Field Painting.

17–22 Color Field painters generally avoid any sense of paint texture in their work.
Helen Frankenthaler, *The Bay*, 1963. Acrylic on canvas, 80 3/4" x 81 3/4" (205.1 x 207.7 cm). The Detroit Institute of Arts, gift of Dr. and Mrs. Hilbert H. DeLawter.

Joseph Albers

(1888–1976)

Joseph Albers became the teacher of many Color Field painters when he came to America from Germany in 1933. Albers began a long series of studies based on the interaction of color. Using the square as a motif, he demonstrated the qualities of color and how they interact when placed next to each other or near other colors. *Homage to the Square: Glow* (fig.17–23) illustrates the format and design of his experiments with color. In most of his works, the squares are placed as they are here. However, with different colors and combinations, the visual results vary. Here, the intensity of the central hue causes that square to come forward and float over the others. Albers published his fascinating studies in a book titled *Interaction of Color* in which he defines his research and explains his findings.

17–23 Especially over the last 200 years, many artists like Josef Albers have developed theories about color and the ways that colors interact. Albers taught at the Bauhaus in Germany before he immigrated to the United States.
Joseph Albers, *Homage to the Square: Glow*, 1966. Oil on fiberboard, 48" x 48" (122 x 122 cm). Hirshhorn Museum and Sculpture Garden, Smithsonian Institution, Washington DC.

Barnett Newman

(1905–1970)

Barnett Newman was part of a movement to produce art totally without any visual or geometrical associations. His color fields are often huge and might be separated by a single, wide or narrow line of contrasting or similar hue. Because he wanted to reduce the content of the painting to virtually nothing, his work was called *Minimal Art*. It has also been called *Cool Art* because of its nonemotional quality and its characteristic precision. It is the direct opposite of the hot and emotional Abstract Expressionism.

Newman's *Adam* (fig.17–24) is a large canvas of two elements. A dark-valued reddish-brown color field is divided by bright red lines. The painting has no specific or hidden meanings. It is the most minimal statement that Newman could make at the time. He wanted the viewer to look at the work and see *it*. He did not want the viewer to see any suggestive subject matter or geometrical organization. Perhaps the work would make the viewer think inwardly, much as the Oriental priest who looks at a blank wall and meditates.

Artists like Ad Reinhardt outminimalized Newman later. Reinhardt painted a solid canvas of only black. He painted it so smoothly that no brushstrokes would show—the ultimate minimal statement.

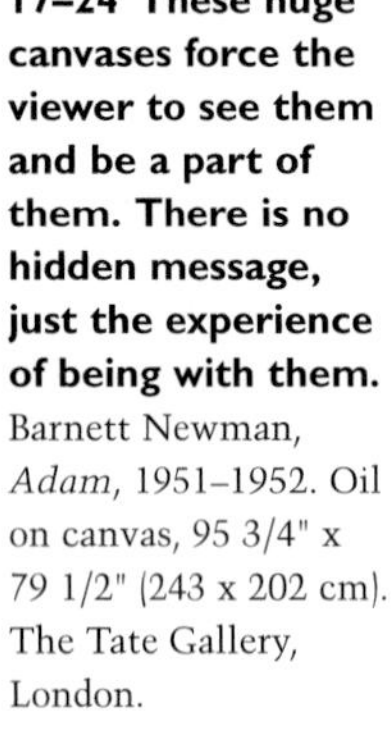

17–24 These huge canvases force the viewer to see them and be a part of them. There is no hidden message, just the experience of being with them.
Barnett Newman, *Adam*, 1951–1952. Oil on canvas, 95 3/4" x 79 1/2" (243 x 202 cm). The Tate Gallery, London.

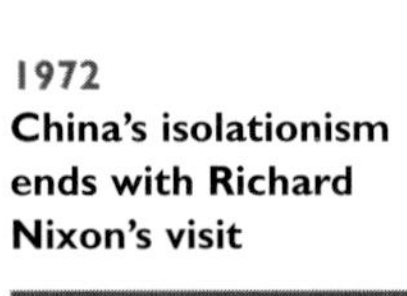

1972
China's isolationism ends with Richard Nixon's visit

1975
The Vietnam Conflict ends and North and South Vietnam reunite

World Cultural Timeline

1973
American Indian movement political protest at Wounded Knee

1979
Mother Teresa of Calcutta receives Nobel Peace Prize

17–26 Many of Kelly's beautiful abstract shapes began as part of sketches of everyday objects such as shadows, doors and windows. Ellsworth Kelly, *Blue Curve III*, 1972. Oil on canvas, 67 3/4" x 166 1/2" (172 x 423 cm). Los Angeles County Museum of Art.

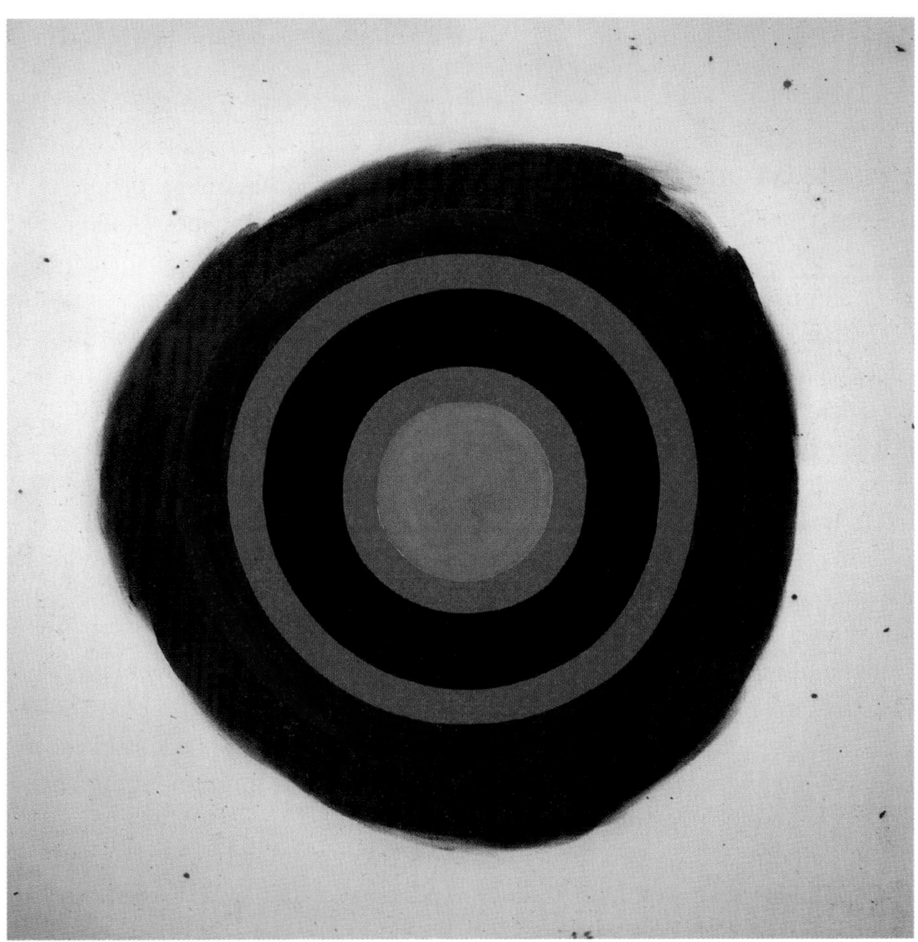

17–25 Noland used very thin pigment to stain his canvases. Kenneth Noland. *Song*, 1958. Oil on canvas, 69" x 69" (175 x 175 cm). Gift of the Friends of the Whitney Museum of American Art, New York. ©1996 Ken Noland/Licensed by VAGA, New York, NY

Kenneth Noland

(b.1924)

Kenneth Noland studied with Albers and continued the Color Field emphasis on the canvas over subject matter or design. He started painting concentric circles on unprimed canvas, which caused a staining process and made the circles seem to pulsate and float. He then moved to gigantic, inverted chevrons of bright colors. Each chevron is made up of several stripes placed against a darkly painted canvas. At first, they were symmetrical, as in *Song* (fig.17–25). But soon he moved the point of the chevron to one side or the other. More recently, he has painted huge canvases of horizontal stripes of flat color. The stripes float against vast white fields, producing the effect of flat landscapes. He was also one of the first artists to work on ***shaped canvases***. Instead of using the rectangular shape, he worked with canvases shaped like diamonds and triangles.

Ellsworth Kelly

(b.1923)

Ellsworth Kelly works with pure colors and geometric shapes. Some of his designs have only two intense colors and several large flat shapes. Large is an apt word because often his simple designs are mural-sized—over 9 feet high and about 20 feet wide. Kelly studied in Paris with the Constructionists, artists who worked abstractly with basic geometric shapes. He often uses acrylic paints to attain the hard, perfect edges of his shapes. Such precision is essential to the concept and style of Hard-Edge painting. It is possible only with the use of masking tape and thinned pigments.

Blue Curve III (fig.17–26) is part of a series of works based on shaped canvases and curved shapes. The edge of the intense blue color appears to bulge forward from the diamond-shaped frame. But, in reality, it is perfectly flat.

17–27 By overlapping and repeating this common shape and varying the color, Frank Stella invites your eye to follow him through the design and complete the forms. Although the protractor is the only shape used, other shapes are implied. Can you find them?
Frank Stella, *Protractor Variation,* 1969. Fluorescent-alkyd on canvas, 120" x 240 1/4" (305 x 610 cm). Los Angeles County Museum of Art.

Frank Stella

(b.1936)

Frank Stella carried the shaped canvas still further. His geometric designs make use of the unframed edges as part of the painting. In *Protractor Variation* (fig.17–27), the interior lines and shapes repeat the curved and flat edges of the canvas itself. Unlike other Color Field painters, Stella used colors that are extremely varied. His protractor series often combines fluorescent paints and metallic colors that are visually jarring. The colors are carefully chosen to cause visual movement. What appear to be white lines are really narrow negative areas of unpainted canvas between the brightly painted shapes. During an earlier period of his development, Stella used these unpainted lines against a solid color field as the main element of the painting.

Adolph Gottlieb

(1903–1974)

Adolph Gottlieb was an Abstract Expressionist whose work became larger and larger. He developed a set of visual symbols in his art. He evolved a way of combining two opposite shapes: a disk and a ragged-edged form. The disk, often a soft-edged roundish shape, is calm and geometric. The ragged shape breaks out of any containment. People have labeled the shapes "bursts" and "blasts." The roundish shapes always float over the irregular ones. Although Gottlieb did not mind other readings of his powerful work, he only wanted to make the two opposite shapes work together as a unit. *Orb* (fig.17–28) illustrates these two visual symbols. The soft edges of the round shape were made by staining the raw canvas. They create a pulsating sensation of forward and backward movement. The powerful black shapes are reminders of Kline's slashing black strokes. However, by combining them with the round shapes, Gottlieb has produced a completely different and personal statement.

17–28 Notice how the powerful black strokes compare with the softness of the circles.
Adolph Gottlieb. *Orb,* 1964. Oil on canvas, 90" x 60" (228.5 x 152.5 cm). Dallas Museum of Art.

Sam Francis

(b.1923)

Sam Francis pours freely applied thin colors onto the canvas. The colors spread, stain and overlap, creating luminous transparent layers. In earlier works, such as *Basel Mural* (fig.17–29), the shapes are clustered in the top part of the gigantic canvas. In later works, the vivid color blobs are arranged around the edges of the canvas and almost slip out of sight. In both arrangements, the white area acts as a powerful, sparkling, positive area of vibrant space. The drips, blobs, lines, stains and bright colors add to the intensity of the unpainted areas. The unpainted areas seem to be space through which one can move. Some of these works by Francis are enormous, over thirty-two feet wide. They enwrap the viewer in sparkling white space.

17–29 The dripping paints, cut-off edges of shapes and open areas of white negative space create a sense of movement in and out of the picture plane as if the artist has given us only a part of a larger subject.
Sam Francis, *Basel Mural*, 1956–58. Oil on canvas, 156 3/4" x 236 1/4" (398 x 600 cm). The Norton Simon Art Foundation, Pasadena, CA.

17–30 Controlling layers of transparency on a huge surface requires a lot of practice and the willingness to take risks to see the idea through.
Morris Louis, *Point of Tranquility*, 1958. Synthetic polymer on canvas, 101 1/2" x 135" (258 x 343 cm). Hirshhorn Museum and Sculpture Garden, Smithsonian Institution, Washington DC.

Morris Louis

(1912–1962)

Morris Louis based his images on the physical movement of color across unprimed canvas. First, he poured diluted acrylic paint on the canvas. Then, he tilted the canvas and let the paint run until it produced superimposed veils of color. Sometimes, the shapes were linear, running from top to bottom. Others, such as in *Point of Tranquility* (fig.17–30), spread in different directions. The overlapping, transparent shapes create a feeling of depth on the huge flat surfaces. Although the work is spontaneous and unplanned, the working process is delicate and careful. Such a gigantic surface required special care in the application of each color. The tilting of the canvas to spread the paint had to be controlled, stopped and shifted to another angle until the supply of color was even. Colors had to run to a satisfactory shape and location. *Point of Tranquility* is a soft, gentle explosion of color. Colors seem to float like colored smoke in the white space of the canvas. It is a painting done completely without a brushstroke.

Lesson 17.3 Review

1 How do the Color Field painters cause viewers to notice their paintings and then to react with them?
2 Why is Barnett Newman's art described as minimal art and cool art?
3 What is the point in minimal art such as Barnett Newman's *Adam*? What is the artist trying to get the viewer to see?
4 Who was one of the first artists to paint on shaped canvases? Which artist use shaped canvases even more extensively?
5 How does Ellsworth Kelly make the hard edges in his paintings such as *Blue Curve III*?
6 How many protractors can you count in Stella's *Protractor Variation*?
7 What was Adolph Gottlieb's design concern as he painted the different shapes in *Orb*?
8 Would either Frank Stella's *Protractor Variation* or Sam Francis' *Basel Mural* fit on your bedroom wall?

17.4 New Realism

AMERICAN INTEREST IN REALISTIC ART never really disappeared from the scene. In the seventies, a revival began in California and spread rapidly throughout the country. The movement goes by various names like *Super-Realism, Photo-Realism, New Realism* and *Hyper-Realism.* Artists used commercial art techniques of airbrush, photography, spray or anything else that might help to produce realistic images. New Realism was based on genre art and the Pop paintings of the fifties. It led directly into the illusionistic paintings of the early eighties that astound the viewer with mind-boggling illusions of reality.

These works are rich in imagery and often function as visual metaphors. Familiar images often are juxtaposed in unusual and sometimes perplexing ways. Subjects are treated with cool, intellectual approaches and, in this way, differ from the Realism of the nineteenth century. New Realism reflects the high energy and variety of contemporary life in America.

Key Notes

- New Realism is based on the Pop Art of the fifties.
- A tremendous variety of images and metaphors reflect contemporary American life.

17–31 How does this compare to the acrylic painting of the same subject? Chuck Close, *Mark, unfinished,* 1978. Watercolor, 53 1/2" x 40 1/2" (136 x 103 cm). Pace Wildenstein, New York.

Special Feature

Chuck Close

(b.1940)

The ultimate research tool of the New Realists is the camera. One of the pioneers of the use of photography as a source of imagery is Chuck Close. Close started gaining attention in the late sixties with his gargantuan, photographically realistic black-and-white portraits of himself and his friends. Like other Realist artists, Close wants to make a very objective rendering of his subjects. He has said that his main objective is to translate photographic information into paint information.

He depicts only the human figure. Usually, the portraits are head and shoulder views seen frontally against a uniform background. These are completely dispassionate studies and do not in any way reflect the inner qualities of the subjects. Close gives equal attention to every physical characteristic. Instead of seeing the sitter's personality, we become very aware of how the artist has presented us with a gigantic illusion.

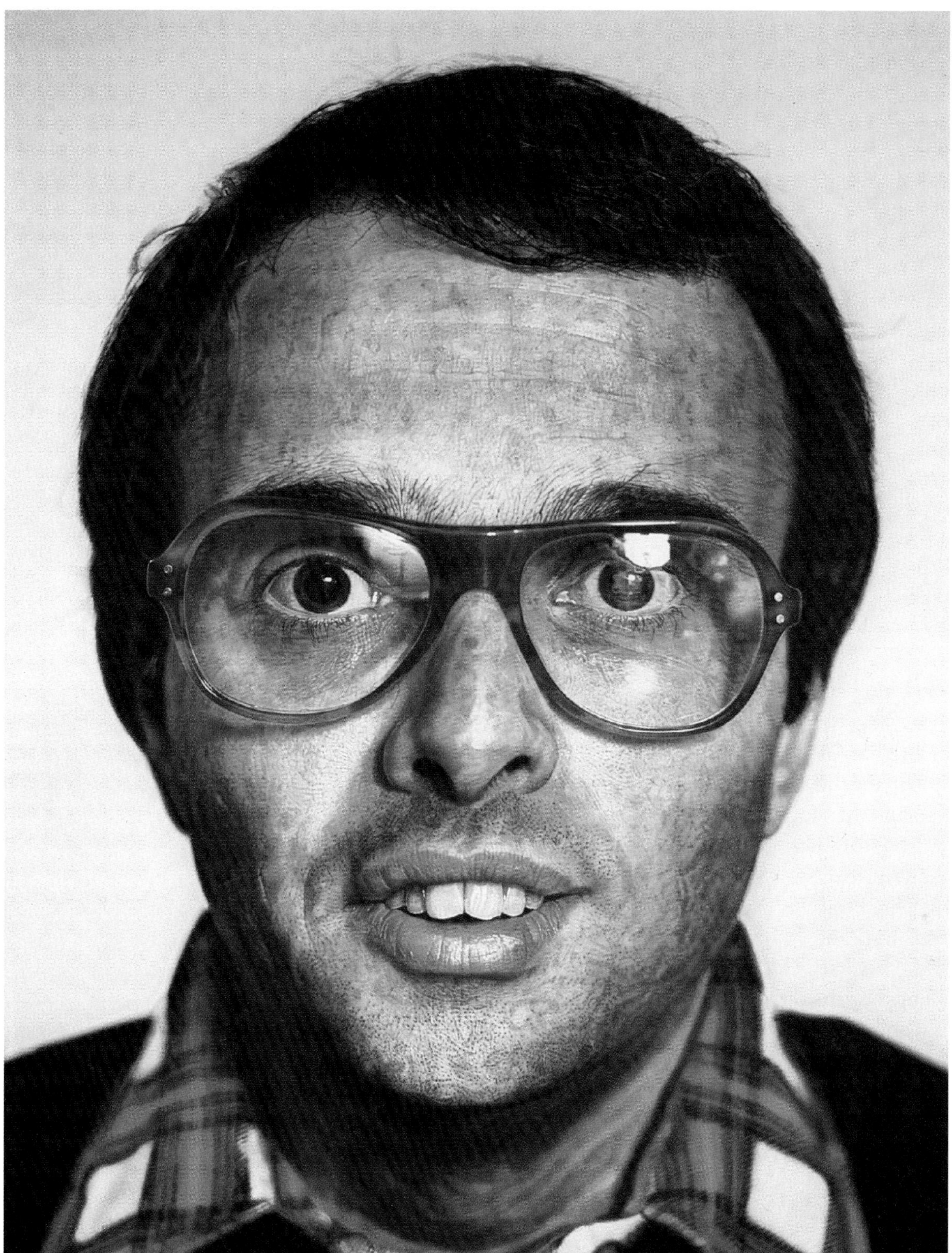

17–32 Would you want Chuck Close to do your portrait? Why or why not?
Chuck Close, *Mark,* 1979. Acrylic on canvas, 9' x 7' (274 x 213 cm). Pace WIldenstein, New York.

From a distance, the portraits appear to be giant blowups of photographs. Up close, they break down into fields of dots and marks.

Two paintings of the same person, Mark, give a good idea of how his technique works. *Mark, unfinished* (fig.17–31) makes use of a mechanistic dot and square technique. It is a gridded image composed of horizontal bands of variegated color.

Mark, (fig.17–32) is a much more factual, realistic painting. This head resembles the way we look under harsh fluorescent light. Pores, hairs, wrinkles and blemishes are nakedly displayed.

Close's work is representative of New Realism. His paintings are both perfect reproduction as well as gigantic illusion.

17–33 Andrew Wyeth's father was a painter and illustrator, and his son Jamie is also an artist. The family tradition in the arts may have given Andrew the self-confidence to follow his own interest and to use traditional techniques such as egg tempera.
Andrew Wyeth, *Christina's World,* 1948. Tempera on gesso panel, 32 1/4" x 47 3/4" (82 x 121 cm). The Museum of Modern Art, New York.

Andrew Wyeth

(b.1917)

Andrew Wyeth has painted in his own realistic way throughout the various isms and developments of twentieth-century art. His work is a continuation of the American Scene painting and portrays the natural environment of Pennsylvania and Maine. In addition to the natural landscape, he also paints portraits of his neighbors. Wyeth works in a natural and easy style, while using the exacting medium of egg tempera. From energetic and emotional sketches, he works to a finished product that seems absolutely real. Yet, the works are based on abstract structuring and design.

In paintings such as *Christina's World* (fig.17–33), he painted in the vast spaces and background first. Then, he added the figure over it. The girl was a crippled neighbor of Wyeth's. Her family's farm, shown in the painting, is next to his in Maine. The painting, like many of Wyeth's works, is a realistic presentation that also creates a mood. He is able to capture a moment in time and a feeling of place, enriched by a touch of the universal experience with life, people and place. He raises commonplace subjects to levels of importance and dignity with immense skill.

17–34 Use the text to help you find all of the images in this painting.
James Rosenquist, *Nomad,* 1963. Oil on canvas with plastic and wood, 84 1/4" x 209 1/2" (214 x 532 cm). Albright-Knox Gallery, Buffalo, New York, gift of Seymour H. Knox. ©1996 James Rosenquist/Licensed by VAGA, New York, NY

James Rosenquist

(b.1933)

James Rosenquist worked as a billboard painter. In the sixties, he began to create king-sized paintings on canvas of billboard proportions. He uses many techniques of commercial and industrial artists, and he mimics the advertising style of art. His work has the feeling of Pop Art in its common subjects, but he combines many such images into one framework. In *Nomad* (fig.17–34), the viewer can see (from left to right) part of a detergent box, two pairs of ballerinas' legs, a redwood picnic table and bench, a gigantic billfold, spaghetti with meatballs and olives, part of a light bulb, a microphone and a patch of grass with a stake in it. He has also included a real plastic trash bag and a pile of sticks he used to mix his paints. Imagine watching a dozen television commercials or zipping by several advertising billboards. The work creates the same kind of impression.

17–36 These sculptures seem so real that passersby often try to interact with them by speaking to them or asking them questions!
Duane Hanson, *Self-Portrait with Model*, 1979. Polyester and fiber glass, life-size. Courtesy of the artist.

Richard Estes

(b.1936)

Richard Estes is a master of the urban scene. His buildings, windows and vehicles sparkle with the brilliance and clarity of a rain-washed day. People are generally absent or an insignificant part of the scene. They are not needed because the shine and reflection of chrome and glass surfaces produce plenty of life and interest. Estes works directly from photographs and slides. Colors, shadows, values and reflections are painstakingly reproduced. As in *Drugstore* (fig.17–35), the result is a cool, impassionate look at the city. *Drugstore* is a matter-of-fact photographic representation of a place. Estes' attitude is derived from Pop Art, but his technique and style are much more sophisticated.

17–35 Estes is particularly interested in reflections. What reflective surfaces do you find in this painting? Can you detect how the illusion of reflection was created?
Richard Estes, *Drugstore*, 1970. Oil on canvas, 59 3/4" x 44 1/2" (152 x 113 cm). The Art Institute of Chicago. ©1996 Richard Estes/Licensed by VAGA, New York, NY

Duane Hanson

(b.1925)

Duane Hanson produces life-size, colored models of people that are dressed and surrounded with actual things. The result is so lifelike that viewers often gape and giggle in disbelief and amusement. His three-dimensional New Realism is flawless and almost frightening at times. Hanson makes plaster casts of people, then creates polyester and fiberglass models from the casts. The models are tinted in natural colors. He works with ordinary people and even himself. In *Self-Portrait with Model* (fig.17–36), he surrounds the realistic sculptures with props that heighten the reality even more. His people and arrangements appear so real and ordinary that some viewers walk right past Hanson's work without realizing they are sculptures, not living people—the ultimate compliment to a Super-Realist artist.

Lesson 17.4 Review

1 Give several names for the extremely realistic art movement that began in the 1970s. List a few artists involved in this movement.
2 How does Chuck Close use photography in his work? What is he trying to achieve in his painting?
3 How does James Rosenquist's *Nomad* differ from Andy Warhol's style of Pop Art?
4 Describe how Duane Hanson creates his sculptures. How are his sculptures like and different from George Segal's?

17.5 Sculpture

During the second half of the twentieth century, sculpture took gigantic steps in the use of new materials, techniques, concepts and directions. The direction of its development is even more varied than that of painting. Contemporary sculpture reflects the excitement and innovative work of artists using these new techniques and materials. The scale of sculpture in the second half of the twentieth century assumed great significance. In addition, there was the development of open sculpture. Open sculpture does not divide or enclose space in any fixed way.

New industrial materials and techniques helped the change in attitude toward sculpture. Many modern sculptors, such as David Smith, worked in factories to learn their skills in metalworking. An endless variety of materials have been used in sculpture: steel, Plexiglas, epoxy, fired clay, leather, wire, plastic, fabrics and rubber.

It is the variety, scale and openness of late-twentieth-century sculpture that makes it elude strict definition.

Key Notes

- New materials and techniques have given sculpture new direction in the second half of the twentieth century.
- Variety and scope of sculpture has made it difficult to strictly define.

Special Feature

Isamu Noguchi

(1904–1988)

Isamu Noguchi produced an amazing variety of sculptures in various materials. Born of Japanese-American parents, he spent his early years in Japan and then two years working with Brancusi in Paris. He later studied in China and Japan and worked in London and Mexico. His international background led to works of international feeling and acceptance. Noguchi was able to use the best modern tradition of Europe without losing himself or fixating on any single style.

During the 1940s, Noguchi emerged as a prominent stone

17–38 The sculpture garden is an example of "sited sculpture." The piece was designed specifically for this site.
Isamu Noguchi. *Sculpture Garden,* Beinecke Rare Book and Manuscript Library at Yale University.

17–37 Compare this sculpture to Brancusi's *Bird in Space* and *The Kiss.*
Isamu Noguchi, *Great Rock of Inner Seeking,* 1975. Granite, 143 3/4" (365 cm) high. National Gallery of Art, Washington, DC.

carver. *Great Rock of Inner Seeking* (fig.17–37) is carved from granite and weighs eight and one-half tons. Like much of his work, it has a primeval feeling. It seems closely related to traditional Japanese garden art and Zen Buddhist contemplation. Some of the textures were made naturally, some by the drill that severed the stone from its parent mass, and some by Noguchi. The cooperative effort is a magnificent and powerful form, exciting in its simplicity and solemn and quiet in its implications.

Noguchi has also designed some environmental spaces. He designed Detroit's Civic Center Plaza and the Sculpture Garden at Jerusalem's Museum of Art, as well as children's playgrounds and stage sets. His sculpture courtyard, or "garden," for the Beinecke Rare Book and Manuscript Library at Yale University (fig.17–38) is a sunken court, closed in by four glass walls, that can be seen either from above or from the rooms level with it. Looking down on it, the viewer sees a marble plaza on which a pyramid, a circle and a diamond are placed. There is a great sense of unity among the three huge forms. The classic simplicity and purity of the forms is striking.

The exploration of pure form and its translation into modern terms and the creation of unified sculptural spaces are Noguchi's contribution to sculpture of the late twentieth century.

Henry Moore

(1898–1986)

Almost all Henry Moore's abstracted works are based on the various forms of the human figure (fig.3–9). His early work was only slightly abstracted. In his later years, his forms became rounded and simplified.

Sheep Piece (figs.17–d, 17–39) is a monumental bronze work of two interacting forms. The forms could be two sheep huddling against a storm. Moore placed this casting in a sheep pasture, where it seems to belong. However, the powerful, smooth, rounded forms would be just as comfortable in front of a skyscraper or in the courtyard of a museum. Moore produced a tremendous body of work that is universally appealing. Its placement in locations around the world has made Moore's work easily recognizable.

17–39 How is this view of the sculpture different from the view seen in fig.17–d?
Henry Moore, *Sheep Piece*, 1972. Bronze, 223 1/2" (568 cm) long. Hertfordshire, England.

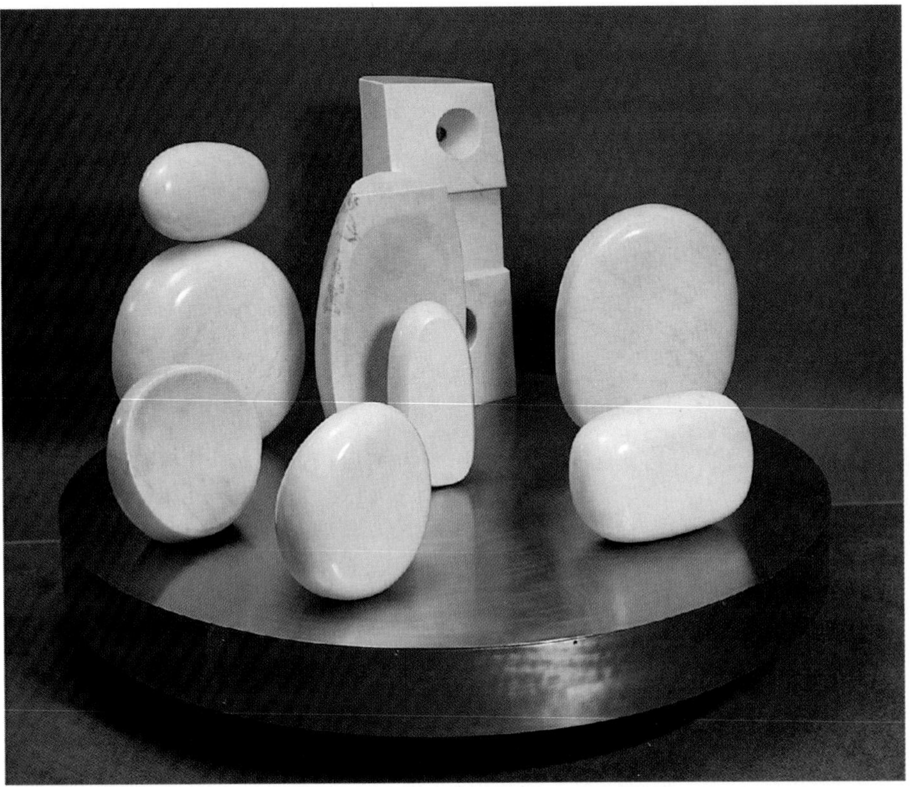

17–40 Imagine what this group sculpture would look like if you were standing in the arrangement.
Barbara Hepworth, *Assembly of Sea Forms*, 1972. White marble, tallest form 42 1/2" (108 cm) high. The Norton Simon Art Foundation, Pasadena, CA.

17–42 The space that it encloses is also a part of this sculpture.
David Smith, *Cubi XII*, 1963. Stainless steel, 109 5/8" x 49 1/4" x 32 1/4" (278 x 125 x 82cm). Hirshhorn Museum and Sculpture Garden, Smithsonian Institution, Washington DC. Gift of Joseph H. Hirshhorn, 1972. ©1996 Estate of David Smith/Licensed by VAGA, New York, NY

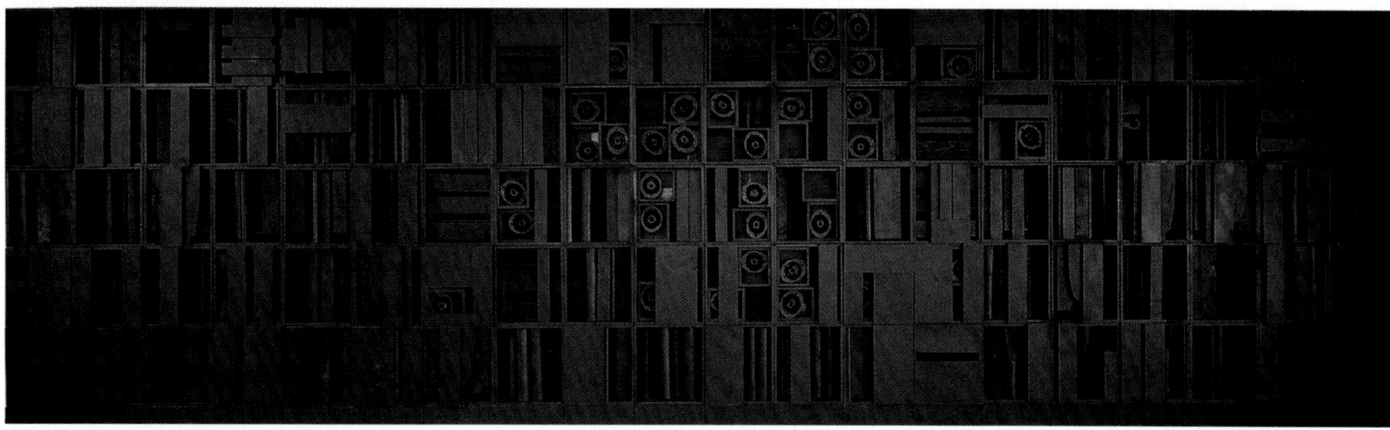

17–41 Identify the various shapes and trace how Nevelson uses their repetition to lead your eye around on the wall.
Louise Nevelson, *Homage to the World*, 1966. Wood, 107 1/2" (273 cm) high. The Detroit Institute of Arts.

Barbara Hepworth

(1903–1975)

Like Henry Moore, Barbara Hepworth was another English sculptor who worked with simplified forms. She created works in wood, bronze or marble. In *Assembly of Sea Forms* (fig.17–40), she used the traditional material of marble. However, she produced a contemporary effect by grouping the pieces to make the completed arrangement. The arrangement may be changed again and again, always producing another complete effect. When a viewer walks around the group, the relationships between each part and the whole change also. In this work, Hepworth has carved marble into the essence of sea forms: rocks, caves, eroded forms, pebbles and cliffs. The simplified units relate perfectly to each other in form and color. They unite to produce a marvelous group sculpture.

Louise Nevelson

(1900–1988)

Louise Nevelson experimented in the forties with all media. By the fifties, she found that her best expression was in wood. She filled boxes with found scraps, boards and pieces of old Victorian houses and arranged them in various configurations. Some were small and some huge, such as *Homage to the World* (fig.17–41). By painting everything a flat black, she unified the many different parts of the work. (Later, she painted them white and even gold.) This gigantic assemblage is an environmental sculpture that occupies two walls of a room.

In later years, Nevelson created an entire chapel of wood, painted white, inside a skyscraper in Manhattan. The chapel is a total environment of benches, walls, altar and vestments. She continued to work with wood into the seventies. But she also added Cor-Ten steel, lucite and aluminum to her list of materials. She produced gigantic outdoor as well as indoor works. A square in New York City is named for her and contains seven mammoth steel sculptures, up to 70 feet high. It is an exterior environmental group of huge proportions.

David Smith

(1906–1965)

David Smith was one of the first American sculptors to weld steel into sculptural forms. He learned to work with metals by working in a locomotive plant and automobile factory. In the late fifties and early sixties, he developed a series of powerful images based on cubes. He welded cubes of various sizes and proportions from stainless steel. The hollow forms were assembled in a variety of combinations and burnished to produce a slightly textured surface. These reflective planes on his geometric structures pleased him because "the surfaces were lightened and unified with the atmosphere." He titled the twenty-eight-piece series *Cubi*. The illustration is *Cubi XII* (fig.17–42). Smith was in a highly productive period of his life when he died in an automobile accident.

Lesson 17.5 Review

1 Where is Isamu Noguchi's *Great Rock of Inner Seeking*? What is its mood or feeling? Of what Asian cultures is the viewer reminded?

2 Write three words that come to mind as you view Henry Moore's *Sheep Piece*. What nationality is Moore?

3 What is unusual about Barbara Hepworth's *Assembly of Sea Forms*?

4 How did Louise Nevelson create unity in her sculpture *Homage to the World*?

5 With what medium did David Smith create? Where did he learn to use these materials? Write a sentence describing *Cubi XII*.

17.6 New Directions

It is extremely hard to define art from the 1960s to the present. So many of the new directions are a far cry from the sculptures, paintings or photographs of the past. The variety of work and the experimental attitude of the artists defy easy classification.

In *Kinetic Art*, sculptors work with materials and motors to create pieces that literally move. Artists use light, sound, computers and electricity to bring their art to life. Videotapes, cinematography and animated film are the language of a new form called *intermedia*.

Artists also devise environments in which spectators participate. When they employ moving equipment to gouge designs in the western deserts, build circular jetties into lakes, or rearrange the ground into mounds, the result is known as *Earth Art*. Still other artists rely on words, diagrams or ideas to communicate concepts that they have in mind, but never intend to carry out. Since there is no finished object, their work is called *Concept Art*.

Artists also use laser beams, span huge valleys with curtains, spray plate glass, and organize mammoth ceramic projects. Finally, there are those who combine technology and art to examine ever-new avenues of expression. In truth, diversity is the only aspect that can be said to unite the many trends of recent decades.

Key Notes

- Art from the 1960s to the present day is so varied it defies classification.
- Kinetic art, intermedia, earth art, conceptual art and computer art are some of its expressions.
- The combination of technology and art opens up new vistas for artists.

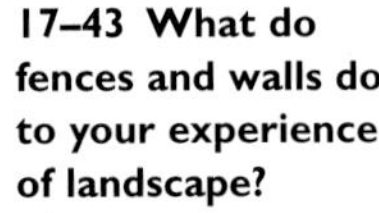

Special Feature

Christo and Jeanne Claude

(both b.1935)

Christo (Javacheff) was born in Bulgaria and lives in New York City with his wife, Jeanne Claude. Together, they have draped unusual objects in several parts of the world. The Christos take something familiar and wrap or curtain it. While wrapping something familiar might sound pretty ordinary, it becomes distinctly astonishing when you think of surrounding anything as large as eleven islands in Miami's Biscayne Bay in pink plastic. Christo and Jeanne Claude have wrapped a bridge (the Pont Neuf in

17–43 What do fences and walls do to your experience of landscape?
Christo and Jeanne Claude, *Running Fence*, 1972–1976. Nylon and cable, 18' (5.5 m) high, 24 1/2 miles (39 km) long. Sonoma and Marin Counties, California. Courtesy of the artists.

17–44 Different colors or new objects in unusual contexts cause us to experience our environment in a different way.
Christo and Jeanne Claude, *The Umbrellas: Japan–USA*, 1984–1991. Fabric, aluminum, paint, steel and concrete. Height including base 19'8 1/4" (6 m), diameter of umbrellas 28' 5" (8.66 m).

Paris), buildings (the German Reichstag), and one million square feet of the Australian coast.

In 1976, they completed *Running Fence* (fig.17–43), a 24 1/2-mile nylon curtain that snaked across California's Marin and Sonoma counties. The piece took four years to complete and, as in all their art, the Christos collaborated with public officials, scientists, environmentalists, artists, townspeople, farmers, construction workers, engineers, clothmakers and seamstresses. How do you feel about a project that cost three million dollars to assemble and was dismantled after several days? The Christos believe that their art is an event that is much more than the final installation. They begin a project with the initial idea, then sell drawings of the project to raise funds for it, and finally coordinate thousands of workers and various equipment to construct the piece itself.

In 1991, the Christos completed their most ambitious endeavor, *The Umbrellas: Japan–USA* (fig.17–44), involving huge areas in both countries. In the United States, the Christos carefully plotted 1760 six-meter-tall yellow umbrellas on grasslands and rolling hills along 17 1/2 miles of Interstate 5, about an hour north of Los Angeles. In Japan, the Christos zigzagged 1340 blue umbrellas for 11 1/2 miles through small towns and farm country just outside of Tokyo. Can you imagine suddenly coming upon one of these sites unexpectedly? The sheer drama of the Christos' installation caused millions of viewers to appreciate their environment in new ways.

Lucas Samaras

(b.1936)

Lucas Samaras has a strong interest in constructing environments, and his *Mirrored Room #2* (fig.17–45) is a prime example. What would it feel like to walk through the door into this many-mirrored space? Where does the floor begin and the tables, walls and ceiling end? The sparkling reflections fragment our vision and trick our senses. There is a sensation of being suspended in space. Samaras integrates the art with outside space by placing mirrors along its exterior that reflect and blend with the surrounding environment.

Dan Flavin

(b.1933)

Instead of paint and canvas, Dan Flavin uses fluorescent lights as his medium. He forms fluorescent lights into abstract geometric shapes, which he then mounts on the walls, floors or ceilings of his environments. Flavin's *Untitled* (fig.17–46) is a two-wall arrangement of circular tubes. The soft, warm light creates an inviting space for us to enter. Light sculptures such as these are best viewed in a darkened environment to sense the original glowing character envisioned by the artist.

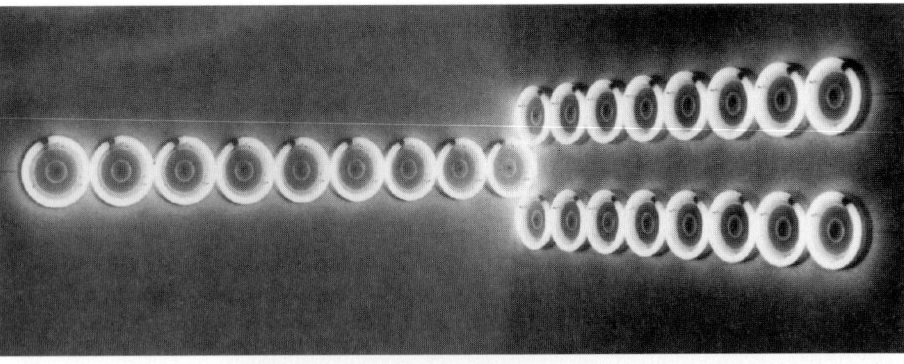

17–46 During the 1960s, many artists began experimenting with lighting as a medium. Flavin has continued to explore the limitations and possibilities of light art.
Dan Flavin, *Untitled,* 1975. Daylight, warm fluorescent light, wall #1: 11 3/4" x 96" (30 x 244 cm); wall #2: 33 3/4" x 96" (86 x 244 cm). Leo Castelli Gallery, New York.

17–45 The artist mounted mirrors on a wooden framework. When a spectator moves into the mirrored environment, there is a sensation of being suspended in space.
Lucas Samaras, *Mirrored Room #2,* 1966. Wood and mirror, 96" x 119 1/4" x 96" (2.44 x 3.03 x 2.44 m). Pace Gallery, New York.

Judy Chicago

(b.1939)

Judy Chicago works in many directions with her art, but is always involved in advancing the cause of women's rights. Her monumental work of 1979 is a gigantic triangular table arrangement called *The Dinner Party* (fig.17–c). Each of the thirty-nine place settings, designed in glazed ceramic and set on an embroidered, handwoven cloth, represents a great, often unrecognized woman in Western history. The ceramic-tile floor below holds the names of 999 additional heroines.

1989
Tian'anmen Square student uprising, China

1995
Sons of Ramses II tombs found in Egypt

World Cultural Timeline

1992
South Africa votes to end apartheid

1994
Israeli-Jordanian peace accord signed

1994
Nelson Mandela elected president of South Africa

Chicago worked in the tradition of women's communal sewing bees, conceiving of the project herself and then relying on the assistance of many volunteers and employees to complete her ambitious task.

Earlier, Chicago painted *Reincarnation Triptych,* three paintings that express the dynamic characteristics of women whose lives are important to her. For *Virginia Woolf* (fig.17–47), Chicago sprayed acrylic paint over stencils to produce the resulting pattern. She added a forty-word statement about Woolf around the border. Chicago's ideas, based upon her personal philosophy of life, are as expressionistic as they are stimulating. Her art defies easy categorization.

17–47 The artist makes a point in all her work of educating the viewer about the role of women in history and art.
Judy Chicago, *Virginia Woolf.* Sprayed acrylic on canvas. 59 3/4" x 59 3/4" (152 x 152 cm). Through the Flower, Albuquerque, New Mexico.

Sidelight

Censorship and the Arts

In general, artists should be able to make any kind of work they like. This is called artistic freedom, and any restrictions on the Constitutionally protected right of free expression amount to censorship. However, when a federal agency or any public commission funds artists whose work may be considered offensive by the viewing public, problems arise.

Nudity is often considered offensive, as in the case of Tom Otterness's 1991 sculpture, *The New World,* commissioned by the General Services Administration (GSA) for a new Los Angeles courthouse and federal building. Otterness's 300-foot-long pergola included a few nude figures. The central statue was a nude baby girl holding a globe. Once the sculpture was installed, there were protests from judges who work in the building. Two offending sections of the piece were removed and put in storage. However, the censorship resulted in widespread press attention, and the GSA agreed to reinstall the pieces.

John Ahearn, *Corey.* Bronze, formerly in front of the 44th Precinct in the Bronx. Lifesize.

John Ahearn's sculptures, however, have not been as fortunate. In 1991, three life-size painted bronze figures were put on pedestals in front of the 44th Precinct Police Headquarters in the Bronx. The statues were funded by the New York City percent-for-art program, which puts aside about one percent of any money for a new public building for the buying of artworks. Using neighborhood people as models, Ahearn depicted a girl on roller skates, a basketball player with a boom box, and a squatting teen wearing a hooded sweatshirt and holding a pit bull. The work underwent a community review and was approved. However, once the sculptures were in place, community residents complained that pit bulls and boom boxes are negative stereotypes. Ahearn voluntarily removed his sculptures and the works are currently in storage.

17–48 Grooms fills entire rooms with papier-mâché figures and objects painted in vivid, sometimes clashing colors.
Red Grooms, *Ruckus Rodeo*, 1980. Sculpture wire, celastic, acrylic, canvas and burlap, 174" x 606" x 294" (442 x 1539 x 747 cm). Commissioned by the Modern Art Museum of Fort Worth. Museum purchase with funds from the National Endowment for the Arts and the Benjamin J. Tillar Memorial Trust.

Red Grooms

(b.1937)

Red Grooms works like no other living artist, although he was an abstract expressionist in his early years. He calls his papier-mâché environments "sculpto-pictoramas," and these colorful installations completely engulf us as we walk through them. Grooms combines sculpture, construction and painting to produce pieces that overflow with detail, exaggerated perspective, verbal and visual puns, and cartoonlike figures. Can you sense the roar and excitement of the crowd inside *Ruckus Rodeo* (fig.17–48)? Grooms spends an average of four months on each project, with some taking up to a year to complete. The artist also makes films, watercolors, prints, oils, drawings, bronzes and mechanized constructions.

Nancy Graves

(b.1940)

As a child, Nancy Graves wandered behind the scenes in Massachusetts' Berkshire Museum, where her father was on staff. She was particularly fascinated by the laboratories that created dioramas and taxidermy habitats. "Later the process of transformation became integral to my own...process...where art and the natural sciences are merged."

Her work *II-11-94* (fig.17–49) is a melding of science and the natural world. The huge starfish and flower dance together at the base, while manufactured items help complete the Z-like form. There are bits of grating and machine parts. A bulging cone of an old-fashioned hand juicer echoes the huge blue blossom below. Graves interjects nature once again with her translucent glass swirl that carries our glance up and out, as though translating the wind into visible form. Her delicate balance of shape, color and texture establishes an overall lyrical quality that defies the actual weight of the metal sculpture. With the exception of the handblown glass, Graves casts all her natural and manufactured objects in bronze.

New Frontiers

In recent years, artists have investigated an astounding multitude of concerns and styles. It is difficult, if not impossible, to identify all of the diverse trends, let alone to predict which ones will be considered important in the future. Artists are currently redefining Abstraction, Realism and Expressionism. They are challenging age-old traditions, exploring global politics and personal beliefs, and also examining the impact of ever-advancing technology on the modern world.

The question of why art has exploded in all these directions at once is both interesting and perplexing. Is this unbridled creativity an outgrowth of the endless possibilities emerging from current technology? Is art simply reflecting the revolutionary spirit that is changing the way people all over the world think, work and communicate? On the other hand, perhaps we are witnessing the storm that will soon give way to a more discernible future. Undoubtedly, artists' knowledge of the past and current experiences of new frontiers greatly enrich their many and diverse expressions.

It is vitally important to approach contemporary art with a sense of inquiry. What is this? How was it made? What does it mean to me? Did the artist perhaps have a different intention? Often, today's artists are concerned not with creating something pretty, but rather with having us consider what we see and what we believe.

17–50 Words are an integral part of the images that this artist creates. Do you think the words provide you with more information about the piece, or do they raise questions in your mind?
Barbara Kruger, *Untitled (We Don't Need Another Hero)*, 1987. Photographic silkscreen/vinyl. Mary Boone Gallery, New York.

Barbara Kruger

(b.1945)

What could be more innocent than a picture of Dick and Jane from the children's reading book that Barbara Kruger uses in *Untitled* (fig.17–50)? Look at Jane's adoring admiration of Dick's bulging preadolescent biceps. But how do Kruger's carefully chosen words, borrowed from Tina Turner's popular song for the movie *Mad Max*, put another possible spin on the piece? Whose voice is making this statement? Does the work's meaning change if you hear the sentence said by a man or a woman? Do the words contradict the stereotypical images of boys and girls usually seen in society?

Kruger typically prints ambiguous statements over familiar imagery as a means of questioning the anonymous authoritarian voice in countless media and advertising campaigns. But her seemingly amusing juxtapositions are also alarming. They jolt us into recognizing how easily we accept these seductive messages, which make us want, buy or believe in nearly anything without so much as a second thought. Perhaps Kruger's skill at criticizing the media's ability to manipulate an unthinking public comes from her early success at *Mademoiselle* magazine, where she worked as chief designer when she was only twenty-two.

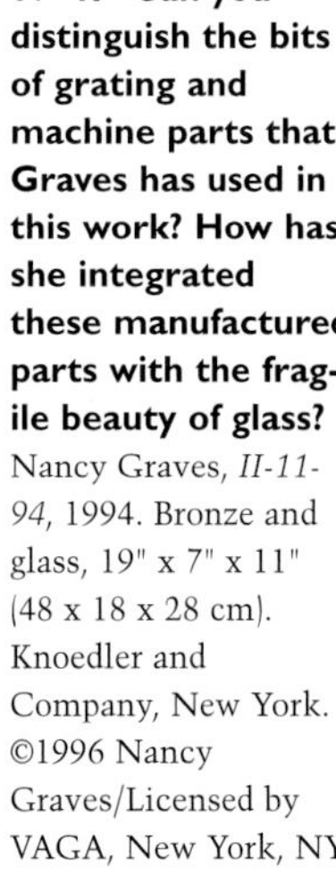

17–49 Can you distinguish the bits of grating and machine parts that Graves has used in this work? How has she integrated these manufactured parts with the fragile beauty of glass?
Nancy Graves, *II-11-94*, 1994. Bronze and glass, 19" x 7" x 11" (48 x 18 x 28 cm). Knoedler and Company, New York. ©1996 Nancy Graves/Licensed by VAGA, New York, NY

Window in Time

Computers and Art

The amazing range of things that computers can do has not been lost on artists. In recent years a whole new computer art form has developed. The origins of computer art can be traced back to 1952 when Ben F. Laposky, in the United States, used an analogic computer and a cathode tube oscillograph for the composition of his *Electronic Abstractions*. In 1956 he followed this up with the creation of a colored electronic image.

Since that time computer art has expanded considerably. In 1993 an International Festival of the Image was put on in Rochester, New York, as part of Montage '93. To reach a broad audience, sixteen group and solo exhibitions were placed in diverse locations, such as a shopping mall and the inner city, to show how art using new technologies can touch different audiences.

The artists involved tackled all kinds of subjects and used the computer in very different ways. Artist Alan Rath gave a riveting account of the *Challenger* space shuttle disaster. A sequence of black-and-white still images on seven monitors traced the development of the Apollo space program up to the 1986 shuttle launch. With flashing LED signs, bouncing ping-pong balls and intermittently blinking lights, Rath evoked the deadly explosion. At the same time, recorded phrases from the media coverage of the disaster were played, such as "technology triumphed," "What went wrong?" and "felt every one of them were my sons and daughter."

Esther Parada, another artist in the festival, began her two-dimensional exhibit with a turn-of-the-century photograph of a Spanish monument in Cuba and her own photographic portraits made in Latin America. Then she scanned, digitized and electronically overlaid the images with text about the European conquest of the Western Hemisphere. Presented as large, color ink-jet prints, her composites attained a great sense of spatial depth through their rich tonal values and the layering of images and typography. The message she was attempting to convey was that cultural identity comes about as a result of similar layering.

In an exhibition of her work at the Julie Saul Gallery in Manhattan, also in 1993, Penelope Umbrico showed yet a different use of the computer. Trained as a painter, Umbrico now uses photography almost exclusively. Umbrico began by photographing ordinary household objects either in blurred motion or out of focus, against a color background. She then scanned the images into a computer and manipulated them until she achieved wildly colorful abstractions. These abstractions were then turned into color prints. *Untitled (computer drawings)* is made up of 196 color prints, each approximately 8 1/2" by 6 1/2". The individual images are amoeba-like blobs, which Umbrico produced by cutting each photograph in half, then rejoining its pieces in a new orientation so as to create a new shape.

Incredible sleight-of-hand is also made possible by the computer. This was very ably demonstrated in Richard W. Maile's *Birth of Elvis*, shown at the Siggraph '90 exhibition in Dallas in August 1990. He presented a digital image based on a reproduction of Botticelli's *The Birth of Venus*, but instead of the figure of Venus, Maile substituted a digitally integrated image of Elvis Presley.

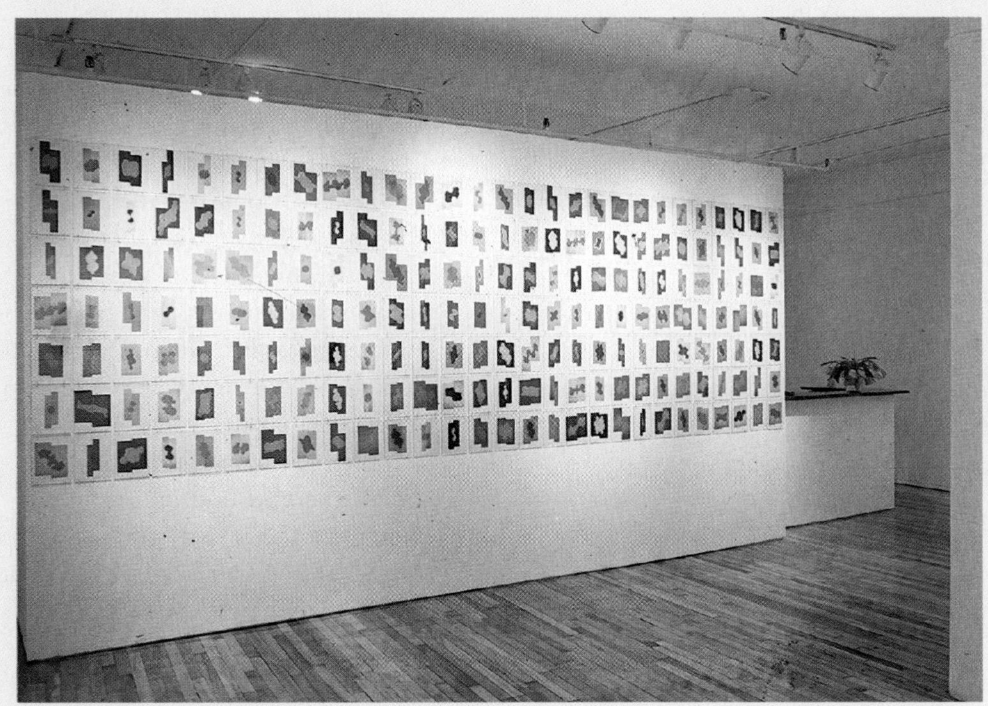

Penelope Umbrico, Exhibition Installation, March 27–May 1, 1993. Julie Saul Gallery, New York.

Jaune Quick-to-See Smith

(b.1940)

Jaune Quick-to-See Smith deliberately uses references to her own Salish, Shoshone and French Cree descent to fight centuries of misconceptions and misrepresentations about the first inhabitants of North America. Her art captures the stinging reality of the discrimination and hardships that many Native Americans have experienced in the United States.

Smith's *I See Red: Ten Little Indians* (fig.17–51) recalls the popular children's nursery rhyme of the same name. Yet, the inclusion of only four figures alludes to the appalling death rate of young native children during her growing-up years. "By all odds, I should not be here today. In 1940, when I was born, one in ten children survived."

Smith writes the rhyme in Salish across notebook paper and a chalkboard, confronting the mistaken belief that native peoples had no written language. At the same time, the classroom image refers to the efforts of government and missionary schools earlier in this century to erase Native American children's sense of heritage. The children were severely punished for speaking their tribal tongues or honoring ancient customs.

17–51 What does the phrase "Ten Little Indians" mean to you? Read the text for a better understanding of the artist's intent.
Jaune Quick-to-See Smith, *I See Red: Ten Little Indians*, 1992. Mixed media, collage on paper. 41 1/2" x 29 1/2" (105.5 x 75 cm). Steinbaum Krauss Gallery, New York.

Edward Kienholz

(1927–1994)

Edward Kienholz used the three-dimensional space of his stage-like environments to draw us into his shockingly personal dramas. What is the "wait" that he refers to in the title (fig.17–52)? Can you guess how this old woman feels? Where are the friends and family whose pictures she has gathered on the tabletop? The trinkets held in the woman's glass-jar necklace are remembrances from the past. In her last days, she clings to the cat for connection with another living being.

Kienholz learned carpentry, plumbing and engineering as a young boy on his family's farm in Washington State, and worked with his hands throughout his life. Kienholz included real objects in his constructed environments to create poignant scenes. Despite their departure from exact reality, they communicate their emotions quite strongly.

17–52 What is this woman waiting for?
Edward Kienholz, *The Wait*, 1964–65. Tableau, 80" x 148" x 78" (203 x 376 x 198 cm). Collection of Whitney Museum of American Art, New York, gift of the Howard and Jean Lipman Foundation, Inc.

17–53 This image documents an event in which the artist spent one week with a coyote in a New York art gallery. Why might the artist have taken this action? Compare your ideas with the reason given in the text.
Joseph Beuys, *I Like America and America Likes Me*, 1974. Performance at Rene Block Gallery, NY, May 23–25, 1974. Courtesy Ronald Feldman Fine Arts, New York.

Joseph Beuys

(1921–1986)

Joseph Beuys decided to dedicate himself to the future of humanity after being shot down as a Nazi pilot in a remote region of Crimea and, subsequently, being saved by Tartars. Beuys' primary outlet became his socially motivated Performance Art. Performance Art is a form similar to theater, but the artist becomes an integral and active ingredient in the work itself. A great deal of Performance Art's impact comes from its shock value, expressed by irreverent humor, incongruity or explicit sexuality.

In *How to Explain Pictures to the Dead Hare*, Beuys covered his head with honey and gold leaf in order to resemble a sculpture. Then, he cradled a dead rabbit in his arms while discussing a painting with the creature. Beuys felt that "a hare comprehends more than many human beings with their stubborn rationalism."

In 1974, Beuys spent a week with a coyote in a New York art gallery (fig.17–53) in order to draw attention to how the animal, which is held sacred by a number of Native American tribes, was being persecuted by white society. He hoped that this event would help heal the rift between two opposing cultures within a single nation.

Jennifer Bartlett

(b.1941)

What happens when nature and the human-made world collide? In *Spiral: An Ordinary Evening in New Haven* (fig.17–b), Jennifer Bartlett explodes the backyard scene, sending birds, fish, tables, pots and chairs flying in all directions. But, do the bright hot flames singe even a single object? For all its destructive potential, Bartlett's fire generates enormous energy without so much as causing a single burn. Her title makes us wonder why she says there is anything "ordinary" about this evening event.

How might it feel to wander among the huge three-dimensional cones and red hexagon tables on the floor that imitate the painted images? Bartlett includes us in her work by encroaching on our own physical space. Since we share the stage with the installation, our entire bodies and not just our minds fully engage in the experience. Bartlett has been surrounding viewers with her investigations of simple, single themes since the 1970s. Her works are always based on recognizable elements. However, the repetition and manipulation of particular images infuse an abstract component into her final pieces.

Lesson 17.6 Review

1 Describe one of the Christos' projects. How do you feel about this creation?
2 Describe Judy Chicago's *The Dinner Party*. What cause does the artist support in this art?
3 What type of art does Red Grooms create? Name some materials he uses in his art.
4 What are some questions the viewer should consider when approaching contemporary art?
5 What are some of the symbols and messages in Jaune Quick-to-See Smith's *I See Red: Ten Little Indians*?
6 Explain what you think *The Wait* means in Edward Kienholz's environment? What are some clues to the woman's feelings?
7 What event in Joseph Beuys' life motivated him to be concerned about the future of humanity?
8 Do you see any similarities in themes shared by some of the art in this New Frontiers section?

Primary Source

"...I wanted to be an artist."

In order to appreciate some forms of contemporary art, it is helpful to hear what artists have to say about their work. Artists speak about their intent, events and people that influenced their art, their relationship with their culture, and why they have selected a particular style, theme or technique.

Other artists refuse to discuss their intentions saying that what you see is what you see and each work's meaning is unique to the viewer.

Jennifer Bartlett:
"I always told everyone I wanted to be an artist. I want to move people. I'd like to be a strong, heartbreaking artist."

Jackson Pollock:
"Most of the paint I use is liquid, flowing...the brushes are used more as sticks and do not touch the surface...I'm able to be more free...and move about...with greater ease...it seems to be possible to control the flow of paint to a greater extent...I deny the accident...I have a general notion of what I'm about and what the results will be...I approach painting in the same sense one approaches drawing, that is it's direct..."

Jaune Quick-to-See Smith:
"I knew I was an artist before I knew the word or the meaning. As a child, I lived on several reservations in very remote places. I didn't have store-bought toys so I entertained myself with whatever was at hand such as rocks, ferns, and dirt. In the woods or field I blotted out a world I didn't know how to deal with and created a small world I could manage."

Chapter Review

Review

1 Compare the brushstrokes and design in Diebenkorn's *Cityscape I* with Hofmann's *Flowering Swamp*. What is the mood of each?

2 How are Picasso's and Braque's collages like Rauschenberg's combine paintings? How are they different?

3 Study Robert Rauschenberg's *First Landing Jump*. What looks like abstract expressionism? What seems more like Pop Art?

4 How are the sculptures of George Segal and Claus Oldenburg alike?

5 Helen Frankenthaler was a friend of Jackson Pollock. What are the differences and similarities in their methods of painting?

6 What are some other terms for Color Field Painting? Which term do you think describes this style best? Explain why.

7 Jackson Pollock studied with both Thomas Hart Benton and Hans Hofmann. Which artist do you think was more influential to his mature painting style?

Interpret

1 Rank the art movements—Abstract Expressionism, Pop Art, Op Art and Color Field Painting—from most emotional to least emotional. (You might want to refer to the chart on page 67).

2 Analyze *Christina's World* by Andrew Wyeth. What is the subject? What medium did he use? Describe the colors, contrasts, and textures. What is the mood? What is the center of interest? Is the balance symmetrical or asymmetrical? How does the artist direct your eye through the picture? Explain why you like or dislike this painting.

3 Compare Richard Estes' *Drugstore* with Edward Hopper's *Nighthawks*. What is the mood in each? How does each artist see the city? Which is more realistic?

4 Which artist in this chapter do you think creates the most realistic art? Use an example of this artist's work in your explanation of your choice.

Other Tools for Learning

Timelines

Consider how familiar you are with the international events on the timelines in this chapter. Do you think your counterparts 100 years ago would have been equally aware of events across the globe? Why or why not?

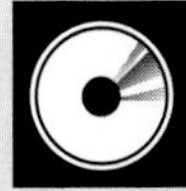

Electronic Research

Videodisc player: *National Gallery of Art*

1 After looking at several works by Henry Moore or David Smith, describe several characteristics that are found in most of the artist's sculptures.

Activity 1

Sculpting with Cloth

Materials

newspaper
pencils
tape
cloth, vinyl (various colors)
needles
thread
foam rubber pillow filling

Take a look.

- Fig.17–10, Claes Oldenburg. *Installation of One-Man Show,* 1970.
- Fig.17–11, Claes Oldenburg. *Shoestring Potatoes Spilling from a Bag.*

Think about it. Change, innovation, and a quest for personal expression have led artists to create art in new and extremely diverse directions. Study the works of contemporary artist Claes Oldenburg, who views the manufactured world around us with a unique and imaginative perspective.

Do it. Design a large soft sculpture using vinyl material, cloth, and foam rubber pillow filling. For example, you might wish to create an artist's palette. The curved palette, exaggerated in size, would include a large hole for the thumb, with large cloth circles sewn onto the vinyl representing the paint colors.

- Select the object you wish to sculpt. Do a few rough sketches from more than one angle to consider how it will look three-dimensionally.
- Draw the object on newsprint at the size you wish to produce it. (In sewing, this is called making a pattern.) If there are pieces in different colors to be added, draw these also. Draw each side of your object to size.
- Fit the pieces together, perhaps holding them together with tape to see if it works. Make any adjustments.
- Lay each piece of the pattern on selected cloth and cut. Sew the pieces together and stuff with foam rubber filling.

Check it.

Is your finished sculpture recognizable as the object you selected? Have you sewn your work together such that the stitches are not distracting? Does your work look "finished"?

Helpful Hint: Choose a common, everyday object and see if you can enlarge it at least ten times its actual size. Have the object in front of you as you work, if possible, so you are working from observations, not memory.

Activity 2

Mimic the Masters

Materials

tempera paints/paper
or acrylic paints/canvas
brushes
water containers

Take a look.

- Fig.17–3, Jackson Pollock. *No. 1, 1950 (Lavender Mist).*
- Fig.17–13, Roy Lichtenstein. *Masterpiece,* 1962.
- Fig.17–14, Andy Warhol. *100 Cans,* 1962.
- Fig.17–21, Helen Frankenthaler. *The Bay,* 1963.
- Fig.17–26, Frank Stella. *Protractor Variation,* 1969.
- Fig.17–29, Morris Louis. *Point of Tranquility,* 1958.

Think about it. Review the work of contemporary artists listed above. Which style do you find most interesting? Why?

Do it. Make a tempera or acrylic painting in the style of one of the following artists (or others of your choice). Use your own design, but work in that artist's style.

- Jackson Pollock: drip painting
- Roy Lichtenstein: current, simple comic style and colored dots
- Andy Warhol: repetition of forms using stencils
- Helen Frankenthaler or Morris Louis: flowing shapes
- Frank Stella: symmetrical designs created with a protractor

Check it.

Pair up with a friend and ask him or her to identify what aspects of style you've adopted and from which artist. Then do the same in response to your friend's work.

Helpful Hints:

Choose as your subject an object that has special meaning for you.

Additional Activities

- Compare the realistic sculpture of Duane Hanson to the monumental abstract works by sculptor Henry Moore. Are they both appealing to you? Explain your reactions. Consider the approach each artist has taken.
- Do a silkscreen self-portrait in the style of Pop artist Andy Warhol.
- Imagine yourself a young Renaissance artist who drops into a contemporary gallery in New York, London, Los Angeles or Paris. If you were a student of Raphael's, how would you feel? Which artists might you enjoy? With what aspects of twentieth century art could you identify? What types of art would be very disturbing to you? Explain why. Could you ever become comfortable in the twentieth century? Why or why not?

Student Profile

Chris Byrd

Age 18
Lake Highlands High School
Dallas, Texas
Favorite kinds of art: Cubism, Abstract
Favorite artists: Max Weber, Juan Gris
Activity 2, Mimic the Masters

I have a fondness for guitars and the music they produce, because I play and enjoy listening to it. From my earlier work progressed to cubism and contemporary styles, using Lichtenstein. The dots and the lines gave this piece more energy and excitement similar to the music. I like this piece because the dots and the lines have created an extension of my cubistic style.

In addition to Picasso, Max Weber has also influenced my work. I tried to separate parts of my art and put them back together in different ways. Weber used patterns in his backgrounds as well as Lichtenstein.

I enjoy distorting the objects, and pushing them to their limits. I also enjoy experimenting and exploring with different media to create many different textures on one surface.

Some advice I have for other students is explore and create with many media, styles and techniques to express themselves.

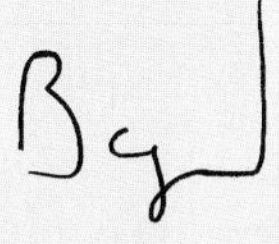

Christina Vicki Ramirez

Age 18
Eastwood High School
El Paso, Texas
Favorite kind of art: Surrealism
Favorite artist: Salvador Dali
Activity 1, Sculpting with Cloth

My project is a soft sculpture of a tennis shoe. I decided to make a tennis shoe, particularly a Converse type tennis shoe, because Converse tennis shoes are so classic. I decided to try and capture that feeling I get when I wear them. I love shoes and think Converse are the one type of shoe that ties everyone together. It doesn't matter what race, sex or any other quality; everyone looks good in them.

My favorite part about the artistic process is the creative process. The area open to the imagination is so vast. You can do anything you want to and there's always going to be someone who likes it. My best advice for other students would be to follow what you want to do because in art nothing is ever right or wrong. It's all up to you.

Christina Vicki Ramirez

Tres Guitars, 1994. Oil, 40 1/2" x 32" (103 x 81 cm).

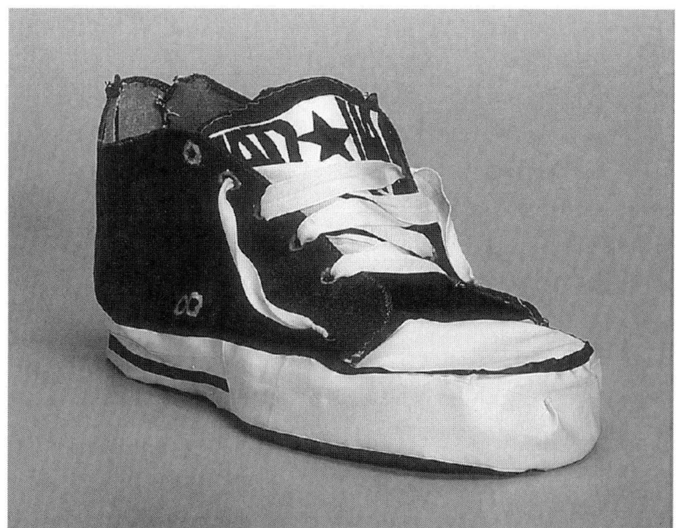

Christina's Shoe, 1994. Fabric and foam stuffing, about 30" x 15" (76 x 38 cm).

Reference

John Frederick Peto, *Job Lot Cheap* (Still Life with Books), detail, after 1900. Oil on canvas, 30" x 40" (76 x 101.7 cm). San Francisco Art Museums.

Map of Today's World

The best way to see what the world looks like is to look at a globe. The problem of accurately depicting the earth on a flat surface has challenged mapmakers for centuries. This map, called a Robinson projection, is designed to show the earth in one piece, while maintaining the shape of the land and size relationships as much as possible. However, any world map has distortions.

This map is also called a *political* map, showing the names and boundaries of countries as they existed at the time of its creation. Political maps, of necessity, change every year as new countries develop. Some of the maps in this book are *physical,* showing where mountain ranges and rivers exist, while some maps combine both physical and political features.

Key to Abbreviations

ALB.	**Albania**
AUS.	**Austria**
B.–H.	**Bosnia–Hercegovina**
BELG.	**Belgium**
CRO.	**Croatia**
CZ REP.	**Czech Republic**
EQ. GUINEA	**Equatorial Guinea**
HUNG.	**Hungary**
LEB.	**Lebanon**
LITH.	**Lithuania**
LUX.	**Luxembourg**
MAC.	**Macedonia**
NETH.	**Netherlands**
RUS.	**Russia**
SLOV.	**Slovenia**
SLVK.	**Slovakia**
SWITZ.	**Switzerland**
YUGO.	**Yugoslavia**

GREENLAND (KALAALLIT NUNAAT) (Den.)
Arctic Ocean
ICELAND
NORWAY
SWEDEN
FINLAND
ESTONIA
LATVIA
LITH.
RUS.
UNITED KINGDOM
IRELAND
DENMARK
NETH.
GERMANY
POLAND
BELARUS
BELG.
LUX.
CZ. REP.
SLVK.
UKRAINE
FRANCE
AUS.
HUNG.
MOLDOVA
SWITZ.
SLOV.
ROMANIA
CRO.
YUGO.
B.-H.
BULGARIA
ITALY
ALB.
MAC.
GREECE
PORTUGAL
SPAIN
AZORES (Port.)
MALTA
TUNISIA
TURKEY
GEORGIA
ARMENIA
AZERBAIJAN
CYPRUS
SYRIA
LEB.
ISRAEL
IRAQ
JORDAN
KUWAIT
BAHRAIN
QATAR
SAUDI ARABIA
UNITED ARAB EMIRATES
OMAN
YEMEN
IRAN
MOROCCO
CANARY IS. (Sp.)
WESTERN SAHARA (Mor.)
ALGERIA
LIBYA
EGYPT
MAURITANIA
CAPE VERDE
SENEGAL
MALI
NIGER
CHAD
SUDAN
ERITREA
DJIBOUTI
GAMBIA
GUINEA-BISSAU
GUINEA
NIGERIA
BENIN
TOGO
SIERRA LEONE
LIBERIA
CÔTE D'IVOIRE
BURKINA FASO
GHANA
CAMEROON
EQ. GUINEA
CENTRAL AFRICAN REP.
ETHIOPIA
SOMALIA
UGANDA
KENYA
CONGO
RWANDA
ZAIRE
BURUNDI
TANZANIA
GABON
SÃO TOMÉ & PRÍNCIPE
ANGOLA
ZAMBIA
MALAWI
COMOROS
SEYCHELLES
MADAGASCAR
MAURITIUS
RÉUNION (Fr.)
NAMIBIA
ZIMBABWE
BOTSWANA
MOZAMBIQUE
SWAZILAND
SOUTH AFRICA
LESOTHO
RUSSIA
KAZAKHSTAN
UZBEKISTAN
TURKMENISTAN
KYRGYZSTAN
TAJIKISTAN
AFGHANISTAN
PAKISTAN
MONGOLIA
CHINA
N. KOREA
S. KOREA
JAPAN
NEPAL
BHUTAN
BANGLADESH
INDIA
MYANMAR (BURMA)
LAOS
THAILAND
VIETNAM
CAMBODIA
TAIWAN
PHILIPPINES
MALDIVES
SRI LANKA
BRUNEI
MALAYSIA
SINGAPORE
INDONESIA
PAPUA NEW GUINEA
Pacific Ocean
NORTHERN MARIANA IS. (U.S.)
GUAM (U.S.)
MARSHALL ISLANDS
PALAU
FEDERATED STATES OF MICRONESIA
KIRIBATI
NAURU
TUVALU
SOLOMON IS.
VANUATU
FIJI
NEW CALEDONIA (Fr.)
Indian Ocean
AUSTRALIA
NEW ZEALAND
ANTARCTICA

Pronunciation Guide for Artists' Names

Italicized syllables are accented.

Abramovitz, Max ah-*bram*-oh-vits
Adams, Ansel *ad*-ams, *an*-sull
Aeschylus *ess*-kul-luss
Aguilar, Rosalie *ah*-gwee-lar, *rose*-ah-lee
Alberti al-*bair*-tee
Angelico, Fra an-*jay*-lee-co, frah
Anuskiewicz, Richard an-*nu*-skah-vich
Anguissola, Sofanisba ahng-gwee-*soh*-lah, soh-fahn-*eez*-bah
Areogun *are*-ee-oh-gun
Arp, Jean (Hans) arp, zhahn (hahns)

Baciccio, Giovanni Battista bah-*chee*-chee-oh, jo-*vahn*-ee bah-*tee*-stah
Barlach, Ernst *bahr*-lock, airnst
Bellini, Giovanni bel-*lee*-nee, jo-*vahn*-nee
Bernini, Gianlorenzo bair-*nee*-nee, jahn-low-*rens*-oh
Beuys, Joseph boyss, *yo*-zef
Bierstadt, Albert *beer*-staht
Boccioni, Umberto bot-cho-nee, oom-*bair*-toe
Bologna, Giovanni boh-*loh*-nyah, jo-*vahn*-nee
Bonheur, Rosa bon-*err*
Boromini, Francesco bore-oh-*mee*-nee, fran-*chess*-co
Bosch, Hieronymus bosh, heer-*ahn*-ni-mus
Botero, Fernando boh-*tay*-roh, fair-*nahn*-doh
Botticelli, Sandro bot-tee-*chel*-lee, *sand*-ro
Boucher, Francois boo-*shay*, fran-*swah*
Brancusi, Constantin bran-*coo*-zee, *con*-stan-tin
Braque, Georges brahk, zhorzh
Bruegel, Pieter *brue*-gl, *pee*-ter
Brunelleschi, Filippo brew-nell-*less*-key, fee-*leep*-poh
Buonarroti, Michelangelo bwoh-na-*roh*-tee, mee-kel-*an*-jay-loh
Burgee, John bur-*ghee*

Campin, Robert cahm-*peh*, roh-*bair*
Canaletto, Antonio can-ah-*let*-toe, an-*toe*-nee-oh
Caravaggio car-ah-*vah*-jyoh
Cartier Bresson, Henri car-*tyay* bre-*sohn*, ahn-*ree*
Cassatt, Mary cah-*saht*
Cellini, Benvenuto chel-*lee*-nee, ben-vay-*noo*-toe
Cézanne, Paul say-*zahn*
Chagall, Marc sha-*gahl*
Chalgrin, J. F. shal-*gren*
Chardin, Jean Baptiste-Simeon shar-*da*, zhahn bah-*teest*-see-may-*on*
Chirico, Giorgio de *key*-ree-coh, *jor*-jyoh day
Christo *kriss*-toe
Claude Lorrain (Claude Gellée, zhuh-*lay*) klohd loh-*ren*
Clouet, Jean *cloo*-eh, zhahn
Copley, John Singleton *kop*-lee
Corbusier, Le kore-boo-zee-*ay*, leh
Corot, Jean-Baptiste-Camille ko-*roh*, zhahn-bah-*teest*-kah-*mee*-yuh
Courbet, Gustave koor-*bay*, goo-*stahv*
Cranach, Lucas crah-*nak* (soft), *loo*-kahs

Dali, Salvador *dah*-lee, *sahl*-vah-door
Daumier, Honoré doe-mee-*ay*, on-noh-*ray*
David, Jacques-Louis dah-*veed*, zjahk-loo-*ee*
Degas, Edgar day-*gah*, ed-*gahr*
Delacroix, Eugene dul-la-*krwah*, oo-*zhen*
DeKooning, Willem deh-*koon*-ing, *vil*-em
Demuth, Charles *day*-mooth,
Devereaux *dev*-er-roh
Diebenkorn, Richard *dee*-ben-korn
Donatello doe-nah-*tell*-oh
Duccio *doo*-chyoh
Duchamp, Marcel doo-*shahn*, mar-*sell*
Dürer, Albrecht *dur*-er, *ahl*-brecht

Eakins, Thomas *ay*-kins
Eiffel, Alexandre-Gustave *ee*-fel, al-ex-*andr*- goo-*stahv*
El Greco (Domenikos Theotocopoulos, thay-oh-toe-*coe*-poo-loss, doe-*may*-nee-coss) el *greh*-koh
Ernst, Max airnst
Estes, Richard *ess*-tess
van Eyck, Hubert fahn *ike*, *hoo*-bert
van Eyck, Jan fahn *ike*, yahn
Exekias ek-*sek*-ee-uhs

Fischer, Johann Michael *fish*-er, *yoh*-hahn
Flavin, Dan *flay*-vin
Fouquet, Jean foo-*kay*, zhahn
Fragonard, Jean-Honore fra-go-*nahr*, zhahn-oh-no-*reh*
Frankenthaler, Helen frank-en-*thal*-er

Garnier, Charles gahr-*nyay*, sharl
Gauguin, Paul go-*gen*
Gaulli, Giovanni Battista Francesco gah-*ool*-lee, jo-*vah*-nee bah-*tees*-tah fran-*chess*-koh
Gentile da Fabriano jen-*tee*-lay da fah-bree-*ah*-no
Gentileschi, Artemisia jen-teel-*ess*-key, ar-tay-*mee*-zee-ah
Gericault, Theodore *zhay*-ree-koh *tay*-oh-dor
Ghiberti, Lorenzo ghee-*bair*-tee, loh-*ren*-zoh
Giacometti, Alberto zhah-co-*met*-ee, al-*bair*-toe
Giotto *jot*-toe
Gislebertus geez-ul-*bair*-tuhs
Giorgione da Castelfranco jor-*joh*-nay dah cah-stell-*frank*-oh
van Gogh, Vincent vahn *go*, *vin*-sent
Gorky, Arshile *gor*-kee, *ar*-shil
Gottlieb, Adolph *got*-leeb, *ay*-dolf
Goujon, Jean goo-*zhahn*, zhahn
Goya, Francisco *goy*-ah, fran-*sis*-co
Gropius, Walter *grow*-pee-us
Grünewald, Mathias *groon*-eh-valt, mah-*tee*-ahs

Hals, Frans hahls, frahns
Hardouin-Mansart, Jules *are*-doo-ehn-mahn-sar zjool
Haussmann, Georges Eugene ohs-*mahn*, zjorzj oo-*zjehn*
Hasegawa Tohaku hah-seh-*gah*-wah, toe-*hah*-coo
Henri, Robert *hen*-rye
Herrera, Juan de er-*ray*-rah, wahn day
Hiroshige, Ando hear-oh-shee-gay, ahn-doe
Hokusai, Katsushika, ho-k'-sy, kaht-soo-she-ka
Holbein, Hans *hole*-bine, hahns
Houdon, Jean Antoine oo-*don*, zhahn an-*twahn*

Iktinus *ick*-tih-nus
Imhotep im-*hoh*-tep
Ingres, Jean-Auguste-Dominique aingr, zhahn-oh-*goost*-doh-min-*eek*
Isozaki, Arata ee-soh-zah-kee, ah-rah-tah

Jahn, Helmut yahn

Kallikrates kal-i-*crate*-ees
Kandinsky, Wassily kan-*dins*-key, *vahs*-i-lee
Kashani, Maqsud kah-shanee, mock-sud
Kienholz, Edward *keen*-hohlts
Kirchner, Ernst Ludwig *kear*-kner, airnst *lood*-vig
Klee, Paul clay
Klimt, Gustav klimt, *goo*-stahf
Kollwitz, Käthe *kahl*-vits, *kay*-teh
Ku K'ai-chih goo kai-juh

Lachaise, Gaston la-*shez*, ga-*ston*
Lange, Dorothea lang, dor-uh-*thee*-uh
Langhans, Karl *lahng*-hahns
La Tour, George de la-*toor*, zjorzj duh
Le Brun, Charles luh-*brun*, sharl
Leonardo da Vinci lay-oh-*nar*-doh dah *vin*-chee
Lescot, Pierre les-*koh*, pee-*air*
Leyster, Judith *lie*-stir, *you*-deet (jew-*dith*)
Lichtenstein, Roy *lick*-ten-stine
Lippi, Filippo *lip*-pee, fi-*lip*-po
Lysippus lie-*sip*-us

Ma Yuan ma you-an
Maderno, Carlo mah-*dair*-noh
Magritte, René mah-*greet*, ren-*ay*
Maillol, Aristide mah-*yahl*, ah-riss-*teed*
Manet, Edouard ma-*nay*, eh-doo-*are*
Mantegna, Andrea man-*ten*-ya, ahn-*dray*-ah
Marin, John *mar*-in
Martinez, Maria and Julian mar-*tee*-nez, *who*-lee-ahn
Martini, Simone mar-*tee*-nee, see-*moh*-nay
Masaccio ma-*zaht*-choh
Matisse, Henri mah-*teess*, ahn-*ree*
Medici, Lorenzo de *meh*-di-chee, loh-*ren*-zo day
Michelangelo mee-kel-*an*-jay-loh
Mies van der Rohe, Ludwig mees van der *roe*, *lood*-vig
Millet, Jean Francois mee-*lay*, zhahn fran-*swah*
Miro, Joan mee-*roh*, *joe*-on
Modersohn-Becker, Paula *moh*-der-sohn *bek*-ker
Modigliani, Amedeo moh-dee-lee-*ah*-nee, ah-may-*day*-oh
Mondrian, Piet *mohn*-dree-ahn, pate
Monet, Claude moh-*nay*, kload
Montenegro, Roberto mohn-tay-*nay*-groh, roh-*bair*-toe
Morisot, Berthe moh-ree-*zoh*, bairt
Mukhuba, Nelson muck-who-bah
Munch, Edvard moonk, *ed*-vard
Murillo, Bartholome Esteban moo-*ree*-yoh, bar-toh-loh-*may* *ess*-tay-bahn
Muybridge, Eadweard *my*-brij, *ed*-wurd

Niccolo dell' Arca *Knee*-Ko-lo dell *ar*-ka
Noguchi, Isamu noh-goo-chee, ees-sah-moo
Nolde, Emil *nohl*-deh, eh *meel*
Oeben, Jean Francois *ur*-buhn, zhahn frahn-swar
Oldenburg, Claes *old*-en-berg, klahss
Oppenheim, Meret *ahp*-uhn-hym, meh-*ray*
Orozco, José Clemente oh-*ross*-coh, ho-*say* cleh-*men*-tay

Palladio, Andrea pah-*lah*-dee-oh, an-*dray*-ah
Panini, Giovanni Paolo pah-*nee*-nee, jo-*vah*-nee *pah*-oh-loh
Peale, Raphaelle peel, *rah*-fay-ell
Pei, I.M. pay
Pelli, Cesar *pel*-lee, *say*-zar
Perrault, Claude pear-oh, klohd
Phidias *fid*-ee-us
Picasso, Pablo pee-*kahs*-oh, *pah*-blo
Pissarro, Camille pee-*sahr*-oh, cah-*meal*
Pollock, Jackson *poll*-lock
Poussin, Nicholas poo-*sahn*, *nick*-oh-lahs
Prandtauer, Jacob *pran*-tower, *yahk*-ob
Pugin, A. Welby *pyu*-jin

Raggi, Antonio *rah*-jee, an-*toe*-nee-oh
Raphael rah-fah-*ell*
Rauschenberg, Robert *rau*-shen-berg
Rembrandt van Rijn *rem*-brant van rhine
Renoir, Pierre Auguste ren-*wahr*, pee-*air* oh-*gust*
Riemenschneider, Tilman *reem*-en-shny-dr, *till*-mahn
Rietveld, Gerrit *reet*-velt, *gair*-it
Rivera, Diego ree-*vay*-rah, dee-*ay*-goh
Rodin, Auguste roh-*dan*, oh-*gust*
Rosenquist, James *roh*-zen-kwist
Rosso, Fiorentino *rohss-soh*, fyor-en-*tee*-noh
Rouault, Georges roo-*oh*, zjorzj
Rousseau, Henri roo-*soh*, ahn-*ree*
Rubens, Peter Paul *roo*-bens
Rude, Francoise rood, fran-*swahz*
Ruisdael, Jacob van *rwees*-dahl, *yah*-cob van
Ruysch, Rachel royss, rah-kel

Saarinen, Eero *sahr*-in-en, *air*-oh
Safdie, Moshe *sahf*-dee, *moh*-shuh
Samaras, Lucas sah-*mah*-ras, *loo*-kus
Schwitters, Kurt *schvit*-urs, kort
Seurat, Georges suh-*rah*, zjorzj
Shen Chou sun-joe
Siqueiros, David Alfaro see-*kayr*-ohss, *day*-vid al-*far*-oh
Sluter, Claus *sloo*-tr, *klows*
Staël, Nicholas de stahl, nee koh *lah* duh
Steen, Jan stain, yahn
Steichen, Edward *sty*-ken
Stieglitz, Alfred *stee*-glits
Suger, Abbot soo-*gay, a*-but

Tao Chi dow-jee
Tiepolo, Giovanni Battista tee-*eh*-po-lo, jo-*vah*-nee bah-*tees*-tah
Tintoretto (Jacopo Robusti) tin-toe-*ret*-toe, (*yah*-coe-poe roe-*booss*-tee)
Titian (Titiano Vecelli) tish-un (tee-tsee-*ah*-noh vay-*chell*-ee)
Toledo, Juan Bautista de toe-*lay*-doe, wahn baw-*tees*-tah day
Toulouse-Lautrec, Henri de too-*looz* low-*trek*, ahn-*ree* duh

Uccello, Paolo oo-*chell*-loh, *pah*-oh-loh

van Dyck, Anthony fahn *dike*, *an*-toe-nee
Vasarely, Victor va-sah-*rell*-ee
Vasari, Giorgio va-*sah*-ree, *jor*-jyoh
Vau, Louis le voh, loo-*ee* le
Velazquez, Diego vay-*lass*-kess, dee-*aye*-goh
Vermeer, Jan fare-*meer*, yahn
Veronese (Paolo Caliari) vay-roe-*nay*-zay, (*pah*-oh-loh kal-ee-*are*-ee)
Vigée-Lebrun, Elizabeth vee-*zhay* luh-*brun*, uh-*lee*-zah-bet
Vignon, Pierre vee-*nyon*, pee-*air*
Villon Jacques vee-*yohn*, zhahk
Warhol, Andy *war*-hall
Watteau, Antoine wah-*toh*, an-*twahn*_
Webster, Elon web ster, eh-lon
van der Weyden, Rogier van der *vay*-den, roh-*jair*
Wright, Frank Lloyd rite, loid
Wyeth, Andrew *why*-eth

Zimmerman, Dominikus *tsim*-ur-mahn, doe-*min*-ih-kus
Zurbaran, Francisco de *zoor*-bah-ran, fran-*sis*-coe day

Pronunciation Guide for Places and Terms

Acropolis ah-*krahp*-uh-lis
Abu Simbel *ah*-boo *sim*-bul
Aegean a-*jee*-un
Aix eks
Altamira ahl-tah-*mee*-rah
Amboise am-*bwahz*
Amiens *ah*-mee-en
Angkor Thom *ang*-kore tahm
Angkor Wat *ang*-kore wot
Arc de Triomphe de l'Etoile ark duh *tree*-omf duh leh-*twahl*
Arezzo ah-*retz*-oh
Argenteuil ahr-zhahn-*toy*
Ashurnasirpal ash-er-*naz*-er-pahl
Asuka ah-soo-*kah*
Avignon ah-veen-*yohn*

Baalbek *bal*-beck
Babylonia ba-bi-*loh*-nyah
Barbizon bahr-bih-*zon*
Baroque ba-*rohk*
Basel *bah*-zel
Bayeux bah-*yuh*
Beijing bay-*zhing*
Benin ben-*een*
Bokhara boh-*cahr*-ah
Bologna boh-*loh*-nyah
Borobodur bor-oh-boh-*duhr*
Breda *bray*-dah
Bruges brooszh
Byzantine *biz*-ahn-teen

Calais cal-*ay*
Casale cah-*sah*-lay
Chambord shan-*boar*
Chartres shartr
Chateau sha-*toe*
Chateaux sha-*toe*
Chenonceaux shen-ahn-*soh*
Cheops *kee*-ahps
Cheyenne shy *an*
Chichen Itza *chee*-chen *eet*-zah
Colmar *coal*-mahr
Cologne coh-*lone*
Colosseum kahl-uh-*see*-uhm
Constantinople *kahn*-stan-tin-*oh*-pul
Cordova kor-*doh*-vah
Cyclades sick-*la*-dees

Dada *dah*-dah
Deir el Bahari dayr el bah-*hah*-ree
Der Blaue Reiter dehr *blah*-way *right*-er
De Stijl deh *sty*-ul
Die Brücke dee *broock*-eh
Dijon dee-*zjohn*
Doge *dojh* (soft)

Eiffel *y*-ful (Eng: *eye*-ful)
El Castillo el cas-*tee*-yoh
El Escorial el eh-skor-ee-*ahl*
Epidauros ehp-eh-*dor*-us
Euphrates you-*fray*-tees

Flemalle fleh-*mahl*
Fontainebleau fohn-ten-*bloh*

Gare Saint Lazare gahr sen lah-*zahr*
Ghent gent (hard g)
Giverny *zhee*-ver-nay
Giza *gee*-zah (hard g)
Gudea goo-*dee*-ah
Guernica *gwer*-ni-ka
Guilin *gwee*-lun

Haarlem *har*-lem
Hagia Sophia *hah*-zhee-ah soh-*fee*-ah
Han dynasty hahn
Heliopolis hee-lee-*ahp*-oh-liss
Herculaneum her-cue-*lay*-nee-um
Holofernes hoe-loh-*fer*-nays
Hue hway

Ife *ee*-fay
Il Gesu ill *jay*-soo
Invalides in-vah-*leed*
Isenheim *iss*-en-hime
Isfahan *iss*-fah-hahn

Jericho *jer*-eh-ko
Jerusalem jeh-*roo*-suh-lem

Kamakura kah-mah-*koo*-rah
Karnak *kahr*-nack
Kiev key-*eff*
Knossos *no*-sohs
Kyoto *kyoh*-toh

La Grande Jatte lah grahnd zhaht
Lascaux lass-*ko*
Las Meninas lahs men-*een*-yahss
Le Havre luh hahv
Leiden *lye*-den
Les Demoiselles d'Avignon lay *dem*-wah-zell dah-veen-*yohn*
Loire River lwahr
Louvain loo-*van*
Louvre loovr

Madeleine mah-duh-*lin*
Maesta mah-aye-*stah*
Magi *may*-jie
Mamallapuram mah-mah-lah-*poor*-um
Mantua *man*-too-ah
Masada mah-*sah*-dah
Medici *meh*-di-chee
Mesopotamia mess-oh-poh-*tay*-mee-ah
Minoan min-*noh*-uhn
Mohenjo-daro moh-hen-jo-*dah*-roh
Monte Alban *mohn*-tay ahl-*bahn*
Monticello mohn-ti-*chell*-oh
Montmartre mon *martr*
Montreux mahn-*truh*
Mont Sainte Victoire mohn sen vik-*twahr*
Moulin de la Galette moo-*lahn* duh lah gah-*lett*
Moulin Rouge moo-*lahn* roozjh
Mughal *mo*-gull
Mycenae my-*see*-nee

Nanzenji nan-*sen*-jee
Nara *nah*-rah
Navajo *nah*-vah-hoh
Naxos *nahx*-ohs
Nevers neh-*vair*
Nijo nee-jo
Nineveh *nin*-eh-vuh
Notre Dame noh-*trah* dahm
Nuremberg *noor*-em-burg

Oaxaca wah-*hah*-cah
Osaka oh-*sah*-kah

Padua *pa*-doo-ah
Paestum pie-*aye*-stum
Pagan *pah*-gahn
Palazzo Ducale pah-*laht*-zoh doo-*kahl*-eh
Palazzo Vecchio pah-*laht*-zoh *veh*-key-oh
Pantheon *pan*-thee-on
Parthenon *par*-then-on
Penang pen-*ang*
Persepolis per-*seh*-poh-lis
Piazza della Signoria pee-*aht*-zah *del*-lah *seen*-yor-*ee*-ah
Piazza Navona pee-*aht*-zah nah-*voh*-nah
Pieta pee-aye-*tah*
Pisa *pee*-sah
Poitiers pwah-*tyay*
Pompeii pahm-*pay*-ee
Port en Bessin port ahn bes-*ehn*
Poseidon poh-*sigh*-dun
Prado Museum *prah*-doh

Qing Dynasty ching

Ravenna rah-*ven*-ah
Reims reemz
Renaissance *ren*-eh-*sahnss*
Rijksmuseum *rikes*-myoo-zee-um
Rococo roh-*koh*-koh
Romanesque *ro*-mahn-esk
Ronchamp roh-*shahn*
Rouen roo-*ahn*

St. Apollinare in Classe saint ah-pahl-in-*ahr*-ay in *klahss*-eh
Sainte Chapelle sant shah-*pell*
St. Denis sahn duh-*nee*
Sakkara (Saqqara) sah-*kahr*-ah
Salisbury *sals*-burr-ee
Samothrace *sam*-oh-thrace
San Francesco san fran-*chess*-coh
San Rocco san *rock*-oh
San Lorenzo san loh-*ren*-zoh
Santa Maria del Carmine *san*-tah mah-*ree*-ah *del* cahr-*mee*-nay
Santa Maria della Grazie *san*-tah mah-*ree*-ah del-lah *graht*-see-eh
San Vitale san vih-*tahl*-ay
San Zavier del Bac san *hahv*-yair del bahk
Sawankhaloke kiln sah-*wahnk*-ah-lock kill
Schoenbrun *show-en*-broon
Scythia *sith*-ee-ah
Segovia seh-*goh*-vee-ah
Seine River sen
Seto *see*-toe
Seville seh-*vee*-yah
Sforza *sfort*-sah
Shekwan *shek*-wahn
Shoshone shoh-*shoh*-nee
Siena see-*en*-ah
Staffelstein *stah*-fell-stine
Stanza della Segnatura *stahn*-zah *del*-la seg-nah-*too*-rah
Sumer *soo*-mur
Sumeria soo-*mair*-ee-uh
Sutton Hoo *suht*-uhn hoo

Tabriz tah-*breeze*
Taj Mahal tazh mah-*hahl*
Tenochtitlan teh-*nok*-tit-lahn
Teotihuacan *tay*-oh-tee-*wah*-kan
Thebes theebs
Tigris *ty*-gris
Todai-ji toe-dah-ee jee
Toledo toe-*lay*-doe
Topkapi *top*-cap-ee
Torgau *tohr*-gow
Toulouse too-*looz*
Tuilleries *twill*-er-ee

Uffizi Gallery oo-*feet*-see
Ur er
Urbino oor-*bee*-noh

Vendome vehn-*dome*
Versailles vehr-*sigh*
Vesuvius vuh-*soo*-vee-uhs
Vetheuil veh-*twahl*
Vezelay *ves*-eh-lay
Vicenza vee-*chen*-zah
Vierzehnheiligen *fear*-tsayn-*high*-li-gen

Wijk by Durstede vike by *duhr*-sted-eh
Worms vhorms
Würzburg *virts*-burg

Xian *chee*-an

Yosemite yoh-*sem*-i-tee

Zaire zy-*ear*
Zhou dynasty jo
Zwiefalten *tswee*-fahl-ten

Glossary

Correct pronunciation of difficult words is Indicated.

Italics indicate emphasis or accent in pronunciation.

abbey A complex of buildings comprised of a monastery and a church.
aborigine (a-bor-*ij*-i-nee) Indigenous or native inhabitants as differentiated from an invading or colonizing people.
abrade To scrape or rub off.
Abstract Expressionism A twentieth-century painting style that features large-scale works and expression of feelings through slashing, active brushstrokes.
abstraction (ab-*strak*-shun) A work of art that emphasizes design and a simplified or systematic investigation of forms. The subject matter may be recognized or may be completely transformed into shape, color and/or line.
acropolis The citadel of a Greek city; its highest point, containing temples and public buildings.
acrylic paint (a-*krill*-ik) A mixture of pigments that can adhere to almost any surface.
adobe (a *doh* bee) A clay brick made of sun-dried earth used as a building material. Any structure made of adobe bricks.
aerial perspective A method of creating the illusion of distance by representing objects further away with less clarity of contour and in diminished color. Also called **atmospheric perspective**.
aesthetic (es-*thet*-ik) Pertaining to the philosophically pleasing, beautiful and emotional nature of man; also, a pattern of thinking so oriented.
aesthetics (es-*thet*-iks) The description and explanation of artistic phenomena and aesthetic experience by means of psychology, sociology, ethnology or history.
agora (ah-*go*-rah) Greek word for assembly; the square or marketplace that was the center of public life in an ancient Greek city.
aisle (*eye*-l) The long, narrow space on each side of the nave of a church, usually between a row of columns and the outer wall. Often referred to as "side aisles."
alabaster A fine-grained gypsum or calcite (like marble), often white and translucent (though sometimes delicately tinted), used for sculpture and architectural columns.
allegorical Symbolic of truths or generalizations about human nature.
altar A structure on which to place or sacrifice offerings to a deity.
altarpiece A painted and/or sculpted work of art that stands above or at the back of the altar. It usually represents visual symbols of the Mass or depicts the saint to whom the chapel is dedicated, and may contain scenes from his or her life. See **retable** and **reredos**.
ambulatory (*am*-byoo-lah-tor-ee) Any passageway around a central space. A place for walking around the apse of a church, often a continuation of the side aisles; also, a covered walkway around a cloister.
Amida (ah-*me*-dah) The Buddha of the Western Paradise, particularly popular in eleventh-century Japan. Pictured with short curly hair, elongated ear lobes, long arms and an urna on his forehead.
amphitheatre (*am*-fi-*the*-a-ter) A double theater or closed arena, such as the Roman Colosseum; an elliptical or circular space surrounded by rising tiers of seats.
amphora (am-*for*-ah) A storage jar having an egg-shaped body, a foot and two handles, each attached at the neck and shoulders of the jar.
Anasazi (ah-nah-*sah*-zee) "The Ancient Ones"; early pueblo-dwelling peoples of the plateaus of the American Southwest.
anatomy The structure of the human body (or of animals or plants).
Andean (an-*dee*-an) Region of the Andes mountains of western South America and the mountain-oriented highland culture of indigenous people there.
Angkor (ong-*kore*) Ancient Khmer temple complex in Northwest Cambodia and center of the ancient Khmer kingdoms from the tenth to thirteenth centuries.
animal style Artistic practice of making objects in the shape of, or with motifs based on, animals; specifically refers to a tradition of art among the nomads of Eastern Europe and Central and Northern Asia.
animism The religious or spiritual attribution of conscious life to natural objects; the belief in the existence of spirits separable from bodies.
anthropomorphic (an-thro-po-*more*-fik) Refers to giving human characteristics to non-human objects or beings. Many Egyptian and Brahmanic gods were animals in the form of humans.
Apache (ah-*patch*-ee) Tribe of Native Americans inhabiting the American Southwest, artistically distinguished by their coiled basketry, large beaded women's collars and decorated fine leatherwork.
Apollo (ah-*pall*-oh) Greek god of the sun, prophecy, music, medicine and poetry; artistically significant as a model of physical beauty, dignity and serenity.
apostle (ah-*pos*-ell) In Christian usage, refers to the twelve followers of Christ who spread his teachings throughout the Mediterranean world. The apostles of Buddha are known as "lohan."
apse A large semi-circular (or polygonal) area at the choir end of a church. Usually contains the altar. May also be found at the ends of transepts or at the ends of smaller chapels.
aqueduct (*ak*-wah-dukt) An artificial channel for carrying water from a distance.
arabesque (*ar*-uh-besk) Intricate and fanciful surface decoration generally based on geometric patterns and using combinations of flowering vines, tendrils, etc.
arcade A series of arches and their supports (columns). When placed against a wall and used mainly as decoration, the result is called a "blind arcade."
arch An architectural construction (semi-circular or pointed) built of wedge-shaped blocks (voussoirs) to span an opening and usually supported by columns or piers. A corbeled arch is made by overlapping layers of stones, each one projecting slightly farther over the opening than the one below it. A building dependent upon arches for its structure is said to be "arculated."
archaeology Unearthing and study of evidences from past cultures which have been hidden from human eyes for centuries.
archaic (ar-*kay*-ik) Referring to the early phase of an artistic development; specifically applies to the span of ancient Greek art prior to the Classical period.

architecture (*ar*-ki-tek-choor) The art and science of designing and erecting buildings.
architrave (*arch*-i-trave) The main horizontal beam at the bottom of an entablature, resting on the capitals of columns. Often made of several lintels to stretch the length of the building.
archivolt (*ar*-ki-volt) The concentric moldings above the arched openings in Romanesque and Gothic churches, often decorated with sculpture; also, the underside of an arch.
Art Nouveau (art new-*voh*) Abstract style in European and American arts from the 1880s to 1930s characterized by the use of undulating waves or flames, flower stalks and flowing lines.
artifact Object, usually simple, that reveals human workmanship and modification.
artisan (*ar*-ti-zen) A person manually skilled in making a particular product; a craftsperson.
artist An individual who professes and practices the manipulation of materials in executing the concepts of his or her imagination. One who reflects the aesthetics and technology of his or her era and a cultural "editor" of the environment.
Ashanti (ah-shahn-tee) A people and former kingdom of West Africa, artistically significant in their use of highly stylized and simplified fertility dolls as well as their mud-built houses with foundations ornamented with curvilinear patterns.
Asoka (ah-*show*-kah) First Indian Emperor and Buddhist enthusiast responsible for the origins of Buddhist art, 274–236 BC.
assemblage (ah-*sem*-blij) A work of art composed of fragments of objects or materials originally intended for other purposes.
Asuka (*ah*-skah) Early Japanese capital city and name of the first Buddhist cultural period there (538–645), artistically significant for importation of Korean and Chinese sculpture and architecture.
atlantes (*at*-lan-teez) Supports or columns in the form of carved male figures.
atrium (*ay*-tree-um) The inner court of a Roman house, open to the sky. Also, the enclosed (but open to the sky) courtyard in front of the main doors of a basilica or church.
Attic Pertaining to Attica, a region of Greece, and the artistic style developed there in pre-Classical times; also, the story above the main colonnade of a building.
Avaloketisvara (ah-vah-lok-eh-*tesh*-vah-rah) The merciful Bodhisattva of Buddhism, manifested in Chinese culture as Guan Yin, the Goddess of Mercy; known to the Japanese as *Kannon*.
avant-garde (ah-vant-*gard*) A style of twentieth-century art; also, any style of contemporary art in any period of time, being the newest form of visual expression and the farthest from the traditional ways of working.
axial (*ak*-si-ell) Describing a building plan that has a strong emphasis along one direction.
Ayuthaya (ah-*you*-tee-ah) Early Thai kingdom, founded 1350, artistically distinguished by its free mixing of Burmese, Khmer and Ceylonese styles.
Aztec People and kingdom of ancient central Mexico, noted for their advanced civilization before their conquest by Cortés in 1521, artistically distinguished by their large temple-oriented cities.
azulejos (ah-jew-*lay*-os) Glazed pottery tiles, usually painted in bright colors and floral or other patterns, used in Spanish, Portuguese and Hispanic architecture.
balance A principle of design that refers to the visual equalization of elements in a work of art. There are three kinds of balance: symmetrical (formal); asymmetrical (informal); and radial.
baldachin (bal-dah-*cheen*) A fixed canopy of wood, stone, fabric, etc., over an altar, throne or doorway. Sometimes portable, as when it is over a movable statue during a parade or procession.
balustrade A row of short pillars or columns topped by a railing.
Bamara (bah-*mar*-ah) A tribe of west Africa, particularly in Mali.
Ban Chiang (bahn cheng) Site of prehistoric burial grounds in northeast Thailand believed to be the oldest remains yet discovered of Bronze Age civilization. Distinguished by a fine grade of earthenware with very thin hand-built walls and curvilinear slip decoration.
baptistry (*bap-ti-stree)* An area in which the Sacrament of Baptism is administered, either within an area of a church or as a separate building.
Baroque (bar-*oak*) A period and style of European art (seventeenth century) which emphasized color and light. Work was characteristically exuberant, large, filled with swirling lines, and required emotional involvement; also refers to any highly ornate style.
barrel vault A semi-cylindrical ceiling spanning an open room, such as in Romanesque churches.
basketry The art of making wickerwork objects by methods of plaiting stalks, cane, rushes, etc.
basket weave Technique of forming a fabric wherein double threads are interlaced to produce a checkered pattern, similar to that of a woven basket.
bas-relief (*bah* ree-*leef*) A low, partially-round sculpture that emerges from a flat panel.
basilica (bah-*sill*-ee-ka) Roman civic building of rectangular form in which the ground plan was divided into nave, side aisles and apse, and was approached through a narthex. In Christian architecture, a church building similar in shape was the major worship form from the third to eighth centuries.
batik (bah-*teek*) A coloring or dyeing process using a wax stencil to protect design areas from coloration by dyeing of cloth or paper.
battlements Parapets built on top of walls with indentations for defense or decoration.
Bauhaus (*bow*-hows) A German art school, begun in 1918, that stressed science and technology as major resources for art and architecture. Many modern concepts of design were originated at the Bauhaus which affect contemporary artistic ideas.
bay A rectangular division (compartment) or a building, marked off by consecutive pairs of piers, columns or other supports. Large stained glass windows were put into the bays of Gothic cathedrals. The size of Chinese and Japanese temples is measured in terms of the number of bays along the facade.
bema (*bee*-mah) The raised sanctuary or chancel space in an early Christian or Eastern Orthodox church. In a synagogue, the elevated pulpit from which scripture is read.
Benin (beh-*neen*) A people and former kingdom of Nigeria, artistically distinguished by their fine-quality bronze castings of the sixteenth and seventeenth centuries.

Bible The collection of sacred writings of the Christian religion that includes Old and New Testaments, or that of the Jewish faith which contains only the Old Testament.
biomorphic shape (by-o-*mor*-fik) Artistic stylization suggested by organic forms.
bishop A spiritual overseer of a number of churches in a diocese of Greek, Roman Catholic and Anglican Church organizations. See **cathedral**.
blue-and-white A general term for the underglaze cobalt-decorated porcelain ware produced in China beginning in the Yuan dynasty. Cobalt produces the blue color, often of various intensities depending upon quality and thickness, and the white is the color of the kaolin body itself. Also, any pottery which seems to duplicate the style of such Chinese ware.
Bodhisattva (bode-he-*saht*-vah) A Buddhist saint, one who has compassionately refrained from entering eternal enlightenment (nirvana) in order to minister to the needs of mortals.
bond Pattern of alternating the directions of individual bricks or stones in a masonry wall.
Borobudor (bore-u-beh-*door)* An Indonesian stupa with ten levels.
Brahma (*brah*-mah) The Indian creator-god of the Hindu trinity; the ultimate basis of all existence; the universal self.
Brahmanism (*brah*-mahn-izm) Orthodox Indian religion adhering to the pantheon of the Vedas, stressing the pre-eminence of Siva, Indra and Vishnu as well as the practice of sacrifices and ceremonies.
broken color The effect produced from the application of optical mixing.
Buddha (*boo*-dah) Gautama Siddhartha, founder of Buddhism, c.563–483 BC; also any Buddhist sage who has achieved enlightenment in accordance with the teachings of Gautama.
Buddhism (*boo*-dizm) Religious belief based on the teachings of Gautama Buddha that suffering is inherent in life and that one can be liberated from it by mental and moral self-purification. Hinayana Buddhism stresses individualistic faith and a simple iconography. Mahayana Buddhism evolved in the second century under the teachings of Nagayana, stressing a complex understanding of the five eons of time, the four levels of creation, and the role of saints or Bodhisattvas.
burnish To polish leather-hard clay with a smooth object, rubbing to seal the porous surface of the clay; also, any such rubbing on any material.
buttress A massive support built against a wall to receive the lateral thrust (pressure) exerted by a vault, roof or arch. See **Flying Buttress**.
caliph (*kay*-liff) Title of an Islamic ruler, functioning in both religious and secular affairs.
calligraphy (kah-*lig*-ra-fee) The art of beautiful writing or printing; fine lettering of elegance, often thought in the West as being similar to the grace of Oriental writing.
campanile (camp-uh-*neel*-ee) A bell-tower either attached to a church or freestanding nearby.
campo santo A cemetery, from the Italian word for "holy field."
camera obscura (ob-*skyoor*-ah) A box with a small opening on one side through which an image was transferred in reverse onto the opposite wall of the box; similar to a modern camera.
cancello (can-*chell*-oh) A latticed screen or grille separating the choir from the nave.
candi (*john*-dee) Javanese commemorative structure, temple or shrine.
canopy (*kan*-ah-pee) An ornamental, roof-like covering placed above a statue, tomb, niche or altar.
cantilever (*kan*-tl-ee-ver) A horizontal projection, canopy, balcony or beam balanced and supported with a fulcrum.
canvas Surface of woven linen or other fiber on which an artist applies paint, and the most common ground or support for an oil painting; also, any painting executed on such material.
capital The top element of a column, pier or pilaster, usually ornamented with stylized leaves, volutes, animal or human forms. The entablature rests on capitals in Doric, Ionic and Corinthian orders.
caricature (*kar*-i-ki-choor) A drawing, painting or sculpture of a person that exaggerates selected characteristics of the subject, such as a prominent chin or large eyes. Often humorous.
cartoon A full-scale drawing from which a painting or fresco is made. Also, a simplified humorous drawing.
carving The subtractive process of sculpture in which parts of a block are cut or chiseled away, leaving the finished work.
caryatid (care-ee-*ah*-tid) A support or column in the form of a human figure, usually female. See **atlantes**.
casting A method of reproducing a three-dimensional object by pouring a hardening liquid or molten metal into a mold bearing its impression.
castle A fortified habitation, primarily used for defense, composed of a central dungeon, or keep, and outer defense works.
catacombs (*kat-i-komz)* Underground burial places made up of passageways and niches for holding the sarcophagi. Some catacombs contained chapels and meeting rooms of the early Christians.
cathedra The chair or throne of a bishop.
cathedral The main church of a diocese, containing the cathedra, or bishop's chair. See **bishop**.
celadon (*sell*-a-don) Pottery glaze characterized by a pale-green to bluish-green color, derived from iron, popularly used during the Sung dynasty in China and later in Korea and Thailand; also, ware covered with such a glaze.
cella (*sell*-ah) The main rectangular room of a temple containing the image of a god, goddess or cult deity.
centaur (*sen*-tor) A creature of Greek mythology with the head and torso of a man and the body and legs of a horse.
center of interest The area of a work of art toward which all visual movement is directed. It is the visual focal point of the work.
centering A wooden framework to support a stone arch or vault during construction.
ceramics Objects made of clay and fired in a kiln; also, the art of producing such objects.
chaitaya (*chah-ee*-tee-ah) A Buddhist sanctuary.
chakra (*shak*-rah) Iconographic wheel symbolizing the first sermon of Buddha and the progression of the law.
Chan (john) Buddhist sect emphasizing contemplation and meditation, self-discipline and the teaching that the Buddha is inherent in all things. Known in Japan as Zen.
chancel (*chan*-sell) The space kept for clergy and the choir in a church, between the nave and the apse. It is usually separated from the nave by steps, a railing or a screen.
Cha-no-yu (cha-*know*-you) The "way tea"; a prescribed ceremony for appreciating the process of making and drinking tea, connected with Zen meditation. This ceremony has inspired the creation of utensils and art objects to be used and appreciated during the tea-making process.

château (sha-*toh*) A French castle or large country house. (plural=châteaux)
Chavin (chow-*veen*) The mother culture of Andean cultures, dating from about 500 BC, centered in the Peruvian highlands.
chedis (*jay*-dee) A tiered, pointed, spire-like Thai pagoda.
cherub One of an order of angelic beings, often visualized in European art as a winged child.
Cheyenne (shy-*enn*) A tribe of North American natives of the north central plains that created unique silverwork in 1870s; this tribe is also noted for its fine leatherwork.
chiaroscuro (key-ah-ross-*kyoo*-roh) A technique for modeling forms in painting by which the lighted parts seem to emerge from surrounding dark areas. Strong contrast of dark and light values in painting.
Chilkat (*chill*-cat) A band of Tlingit Indians of southern Alaska, artistically unique in their woven, twined and plaited blankets in symbolic bear and other animal patterns.
Chimu (*chee*-moo) An urbanist culture of Andean peoples, reaching a zenith of creative activity about 1200, noted for their heavy adobe architecture on terraced sites, their use of interlocking fish designs, and stirrup pottery vessels in representations of birds and humans.
Chinoiserie (chee-nwa-*sree*) Style of European arts and crafts growing from a fanciful and idealized concept of "exotic" China based on travelers' accounts and isolated objects of Chinese art.
choir (kwire) The part of the church in which the service is sung, usually the apse; also, a group of trained singers.
Chola (*cho*-la) Dynasty of Indian rulers powerful from 846–1279, artistically distinguished by excellent graceful bronze castings, mostly notably of the Nataraja.
chops In Chinese art, the signature seal of the artist stamped on the work.
Churrigueresque (chur-*ig*-er-esk) Extravagantly ornamented architecture of Baroque Spain and the Hispanic world characterized by abundant and indiscriminate use of decorative motifs, twisted columns and complex ornamentation.
cityscape A work of art that shows views of city streets, plazas, courtyards, buildings and activities taking place in the urban environment.
cire perdue (sear per-*dew*) Method of casting molten metal into a cavity originally filled with a wax model. The resulting casting is an exact replica of the wax original.
Classical Relating to form regarded as having reached its greatest standard of excellence before modern times, i.e., Classical Greek or Classical Inca architecture.
Classical Abstraction Another name for Color Field Painting.
Classicism The practice of using stylistic elements and/or myths derived from the Greek Classical period.
clay Fine-grained earth, chiefly composed of aluminum silicate and formed by natural water deposition which is plastic, easily formed, and becomes hard and brittle upon treatment by high heat (firing).
clerestory (*clear*-story) The upper section of a wall (windowed or open) used for fighting and ventilation; also, the upper story of the nave of a church building.
cloisonné (kloy-soh-*nay*) Technique for setting colored glass, stones or enamel between thin strips of metal on a metal surface.
cloister (*kloy*-ster) A covered walkway or ambulatory around an open court or garden. Usually, a colonnade faces the garden, allowing light to enter.
Cochise Culture (ko-*cheese*) Ancient Southwest Native American society noted for unfired clay pottery.
codex (*ko*-decks) A manuscript in book form, often with pages arranged in an accordion-fold, as distinguished from a scroll.
coelanoglyph (koh-eh-*lan*-oh-gliff) A low-relief carving set into a flat panel, below the surface as distinguished from a bas-relief.
coffer In architecture, a square, rectangular or polygonal recess in a ceiling to reduce the weight of the structure.
coiling To build up with concentric rings.
Colima (ko-*lee*-ma) Culture of Western Mexico, artistically distinguished by superior free-hand molded clay vessels in animal and human forms, some with stirrup handles.
collage A technique in which the artist glues materials such as paper, cloth or found materials to some type of ground.
colonnade A series of columns, usually supporting lintels or arches.
color An element of design that identifies natural and manufactured things as being red, yellow, blue, orange, etc.
Color Field Painting A style of painting that relies solely on flat fields of color.
column (*kol*-um) An upright post, bearing the load of the upper part of a building. It consists of a base, a shaft and a capital. An engaged column is half a column, attached to a wall, and non-weight bearing.
combine Painting Technique developed by Robert Rauschenberg in which artworks are made by fastening objects to abstract canvases, mixing reality with abstraction.
Commanche (ko-*man*-she) Native American tribe of western Texas and New Mexico, artistically distinguished by its tipis, leather boots, clothing and elaborate beadwork.
complementary colors Any two colors that are located opposite each other on a color wheel. When mixed together they will tend to subdue the intensities and produce a grayed hue. When placed side by side, they produce optical vibrations.
composition The ordered arrangement of the elements (colors, shapes, lines, etc.) in a work of art, usually according to the principles of design.
computer art Artwork created on computer screens with computer software programs and printed on computer printers.
concept art A style of art in which the artist expresses the idea concept of a proposed work of art in verbal or diagram form. The actual work will probably not be carried out.
Confucianism (kun-*few*-shun-izm) System of social interaction based on the teachings of Confucius (551–479 BC) who preached reforms of Chinese society during the Zhou dynasty. Stresses order and loyalty; personal virtue; devotion to family and to the spirits of ancestors and justice.
connoisseur (kon-i-soor) A person with expert knowledge or training; a person of informed and discriminating taste.
contemporary art Refers to the art of today; the methods, styles and techniques of artists living now.
content The subject matter in a painting or other work of art.
contour (*kon*-toor) A single line or lines that define the outer and often the inner edges and surfaces of objects or figures.
contrapposto (kon-tra-*pohs*-toh) Technique of sculpting a human figure in a pose that shows the weight of the body in balance. With weight on one leg, the shoulders and hips counterbalance each other in a natural way so that the figure does not fall over. Developed in the late Greek period.

contrast A principle of design that refers to differences in values, colors, textures and other elements to achieve emphasis and interest.
Cool Art Another name for Minimal Art.
cool colors The hues on one side of the color wheel which contain blue and green.
Coptic Native of Egypt; descended from ancient Egyptians.
corbel (*kore*-bell) An overlapping arrangement of stones, each layer projecting a bit beyond the row beneath it; also, a bracket of stone, wood or brick projecting from the face of a wall which may support a cornice or arch.
Corinthian (koh-*rin*-the-en) One of the Classical styles of architecture of ancient Greece (fourth century BC) that features tall, slender columns topped with ornate capitals decorated with stylized acanthus leaves.
cornice (*kor*-niss) Any projecting ornamental molding along the top of a building, wall, arch, etc.; also, the topmost projecting part of an entablature in a Classical Greek building.
course Rows of stones or bricks that form a horizontal layer of a wall.
crafts Works of art that generally have a utilitarian purpose, including ceramics, macramé, leatherwork, metals, weaving, fabrics, jewelry, furniture, basketry, etc.
craftsperson One who fabricates useful and well-designed objects of quality, durability and function. **Craftsmanship** implies the skillful practice of this process.
crenelations (*kren*-i-lay-shens) Indentations or notches such as in battlements.
cromlech (*krom*-lek) A circle of monoliths, usually enclosing a type of altar.
crossing The area of a church where the transept intersects the nave. Sometimes a dome or tower is built over this area, further emphasizing it as the focal area of the worship space.
crucifix (*kroo*-sih-fiks) A representation of a cross with the figure of Christ's crucifixion placed on it.
cruciform (*kroo*-sih-form) In the shape of a cross; usually a floorplan of building in such an arrangement.
crypt (kript) A vaulted space below ground level, usually beneath the raised choir or apse of a church, or under a temple or shrine.
Cubism (*kyoo*-biz-em) A style of art in which the subject is broken apart and reassembled in an abstract form, emphasizing geometric shapes.
cult figures Figures of religious devotion or ritualistic value.
cult magic Mystic practices of a system of religious beliefs and rituals.
culture Elements that add to the aesthetic aspects of life, enriching it with beauty and enjoyment; also, a society or civilization marked by distinctive concepts, habits, skills, implements and art forms.
cupola (*coop*-oh-lah) A rounded convex roof on a circular base; a dome of small size.
curtain wall A wall that carries no weight other than its own; a nonstructural panel set between weightbearing pillars in a building.
dagob (duh-*gobb*) A small stupa-like architectural form which symbolically represents the commemorative function of the Buddhist stupa.
dais (*day*-ahs) A raised platform, usually at one end of a long room.
Dao See **Taoism**.
Dayak (*die*-yak) Coastal and Highland people of Borneo, known for their bold graphic designs in painting and carving.
Delftware Blue-and-white faience pottery made in the Dutch city of Delft, inspired by Ming porcelain, which reached a peak in quality and production between 1650 and 1750; also, a term generally applied to any such European-produced blue-and-white china.
descriptive perspective shows more important objects larger than less important objects.
Deva Raja (day-va *rah*-jah) A god-king; the concept in Javanese and Southeast Asian culture that the ruler is an earlier counterpart of a divine being, usually Siva or Buddha.
diaper (*die*-uh-per) Decorative unit or motif, often abstract or symbolic, repeated to create intricate surface decoration.
Dibutsu (*die*-boot-sue) Japanese name for Buddha.
Ding Zhou (ding jshoo) Region of Henan and Hebei provinces of China, producing non-Imperial pottery, especially during the Song dynasty, decorated with typical dark brown free-flowing floral designs; also the pottery made there.
diocese. See **bishop**.
diptych (*dip*-tik) A pair of wood, ivory or metal panels (large or small) usually hinged together, with painting or carving on the inside surfaces. Usually placed over an altar.
distort To deform or stretch something out of its normal shape.
Doge (*doe*-jshay) Italian word for the chief magistrate in the former republics of Venice and Genoa.
dolmen A grouping of huge, uncut stones, set on end and covered with a large single stone, apparently used by Neolithic peoples as a burial altar.
dome A hemispherical or beehive-shaped vault or ceiling over a circular opening. May be elevated further by placement on a drum. If placed over a square opening, the transition to a round shape is made by use of pendentives in the four corners.
Doric The earliest of the classical style of ancient Greek architecture, characterized by sturdy columns that have no base and are terminated by simple, undecorated capitals.
dormer A window placed vertically in a sloping roof, and with a roof of its own.
dragon Legendary animal usually represented as a monstrous winged and scaly serpent or lizard with a crested head and enormous claws. Symbolic to the Chinese of Imperial power.
Dravidian The people, language and culture of much of South India, often regarded as the native people of the subcontinent.
dress To prepare stone for architectural purposes by carving or decorating.
drip painting Technique developed by Jackson Pollock in which he walked over a canvas with a can of paint, dripping and spilling paint about the canvas.
drolleries (*drole*-er-ees) The marginal designs, usually whimsical or fanciful, found on medieval European manuscripts.
drum The cylindrical wall supporting a dome; also, one of several sections composing the shaft of a column.
Dvaravati (dvar-ah-*vaht*-tee) The earliest known period of Thai Buddhist culture and art, flourished in the sixth to eleventh centuries.
earth art Artworks which involve the natural environment and in which spectators participate.
earth works Large formations of moved earth, excavated by artists in the surface of the earth and best viewed from a high vantage point.

earthenware Vessels of a coarse nature made from clay fired at a low temperature. Commonly left unglazed.
easel painting Any kind of painting done in a studio (on an easel) which can be transported from place to place.
eclecticism (e-*klek*-ti-*siz*-em) The practice of using compositional elements or artistic styles derived from a variety of sources.
edge A linear separation between two color areas; also, the outer contour of a shape or form.
Edo (ay-doe) Japanese capital city (Tokyo) and name often given to the rule of the Tokugawa shogunate (1615–1867), significant as a period when Japan essentially closed itself to the outside world.
egg tempera See **tempera**.
element The graphic devices with which the artist works, such as line, shape, color, texture, etc.
elevation The external faces of a building; also, a side or front view of a structure, painted or drawn to reveal each story with equal detail.
ellipse (ih-*lips*) A curved line that is drawn to produce an oval shape with specific geometric proportions.
elongated Stretched out lengthwise; drawn in a way as to exaggerate height or length.
embroider (em-*broy*-der) To ornament textiles with stitching of colored thread or other fine material.
emphasis (*em*-fah-sis) A principle of design by which the artist or designer may use opposing sizes, shapes, contrasting colors or other means to place greater attention on certain areas, objects or feelings in a work of art.
enamel Powdered colored glass that is fused by heating to a ceramic or metal ground; a work of art created by this method. Overglaze enamels are applied over previous glazes.
encaustic (en-*koz*-tik) A method of painting on a ground, with colors dissolved in hot wax; also, a work of art produced by this technique.
engaged To be partially set into a larger mass; not fully freestanding.
engaged column See **column**.
engraving The process of incising lines into a surface to create an image; also, a print made by inking such an incised surface.
Enlarged Field Painting Style of painting which uses large-scale canvases designed to draw the viewer into active visual participation with the work.
entablature (en-*tab*-li-*choor*) The upper part of an architectural order, being the part placed above the columns, usually consisting of architrave, frieze and cornice.
entasis (*en*-tah-sis) The subtle convex swelling of a Classical Greek column shaft.
epistle (i-*pis*-el) A message; in Christian usage, one of the letters of the apostles that make up twenty-one books of the Biblical New Testament.
espadaña (es-pah-*dahn*-ya) A gable wall on the facade of a building in which the curved top extends above the roof line; characteristic of Spanish and Hispanic architecture.
etching A technique in which a metal plate is incised by acid through needle-thin scratches in a waxed coating. The image is inked and printed on paper; also, the print made by this process.
Eucharist (*you*-cah-rist) From the Greek word for *thanksgiving*: the Sacrament of the Lord's Supper. Also, the consecrated bread and wine used in this sacrament; also, the sacrament itself.
Evangelists (i-*van*-je-lists) The four writers of the Gospels in the New Testament: Matthew, Mark, Luke and John; frequently visualized by their respective symbols of an angel, a lion, a bull and an eagle.
export ware Objects made expressly for the tastes of a foreign market; in ceramics, shapes and designs may be made to order which are alien to the native aesthetics of the producing craftspersons.
Expressionism (ex-*spresh*-a-*niz*-em) Style of art begun in Germany early in the twentieth century. The artists working in this style sought to communicate strong personal and emotional feelings to the viewer.
expressionists (ex-*spresh*-a-nists) Any style of art in which the artist tries to communicate strong personal and emotional feelings to the viewer.
eye level A horizontally drawn line that is even in height with the viewer's eye. In perspective drawing and painting, it can be the actual distant horizon line, but it can also be drawn in a close-up still life.
facade (fah-*sahd*) The front of a building.
faience (fay-*ahns*) Opaque low-firing colored ceramic glaze; also, earthenware decorated with such glaze.
famille rose (fa-*meal* rose) Chinese porcelain decorated in the Qing dynasty under European influence, using a mixture of opaque whites to paint scenery of court life, birds, flowers, etc.
famille verde (fah-*meal vehr*d) Chinese porcelain developed in the Qing dynasty, decorated with overglaze enamels, principally greens and weaker reds and yellows.
fan vault A complex vault with radiating ribs, characteristic of late English Gothic (perpendicular) architecture.
Fates, Three In Greek and Roman mythology, the goddesses Clotho, Lachesis and Atropos, who were believed to have the ability to determine the course of human life.
Fauvism (*foe*-vism) A style of painting which used brilliant colors for expressive purposes in France of the early twentieth century.
feldspathic Crystalline silica-based minerals used in the formulation of high firing ceramic glazes.
ferroconcrete See **reinforced concrete**.
fertility The capability to produce abundantly; the successful breeding and reproduction of the species.
fête galante (fet gah-*lahnt)* Elegant entertainment.
fetish An object to which magical powers are ascribed; a good luck charm.
field The area in which a design, decoration or painting is applied.
filigree (*fill*-i-gree) Ornamental openwork of thinly hammered ribbons of metal; the process of making such openwork; also, any delicate design resembling delicate work.
finger weaving Technique of forming fibers, rushes, cornhusks and bark into fabric by twining, braiding without a loom.
flamboyant Decoration or style characterized by waving curves suggesting flames; also, any ornate style in a flashy or resplendent style. Specifically, a decorative architectural style of mid-thirteenth century Europe stressing curving tracery in flame-like patterns.
flash-firing Method of firing coarse pottery in an open pit with highly combustible fuel, much like a bonfire.
Flemish Characteristic of Flanders (Belgium); usually refers to the culture of this area from the fourteenth to seventeenth centuries.
flint A very hard quartz or silica stone.
fluting The shallow, rounded, concave, vertical grooves in the shaft of a column.
flying buttress A supportive structure consisting of a tower buttress and a flying arch which spans the side aisles and supports the upper wall of the nave of a Gothic church.

folk art Objects made by untrained artists with a combined goal of being functional and pleasing to the eye.
foreshortening A method of drawing or painting an object or person that is not parallel to the picture plane so that it seems to recede in space, giving the illusion of three dimensions. Parts get smaller as they recede in space.
forge To shape metal by hammering heated pieces with directed blows of a mallet or other driving tool.
form An element of design that is three-dimensional and encloses volume, such as a cube, sphere, pyramid, cylinder. Also, in metalworking, to shape metal with hammered strokes.
Formalism Stylization based on traditionally accepted forms.
format The shape, size and general composition of a work of art or publication.
fortress church A strongly fortified worship building in which Christianity faced military threats from local opponents.
forum A central gathering place for the people of a town, particularly of ancient Rome. A place for judicial and public business.
Franciscan A member of the monastic order founded in 1209 by Francis of Assisi; peaceful proselytizers of native coastal Indians who built missions—each a day's walk apart along the southern California coast—as stations for their work in the late eighteenth century
friar A brother or member of one of four Mendicant Roman Catholic Orders—Franciscan, Augustinian, Dominican and Carmelite.
free form Not having prescribed geometric proportions.
fresco A method of painting in which pigments suspended in water are applied to a thin layer of wet plaster so that the plaster absorbs the color and the painting becomes part of the wall.
frieze (freeze) Any horizontal band, decorated with moldings or patterns, either painted or carved, usually at the upper end of a wall; specifically in Greek architecture, the middle layer (plain or carved) of an entablature.
frontal A pose in figure drawing or sculpture in which figures face forward.
Fu-nan (foo-nahn) Ancient Southeast Asian empire (c. 100–525), typified by their worship of Harihara, their early sculpture of Buddha and Vishnu, and their use of canals to drain the rice lands of Cambodia.
Futurism (*fyoo*-cha-riz-em) A style of painting and sculpture that emerged in Italy, early twentieth century. Futurism emphasized the machine-like quality of "modern" living.
gable A shaped piece of a wall, generally triangular, at the end of a ridged roof; called a pediment in Classical Greek architecture.
gallery A story over the aisle and open to the nave through an arcade in Christian church architecture. Also, a contemporary commercial enterprise that exhibits works of art for sale.
gamelon (*gam*-eh-lahn) A Javanese orchestra incorporating bronze gongs, wooden xylophone-like chimes, drums and wind instruments. Used to accompany puppet and human theatrical performances.
Gandhara (gahn-*dar*-ah) School of earliest Buddhist sculpture in the Indian province of Bactria distinguished by the use of Hellenistic and Persian anatomical representation. Also known as the Indo-Greek or Greco-Buddhist School.
Ganges civilization (*gan*-jeez) Society of the Indo-Gangetic plains of northern India from about 1500 BC, noteworthy for the evolution of the Vedic writings fundamental to Brahmanic religion.
Gautama (gow-*tah*-mah) The historical Buddha, Sakyamuni. See **Buddhism**.
genre (*zhahn*-ra) Referring to the common, ordinary; also, a type of localized art.
genre painting The representation of acts and/or scenes from everyday life.
geodesic (jee-oh-*des*-ik) A form of geometry (solid) which forms the basis for structures built of interlocking polygons.
geometric Referring to mechanical, human-made shapes such as squares, zigzags, circles, spirals, checkerboard patterns, bands, etc.; also, a period of ancient history when decorative motifs of such patterns were commonly used on pottery (i.e., Geometric Greek pottery).
gesso (*jess*-oh) A mixture of finely ground plaster and glue that is often spread on a surface prior to painting.
gilding A covering of gold leaf over inexpensive or perishable materials.
glaze In pottery, the thin coating of minerals which provides the glassy coloring and waterproof gloss for the final ware. In painting, a transparent mixture of a small amount of color dissolved in a large amount of the vehicle (such as linseed oil mixed with turpentine in oil painting) that changes the hues of previously painted surfaces.
gopura (*go*-poor-uh) Elaborate, pyramidal, tapered gateway towers typical of South Indian Hindu temple architecture.
gospel In Christian usage, the story of Christ's life and teaching, as found in the writings of the first four books of the New Testament.
Gothic A style of art in Europe of the twelfth–fifteenth centuries, emphasizing religious architecture and typified by pointed arches, spires and verticality.
gouache (gwash) Any opaque water-soluble paint or opaque watercolor.
Great Pueblo An era of Southwestern Native American culture (1050–1300) marked by large communities of multistoried buildings and the first appearance of polychrome painted pottery in the region.
Great Wall A massive fortification built during the Qin dynasty of China to keep out the nomads of Mongolia and Manchuria.
Greco-Buddhist See **Gandhara**.
Greek cross A cross with four arms of equal length.
grid-iron A design consisting of a network, i.e., a street pattern or the regular divisions of a decorative surface.
groin (groyn) The sharp edge formed by two intersecting vaults.
groined vault A vault formed by the intersection (at right angles) of two barrel vaults of equal size so that the groins form a diagonal cross.
ground (grownd) The surface on which a painting is made.
Guan Yin (gwahn yin) The Chinese Buddhist goddess of mercy, an interpretation of the Indian Bodhisattva Avaloketisvara. A compassionate goddess, benevolent to children and protective of sailors.
guilds (gilds) Independent associations of artisan-manufacturers and bankers in Renaissance Florence. The Italian word is *arti*, from which the word *art* comes.
Gupta (*goop*-tah) The ruling dynasty (320–600) synonymous with the golden age of Indian art, artistically significant for its Indianization of Buddhist images, the evolution of Mahayana Buddhist iconography and the digging of early cave temples (Chaitya).
gypsum (*jip*-some) A white, calcium-sulphate mineral, useful as a painting pigment.
Haida (*high*-dah) Coastal Indians of British Columbia, artistically known for their symbolic and abstract wood carvings, totem poles and plank houses.

halo The circle of light shown around the head of a saint or of a holy person; also used to identify the divinity of a god. Also known as a nimbus.
Han (han[d]) The second longest Chinese dynasty (206 BC–221 AD), divisible into a number of phases. Artistically typified by aristocratic tomb art; sophisticated silk, lacquer, glazed ceramics; and clay models of architecture and daily-use objects.
handbuilt (hand-bilt) Ceramic objects formed without the use of a potter's wheel, typically using slabs or coils of clay to construct vessels.
Haniwa (*hahn*-ee-wah) The late Neolithic culture of the Japanese Tumulus Age (300–700), named for the sculptured cylinder-like clay guardian figures typically found at burial sites of the period; also, the sculptures of humans, architecture and animals made during the period.
Hanuman (*hahn*-oo-*mahn*) The mythological king of the monkeys in the *Ramayana*, responsible for Rama's successful recovery of his kingdom.
Hard-Edge Painting A style of art in which the artist uses crisp, clean edges and applies the values and colors so they are even and flat.
harmika (har-*meek*-ah) The small railed balcony surmounting the dome of a stupa.
hatching The use of parallel lines to create shading. When lines are overlapped at angles to each other, the technique is called crosshatching.
Heian (*hey*-on) The long-lived Japanese dynasty (794–1185) named for the new capital city at Kyoto. The later phase (894–1185) is known as the Fujiwara period. The Heian dynasty is significant for the establishment of Amida Buddhist sects, aristocratic refinement at court and the flowering of the arts.
Hellenistic An era of Mediterranean culture influenced by the Greek world following the conquest of Alexander the Great.
heraldic (heh-*ral*-dik) Relating to coats of arms and family crests or emblems.
hieroglyphs (high-row-*gliffs*) Characters in the picture-writing system of many ancient cultures that use pictures or symbols representing sounds, words or ideas.
Hindu (*hin*-doo) The dominant religion of India, acknowledging a pantheon of earth spirits, the foremost of which are Brahma (the creator), Vishnu (the Preserver) and Siva (the Destroyer).
Hispanic (hiss-*pan*-ick) Pertaining to Spain or its people throughout the world.
Hohokam (ho-*ho*-kahm) An ancient Southwestern American culture (100–1400) that developed from contacts with Mexico, typified by their use of irrigation canals, and artistically marked by red-on-buff pottery, the use of copper, and fine textiles and stonework.
Hopi (*ho*-pee) A pueblo-dwelling people of the Shoshone group of Arizona, considered the finest Native American weavers. Their pottery of ancient times was decorated with abstract stylized animals. Modern distinction is in repoussé silverwork and turquoise and shell settings.
horizon line (hor-*ize*-on) The division between earth and sky, as seen by an observer.
Hours, Book of A book for private devotions, containing the prayers for the seven canonical hours of the Roman Catholic Church. Often executed in illuminated manuscript form.
Huaxtec (*wahx*-tec) The war-like culture of Northern Veracruz which peaked between 600 and 900 but survived through Aztec times. Artistically noted for miniature and large sculptures of human and anthropomorphic gods.
hue (hyoo) The attribute of a color that gives it its name. The spectrum is usually divided into six basic hues: violet, blue, green, yellow, orange and red.
humanism The renewed interest at the beginning of the Italian Renaissance in the art and literature of antiquity. Also, any concern with the study of humanity and its writings and activities.
hydria (*heye-dree-ah)* A large jug used to carry water.
hypostyle (*hip*-oh-stile) A building having a roof or ceiling supported by rows of columns; used to describe a hall constructed of many columns; also, a row of columns.
Iban (*eh*-bahn) A tribe of coastal rice farmers in Northern Borneo, artistically distinguished by their stilted communal longhouses, finger weaving and fine basketry.
Iberia (eye-*beer*-ee-ah) The European peninsula composed of the Spanish, Portuguese and Basque peoples.
Ibibo (*ee*-bee-bo) An African tribe of the Nigeria region, artistically noted for their ritual wooden masks.
Ica (*ee*-ka) The coastal people of Southern Peru, noted for their thin polychromatic pottery in the tradition of the Nazca culture, 1200–1500.
icon (*eye*-kon) A religious image or likeness; in the Eastern Orthodox religion, usually a panel painting of a saint or of Christ.
iconoclasm (eye-*kon*-oh-klasm) Destruction of images or icons; historical examples include the Iconoclastic Controversy (eighth–ninth centuries), the Protestant purges (sixteenth–seventeenth centuries), the Tang repression (845) and the Japanese persecution of Christians (1580–1640).
iconography (eye-kon-*ah*-gra-fee) The system of symbolic elements in a work of art; the system of symbols traditionally used to identify a deity, illustrated by pictures or other visual representations; also, the study of symbols and their meanings.
iconostasis (eye-kon-*ah*-stah-sis) A decorated screen (often of icons) in Eastern Orthodox churches, separating the main part of the church from the sanctuary.
idealization The representation of objects or people in a stylized and perfected way, often following a preconceived model. Greek and Indian gods idealized human forms.
idiom (*id*-eum) A style or design peculiar to a specific place or time.
idol (*eye*-dul) A representation or symbol of a deity used as an object of worship.
Ife (*ee*-fay) The African civilization of the Nigerian coast, flourishing 1200-1500.
ikebana (ee-kay-*bahn*-ah) Japanese art of flower arranging, using flowers and other organized objects to depict mood and movement.
illumination (i-*loo*-mi-*nay*-shun) Colored illustrations, often containing gold and silver, that decorated manuscripts in medieval times in Europe.
imari (ee-*mar*-ee) Porcelain produced in the Azita region of Kyushu Island, Japan, decorated with underglaze blue and overglaze red enamels. Often gilded.
impasto (im-*pass*-toe) A thick, heavy application of paint, with either brush or knife.
imperial art (im-*peer*-i-al) Objects of beauty and high value produced by workers hired by a ruler or the court; usually the finest products become the property of the crown for use at court or as royal gifts.

impress To push into; in ceramics, patterns are made in soft or leather-hard clay by pressing with textured tools, stamps or chops.
Impressionism (im-*presh*-ah-*niz*-em) A style of painting begun in France about 1875. It stresses a candid glimpse of the subject, spontaneity and an emphasis on the momentary effects of light on color.
Inca (*ing*-kah) An ancient imperialist Peruvian culture (1200–1532) unifying many local cultures of the Andes and ruled by a king (inca). Artistically noted for their encouragement of native traditions and their expert construction of fortified cities.
incise (in-*size*) To cut into a surface with a sharp tool.
Indo-Greek See **Gandhara**.
Indra (*in*-druh) King of the Vedic gods of India, personification of the Aryan warrior, and the god of thunder and the atmosphere.
Indus Valley civilization A sophisticated early civilization of Northern India and Pakistan, probably influenced by Mesopotamian cultures, flourishing about 4000–1500 BC; distinguished by their water-worship, grid-iron pattern streets and early bronze casting.
inlay To set one material into recessed areas of another substance; to decorate with such insertions.
intaglio (in-*tahl*-ee-oh) A printmaking technique in which ink is transferred from areas beneath the surface (etched, engraved or scratched) onto paper, resulting in a print.
intensity (in-*ten*-si-tee) The strength, brightness or purity of a color. The more intense the color, the less it is weakened with admixtures of neutrals or its complementary color.
intermedia (*in*-ter-*meed*-ee-ah) An art form that uses videotapes, cinematography and animated film.
Ionic (eye-*ahn*-ik) A Classical Greek style of architecture characterized by slender columns with fluted shafts and capitals, decorated with scroll-like devices (volutes).
Iroquois (*eer*-oh-coy) The native people of Northeastern America whose hunting and fishing economy produced significant carved-bone tools; masks; carved, painted, wooden weaponry; and bark canoes.
Islam (is-*lahm*) A religious faith based on belief in Allah as the sole deity as revealed to the prophet Mohammed (570–632); also, the civilization based on that Arabic faith.
ivory (*eye*-vah-ree) A hard, white dentine substance of the tusk of elephant, hippopotamus, walrus and narwhal; also, an article made of that substance, usually by carving.
jade (jayd) Highly valued opaque-to-translucent stone, usually nephrite or jadite; known to the Chinese as *Yu*; also, a carved object made of such material.
Jain (jayn) The Indian religion following the teachings of Vardhamana Mahavira (sixth century BC), based on a doctrine of peace, harmony and non-violence.
Jalisco (hah-*lees*-ko) An ancient culture of West Mexico more attuned to Peruvian and Hohokam influences than other Mexican cultures. Thrived 100–300. Artistically known for ceramic figures of natural proportion in brown and gray clay.
jamb (jam) The upright piece, forming the side of a doorway or window frame. In Romanesque and Gothic cathedrals, the jambs were the location for tall, sculptural figures.
Jesuit (*jeh*-zoo-it) A member of the Roman Catholic "Society of Jesus," founded by Loyola in 1534, and responsible for much of the spread of Christianity in the post-Reformation period.
Jesus (*jeez*-us) Christian Son of God and Savior of the world (4 BC–30 AD) whose teachings stressed peaceful co-existence, salvation based on His dying for humanity's sins, and a resurrection to eternal life. Also known as The Christ.
jewelry (*joo*-el-ree) Objects of precious materials, usually metals and gems, worn for personal adornment.
Jomon (jo-*mahn*) Neolithic hunting society of prehistoric Japan (7000–200 BC), artistically typified by rope-designed pottery and clay fertility dolls.
Judaism (*joo*-day-*iz*-em) The Jewish religion, characterized by belief in one God and by a religious life in accordance with scriptures and rabbinic traditions; the Hebrew culture.
Judeo-Christian (*joo*-day-oh) Culture originating with Biblical Abraham and continuing through the periods of prophecy into the Christian era; the common culture shared by Christians and Jews and their heritage of religious and societal values.
jun (chun) Chinese celadon ware and kiln site in Henan Province, typified by glazes of lavender and greenish blue, frequently splashed and suffused with purple and crimson, produced by copper which has been reduced in firing.
kabuki (kah-*boo*-kee) Popular Japanese drama, both tragic and comic, involving highly costumed male actors.
kachina (kah-*chee*-nah) Small dolls or figures made by Pueblo Indians which represent the gods and are used to teach religion.
Kamakura (kah-mah-*koo*-rah) The military government in Japan (1192–1338) with a capital city at Kamakura, whose arts reflect military austerity and the growth of Buddhist salvation sects.
Kannon (*kan*-on) Japanese equivalent of the Bodhisattva Avaloketisvara and the Chinese Guan Yin. The goddess of mercy.
Karen (*kar*-en) Tribal hill people of Tibeto-Burman stock living in North Thailand, Laos and Burma, noted for their embroidered clothing and handicrafts.
keep The massive central tower of a castle and the final point of defense; also, a tower-like fortress.
Kenyah (*ken*-yah) The tribal people of Borneo, artistically noted for fine basketry.
keystone The topmost stone in an arch, and the last stone to be placed in the construction of the arch; the stone that balances the gravitational forces pulling on the arch.
Khmer (kmair) The ancient kingdom and people of Cambodia, emerging as a distinct cultural group in the sixth century, climaxing in the twelfth century with the construction of huge god-king temple complexes at Angkor and Angkor Thom.
kiln (kill) An oven capable of controlled high temperatures in which clay objects are fired or baked; also, the complex of a pottery-producing site, including workshops, studios and firing chambers.
kinetic art (ki-*net*-ik) Any three-dimensional art that contains moving parts and can be set in motion either by air currents or some type of motor. Also may refer to art in which changing light patterns are controlled by electronic switches.
Kiowa (*ky*-oh-wah) A nomadic tribe of the Oklahoma region noted for fine leather garments ornamented with beadwork.

kiva (*kee*-vah) A subterranean chamber ceremonially used by Southwestern Native Americans as a worship center; kivas were square in early phases of Pueblo culture and round during the Great Pueblo era. Roofs are low and slightly domed.
Koran (koh-*rahn*) The sacred writings as revealed by Allah to Mohammed, and the foundation of the Islamic faith.
kore (*kor*-ay) A female figure, a clothed sculpture in archaic Greek art.
krater (*kray*-ter) A tall, wide-mouthed vase, usually of earthenware, in ancient Greece and Rome. It had two handles and was used for mixing water and wine. **kraton** (kray-*tahn*) An Islamic royal palace complex.
kris (kreese) An Islamic dagger with a wavy blade, held with a decorated pistol-grip handle. Commonly associated with Southeast Asia and Javanese arts.
Krishna (*krish*-nah) A Hindu god and incarnation of Vishnu, the Preserver.
kufic script (*koo*-fik) An early Arabian writing form, used in the region south of Babylon.
kutani (koo-*tah*-nee) Kiln site and name of Japanese seventeenth-century porcelain richly decorated in overglaze enamels in patterns of birds, plants, landscapes and textiles.
kylix (*ky*-lix) An ancient Greek, two-handled, shallow wine cup, often with a stem and foot.
lacquer (*lack*-er) A durable natural resin which, when applied in many thin layers over a base of clay, wood, cloth or basketry, forms a tough and permanent object. Objects so made are called lacquer or lacquerware.
landscape A work of art that shows the features of the natural environment (trees, lakes, mountains, etc.).
lantern A small dome, usually with windows around its drum, built atop a larger dome or on a roof to allow light to enter the structure.
Lao (lau) The hill tribe people of Indo-China, noted artistically for colorful patchwork stitchery and heavy silver jewelry.
Latin cross A cross in which the vertical member is longer than the horizontal one.
leather-hard The stage in the drying process of a clay object when designs are carved and impressed, handles and other appliqués added and coatings of colored clay slips applied.
limners Early American artists who painted portraits without faces and later found patrons who wanted their faces filled in.
line An element of design that may be two-dimensional (pencil on paper), three-dimensional (wire) or implied (the edge of a shape or form).
linear perspective (*lin*-ee-ar) A system of drawing or painting to give the illusion of depth on a flat surface. All parallel lines receding into the distance are drawn to one or more imaginary vanishing points on the horizon in such a work.
linocut (*lin-oh-cut)* A relief print made by cutting a design into a block of linoleum and applying ink to the surface.
lintel (*lin*-tl) Horizontal structural member that spans an opening between two walls or posts.
lithography (li-*thog*-ra-fee) A printmaking process in which a flat stone, previously marked with a greasy substance (either a special ink or crayon) that will retain the ink, is charged with ink, placed against paper and run through a press, producing a print known as a lithograph.
live rock Stone carved where it is found in nature; rock still in its original location.
local color The color of an object seen in white (or natural) light and free from reflected colors and shadow.
Lokeshvara (low-kesh-*vahr*-ah) The Khmer equivalent of the compassionate Bodhisattva Avaloketisvara (See **Guan Yin** and **Kannon**). Depicted with a turban and four arms that carry a lotus, a rosary, a flask and a book.
longhouse Communal dwelling for an entire tribe in Borneo. The front half of the structure is a common verandah, and the back half is divided into individual dwellings for each family.
Long Shan (loong shahn) The Neolithic Chinese culture (c. 3000–1600 BC) of Gansu province, artistically typified by thin black pottery made with a potter's wheel and burnished by hand.
loom A frame or device in which yarn or other threadlike material is woven into fabric by the crossing of threads, called weft, over and under stationary warp threads.
lost-wax process See **cire perdue**.
lotus A variety of water lily popular in Egyptian, Hindu and Buddhist iconography as a symbol of purity.
low relief A surface that has only slight variations between the highest and lowest parts. Bas-relief is sculpture of low relief on a wall, and a coelanoglyph is a sculpture of low relief carved into a wall surface.
lunette (loo-*net*) A semi-circular area, such as the space at the end of a vaulted room or over a door, niche or window. When it is over the portal (main door) of a church, it is called a tympanum.
lustre (*luss*-ter) An iridescent metallic ceramic glaze or surface on glass; this effect may be created intentionally or may occur when pieces are buried in certain soils for long periods of time.
Madonna Mary, the mother of Jesus Christ.
madrasah (mah-*drahs*-ah) A style of mosque using an enclosed courtyard, but open to the sky.
maesta (my-*ays*-tah) An altarpiece with a central panel representing the enthroned Madonna adored by saints. From the Italian word for "majesty."
Mahayana (mah-hah-*yan*-ah) See **Buddhism**.
majolica (mah-*yall*-ikah) Earthenware with an opaque, low-fired, tin, enamel glaze, ornamented with colors of mineral oxides.
Manchu (*mahn*-chew) See **Qing**.
mandala (*mahn*-dahl-uh) A mystical geometric design symbolizing a supernatural understanding of the universe. Called a *mandara* in Japan.
mandorla An almond-shaped outline enclosing the full figure of a person endowed with divine light, usually Christ.
Mannerism A style and period of European art (sixteenth century) notable for its deliberate reaction against the balance of High Renaissance art. It is characterized by subjective expression, distortion of the figure, peculiar placement of figures in the composition, exaggerated perspective view and a crisp and harsh treatment of light and shadow.
Maori (*mou*-ree) Native peoples of New Zealand, artistically distinguished by totemic carvings, shellwork and finely-plaited house walls.
mask A covering worn over the face, often ascribed with supernatural powers, worn during rituals in animistic societies.
masonry (*may*-son-ree) Stone or brickwork in architecture; also, the pattern of bricks laid vertically or horizontally by courses to build up a wall.

mass The physical bulk, weight and density of a three-dimensional object; also, the celebration of the Eucharist in a Christian Church.
mastaba (mah-*stah*-bah) A rectangular Egyptian tomb of mud brick and masonry with sloping sides and a flat top used to cover the burial chamber.
mat (matt) A dull or non-reflecting surface. Also, a cardboard frame surrounding a print, drawing, watercolor or photograph.
Mauryan (*moo*-ree-un) An early Indian kingdom, founded by Chandragupta Maurya about 322 BC, uniting India for the first time. Artistically distinguished by the evolution of the stupa and the Ashokan pillar.
mausoleum (*maw*-sa-*lee*-um) A magnificent and stately tomb.
Maya (*my*-uh) An ancient Classical civilization of Eastern Mexico and the Yucatan (300–800), artistically distinguished by colored frescoes, excellent weavings, iconographic sculpture and boldly illustrated codices.
medallion (mi-*dal*-yen) A tablet or panel in a wall or window bearing a figure in relief; a portrait or a symmetrical ornament.
medium A material used by an artist and often implying the technique of using that material. The plural is **media**. Also, the solvent which suspends pigments in a paint.
megalithic Consisting of huge undressed stones, usually arranged by prehistoric peoples.
megaron (*meg*-a-rahn) In Minoan and Mycenaean culture, a large rectangular space with a hearth at the center and four columns supporting the roof. The main hall or room in palaces or houses of these early Greek cultures.
Meiji (may-jee) The Japanese era (1868–1912) of enthusiastic learning from the West.
mei-ping (may-ping) Shape of a tall Chinese vase typified by a gently tapering body toward a broad shoulder and a short narrow neck.
Melanesia (mel-ahn-*ee*-shah) The cultural area of the South Pacific, east of Fiji, artistically distinguished by painted wooden images, totemism and the tribal arts of New Guinea.
menhir (*men*-eer) A single, upright, undressed monolith, usually of prehistoric origin.
Meo (meow) The hill tribe people of Northern Thailand, Laos and Burma, artistically noted for their fine embroidery and heavy textured silverwork.
Meso-America The cultural areas of Central America and Mexico.
metallurgy (*met*-al-ur-gee) The science and technology of working with metals.
metope (*met*-oh-pee) The carved or plain areas between the triglyphs in the frieze of a Doric building.
Micronesia (my-crow-*nee*-shah) Islands of the Pacific north of the Equator and east of the Philippines where colorful weavings are produced.
minaret (min-a *ret*) A tall, slender tower attached to a mosque from which the muezzin (crier) calls people to prayer.
Ming dynasty The Chinese dynasty (1368–1644), significant for its achievements in foreign trade, scholarship and the arts (particularly in porcelain)
miniature (*min*-ee-a-*choor*) A small painting executed with great detail; a small portrait, picture or decorative letter on an illuminated manuscript.
Minimal Art Usually a wood or metal sculpture (but also a painting) using flat areas or planes in what seems a simple, geometric composition. Also, any non-representational art form using very simplified forms and colors.
mishima (mih-*shee*-mah) A Korean technique of applying colored slip into textured or etched surfaces of leather-hard pottery, developed during the twelfth century. Resulting decorative patterns are exposed after the excess slip is scraped away and the piece is glazed and fired.
Mission Indians (*mish*-en) Native tribes of Southern California who were served by the missions of San Diego, San Gabriel and San Fernando, noted for their soft-coiled baskets and fine featherwork.
Mission Style An architectural tradition of the Southwest United States, inspired by Franciscan-built churches and dormitories, typified by thick white adobe walls, arcaded or pillared verandahs, curvilinear gable walls and unglazed red tile roofing.
mixed media A two-dimensional art technique that uses more than one medium, for example, a crayon and watercolor work.
Mixtec (*mix*-teck) An ancient Mexican culture in the Puebla and Oaxaca region, flowering in the sixth-seventh centuries, but contemporary with Toltec and Aztec peoples. Significant artistically for their immense pyramid at Cholula and their fine manuscripts painted on animal skins.
mobile (*mow*-beel) A balanced construction with moving parts, suspended from above, and moving freely in the air currents. May be set in motion by a motor. Invented by Alexander Calder in 1932.
Mochica (moh-*cheek*-ah) A coastal South American culture noted for fine pottery and adobe pyramidal temples (500 BC–900 AD).
modeling (*mod*-al-ing) The forming of a three-dimensional form in a soft substance such as clay or wax. Also, the effect of light falling on a three-dimensional form, delineating its form by means of shadow and light. Also, representing this three-dimensionality of forms in a painting by means of light and dark values.
Mogollon Culture (*moh*-gull-on) The first ancient American culture of the Southwest to produce fired clay objects, from about 200 BC–1400 AD; influential on later Pueblo cultures.
Mohammed (moh-*hahm*-ed) The prophet and founder of the Islamic faith who lived in Arabia (570–632).
mold The hollow form into which molten materials (gold, lead, plaster, etc.) are poured to create a cast sculpture.
molding An ornamental strip that gives variety to the surface by creating light and shadow.
Momoyama (mo-mo-*yahm*-ah) The exuberant and vital Japanese shogunate (1573–1615) which was the pinnacle of the Samurai culture, Zen-inspired arts and political unification. The era characterized by castle construction and use of feudal armament.
monastery (*mohn*-i-*ster*-ee) Living quarters for monks.
Mongol See **Yuan**.
monochromatic (*mohn*-ah-kro-*mat*-ik) One color; refers to colors formed by changing the values of a single hue by adding the neutrals (black, white and gray).
monolith (*mohn*-oh-*lith*) A large single block of stone used in architecture or sculpture; also, a structure made of such large stones.
monotype (*mohn*-oh-tipe) Any of several printmaking techniques where the image printed is unique and not able to be reproduced.
montage (mohn-*tazh*) A composition composed of several pictures, usually pasted together; also, a painting that has that appearance.

Monte Alban (*mohn-tay ahl*-bahn) A classical Mexican civilization (200-500) of Zapotec origins, artistically distinct for burial urns in the form of gods; also, the sacred urban and necropolis center of many later Mexican civilizations.
monumental (*mohn*-you-*men*-tal) A work of art that is huge in size, often displayed in public squares. By extension, it refers to the quality of a work of art that may be small in actual size, but has the characteristics and feeling of a huge work.
Moorish Referring to the Moors, the Islamic rulers of Spain (710–1492), particularly their architecture, typified by the use of arches, stucco, tile roofing and polychromatic majolica.
mosaic (mo-*zay*-ik) A work of art consisting of pieces of colored marble or glass (tesserae) embedded in a layer of adhesive material.
mosque (mosk) An Islamic temple or place of worship.
mother-of-pearl The hard, pearly, iridescent substance forming the inner layer of a mollusk shell, used in inlay work in jewelry and furniture.
motif (mo-*teef*) The main subject or idea of a work of art, such as landscape or still life; also, the two- or three-dimensional configuration repeated in a pattern.
mound builders Early Native Americans of the Middle West and Southeast who formed large earthen burial mounds and fortifications thus creating the first earth works in America (100–1000).
movement A principle of design referring to the arrangement of parts in a work of art to create a slow-to-fast movement of one's eye through the work. Also, a style, school or artistic thought and practice, i.e., the Impressionist movement.
Mudéjar (*mood*-ay-yar) The style of Moorish architecture.
mudra (*moo*-druh) A ritual gesture which grew out of a simple gesture of the Buddha, symbolizing mystical power or action in mime or dance.
muezzin (moo-*zeen*) See **minaret**.
Mughal (*moh*-gull) The Islamic empire in India, which was founded by Baber in 1526 and flourished until 1857. Also spelled Mongul.
mullion (*mull*-yen) A vertical member separating two areas of a window.
mummification (*mum*-i-*fi*-kay-shun) The embalming of a dead body in preparation for burial as done by the ancient Egyptians.
mural (*myoor*-ul) A painting on a wall, usually large in format.
Muromachi (mur-oh-*motch*-ee) The Japanese shogunate (1338–1578) whose capital city was Kyoto, characterized aesthetically by the growth of Zen-related concepts of simplicity, restraint, subtlety, and artforms such as ikebana, sumi-e and the cha-no-yu.
Muses (*myoos*-ez) The nine sister-goddesses of Classical Greek mythology who presided over learning and the arts. There were Muses for epic poetry, history, love poetry, music, tragedy, sacred song, dance, comedy and astronomy.
Muslim (*muz*-lim) A believer in the Islamic faith.
mysticism (*miss*-ti-*siz*-um) A spiritual discipline of communion and unity with the divine, often achieved through meditation or trance-like contemplation.
Nabis (nah-*bee*) A small group of French artists who painted (1889–1899) in a style of flat, bold colors and were unconcerned with naturalism.
Naga (*nah*-gah) A divine serpent in Hindu mythology representing water spirits, guardians of cisterns and sacred water; a favorite motif in Thai, Indian and Southeast Asian Hindu art.
Nandi (*nahn*-dee) The mythological bull upon which Siva rides; hence, a symbol of Siva's fertility and reincarnation powers.
Nara (*nah*-rah) The city associated with the early Buddhist Japanese era (646–794), subdivided into the Hakuho (646–710) and the Tempyo (710–794). The period is artistically significant for its Chinese-style architecture, iconographic Buddhist sculpture in the Tang style, and the inculcation of Confucian and Buddhist ideals.
narthex A porch or vestibule, sometimes enclosed, preceding the main entrance of a church.
Nataraja (nah-tah-*rah*-jah) The "Lord of the Dance" aspect of Siva who dances the Nataraj in the frenetic art of eternal reincarnation; a popular motif in Hindu sculpture.
naturalism (*nach*-er-i-*liz*-em) The suggestion, in a work of art, of the direct observation of a scene or of a figure; also, an Italian Renaissance concept of interest in the world of nature including exploration of it scientifically.
Navajo (*nah*-vah-ho) A tribe of Native American Indians, related to the Pueblo group of the American Southwest, artistically noted for their unpainted pottery, use of the true loom in weaving outstanding blankets and rugs, and excellent hammered silverwork.
nave The central section of a church where the congregation assembles. In a basilican plan, the space extends from the main entrance to the apse or the crossing. The nave is usually flanked by side aisles.
Nayarit Mexican culture of Western coastal Mexico, artistically distinguished by the creation of ceramic figures of exaggerated features.
Nazca The coastal culture of Peru, noted for thin polychrome pottery produced from 100–1200.
necropolis (neh-*crop*-oh-liss) A cemetery of an ancient city.
negative space The area around the objects in a painting, sometimes called the background.
Neoclassicism (*nee*-oh-*klass*-i-*siz*-em) A style of art in nineteenth-century France that was a reaction to Baroque. This style was derived from the art and culture of ancient Greece and Rome and imitated this period's architecture and fascination for order and simplicity. Also, any revival of Classical ideas in the arts..
Nestorian (nest-*or*-ee-an) A sect of Christianity following the teaching of Nestorius (d. 451) who believed that the divine and human aspects of Christ are separate.
neutral A color not associated with any hue, such as black, white and gray; a neutralized color made by combining complementary colors to produce a grayish hue.
Nevers (neh-*vehr*) The center of French faience manufacture, originally established by Italian potters about 1565, typified by large plates decorated with engraving-like scenes and rich borders.
N'gere (nn-jerry) The tribal people of Nigeria, noted artistically for ritual masks.
niche (nitch) A recess in a wall, usually intended to hold a statue.
nimbus See **halo**.
Noh (no) Classical Japanese drama, originating in the fourteenth century and derived from temple dances; the stylized presentation by two richly costumed actors performing against no scenery.

Nok Ancient Nigerian civilization of about 500 BC, noted for its large sculptural figures.
nonobjective art Art that has no recognizable subject matter such as trees, flowers or people. The actual subject matter might be color or the composition of the work itself.
nonrepresentational art See **nonobjective art**.
obelisk (ob-eh-lisk) A tapering four-sided shaft of stone (usually one piece) topped by a pyramidal form, typical of Egyptian art. Sometimes called "Cleopatra's Needles."
Oceania (*o*-shee-*ahn*-ee-ah) Geographic region comprising the islands of the Pacific, artistically characterized by totemic and mystic sculptures of perishable materials, the general use of bright colors and fetishes.
oculus (*ah*-cue-lus) A circular opening in a wall or in the top of a dome, from the Latin for "eye."
odalisque (*oh*-dah-lisk) Any reclining female figure used as the subject for a painting or sculpture, from the French for "harem slave."
oil paint An opaque mixture of pigments dissolved in linseed oil using turpentine as a solvent; applied to a gessoed panel or canvas ground.
Olmec (*ohl*-mek) The mother culture of ancient Mexico (2000 BC-700 AD), centered in the Gulf coastal area, noted for the construction of the sacred city of Monte Alban and for the buildings and sculptures at La Venta.
Oneida (oh-*ny*-dah) An Iroquois tribe that moved to the Wisconsin area (1822–1827) where they became noted for fine silverwork.
Op Art A style of art that confuses the visual senses by generating optical vibrations or ambiguous or undulating spatial relationships.
optical mixing (*op*-ti-kul) Technique used by Impressionist artists in which the viewer's eye blends juxtaposed dots of color from a distance.
oracle bone (*or*-ah-kul) Large, usually flat, mammal bones or tortoise shells upon which prehistoric Chinese shamans drew picture messages. When heated, the bones cracked, revealing the response of the mystic forces, and were interpreted by the shamans who were acting as the voice of god, or oracle.
order An architectural system based on the prescribed style of column and entablature, such as the Greek Doric, Ionic and Corinthian. Also, the organization of the parts of a work of art.
overglaze Design or color applied onto a piece of ceramic after it has been glaze fired, usually made permanent by firing to a low temperature.
overlapping planes A perspective technique involving the placement in a flat composition of one object in front of another, thus creating an illusion of depth.
Paekche (*pahk*-shay) An ancient kingdom of Southwestern Korea (18 BC–663 AD) noted for its adoption and promotion of Buddhism and associated Chinese-style aristocratic arts.
pagoda (pah-*go*-dah) A circular or octagonal structure built to preserve relics, commemorate unusual acts of devotion, act as an omen of good fortune or as a water tower. Based on the Indian stupa, the form was modified when introduced to China in the third century, and again when introduced into Japan in the sixth century. Usually built of an odd number of stories.
painterly style or **painterly quality** A technique of painting in which forms are depicted by patches of color rather than by hard and precise edges. Brushstrokes are left visible as part of the surface of the painting.
painting A picture or other image composed of applied colors; the art or occupation of producing such works.
painting knife A small, shaped blade made expressly for applying paint to canvas, creating a textural surface.
palette (*pal*-it) A board or flat surface on which a painter places (and mixes) the supply of paint to be used. Also, the typical group of colors that a particular artist (or school of art) uses.
palette knife A small spatula used for mixing colors on the palette and for cleaning paints from the palette. It may be used as a painting knife.
palisade A raised earthen embankment held in place by closely set posts which act as a retaining wall.
Palladian (peh-*lay*-dee-en) An architectural style based on Renaissance motifs revived and altered by Andrea Palladio (1518–1580) which typify the buildings of Georgian England and British colonies in Asia and America.
Pallava (*pau*-lah-vah) A Southeast Indian kingdom that flourishing about 600–750, artistically distinguished by its rock-cut freestanding temples.
Pantheon Greek for "all the gods"; therefore, a temple dedicated to all the gods. Specifically, the round-domed structure built in Rome in 25 AD.
Paracas (pah-*rock*-us) An ancient culture of the south coast Peru, noted for excellent thin sculptural pottery, often in human form.
Paracas (pah-*rock*-us) **Necropolis** An ancient Peruvian culture named for burial mounds. This culture yielded weavings of superb quality.
paradigm (*pair*-ah-dime) An exceptional example or outstanding object, representative of an entire group of similar pieces.
parchment The treated skin of a lamb or goat, processed to make a smooth, flexible surface for manuscript writing and illumination.
Passion (*pash*-un) The suffering of Jesus Christ during the last week of His earthly life.
pastel A chalky, colored crayon. Also, a chalky, light-valued color.
patina (pah-*tee*-nah) The thin surface coloration on an old object or metal sculpture resulting from natural oxidation or from the careful treatment by heat, chemicals or polishing agents.
pattern A principle of design in which combinations of lines, colors and shapes are used to show real or imaginary things. Pattern may also be achieved by repeating a shape, line or color.
pavilions (pah-*vill*-yens) Protrusions of central entrance and corner sections from the facade of a building.
pediment The triangular area over the entablature in Classical Greek architecture, formed by the ends of a sloping roof and the cornice.
pendentive (*pen*-den-tiv) A triangular piece of vaulting springing from the comer of a rectangular area to support a round or polygonal dome. Usually four pendentives spring from the four comers of a crossing to support the dome.
Pentateuch (*pen*-tah-took) The first five books of the Old Testament containing early history and law of Judeo-Christian culture.
permutation (*per*-myoo-*tay*-shun) The complete change in the nature of a constituent mineral in a ceramic glaze during the firing process.
perspective The representation of three-dimensional objects and space on a flat surface to produce the same impression of distance and relative size as that received by the human eye. **Aerial** or **atmospheric perspective** creates the illusion of distance by muting color and blurring detail as objects get farther away. **Descriptive perspective** shows more important objects larger than less important objects. **Linear perspective** employs sets of parallel lines moving

closer together in the distance until they merge as an imaginary vanishing point on the horizon. Overlapping planes create distance by placing objects in front of other objects. **Worm's eye perspective** creates a feeling of majesty and distance by looking up at subject matter from a low point in the composition.

petroglyph (*pet*-row-glif) A carving on rock, usually of a stylized image or message in such images.

phoenix (*fee*-niks) A legendary bird which rises in youthful reincarnation from its own ashes of destruction. Regarded by the Chinese as the emperor of all birds and as an emblem of beauty.

photography (fa-*tog*-ra-fee) The art or process of producing images on photosensitive paper.

Photo-Realism A revival of realistic art that occurred in the 1970s.

pictograph (*pik*-ta-graf) A drawing or painting stylizing or simplifying a real image; picture-writing, thus the basis of hieroglyphics and ideographs.

picture plane The flat surface which the artist uses as a starting point for a painting. It is not the paper or canvas itself, but an imaginary flat plane that the artist uses as a visual reference, and which is at the same level or depth as the surface itself.

pier (peer) A massive vertical masonry pillar that supports an arch, vault or other kind of roof. Also used under pendentives to support a dome. A square area in a Gothic church marked by a pier at each corner is known as a "bay."

pieta (pee-ay-*tah*) The scene of Mary holding and mourning over the body of the dead Christ, her son. From the Italian word for "pity."

pigment A dry powder that supplies the coloring agent for paint, crayons, chalk and ink.

pilaster (pih-*las*-ter) A rectangular engaged column, sometimes decorative, but at other times used to buttress a wall.

pillar Any vertical architectural member, such as a column, pier or pilaster.

Plains Indians Semi-nomadic horsemen of the Western Mississippi basin, including the Blackfoot, Crow, Sioux, Cheyenne, Arapaho, Kiowa and Comanche tribes. Artistically significant for excellent leatherwork, bone and horn carving, and symbolically decorated rawhide tipis.

plane A flat surface that can be measured by length and width (two dimensions).

plastic The quality that describes material that can be shaped or manipulated, such as clay or wax; flexibility. Also, the three-dimensional quality (roundness) of an artwork. Also, any of a number of synthetic materials with various physical characteristics.

Plateresque (pla-ter-*esk*) A rich, ornate style of decoration resembling overdecorated silverwork, typical of the Spanish Baroque era.

plaza A public square or assembly space.

plinth The base of a building, column, pedestal or wall which is usually marked on top by a molding.

pointillism (*point*-till-iz-em) A style of nineteenth-century French painting in which colors are systematically applied to canvas in small dots, producing a vibrant surface.

polychrome (*pol*-ee-*krom)* Several colors rather than one (monochrome).

Polynesia (pahl-ee-*nee*-zha) A scattered island group of the East Pacific with an artistic tradition characterized by the use of perishable materials and shells, and by large mystic sculptures in wood and stone.

polyptych (pah-*lip*-tik) An altarpiece or devotional painting consisting of more than three panels joined together.

Pomo (*poh*-moh) A Native American tribe of central coastal California, regarded as the finest basketmakers in the world, although their other arts are not highly developed. Typical of their baskets are fine, water-tight weaving, and ornamentation with polychromatic feather work.

Pop Art A style of art in the 1950s that used popular, mass-media symbols (such as a Coke bottle) as subject matter, treating them in both serious and satirical ways.

porcelain (*por*-sell-in) Fine white clay, made primarily of kaolin; also, an object of such clay which is hard, translucent, sonorous, non-porous and, usually, very thin. Porcelain may be decorated with mineral colorants under the glaze or with overglaze enamels.

portal A door or gate, usually of importance or large in size. In Gothic cathedrals, there were usually three portals in the main facade.

portico (*por*-tih-ko) A porch with a roof, supported by columns and usually having an entablature and a pediment.

portrait The image of a person's face, made of any sculptural material or any two-dimensional medium.

positive design A pattern or image created by painting or carving.

positive space The objects in a work of art as opposed to the background or space around the objects.

post and lintel The oldest and simplest way of building an opening: two vertical members (posts) support a horizontal beam (lintel) above them, creating a covered space. The structure can be part of a wall or can be freestanding.

poster A form of graphic art, created for the purpose of making a public announcement.

Post-Impressionism The style of late nineteenth-century French art that immediately followed the Impressionists. Paul Cézanne was a leader of this style which stressed more substantial subjects than those of the Impressionists, and a conscious effort to design the surface of the painting.

Post-Painterly Abstraction Another name for Color Field Painting.

potter's wheel A weighted horizontal disc that revolves on a vertical spindle, upon which clay is symmetrically shaped by a potter as the wheel spins.

pottery Ceramic ware made from clay that is shaped while moist and soft, and made hard and brittle by firing; also, coarser ware so made.

prang A tiered, rounded spire, used in Thai architecture.

pre-Columbian The culture of Meso-America and South America prior to the European colonization period initiated by Columbus' voyage of 1492.

primary colors The hues from which all other spectrum colors can be made: red, yellow and blue (in painting): red, green and blue (in light waves).

primitive The native arts of any culture, usually on a less sophisticated level than that of modern times; a culture before it adopts the ways of another. Also used to describe the art produced by untrained or naive artists.

print A multiple impression made from a master plate or block, produced and printed by the artist (or under his/her supervision).

printmaking The art of producing prints.

proofs The trial prints produced by a printmaker prior to making the final edition (completed set of prints).

proportion (prah-*por*-shen) A comparative size relationship between several objects or between parts of a single object or person. In figure drawing and painting, the correct relationship between the size of head and body.
prototype An original model on which other similar objects are patterned; the first in a series; a piece which inspires future creations.
Pueblo (*pweb*-lo) A communal dwelling consisting of groups of continuous flat-roofed stone or adobe houses; the Native American culture of the Southwestern United States typified by its use of such dwellings, and artistically noted for its excellent slip-painted pottery, loom-woven clothing and blankets, and kachinas.
pylon (*pie*-lahn) The huge entrance structure for an Egyptian freestanding temple, formed by a pair of square tapering piers with a flat top and no connecting lintel. From the Greek word for "gateway." Also, significant pillars in contemporary architecture.
qibla (*kee*-blah) A niche in the inner wall of a mosque, facing toward Mecca.
Qin (chin) A short-lived Chinese dynasty (221–206 BC) responsible for the unification of China, artistically noted for the standardization of Chinese writing and the unification of the Great Wall.
Qing (ching) The final dynastic era of China (1644–1911) also known as the Manchu named for the foreign ruling family. Artistically responsible for few innovations in the major arts, although new forms of ceramic decoration evolved and production of trade goods expanded as a result of contacts with European traders.
quatrefoil (*kwa*-trah-foyl) A four-lobed form used for ornamentation.
Quetzalcoatl (kwet-sah-*kwah*-tel) A Meso-American god representing the dual forces of nature as a bird (sky) and serpent (earth) combination. Called the Feathered Serpent.
radial balance A design based on a circle with features radiating from a central point.
Rama (*rah*-mah) The king and hero of the Ramayana epic and one of the incarnations of Vishnu (the Preserver).
Ramayana (rah-mah-*yah*-nah) The Hindu epic tale of King Rama and his wife Sita, which teaches morality and worthy human behavior. Known in Thailand as the *Ramakien.*
Ravana (rah-*vah*-nah) A mythological demon-king, depicted with multiple heads and arms in Hindu iconography.
realism A mid-nineteenth-century style of art based on the belief that the subject matter should be shown true to life, without any stylization or idealization. By extension it can refer to realistically painted work of any time.
reduction (re-*duk*-shun) The stage in the firing process of glazed ceramics that results in insufficient oxygen for combustion, causing chemical changes in the oxides in clay and glaze.
Regency (*re*-jen-see) The period during which George, Prince of Wales, ruled England in the stead of his father (1811–1820), typified artistically by a taste for exotic Indian and Chinese motifs in art and architecture.
register (*rej*-i-ster) One of a series of horizontal bands placed one above the other, usually a format for painting. Commonly used in Egyptian tomb painting, medieval church sculpture, Aztec codices and manuscript illumination.
reinforced concrete Building material composed of concrete with rods or webs of steel embedded in it; ferroconcrete.
relief (re-*leef) A* sculptural surface which is not freestanding, but projects from a background of which it is a part. High relief or low relief describes the amount of the projection. See **bas-relief**.
reliquary (*reh*-li-kweh-ree) A container for religious relics.
reliquary figures are carved guardians that stand above basket receptacles for ancestral remains.
Renaissance A revival or rebirth of cultural awareness and learning: specifically in Europe, a period of time (about 1400–1600) following the middle ages that featured an emphasis on human beings and their environment, on science and on philosophy, all of which directed the interest back to the culture of ancient Greece and Rome.
rendering The careful and complete drawing or painting of an object, place or person to make it appear realistic.
repoussé (ree-*pooh*-say) The technique of hammering or pressing sheet metal from the reverse side to raise up a shaped or ornamented pattern; a piece of metalwork so made.
representational (*rep*-re-zen-*tay*-shun-ul) Any artistic style in which objects or figures are easily identified.
reredos (*reer*-dahs) An ornamental facing or screen of stone or wood covering the wall at the back of an altar; a hanging of velvet or silk for the same purpose.
resin (*rez*-in) A tree gum substance used to waterproof unglazed fired pottery by rubbing it into the porous surface.
retable (ree-*tay*-bull) A large ornamental wall behind an altar with shelves or frames enclosing decorated panels.
rhythm (*rith*-em) A principle of design that indicates a type of movement in an artwork or design, often by repeated shapes, lines or colors.
rib A slender projecting arch, used as support in Romanesque and Gothic vaults. In late Gothic architecture, the ribs are often ornamental as well as structural, forming lace-like patterns.
ribbed vault A vault constructed of a system of self-supporting ribs and a web of thinner material, filling the spaces between the ribs.
ritual (*rich*-oo-al) A formal procedure or act in a religious observance.
rococo (roh-*koh*-koh) A late Baroque style (about 1715–1775) that can be described as pretty, private and, often, erotic and effete; also, any such elaborate or overdone phase in any culture.
Romanesque A style of architecture, painting or sculpture popular in the eleventh and twelfth centuries.
Romanticism (ro-*man*-ti-*siz*-em) A style of art that emphasizes the personal, emotional and dramatic aspects of exotic, literary and historical subject matter. Specifically, a European style from the mid-eighteenth century onward.
rosary (*ro*-zeh-ree) A string of beads used as a memory aid in the recitation of prayers in any religion; specifically refers to a series of prayers to the Virgin Mary aided by such a device.
rosette (ro-*zet*) A circular decorative element, suggestive of a flattened rose.
rose window A circular window with stone tracery radiating from the center and a characteristic feature of Gothic church architecture.
rotunda (ro-*tun*-dah) A round building or interior hall, topped by a dome.
roundel A circular decorative element.
rustication (russ-tee-*kay*-shun) A surface of massive stonework, having a rough contour with deep joints, with a resultant appearance of strength and solidity.

salon (sah-*lon*) A reception room. Also, an exhibition of the works of living artists and, specifically, the annual exhibition of French art in Paris.
samurai (*sah*-moo-ry) A member of the feudal warrior class of medieval Japan.
sanctuary (*sangk*-choo-*er*-ee) A sacred or holy place, usually enclosed within a temple or church building, often housing an altar and other worship aids.
sarcophagus (sar-*koff*-ah-gus) A stone coffin, often elaborately carved.
saturation (*sach*-ah-*ray*-shun) Also called intensity. The measure of the brilliance and purity of a color. Saturation decreases as the hue is neutralized.
scale The relative size of an object when compared to others of its kind, to its environment or to humans.
school Artists who have a similar philosophy and style or who work under a common influence.
script Written or printed lettering.
sculpture (*skulp*-cher) A three-dimensional work of art.
Scytho-Parthians (*sith*-oh-*par*-thee-uns) Ancient nomadic peoples of Southeast Europe and Central Asia before 100 BC, artistically significant for their development of the "animal style."
secondary colors Orange, green and violet: hues produced by the mixing of equal parts of two primary colors.
section (*sek*-shun) A diagram of a building, showing how it would look if it were cut open on a vertical plane.
secular (*sek*-yew-lar) Non-religious.
self-portrait A portrait of the artist created by the artist.
sepia (*see*-pee-ah) A warm dark-brown color.
sepulchre (*sep*-uhl-ker) A place of burial; a tomb.
serape (sehr-*ah*-pee) A blanket-like shawl worn in Hispanic cultures.
seraph (*sehr*-ahf) An angel; a celestial being.
series Many paintings exploring the same theme over a period of time.
serigraphy (seh-*rig*-raff-ee) A form of printmaking using stencils attached to a porous screen of silk through which the ink is forced. Also called silk screen printing.
serpentine (*sir*-pen-teen) A mineral with a dull green color, composed of magnesium silicate, usually with a mottled appearance closely resembling jade; also, a winding, snake-like line or design.
sfumato (sfoo-*mah*-toh) A slight blurring of the edges of figures and objects in a painting, creating a hazy feeling and aerial perspective.
sgraffito (skrah-*fee*-toh) The process of scratching lines into the surface of a work of art to expose the surface underneath.
shade A low-valued color, made by adding black to a hue.
shading Graduated variations in value, often used in painting to give a feeling of volume, form and depth.
shaft The main part of a column, between the base and the capital, which may be plain, fluted or twisted.
Shailendra (shy-*lynn*-druh) The Buddhist kingdom of ancient central Java (700–850) artistically noted for the construction of the ten-layered cosmic mountain stupa at Borobudor.
shaman (*shah*-mun) A priest who uses magic to cure the sick, predict the future or control nature.
Shang The Bronze-age culture in northern China (about 1600–1027 BC), artistically distinguished by their fine ritual containers made by the cire-perdue process.
shape An element of design that is an enclosed space, having only two dimensions. Shapes can be geometric (triangular, square, etc.) or organic (free form, with curving and irregular outlines).
shaped canvases Canvases in other shapes besides the traditional rectangle.
Shingon (*shin*-gon) A sect of Japanese Buddhism, and the major esoteric philosophy of Japan.
Shinto (*shin*-to) The native religion of Japan, marked by veneration of nature spirits.
shogun (*show*-gun) A generalissimo; military rulers who controlled Japan beginning with the Kamakura era, leaving the Emperor as a figurehead.
Shoshone (show-*show*-nee) A Native American tribe of the Central Basin; a basketmaking group of nomadic seed-gatherers.
side aisle The arcaded walkways on either side of the nave of a Christian church.
sikhara (*sick*-ah-rah) The tall curved roof of an Indian sanctuary.
silk screen See **serigraphy**.
simultaneity (*si*-mul-*ta*-nay-*i*-tee) The technique of depicting objects from separate vantage points in one work of art.
sinicization (sin-uh-siz-*ay*-shun) The process of acquiring Chinese culture.
Sioux (soo) Native Americans of the Plains, living in tipis and artistically noted for colored and beaded leatherwork, silversmithing and quillwork.
Sita (*see*-tah) The legendary wife of the epic-king, Rama.
Siva (*shee*-vah) The third member of the Hindu trinity and controller of great destructive and procreative powers. Also known as Bhairava (The Frightful); Nataraja (Master of the Dance); and Vinadhara (Master of the Arts). Represented with one of two wives (Parvati or Uma); with Nandi (the bull upon which he rides); as a man with a third eye; or as a phallic symbol known as a *lings* (which looks like a fire hydrant).
Six Dynasties An era of political turmoil in China (256–589) during which various dynasties ruled parts of China, and Buddhism from India became well established, especially in the sculpture of the Northern Wei (about 400–550).
sketch A quick drawing that catches the immediate feeling of action or the impression of a place or situation.
slip A thin mixture of clay and water, used both as a clay glue and as a paint on leather-hard ware.
soft sculpture (*skulp*-cher) Sculpture made with fabric and stuffed with soft material.
Song (sung) The Chinese dynasty (960–1127 in the North, continuing until 1279 in the South) during which Chinese aesthetics reached a zenith of sophistication, notably in architecture, painting and ceramics.
space An element of design that indicates areas in a painting (positive and negative); also, the feeling of depth in a two-dimensional work of art.
spandrel A space between two arches and a horizontal molding or cornice above them.
spectrum Bands of colored light, created when white light is passed through a prism; the full range of color.
sphinx (sfinks) A creature of Egyptian art with the body of a lion and the head of a man. In Greek mythology, a monster with the winged body of a lion and the head of a woman.
sprigging The attaching of pre-formed, leather-hard clay ornaments to a larger form; these ornaments are usually plant forms, human or animal bas-reliefs, or geometric bands.

squash blossom (skwash *bloss*-um) A popular motif among Southwestern Native American silversmiths, resembling an open trumpet-like flower and representing abundance.
Sri Vijaya (sree vih-*jih*-ah) An ancient Hindu-Buddhist kingdom of Southeast Asia (eighth–thirteenth centuries) stretching from Java to Southern Thailand, significant for early bronze images and as a Buddhist monastic center.
stabile (*stay*-bile) A standing sculpture with moveable parts.
stain painting The technique used by Helen Frankenthaler in which she stained her canvases with paint.
statue (*stach*-oo) A freestanding sculpture.
stele (*stee*-lee) An upright slab, bearing sculptured or painted designs or inscriptions. From the Greek for "standing block."
stencil (*sten*-sill) A method of producing images by cutting openings in a mask of paper, wax or other material so that paint or dye may go through the openings to the material beneath. Used in serigraphy, batik and ceramic decoration.
step pyramid A solid stone structure built of six huge steps and used as a tomb for an Egyptian Pharaoh.
still life A group of inanimate objects arranged to be painted or drawn; also, a painting or drawing of such an arrangement.
stirrup handle A hollow, loop-like handle resembling in shape the inverted U-shaped metal holder for a horseman's foot. Common in pre-Columbian pottery.
stoa (*stow*-ah) A large porch or covered colonnade in Greek architecture, used for a meeting place, walkway or place for small businesses and offices.
structure (*struk*-cher) The compositional relationships in a work of art; also, a building.
stucco (*stuk*-oh) Any of several types of plaster used for decorative cornices, moldings or ceilings; also, a cement coating for the exterior of a building.
stupa (*stew*-pah) A reliquary structure based on the Vedic funerary mound which represents the Buddhist cosmic mountain and commemorates sacred places, events or people (especially Buddha and Buddhist monks).
stupa-temple A Burmese modification of the Buddhist monument, incorporating a worship space underneath the bell-shaped stupa.
style (stile) The distinctive characteristics contained in the works of art of a person, period of time or geographic location.
stylization (*stile*-i-*zay*-shun) The simplification or generalization of forms found in nature to present a personal and more decorative feeling in a work of art or lettering.
stylobate (*sty*-low-bayt) The immediate foundation for a row of columns, often set on a foundation.
subject That which is represented in a work of art.
subtractive sculpture Sculpture formed by cutting away excess material from a block, leaving the finished work.
Sui (swee) A short-lived Chinese dynasty (581–618) during which Buddhist art and architecture evolved into a more Chinese and less Indian style.
Sukothai (*soo*-koh-ty) An early Thai kingdom (1238–1349) during which national architectural and sculptural styles became established; the golden age of Thai Buddhist sculpture and ceramics.
sultan A local Muslim sovereign; a ruler of both secular and Islamic aspects of society.
sumi-e (*soo*-mee-ay) Japanese black ink painting on white paper in the Chinese style.
Super-Realism A twentieth-century style of painting that emphasizes photographic realism. Many times the objects are greatly enlarged, yet keep their photographic appearance.
support The material in a painting upon which the work is done (canvas, panels, paper, etc.).
Surrealism (seh-*ree*-a-*liz*-um) A style of twentieth-century art in which artists combine normally unrelated objects and situations. Scenes are often dream-like or set in unnatural surroundings.
Sutra (*soo*-trah) Buddhist scripture.
symbol A form, image, sign or subject representing a meaning other than its outward appearance.
symmetry (*sim*-i-tree) A formally balanced composition.
tabard A tunic with open sides.
Tang (tang) Classical Chinese dynasty (618–906) typified by a cosmopolitan character which encouraged the growth of new ideas. Artistically significant for the development of the pagoda form, glazed and unglazed tomb figures and other pottery masterpieces; the final Chinese influence on Buddhist sculpture and sophisticated ink paintings.
Tao (*dah*-oh) The Chinese philosophy regarding the relationships of nature and its forces, based on the teachings of Lao zi in the sixth century BC; means "The Way"; Taoism.
tapestry (*tap*-i-stree) A wall hanging of textile fabric painted, embroidered or woven with colorful ornamental designs or scenes.
tapestry weave A plain or basketweave fabric in which the weft threads are compressed so as to completely cover all warp threads.
Tarascan (tah-*rass*-kan) A culture of West Mexico that maintained independence during the reign of the Aztecs, significant for its claywork.
tatami (tah-*tah*-mee) Rice-straw flooring mats, 36" x 72", about 2" thick, used in Japan.
tattoo An indelible mark or design fixed upon the body by production of sores or insertion of pigment under the skin. From the Tahitian word *tatu* for "a mark."
technology (tek-*nahl*-oh-gee) The understanding and systematic use of materials, tools and processes.
tempera A water-based paint in which egg yolk is used as a vehicle. Some commercially made paints are called tempera, but are actually gouache.
tenebrism A late-sixteenth-century Italian painting technique which exaggerated strong contrasts of light and dark. (tenebroso in Italian)
Teotihuacan (tee-oh-*tee*-hwah-kahn) A classic Mexican civilization (about 350–850) and sacred city of temple pyramids, typified by the use of colored frescoes of gods, symbols and human subjects.
terra cotta Baked earth-red clay, used in ceramics and sculpture. Often glazed, it is used in both architectural decoration and tableware.
tessera (*tess*-ah-rah); pl. tesserae (*tess*-ah-ree) Bits of colored glass or stone used in making mosaics.
texture (*teks*-chur) The element of design that refers to the quality of a surface, both tactile and visual.
Thai (ty) Ancient and contemporary people of the Chao Phaya basin, emerging as a culturally distinct group in the thirteenth century, artistically distinguished by their Buddhist architecture, sculpture and mosaics.
therianthropic (theer-ee-an-*throp*-ic) The combination of human and animal forms into one being, such as a centaur or sphinx.

theriomorphic (theer-ee-ah-*mor*-fik) Having the form of an animal, such as a god taking the form of a jaguar or falcon.
thrust A strong, continued pressure, as the outward force exerted by an arch or vault that must be counterbalanced by buttressing.
thunderbird A mythological bird of North American Indian culture, responsible for thunder, lightning and rain; depicted in a stylized geometric pattern with outstretched wings.
Tiahuanaco (tee-a-*wan*-ah-ko) The Andean culture that united the region's various cultures (about 900–1200).
Ting A Chinese three-legged vessel made of clay, lacquer or bronze for ceremonial purposes.
tint A light value of a hue made by adding white to the original color.
tipi (*tee*-pee) A conical, rawhide dwelling consisting of groups of buffalo hides stretched over a framework of poles, its base diameter ranging from 12 to 30 feet. Characteristic dwelling of the Plains Indians of America.
tokonoma (toh-koh-*noh*-mah) An alcove in a Japanese interior, wherein are placed single objects of beauty for appreciation.
Toltec (*toll*-teck) A war-like people of semi-nomadic origin who unified northern Mexico about 947. Their capital at Tula is characterized by a temple with a pyramidal base and columns of atlantes.
tondo A round-shaped painting.
tone The modification of a color (hue) through the addition of neutrals.
Torah Jewish religious literature.
torii (*tore*-ee) The freestanding gateway at the entrance to a Japanese Shinto temple, consisting of two upright posts supporting a curved lintel, with a straight crosspiece below.
totem (*toe*-tem) An animal or natural object which symbolizes a clan or family. **totem pole** A tall post or pillar carved with the heredity marks, emblems or badges of a tribe or clan, functioning as a type of family tree.
Totonac (toe-*toe*-nack) The classic Mexican civilization of Veracruz (100–1000) typified artistically by the great religious pyramid temple center of El Tajin and light-hearted terra-cotta sculpture.
tracery Ornamental stonework in a decorative pattern with a lace-like effect; a decorative interlacing of lines suggestive of such stonework.
transept The part of a cross-shaped church at right angles to the long nave, usually with one arm on each side of the crossing.
transitional (tran-zish-en-l) A style of art in which influences and tastes are changing from an established practice to a distinctly different form.
transmutation (*tranz*-myoo-*tay*-shun) The conversion of one element into another; a process in the firing of some specialized ceramic glazes.
trefoil (*tree-foyl)* A three-lobed form or ornamentation.
triforium (try-*for*-ee-um) An arcade, often blind, below the clerestory of the nave in a Gothic church.
triglyph (*try*-glif) A group of three vertical ridges alternating with a plain metope in the frieze of a Doric Greek building.
triptych (*trip*-tik) An altarpiece consisting of three panels joined together. Often, the two outer panels are hinged to close over the central panel.
triumphal arch (try-*um*-fal) A monument built to commemorate a great victory with an open vaulted passageway through it. Also, in the Christian church, the large arched opening that separates the chancel (apse) from the nave of the church.
trompe-l'oeil (tromp loy) A type of painting that is so realistic (in form, color, size and lighting) that the viewer may be convinced that it is the actual subject and not a painting. From the French for "fool the eye."
true arch A round arch that actually supports the weight of a wall as opposed to a blind arch which is a surface motif in a wall.
truss An assemblage of structural members forming a rigid framework under a roof; also used in bridge design.
turret A small tower, which may be functional or ornamental, at the outside angle of a larger structure.
twining To wind or twist.
tympanum (*tim*-pa-num) A carved or decorated space over the door and under the arch of a Romanesque or Gothic church facade.
ukiyo-e (oo-key-*oh*-eh) Japanese pictures of the "floating world" pleasure district of Edo. These were first made in paint, but were more commonly produced in editions of polychrome woodcuts. They are the unique creation of the Edo period.
unity A principle of design that relates to the sense of oneness or wholeness in a work of art.
urna (*urn*-ah) The third eye of Buddha, iconographically depicted as a curl of hair on the forehead.
ushnisha (ush-*neesh*-ah) The knot of hair at the crown of Buddha's head or a bulge in the back of his skull which symbolically represents his wisdom.
value (*val*-yoo) An element of design that relates to the lightness and darkness of a color or tone.
vanishing point An imaginary point or points at eye level, toward which parallel lines recede and where they will eventually meet in perspective drawing and painting.
vault (vawlt) An arched roof or covering made of brick stone or concrete. A barrel vault
or tunnel vault is semi-circular. A corbeled vault is made by having each course protrude a little beyond the course below it until the two sides meet. See **groined vault**.
Vedas (*vay*-dahs) Sacred writings of Hindu philosophy, including the hymns to nature (Sanhitas); ethical and moral writings (Brahmanas); treatises on metaphysics (Aranyatas); and the quest for truth (Upanisads). Formulated during the centuries before 600 BC giving the name "Vedic Era" to the previous millennium.
vehicle (*ve*-i-kull) The binding agent in paint that holds the pigment together and forms a film that adheres to the support or ground.
velarium An awning at the top of the Colosseum in Rome that protected spectators from sun and rain.
vellum A fine parchment made from calfskin and used for writing, manuscript illumination and book binding.
view painting An eighteenth-century style of painting depicting city views with incredible accuracy.
Vishnu (*vee*sh-noo) The preserver god of the Hindu trinity, often incarnated as the mild and benevolent Krishna.
volute (voh-*loot*) A spiral ornament, resembling a rolled scroll.
voussoir (voo-*swahr*) A wedge-shaped stone block used in the construction of an arch.
walkabout An initiation ritual for Australian aborigines entering adulthood involving survival skills against nature.

ware A general term for pottery, particularly pottery made for export or sale; by extension, anything made for sale or barter.
warm color A hue in the red to yellow range in the spectrum.
wash A thin transparent layer of paint; also, a thinned mixture of solvent and paint.
wat (wot) A Thai or Laotian temple; a Khmer pagoda.
watercolor Any paint that uses water as a medium, including acrylic, gouache, casein, tempera and transparent watercolor. In a more restricted sense, a paint which has gum arabic as a vehicle and water as a medium (called transparent watercolor or aquarelle). Also, a painting done with this paint.
wattle-and-daub (dawb) A building technique for filling in walls between structural members using a fabrication of poles interwoven with slender branches, reeds, etc., and imbedded with mud.
Wayang Style (*wy*-yong) Indonesian painting of figures which duplicates the flat side views of local shadow puppets; also, relief carving in a form similar to the wooden puppets of local plays. While this style originated in the Hindu-Javanese kingdoms, the plays (Wayang) are part of the Islamic culture as well.
web The thin masonry surface between the ribs of a vault.
Wei (way) Name of a number of dynastic eras in China between 220 and 535, controlling various regions of the country, artistically distinguished by early Buddhist sculptures in the Gandharan style.
westwork The western facade of a medieval European church that includes the main entrance and usually several towers.
wheel-thrown Ceramic objects made by forming clay on a spinning disc, producing a symmetrical round form. See **potter's wheel**.
woodcut A relief print made by cutting a design into the flat surface of a block of wood and applying ink only to the raised surface.
wood engraving A relief print made from a design cut into the end grain of a hardwood block and applying ink only to the raised surface.
Xia (*she*-ah) An ancient Chinese culture (1500–1200 BC) typified by the evolution of oracle bones on which pictographic symbols were inscribed as messages to the gods; also spelled Hsia.
Yamato (ya-*mah*-toh) The cultural area of old Japan, being the plain where Nara, Kyoto and Osaka are located.
yamato-e (ya-*mah*-toh-ay) Japanese style painting, an indigenous response to Chinese brush painting, typified by Japanese genre subjects in a delicate linear style.
Yang Shao (yang show) A Neolithic culture of central China (about 7000–1600 BC), typified artistically by handbuilt terra-cotta pottery with impressed designs or slip-painted spiral motifs.
Yaqui (*yah*-kee) A tribe of Uto-Aztec Indians of Sonora, Mexico.
Yayoi (*yah*-yoy) An agricultural society in pre-historic Japan (200 BC–300 AD) typified artistically by thin-walled, footed pottery.
Yuan (*you*-un) The Mongol dynasty of Chinese history which controlled all of China (1279–1368), artistically significant for the development of blue-and-white porcelain, an infusion of Central Asian culture and a revival of Tang artistic practices.
Zapotec (za-*poh*-tek) Ancient Mexican people in the Valley of Oaxaca (wah-*hah*-kah) (about 200–1000) centered at Monte Alban, typified by their architecture of stuccoed and painted temples and pyramids.
Zen A Buddhist sect emphasizing contemplation and meditation, self-discipline, and that the Buddha is inherent in all things. More commonly known by the Japanese spelling (Zen), it originated in China as Chan.
Zhou (zhoh) Chinese dynasty (1111–256 BC) typified artistically by elaborate cast bronze ritual vessels and sophisticated jade carving; Chou.
ziggurat (*zig*-oo-rat) The high temple platform, built of mud brick, of Sumerian and Assyrian architecture. Usually built in the form of a truncated stepped pyramid with ramp-like stairways leading to the sanctuary at the top.
zoopraxiscope A photographic device invented by Eadweard Muybridge in the late 1870s which produced a series of images of a moving subject.
Zuni (*zoo*-nee) A tribe of Southwestern Native Americans, artistically distinguished as the finest of Pueblo silversmiths and typified by their use of turquoise.

Bibliography

Further Reading

There are literally hundreds of books on the shelves of libraries and bookstores that offer both general and detailed information about art and art history. Some are technical while others feature many pictures; some are written for art specialists, others for the general public. The authors found the following books useful, but by all means explore school, university (if accessible) and public libraries for more information.

General Reference

Boorstin, Daniel J. *Creators: A History of Heroes of the Imagination.* New York: Random House Inc., 1992.

Carey, John, ed. *Eyewitness to History.* New York: Avon, 1990.

Chapman, Laura. *A World of Images.* Worcester, MA: Davis Publications, Inc., 1992.

———. *Art: Images and Ideas.* Worcester, MA: Davis Publications, Inc., 1992.

Chilvers, Ian. *The Concise Oxford Dictionary of Art and Artists.* New York: Oxford University Press, 1990.

Cooke, Jean, et al. *History's Timeline.* London: Grisewood and Dempsey, 1981.

Cunningham, Lawrence, and Reich, John. *Culture and Values: A Survey of the Western Humanities.* 2 vols. New York: Holt, Rinehart and Winston Inc., 1982.

de la Croix, Horst, and Tansey, Richard G. *Gardner's Art through the Ages.* 10th ed. Orlando: Harcourt Brace Jovanovich, 1995.

The Dictionary of Art. Jane Shoaf Turner, Ed. 34 vols. New York: Grove's Dictionaries, Inc., 1996

Fine, Elsa H. *Women and Art: A History of Women Painters and Sculptors from the Renaissance to the Twentieth Century.* Montclair, NJ: Allanheld and Schram, 1978.

Finn, David. *How to Look at Sculpture.* New York: Harry N. Abrams Inc., 1989.

Fleming, William. *Arts and Ideas.* 8th ed. Orlando: Harcourt Brace Jovanovich, 1991.

Fletcher, Banister. *A History of Architecture.* Ed. J.C. Palmes, 18th ed., rev. New York: Macmillan, 1975.

Friedenthal, Richard, trans., et al. *Letters of the Great Artists.* Vol. 1, *From Ghiberti to Gainsborough.* Vol. 2, *From Blake to Pollock.* London: Thames and Hudson Inc., 1963.

Goldwater, Robert, and Treves, Marco. *Artists on Art: From the Fourteenth to the Twentieth Century.* New York: Pantheon Books, 1974.

Grun, Bernard. *The Timetables of History: A Horizontal Linkage of People and Events.* Updated ed. New York: Touchstone, 1987.

Harris, Ann S. *Women Artists, 1550–1950.* New York: Alfred A. Knopf Inc., 1977.

Hartt, Frederick. *History of Art: Painting, Sculpture, Architecture.* 3rd ed. New York: Harry N. Abrams Inc., 1989.

Hobbs, Jack A., and Duncan, Robert L. *Arts, Ideas and Civilization.* Englewood Cliffs, NJ: Prentice Hall, 1989.

Hobbs, Jack and Salome, Richard A. *The Visual Experience.* 2nd ed. Worcester, MA: Davis Publications, Inc., 1995.

Holt, Elizabeth G. *A Documentary History of Art: The Middle Ages and The Renaissance* , vol I: *Michelangelo and The Mannerist–The Baroque and The Eighteenth Century,* vol II, 2nd ed. Princeton: Princeton University Press, 1983.

———, ed. *Impressionist: Art and Architecture in the Nineteenth Century.* Vol. 3 of *Documentary History of Art.* New Haven: Yale University Press, 1986.

Honour, Hugh, and Fleming, John. *The Visual Arts: A History.* 3rd ed. Englewood Cliffs, NJ: Prentice Hall, 1991.

Jacobus, Lee A. *Humanities.* New York: McGraw-Hill Inc., 1986.

Janson, H. W. with contributions by Anthony F. Janson. *The History of Art.* New York: Harry N. Abrams Inc., 1995.

Murray, Peter, and Murray, Linda. *A Dictionary of Art and Artists.* 5th ed. London: Penguin, 1984.

Phipps, Richard, and Wink, Richard. *Invitation to the Gallery: An Introduction to Art Appreciation.* Carmel, IA: Brown and Benchmark, 1987.

Piper, David, ed. *Random House Dictionary of Art and Artists.* New York: Fodor's Travel Publications Inc., 1990.

Read, Herbert, and Stangos, Nikos, eds. *The Thames and Hudson Dictionary of Art and Artists.* Rev. ed. London: Thames and Hudson, Inc. Inc., 1988.

Slatkin, Wendy. *The Voices of Women Artists.* Englewood Cliffs, NJ: Prentice Hall, 1993.

———. *Women Artists in History.* 2nd ed. Englewood Cliffs, NJ: Prentice Hall, 1989.

Vidal-Naquet, Pierre. *The Harper Atlas of World History.* New York: Harper and Row, 1987.

Prehistoric Art, Mesopotamia and Egypt

Aldred, C. *Akhenaten and Nefertiti.* New York: Brooklyn Museum/Viking Press, 1973.

———. *Art of Ancient Egypt.* 3 vols. New York: Trans-Atlantic Publications Inc., 1974.

———. *Development of Ancient Egyptian Art from 3200 to 1315 BC.* New York: Trans-Atlantic Publications Inc., 1975.

Amiet, P. *Art of the Ancient Near East.* New York: Harry N. Abrams Inc., 1980.

Childe, V. G. *The Dawn of European Civilization.* 6th ed. New York: Alfred A. Knopf Inc., 1958.

El Mahdy, Christine, ed. *The World of the Pharaohs: A Complete Guide to Ancient Egypt.* London: Thames and Hudson Inc., 1989.

Frankfort, H. *The Art and Architecture of the Ancient Orient.* 4th rev. New Haven: Yale University Press, 1992.

Grand, P. M. *Prehistoric Art: Paleolithic Painting and Sculpture.* Greenwich: New York Graphic Society, 1967.

Graziosi, P. *Paleolithic Art.* New York: McGraw-Hill Inc., 1960.

Groenewegen-Frankfort, H. A., and Ashmole, B. *Art of the Ancient World.* Englewood Cliffs, NJ: Prentice Hall, 1971.

Leroi-Gourhan, A. *Treasures of Prehistoric Art.* New York: Harry N. Abrams Inc., 1967.

Lloyd, Seton, Müller, H. W., and Martin, R. *Ancient Architecture: Mesopotamia, Egypt, Greece.* New York: Harry N. Abrams Inc., 1974.

Mekhitarian, A. *Egyptian Painting.* New York: Rizzoli International Publications Inc., 1977.

Mellaart, J. *Earliest Civilizations of the Near East.* New York: McGraw-Hill Inc., 1965.

———. *The Neolithic of the Near East.* New York: Scribner, 1975.

Michalowski, K. *Art of Ancient Egypt.* New York: Harry N. Abrams Inc., 1985.

Moortgat, A. *The Art of Ancient Mesopotamia.* New York: Phaidon, 1969.

Poulsen, V. *Egyptian Art.* Greenwich: New York Graphic Society, 1968.

Powell, T. G. E. *Prehistoric Art.* New York: Praeger Publishers, 1966.

Sandars, N. K. *Prehistoric Art in Europe.* New Haven: Yale University Press, 1992.

Smith, W. S., and Simpson, W. K. *The Art and Architecture of Ancient Egypt.* New Haven: Yale University Press, 1992.

Strommenger, E., and Hirmer, M. *Five Thousand Years of the Art of Mesopotamia.* New York: Harry N. Abrams Inc., 1964.

Thom, A. *Megalithic Sites in Britain.* Oxford: Clarendon Press, 1967.

Wainwright, Geoffrey. *The Henge Monuments: Ceremony and Society in Prehistoric Britain.* London: Thames and Hudson Inc., 1990.

Wolff, Walther. *The Origins of Western Art: Egypt, Mesopotamia, the Aegean.* New York: Universe Publishing, 1989.

Ancient Greece and Rome

Adam, S. *The Technique of Greek Sculpture in the Archaic and Classical Periods.* New York: Thames and Hudson Inc., 1967.

Andreae, B. *The Art of Rome.* New York: Harry N. Abrams Inc., 1977.

Banti, L. *Etruscan Cities and Their Culture.* Berkeley: University of California, 1973.

Boardman, John. *Greek Art.* Rev. ed. New York: Thames and Hudson Inc., 1985.

Boethius, A. *Etruscan and Early Roman Architecture.* 2nd integrated ed., rev. New Haven: Yale University Press, 1992.

Brendel, O. J. *Etruscan Art.* Harmondsworth, NY: Penguin USA, 1978.

Brilliant, R. *Arts of the Ancient Greeks.* New York: McGraw-Hill Inc., 1973.

———. *Roman Art from the Republic to Constantine.* New York: Phaidon, 1974.

Bulfinch, Thomas. *The Age of Fable.* Reprint of 1855 ed. Irvine: Reprint Services, 1989.

Carpenter, R. *The Architects of the Parthenon.* Baltimore: Penguin USA, 1970.

Charbonneaux, J., Martin, R., and Villard, F. *Classical Greek Art.* New York: George Braziller Inc., 1973.

Christ, Karl, and Holme, Christopher, trans. *The Romans.* Berkeley, CA: University of California Press, 1984.

Coolidge, Olivia. *Trojan War.* Boston: Houghton Mifflin Co., 1990.

Hamilton, Edith. *Mythology: Timeless Tales of Gods and Heros.* New York: New American Library, 1989.

Hampe, R., and Simon, E. *The Birth of Greek Art from the Myceanean to the Archaic Period.* New York: Oxford University Press, 1981.

Hood, S. *The Arts in Prehistoric Greece.* Harmondsworth, NY: Penguin USA, 1978.

———. *The Minoans: The Story of Bronze Age Crete.* New York: Praeger Publishers, 1981.

Kleiner, Diana E. E. *Roman Sculpture.* New Haven: Yale University Press, 1992.

Lawrence, A. W. *Greek and Roman Sculpture.* New York: Harper and Row, 1972.

———. *Greek Architecture.* 4th ed., rev. New York: Penguin USA, 1983.

MacDonald, W. L. *The Architecture of the Roman Empire.* New Haven: Yale University Press, 1982.

MacKendrick, Paul. *The Greek Stones Speak: The Story of Archaeology in Greek Lands.* New York: W.W. Norton, 1983

Martin, Roland. *Greek Architecture: Architecture of Crete, Greece, and the Greek World.* New York: Electa/Rizzoli International Publications Inc., 1988.

Mayani, Zacharie. *The Etruscans Begin to Speak.* New York: Simon and Schuster, 1962.

Nash, E. *Pictorial Dictionary of Ancient Rome.* 2 vols., 2nd ed., rev. New York: Hacker, 1980

Papaioannou, Kostas. *The Art of Greece.* New York: Harry N. Abrams Inc., 1989.

Perowne, S. *The Archaeology of Greece and the Aegean.* New York: Viking, 1974.

Pollitt, J. J. *The Art of Rome and Late Antiquity: Sources and Documents.* Englewood Cliffs, NJ: Prentice Hall, 1966.

Renfrew, C. *The Emergence of Civilization: The Cyclades and the Aegean in the Third Millennium* BC. London: Methuen, 1972.

Richardson, E. *The Etruscans: Their Art and Civilization.* Chicago: University of Chicago Press, 1964.

Richter, G. M. A. *A Handbook of Greek Art.* 9th ed. New York: DaCapo, 1987.

———. *The Sculpture and Sculptors of the Greeks.* 4th ed., rev. New Haven: Yale University Press, 1970.

Sprenger, M., Bartolini, G., Hirmer, M., and Hirmer, A. *The Etruscans, Their History, Art, and Architecture.* New York: Harry N. Abrams Inc., 1983.

Stewart, Andrew. *Greek Sculpture: An Exploration,* 2 vols. New Haven: Yale University Press, 1990.

Strong, Donald, and Ling, Roger. *Roman Art.* 2nd rev. ed. New Haven: Yale University Press, 1992.

Veyne, Paul et al eds. *A History of Private Life.* Vol. 1: *From Pagan Rome to Byzantium.* Trans. Arthur Goldhammer. Cambridge: Harvard University Press, 1987.

Ward-Perkins, John B. *Roman Architecture.* New York: Rizzoli International Publications Inc., 1988.

———. *Roman Imperial Architecture.* New Haven: Yale University Press, 1992.

Early Christian, Byzantine Art and Early Medieval Art

Arnold, Bruce. *Irish Art: A Concise History.* Rev. ed. London: Thames and Hudson Inc., 1989.

Beckwith, J. *The Art of Constantinople: An Introduction to Byzantine Art.* 2nd ed. New York: Phaidon, 1968.

———. *Early Christian and Byzantine Art.* 2nd ed. New Haven: Yale University Press, 1992.

Dodwell, C. R. *Painting in Europe, 800–1200.* New Haven: Yale University Press, 1992.

Grabar, A. *The Beginnings of Christian Art, 200–395.* London: Thames and Hudson Inc., 1967.

———. *Early Christian Art.* New York: George Braziller Inc., 1971.

———. *The Golden Age of Justinian, from the Death of Theodosius to the Rise of Islam.* New York: George Braziller Inc., 1971.

Krautheimer, R. *Early Christian and Byzantine Architecture.* 4th ed. New Haven: Yale University Press 1984.

MacDonald, William L. *Early Christian and Byzantine Architecture.* New York: George Braziller, 1963.

Mango, C. Ed. *The Art of the Byzantine Empire, 312–1453: Sources and Documents.* Toronto: University of Toronto Press, 1986.

———. *Byzantine Architecture.* New York: Rizzoli International Publications Inc., 1985.

Marzials, Sir Frank, trans. *Memoirs of the Crusades.* London: Dent and Sons, 1955.

Mathews, T. J. *Byzantine Churches of Istanbul: A Photographic Survey.* University Park: Pennsylvania State University Press, 1976.

Mayer, Hans Eberhard. *The Crusades.* New York: Oxford University Press, 1993.

McEvedy, Colin. *The New Penguin Atlas of Medieval History.* London: Penguin, 1992.

Megaw, Ruth, and Megaw, Vincent. *Celtic Art: From Its Beginnings to the Book of Kells.* London: Thames and Hudson Inc., 1989.

Milburn, Robert L. P. *Early Christian Art and Architecture.* Berkeley: University of California Press, 1991.

Nordenfalk, C. *Early Medieval Book Illumination.* Geneva/New York: Skira/Rizzoli International Publications Inc., 1988.

Runciman, S. *Byzantine Style and Civilization.* Baltimore: Penguin USA, 1975.

Snyder, James. *Medieval Art: Painting, Sculpture, Architecture, Fourth to Fourteenth Century.* New York: Harry N. Abrams Inc., 1989.

Weitzmann, K. *Byzantine Book Illumination and Ivories.* London: Vriorum Reprints, 1980.

———. *Late Antique and Early Christian Book Illumination.* New York: George Braziller Inc., 1977.

White Jr., Lynn. *Medieval Technology and Social Change.* London: Oxford University Press, 1964.

Zarnecki, G. *Art of the Medieval World: Architecture, Sculpture, Painting, The Sacred Arts.* Englewood Cliffs, NJ: Prentice Hall, 1976.

Romanesque and Gothic

Aries, Philippe, and Duby, Georges, gen. eds. *A History of Private Life: Revelations of the Medieval World.* Cambridge, MA: Belknap Press, 1988.

Bowie, T., ed. *The Sketchbook of Villard de Honnecourt.* 3rd ed. Bloomington: Indiana University Press, 1968.

Cennini, C. D. *The Craftsman's Handbook (Il Libro dell'Arte).* New York: Dover Publications Inc., 1933.

Cole, B. *Giotto and Florentine Painting, 1280–1375.* New York: HarperCollins, 1977.

Conant, K. J. *Carolingian and Romanesque Architecture, 800–1200.* 4th ed. New Haven: Yale University Press, 1992.

Erlande-Brandenburg, Alain. *Gothic Art.* New York: Harry N. Abrams Inc., 1989.

Frankl, P. *Gothic Architecture.* Baltimore: Penguin USA, 1962.

Gies, Joseph, and Gies, Frances. *Life in a Medieval Castle.* New York: Harper and Row, 1979.

———. *Life in a Medieval City.* New York: Harper Perennial, 1981.

Grabar, Oleg. *The Formation of Islamic Art.* New Haven: Yale University Press, 1987.

Kubach, H. E. *Romanesque Architecture.* New York: Rizzoli International Publications Inc., 1988.

Martindale, A. *Gothic Art.* New York: Praeger Publishers, 1967.

Von Simson, Otto Georg. *The Gothic Cathedral: Origins of Gothic Architecture and the Medieval Concept of Order.* 3rd enl. ed. Princeton: Princeton University Press, 1988.

White, J. *Art and Architecture in Italy, 1250–1400.* 2nd ed. New Haven: Yale University Press, 1992.

Renaissance Art

Andres, Glenn, et al. *The Art of Florence.* 2 vols. New York: Abbeville Publishing Group, 1989.

Avery, C. *Florentine Renaissance Sculpture.* Trafalgar Square Publishing, 1989.

Baxandall, Michael. *Painting and Experience in Fifteenth-Century Italy: A Primer in the Social History of Pictorial Style.* 2nd ed. New York: Oxford University Press, 1988.

Beck, James. *Italian Renaissance Painting.* New York: HarperCollins, 1981.

Benesch, O. *The Art of the Renaissance in Northern Europe.* Rev. ed. London: Phaidon, 1965.

Blunt, Anthony. *Art and Architecture in France, 1500–1700.* 4th ed. New Haven: Yale University Press, 1992.

Bull, George, trans. *Lives of the Artists.* Vol. 1. New York: Viking Penguin, 1988.

Cole, B. *Masaccio and the Art of Early Renaissance Florence.* Bloomington: Indiana University Press, 1980.

Cutler, C. D. *Northern Painting: From Pucelle to Bruegel.* New York: Holt, Rinehart and Winston, Inc., 1968.

Earls, Irene. *Renaissance Art: A Topical Dictionary.* New York: Greenwood Publishing Group Inc., 1987.

Freedberg, S. J. *Painting in Italy: 1500–1600.* 3rd ed. New Haven: Yale University Press, 1992.

Friedlander, M. J. *Early Netherlandish Painting.* 14 vols. New York: Praeger Publishers, 1967–1973.

———. *From Van Eyck to Bruegel: Early Netherlandish Painting.* Ithaca: Cornell University Press, 1981

Gilbert, Creighton. *History of Renaissance Art throughout Europe: Painting, Sculpture, Architecture.* New York: Harry N. Abrams Inc., 1973.

Hartt, Frederick. *History of Italian Renaissance Art: Painting, Sculpting, Architecture.* 4th ed. Ed. David G. Wilkins. New York: Harry N, Abrams Inc., 1994.

Hibbard, H. *Michelangelo.* 2nd ed. New York: HarperCollins, 1985.

Hills, Paul. *The Light of Early Italian Painting.* New Haven: Yale University Press, 1990.

Murray, Peter. *Renaissance Architecture.* New York: Rizzoli International Publications Inc., 1982.

Panofsky, E. *Early Netherlandish Painting.* 2 vols. New York: HarperCollins, 1971.

Seymour Jr., Charles. *Sculpture in Italy, 1400–1500.* New Haven: Yale University Press, 1992.

Shearman, J. K. G. *Mannerism.* New York: Viking Penguin, 1978.

Snyder, J. *Northern Renaissance Art: Painting, Sculpture, the Graphic Arts from 1350 to 1575.* New York: Harry N. Abrams Inc., 1985.

Symonds, John Addington. Trans. *The Life of Benvenuto Cellini.* Oxford: Phaidon Press, 1995.

Vasari, G. *The Lives of the Most Eminant Painters, Sculptors and Architects.* 10 vols. Reprint of 1915 ed. New York: AMS Press.

Waterhouse, E. K. *Painting in Britain, 1530–1790.* 4th ed. New Haven: Yale University Press, 1992.

Baroque and Rococo Art

Bazin, Germain. *Baroque and Rococo.* New York: Thames and Hudson Inc., 1992.

Gaunt, W. *The Great Century of British Painting: Hogarth to Turner.* London: Phaidon, 1971.

Gerson, H., and Ter Kuile, E. H. *Art and Architecture in Belgium, 1600–1800.* Baltimore: Penguin USA, 1978.

Held, J., and Posner, D. *Seventeenth and Eighteenth Century: Baroque Painting, Sculpture, Architecture.* Ed. H.W. Janson. Englewood Cliffs, NJ: Prentice Hall, 1972.

Hempel, E. *Baroque Art and Architecture in Central Europe.* Baltimore: Penguin USA, 1977.

Kalnein, W. Graf, and Levey, M. *Art and Architecture of the Eighteenth Century in France.* Harmondsworth, NY: Penguin USA, 1972.

Levey, M. *Rococo to Revolution: Major Trends in Eighteenth Century Painting.* New York: Oxford University Press, 1977.

Nash, J. M. *The Age of Rembrandt and Vermeer: Dutch Painting in the Seventeenth Century.* New York: Holt, Rinehart and Winston, Inc., 1972.

Rosenberg, J. *Rembrandt, Life and Work.* Rev. ed. Ithaca, NY: Cornell University Press, 1980.

———, Slive, S., and Ter Kuile, E. H. *Dutch Art and Architecture, 1600–1800.* 3rd ed. New Haven: Yale University Press, 1992.

Stechow, W. *Dutch Landscape Painting of the Seventeenth Century.* Ithaca, NY: Cornell University Press, 1981.

Waterhouse, Ellis. *The Dictionary of Sixteenth and Seventeenth Century British Painters.* Woodbridge, England: Antique Collectors' Club, 1988.

Wittkower, R. *Art and Architecture in Italy, 1600–1750.* 3rd ed. New Haven: Yale University Press, 1992.

Nineteenth Century Art

Brown, M. W. *American Art to 1900.* New York: Harry N. Abrams Inc., 1977.

Clark, T. J. *The Painting of Modern Life: Paris in the Art of Manet and His Followers.* Princeton: Princeton University Press, 1986.

Driskell, D. C. *Two Centuries of Black American Art.* California: Los Angeles County Museum of Art/New York: Alfred A. Knopf Inc., 1976.

Harris, Neil. *The Artist in American Society: The Formative Years, 1790–1860.* Chicago: University of Chicago Press, 1982.

Herbert, Robert L. *Impressionism—Art, Leisure and Parisian Society.* New Haven: Yale University Press, 1988.

Holt, Elizabeth G., ed. *Impressionist: Art and Architecture in the Nineteenth Century.* Vol. 3 of *Documentary History of Art.* New Haven,: Yale University Press, 1986.

Honour, H. *Neoclassicism.* Baltimore: Penguin USA, 1968.

———. *Romanticism.* New York: Harper and Row, 1979.

Janson, H. W. *Nineteenth Century Sculpture.* New York: Harry N. Abrams Inc., 1985.

Nochlin, L. *Realism.* Baltimore: Viking Penguin USA, 1972.

Novotny, F. *Painting and Sculpture in Europe, 1780–1880.* New Haven: Yale University Press, 1992.

Rosenblum, R., and Janson, H. W. *Nineteenth-Century Art.* Englewood Cliffs, NJ: Prentice Hall, 1983.

Wilmerding, J. *American Art.* Baltimore: Penguin USA, 1976.

Twentieth Century Art

Ades, Dawn. *Art in Latin America: The Modern Era, 1820–1980.* New Haven: Yale University Press, 1989.

Arnason, H. H. *History of Modern Art: Painting, Sculpture, Architecture, Photography.* 3rd rev. and enl. ed. New York: Harry N. Abrams Inc., 1986.

Baker, Kenneth. *Minimalism: Art of Circumstance.* New York: Abbeville Publishing Group, 1989.

Beardsley, John, and Livingston, Jane. *Hispanic Art in the United States: Thirty Contemporary Painters and Sculptors.* Houston: Museum of Fine Arts/New York: Abbeville Publishing Group, 1987.

Braun, Emily, ed. *Italian Art in the Twentieth Century.* Munich: Prestel-Verlag, 1989.

Brown, Milton W. *The Story of the Armory Show.* New York: Abbeville Publishing Group, 1988.

Campbell, Mary Schmidt; Driskell, David C.; Levering, David Lewis; and Ryan, Deborah Willis. *Harlem Renaissance: Art of Black America.* New York: Studio Museum, Harlem/Harry N. Abrams Inc., 1987.

Celant, Germano. *Un-Expressionism: Art Beyond the Post-Modern Era.* New York: Rizzoli International Publications Inc., 1988.

Crane, Diana. *The Transformation of the Avant-Garde: The New York Art World, 1940–1985.* Chicago: University of Chicago Press, 1989.

Doty, R., ed. *Contemporary Black Artists in America.* New York: Whitney Museum of Art, 1971.

Dube, W. D. *The Expressionists.* New York: Thames and Hudson, 1985.

Geldzahler, H. *American Painting in the Twentieth Century.* New York: Metropolitan Museum of Art, 1965.

Godfrey, T. *The New Image: Painting in the 1980s.* New York: Abbeville Publishing Group, 1986.

Goldberg, Rose Lee. *Performance Art: From Futurism to the Present.* Rev. and enl. ed. New York: Harry N. Abrams Inc., 1988.

Golding, John. *Cubism: A History and Analysis, 1907–1914.* 3rd. ed. Cambridge: Harvard University Press, 1988.

Green, Chris. *Cubism and Its Enemies: Modern Movements and Reaction in French Art, 1916–1928.* New Haven: Yale University Press, 1987.

Hammacher, A. M. *Modern Sculpture: Tradition and Innovation.* New York: Harry N. Abrams Inc., 1988.

Herbert, R. L., ed. *Modern Artists on Art.* Englewood Cliffs, NJ: Prentice Hall, 1965.

Hunter, S., and Jacobus, J. *American Art of the Twentieth Century: Painting, Sculpture, Architecture.* Englewood Cliffs, NJ: Prentice Hall, 1974

Jaffe, H. L. C. *De Stijl, 1917–1931: Visions of Utopia.* New York: Abbeville Publishing Group, 1982.

Jencks, Charles. *Post-Modernism: The New Classicism in Art and Architecture.* New York: Rizzoli International Publications Inc., 1987.

Leymarie, Jean. *Fauves and Fauvism.* New York: Rizzoli International Publications Inc., 1987.

Lippard, L. R. *Pop Art.* New York: Thames and Hudson, 1985.

Lynton, Norbert. *The Story of Modern Art.* 2nd ed. Englewood Cliffs, NJ: Prentice Hall, 1989.

Mahsun, Carol A., ed. *Pop Art: The Critical Dialogue.* Ann Arbor: University of Michigan Press, 1988.

McShine, Kynaston. *Andy Warhol: A Retrospective.* New York: Museum of Modern Art, 1991.

Meisel, Louis K. *Photorealism.* New York: Harry N. Abrams Inc., 1989.

Motherwell, Robert, ed. *The Dada Painters and Poets: An Anthology.* 2nd ed. Cambridge: Harvard University Press, 1989.

Nadeau, Maurice. *History of Surrealism.* Cambridge: Harvard University Press, 1989.

Norris, Christopher, and Benjamin, Andrew. *What Is Deconstruction?* New York: St. Martin's Press Inc., 1989.

Pincus-Witten, Robert. *Postminimalism into Maximalism: American Art, 1966–1986.* Ann Arbor: University of Michigan Press, 1987.

Rosenblum, R. *Cubism and Twentieth-Century Art.* Rev. ed. New York: Harry N. Abrams Inc., 1976.

Rubin, W., ed. *Pablo Picasso, A Retrospective.* Greenwich: New York Graphic Society for the Museum of Modern Art, NY, 1980.

Shikes, Ralph E. *The Indignant Eye.* Boston: Beacon Press, 1969.

Twentieth Century Architecture

Cole, D. *From Tipi to Skyscraper: A History of Women in Architecture.* Cambridge: MIT Press, 1978.

Hitchcock, H. R. *Architecture: Nineteenth and Twentieth Centuries.* 2nd ed. Baltimore: Penguin USA, 1971.

Klotz, Heinrich. *History of Postmodern Architecture.* Cambridge: MIT Press, 1988.

Pevsner, Nikolaus, Sir. *A History of Building Types.* London: Thames and Hudson Inc., 1987.

———. *The Sources of Modern Architecture and Design.* New York: Oxford University Press, 1968

Scully, Vincent. *Architecture.* London: Harvill, 1991.

———. *Modern Architecture.* Rev. ed. New York: Braziller, 1974.

Trachtenberg, M, and Hyman, I. *Architecture: From Prehistory to Post-Modernism.* New York: Harry N. Abrams Inc., 1985.

Photography

Buckland, Gail. *Fox Talbot and the Invention of Photography.* Boston: David R. Godine Publisher, Inc., 1980.

Daval, J. L. *Photography: History of an Art.* Skira/Rizzoli International Publications Inc., 1982.

Gernsheim, H., and Gernsheim, A. *The History of Photography from the Camera Obscura to the Beginning of the Modern Era.* 2nd ed. New York: McGraw-Hill, 1969.

Greenough, Sarah, et al. *On the Art of Fixing a Shadow: One Hundred and Fifty Years of Photography.* Washington, DC: National Gallery of Art/Chicago: Art Institute of Chicago, 1991.

Jeffrey, Ian. *Photography: A Concise History.* New York: Thames and Hudson, 1982.

Newhall, Beaumont. *The History of Photography from 1839 to the Present Day.* 5th rev. ed. New York: Museum of Modern Art, 1982.

Phillips, Christopher, ed. *Photography in the Modern Era: European Documents and Critical Writings, 1913–1940.* New York: Metropolitan Museum of Art, 1989

Rosenblum, Naomi. *The History of Women Photographers.* New York: Abbeville Publishing Group, 1994.

Szarkowski, John. *Photography Now.* New York: Museum of Modern Art, 1990.

Nonwestern Art and Cultures

Barrow, Terrence. *An Illustrated Guide To Maori Art.* Honolulu: University of Hawaii Press, 1984.

———. *The Art of Tahiti and the Neighbouring Society, Austral and Cook Islands.* New York: Thames and Hudson Inc., 1979.

Ben-Amos, Paula. *The Art of Benin.* Thames and Hudson Inc., 1980.

Braun, Barbara. *Pre-Columbian Art and the Post-Columbian World: Ancient American Sources of Modern Art.* New York Harry N. Abrams Inc., 1993.

Chanda, Jacqueline. *African Arts and Cultures.* Worcester, MA: Davis Publications, Inc., 1993.

Corbin, George A. *Native Arts of North America, Africa, and the South Pacific: An Introduction.* Harper & Row, 1988.

Courtney-Clarke, Margaret. *African Canvas: The Art of West African Women.* New York: Rizzoli International Publications Inc., 1990.

Creswell, K. A. C. *A Short Account of Early Muslim Architecture.* Rev. and enl. ed. Aldershot, England: Scolar, 1968.

D'Alleva, Anne. *Native American Arts and Cultures.* Worcester, MA: Davis Publications, Inc., 1993.

Exploring the Visual Art of Oceania: Australia, Melanasis, Micronesia, and Polynesia. Honolulu: University of Hawaii Press, 1979.

Goodwin, Godfrey. *A History of Ottoman Architecture.* New York: Thames and Hudson Inc., 1992.

Guidoni, Enrico. *Primitive Architecture.* New York: Rizzoli International Publications Inc., 1987.

Heyden, D. and Gendrop, P. *Pre-Columbian Architecture of Mesoamerica.* New York: Rizzoli International Publications Inc., 1988.

Hoag, John D. *Islamic Architecture.* New York: Rizzoli International Publications Inc., 1987.

Hutt, Julia. *Understanding Far Eastern Art: A Complete Guide to the Arts of China, Japan, and Korea.* New York: Dutton, 1987.

Myth of Primitivism: Perspectives on Art, The. New York: Routledge, 1991.

National Museum of African Art. *The Art of West African Kingdoms.* Washington D.C.: Smithsonian Institution Press, 1987.

Thomas, Nicholas. *Oceanic Art.* London: Thames and Hudson Inc., 1995.

Thorp, Robert L. *Son of Heaven: Imperial Arts of China.* Seattle: Son of Heaven Press, 1988.

Sabloff, Jeremy A. *The Cities of Ancient Mexico.* New York: Thames and Hudson Inc., 1989.

Individual Artists/ Museum Catalogues

Many books on individual artists and museum catalogues from various specialized exhibitions can be found. Museum libraries and bookstores are well stocked with such publications.

Electronic Media

CD-ROM Disks

American Visions

Ancient Egyptian Art: The Brooklyn Museum. Digital Collections, Inc.

A Passion for Art: Corbis

Art Gallery: The Collection of the National Gallery, London. Microsoft Corporation.

Ancient Lands. Microsoft Corporation.

Encarta: The Complete Multimedia Encyclopedia. Microsoft Corporation.

The Great Buildings Collection. Van Nostrand Reinhold.

Great Paintings: Renaissance to Impressionism—The Frick Collection. Digital Collections, Inc.

Masterworks of Japanese Painting: The Etsulo and Joe Price Collection: Digital Collections, Inc.

Tate Gallery: ATTICA Cybernetics

The New Grolier Multimedia Encyclopedia. Grolier Electronic Publishing.

Perseus 1.0. Yale University Press.

Videodiscs

American Art from the National Gallery of Art. National Gallery of Art.

Art of the Western World Series. The Annenberg/CPB Project.

A Day in the Country: Impressionism and the French Landscape. Comco Productions.

Dream Machine Series. Voyager Company.

The First Emperor of China. Voyager Company.

The Louvre Videodisc Series. Voyager Company.

Masterpieces of Italian Art Series. Crystal Productions.

Masterpieces of the Met. Metropolitan Museum of Art.

Musée d'Orsay.National Gallery of Art. Videodisc Publishing Inc.

New Ways of Seeing: Picasso, Braque and the Cubists. Home Vision.

Perseus 1.0. Yale University Press.

Regard for the Planet. Voyager Company.

Salamandre: Châteaux of the Loire. Voyager Company.

With Open Eyes: Images from the Art Institute of Chicago.

Videos

Abstract Expressionism. Crystal Productions.

American Art from the National Gallery of Art. National Gallery of Art.

Ancient Egypt. Time-Life Films.

Ancient Greece. BBC Television.

Art Appreciation. Crystal Productions.

Art of the Western World. The Annenberg/CPB Project.

At the Louvre with the Masters. Home Vision Cinema.

At the Met: Curators' Choice. NVC.

Centre Georges Pompidou: The Big Escalator. RM Arts.

Footloose in History. Crystal Productions.

Introduction to Sculpture. National Gallery of Art.

Light of the Gods. National Gallery of Art.

Masterpieces of British Art. Crystal Productions.

Masterpieces of Italian Art Series. Crystal Productions.

Masterpieces of the Met. Metropolitan Museum of Art.

Masters of Illusion. National Gallery of Art.

Masterworks of Painting. Crystal Productions.

The Mind's Eye. BBC Horizon.

National Gallery of Art. Videodisc Publishing Inc.

New World Visions: American Art and the Metropolitan Museum. WNET, BBC.

20th Century American Art. Crystal Productions.

Sources and Credits

Primary Source Citations

Ch. 1, page 15: Holt, Elizabeth G. *A Documentary History of Art: The Middle Ages & The Renaissance,* vol. I, expanded ed. Princeton: Princeton University Press, 1981. **Ch. 2, page 55**: Nevelson, Louise. *Dawns and Dusks: Taped Conversations with Diana MacKown.* New York: Helen Merill Ltd., 1976. **Ch. 3, page 73**: Goldwater, Robert, Marco Treves, eds. *Artists on Art.* New York: Pantheon, 1972. Shikes, Ralph E. *The Indignant Eye.* Boston: Beacon Press, 1969. **Ch. 4, page 143**: Fong, Wen. *Summer Mountains: The Timeless Landscape.* New York: The Metropolitan Museum of Art, 1975. **Ch. 6, page 201**: Alberti, Leon Battista. *Ten Books on Architecture.* New York: Transatlantic Arts [c.1966]. **Ch. 7, page 227**: Reprinted by permission of the publishers and the Loeb Classical Library from Procopius: *The Buildings*, vol. 7, translated by H.B. Dewing, Cambridge, Mass.: Harvard University Press, 1935. **Ch. 8, page 257**: Evans, Joan. *Monastic Life at Cluny 910-1157.* London: Archon Books, 1968. **Ch. 9, page 299**: Symonds, John Addington. *The Life of Michelangelo Buonarroti.* 3rd ed., 2 vols., New York: Scribners, 1899. **Ch. 10, page 327**: Holt, Elizabeth G. *A Documentary History of Art: The Middle Ages & The Renaissance,* vol. I, expanded ed. Princeton: Princeton University Press, 1981. **Ch. 11, page 377**: Ireland, John. *Hogarth Illustrated,* 3 vols., London: 1791-1798; 1805 edition. **Ch. 12, page 413**: Le Brun, Madame Vigeé. *Souvenirs.* New York: R. Worthington, 1879. **Ch. 13, page 445**: Whistler, J.A. McNeill. *The Gentle Art of Making Enemies.* New York: 1893. **Ch. 14, page 489**: Monks, Noel. *Eyewitness.* Frederick Muller, 1955. **Ch. 15, page 519**: Lawrence, Jacob. "Philosophy of Art," statement solicited by the Whitney Museum of American Art, to relate to the Lawrence painting *Depression* (1950), which they own, May 30, 1951. Whitney Museum Library, Jacob Lawrence Artist File. **Ch. 16, page 531**: Fitch Manes Marston. "Frank Lloyd Wright's War on the Fine Arts." *Horizon* volume 3 no.1, September 1960. **Ch. 17, page 587**: Goldwater, Marge et al. *Jennifer Bartlett* rev. ed. New York: Abbeville Press, 1990. O'Connor, Francis Valentine and Eugene Victor Thaw eds. *Jackson Pollock: A Catalogue Raisonné of Paintings, Drawings, and Other Works* vol 4. New Haven: Yale University Press, 1978. Jaune Quick-To-See Smith from an interview with Trinkett Clark, Curator of Twentieth-Century Art at The Chrysler Museum, Norfolk, VA for the *Parameters* brochure and exhibitiion, October 9, 1992.

Special Feature Artist Portraits and Icons

Ch. 9, page 262: Death Mask of Filippo Brunalleschi, 1446, clay, Museo dell'Opera del Duomo, Florence. **Ch. 9, page 276**: Leonardo da Vinci, Self-Portrait, drawing, Biblioteca Reale, Turin. **Ch. 9, page 288**: El Greco, *Portrait of a Man* (Self-Portrait), oil on canvas, 16" x 12" (40.6 x 30.5 cm), The Metropolitan Museum of Art, New York. **Ch. 10, page 304:** Robert Campin, Flower vase, detail of fig. 10-1, *Mérode Alterpiece*, about 1425-1426, oil on panel, 25" x 10" (64 x 27 cm), The Metropolitan Museum of Art, New York, The Cloisters Collection, 1956. (56. 70). **Ch. 10, page 314:** Albrecht Durer, *Self-Portrait as a Boy,* drawing, The Albertina Museum, Vienna. **Ch. 10, page 322:** Juan Bautista De Toledo, El Escorial, tower, c. 1563-1584, outside Madrid. **Ch. 11, page 332:** Gian Lorenzo Bernini, Self- Portrait, oil on canvas, Galleria Borghese, Rome. **Ch. 11, page 340:** Georges de La Tour, *Magdalen with a Smoking Flame,* detail of fig. 11-14, about 1630-1635, oil on canvas, 46" x 36 1/4" (117 x 92 cm), Los Angeles County Museum of Art, gift of the Ahmanson Foundation. **Ch. 11, page 360:** Diego Velazquez, *Las Meninas,* detail of fig. 11-37, self -portrait of Diego Velazquez, oil on canvas, 124 3/4" x 107 3/4" (317 x 274 cm), Prado Museum, Madrid. **Ch. 11, page 364:** Rosalba Carriera, *Antoine Watteau,* oil on canvas, Museo Civico, Treviso, Italy. **Ch. 12, page 382:** Jacques Louis David, Self-Portrait, oil on canvas, Uffizi Gallery, Florence. **Ch. 12, page 390:** Francisco Goya, Self-Portrait, 1815, oil on canvas, Prado Museum, Madrid. **Ch. 12, page 400:** Anna Elizabeth Klumpke, *Rosa Bonheur,* 1869, oil on canvas, 46 1/8" x 38 5/8" (117.2 x 98.1 cm), The Metropolitan Museum of Art, New York, Gift of the artist in memory of Rosa Bonheur, 1922. **Ch. 12, page 410:** Edward J. Steichen, Self-Portrait, photograph, National Portrait Gallery, Washington, DC. **Ch. 13, page 418:** Claude Monet, photograph, Caisse Nationale des Monuments Historiques et des Sites, Paris. **Ch. 13, page 430:** Laurent, *Georges Seurat,* 1883, conté crayon, 15 1/4" x 11 1/2" (38.75 x 29.25 cm), Département des Arts Graphiques, Paris. **Ch. 13, page 440:** Edward Munch, *Self-Portrait with Female Mask,* 1892, oil on wood, 27 1/2" x 17 1/2" (70 x 44.5 cm), Munch Museum, Oslo. **Ch. 14, page 450:** Juley, Peter A., Diego Rivera, photograph, Peter A. Juley & Son Collection, National Museum of American Art , Washington, DC. **Ch. 14, page 464:** Stella, Joseph, Self-Portrait, 1920's, drawing, Philadelphia Museum of Art: Alice Newton Osborne Fund, Katharine Levin Farrell Fund, Margretta S. Hinchman Fund, Joseph E. Temple Fund and funds contributed by J. R. Massey and Marion Stroud Swingle. **Ch. 14, page 472:** Constantin Brancusi, photograph. **Ch. 14, page 476:** Juley, Peter A., Salvadore Dali, photograph, Peter A. Juley & Son Collection, National Museum of American Art, Washington, DC. **Ch. 14, page 484:** Van Der Zee with Violin, 1931, photograph. **Ch. 15, page 494:** Bellows, George Wesley, Self-Portrait, lithograph, 10 1/2" x 7 7/8 " (26.7 x 20 cm), National Portrait Gallery, Washington, DC. **Ch. 15, page 502:** Georgia O'Keeffe, photograph. **Ch. 15, page 508:** Thomas Hart Benton, photograph. **Ch. 15, page 514:** Jacob Lawrence, photograph, Francine Seders Gallery Ltd. **Ch. 16, page 524:** Mies van der Rohe, photograph, Courtesy of Illinois Institute of Technology. **Ch. 16, page 536:** Michael Graves, photograph. **Ch. 17, page 550:** Portrait of W. de Kooning, photograph, Collection of the Center for Creative Photography, Tuscon, AZ. **Ch. 17, page 556:** Robert Mapplethorpe, Claes Oldenburg , 1989, photograph, Courtesy PaceWildenstein, photograph. **Ch. 17, page 564:** Arkatov, J., Helen Frankenthaler, photograph. **Ch. 17, page 570:** Close, Chuck, Self-Portrait, oil on canvas, 100 x 84 " (254 x 213 cm), Courtesy PaceWildenstein. **Ch. 17, p. 574:** Isamu Noguchi, photograph, Isamu Noguchi Foundation, Inc., Long Island City, NY. **Ch. 17, page 578**: Christo and Jeanne-Claude in front of the Reichstag, Berlin 1991, photograph.

Photo Credits

Peter Accettola, 2-29; The Albertina Museum, Vienna, 10.IC.2, 10-15; Albright-Knox Art Gallery, Buffalo, New York, 2-52, 15-17, 17-4, 17-13, 17-15, 17-20, 17-34; Alinari/Art Resource, NY, 6-29, 8-43, 12-16; American Museum of Natural History, 4-89; Courtesy Amon Carter Musuem, Ft. Worth, 14-54; Courtesy of the Ansel Adams Publishing Rights Trust, 14-56; Archiv Cameraphoto Venizia/Art Resource, NY, 9-34; James Arkatov,17.IC.3; ©ARS, Scala/Art Resource, NY, 13-31; Museum of Art and Archaeology, University of Missouri, Columbia, 5T-b; Art Institute of Chicago, 11-51, 12-18, 12-20, 12-38, 13-19, 13-c, 13-30, 14-25, 14-33, 15-4, 15-11, 15-25, 15-b, 17-35; Art Resource, NY, 8-13, 6-b, 6-d, 7-33, 8-26, 10-16, 12-a, 16-13; Baltimore Museum of Art, 1-6; Bettmann, 8T-d, 11.WT.2, 13T-4, 16T-3, 16T-4, 17T-2, 17T-5, 17T-6; Tom Bernard, 16-26; Michael Bodycomb, 2-d, 8-44, 8-d; Mary Boone Gallery, New York, 17-50; David L. Ryan/The Boston Globe, 14.SL; Bowdoin College Museum of Art, Brunswick, ME, 11-57; Bridgeman/Art Resource, NY, 9T-2, 11T-6, 13-b, 14-30; British Library, London, 7-28, 7-29; British Museum, 1-9, 2-3, 2-42, 4-2, 4-6, 4-35, 4-81, 4-82, 4-c, 5-10, 5-11, 5-13, 5-16, 5-22, 5-29, 5-30, 6-14, 6-15, 6-40, 7.IC.1, 7-1, 7-2, 7-30, 7-34; British Tourist Authority, 8-33; Gerald F. Brommer, 4-57; The Brooklyn Museum, 4-110, 4-86, 4-93; Courtesy Malcolm Brown Gallery, Cleveland, 2-32; Brown Brothers, Sterling, PA, 15T-1; Suzanne Brown Gallery, Scottsdale, AZ, 4-101; Bryn Mawr College Archives, 1-11; Dan Budnik, 4-16; Hillel Burger, Peabody Museum, Harvard University, 2-40, 2-43, 2-58, 3-3, 4-60, 4-61, 4-62, 4-100, 4-60, 4-61, 4-62, 4-5; Michele Burgess, 2-66, 11T-8, 15T-4; Kimberly Burnham, 4-47; Cameraphoto/Art Resource, NY, 9-45; Camerique/H. A. Roberts, 11.WT.1; Museo e Gallerie di Capodimonte, Naples, 9-40; Richard Carafelli, 2-9, 17-3; Casimir, 8-23; Leo Castelli, Inc., 17-14, 17-a; ©Judy Chicago, 1973,17-47; © Christo, 17-43; Courtesy Circle Fine Arts Corporation, Chicago, IL, 3-10; ©The City of Oakland, The Oakland Museum, 14-57; Geoffrey Clements, 1-a, 3-8, 17-25; Cleveland Museum of Art, 2-21, 2-30, 4-8, 4-28, 4-43, 15-2; ©Stuart Cohen, 11-7; Paula Cooper, Inc., NY, 17-b; In the collection of the Corcoran Gallery of Art, 15.WT; Cranbrook Institute of Science, 4-112; Culver Pictures Inc., 11.SL.1, 11T-b, 12T-3, 12T-5, 12T-6, 13T-2, 14T-5, 15T-c, 15T-d, 17T-3; Daitokuji, Kyoto, Japan, 2-14; Dallas Museum of Art, 13-14, 17-28; Friedmar Damm, 3-20, 8-29, 12-11; Bevan Davies, courtesy of Pace Wildenstein, 17-31; Bob Davis, 4-33; The Detroit Institute of Arts, 3-e, 14-10, 6-33, 11-6, 13-16, 14-b, 15-27, 17-22, 17-41; Mark Downey, 4-52, 4-55; Dumbarton Oaks, Washington, DC, 4-87, 4-88; Karen Durlach, 3-4, 3-d, 4-90; Timothy Eagan, 4-40; Ecole des Beaux-Arts, Paris, 6.SL.2; John Elk Photography, 4-22; Bonnie Elliott, SP.17.6; Lorene Emerson, National Gallery of Art, Washington, DC,11-22; Foto Marburg/Art Resource, NY, 7-31; Fratelli Alinari/Art Resource, NY, 6-32; Fratelli Fabri, Milan/Art Resource, NY, 10.WT.2; Freer Gallery of Art, Smithsonian Institution, Washington, DC, 4.PS.1, 4-27a, 4-27b, 4-30, 4-37, 4-41; Robert Frerck, 6T-2, 1-14, 4-94; © The Frick Collection, New York, 2-62, 10-21, 10-a, 11-45; Isabella Stewart Gardner Museum, Boston, 13.WT; Gemaldegalerie, Staatliche Museen, Berlin-Dahlem,

10-25; Germanishes Nationalmuseum, Nuremburg, Germany, 9T-4; George Gerster, 10-23; Giraudon/Art Resource, 1-3, 3.PS.1, 5-14, 5-17, 5-23, 5-b, 7-20, 8-15, 8-a, 10-4, 10-17, 10-18, 10-19, 10-26, 11-15, 11-43, 11.IC.5, 12-4, 12-6, 12-7, 12-28, 12-34, 12-37, 13-15; Glasgow Museums, 14-42; Jeff Greenberg, 16-35; Richard Gross, 14-6; George Hall, 16-18; Hampton University Museum, Hampton, VA 15-9; Hartill Art Associates, Canada, 6-30, 8-4, 8-5, 8-11, 8-20, 8-31, 12-12, 12-13; Anthony Haruch, 4-15, 4-65; David Heald ©The Solomon R. Guggenheim Foundation, New York, 14-15, 14-3; Lindsay Hebberd, 4-45; ©The Henry Moore Foundation, 17-d; John Hicks, 4-53, 4-a; Jean Higgins, 1-12; Hans Hinz, 5-1, 5-2; The Hispanic Society of America, NY, 12-15; Anthony Howarth, 5-8; Michael J. Howell, 5-d; William Hubbell, 6-22; Hurst Gallery, Cambridge, MA, 4-98; International Society for Educational Information, 4-42, 4-46; The J. Paul Getty Museum, 2-45, 6-16, 11-44; Bill Jacobson, courtesy of PaceWildenstein, 17.IC.4; The Japanese Consulate, Boston, 3-5; Jefferson Medical College of Thomas Jefferson University, Philadelphia, PA, 12-41; Joslyn Art Museum, Omaha, NE,15-22; Wolfgang Kaehler, 4-17, 4-24, 4-49, 4-50, 4-51, 4-72, 6.IC.1, 6-2; Kimbell Art Museum, 4-54, 13-32, 13-d, 16-15; Knoedler & Company, New York, 17-49; R. Kord/H. Armstrong Roberts, 8-38; Balthazar Korab, 16-14; Robert Landau, 16.WT.A, 16.WT.B; Eric Lessing/Art Resource, NY, 1-4, 2-1, 2-35, 3-12, 5-4, 6-1, 6-3, 6-17, 6T-b, 8.IC.2, 8-9, 8-39, 9.SL.3, 9-11, 9-29, 9-30, 10-12, 11-21, 11-25, 11-31, 13-3, 13-11, 14T-3, 15T-3; Reproduced from the Collections of the Library of Congress, 2-10; Museum Associates, Los Angeles County Museum of Art, 1-1, 2-19, 2-27, 2-36, 2-65, 2-67, 3-21, 4-10, 4-11, 4- 18, 4-26, 4-56, 4-69, 4-74, 4-76, 4-95, 5-15, 10.WT.1, 11-14, 11-35, 12-31, 13-6, 13-7, 14-7, 14-47, 14-48, 15-1, 15-2, 15-26, 17-18; Joseph J. Lucas Jr., 16.IC.1; McNay Art Museum, San Antonio, TX, 15-12; Spike Mafford, 15.IC.4; Francie Manning, 6-7; Robert Mapplethorpe, courtesy PaceWildenstein, 17.IC. 2; ©1995 Ari Marcopoulos, 17.SL; Robert Mates, The Solomon R. Guggenheim Museum, New York, 14-16; Metropolitan Museum of Art, 2-16, 2-31, 2-33, 2-61, 3-16, 3-19, 4-32, 4-80, 6-12, 6-19, 6-46, 7-9, 8-12, 8-36, 10.IC.1, 10-1, 10-2, 10-3, 11-16, 11-29, 12.IC.3, 12-23, 12-24, 12-25, 12-31, 12-36, 12-43, 12-44, 12-b, 13-2, 13-9, 15-5, 15-15, 15-30, 15-34, 17-1; Midtown Payson Galleries, 15-31; Michael Moran, 16-32, 16-d; Murphy/Jahn, Inc. Architects, 16-31; Museum of Art, Carnegie Institute, Pittsburgh,12.WT, 14-32; Museum of Fine Arts, Boston, 2-b, 3-7, 3-b, 4-31, 4-36, 4-70, 4-73, 4-d, 5-21, 6T-3, 11-54; Museum Folkwang, 14-9; Museum of Modern Art, NY, 2-13, 2-17, 2-18, 2-20, 2-49, 2-51, 2-53, 13-18, 14-31, 14-36, 14-39, 14-40, 14-45, 14-46, 14-51, 15-18, 15-19, 15-28, 15-c, 17-2, 17-12, 14T-b, 3-a; Hans Namuth, ©Hans Namuth Estate, 17.IC.1; Jose A. Naranjo, 2-4; Reproduced by courtesy of the Trustees, The National Gallery, London, 2-8, 3-c, 9-15, 9-21, 9-b, 10-6, 10-22, 10-c, 11-4, 11-18, 11-24, 11-39, 11-41, 11-42, 12-19, 12-21, 13-5, 16-27; National Gallery of Art, Washington, DC, 2-55, 6-35, 7-19, 8-14, 9-31, 9-32, 9-33, 9-36, 9-42, 9-44, 9T-a, 10-5, 10-9, 11.IC.3, 11-17, 11-30, 11-46, 11-56, 12-2, 12-33, 12-39, 12-40, 13-1, 13-4, 13-22, 14-5, 14-18, 14-28, 14-37, 14-41, 15-10, 16-21, 17-21, 17-37, 12T-b; National Gallery of Canada, Ottawa, 11-55; National Museum of American Art, Washington, DC/Art Resource, NY, 2-54, 2-63, 15-6, 15-7, 15-8; National Museum of Korea, Seoul, 2-12; The National Museum of Women in the Arts , 2-28, 12-30, 15-13; National Portrait Gallery, Smithsonian Institution/Art Resource, NY, 12.IC.4, 15.IC.1; Les Nelken, 5-24, 5-27, 07-24, 16.PS, 16-4, 16-a; Nelson-Atkins Museum of Art, Kansas City, MO, 1-b, 2-5, 2-37, 2-46, 2-68, 3-22, 4-14, 4-108, 4-34, 4-b, 5.IC.2, 5-12, 6-41, 6-42, 8-35, 12-8, 14-14, 14-17, 14-38, 14-49, 14-c, 4-29, 4-59, 4-12; New Britain Museum of American Art, CT, 15-21; ©Nijo Castle, 4-48, Nimatallah/Art Resource, NY, 6. IC.2, 6-13, 9.IC2; Nippon Television Network Corporation, Tokyo, 1994, 9.WT; The Norton Simon Museum, Pasadena, CA, 2-57a, 2-57b, 2-6, 13-26, 17-40; PaceWildenstein, 17-10, 17-45; Richard Payne, 16-19, 16-20, 16-28, 16-29; Cesar Pelli, 16-36; Philadelphia Museum of Art, 2-25, 2-60, 13-21, 14-1, 14-26, 14-34, 14-35, 15-14, 15-a; The Pierpoint Morgan Library, Art Resource, NY, 1-7; Prado Museum, Madrid, 2-26; ProFiles West, 8T-7; Carl Purcell, 4-68; Oliver Radford, 3-6, 6.SL3, 6-21, 6-31, 6-38, 6-45, 6-c 7.IC.3, 7-21, 7-22, 7-23, 8-19, 8-27, 9-1, 9-28, 10.IC.3, 10-24, 10-28, 10-b, 11-9, 11-19, 11-a, 12-26, 12-29, 16-1, 16-3, 16-6, 16-7, 16-8, 16-9, 16-10, 16-11, 16-12, 16-22, 16-30; A. Ramey, 17T-1, 17T-8; Reuters/Bettmann, 17T-7; Rijksmuseum, Amsterdam, 11-26, 11-27, 11-36; RMN, Paris, 5-3, 5-5, 12-3, 13.IC.2; Helen Ronan, 4-3, 4-4, 4-102, 4-103, 5-26, 5-28, 6.WT, 6-39, 7-b, 8-8, 8-28, 8-30, 8T-4, 9-26, 16.SL.2, 16-16, 16-17, 16-24, 16-b; The Royal Collection, Her Majesty Queen Elizabeth II, 11-48, 11-b; San Francisco Museum of Modern Art, 2-22; Sandak, 8.IC.1, 8-1, 8-2, 8-7, 8-10, 8-21, 8-24, 8-25, 8-37, 8-b, 16.SL.1, 16-2, 16-5; Nicolas Sapieha/ Art Resource, 17-39; Saskia, Ltd., 2-2, 6-5, 6-6, 6-10, 6-11, 6-25, 10-13, 10-14, 11.SL.3, 11-28, 11-37, 11-38; Julie Saul Gallery, New York, 17.WT; Scala/Art Resource, NY, 2-7, 2-44, 2-64, 2-69, 2-c, 3-11, 4-20, 5-a, 6-49, 6T-5, 6-8, 6-9, 6-18, 6-34, 6-36, 6-43, 6-44, 6-47, 6-48, 7.IC.2, 7-6, 7-7, 7-8, 7-10, 7-11, 7-12, 7-17, 7-a, 7-c, 8-c, 8.WT, 8-6, 8-16, 8-17, 8-18, 8-40, 8-45, 8-46, 9.IC.1, 9.IC3, 9-2, 9-3, 94, 9-5, 9-6, 9-7, 9-8, 9-9, 9-10, 9-12, 9-14, 9-16, 9-17, 9-18, 9-19, 9-20, 9-22, 9-23, 9-25, 9-27, 9-37, 9-38, 9-39, 9-41, 9-43, 9-46, 9-47, 9-48, 9-a, 9-c, 10-7, 10-10, 10-11, 11.IC.1, 11.IC.2, 11.IC.4, 11-2, 11-3, 11-5, 11-10, 11-13, 11-23, 11-40, 11-c, 12.IC.1, 12.IC.2, 12-1, 12-14, 12-17, 12-27, 12-c, 13.IC.3, 13-a; Schmeiser, 11-12; Collection of Stephen S. Schwartz, OH, 1-10; Douglass G. Scott, 11T-7, 13T-d, 4-25, 4-38; SEF/Art Resource, NY, 2-24, Mark Sexton, 12T-01; Robin Shahid, 4-7, 4-23, 5T-7, 6-24, 6-26, 6T-a; Collection of Bertha and Mitchel Siegel, NM, 4-1, 4-e; Smithsonian Institution, 14.IC.1, 14.IC. 4; Courtesy of Sotheby's Inc., 12-45, 14-55; ©SPARC, 14.WT; Mike Spinelli for *Sprits in Stone* by Anthony and Laura Ponter, Ukama Press, Sebastopol, CA 1992, 4-84; Lee Stalsworth, Hirshorn Museum and Sculpture Garden, 2-38, 17-8, 17-30, 17-42; Steinbaum Krauss Gallery, 17-51; Paul Stopforth and Carol Marshall Collection, 4-77, 4-85; Rick Strange, 5-19; Tim Street-Porter, 16-34; © 1993 Succession H. Matisse/ ARS, New York, 14-4; Tate Gallery, London/Art Resource, NY, 11-50, 11-53, 13-20, 17-06, 17-24; John Bigelow Taylor, New York, 2-15, 4-96; William Taylor, Taylor Photography, 16.IC.2; Ron Testa, 4-109; Texas Memorial Museum, The University of Texas, Austin, 1-5; The Textile Museum, Washington, DC, 3-2; Caroline Tisdall, Courtesy Ronald Feldman Fine Art Inc., 17-53; © The Tokunaga Reimeikai Foundation, 8T-5; Jerry L. Thompson, NY, 17-16, 17-52; Topkapi Palace Musuem, Istanbul, 7-26; UPI Photo, 16T-b; UPI/Bettmann, 14.IC.3, 15.IC.2, 15.IC.3, 17T-c; Vanni, Berlin/Art Resource, 5-31; Venturi, Scott Brown and Associates, Inc. 16-26; Hirmer Verlag München Fotoarhiv, 5.IC.1, 5-9; Steve Vidler, 4-71; Sylvia Volz, 1991, 17.IC.6; Wolfgang Volz, © Christo, 1984-1991, 17-44; Wyatt Wade, 16-25; David Wakely, 14-2; Collection of The Walker Art Center, Minneapolis, 17-11; Werner Forman Archive, 9T-7; Werner Forman/Art Resource, NY, 7T-c; Whitney Museum of American Art, 1-a, 2-29, 15-24; Wichita Art Museum Collection, 2-23; Ellen Page Wilson, Courtesy of PaceWildenstein, 17-32; Don F. Wong Photography, 16-33; Graydon Wood, 1994, Philadelphia Museum of Art, 14-29; ©Donald Woodman, 17-c, Adam Woolfit, 5-e; Worcester Art Museum, 15-16; Yale University Art Gallery, 14-22, 14-23, 17-38; Michael S. Yamashita, 3-1; Courtesy Donna Mussenden Van Der Zee, 14.IC.5, 14-52, 14-53; ZEFA/H. Armstrong Roberts, 7-18; Octave Zimmermann, 10-20.

Front Matter and Part Opener:
Museum of Modern Art, NY, half title page; National Gallery of Art, Washington, DC, tiltle page; Saskia, Ltd., p. IV; Hans Hinz, p. V top right; Art Resource, NY, p. V bottom; Art Resource, NY, p. V left; Art Resource, NY, p.VI top left; Museum of Modern Art, NY, p. VI bottom left; Mark Downey, p. VI right; Helen Ronan, p. VII top left; Oakland Museum, p. VII bottom left; Through the Flower, p. VII right; San Francisco Art Institute, photo by David Wakely, p. 2-3; Textile Museum, Washington, DC, p. 58-59; National Gallery of Art, Washington, DC, photo by Richard Carafelli, p. 146-147; Saskia, Ltd., p. 590-591.

Index

Acknowledgments

My grateful thanks to the many artists and their representatives who provided both permission and illustration of their works, including Christo and Jeanne-Claude, Chuck Close, Judy Chicago, Duane Hanson, and Bridget Riley. PaceWildenstein, Julie Saul and Mary Boone Galleries in New York provided gratis materials for this book. Dr. Henri Dorra gave permission to use several of his excellent diagrams which add to the book's clarity.

Many museums were helpful in providing photographic materials and documentary information for which I am grateful. They include The Metropolitan Museum of Art, New York, National Gallery, Washington, The Museum of Modern Art, New York, The Nelson-Atkins Museum of Art, Kansas City, Museum of Fine Arts, Boston, Kimbell Art Museum, Fort Worth, Texas, Peabody Museum, Harvard University, Art Institute of Chicago, Philadelphia Art Museum, Detroit Institute of Arts and Los Angeles County Museum of Art. Also the following photo suppliers: Art Resource, New York, Derin Tanyol, Saskia Ltd., Bettmann, Culver Pictures, Oliver Radford, Cambridge, MA, embassy of Zimbabwe, Consulate General of Japan, Boston and International Society for Informational Education, Tokyo.

I would like to thank the following teachers for editorial consultation: Merceda Saffron, West Springfield High School, Springfield VA, Kaye Passmore, Notre Dame Academy, Worcester, MA, Sandi Hammonds, Woodson High School, Fairfax, VA, Sallye Mahan-Cox, Robinson Secondary School, Fairfax, VA, Roger Tomhave, Art Curriculum Specialist, Fairfax County Public Schools, Fairfax, VA, Virginia Fitzpatrick, Moore College of Art, Philadelphia, PA, and Trinket Doty, McLane High School, Fairfax, VA.

I express my special thanks to those who went out of their way to help, encourage, and express interest in the book as it developed. To Dave Kohl who supplied many visuals and the basic text for Chapter 4. His knowledge and friendship are deeply appreciated. To Davis Publications, who for so long have supported art education and who eagerly and consistently supported this project from its initial stages to this third edition. To Gerald Stashak and Wyatt Wade who have always supported my efforts in working with Davis Publications. To Helen Ronan who worked mightily on this third edition, and whose insight, editorship and perseverance were vital in this evolving process of revision and publication. Thanks also to Douglass Scott, WGBH Design, for superb workmanship and a very positive approach to this project.

And to my wife, Georgia, whose patience, understanding, and constant help in many ways are most appreciated.

I thank you all!

Gerald F. Brommer

Studio City, California
December, 1995

Managing Editor: Wyatt Wade
Associate Editor: Helen Ronan
Production Editors: Nancy Bedau, Nancy Burnett
Production: Steven Vogelsang
Copyeditor: Janet Stone
Contributing Editors: Carol Marshall, Abby Remer
Photo Research: Ewa Moncure
Editorial Assistance: Jane Boland

Design: Douglass Scott, Cathleen Damplo, WGBH Design

Editorial Consultants:

Trinket Doty
McLane High School, Fairfax, VA

Virginia Fitzpatrick
Moore College of Art, Philadelphia, PA

Sandi Hammonds
Woodson High School, Fairfax, VA

Sallye Mahan-Cox
Robinson Secondary School, Fairfax, VA

Kaye Passmore
Notre Dame Academy, Worcester, MA

Merceda Saffron
West Springfield High School, Springfield, VA

Roger Tomhave, Art Curriculum Specialist
Fairfax County Public Schools, VA

Front Cover: *Funerary Mask of Tutankhamun*, 1352 B.C., 18th Dynasty. Gold, lapis, cloisonné, quartz. 21 1/4" (54 cm) tall. Thebes. Cairo Museum, Egypt. Photo by Fred J. Maroon.
Back Cover: *Funerary Mask of Tutankhamun*. Photo by Giraudon/Art Resource, New York.